This book presents a sobering analysis of the secular growth slowdown based on the most comprehensive database of potential growth estimates available to date. With nearly all the forces that have driven growth and prosperity in recent decades now weakened, the book argues that a prolonged period of weakness is under way, with serious implications for emerging market and developing economies. The authors call for bold policy actions at both the national and global levels to lift growth prospects. The book is essential reading for policy makers, economists, and anyone concerned about the future of the global economy.

Beatrice Weder di Mauro
Professor of International Economics, Geneva Graduate Institute
and President of the Centre for Economic Policy Research

A terrific book that couldn't be published at a better time. As economic growth is in the midst of a sustained slowdown across regions, there is an urgent need for understanding the factors behind these developments and for identifying policy solutions. This volume tremendously delivers on both fronts and more as it also introduces a comprehensive global database on potential growth that will facilitate much needed research in this area. Undoubtedly, the book's insightful analysis and policy recommendations will be a useful tool for policy makers around the world for years to come. A tour de force that is a must read!

Liliana Rojas-Suarez
Director of the Latin America Initiative and Senior Fellow
Center for Global Development

Economic policy making is becoming increasingly complicated in the 2020s. In addition to tackling traditional trade-offs in aggregate demand management and improving efficiency on the supply side, policy makers need to address new priorities and challenges, from addressing climate change and its impacts to improving income distribution, all in the context of lower growth rates, waning productivity growth, and flattening of the globalization process that has brought unprecedented prosperity across the globe and lifted more than a billion people out of poverty. In *Falling Long-Term Growth Prospects*, the authors do a phenomenal job of assessing these trends at the global and regional levels, identifying and unpacking salient twenty-first-century policy challenges, and providing thoughtful and evidence-based policy prescriptions for leaders in advanced, emerging market, and developing economies. Importantly, the book underscores that these challenges tend to be global and, hence, global cooperation at all levels is necessary to achieve optimal results. Alas, we seem to be going in the opposite direction; this book offers a road map to put us back on the path to creating a more integrated, prosperous, and equitable global community.

Michael G. Plummer
Director, SAIS Europe and Eni Professor of
International Economics, Johns Hopkins University

The book is a timely, lucid, and comprehensive compendium of papers analyzing the growth experiences of emerging and developing economies during the last three decades. It especially focuses on the economic slowdown of the last decade and predicts that the slowdown could easily continue for at least another decade. The prognosis is thus stark, and urges timely policy actions. Not just policy makers and practitioners, but equally academics and students, will find the book to be a compelling resource for better comprehending the dynamics of the ongoing structural slowdown around the world, specifically in the developing world. This will also enable all the key stakeholders to come up with innovative ways and out-of-the-box solutions to address this worrisome issue. All in all, the book therefore offers compelling reading as well as a road map for future policies.

Poonam Gupta
Director General of the National Council of Applied Economic Research
and Member of the Economic Advisory Council to India's Prime Minister

As if the convulsions of COVID, extreme weather events, and the Russia-Ukraine war were not enough, developing countries are facing a silent crisis: their long-term growth prospects are declining. This carefully researched and compellingly argued book shows that, thanks mainly to demographic and climate change, potential growth will be significantly lower in the future than in the past. The book also identifies policies that can reverse this trend. We must adopt these policies now; we owe it to our children.

Shanta Devarajan
Professor of the Practice of International Development,
Edmund A. Walsh School of Foreign Service, Georgetown University

Nobel Laureate Robert Lucas once wrote that the consequences of economic growth for human welfare are staggering and that once one starts thinking about what drives growth *"it is hard to think about anything else."* In the aftermath of the global financial crisis, economic growth in emerging and developing economies started slowing down. This important volume shows that this growth slowdown was not fully driven by cyclical factors and that, absent a massive effort, in terms of structural policy reform it may persist for the remainder of this decade. Without sustained growth and investment, it will be impossible to reach global development goals in terms of poverty reduction or addressing climate change. The volume provides a unified framework centered on the concept of potential growth and, by identifying the drivers of potential growth, it provides a set of empirically grounded policy suggestions aimed at increasing potential growth. It also develops and describes a novel data set of measures of potential growth covering more than 170 countries for a 40-year period. The book and the associated data will be invaluable tools for researchers who are trying to uncover what Lucas called the *"mechanics of economic development."*

Ugo Panizza
Pictet Chair in Finance and Development, Geneva Graduate Institute
and Vice President, Centre for Economic Policy Research

This is timely and important work. It breaks new ground by assembling and analyzing the most comprehensive international database to date on potential growth and its drivers. It offers valuable advice on policy options to countries as they face the prospect of slowing long-term economic growth and a range of shocks. An essential reading for policy makers and more broadly for those interested in current global economic trends and challenges.

Zia Qureshi
Senior Fellow, Brookings Institution

This book is a must read for economists and policy makers alike. It provides a new and unique database for potential output growth covering a large set of countries. The book also offers a thorough analysis of the drivers of potential output growth. It argues that the recent weakness in growth will continue for the remainder of the present decade and comes up with policy conclusions to reverse this trend.

Jakob de Haan
Professor of Political Economy
University of Groningen

Falling Long-Term Growth Prospects

Falling Long-Term Growth Prospects

Trends, Expectations, and Policies

Edited by

M. Ayhan Kose and Franziska Ohnsorge

 **WORLD BANK GROUP**

Summary of Contents

Contents

Figures

Tables

Foreword

The overlapping crises of the past few years have ended a span of nearly three decades of sustained economic growth that brought the world a massive reduction in extreme poverty. Starting in 1990, productivity surged, incomes rose, and inflation fell. Within a generation, about one out of four developing economies leaped to high-income status.

Today, nearly all the economic forces that drove economic progress are in retreat. In the decade before COVID-19, a global slowdown in productivity—which is essential for income growth and higher wages—was already adding to concerns about long-term economic prospects. In this decade, total factor productivity is expected to grow at its slowest clip since 2000. Investment growth is weakening: The 2022-24 average will be half that of the previous two decades. The global labor force is also growing sluggishly as populations age in advanced economies and many emerging market and developing economies (EMDEs). In addition, reversals in human capital triggered by the health shock delivered by COVID-19, school closures, and learning losses will have long-lasting effects on the growth of potential output. International trade—which from the 1990s through 2011 grew twice as fast as GDP growth—is now barely matching it.

The result could be a lost decade in the making—not just for some countries or regions as has occurred in the past, but for the whole world. Without a big and broad policy push to rejuvenate it, the global average rate of potential GDP growth—the theoretical growth rate an economy can sustain over the medium term based on investment and productivity rates without risking excess inflation—is expected to fall to a three-decade low of 2.2 percent a year between now and 2030, down from 2.6 percent in 2011-21. That is a steep drop of nearly a third from the 3.5 percent rate that prevailed in the first decade of this century. Potential GDP growth will also decline sharply for developing economies, largely because of low investment rates: from an annual average of 6 percent between 2000 and 2010 to an average of 5 percent in 2011-21 and 4 percent over the remainder of this decade.

This broad-based slowdown in the growth rate of potential GDP has profound implications for the world's ability to tackle the growing array of challenges unique to our times. An economy's potential GDP growth rate sets boundaries for key policies affecting development, including the level of benchmark interest rates, the range of possible government spending, and the expected size of returns to investors.

The rate of potential growth *can* be raised through policies that grow the labor supply, increase productivity, and provide incentives for investment. The analysis in this volume shows that, if all countries make a strong push, potential global GDP growth can be boosted by 0.7 percentage point—to an annual average rate of 2.9 percent. That would convert an expected slowdown in potential GDP growth into an acceleration. This book lays out an extensive menu of policies to boost growth and highlights six priority interventions:

- **Increasing investment:** A major global push for greater investment to achieve development and climate goals, without undermining fiscal sustainability, could boost rates of potential growth by as much as 0.3 percentage point per year. Business-enabling reforms can be carried out to address a range of impediments to private sector development, such as high business start-up costs, weak property rights and corporate governance, inefficient labor and product market policies, and shallow financial sectors. Investments aligned with climate goals—such as in transportation and energy, climate-smart agriculture and manufacturing, and land and water systems—can increase long-term growth and economic resilience to natural disasters.

- **Aligning monetary and fiscal frameworks:** Robust macroeconomic policy frameworks are critical to support investor confidence and can moderate the ups and downs of business cycles. They help countries attract investment by instilling confidence in investors regarding national institutions, policy making, and currencies. Such frameworks are most effective when monetary and fiscal policies are aligned in their purpose. They should make inflation, debt, fiscal prudence, and financial sector stability priorities.

- **Cutting trade costs:** Trade costs—mostly those associated with shipping, logistics, and regulations—can double the cost of internationally traded goods. Countries with the highest shipping and logistics costs could cut their trade costs in half by adopting the trade facilitation practices of countries with the lowest shipping and logistics costs. Moreover, trade costs can be reduced in climate-friendly ways—by removing the current bias toward carbon-intensive goods inherent in many countries' tariff schedules and by eliminating restrictions on access to environmentally friendly goods and services.

- **Capitalizing on services:** As international trade in goods has ebbed, the services sector has become an increasingly important engine of growth for developing economies. Exports of digitally delivered professional services related to information and communications technology climbed to more than 50 percent of total exports of services in 2021, up from 40 percent in 2019. Developing economies enjoy significant room to grow in this area because of their limited use of such technology in everyday interactions. This requires a renewed focus on education and skills, particularly language and digital skills.

- **Upping labor force participation:** If overall labor force participation rates, especially among women and older workers, could be boosted to match the best 10-year increase on record, this could increase global rates of potential growth by 0.2 percentage point on average by 2030. Globally, average female labor force participation remains three-quarters that of men, and the gap is even larger in EMDEs. In some regions, such as the Middle East and North Africa and South Asia, an increase in female labor force participation rates to match the EMDE average could boost EMDEs' potential GDP growth by as much as 1.2 percentage points a year by 2030. Increasing the average participation rate of workers aged 55 years or older—which is about half that of 30- to 45-year-old workers—is similarly valuable but will require further investments in work ability, retraining, and new skills.

- **Strengthening global cooperation:** From 1990 through the mid-2010s, the global economy fired on nearly all cylinders partly because of broad-based international cooperation following the breakup of the Soviet Union. That cooperation has since faltered. Effective new methods of cooperation—on trade, climate, finance, debt transparency, fragility, health, and infrastructure, to name a few—will be essential if the world is to mobilize the investment that will be needed to achieve sustainable growth and poverty alleviation.

An extraordinary series of setbacks has brought the world to another crossroads. It will take an exceptional mix of focused policies and effective international cooperation to revive growth. The World Bank Group is fully engaged in helping countries design and implement policies and projects that boost growth and median incomes while fostering environmental sustainability and resilience.

David Malpass
President
The World Bank Group
March 27, 2023

Acknowledgments

As Robert Lucas once wrote: "Once one starts to think about [economic growth], it is hard to think about anything else." We are extremely fortunate to have worked with many outstanding colleagues who helped us to think through complex growth challenges confronting the global economy, put together a brand-new data set of potential growth, and formulate policy responses to deliver better growth outcomes. It would not have been possible to finalize a study of this magnitude without such a dedicated group of collaborators. We are deeply grateful for their insightful contributions.

The seven chapters of this book were produced by our tireless coauthors: Elwyn Davies, Sergiy Kasyanenko, Philip Kenworthy, Sinem Kilic Celik, Gaurav Nayyar, Lucia Quaglietti, Franz Ulrich Ruch, Kersten Stamm, Ekaterine Vashakmadze, Dana Vorisek, and Collette Wheeler. We are also thankful to Hayley Pallan, Cordula Rastogi, and Shu Yu for their contributions to annexes, boxes, and background literature reviews.

We would like to thank Indermit Gill for his support of our work program on economic growth. We owe a debt of gratitude to colleagues who reviewed the preliminary drafts, provided detailed comments, discussed our findings, and patiently answered our many questions: Amat Adarov, Carlos Arteta, Dilek Aykut, Martin Bailey, Valerie Mercer Blackman, Eduardo Borensztein, Natalie Chen, Ajai Chopra, Ibrahim Chowdhury, Kevin Chua, Kevin Clinton, Brahima Coulibaly, Kevin Cruz, Antonio Fatas, Erik Feyen, Poonam Gupta, Jakob de Haan, Graham Hacche, Thomas Helbling, Elena Ianchovichina, Ergys Islamaj, Bradley Jensen, Gerard Kambou, Jean Pierre Lacombe, Yusha Li, Dorsati Madani, Aaditya Mattoo, Joseph Mawejje, Dennis Novy, Ugo Panizza, Zia Qureshi, David Robinson, Apurva Sanghi, Sudhir Shetty, Naotaka Sugawara, Jonathan Temple, Christopher Towe, and Garima Vasishtha.

We also would like to thank the participants in many internal seminars and in the World Bank Group-wide review process of *Global Economics Prospects* reports for useful suggestions on the preliminary chapters and numerous policy makers and researchers for conversations on topics covered here.

We are deeply grateful to Kaltrina Temaj for shouldering the lion's share of research assistance responsibilities. We are also thankful to Lule Bahtiri, Mattia Coppo, Hrisyana Stefanova Doytchinova, Jiayue Fan, Arika Kayastha, Maria Hazel Macadangdang, Rafaela Martinho Henriques, Muneeb Ahmad Naseem, Mohamad Nassar, Julia Roseman Norfleet, Vasiliki Papagianni, Lorez Qehaja, Juan Felipe Serrano Ariza, Shijie Shi, Yujia Yao, and Juncheng Zhou for excellent research support.

We are indebted to our colleagues who worked on the production process, media relations, and dissemination. We truly appreciate the herculean efforts of Adriana Maximiliano in assembling the print publication and designing the cover, with assistance from Hazel Macadangdang. Graeme Littler produced the website (www.worldbank.org/potential-growth) and provided editorial support, with contributions from Adriana Maximiliano. Therese Reginaldo provided extensive logistical support. Chisako Fukuda, Patricia Katayama, Jewel McFadden, Koichi Omori, Joseph Rebello, and Nandita Roy managed media relations and dissemination.

The production of this book was managed by the Prospects Group of the Development Economics Vice Presidency of the World Bank. The Prospects Group gratefully acknowledges financial support from the Policy and Human Resources Development Fund provided by the Government of Japan.

Authors and contributors

Elwyn Davies, Senior Economist, World Bank

Sergiy Kasyanenko, Economist, World Bank

Philip Kenworthy, Economist, World Bank

Sinem Kilic Celik, Economist, International Monetary Fund

M. Ayhan Kose, Director and Deputy Chief Economist, World Bank

Gaurav Nayyar, Lead Economist, World Bank

Franziska Ohnsorge, Manager, World Bank

Hayley Pallan, Economist, World Bank

Lucia Quaglietti, Economist, Organisation for Economic Co-operation and Development

Cordula Rastogi, Senior Economist, World Bank

Franz Ulrich Ruch, Senior Economist, World Bank

Kersten Stamm, Economist, World Bank

Ekaterine Vashakmadze, Senior Economist, World Bank

Dana Vorisek, Senior Economist, World Bank

Collette Wheeler, Senior Economist, World Bank

Shu Yu, Senior Economist, World Bank

Abbreviations

AEs	advanced economies
ASEAN	Association of Southeast Asian Nations
CA	Central Asia
CE	Central Europe
COVID-19	coronavirus disease 2019
EAP	East Asia and Pacific
EBRD	European Bank for Reconstruction and Development
ECA	Europe and Central Asia
EE	Eastern Europe
EMDEs	emerging market and developing economies
EU	European Union
excl.	excluding
FDI	foreign direct investment
FY	fiscal year
G7	Group of Seven
GCC	Gulf Cooperation Council
GDP	gross domestic product
ICT	information and communications technology
IMF	International Monetary Fund
LAC	Latin America and the Caribbean
LICs	low-income countries
LPI	Logistics Performance Index [World Bank]
LSCI	Liner Shipping Connectivity Index [United Nations Conference on Trade and Development]
MERS	Middle East Respiratory Syndrome
MICs	middle-income countries
MNA	Middle East and North Africa
MVF	multivariate filter
NEET	neither employed nor in education or training
OECD	Organisation for Economic Co-operation and Development
PF	production function approach
PISA	Programme for International Student Assessment
PMI	purchasing managers' index
R&D	research and development
RTA	regional trade agreement
SAR	South Asia
SARS	Severe Acute Respiratory Syndrome
SCC	South Caucasus

SDGs	Sustainable Development Goals
SSA	Sub-Saharan Africa
TFP	total factor productivity
UCM	unobserved-components model
UNESCAP	United Nations Economic and Social Commission for Asia and the Pacific
UVF	univariate filter
WBK	Western Balkans
WEO	*World Economic Outlook*

Across the world, a structural growth slowdown is under way: If current trends continue, the global rate of potential growth—the maximum rate at which an economy can grow without igniting inflation—is expected to fall to a three-decade low over the remainder of the 2020s. Nearly all the forces that have powered growth and prosperity since the early 1990s have weakened, not solely because of a series of shocks to the global economy over the past three years. The rates of growth of investment and total factor productivity are declining. The global labor force is aging—and expanding more slowly. International trade growth is much weaker now than it was in the early 2000s. The slowdown could be even more pronounced if financial crises erupt in major economies and spread to other countries, as these types of episodes often lead to lasting damage to potential growth. A persistent and broad-based decline in long-term growth prospects imperils the ability of emerging market and developing economies (EMDEs) to combat poverty, tackle climate change, and meet other key development objectives. These challenges call for an ambitious policy response at the national and global levels. The slowdown can be reversed by the end of the 2020s—if all countries replicate some of their best policy efforts of recent decades and accompany them with a major investment push grounded in robust macroeconomic frameworks. Boosting human capital and labor force participation and making sound climate-related investments can also make a measurable difference in lifting growth prospects. Increased cross-border cooperation and substantial financing from the global community will need to support bold policy actions at the national level.

Slowing growth, dimming prospects

In 2015, Kaushik Basu, the World Bank Group's Chief Economist at the time, asked us to assess the long-term growth prospects of emerging market and developing economies (EMDEs). His request inspired us to prepare the study "Slowdown in Emerging Markets: Rough Patch or Prolonged Weakness?"[1] The question in the title was a deliberate choice, since the study documented a synchronous slowdown in these economies during 2010-15 but concluded that cyclical factors played a partial role and that policies could reverse the decline in growth. We now have a definitive answer to the question we posed in the title: These economies are in the midst of a prolonged period of weakness.

Note: This overview was prepared by M. Ayhan Kose and Franziska Ohnsorge.

[1] Our earlier study focused on both cyclical and structural drivers of the slowdown (Didier et al. 2015). This study also acknowledges the importance of cyclical factors but focuses on structural drivers that have become more prominent in explaining the decline in growth. It is much more comprehensive than our earlier study, as it builds on, and expands, multiple studies we have conducted since then. Some of these have been featured in the World Bank Group's flagship *Global Economic Prospects* report in which we have examined different aspects of growth in EMDEs.

This book argues that the current weakness in growth in EMDEs will likely extend through the remainder of the 2020s. It could be even more pronounced if financial crises erupt in major economies and, especially, if they trigger a global recession. The experience of the past two decades has shown that financial crises and recessions cause lasting damage to growth; this damage would compound the weaknesses in the main drivers of growth that are already embedded in current trends. In addition, the necessary policy interventions could be delayed, as has often happened during the past decade, such that global growth over the 2020s could disappoint once again.

It will take a herculean collective policy effort to restore growth in the next decade to the average of the previous one. At the national level, this effort will require these economies to repeat their own best 10-year records in a wide range of policy results. At the global level, given the cross-border nature of many challenges confronting growth, the policy response requires stronger cooperation, larger financing, and a reenergized push for mobilization of private capital.

Major shocks have battered the global economy over the past three years—including the coronavirus disease 2019 (COVID-19) pandemic and the war in Ukraine. After countries had provided the necessary support for businesses and individuals hurt by the pandemic, cyclical policies turned contractionary. A steep rise in inflation over the past two years has led to the sharpest tightening of global monetary policy in four decades. Fiscal policy has also become less supportive following a significant deterioration of government budget balances during the 2020 global recession, when debt levels reached historic highs. Amid these multiple adverse shocks and limited policy space, the global economy has experienced, over the past three years, the sharpest growth slowdown ever following a global recession.

Even as policy makers confront these short-term challenges, a longer-term setback of considerable importance has been brewing quietly: a persistent decline in long-term growth prospects. In the past decade, growth in EMDEs has slowed sharply (table OA.1). Global growth declined from a recent peak of 4.5 percent in 2010 to a projected low of 1.7 percent in 2023 (figure O.1). The slowdown was widespread: in 80 percent of advanced economies and 75 percent of EMDEs, average annual growth was lower during 2011-21 than during 2000-10.

The slowdown was particularly pronounced in EMDEs. As a result, the pace at which the per capita incomes of these economies are catching up to those of advanced economies (so-called income convergence) has fallen: In 2011-21, EMDE per capita incomes grew more rapidly than per capita incomes in advanced economies by 2.0 percentage points a year. But that was considerably smaller than the differential of 3.4 percentage points a year during 2000-10. The income convergence process was set back in all EMDE regions (that is, regions with EMDEs). Middle-income EMDEs were hit somewhat harder than low-income countries (LICs). Per capita income growth slipped by 1.4 percentage points in middle-income countries, from 4.9 percent in 2000-10 to 3.5 percent in 2011-21 (table OA.2). LIC per capita income growth also slowed, by 1.2 percentage points, to 1.7 percent in 2011-21 from 2.9 percent in 2000-10.

FIGURE O.1 **Growth**

Growth has slowed sharply—in aggregate and per capita terms and in the majority of countries— from its elevated rates in the early 2000s. The pace at which per capita incomes are converging toward those in advanced economies has slowed in all EMDE regions.

A. Growth

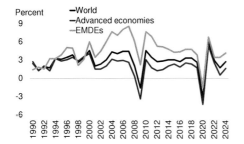

B. Per capita growth

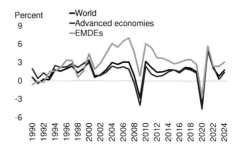

C. Share of countries with slower growth than in the previous decade

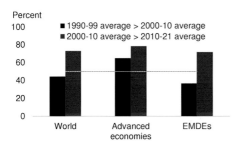

D. Annual average per capita income growth relative to advanced economies

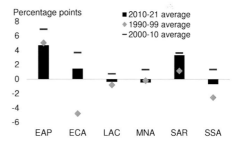

E. Growth

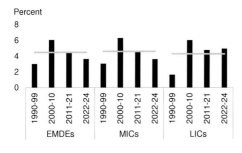

F. Per capita growth relative to advanced economies

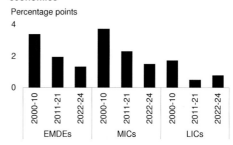

Source: World Bank.
Note: EMDEs = emerging market and developing economies.
A.B. Projections for 2023-24. Averages weighted by gross domestic product (GDP) (at 2010-19 average exchange rates and prices).
C. Yellow horizontal line indicates 50 percent.
D. EAP = East Asia and Pacific; ECA = Europe and Central Asia; LAC = Latin America and the Caribbean; MNA = Middle East and North Africa; SAR = South Asia; SSA = Sub-Saharan Africa.
E.F. GDP-weighted averages (at 2010-19 average exchange rates and prices). Unbalanced sample of up to 105 MICs and 26 LICs. Projections for 2022-24 from the World Bank's January 2023 *Global Economic Prospects* report. LICs = low-income countries; MICs = middle-income countries.

The slowdown represents a deepening crisis of development—because all the fundamental drivers of economic growth have faded (figure O.2). Ordinarily one of the most powerful drivers of economic growth, global trade in 2010-19 grew only as fast as overall economic growth, down from twice as fast during 1990-2011. Factor reallocation from less to more productive firms and sectors has also slowed. Gains from better education and health have faded as improvements in education and health care systems have leveled off. Continuing a decade of weakness prior to the pandemic, average growth of investment in EMDEs is projected at 3.5 percent per year, about half its 2000-21 average.[2] After rising over the preceding decades, the growth of the working-age population relative to overall global population growth declined to a three-decade low in 2017. Global policy uncertainty has risen, while attitudes toward trade integration have turned more cautious.

On top of this fading growth momentum, a series of shocks—including the pandemic and climate-related disasters—over the past decade have done lasting damage to the development process. This damage has been reflected in stalling poverty reduction.

Magnifying challenges

Weaker long-term growth gives rise to a wide range of challenges. First, it slows the pace of poverty reduction. At projected growth rates, the goal of reducing global extreme poverty to 3 percent of the population by 2030 is now out of reach. Second, slower output growth tends to reduce the resources available to invest in solving problems confronting the global economy. Without sustained investment growth, it will be difficult, if not impossible, to address climate change and make material progress toward other development goals. Third, slower long-term output growth implies limited job creation and wage growth, which provides fertile ground for social tensions and is likely to entail slower transitions from informal to formal economic activity. Finally, weaker long-term output growth curtails the resources available to pay off mounting debt loads, potentially undermining debt sustainability and leading to financial stress.

One tool for meeting multiple policy priorities

A raft of sometimes competing policy priorities accompany the intensifying development challenges the world faces: eliminating extreme poverty, reducing inequality, achieving higher growth, and combating climate change. The good news is that addressing each of these priorities requires the same recipe: sustained and robust investment and productivity growth. Through this mechanism, policy makers can overcome these enormous challenges and deliver sustained, sustainable, and inclusive growth. Measures to promote investment in human capital, foster gender equality, and strengthen social protection systems will need to accompany efforts along these lines.

---

[2] Throughout this book, unless otherwise specified, "investment" refers to real gross fixed-capital formation (public and private combined).

FIGURE O.2 **Drivers of output growth**

All the fundamental drivers of output growth have slowed in the past decade. Improvements in human capital, growth of the labor force, investment (including because of policy uncertainty), and total factor productivity (including through factor reallocation) all decelerated. These drivers of growth are expected to slow further in the remainder of the current decade.

A. Working-age population

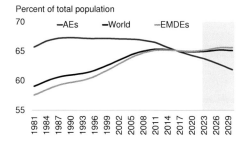

B. TFP growth

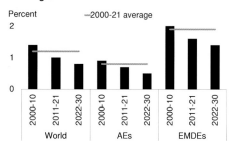

C. Investment growth

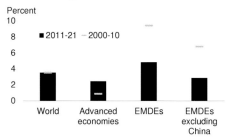

D. Contributions to labor productivity growth

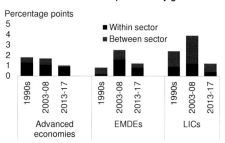

E. Improvement in human capital indicators

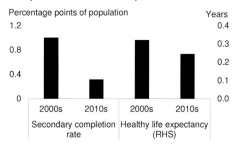

F. Global policy uncertainty

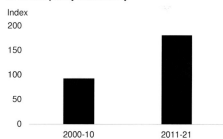

Sources: Baker, Bloom, and Davis (2016); Barro and Lee (2013); Dieppe and Matsuoka (2021); UN population statistics; World Bank.

Note: AEs = advanced economies; EMDEs = emerging market and developing economies; LICs = low-income countries; RHS = right-hand scale; TFP = total factor productivity.

A. Population-weighted averages. The working-age population is defined as people aged 15-64 years.

B. GDP-weighted arithmetic average of total factor productivity growth. Includes 53 EMDEs and 29 advanced economies.

B.-E. Arithmetic annual averages.

C. Averages weighted by gross domestic product (GDP) for the period indicated.

D. Based on samples of 94 countries during 1995-99 and 103 countries during 2003-17. Median of country-specific productivity contributions. Within-sector growth shows the contribution of initial productivity growth weighted by real value added, and between-sector growth shows the contribution from changes in the employment share.

E. For healthy life expectancy at birth, annual average change in population-weighted average for 179 countries between 2000 and 2010 and between 2011 and 2019. For lower secondary school completion rate (in percent of relevant age group), annual average change in world aggregate between 2000 and 2010 and between 2010 and 2019.

F. Period averages. The global policy uncertainty index is a GDP-weighted average of national economic policy uncertainty indexes for 21 countries: Australia; Brazil; Canada; Chile; China; Colombia; France; Germany; Greece; India; Ireland; Italy; Japan; Korea, Rep.; Mexico; the Netherlands; the Russian Federation; Spain; Sweden; the United Kingdom; and the United States (Baker, Bloom, and Davis 2016).

Achieving this goal is not easy: policies that are effective in lifting long-term growth and investment are often difficult to design and even more difficult to implement. They tend to involve structural interventions that can sometimes impose substantial, asymmetric costs on parts of society and therefore can face stiff resistance from vested interests. Some need to be accompanied by supportive measures to ensure inclusive growth. Moreover, their growth dividends often take time to accrue. Nonetheless, achieving strong and sustained growth is the only plausible path to durably addressing climate change, poverty, and a wide range of other development challenges.

Understanding long-term growth: A framework

This book frames long-term growth around the concept of potential growth: the maximum gross domestic product (GDP) growth rate that an economy can sustain in the long term at full employment and full capacity without igniting inflation. An economy's potential growth rate is effectively its speed limit. It influences the full spectrum of policies that determine economic and development outcomes: the level of benchmark interest rates, the scale of government spending, and even the expected size of returns to investors. The speed limit can be raised—through policies that expand the labor supply, boost productivity, and ramp up investment.

Although the concept of potential growth has been much explored, potential growth itself is not directly observable and must be inferred from other data. The book develops a variety of measures of potential growth and examines their evolution over time. It presents a detailed discussion of linkages between potential growth and its underlying drivers: capital accumulation (through investment growth), labor force growth, and the growth of total factor productivity (TFP), which is the part of economic growth that arises from more efficient use of inputs and often results from technological changes. The book also pays special attention to developments in the trade and services sectors, both of which have been key contributors to productivity growth and changes in labor markets.

Contributions to the literature

There is a rich literature on policies to improve long-term growth prospects.[3] This book makes three key contributions with its introduction of a new database of potential

---

[3] Several studies have examined the links between growth and inequality (for example, Cerra et al. 2021) or between short-term shocks and long-term output trends (for example, Cerra, Fatás, and Saxena 2020). Others have looked in depth at specific drivers of growth, such as innovation (Aghion, Akcigit, and Howitt 2015; Aghion, Antonin, and Bunel 2021; Aghion and Howitt 2005), institutions (Acemoglu 2012; Acemoglu, Johnson, and Robinson 2005), culture (Gorodnichenko and Roland 2011), political economy (Acemoglu and Robinson 2012; Allen et al. 2014), trade (Rodrik 2016), finance (Arcand, Berkes, and Panizza 2015; Obstfeld 2009), digitalization (Brynjolfsson and McAfee 2014, 2017), and human capital (Schady et al. 2023). Some studies have examined growth prospects in different regions, such as Europe (Gill and Raiser 2012), Central America (Ulku and Zaourak 2022), Latin America (Alvarez and de Gregorio 2014), and Africa, Asia, and Latin America (seven country case studies by McMillan, Rodrik, and Sepúlveda 2017). Others, such as Loayza and Pennings (2022), have developed tools for modeling long-term growth. Finally, a group of studies has examined firm-level drivers of growth prospects (for example, Comin and Mulani 2009; Fisman and Svensson 2007; and Goedhuys and Veugelers 2012).

growth, emphasis on global and region-specific growth trends and prospects, and presentation of a rich menu of policies for delivering better growth outcomes.

Comprehensive database of potential growth. The book introduces the first comprehensive database of the nine most commonly used estimates of growth in potential output for the largest available country sample, up to 173 economies (37 advanced economies and 136 EMDEs) over 1981-2021 (chapter 1). These estimates are based on multiple methodologies. The book also examines prospects for potential growth based on projections of its structural drivers: growth of physical and human capital, growth of labor supply, and growth of TFP.[4] In addition, using the new database, it presents the first detailed analysis of the damage to potential growth from many adverse developments in EMDEs, including recessions, banking crises, epidemics, and natural disasters (chapters 1 and 5).[5]

Regional aspects of potential growth and investment. This book is the first to examine regional trends in EMDEs and the prospects for the growth of potential output and investment since the onset of the COVID-19 pandemic. In dedicated chapters, the book also discusses regional policy priorities and options to strengthen investment and potential growth (chapters 2 and 4). Its analysis draws on specific literature and data for each of the six World Bank Group regions: East Asia and Pacific (EAP), Europe and Central Asia (ECA), Latin America and the Caribbean (LAC), the Middle East and North Africa (MNA), South Asia (SAR), and Sub-Saharan Africa (SSA).

Policies. The book explores, in a consistent framework, policy options to lift potential growth. In contrast to those in earlier studies, the discussion of policy options is directly based on empirical analysis.[6] Some of these policies include reforms of education and health care systems as well as labor markets (chapter 5). The book also presents an extensive menu of policies for boosting investment and productivity growth and examines policy interventions geared toward promoting growth in services activity and international trade.

- *Investment as a key driver of potential growth.* As noted earlier, investment is essential for delivering sustained growth in potential output, improving living standards, and making progress in achieving the Sustainable Development Goals (SDGs) and fulfilling commitments made under the Paris Agreement on climate change. This

---

[4] Previous studies have been confined to a single methodology, such as the production function approach (OECD 2014) or multivariate filters (ADB 2016; IMF 2015). Some earlier studies estimated trends for only a subset of measures of potential growth (for example, Chalaux and Guillemette 2019; Kilic Celik, Kose, and Ohnsorge 2020). The book's focus on long-term potential growth projections also contrasts with the previous literature, which has examined past trends (ADB 2016; Dabla-Norris et al. 2015; IMF 2015; OECD 2014).

[5] Earlier work has estimated the effects of recessions on potential growth, but those recessions were primarily confined to member countries of the Organisation for Economic Co-operation and Development and to one specific measure of potential growth (Furceri and Mourougane 2012; Mourougane 2017).

[6] Previous studies have investigated the link between actual growth of output or productivity and structural reforms, focusing on the near-term benefits (Prati, Onorato, and Papageorgiou 2013), productivity effects (Adler et al. 2017; Dabla-Norris, Ho, and Kyobe 2016), or a sample consisting of mostly advanced economies (Banerji et al. 2017; IMF 2015, 2016b).

book provides the first comprehensive analysis of investment growth in a large sample of EMDEs since the pandemic and the Russian Federation's invasion of Ukraine. It examines the likely medium- and long-term consequences of the damage to investment in EMDEs from recent adverse shocks, focusing on the effects on productivity, growth in potential output, trade, and the ability to achieve the SDGs and climate-related goals. It also describes a rich menu of policies to revive investment growth.

- *Trade as a traditional engine of growth.* Trade has been a powerful engine for EMDE growth over the past four decades, but its role is now under threat. The book presents a comprehensive analysis of trade costs and avenues for promoting trade growth (chapter 6). It goes beyond previous research in assessing the role of trade policy—including policy regarding tariffs and participation in trade agreements—in determining trade costs (Arvis et al. 2016; Chen and Novy 2012; World Bank 2021). An event study of the evolution of trade in goods and services around global recessions, including the pandemic-induced global recession of 2020, complements this analysis. Building on the econometric analysis, the chapter derives policy options to lower trade costs.

- *Services as a new engine of growth.* High hopes have been placed on the services sector as a new engine of economic growth as traditional engines of growth such as goods trade and resource sectors sputter.[7] This book establishes a set of stylized facts that summarize the role of the services sector in growth and development over the past three decades (chapter 7). It presents growth decompositions that estimate the contributions of subsectors of services as well as the contributions of the growth of factor inputs versus TFP. The book also documents how the pandemic has affected prospects and policy priorities for services-led growth, building on some recent studies. It assesses future growth opportunities linked to the acceleration in digitalization, taking as a starting point the literature on how the digital economy is expanding opportunities to boost productivity in the services sector.

Key findings and policy messages

Using a comprehensive database of multiple measures of potential growth, this book examines trends in potential growth and its drivers (especially investment), global and regional prospects for potential growth and investment over the 2020s, and a range of policy options for lifting potential growth. It documents three major findings. First,

---

[7] Major shifts are under way in commodity markets as part of the energy transition, as discussed in Baffes and Nagle (2022). Recent work considers the potential of services as an engine of growth and trade (Lee and McKibbin 2018; Nayyar, Hallward-Driemeier, and Davies 2021a, 2021b; OECD 2005; Park and Noland 2013) and trade (Baldwin 2016; Francois and Hoekman 2010). Some recent studies also consider the effects of the pandemic on growth and household income or firm sales distribution (Apedo-Amah et al. 2020; Chetty et al. 2020; Narayan et al. 2022). The book expands on the growing literature on structural change and productivity growth in EMDEs, which highlights changes in the relative contributions of the broader manufacturing and services sectors and demand- and supply-side factors (Fan, Peters, and Zilibotti 2021; Kinfemichael and Morshed 2019; McMillan and Rodrik 2011; Nayyar, Hallward-Driemeier, and Davies 2021a, 2021b; Rodrik 2016).

potential growth and its underlying drivers have declined in a protracted, broad-based way. Major adverse shocks have also reduced potential growth by leaving a lasting impact on these drivers. Second, the slowdown in potential growth is expected to persist for the rest of this decade. Finally, while these two matters are significant challenges confronting EMDEs, they are not insurmountable. It is possible to reverse the slowdown in potential growth and chart a sustained, sustainable, and inclusive growth path by implementing ambitious, broad-based, and forceful policies at the national and global levels.

Long-standing, widespread decline in potential growth

All measures document a widespread decline in potential growth in the decade 2011-21, relative to the preceding decade (chapter 1). Global potential growth fell to 2.6 percent a year during 2011-21 from 3.5 percent a year during 2000-10; meanwhile, EMDE potential growth fell to 5.0 percent a year during 2011-21 from 6.0 percent a year during 2000-10 (table OA.3).

The weakening of potential growth was highly synchronized across countries: during 2011-21, potential growth was below its 2000-10 average in almost all advanced economies and nearly 60 percent of EMDEs. Among EMDE regions, the steepest slowdown occurred in MNA, followed by that in EAP, although potential growth in EAP remained higher than that in all other EMDE regions except SAR, where potential growth remained broadly unchanged (chapter 2).

This slowdown in potential growth can be attributed to many factors, as all fundamental drivers of growth faded. Globally, slower growth in TFP, labor supply, and investment than in the period 2000-10 marked the period between 2011 and 2021. The period between 2011 and 2021 was marked globally by slower TFP growth, slower labor supply growth, and slower investment growth than in the period 2000-10. In addition, financial crises, global recessions, bouts of inflation, health crises such as epidemics and a pandemic, climate-related disasters, and wars and conflict of varying severity rocked the global economy. Almost all of these shocks, and especially the global recessions, left lasting legacies of damaged drivers of, and slower rates of, potential growth (figure O.3). Using a series of econometric approaches, this book quantifies this damage.

- *Recessions* resulted in lasting damage to the productivity capacity of the global economy. National recessions were associated with potential growth that was 1.4 percentage point slower, on average, even five years later (chapter 1). Over the medium term, recessions tended to have a somewhat more severe impact than did other adverse events—such as banking crises, epidemics, and other natural disasters. The effect of recessions on potential growth operated through multiple channels. Four to five years after a typical recession, investment growth, employment growth, and TFP growth remained significantly lower than in "normal" years—by 3.0 percentage points for investment, 0.7 percentage point for employment, and 0.7 percentage point for TFP.

FIGURE O.3 Recessions' lasting damage to potential growth

Potential growth fell during the global recessions of 2009 and 2020, reflecting declines in investment growth, labor force growth, and total factor productivity growth. The decline was particularly steep in the COVID-19-induced global recession of 2020, which was unusual also in regard to the disproportionately large loss in services activity.

A. World: Potential growth

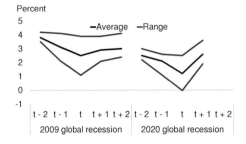

B. Advanced economies: Potential growth

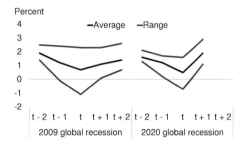

C. EMDEs: Potential growth

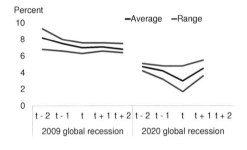

D. World: Contributions to potential growth

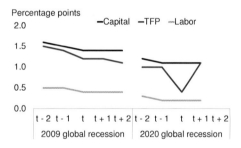

E. National recessions before 2020

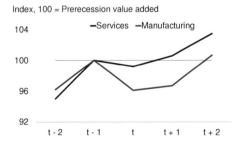

F. National recession in 2020

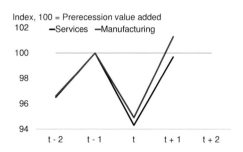

Source: World Bank.
Note: In each panel, the horizontal axis shows years, with t representing the recession year. COVID-19 = coronavirus disease 2019; EMDEs = emerging market and developing economies.
A.-C. "Average" is an unweighted average of seven measures of potential growth (excluding forecasts). "Range" reflects the maximum and minimum. Figures show potential growth around t = 2009 and t = 2020.
D. Figures show the contributions of growth in capital, total factor productivity (TFP), and labor to potential growth around t = 2009 and t = 2020.
E.F. Figures show the unweighted average level of real value added in services (blue) and manufacturing (red) in the years around the recession year t, indexed to 100 for the year preceding the recession.

- *Banking crises* were associated with initially larger declines in potential growth than recessions, with the declines peaking at 1.8 percentage points after two years as a result of collapses in investment. However, quick recoveries in investment generally followed, such that the damage to potential growth after five years was only 1.2 percentage points—less than after recessions. In contrast to recessions, banking crises tended to be mainly associated with lasting productivity losses.

- *Climate change* has increased the frequency and severity of weather-related natural disasters. Over the past two decades, these natural disasters have caused a significant decline in potential growth (chapter 5). For example, over the medium term, depending on the magnitude and speed of reconstruction efforts, damage to potential growth varied from nil to 10 percent three years after the disaster. Some countries, especially small states, have suffered much larger damage than the average effect suggests: on average 5 percent of GDP per year. These losses have not occurred in a predictable pattern. Instead, it has not been uncommon for the damages from a single climate-related disaster to cost a substantial portion of a country's GDP, or even multiples of GDP in extreme cases.

A lost decade in the making? Weaker growth prospects

The slowdown in potential growth during 2011-21 is projected to extend into the remainder of the current decade (figure O.4). Projections for its fundamental drivers suggest that global potential growth will slow further, by 0.4 percentage point a year from 2011-21 to an average of 2.2 percent a year in 2022-30, the slowest pace since 2000 (chapter 5). About half of the projected slowdown will be due to demographic factors from an aging population, including slowing growth in the working-age population and declining labor force participation. EMDE potential growth is projected to slow by 1.0 percentage point a year to an average of 4.0 percent a year in 2022-30. The decline will be internationally widespread: Economies accounting for nearly 80 percent of global GDP, including most EMDEs, are projected to experience a slowdown in potential growth between 2011-21 and 2022-30. All traditional drivers of growth, including trade, are expected to weaken in the remainder of this decade. However, relatively healthier growth is expected in the services sector.

Investment. The slowdown in investment during 2011-21 will likely extend into the remainder of the current decade because of the effects of the COVID-19 pandemic, Russia's invasion of Ukraine, limited policy space, and tight financial conditions (figure O.5; chapter 3). In 2022-24, investment growth in EMDEs is projected to average 3.5 percent per year, about half its average annual growth during 2000-21 (chapter 3). Projected investment growth through 2024 will be insufficient to return aggregate EMDE investment to its prepandemic trend from 2010 to 2019 (the period between the highly disruptive 2009 and 2020 global recessions). Annual average investment growth in 2022-30 is now forecast to be 0.3-1.8 percentage points lower, on average, than in 2011-21 in all regions except in LAC and SAR, where adverse shocks that depressed investment growth in the 2010s are not expected to recur. After a gradual decline over

FIGURE O.4 **Potential growth**

A broad-based weakening of potential growth in the past decade is expected to continue in the remainder of the current decade. In part, this reflects a weakening of investment growth that downgrades to consensus forecasts have reflected.

A. Potential growth

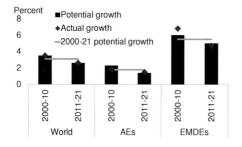

B. Potential growth

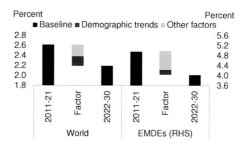

C. Contributions to potential growth

D. Contributions to potential growth

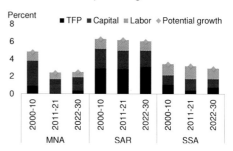

E. Investment growth, by region

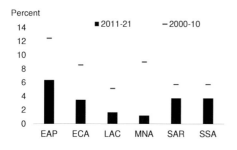

F. Five-year-ahead consensus forecasts of investment growth

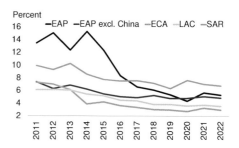

Sources: Consensus Economics; Penn World Table; World Bank.

Note: AEs = advanced economies; EAP = East Asia and Pacific; ECA = Europe and Central Asia; EMDEs = emerging market and developing economies; LAC = Latin America and the Caribbean; MNA = Middle East and North Africa; RHS = right-hand scale; SAR = South Asia; SSA = Sub-Saharan Africa; TFP = total factor productivity.

A.-E. Arithmetic annual averages.

A.B. Based on production function approach. Averages weighted by gross domestic product (GDP) for a sample of 29 advanced economies and 53 EMDEs.

C.D. Based on production function approach. Sample includes 4 countries in EAP, 9 in ECA, 15 in LAC, 7 in MNA, 2 in SAR, and 13 in SSA. Data for 2022-30 are forecasts.

E. Weighted averages by real annual fixed investment in constant U.S. dollars. Sample includes 8 economies in EAP, 12 economies in ECA, 19 economies in LAC, 9 economies in MNA, 3 economies in SAR, and 19 economies in SSA.

F. Includes data for six economies in EAP (China, Indonesia, Malaysia, Philippines, Thailand, Vietnam), seven economies in ECA (Bulgaria, Croatia, Hungary, Poland, Romania, Russian Federation, Ukraine), six economies in LAC (Argentina, Brazil, Chile, Colombia, Mexico, Peru) and one economy in SAR (India). Single-year missing data are interpolated.

FIGURE O.5 **Global trade and investment**

Global trade growth has slowed, in part on account of growing use of restrictive trade measures. Foreign direct investment inflows to EMDEs have weakened since the early 2000s. The recovery in EMDE investment from the 2020 global recession is expected to be less robust than that after the global recession of 2009.

A. Global trade

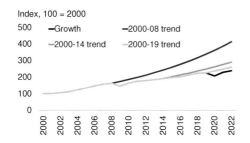

B. Policy interventions affecting trade

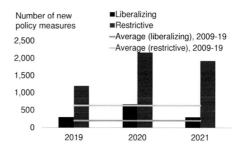

C. EMDE investment

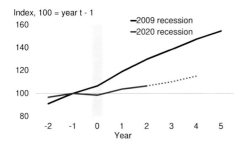

D. Foreign direct investment in EMDEs

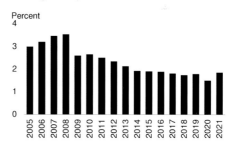

Sources: Global Trade Alert database; Haver Analytics; United Nations Conference on Trade and Development; World Bank.
Note: EMDEs = emerging market and developing economies.
A. Trade defined as exports and imports of goods and nonfactor services.
B. Data exclude late reports for the respective reporting years (the cut-off date is December 31 of each year).
C. Investment-weighted average (at 2010-19 average exchange rates and prices), indexed to 100 in the year before the global recession. "0" indicates the year of the global recession (2009 or 2020).
D. Last observation in 2021.

the past decade, foreign direct investment (FDI) will also likely remain weak over the remainder of the 2020s.

Trade. Global trade growth may weaken by another 0.4 percentage point per year, on average, during the remainder of the current decade compared with 2011-21, owing partly to slower global output growth and partly to the further waning of structural factors that have supported rapid trade expansion in recent decades (chapter 6). Fragmentation of trade and investment networks loom large over trade prospects amid policies that favor suppliers from allied countries (friend-shoring) or nearby countries (near-shoring). The historical record also shows that persistently weak investment growth tends to be associated with slow trade growth.

Services. A possible bright spot may be the services sector—provided its productivity potential can be unlocked (chapter 7). In particular, the pandemic has ushered in a pronounced shift toward digitalization as firms have moved many of their activities online. This shift promises productivity gains if it can be harnessed for better delivery of services. Since the pandemic, there has also been a shift toward high-skilled offshorable services activities, such as digitally deliverable information and communications technologies (ICTs) and professional services.

From technological innovations to the "roaring 2020s"?

The implications of technological innovations for future growth prospects have been a subject of intense debate. Some claim that the global economy will enjoy a surge in economic growth in the coming decades, with that surge driven by improvements in productivity thanks to new technologies (for example, Brynjolfsson and McAfee 2014). Others caution that future growth could stall, or even fall, because new technologies will likely have a declining marginal impact on productivity and structural challenges associated with aging and sluggish growth of investment will adversely affect prospects (for example, Gordon 2017).

As the world gradually emerges from the pandemic-induced recession of 2020, it is tempting to look back to the 1918 Spanish flu epidemic and hope for a decade of rapid global growth reminiscent of the "Roaring Twenties" of that era because of recent technological innovations. Building on technological breakthroughs in earlier decades, Europe and North America enjoyed rapid modernization and strong economic growth in the 1920s. Automobiles replaced horse-drawn transportation and became ubiquitous as improvements in assembly lines cut costs. Newly built electrical grids paved the way for rapid industrial and household electrification. The economies of Japan, the United States, and some European countries became more productive. Global growth averaged 3.6 percent in the 1920s, double that of the preceding two decades.

There is no question about the potential of recent technological innovations to transform lives across the world, in many dimensions. However, in light of the trends of the past two decades and the persistent slowdown in the fundamental sources of growth, our analysis concludes that the 2020s are more likely to be "disappointing" than "roaring" for the global economy, unless a comprehensive set of policies are put in place.

Trends are not destiny: Policies to boost potential growth

It is possible to reverse the slowdown in potential growth through structural policy interventions. Structural policies associated with higher investment in physical capital, improved human capital, and faster growth of the labor supply could raise potential growth by 0.7 percentage point a year in 2022-30—both globally and in EMDEs. This would offset the 0.4 percentage-point decline in global potential growth between 2011-21 and 2022-30 projected in the baseline scenario and most of the 1.0 percentage-point slowdown projected for EMDEs (figure O.6). Global potential growth would rise to 2.9 percent per year—above its 2011-21 average of 2.6 percent, but still well below its 2000-10 average of 3.5 percent; EMDE potential growth, at 4.7 percent per year, would remain below its 2011-21 average of 5.0 percent but by a much-reduced margin. Robust policy frameworks involving fiscal, monetary, and financial sector policies would need to

FIGURE O.6 **Policy options**

Economic reforms comparable with past achievements, or a major investment boost to meet climate change-related goals, could lift potential growth. EMDEs have room for services sector productivity improvements. Broad-based reforms to shipping and logistics as well as border procedures could lower the costs of goods trade.

A. Global potential growth under reform scenarios

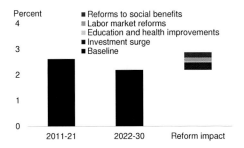

B. Potential growth in EMDEs in scenarios involving investment in climate-related infrastructure

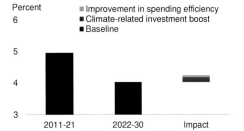

C. Composition of output and employment

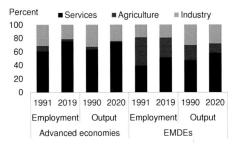

D. Reduction in overall trade costs associated with policy improvements

Sources: Nayyar, Hallward-Driemeier, and Davies (2021a); Penn World Table; World Bank.
Note: Averages weighted by gross domestic product (GDP). AEs = advanced economies; EMDEs = emerging market and developing economies.
A.-C. Arithmetic annual averages.
A. Scenarios assume a repeat, in each country, of each country's best 10-year improvement.
B. "Climate-related investment boost" assumes an increase in average annual investment over the course of 2022-30 of 2.3 percentage points of GDP, in line with the average of 13 countries covered in World Bank *Country Climate and Development Reports* (Argentina; China; Egypt, Arab Rep.; Ghana; Iraq; Jordan; Kazakhstan; Morocco; Peru; the Philippines; South Africa; Türkiye; and Vietnam). The regional differences are in line with Rozenberg and Fay (2019). "Improvement in spending efficiency" assumes that each EMDE moves up two quartiles in the distribution of spending efficiency.
C. Sample for employment includes 35 advanced economies and 143 EMDEs, with data until 2019. Sample for output includes 31 advanced economies and 140 EMDEs, with data until 2020.
D. Bars show the fraction of goods trade costs that would remain after policy improvements. Policy improvements assume that the average EMDE in the quartile of EMDEs with the poorest scores on the United Nations Conference on Trade and Development's Liner Shipping Connectivity Index and the World Bank's Logistics Performance Index improves to match the score of the average EMDE in the quartile of EMDEs with the best scores for the Liner Shipping Connectivity Index and Logistics Performance Index. The comprehensive package assumes that all three scores improve simultaneously. Data refer to 2018. Yellow line indicates 1 (that is, unchanged trade costs in 2018) among the sample of EMDEs scoring in the poorest quartile on these indicators.

accompany these policies. Interventions by the global community would also need to support them.

The book discusses measures to boost human capital, labor supply, and productivity and explores in depth policies to promote investment, services, and trade. It also explains the importance of strong macroeconomic policy frameworks and the need for support from the global community.

Investment. Policy makers in EMDEs can tap into opportunities to raise potential growth by focusing on interventions that can boost investment. Given the enormous challenges associated with climate change, there is a well-defined need for an ambitious investment push. Climate change is expected to exacerbate extreme poverty by reducing agricultural output, increasing food prices, and worsening food and water insecurity in EMDEs and increasing the disaster-related damages to the physical environment. As discussed earlier in this overview, climate-related disasters are becoming more common, and they weigh particularly heavily on vulnerable countries such as small states. They can also worsen government fiscal positions through lower tax receipts and lower productivity alongside increased spending on reconstruction and public services.

Addressing gaps between current spending on infrastructure and the level needed to meet development goals can promote investment growth. Making investment a priority in green infrastructure projects with high economic returns and fostering the widespread adoption of environmentally sustainable technologies can support higher growth levels in the long run while contributing to climate change mitigation. Sound investments aligned with climate goals in key areas—such as transport and energy, climate-smart agriculture and manufacturing, and land and water systems—can all boost long-term growth, while also enhancing resilience to future natural disasters.

Although green transitions need to be carefully managed, sustainable investments—including those by the private sector—offer significant opportunities. Besides their broader benefits, green investments may represent an important engine for job creation, as they tend to be labor intensive. Addressing climate change and other development challenges also requires structural reforms that encourage the mobilization of private capital and lower barriers of access for the private sector. In many EMDEs, governance and institutional reforms are necessary to improve and unify often-fragmented regulatory and institutional environments. Reforms that improve the business climate can stimulate private investment directly and amplify the positive effects of investment, such as less informality and more job creation. All of these policy interventions also help attract FDI.

All EMDE regions need to invest more heavily in infrastructure (chapter 4). This may be infrastructure intended to improve climate resilience, including that to protect against floods, storms, and drought and dampen their impact, especially in small states (EAP and LAC) and heavily agriculture-reliant economies (SAR and SSA). It may be infrastructure to improve chronically low levels of infrastructure development (SAR and SSA) or to accommodate rising levels of urbanization (EAP, LAC and SAR). Or it may be infrastructure to support productivity in sectors that employ a large proportion of the population (for example, agriculture in SSA) or to rebuild following conflict (ECA, MNA, and SSA) or to improve trade linkages (LAC and SAR).

The investment needed to achieve climate and development goals exceed many governments' ability to finance it. Hence, successfully leveraging private sector capital to boost investment requires a set of policies to balance the risks, costs, and returns of investment projects and overcoming common obstacles to private investment, such as poor business conditions, insufficient project pipelines, and underdeveloped domestic capital markets.

Labor supply and human capital. Policies can aim to raise the active share of the working-age population, in particular policies to "activate" discouraged workers or groups with historically low participation rates, such as women and younger and older workers. Globally, average female labor force participation in 2011-21, at 54 percent, was three-quarters that of men, which stood at 72 percent; the gap between male and female participation was even larger in EMDEs, at 25 percentage points. Similarly, in both EMDEs and advanced economies, the average participation rate of workers aged 55 years or older was about half that of 30- to 45-year-old workers, and labor force participation among those aged 19-29 years was only four-fifths that of 30-45 year olds.

A set of reforms that gradually raises participation rates in each five-year age group from 55-59 years onward and that lifts female labor force participation rates by their best 10-year improvement on record could increase global rates of potential growth by as much as 0.2 percentage point per year on average during 2022-30. Regions such as MNA and SAR could achieve considerably greater boosts to potential growth, in excess of 1 percentage point per year, if they raised female labor force participation from their current levels of about half of the EMDE average to the EMDE average.

Improvements to health and—especially—education could be one prong of such a set of reforms to boost labor force participation, since better-educated workers tend to be more firmly attached to labor markets. In addition, improvements in education and health outcomes on par with the best 10-year improvement on record could boost productivity and lift EMDE potential growth by an additional 0.1 percentage point per year, on average, for the remainder of this decade and more over the longer term.

Trade. Trade has flagged over the past decade. A major effort to rekindle it could yield large growth dividends over the next one. The costs added to internationally traded goods remain high: on average, they are almost equivalent to a 100 percent tariff, roughly doubling the costs of internationally traded goods relative to domestic goods (chapter 6). Transportation and logistics, non-tariff barriers, and policy-related standards and regulations account for the bulk of the costs; tariffs amount to only 5 percent of average costs of trade in goods. Trade costs for services tend to be even higher than those for goods, largely reflecting regulatory restrictions.

To reduce elevated trade costs in EMDEs will require comprehensive reform packages. Trade agreements can reduce trade costs and promote trade, especially if they lower non-tariff barriers as well as tariffs and generate momentum for further domestic reforms (Baldwin and Jaimovich 2010; Plummer 2007). However, even if the global environment is not conducive to progress in regard to such agreements, countries can take action at home to rekindle trade. For example, they can streamline trade processes and customs clearance requirements, enhance domestic trade-supporting infrastructure, increase competition in domestic logistics and in retail and wholesale trade, reduce tariffs, lower the costs of compliance with standards and regulations, and reduce corruption. Empirical analysis suggests that reforms that lift an EMDE in the quartile of countries with the highest shipping and logistics costs to the quartile of those with the lowest costs could cut its trade costs in half. For maximum effect, such reforms need to be embedded in broader improvements such as those in human capital and digital connectivity (Devarajan 2019; Okonjo-Iweala and Coulibaly 2019).

Trade can also play a critical role in climate-related transition (Devarajan et al. 2022). It has the potential to promote the production of goods and services necessary for transitioning to low-carbon economies. In addition, trade delivers goods and services that are key to helping countries recover from extreme weather events. However, evidence indicates that in some countries, greater carbon emissions have accompanied entry into global value chains in manufacturing and that global value chains have contributed to greater waste and increased shipping (World Bank 2020). Shipping accounts for 7 percent of global carbon emissions and 15 percent of global emissions of sulfur and nitrogen (World Bank 2020).

A number of policies can be implemented to reduce trade costs in a climate-friendly way. For example, policies can be designed to remove the current bias in many countries' tariff schedules favoring carbon-intensive goods and to eliminate restrictions on access to environmentally friendly goods and services (Brenton and Chemutai 2021; World Bank 2020). In addition, multilateral negotiations can focus not only on tariffs on environmental goods but also on nontariff measures and regulations affecting services—access to which is often vital for implementing the new technologies embodied in environmentally friendly goods.

Services. Policy interventions can also help countries unlock the potential of the services sector to drive economic growth (chapter 7). Supporting the diffusion of digital technologies in EMDEs remains central to delivering better growth outcomes. In this context, investing in ICT infrastructure, updating regulatory frameworks around data, and strengthening management capabilities and worker skills are important. Countries can promote the expansion of productive, high-skilled, offshorable services by enabling greater use of online communications and digital platforms, reducing barriers to services trade, and supporting training in relevant skills. Where education systems are weak, but reliable and widespread internet access exists, it would be possible to increase use of higher-quality online schooling and training. Digital technologies may expand access to finance in the poorest countries, enable more effective delivery of government services, and accelerate the trend toward the automation of some routine occupations. In addition, regulatory reforms can support investment to revive low-skilled contact services, such as transportation, that employ large numbers of people.

Climate change considerations will also influence the prospects for services-led growth. The services sector can play an important role in climate mitigation and adaptation. For instance, financial services can play a fundamental role in mobilizing the resources needed for necessary investments (Grippa, Schmittmann, and Suntheim 2019). Similarly, engineering and environmental consulting services will likely be central to enabling improvements in energy efficiency (World Economic Forum 2022).

Macroeconomic policies. Robust macroeconomic policy frameworks play an important role in boosting long-term growth prospects. They can help proactively smooth business cycles to avert the disruptions and distortions associated with adverse shocks. They can ensure that social protection systems are geared toward minimizing long-term damage from such shocks. In addition, they can instill confidence in sound policy making and buttress the credibility of institutions.

Robust fiscal and monetary policy frameworks are founded on transparent and rules-based approaches. Fiscal rules and medium-term budget frameworks can help countries maintain sustainable finances and accumulate reserves when their economies are doing well. These types of disciplined fiscal policy frameworks are especially critical nowadays to support growth prospects amid elevated debt levels and tight global financial conditions. In a deficit-neutral manner, they can guide government spending toward policies with long-term growth benefits, such as those in health, education, or transport, or expand revenue bases to increase financing for such priority policies. Better fiscal frameworks also assist monetary policy by restraining procyclical spending that could contribute to demand pressures.

A transparent and independent central bank will be better placed to maintain price stability, thereby helping to create a macroeconomic environment that is conducive to strong growth. In particular, by establishing an environment of low and stable inflation over the medium term, and thus fostering confidence in macroeconomic stability, central banks can support growth in private investment (World Bank 2022). Strong monetary policy frameworks are currently particularly important to overcome inflation and stabilize inflation expectations. Monetary policy can also play a countercyclical role through its management of interest rates and credit growth, thereby supporting investment growth when activity is weak and inflation is low but helping to contain investment when the economy is overheating.[8]

To avoid boom-bust cycles that do lasting damage to investment and potential growth, proactive financial sector supervision and regulation can mitigate risks—especially in countries with financial markets that are developing rapidly and becoming more integrated globally. In EMDEs without a prudential authority or prudential powers, creating or empowering institutions in these areas is a priority. In EMDEs with the appropriate institutions, flexible and well-targeted tools are needed to manage balance sheet mismatches, risk related to flows of foreign currency and capital, and misalignment of asset prices with economic fundamentals.

Global cooperation. Since many of the challenges EMDEs face transcend national borders, it is essential to strengthen global cooperation to address them. The increasing frequency and severity of climate-related disasters in recent years highlights the escalating costs of climate change: The global community must therefore work together to accelerate progress toward meeting the goals of the Paris Agreement. In addition, there is

---

[8] Fiscal challenges combined with weak growth prospects complicate monetary policy when inflation is high (Ha, Kose, and Ohnsorge 2022) and increase the risk of recession (Guenette, Kose, and Sugawara 2022).

a pressing need to reduce the economic, health, and social costs of climate change, many of which vulnerable populations in EMDEs, particularly LICs, bear disproprotionately. More pressingly, the global community can help expand the financing and capacity building needed to promote growth in EMDEs—including expanding it by scaling up adaptation to climate change, increasing green investments, and facilitating a green-energy transition (Bhattachariya, Kharas, and MacArthur 2023). The increase in investment spending (relative to GDP) needed to achieve the SDGs will be much larger for LICs than for the average EMDE. That implies that substantial additional financing from the global community and the private sector will be needed to close investment gaps in LICs. For some LICs that are already in—or at high risk of—debt distress, debt relief may need to accompany such financing to allow them to steer spending toward development goals instead of debt service.

Synopsis

The book features three interconnected parts. Part I analyzes the evolution of global and regional potential growth using a new comprehensive database. Part II focuses on global and regional investment dynamics and policies to promote investment growth. Part III presents a detailed analysis of prospects for potential growth and policy measures that can lift it. It turns to the roles of services and trade as engines of long-term economic growth. The book presents a wide menu of policy options for improving growth prospects in each chapter.

The remainder of this introduction presents a summary of each chapter. After establishing the motivation of the chapter, each summary explains the main questions the chapter explores, its contributions to the literature, and its analytical findings. It then discusses future research directions.

Part I. Potential Growth: An Economy's Speed Limit

Chapter 1 explores the conceptual framework and measurement of potential growth. Based on a new database introduced in the chapter, it describes the slowdown in potential growth in the past decade and its sources. Chapter 2 delves deeper into regional differences in the evolution of potential growth, describes regional prospects, and offers region-specific policy options.

Chapter 1. Potential Not Realized: An International Database of Potential Growth

In this chapter, Kilic Celik, Kose, Ohnsorge, and Ruch introduce the most comprehensive database of estimates of potential growth available to date. Potential growth is critical to reducing poverty; raising the resources needed to invest in solving global challenges; creating jobs and generating wage growth, especially in the formal sector; and achieving or sustaining debt sustainability.[9]

---

[9] Ohnsorge and Yu (2022) discuss more broadly the challenges in shifting informal activity into the formal economy. For a discussion of the challenges of low growth for debt sustainability, see Kose, Ohnsorge, and Sugawara (2022), and of government debt reduction, see Kose et al. (2022).

Based on an extensive analysis of the earlier literature, the authors present three main approaches to estimating growth in potential output—each of which has its advantages and disadvantages.

- *Production function approach.* The first approach measures potential growth based on production function estimates. This makes it possible to study the contributions of what theory suggests are the fundamental drivers of growth—the growth of inputs of the factors of production (labor and capital) and technological progress—but involves assumptions that may be viewed as restrictive.

- *Time-series methods.* The second approach obtains measures of potential growth from statistical filters that generate smoothed versions of actual output growth data as measures of potential output. This may provide the most consistency between estimates of potential growth and output gaps, on the one hand, and indicators of domestic demand pressures, on the other. However, it provides no links between estimated potential growth and its plausible fundamental drivers.

- *Long-term growth expectations.* A third approach uses long-term (say, five-year-ahead) forecasts of output growth from economic analysts, which may be assumed to incorporate the forecasters' judgments about potential growth but whose drivers are highly uncertain.

Chapter 1 introduces the most comprehensive international database for the nine most common measures of potential growth based on these three approaches. This database and the analysis in this chapter serve as the foundation for chapters 2 and 5—which examine past and prospective potential growth globally, by country group, and by region and policies that can be implemented to improve them. Specifically, this chapter addresses the following questions.

- How has global potential growth evolved in the past three decades?

- How have recessions and other adverse events affected potential growth?

- Through which channels have such events affected potential growth?

Contributions. Chapter 1 makes the following contributions to the literature. First, it introduces the first comprehensive database for the nine most commonly used measures of potential growth for the largest-available country sample, up to 173 economies (37 advanced economies and 136 EMDEs) over 1981-2021. One of the nine measures is based on the production function approach, five are based on the application of univariate time-series filters (Hodrick-Prescott, Baxter-King, Christiano-Fitzgerald, Butterworth, and unobserved-components filters), one applies a multivariate Kalman filter, and two are based on analysts' long-term growth forecasts.[10]

---

[10] Univariate filters are applied only to actual output; multivariate filters are applied to multiple series, including actual output. Both types of filters generate smoothed output series that are considered estimates of potential output.

By including a measure that builds potential growth from its fundamental drivers, the database allows later chapters to examine the role of policy initiatives such as an investment push to address climate change. Previous studies have limited themselves to a single method of measuring potential growth, such as the production function approach (OECD 2014) or multivariate filters (ADB 2016; IMF 2015). The database updates an earlier version published before the pandemic (Kilic Celik, Kose, and Ohnsorge 2020).

Second, chapter 1 documents that all measures of potential growth show a decline in global potential growth in 2011-21, relative to 2000-10, and that this decline was internationally widespread. Earlier studies have documented the decline for only a subset of measures (for example, Chalaux and Guillemette 2019; Kilic Celik, Kose, and Ohnsorge 2020).

Third, chapter 1 describes the first systematic study of the long-term damage to potential growth from a range of short-term economic disruptions—such as recessions, banking crises, and epidemics—in a large set of countries and for a wide range of measures of potential growth. Only a few earlier studies have estimated the effects of recessions on growth in potential output, and they were confined to a smaller sample of countries and the production function approach (Furceri and Mourougane 2012; Mourougane 2017). Chapter 1 broadens the earlier research by estimating the effects of recessions, banking crises, and epidemics in a large sample of advanced economies and EMDEs and for a wide range of measures of potential growth.

Fourth, chapter 1 uses a set of local-projection models to estimate empirically the channels through which short-term economic disruptions dampen long-term potential growth. Specifically, it estimates, in a consistent framework, the effects of disruptions on the growth of the labor force, the growth of the capital stock (through investment), and the growth of TFP. Previous studies have typically examined overall effects on output growth or effects through individual channels only.[11]

Findings. Chapter 1 reports several novel findings. First, an internationally widespread decline in potential growth occurred in 2011-21 relative to 2000-10 (figure O.7). All estimates of potential growth, globally and for both advanced economies and EMDEs, show this decline. Global potential growth, as estimated using the production function approach, fell to 2.6 percent a year during 2011-21 from 3.5 percent a year during 2000-10; advanced-economy potential growth fell to 1.4 percent a year during 2011-21 from 2.2 percent a year during 2000-10; and EMDE potential growth fell to 5.0 percent a year during 2011-21 from 6.0 percent a year during 2000-10. The weakening of

---

[11] The theoretical literature has modeled several mechanisms through which output disruptions may cause lasting damage: lower expected profitability of productivity-increasing research and development (Fatás 2000) or of the adoption of new, productivity-increasing technology (Anzoategui et al. 2017); lower asset prices (Caballero and Simsek 2017); restricted firm access to credit and start-up capital (Queralto 2013; Wilms, Swank, and de Haan 2018); resource misallocation (Furceri et al. 2021); and human capital losses (Blanchard and Summers 1987; Lockwood 1991). Empirical estimates have shown some of these mechanisms at work during past recessions (Nguyen and Qian 2014; Oulton and Sebastia-Barriel 2016). None of these studies, however, systematically estimates and compares the various channels through which short-term disruptions reduce potential growth.

FIGURE O.7 Evolution of potential growth

Potential growth slowed in 2011-21 from 2000-10 across country groups, with all major drivers of growth weakening. Adverse events—such as banking crises, recessions, and epidemics—damaged potential growth by persistently lowering total factor productivity growth, investment growth (recessions and epidemics), and employment growth (epidemics).

A. Estimates of potential growth (range across methodologies)

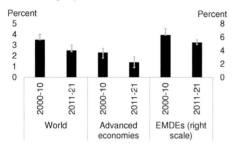

B. Contributions to potential growth

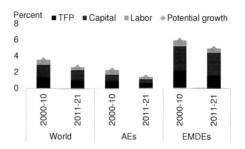

C. Response of growth in potential output five years after events

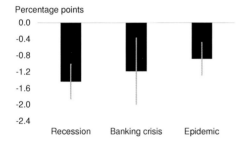

D. Response of potential TFP growth five years after events

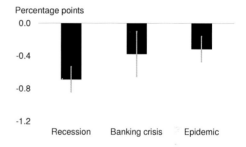

E. Response of investment growth five years after events

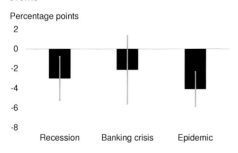

F. Response of employment growth five years after events

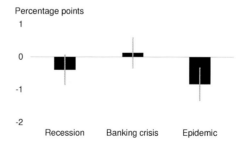

Sources: Penn World Table; World Bank.
Note: AEs = advanced economies; EMDEs = emerging market and developing economies; TFP = total factor productivity.
A. Blue bars denote production function-based estimates. Vertical lines indicate range of eight filter- or expectations-based estimates. Decade averages of average estimates, weighted by gross domestic product (GDP), of potential growth of varying samples.
B. Based on production function approach.
C.-F. Blue bars are coefficient estimates from local-projections model. Vertical lines indicate 90 percent confidence intervals. Chapter 1 describes sample and methodology.

potential growth was highly synchronized across countries: during 2011-21, potential growth was below its 2000-10 average in 96 percent of advanced economies and 57 percent of EMDEs. This widespread decline reflected a multitude of factors. In terms of the production function framework, all the fundamental drivers of growth faded in 2011-21: TFP growth slowed, investment growth weakened, and labor force growth declined.

Second, recessions were associated, on average, with a decline of about 1.4 percentage points in potential growth even after five years. This refers to potential growth estimated using the production function approach; other measures yielded different estimates (with a range of 0.2-1.4 percentage points), but all were statistically significant. The effect was somewhat stronger in EMDEs—with potential growth 1.6 percentage points lower five years after the average recession—than in advanced economies, in which potential growth was, on average, 1.3 percentage points lower.

Third, recessions tended to have a more severe medium-term impact on potential growth than other adverse events. Banking crises were associated with initially larger falls in potential growth, with those falls peaking at 1.8 percentage points after two years, as a result of collapses in investment. However, rapid recoveries in investment tended to follow these declines, such that the fall in potential growth after five years was only 1.2 percentage points. Epidemics were associated with more modest, but still statistically significant, short- and medium-term declines in potential growth. These effects were more severe in EMDEs than in advanced economies, possibly reflecting the greater ability of advanced economies to limit the economic damage with fiscal and monetary policy support as well as their better-developed health care systems.

Fourth, the chapter provides evidence that recessions affected potential growth through multiple channels. Five years after an average recession, the growth rate of investment was 3 percentage points lower than in "normal" years, and those of employment and TFP were both 0.7 percentage point lower. This contrasts with what took place in respect to banking crises, which tended to be associated with lasting losses of TFP growth, and in respect to epidemics, which were often associated only with lasting employment losses. These losses possibly reflected prolonged effects on the health of the labor force and behavioral responses to epidemics.

Fifth, different estimates of potential growth were found to display different features. Estimates based on forecasts tended to be the highest, and those based on univariate filtering techniques the lowest. Estimates based on filtering techniques tended to be the most volatile and to track actual growth most closely, as expected. Estimates based on the production function approach tended to be the most stable and the least correlated in the short term with actual growth.

Chapter 2. Regional Dimensions of Potential Growth: Hopes and Realities

In chapter 2, Kasyanenko, Kenworthy, Kilic Celik, Ruch, Vashakmadze, and Wheeler build on chapter 1 to explore regional dimensions of potential growth. Their starting point is the finding that potential growth slowed in 2011-21 relative to the preceding decade in almost all of the World Bank's six EMDE regions. Yet wide differences are apparent in recent developments and prospects across the regions, and these have implications for regional policy priorities. Chapter 2 explores these regional differences by considering the following questions.

- How have potential growth and its drivers evolved in each region since the turn of the century?

- What are the prospects for regional potential growth?

- What policies would lift regional potential growth?

Contributions. Chapter 2 adds regional detail to the analysis of global potential growth in chapters 1 and 5 and does so in a consistent manner across the EMDE regions. Drawing on a rich body of regional studies and using the new database introduced in chapter 1, the chapter provides the first systematic analysis of potential growth in all six EMDE regions. Other major cross-country studies of potential growth have largely focused on advanced economies (Dabla-Norris et al. 2015; IMF 2015; OECD 2014) or Asian economies (ADB 2016). Chapter 2 examines data for up to 53 EMDEs—6 in EAP, 9 in ECA, 16 in LAC, 5 in MNA, 3 in SAR, and 14 in SSA—over the past two decades (2000-2021) and considers prospects for the remainder of this decade (2022-30).

Findings. Chapter 2 documents an array of regional differences (figure O.8). First, the slowdown in potential growth between 2000-10 and 2011-21 was steepest in MNA, followed by EAP, although potential growth in EAP remained higher than in all other regions except SAR. ECA and LAC experienced less pronounced slowdowns, but potential growth in LAC remained the lowest among all EMDE regions. In SAR, potential growth was almost unchanged, at the highest rate among EMDE regions, while in SSA, potential growth weakened only moderately but remained one of the lowest among EMDE regions, at about half the average for SAR.

Second, EAP is expected to show the sharpest decline among EMDE regions in the growth of both aggregate and per capita potential output during 2022-30. The decline is expected to amount to about 1.6 percentage points a year, on average, and mainly reflects slower projected capital accumulation and TFP growth in China as the country implements policies to shift from an investment-led to an increasingly consumption-led growth model. ECA is projected to experience the second-largest decline in potential growth in 2022-30, with that decline resulting in part from the fallout of the war in Ukraine, but also from continued weakness in labor force growth. In SSA, potential growth is expected to decline moderately as strengthening TFP growth is expected to partially offset slowing investment and population growth. Elsewhere, potential growth is projected to be broadly unchanged in LAC and SAR and to rise in MNA in 2022-30 as strengthening TFP growth offsets demographic headwinds to potential growth.

FIGURE O.8 Potential growth in EMDE regions

The Middle East and North Africa (MNA) experienced the steepest slowdown in potential growth between 2000-10 and 2011-21, followed by East Asia and Pacific (EAP), although potential growth in EAP remained higher than in all other regions except South Asia (SAR). In 2022-30, EAP is expected to have the sharpest declines in growth of aggregate and per capita gross domestic product (GDP), mainly reflecting slower capital accumulation in China. Potential growth is projected to be broadly unchanged in LAC, SAR, and SSA and to rise in MNA; stronger total factor productivity (TFP) growth and, in SAR and SSA, stronger investment growth are expected to offset demographic headwinds.

A. Changes in potential growth between 2000-10 and 2011-21 (across methodologies)

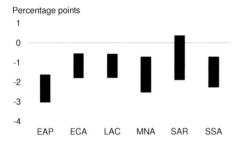

B. Potential growth

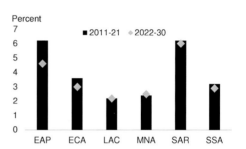

C. Contributions to potential growth

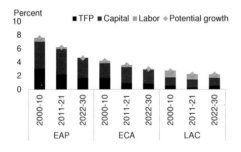

D. Contributions to potential growth

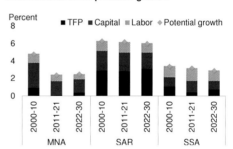

Sources: Penn World Table; World Bank.

Note: ECA = Europe and Central Asia; LAC = Latin America and the Caribbean; MNA = Middle East and North Africa; SSA = Sub-Saharan Africa. Period averages of annual GDP-weighted averages.

A. Samples differ across measures, depending on data availability. PF = production function approach. MVF = multivariate filter-based. UVF = univariate filter-based (specifically, the Hodrick-Prescott filter). "Exp." = estimates based on five-year-ahead *World Economic Outlook* growth forecasts. For SAR, insufficient data available for filter-based estimates until 2010. The sample includes three countries in EAP (China, Philippines, and Thailand), six countries in ECA (Bulgaria, Croatia, Hungary, Kazakhstan, Poland, and Romania), ten countries in LAC (Bolivia, Brazil, Chile, Colombia, Costa Rica, Honduras, Mexico, Paraguay, Peru, and Uruguay), three countries in MNA (Jordan, Morocco, and Tunisia), four countries in SAR (Bangladesh, India, Pakistan, and Sri Lanka), and three countries in SSA (Cameroon, Namibia, and South Africa). Due to the limited sample, other measures are excluded from the SAR region.

B. C.D. Based on production function approach. Sample includes 4 countries in EAP, 9 in ECA, 15 in LAC, 7 in MNA, 2 in SAR, and 13 in SSA. Note that quantitative estimates may differ from those presented in panels A and B because of sample differences. Panels A and B ensures sample consistency across measures; panels C and D ensure sample consistency across time. 2022-30 are forecasts.

Third, persistently weak TFP growth in LAC, MNA, and SSA makes policy action to raise productivity growth especially important for these regions. There is also considerable room to boost labor force growth in MNA and SAR by encouraging female labor force participation and, in EAP and ECA, by raising participation among older workers. SAR and MNA lag especially far behind other EMDE regions in female labor force participation (Klasen 2019). LAC and SSA have particularly weak prospects for investment growth, and a wide range of measures is likely to be required to reignite it. Chapter 4 discusses such measures. A climate-related investment push could catalyze a boost to potential growth in all EMDE regions.

Part II. Investment: Time for a Big Push

Part II of this volume describes the weakening of investment growth in EMDEs in the past decade, examines its causes, and considers policy options to help lift investment growth. Chapter 3 examines trends in a broad group of EMDEs, and chapter 4 delves deeper into regional characteristics and identifies region-specific policy priorities for lifting investment growth.

Chapter 3. The Global Investment Slowdown: Challenges and Policies

In this chapter, Stamm and Vorisek draw attention to the weakening of investment growth in EMDEs even before the onset of the COVID-19 pandemic (figure O.9).[12] By the time the pandemic began in early 2020, investment growth had already slowed in EMDEs over the previous decade, from nearly 11 percent in 2010 to less than 4 percent in 2019. When China is excluded from the EMDE group, investment growth had fallen more sharply: from about 9 percent in 2010 to just under 1 percent in 2019. The slowdown occurred in all regions, in both commodity-importing and commodity-exporting country groups, and in a large portion of individual economies. In advanced economies, by contrast, investment growth was more sluggish but also more stable, hovering around its long-term average of 2 percent per year.

In 2020, the pandemic triggered a severe investment contraction in EMDEs excluding China—a far deeper decline than in the 2009 global recession triggered by the global financial crisis. Even when China is included, EMDEs did not avoid an investment contraction in 2020, as they had in 2009. In advanced economies, however, because large-scale fiscal support packages and expansionary monetary policies buttressed investment, it shrank less in 2020 than in 2009. After having rebounded sharply in 2021, investment growth in EMDEs is projected to slow back to rates that are about half the average of the previous two decades.

Slowing investment growth is a concern because it is critical to sustaining growth of potential output and per capita income. Capital accumulation raises labor productivity,

---

[12] Throughout the book, "investment" refers to real gross fixed-capital formation (public and private combined). Investment growth is measured as the annual percent change in real investment. In international averages, investment growth rates are weighted by average 2010-19 investment levels. For a discussion of factor reallocation across firms and sectors, see Dieppe (2021).

FIGURE O.9 **Global investment**

The pandemic-induced 2020 global recession was associated with steep investment contractions and more muted subsequent recoveries than was the 2009 global recession. The weakening of investment growth in the 2010s reflected a range of factors, including slower credit growth, deteriorating terms of trade for commodity exporters, slowing reform momentum, and a shift in China's growth strategy away from reliance on fixed investment.

A. Investment growth

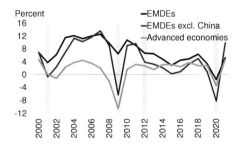

B. Contributions to EMDE investment growth, by country

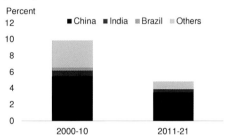

C. Growth in private investment

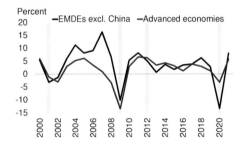

D. Investment in EMDEs around global recessions

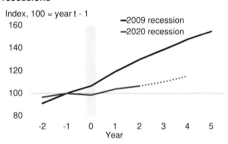

E. Investment growth in EMDEs with high and low credit growth, 2000-21

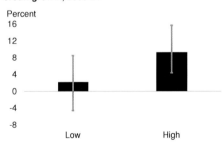

F. Total factor productivity growth in EMDEs with high and low investment growth, 2000-21

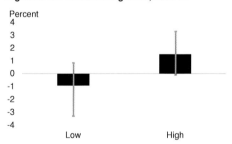

Sources: Haver Analytics; World Bank.
Note: Period averages of annual GDP-weighted averages. Investment refers to gross fixed-capital formation. EMDEs = emerging market and developing economies.
A.C. Investment-weighted averages. Shaded areas indicate global recessions (in 2009 and 2020) and slowdowns (in 2001 and 2012). Sample for aggregate investment (panel A) includes 69 EMDEs and 35 advanced economies. Sample for private investment (panel C) includes 32 EMDEs (China is excluded) and 11 advanced economies.
B. Bars show the percentage-point contribution of each country or country group to EMDE investment growth during the indicated years. Height of the bars is average EMDE investment growth during the indicated years. Sample includes 69 EMDEs.
D. On the horizontal axis, year 0 refers to the year of global recessions in 2009 and 2020. Dotted portion of red line represents forecasts. Sample includes 69 EMDEs.
E.F. Bars show group medians; vertical lines show interquartile ranges. "Low" and "High" indicate years when real growth in private sector credit observations (panel E) or investment growth observations (panel F) were in the bottom and top third of the distribution, respectively, during 2000-21. Difference in medians between "Low" and "High" subsamples is significant at the 1 percent level. Sample includes 69 EMDEs.

the key determinant of real wages and household incomes, both through capital deepening—equipping workers with more capital—and by embodying productivity-enhancing technological advances.

Slowing investment growth has held back progress toward meeting the SDGs and fulfilling commitments made under the Paris Agreement on climate change. Meeting these goals and commitments will require filling substantial unmet infrastructure needs, including growing needs for climate-resilient infrastructure and infrastructure that reduces net emissions of greenhouse gases. Given limited fiscal space in EMDEs, such scaling up of investment will require additional financing from the private sector and the international community.

Against this backdrop, chapter 3 addresses four questions:

- How has investment growth evolved over the past decade, and how does the performance of investment during the 2020 global recession compare with its performance during previous recessions?

- What are the key factors associated with investment growth?

- What does weak investment growth imply for development prospects?

- Which policies can help promote investment growth?

Contributions. Chapter 3 makes several contributions to the literature on investment. It provides the first analysis of investment growth in a large sample of EMDEs since the pandemic and Russia's invasion of Ukraine. Moreover, because FDI is a potentially critical source of technology spillovers and financing, the chapter reviews a large set of studies on the link between FDI and output or aggregate domestic investment.

In addition, the chapter examines the likely medium- and long-term consequences of the damage to investment in EMDEs from the pandemic and from Russia's invasion of Ukraine, focusing on the effects on productivity, growth in potential output, trade, and the ability to achieve the SDGs and climate-related goals. Finally, the chapter describes policies to revive investment growth, including identifying opportunities the pandemic created.

Previous studies of investment in EMDEs have generally been based on pre-global financial crisis data, confined to analysis of the behavior of investment around the global financial crisis, or focused on specific regions.[13] A number of studies have explored

---

[13] See, for example, the analysis of the drivers of investment in Anand and Tulin (2014); Bahal, Raissi, and Tulin (2018); Caselli, Pagano, and Schivardi (2003); Cerra et al. (2017); and Qureshi, Diaz-Sanchez, and Varoudakis (2015). Firm-level studies include Li, Magud, and Valencia (2015) and Magud and Sosa (2015). On investment weakness, see Banerjee, Kearns, and Lombardi (2015); IMF (2015); Leboeuf and Fay (2016); and Ollivaud, Guillemette, and Turner (2016).

investment weakness in advanced economies. This study updates and extends two previous studies of investment trends and correlates in a large sample of EMDEs (World Bank 2017a, 2019a).

Findings. Chapter 3 presents four main findings. First, investment in EMDEs has recovered more slowly from the trough of the COVID-19 pandemic in 2020 than it did from the 2009 recession that followed the global financial crisis. In EMDEs excluding China, investment shrank by about 2 percentage points more in 2020 than during the 2009 global recession, despite easier financial conditions and the provision of sizable fiscal stimulus in many large EMDEs. This partly reflects the more widespread impact of the pandemic on investment: investment shrank in nearly three-quarters of EMDEs in 2020, compared with just over 50 percent of EMDEs in 2009. The effects of the pandemic, the war in Ukraine, and monetary policy tightening by major central banks have extended the prolonged and broad-based slowdown in investment growth in EMDEs in the 2010s, which occurred in all regions and in both commodity-exporting and commodity-importing economies. Growth in both private and public investment was more sluggish during the 2010s than in the previous decade.

Second, the weakening of investment growth in EMDEs over the past decade has reflected a wide range of headwinds. It has been correlated with weaker output growth, declining net capital inflows relative to GDP, slower real growth in private sector credit, and a deterioration of the terms of trade energy exporters face. Conversely, spurts in reform of the investment climate tended to be associated with stronger real investment growth.

Third, after a robust rebound in 2021, investment growth is projected to average 3.5 percent per year in 2022-24 in EMDEs, about half its 2000-21 average, and 4.1 percent a year in EMDEs excluding China—one-fifth less than the 2000-21 average. For all EMDEs, projected investment growth through 2024 will be insufficient to return investment to its prepandemic (2010-19) trend. This investment outlook dampens long-term prospects for the growth of output and productivity as well as global trade and makes meeting development and climate goals even more challenging.

Fourth, a sustained improvement in investment growth in EMDEs will require both the use of domestic policy tools and, for some of them, international financial support—with appropriate prescriptions dependent on country circumstances. Macroeconomic policies can support investment in a number of ways, but particularly by encouraging private investment through establishing confidence in macroeconomic stability and improving business climates. Reducing unproductive expenditures and subsidies and strengthening spending efficiency and revenue collection can increase public investment. To boost private investment, institutional reforms could address a range of impediments and inefficiencies, such as high business start-up costs, weak property rights, inefficient labor and product market policies, weak corporate governance, costly trade regulation, and small financial sectors. Setting appropriate, predictable rules governing investment, including rules for public-private partnerships, is also important.

Fifth, a review of the literature since 1990 finds mixed evidence on the relationship between FDI and output growth but a mostly positive relationship between FDI and domestic investment. That said, several country characteristics, time period specifics, and features of FDI have influenced the relationship between FDI, output growth, and investment. Greenfield investment in upstream and export-intensive, nonprimary sectors has tended to be more conducive to growth and aggregate investment. FDI has also tended to raise growth and investment more in countries with better institutions, more skilled labor forces, greater financial development, and trade openness.

Chapter 4. Regional Dimensions of Investment: Moving in the Right Direction?

In chapter 4, Kasyanenko, Kenworthy, Ruch, Vashakmadze, Vorisek, and Wheeler note that slowdowns in investment growth between the periods 2000-10 and 2011-21 occurred in all six EMDE regions. Several of these regions have mediocre outlooks for investment growth, with 2021's strong rebound from the 2020 investment collapse having subsided. Given the importance of investment growth for growth in potential output, this puts a premium on policies that can help meet the large and diverse investment needs of countries across all six EMDE regions.

Chapter 4 explores cross-regional differences in investment growth by addressing the following questions:

- How has investment growth evolved in each of the six EMDE regions?

- What are the current and prospective investment needs of each EMDE region?

- Which policies can help address investment needs in each EMDE region?

Contributions. Chapter 4 adds regional detail to the analysis of global investment growth in the previous chapter, applying a consistent framework across all EMDE regions. It draws on a rich body of regional studies that have examined the constraints on investment and possible policy solutions.

Findings. Chapter 4 identifies several regional patterns. First, investment growth slowed in the past decade in all EMDE regions, but most sharply in EAP and MNA (figure O.10). In EAP, a policy shift in China aimed at reducing reliance on credit-fueled investment for economic growth and mitigating risks to financial stability was largely responsible for the slowdown. In MNA, an oil price slide in 2014-16, armed conflicts, and persistent policy uncertainty in several countries contributed to the slowdown.

Second, investment growth is projected to remain well below its 2000-21 average in the near term in EAP, ECA, LAC, and SAR but to be close to its two-decade average in MNA and SSA. Consensus long-term (five-year-ahead) forecasts for investment growth have been downgraded repeatedly. Annual average investment growth in 2022-30 is now forecast to be 0.3-1.8 percentage points lower, on average, than in 2011-21 in all regions except in LAC and SAR, where adverse shocks that depressed investment growth in the 2010s are not expected to recur.

FIGURE O.10 Investment in EMDE regions

Investment growth slowed sharply in all EMDE regions in 2011-21 but most sharply in East Asia and Pacific (EAP) and the Middle East and North Africa (MNA). It is expected to remain below its 2011-21 average in 2022-30 except in Latin America and the Caribbean (LAC) and South Asia (SAR), where it is assumed that the adverse shocks that depressed investment growth in the 2010s will not be repeated.

A. Investment growth, by region

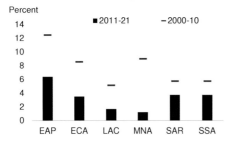

B. Investment growth by region

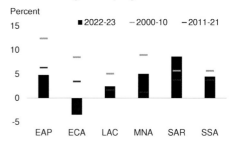

C. Regional shares of EMDE investment

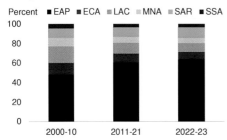

D. Contribution to EMDE investment growth

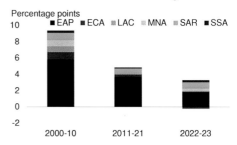

E. Five-year-ahead forecasts for investment growth

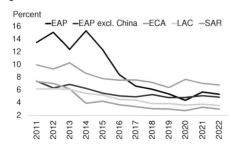

F. Actual and forecast investment growth

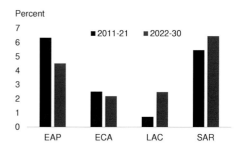

Sources: Consensus Economics; World Bank.

Note: Geometric means over indicated time spans of investment-weighted averages (at real fixed investment in constant U.S. dollars). ECA = Europe and Central Asia; EMDEs = emerging market and developing economies; SSA = Sub-Saharan Africa.

A.B. Sample includes 8 economies in EAP, 12 economies in ECA, 19 economies in LAC, 9 economies in MNA, 3 economies in SAR, and 19 economies in SSA.

C.D. Shares for 2000-10, 2011-21, and 2022-23 are simple averages of weighted real investment growth. Sample includes 8 economies in EAP, 12 economies in ECA, 19 economies in LAC, 9 economies in MNA, 3 economies in SAR, and 19 economies in SSA.

E.F. Include data for six economies in EAP (China, Indonesia, Malaysia, Philippines, Thailand, Vietnam), seven economies in ECA (Bulgaria, Croatia, Hungary, Poland, Romania, Russian Federation, Ukraine), six economies in LAC (Argentina, Brazil, Chile, Colombia, Mexico, Peru) and one economy in SAR (India). Single-year missing data are interpolated.

F. Geometric mean of actual investment growth in 2011-21 and of current-year to eight-year-ahead consensus forecasts for investment growth for 2022-30, as of September 2022. Includes six economies each in EAP, ECA, and LAC, and one economy in SAR.

Third, all regions have large needs for investment in physical and human capital, whether it is to mitigate and adapt to climate change and reverse pandemic-related learning losses (all regions); improve very low levels of infrastructure development (SAR and SSA); accommodate rising levels of urbanization (EAP, LAC, and SAR); support productivity growth, particularly in sectors that employ large proportions of the population (for example, agriculture in SSA); rebuild following conflicts (ECA, MNA, and SSA); improve trade linkages (LAC and SAR); or prepare for future public health crises (EAP and SSA).

Fourth, a range of policies is required to lift investment. Priorities include strengthening the efficiency of public investment (especially in SAR and SSA), boosting private investment (especially in LAC and MNA), and expanding the availability of financing for investment, which is a significant need in all regions.

Part III. Policies: Recognition, Formulation, and Implementation

Part III of this volume examines policy options for improving long-term growth prospects. Using the conceptual framework provided by the production function, chapter 5 develops scenarios that enable the benefits to potential growth from a range of possible policy actions to be quantified. Chapters 6 and 7 focus on two areas in which there may be considerable untapped growth potential that the right policies could unlock: international trade (chapter 6) and the services sector (chapter 7).

Chapter 5. Prospects for Potential Growth: Risks, Rewards, and Policies

In this chapter, Kilic Celik, Kose, and Ohnsorge start from the observation in chapter 1 that global potential growth in 2011-21 was significantly lower than that in 2000-10. This weakening of growth was widespread globally, across country groups, and in the majority of countries.

This trend decline raises concerns about the underlying strength of economic growth over the next several years, following the recovery from the pandemic-related recession of 2020. The chapter sets out a baseline projection that shows a further slowing of global potential growth in 2022-30. This baseline projection is subject to downside risks from a number of adverse events, including climate-related disasters. In some EMDEs, especially commodity-exporting economies in ECA and MNA, a further slowing of potential growth could set back convergence of per capita incomes with those of advanced economies. The projected slowdown in potential growth is therefore a major concern in regard to prospects for growth and income convergence in EMDEs and a formidable challenge to the international community's ability to meet its development goals.

Chapter 5 explores these issues by addressing the following questions:

* What are the prospects for growth in potential output?

* What are the main risks that could lower future potential growth?

* What policy options are available to lift growth in potential output?

Contributions. Chapter 5 makes three key contributions to the literature on potential growth. It presents the first comprehensive set of projections of growth in potential output for the largest sample of countries for which data are available—83 countries (30 advanced economies and 53 EMDEs) that account for 95 percent of global GDP. The chapter's estimates of and projections for growth in potential output are based on the production function approach presented in chapter 1.

Second, the chapter analyzes the possible effects of weather-related disasters, which are expected to become even more frequent because of climate change. It also examines the possible effects that investment to alleviate the effects of climate change may have on potential growth. Several studies—reviewed in Botzen, Deschenes, and Sanders (2019); Klomp and Valckx (2014); and Shabnam (2014)—have found mixed evidence for both short-term and long-term effects of natural disasters on incomes and output growth, with possibly larger and more lasting effects in LICs. Broadly consistent with this literature, chapter 5 documents small, but statistically significant, damage to growth in the short term, which dissipates quickly. The chapter goes on to estimate the impact that investment to mitigate, or reduce the damage from, climate change may have on potential growth, drawing on the investment needs estimated in chapter 3.

Third, chapter 5 explores, in a consistent framework, policy options to lift growth in potential output. A large literature has considered the impact of different policies and other factors on growth, including human capital improvements (World Bank 2018), governance improvements (World Bank 2017b), increased international trade and integration into global value chains (World Bank 2020), new technologies (World Bank 2016, 2019b), and labor market changes (World Bank 2013). In contrast to the analysis in these and other earlier studies, the discussion of growth-enhancing policy options in chapter 5 is based on the framework provided by the production function approach.[14]

Findings. Chapter 5 presents several findings. First, the slowdown in potential growth in the past two decades, described in chapter 1, is projected to extend into the remainder of this decade. Trends in the fundamental drivers of growth suggest that potential growth in global output will slow further, by 0.4 percentage point a year on average, to 2.2 percent a year during 2022-30 (figure O.11). About half of this projected slowdown is due to demographic factors from an aging population, including slowing growth in the working-age population and declining labor force participation.

EMDE potential growth is projected to weaken considerably more, by about 1.0 percentage point a year, to 4.0 percent a year during 2022-30. In advanced economies, potential growth is expected to slow by 0.2 percentage point a year, to 1.2 percent a year, on average, during 2022-30. The slowdown will be internationally widespread: Economies accounting for nearly 80 percent of global GDP, including most EMDEs,

---

[14] Several studies have investigated the link between the growth of output or productivity and structural reforms, focusing on the near-term benefits (Prati, Onorato, and Papageorgiou 2013) or productivity effects (Adler et al. 2017; Dabla-Norris, Ho, and Kyobe 2016). In some of these studies, the sample has consisted mostly of advanced economies (Banerji et al. 2017; de Haan and Wiese 2022; IMF 2015, 2016b).

are projected to experience a slowdown in potential growth between 2011-21 and 2022-30. Global potential growth over the remainder of this decade could be even slower than projected in this baseline scenario, by another 0.2-0.9 percentage point a year, if investment growth, improvements in health and education outcomes, or developments in labor markets disappoint or if unforeseen adverse events materialize.

Second, climate change is likely to have a sizable adverse effect on growth in potential output over the remainder of this decade, given that the frequency and intensity of weather-related disasters is expected to increase. Over the past two decades, the average natural disaster has lowered potential growth in the affected country by 0.1 percentage point in the year of the disaster. Over the medium term, however, the damage to potential growth has varied widely depending on the speed and magnitude of reconstruction efforts. For example, three years after a climate disaster, TFP growth has been anywhere between nil and 10 percent lower than in countries and years without disasters (Dieppe, Kilic Celik, and Okou 2020). The average small state has suffered losses and damages from climate-related disasters of about 5 percent of GDP per year, on average (World Bank 2023). However, increased infrastructure investment to alleviate the effects of climate change could more than offset this damage. For example, the literature review in chapter 3 summarizes estimates of climate-related investment needs averaging 2.3 percentage points of GDP per year; for EMDEs, this is equivalent to about one-third of the investment boost that would occur if they repeated their best 10-year investment growth performance.[15] Such additional investment over the remainder of this decade could raise global potential growth by 0.1 percentage point and EMDE potential growth by 0.3 percentage point a year.

Third, a number of policies could help reverse the projected further weakening of global potential growth and return it to its 2011-21 average rate. Reforms associated with higher investment in physical capital, enhanced human capital, and faster growth of the labor supply could raise potential growth by 0.7 percentage point a year in 2022-30, both globally and in EMDEs. This would offset the 0.4 percentage-point decline in global potential growth between 2011-21 and 2022-30 projected in the baseline scenario and most of the 1.0 percentage-point slowdown projected for EMDEs. The policy options considered here could raise potential growth even more in EAP, ECA, and SSA, where large investment needs remain or where countries have strong track records of boosting investment.

Chapter 6. Trade as an Engine of Growth: Sputtering but Fixable

In chapter 6, Ohnsorge and Quaglietti note that the growth of international trade, powered by trade liberalization and falling transport costs, has historically been an important engine of output and productivity growth. In recent decades, it has helped about a billion people to escape poverty and many EMDEs to integrate into the world economy. Empirical studies indicate that an increase of 1 percentage point of GDP in an

---

[15] Stern and Romani (2023) have also put climate-related investment needs globally at 2-3 percent of GDP.

FIGURE O.11 **Prospects for potential growth and policies to lift it**

Forces similar to those that slowed global potential growth in the past decade are expected to depress it further in the remainder of the current decade. The slowing could be steeper than projected in the baseline if adverse shocks recur or if, for other reasons, current expectations again turn out to be overly optimistic. A menu of policy options is available to help reverse the slowing trend, including initiatives to lift the growth of physical and human capital—such as an investment boost to mitigate and adapt to climate change—and encourage labor force participation by women and older workers.

A. Potential growth

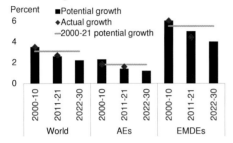

B. Potential growth

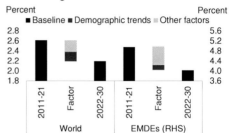

C. Global potential growth, corrected for potential forecast disappointments

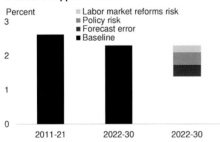

D. Potential growth with more frequent natural disasters

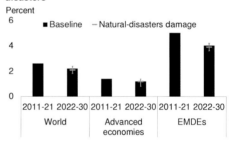

E. Global potential growth under reform scenarios

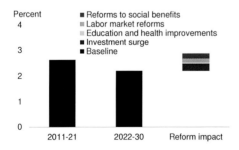

F. EMDE potential growth under scenarios involving investment in climate-related infrastructure

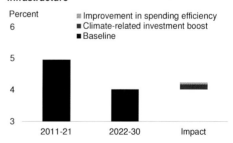

Sources: Penn World Table; World Bank.
Note: Period averages of annual averages weighted by gross domestic product (GDP). AEs = advanced economies; EMDEs = emerging market and developing economies; RHS = right-hand scale.
A. Based on production function approach. Sample includes 29 advanced economies and 53 EMDEs.
B. Derived using production function-based potential growth. "Other factors" reflects declining population growth, convergence-related productivity growth, policy changes, cohort effects, and a slowdown in investment growth relative to output growth. "Factor" reflects the percentage-point changes between the averages for 2011-21 and 2022-30.
C. Baseline and corrections as defined in chapter 5.
D. Impact of damage from natural disasters assumes that the number of climate disasters in 2022-30 will increase as much as it rose between 2011-21 and 2000-10 for each country, that is, from once every two years to twice every three years, on average. Orange whiskers display one standard deviation of the impact of climate disasters.
E. Scenarios assume a repeat, in each country, of each country's best 10-year improvement.
F. Climate-related investment boost and improvement in spending efficiency as described in chapter 5.

economy's trade openness has tended to lift per capita income by 0.2 percent (World Bank 2020).

The expansion of global value chains can account for a large part of the gains from trade in recent decades (World Bank 2020). Participation in global value chains generates efficiency gains and supports the transfer of knowledge, capital, and other inputs across countries—which boosts productivity. Integration into global value chains has also been associated with reduced vulnerability of economic activity to domestic shocks, although it has come with increased sensitivity to external shocks (Constantinescu, Mattoo, and Ruta 2020; Espitia et al. 2021).

In the past decade and a half, global trade growth has slowed as global value chains have matured, weaker investment growth has weighed on goods trade, political support for trade liberalization has waned, and trade tensions have emerged between major economies (World Bank 2015, 2017a). As a result, instead of growing twice as fast as global output growth, as it did during 1970-2008, global trade in goods and services grew less than one-half as fast in 2011-19 as global output growth.

The COVID-19 pandemic hit global trade particularly hard, and the latter fell by nearly 16 percent in the second quarter of 2020. It subsequently rebounded swiftly, however, especially global trade in goods, and much more quickly than it did after the 2007-09 global financial crisis. That said, since 2021, global trade growth has slowed again, amid COVID-19 outbreaks, supply chain strains, and Russia's invasion of Ukraine in February 2022.

Unless there is a major policy push, trade growth is likely to weaken further in the remainder of the current decade, not only because of the prospect of slower output growth, but also because some of the key structural factors that supported rapid trade expansion in the past seem, at least for now, to have run their course. Supply chains have been remarkably resilient given the magnitude of recent shocks. However, the COVID-19 pandemic and Russia's invasion of Ukraine could accelerate the erosion of globally integrated supply chains that was already underway, including by leading to further in-sourcing and regionalization of production networks and by increasing digitalization. Multinational corporations operating in EMDEs have already increased their use of digital technologies and diversified suppliers and production sites to increase their resilience to supply chain shocks (Saurav et al. 2020). As multinationals seek to diversify, EMDEs with business environments, institutions, and governance of the prerequisite quality may have new opportunities to integrate into global supply chains.

As discussed in chapter 1, growth in potential output is expected to slow in many EMDEs in the remainder of the current decade amid unfavorable demographics and weak investment and TFP growth. One way policy makers in EMDEs can boost the long-term growth of output and productivity is by promoting trade integration through measures to reduce trade costs.

Chapter 6 examines the following questions:

- What is the link between trade growth and long-term output growth?

- What are the prospects for trade growth in the coming decade?

- How large are trade costs?

- What are the correlates of trade costs?

- Which policies can help reduce trade costs?

Contributions. Chapter 6 contributes to the literature in several ways. First, the chapter expands on an earlier study with a new, comprehensive review of the theoretical and empirical literature on the links between trade and output growth (World Bank 2021). Second, it shows the evolution of trade in goods and services through global recessions, including the pandemic-induced global recession of 2020.

Third, the chapter revisits estimates of trade costs and their correlates in some earlier studies (Arvis et al. 2016; Novy 2013; World Bank 2021). The chapter uses estimates of the costs of goods trade for up to 180 countries (29 advanced economies and 151 EMDEs) from the UN Economic and Social Commission for Asia and the Pacific (ESCAP)-World Bank Trade Cost Database for 1995-2019. It estimates the determinants of the costs of goods trade, which accounts for about 75 percent of world and EMDE trade in goods and services, econometrically. The chapter also quantifies the costs of one type of services trade—logistics and shipping services—relative to the costs of goods trade. In addition, the chapter goes beyond previous research in assessing the role of trade policy—tariffs, participation in trade agreements, and nontariff barriers—in trade costs.

Fourth, the chapter discusses policy options for lowering trade costs. In particular, it offers scenarios that indicate the potential effects of various policy measures on trade costs.

Findings. Chapter 6 offers several findings. First, the theoretical literature indicates that international trade boosts long-term growth of output and productivity by promoting a more efficient allocation of resources, technological spillovers, and human capital accumulation. The empirical literature supports the theory by finding statistically significant positive relationships between trade openness and output growth, although these relationships may be conditional on the presence of sound institutions and a supportive business environment in exporting countries. Overwhelmingly, empirical studies find that international trade enhances productivity growth.

Second, the COVID-19-induced global recession of 2020 triggered a collapse of global trade in goods and services that was followed by a rapid rebound (figure O.12). Before the end of 2020, global goods trade had recovered to prepandemic levels, and by

FIGURE O.12 Reducing trade costs to boost growth prospects

World trade growth has slowed sharply since the early 2000s. The pandemic hit services trade particularly hard. Trade costs, on average, roughly double the cost of internationally traded goods relative to domestically traded goods. Tariffs amount to only one-twentieth of average trade costs. Comprehensive reform packages to lower trade costs could yield large dividends: EMDEs with the most challenging business climates could halve their trade costs by implementing reforms that improve logistics performance and maritime connectivity to the standards of EMDEs with the least challenging business climates.

A. Global trade and output growth

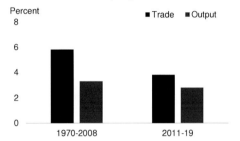

B. Composition of global trade, 2010-19

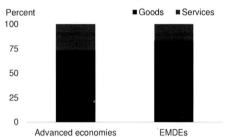

C. Trade costs

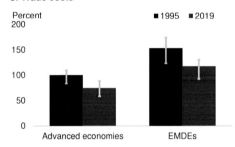

D. Tariff rates

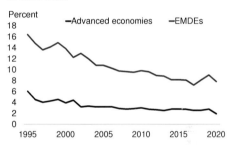

E. Goods and services trade around global recessions

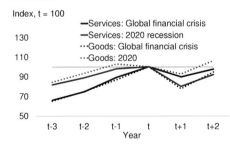

F. Reduction in overall trade costs associated with policy improvements

Sources: UN Comtrade (database); UN Economic and Social Commission for Asia and the Pacific (ESCAP)-World Bank Trade Cost Database; World Bank; World Trade Organization.

Note: EMDEs = emerging market and developing economies.

A. Annual average growth. Trade growth refers to the average growth of import and export volumes of goods and services.

C. Bilateral trade costs are aggregated into individual-country measures using 2018 shares of bilateral country exports from the UN Comtrade database. Bars show unweighted cross-country averages; whiskers show interquartile ranges. Sample for 1995 includes 33 advanced economies and 46 EMDEs. Sample for 2019 includes 23 advanced economies and 53 EMDEs.

D. Unweighted cross-country averages of applied weighted tariff rates. Sample includes up to 35 advanced economies and 123 EMDEs. Primary tariffs are used as a proxy for agriculture tariffs.

E. Levels of goods and services trade around past recessions and in 2020. *t* refers to the year before the recession.

F. Fraction of trade costs that would remain after policy improvements, as described in chapter 6. Data refer to 2018. Orange line indicates 1 (that is, unchanged trade costs in 2018) among the sample of EMDEs scoring in the poorest quartile on these indicators.

September 2021, global services trade had reached prepandemic levels, even though trade in travel and tourism services was still 40 percent lower than before the pandemic. The decline in services trade was considerably more pronounced and its recovery more subdued than in past global recessions, whereas movements in goods trade were broadly comparable to those in past global recessions.

Third, global trade growth is likely to weaken by another 0.4 percentage point per year in the remainder of the current decade as a result of slower global output growth as well as of the further waning of structural factors that supported rapid trade expansion in the past, such as the expansion of global value chains. The disruptions caused by the pandemic and the war in Ukraine may also continue to dampen trade growth over the medium term. A major policy effort to reduce trade costs could help reverse the trade slowdown.

Fourth, trade costs for goods are high: on average, they are almost equivalent to a 100 percent tariff—making internationally traded goods cost roughly twice as much as domestic goods. Tariffs amount to only one-twentieth of average trade costs; transportation and logistics, nontariff barriers, and policy-related standards and regulations account for the bulk of trade costs. Despite a one-third decline since 1995, trade costs in EMDEs remain about one-half higher than those in advanced economies. Higher shipping and logistics costs can explain about two-fifths of the explained difference in trade costs between EMDEs and advanced economies, and trade policy (including trade policy uncertainty) can explain a further two-fifths. Services trade tends to have considerably higher costs than goods trade; those higher costs can, to large extent, be attributed to regulatory restrictions.[16]

Fifth, reducing elevated trade costs in EMDEs requires comprehensive reform packages, including reforms to streamline trade processes and customs clearance requirements, enhance domestic trade-supporting infrastructure, increase competition in domestic logistics and in retail and wholesale trade, lower tariffs, lower the costs of compliance with standards and regulations, and reduce corruption. Trade agreements can also reduce trade costs and promote trade, especially if they lower nontariff barriers as well as tariffs. The chapter's empirical analysis suggests that an EMDE in the 25 percent of EMDEs with the highest shipping and logistics costs can cut its trade costs in half if it improves conditions in these areas to match those in the 25 percent of EMDEs with the lowest costs of shipping and logistics.

Chapter 7. Services-Led Growth: Better Prospects after the COVID-19 Pandemic?

In chapter 7, Nayyar and Davies document that services, generally the largest sector of economic activity, have also been the main source of growth over the past three decades. In 2019, services accounted for 63 percent of global output and 57 percent of global employment. Between 1995 and 2019, services accounted for two-thirds of global

---

[16] That said, there is some evidence that professional services now have trade costs comparable to those in manufacturing industries (Gervais and Jensen 2019).

output growth and almost three-quarters of global employment growth. Although the services sector accounts for a smaller part of economic activity in EMDEs than in advanced economies, the difference is not large: even in EMDEs, services accounted for 60 percent of output and 52 percent of employment in 2019.

The services sector is diverse. It includes high-skilled offshorable services (such as information and communications technologies, finance, and professional services) that have been internationally traded much like goods since the ICT revolution in the 1990s. It also includes low-skilled contact services (transportation, hospitality, retail, personal, arts, entertainment and recreation, and administrative and support) that have typically required physical proximity of providers and consumers. Many services in both of these categories provide important inputs for non-services-sector activity. For example, transportation and logistics services are essential for international trade in agricultural commodities and manufactured goods, while ICT services are central to increasingly data-intensive production processes, including those in manufacturing.[17]

Chapter 7 shows the uneven blows that the pandemic has dealt to different activities in the services sector. Social-distancing regulations and precautions against the spread of the virus have hit low-skilled contact services, such as transportation and hospitality, particularly hard. But it has affected high-skilled offshorable services, such as ICT and professional services, much less, because they are amenable to home-based work. The productivity benefits resulting from high-skilled services and ICT can boost economic growth more broadly through the important linkages between services and other sectors of the economy.

To explore these issues, chapter 7 addresses the following questions:

- How has the services sector shaped global economic growth over the past three decades?

- How has the pandemic affected the services sector?

- How can digitalization enhance the services sector's growth as countries recover from the pandemic?

- Which policies can help harness the services sector's growth potential?

Contributions. Chapter 7 makes several contributions to the literature. First, it establishes a set of stylized facts that describe the role of the services sector in the global economy over the past three decades. These stylized facts complement a growing literature on structural change and productivity growth in EMDEs that highlights the shifting contributions of the manufacturing and services sectors.[18] In particular, a set of decompositions by services subsector compares the contributions of growth in different

---

[17] Chapter 7 does not focus on social services (education and health care), which are largely publicly provided.

[18] On the contributions of manufacturing and services sectors to economic growth, see, for example, Fan, Peters, and Zilibotti (2021); Kinfemichael and Morshed (2019); McMillan and Rodrik (2011); Nayyar, Hallward-Driemeier, and Davies (2021a, 2021b); and Rodrik (2016).

categories of demand—private domestic demand, exports, and government consumption—and, on the supply side, the contributions of growth in factor inputs and TFP.

Second, the chapter analyzes how the pandemic has affected prospects for services-led growth by tracing patterns of recovery and assessing growth opportunities linked to the acceleration in digitalization. This builds on recent studies that examine the effects of the pandemic on growth and income distribution (Apedo-Amah et al. 2020; Chetty et al. 2020; Narayan et al. 2022).

Third, the chapter discusses policies that can leverage the services sector's potential growth after the pandemic. This adds to the policy discussion in Nayyar, Hallward-Driemeier, and Davies (2021a, 2021b) by focusing on what has changed since the pandemic. Policies discussed include reducing regulatory barriers and improving skill development, not only for high-skilled offshorable services that have best withstood the pandemic, but also for low-skilled services such as transportation that have important linkages with other sectors.

Findings. Chapter 7 presents several novel findings. First, the services sector has led economic growth over the past three decades, accounting for more than half of the growth in GDP and employment in both advanced economies and EMDEs between 1995 and 2018-19 (figure O.13). However, the composition of services sector growth has differed between advanced economies and EMDEs. While low-skilled contact services have made a similar contribution to growth in EMDEs and advanced economies, high-skilled offshorable services have contributed about twice as much to growth in advanced economies as in EMDEs. High-skilled offshorable services have accounted for about one-third of GDP growth in advanced economies, but only one-sixth of GDP growth in EMDEs, and for about one-half of employment growth in advanced economies compared with one-ninth in EMDEs. The difference will matter for productivity growth, because low-skilled contact services have been associated with slower export growth than growth in domestic demand and with slower TFP growth than growth of labor and capital inputs.

Second, although overall services activity collapsed during the pandemic, the impact on low-skilled contact services reliant on face-to-face interactions with consumers was far more severe than the impact on high-skilled offshorable services, which are more amenable to remote communication through digital delivery, such as ICT and professional services. The latter were among the activities the pandemic affected least adversely; indeed in some cases, especially that of ICT services, output and investment expanded.

Third, the increased digitalization that occurred during the pandemic augurs well for growth prospects in the services sector. Among high-skilled offshorable services, digitally deliverable ICT and professional-services exports from EMDEs have increased sharply, to more than 50 percent of their total services exports in 2021 from 40 percent in 2019. Even where physical proximity remains important, digitalization has expanded

FIGURE O.13 **The role of services in the global economy**

The services sector accounted for more than half of the growth in gross domestic product (GDP) and employment in both advanced economies and EMDEs in 1995-2018. Services include both high-skilled offshorable services, such as information and communications technology, and low-skilled contact services, such as retail and hospitality. Most labor productivity growth in EMDEs during 1995-2018 was due to within-sector improvements rather than intersectoral shifts. The pandemic-induced recession of 2020 was unusual in the disruptions it caused to services activity.

A. Sectoral contributions to value-added growth, 1990-2019/20

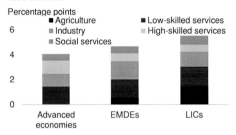

B. Productivity growth, 1995-2018

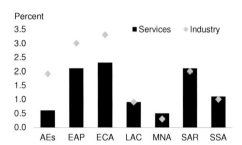

C. Total factor productivity in services relative to that in manufacturing

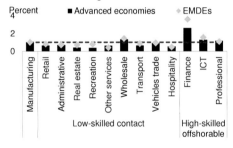

D. Contributions to labor productivity growth, 1995-2018

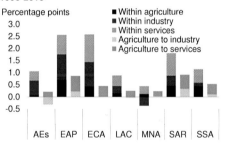

E. Recessions before 2020

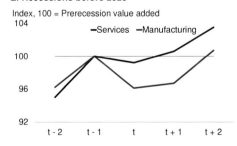

F. Recessions in 2020

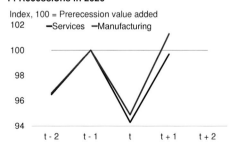

Sources: Groningen Growth and Development Centre (GGDC); Nayyar, Hallward-Driemeier, and Davies (2021a, 2021b); World Bank.
Note: AEs = advanced economies; EAP = East Asia and Pacific; ECA = Europe and Central Asia; EMDEs = emerging market and developing economies; ICT = information and communications technology; LAC = Latin America and the Caribbean; LICs = low-income countries; MNA = Middle East and North Africa; SAR = South Asia; SSA = Sub-Saharan Africa.
A. Bars represent the average contribution of individual sectors to value-added growth between 1990 and 2018. Sample from the GGDC/United Nations University-World Institute for Development Economics Research (UNU-WIDER) Economic Transformation Database includes 6 advanced economies, 39 EMDEs, and 6 LICs.
B. Average compounded annual growth rates in labor productivity (value added per worker) across each region between 1995 and 2018. Unweighted average across country groups.
C. Total factor productivity relative to manufacturing sector in the same country, estimated as in chapter 7. Data are from 56 countries, including 35 EMDEs across all regions, and are for the latest available year between 2010 and 2017.
D. Bars represent labor productivity growth attributed to each sector and movement between sectors for the period 1995-2018.
E.F. Recessions are defined as in chapter 7. Figures show the unweighted average level of real value added in services (blue) and manufacturing (red) in the years around the recession year *t*, indexed to 100 for the year preceding the recession.

opportunities, including opportunities for scale economies. For example, e-commerce platforms have enabled retailers and restaurants to reach beyond their local neighborhoods, while ICT and management practices have enabled the standardization of production over many establishments. Greater reliance on services sectors for growth may also help mitigate the adverse impacts of climate change on agricultural production.

Fourth, policy interventions can help countries leverage the potential of the services sector to drive economic growth as they continue to recover from the pandemic. Policy support for the diffusion of digital technologies in EMDEs remains central, given that the share of firms using email to communicate with clients was less than one-third as recently as 2018. Investing in ICT infrastructure, updating regulatory frameworks around data, and strengthening management capabilities and worker skills all matter. Countries can target the expansion of productive high-skilled offshorable services by reducing barriers to market access and promoting the improvement of skills. They can also support investments and regulatory reforms to revive low-skilled contact services, such as transportation, that employ large numbers of people.

Future research directions

The book suggests several directions for future research. These directions range from improvements in estimates of potential growth to more granular estimates of the effects of climate change and various structural policy measures.

Improvements in measurement

Estimates of potential growth could be improved in a number of ways. In particular, several refinements would be useful in applications of the production function approach (chapter 1):

- Especially for countries that rely heavily on natural resources, the estimation of production function-based potential growth could take into account natural resources as a factor of production.

- TFP growth estimates should take into account the role of new drivers of productivity, such as digital technologies, foreign direct investment, and integration into global value chains.

- Application of the production function approach could be improved by estimation of a broader measure of human capital, beyond the enrollment and completion metrics and life expectancy used in the analysis in this book. The World Bank's Human Capital Index offers one such measure, but currently covers only a few recent years (World Bank 2020).

Other estimates of potential growth could also be refined. For example, estimates of potential growth based on multivariate filters could be extended to calculate output gaps and their relationship with inflation and other measures of demand pressures. External drivers of business cycles—such as global tourism for tourism-reliant countries and global liquidity for financial centers—could also be included.

Data improvements could also benefit the analysis of the role of services in the global economy (chapter 7). Addressing several methodological challenges in measuring services outputs, inputs, and trade flows could improve estimates of the contribution of the services sector to economic growth.

International trade in services has particularly poor data availability (chapter 6). Measures of the costs of trade in services remain scant, which makes it difficult to assess and quantify their determinants. Since these costs are largely associated with regulatory barriers, further analysis of the implications for trade costs of variations in regulations across sectors, countries, and regions is warranted. This would allow a more in-depth analysis of patterns and correlates of the costs of trade in services.

Effects of climate change

Chapter 5 outlines one approach for quantifying the effects of various factors related to climate change on long-term output growth. Estimates of these effects could be refined to identify how country characteristics, circumstances, and policy responses are related to the extent of damage to growth from extreme weather events. In addition, the channels through which climate change affects economic growth could be explored in greater detail. This is particularly im-portant for understanding long-standing growth weakness in small states (World Bank 2023).

Spillovers from natural disasters in one country to its trading partners could also be examined. For example, natural disasters may cause the largest domestic damage in small island states but may have limited international spillovers, whereas disasters that disrupt production of an internationally traded commodity in a major producer can have substantial global repercussions.

Transportation associated with international trade is one of the largest contributors to global emissions of greenhouse gases (chapter 6). Depending on their impact on global patterns of trade, reforms to reduce trade costs may therefore increase or reduce such emissions. Further research could aim to provide a better understanding of the climate-related effects of reducing trade costs.

Effects of other structural policies

Several structural policy changes not considered in this book could be explored, drawing on longer-term data. In the 1970s, 1980s, and 1990s, labor markets, product markets, financial sectors, and fiscal and monetary policy frameworks underwent major structural changes and widespread reforms. These changes and reforms could not be explored with the large cross-country sample used in this study, because it extends only as far back as 2000. However, for at least a subset of countries, data might be available that go further back in time. This could facilitate the analysis of the longer-term effects of the structural changes that occurred in the 1970s, 1980s, and 1990s. A longer time period may also allow a better assessment of the "cleansing" effects of adverse shocks in raising overall productivity.

Many EMDEs host large state-owned and private enterprises in which activity is excessively concentrated, with associated market power. Reforms of state-owned enterprises and measures to break up monopolies, where appropriate, or otherwise reform their regulation could trigger higher productivity growth by reallocating capital and labor toward more productive uses. A better understanding of the quantitative impact on potential growth in EMDEs as well as the identification of conducive preconditions and complementary reforms would be helpful.

Many EMDEs have weak governance and business climates. An assessment of the effects of improvements in various dimensions of governance and business climates on potential growth, including on firm productivity and household employment decisions, would be helpful.

As noted previously, the pandemic has triggered a sharp increase in digitalization. Several countries have launched policy initiatives to encourage further digitalization. Future research could analyze the effects of such digitalization efforts on trade and innovation and how digitalization has changed growth patterns in the services sector.

Finally, the pandemic has highlighted the challenges that disruptions in global value chains can present. Through complex global value chains, with multiple border crossings, trade costs and disruptions can snowball. Future research could investigate which policy measures can be most effective in reducing trade costs in the context of global value chains.

ANNEX OA Tables

TABLE OA.1 Actual GDP growth (percent)

Country group	Period	Growth	Country group	Period	Growth	Country group	Period	Growth
EMDEs	2000-10	6.0	EMDEs	2000-09	5.9	EMDEs	2000-08	6.3
	2011-21	4.4		2010-19	5.1		2011-19	4.9
	2022-24	3.6		2022-24	3.6		2022-24	3.6
MICs	2000-10	6.3	MICs	2000-09	6.1	MICs	2000-08	6.5
	2011-21	4.6		2010-19	5.3		2011-19	5.0
	2022-24	3.6		2022-24	3.6		2022-24	3.6
LICs	2000-10	6.0	LICs	2000-09	5.9	LICs	2000-08	6.0
	2011-21	4.8		2010-19	5.4		2011-19	5.2
	2022-24	4.9		2022-24	4.9		2022-24	4.9

Source: World Bank.
Note: EMDEs = emerging market and developing economies; GDP = gross domestic product; LICs = low-income countries;
MICs = middle-income countries.

TABLE OA.2 Per capita growth (percent)

Country group	Period	Growth	Country group	Period	Growth	Country group	Period	Growth
EMDEs	2000-10	4.6	EMDEs	2000-09	4.4	EMDEs	2000-08	4.8
	2011-21	3.2		2010-19	3.5		2011-19	3.5
	2022-24	2.7		2022-24	2.7		2022-24	2.7
MICs	2000-10	4.9	MICs	2000-09	4.7	MICs	2000-08	5.1
	2011-21	3.5		2010-19	4.1		2011-19	3.8
	2022-24	2.8		2022-24	2.8		2022-24	2.8
LICs	2000-10	2.9	LICs	2000-09	2.8	LICs	2000-08	2.9
	2011-21	1.7		2010-19	2.3		2011-19	2.1
	2022-24	2.1		2022-24	2.1		2022-24	2.1

Source: World Bank.
Note: EMDEs = emerging market and developing economies; GDP = gross domestic product; LICs = low-income countries; MICs =
middle-income countries.

TABLE OA.3 Potential GDP growth (percent)

Country group	Period	Growth	Country group	Period	Growth	Country group	Period	Growth
World	2000-10	3.5	Advanced economies	2000-10	2.2	EMDEs	2000-10	6.0
	2011-21	2.6		2011-21	1.4		2011-21	5.0
	2022-24	2.2		2022-24	1.2		2022-24	4.0

Source: World Bank.
Note: EMDEs = emerging market and developing economies; GDP = gross domestic product.

References

Acemoglu, D. 2012. "Introduction to Economic Growth." *Journal of Economic Theory* 147 (2): 545-50.

Acemoglu, D., S. Johnson, and J. A. Robinson. 2005. "Institutions as a Fundamental Cause of Long-Run Growth." In *Handbook of Economic Growth*, vol. 1, edited by P. Aghion and S. N. Durlauf, 385-472. Amsterdam: Elsevier.

Acemoglu, D., and J. A. Robinson. 2012. *Why Nations Fail: The Origins of Power, Prosperity and Poverty.* New York: Norton.

ADB (Asian Development Bank). 2016. *Asian Development Outlook 2016: Asia's Potential Growth.* Manila: Asian Development Bank.

Adler, G., R. Duval, D. Furceri, S. Kilic Celik, K. Koloskova, and M. Poplawski-Ribeiro. 2017. "Gone with the Headwinds: Global Productivity." Staff Discussion Note 17/04, International Monetary Fund, Washington, DC.

Aghion, P., U. Akcigit, and P. Howitt. 2015. "The Schumpeterian Growth Paradigm." *Annual Review of Economics* 7 (1): 557-75.

Aghion, P., C. Antonin, and S. Bunel. 2021. *The Power of Creative Destruction.* Cambridge, MA: Harvard University Press.

Aghion, P., and P. Howitt. 2005. "Growth with Quality-Improving Innovations: An Integrated Framework." In *Handbook of Economic Growth*, vol. 1, edited by P. Aghion and S. N. Durlauf, 67-110. Amsterdam: Elsevier.

Allen, F., J. R. Behrman, N. Birdsall, S. Fardoust, D. Rodrik, A. Steer, and A. Subramanian. 2014. *Towards a Better Global Economy: Policy Implications for Citizens Worldwide in the Twenty-First Century.* Oxford, U.K.: Oxford University Press.

Alvarez, R., and J. De Gregorio. 2014. "Understanding Differences in Growth Performance in Latin America and Developing Countries between the Asian and the Global Financial Crises." *IMF Economic Review* 62 (4): 494-525.

Anand, R., and V. Tulin. 2014. "Disentangling India's Investment Slowdown." Working Paper 14/47, International Monetary Fund, Washington, DC.

Anzoategui, D., D. Comin, M. Gertler, and J. Martinez. 2017. "Endogenous Technology Adoption and R&D as Sources of Business Cycle Persistence." NBER Working Paper 22005, National Bureau of Economic Research, Cambridge, MA.

Apedo-Amah, M. C., B. Avdiu, X. Cirera, M. Cruz, E. Davies, A. Grover, L. Iacovone, et al. 2020. "Unmasking the Impact of COVID-19 on Businesses: Firm-Level Evidence from across the World." Policy Research Working Paper 9434, World Bank, Washington, DC.

Arcand, J. L., E. Berkes, and U. Panizza. 2015. "Too Much Finance?" *Journal of Economic Growth* 20 (2): 105-48.

Arvis, J.-F., Y. Duval, B. Shepherd, C. Utoktham, and A. Raj. 2016. "Trade Costs in the Developing World: 1996-2010." *World Trade Review* 15 (3): 451-74.

Baffes, J., and P. Nagle. 2022. *Commodity Markets: Evolution, Challenges and Policies.* Washington, DC: World Bank.

Bahal, G., M. Raissi, and V. Tulin. 2018. "Crowding-Out or Crowding-In? Public and Private Investment in India." *World Development* 109 (September): 323-33.

Baker, S. R., N. Bloom, and S. J. Davis. 2016. "Measuring Economic Policy Uncertainty." *Quarterly Journal of Economics* 131 (4): 1593-636.

Baldwin, R. 2016. *The Great Convergence: Information Technology and the New Globalization.* Cambridge, MA: Harvard University Press.

Baldwin, R., and D. Jaimovich. 2010. "Are Free Trade Agreements Contagious?" NBER Working Paper 16084, National Bureau of Economic Research, Cambridge, MA.

Banerjee, R., J. Kearns, and M. Lombardi. 2015. "(Why) Is Investment Weak?" *BIS Quarterly Review* (March): 67-82.

Banerji, A., C. H. Ebeke, D. Furceri, E. Dabla-Norris, R. A. Duval, T. Komatsuzaki, T. Poghosyan, and V. Crispolti. 2017. "Labor and Product Market Reforms in Advanced Economies: Fiscal Costs, Gains, and Support." IMF Staff Discussion Note 17/03, International Monetary Fund, Washington, DC.

Barro, R. J., and J. W. Lee. 2013. "A New Data Set of Educational Attainment in the World, 1950-2010." *Journal of Development Economics* 104 (September): 184-98.

Bhattacharya, A., H. Kharas, and J. W. McArthur. 2023. *Keys to Climate Action: How Developing Countries Could Drive Global Success and Local Prosperity.* Washington, DC: Brookings Institution.

Blanchard, O. J., and L. H. Summers. 1987. "Hysteresis in Unemployment." *European Economic Review* 31 (1-2): 288-95.

Botzen, W. W., O. Deschenes, and M. Sanders. 2019. "The Economic Impacts of Natural Disasters: A Review of Models and Empirical Studies." *Review of Environmental Economics and Policy* 13(2): 167-88.

Brenton, P., and V. Chemutai. 2021. *The Trade and Climate Change Nexus: The Urgency and Opportunities for Developing Countries.* Washington, DC: World Bank.

Brynjolfsson, E., and A. McAfee. 2014. *The Second Machine Age: Work, Progress, and Prosperity in a Time of Brilliant Technologies.* New York: Norton.

Brynjolfsson, E., and A. McAfee. 2017. *Machine, Platform, Crowd: Harnessing Our Digital Future.* New York: WW Norton & Company.

Caballero, R. J., and A. Simsek. 2017. "A Risk-Centric Model of Demand Recessions and Macroprudential Policy." NBER Working Paper 23614, National Bureau of Economic Research, Cambridge, MA.

Caselli, F., P. Pagano, and F. Schivardi. 2003. "Uncertainty and the Slowdown in Capital Accumulation in Europe." *Applied Economics* 35 (1): 79-89.

Cerra, V., A. Cuevas, C. Goes, I. Karpowicz, T. Matheson, I. Samake, and S. Vtyurina. 2017. "Determinants of Infrastructure and Its Financing." *Emerging Economy Studies* 3 (2): 113-26.

Cerra, V., B. Eichengreen, A. El-Ganainy, and M. Schindle, eds. 2021. *How to Achieve Inclusive Growth.* Oxford, U.K.: Oxford University Press.

Cerra, V., A. Fatás, and M. S. C. Saxena. 2020. "Hysteresis and Business Cycles." IMF Working Paper 20/73, International Monetary Fund, Washington, DC.

Chalaux, T., and Y. Guillemette. 2019. "The OECD Potential Output Estimation Methodology." OECD Economics Department Working Paper 1563, OECD Publishing, Paris.

Chen, N., and D. Novy. 2012. "On the Measurement of Trade Costs: Direct vs. Indirect Approaches to Quantifying Standards and Technical Regulations." *World Trade Review* 11 (3): 401-14.

Chetty, R., J. N. Friedman, N. Hendren, and M. Stepner. 2020. "The Economic Impacts of COVID-19: Evidence from a New Public Database Built Using Private Sector Data." NBER Working Paper 27431, National Bureau of Economic Research, Cambridge, MA.

Comin, D., and S. Mulani. 2009. "A Theory of Growth and Volatility at the Aggregate and Firm Level." *Journal of Monetary Economics* 56 (8): 1023-42.

Constantinescu, C., A. Mattoo, and M. Ruta. 2020. "The Global Trade Slowdown: Cyclical or Structural?" *World Bank Economic Review* 34 (1): 121-42.

Dabla-Norris, E., M. S. Guo, V. Haksar, M. Kim, M. K. Kochhar, K. Wiseman, and A. Zdzienicka. 2015. *The New Normal: A Sector-Level Perspective on Productivity Trends in Advanced Economies.* Washington, DC: International Monetary Fund.

Dabla-Norris, E., G. Ho, and A. Kyobe. 2016. "Structural Reforms and Productivity Growth in Emerging Market and Developing Economies." IMF Working Paper 16/15, International Monetary Fund, Washington, DC.

de Haan, J., and R. Wiese. 2022. "The Impact of Product and Labour Market Reform on Growth: Evidence for OECD Countries Based on Local Projections." *Journal of Applied Econometrics* 37(4): 746-70.

Devarajan, S. 2019. "Has Globalization Gone Too Far—Or Not Far Enough?" *Future Development* (blog), September 3, 2019. https://brookings.edu/blog/future-development/2019/09/03/has-globalization-gone-too-far-or-not-far-enough

Devarajan, S., D. Go, S. Robinson, and K. Thierfelder. 2022. "Which Trade Policies Are Most Effective at Spurring Countries to Decarbonize?" PIIE Charts, September 16, Peterson Institute for International Economics, Washington, DC. https://piie.com/research/piie-charts/which-trade-policies-are-most-effective-spurring-countries-decarbonize

Didier, T., M. A. Kose, F. Ohnsorge, and L. S. Ye. 2015. "Slowdown in Emerging Markets: Rough Patch or Prolonged Weakness." Policy Research Note 4, World Bank, Washington, DC.

Dieppe, A., ed. 2021. *Global Productivity: Trends, Drivers, and Policies.* Washington, DC: World Bank.

Dieppe, A., S. Kilic Celik, and C. Okou. 2020. "What Happens to Productivity during Major Adverse Events." In *Global Productivity: Trends, Drivers, and Policies,* edited by A. Dieppe, 141-200. Washington, DC: World Bank.

Dieppe, A., and H. Matsuoka. 2021. "Sectoral Sources of Productivity Growth." In *Global Productivity: Trends, Drivers, and Policies,* edited by A. Dieppe, 357-89. Washington, DC: World Bank.

Espitia, A., A. Mattoo, N. Rocha, M. Ruta, and D. Winkler. 2021. "Pandemic Trade: COVID-19, Remote Work and Global Value Chains." Policy Research Working Paper 9508, World Bank, Washington, DC.

Fan, T., M. Peters, and F. Zilibotti. 2021. "Service-Led or Service-Biased Growth? Equilibrium Development Accounting across Indian Districts." NBER Working Paper 28551, National Bureau of Economic Research, Cambridge, MA.

Fatás, A. 2000. "Do Business Cycles Cast Long Shadows? Short-Run Persistence and Economic Growth." *Journal of Economic Growth* 5 (2): 147-62.

Fisman, R., and J. Svensson. 2007. "Are Corruption and Taxation Really Harmful to Growth? Firm-Level Evidence." *Journal of Development Economics* 83 (1): 63-75.

Francois, J., and B. Hoekman. 2010. "Services Trade and Policy." *Journal of Economic Literature* 48 (3): 642-92.

Furceri, D., S. Kilic Celik, J. T. Jalles, and K. Koloskova. 2021. "Recessions and Total Factor Productivity: Evidence from Sectoral Data." *Economic Modelling* 94 (January): 130-38.

Furceri, D., and A. Mourougane. 2012. "The Effect of Financial Crises on Potential Output: New Empirical Evidence from OECD Countries." *Journal of Macroeconomics* 34 (3): 822-32.

Gervais, A., and J. B. Jensen. 2019. "The Tradability of Services: Geographic Concentration and Trade Costs." *Journal of International Economics* 118 (May): 331-50.

Gill, I. S., and M. Raiser. 2012. *Golden Growth: Restoring the Lustre of the European Economic Model.* Washington, DC: World Bank.

Goedhuys, M., and R. Veugelers. 2012. "Innovation Strategies, Process and Product Innovations and Growth: Firm-Level Evidence from Brazil." *Structural Change and Economic Dynamics* 23 (4): 516-29.

Gordon, R. J. 2017. *The Rise and Fall of American Growth: The U.S. Standard of Living since the Civil War.* Princeton, NJ: Princeton University Press.

Gorodnichenko, Y., and G. Roland. 2011. "Which Dimensions of Culture Matter for Long-Run Growth?" *American Economic Review* 101(3): 492-98.

Grippa, P., J. Schmittmann, and F. Suntheim. 2019. "Climate Change and Financial Risk." *Finance and Development* (December): 26-29.

Guenette, J. D., M. A. Kose, and N. Sugawara. 2022. "Is a Global Recession Imminent?" Equitable Growth, Finance, and Institutions Policy Note 4, World Bank, Washington, DC.

Ha, J., M. A. Kose, and F. Ohnsorge. 2022. "Global Stagflation." Discussion Paper 17381, Centre for Economic Policy Research, London, U.K.

IMF (International Monetary Fund). 2015. *World Economic Outlook: Uneven Growth: Short- and Long-Term Factors.* April. Washington, DC: International Monetary Fund.

IMF (International Monetary Fund). 2016a. "Fiscal Policies for Innovation and Growth." In *Fiscal Monitor: Acting Now, Acting Together.* April. Washington, DC: International Monetary Fund.

IMF (International Monetary Fund). 2016b. "Time for a Supply-Side Boost? Macroeconomic Effects of Labor and Product Market Reforms in Advanced Economies." In *World Economic Outlook: Too Slow for Too Long.* April. Washington, DC: International Monetary Fund.

Kilic Celik, S., M. A. Kose, and F. Ohnsorge. 2020. "Subdued Potential Growth: Sources and Remedies." In *Growth in a Time of Change: Global and Country Perspectives on a New Agenda*, edited by H.-Y. Kim and Z. Qureshi, 25-74. Washington, DC: Brookings Institution.

Kinfemichael, B., and A. K. M. M. Morshed. 2019. "Unconditional Convergence of Labor Productivity in the Service Sector." *Journal of Macroeconomics* 59 (March): 217-29.

Klasen, S. 2019. "What Explains Uneven Female Labor Force Participation Levels and Trends in Developing Countries?" *World Bank Research Observer* 34 (2): 161-97.

Klomp, J., and K. Valckx. 2014. "Natural Disasters and Economic Growth: A Meta-analysis." *Global Environmental Change* 26 (1): 183-95.

Kose, M. A., F. Ohnsorge, C. M. Reinhart, and K. S. Rogoff. 2022. "The Aftermath of Debt Surges." *Annual Review of Economics* 14: 637-63.

Kose, M. A., F. Ohnsorge, and N. Sugawara. 2022. "A Mountain of Debt: Navigating the Legacy of the Pandemic." *Journal of Globalization and Development* 13 (2): 233-68.

Leboeuf, M., and R. Fay. 2016. "What Is Behind the Weakness in Global Investment?" Working Paper 2016-5, Bank of Canada, Ottawa.

Lee, J. W., and W. J. McKibbin. 2018. "Service Sector Productivity and Economic Growth in Asia." *Economic Modelling* 74 (August): 247-63.

Li, D., N. Magud, and F. Valencia. 2015. "Corporate Investment in Emerging Markets: Financing vs. Real Options Channel." Working Paper 15/285, International Monetary Fund, Washington, DC.

Loayza, N., and S. Pennings. 2022. *The Long Term Growth Model: Fundamentals, Extensions, and Applications.* Washington, DC: World Bank.

Lockwood, B. 1991. "Information Externalities in the Labour Market and the Duration of Unemployment." *Review of Economic Studies* 58 (4): 733-53.

Magud, N., and S. Sosa. 2015. "Investment in Emerging Markets: We Are Not in Kansas Anymore . . . Or Are We?" IMF Working Paper 15/77, International Monetary Fund, Washington DC.

McMillan, M. S., and D. Rodrik. 2011. "Globalization, Structural Change and Productivity Growth." NBER Working Paper 17143, National Bureau of Economic Research, Cambridge, MA.

McMillan, M. S., D. Rodrik, and C. Sepúlveda. 2017. *Structural Change, Fundamentals, and Growth: A Framework and Case Studies.* Washington, DC: International Food Policy Research Institute and World Bank.

Mourougane, A. 2017. "Crisis, Potential Output and Hysteresis." *International Economics* 149 (May): 1-14.

Narayan, A., A. Cojocaru, S. Agrawal, T. Bundervoet, M. Davalos, N. Garcia, C. Lakner, et al. 2022. "COVID-19 and Economic Inequality." Policy Research Working Paper 9902, World Bank, Washington, DC.

Nayyar, G., M. Hallward-Driemeier, and E. Davies. 2021a. *At Your Service? The Promise of Services-Led Development.* Washington, DC: World Bank.

Nayyar, G., M. Hallward-Driemeier, and E. Davies. 2021b. "The Promise of Services-Led Development." *Future Development* (blog), October 13, 2021. https://brookings.edu/blog/future-development/2021/10/13/the-promise-of-services-led-development

Nguyen, H., and R. Qian. 2014. "Demand Collapse of Credit Crunch to Firms? Evidence from World Bank's Financial Crisis Survey in Eastern Europe." *Journal of International Money and Finance* 47: 125-44.

Novy, D. 2013. "Gravity Redux: Measuring International Trade Costs with Panel Data." *Economic Inquiry* 51 (1): 101-21.

Obstfeld, M. 2009. "International Finance and Growth in Developing Countries: What Have We Learned?" *IMF Staff Papers* 56 (1): 63-111.

OECD (Organisation for Economic Co-operation and Development). 2005. *Growth in Services: Fostering Employment, Productivity, and Innovation.* Paris: OECD.

OECD (Organisation for Economic Co-operation and Development). 2014. "Growth Prospects and Fiscal Requirements over the Long Term". In *OECD Economic Outlook*, Vol. 2014/1. Paris: OECD.

Ohnsorge, F., and S. Yu., eds. 2022. *The Long Shadow of Informality: Challenges and Policies.* Washington, DC: World Bank.

Okonjo-Iweala, N., and B. Coulibaly. 2019. "Making Globalization Work for Africa." Op-Ed, May 30, 2019, Brookings Institution, Washington, DC. https://brookings.edu/opinions/making-globalization-work-for-africa

Ollivaud, P., Y. Guillemette, and D. Turner. 2016. "Links between Weak Investment and the Slowdown in Productivity and Potential Output Growth across the OECD." Working Paper 1304, Organisation for Economic Co-Operation and Development, Paris.

Oulton, N., and M. Sebastia-Barriel. 2016. "Effects of Financial Crises on Productivity, Capital and Employment." *Review of Income and Wealth* 63 (s1): S90-S112.

Park, D., and M. Noland. 2013. *Developing the Service Sector as an Engine of Growth for Asia.* Manila: Asian Development Bank.

Plummer, M. G. 2007. "'Best Practices' in Regional Trading Agreements: An Application to Asia." *World Economy* 30 (12): 1771-96.

Prati, A., M. G. Onorato, and C. Papageorgiou. 2013. "Which Reforms Work and Under What Institutional Environment?" *Review of Economics and Statistics* 95 (3): 946-68.

Queralto, A. 2013. "A Model of Slow Recoveries from Financial Crises." International Finance Discussion Papers 1097, Board of Governors of the Federal Reserve System, Washington, DC.

Qureshi, Z., J. L. Diaz-Sanchez, and A. Varoudakis. 2015. "The Post-crisis Growth Slowdown in Emerging Economies and the Role of Structural Reforms." *Global Journal of Emerging Market Economies* 7 (2): 179-200.

Rodrik, D. 2016. "Premature Deindustrialization." *Journal of Economic Growth* 21 (1): 1-33.

Rozenberg, J., and M. Fay. 2019. *Beyond the Gap: How Countries Can Afford the Infrastructure They Need While Protecting the Planet.* Washington, DC: World Bank.

Saurav, A., P. Kusek, R. Kuo, and B. Viney. 2020. "The Impact of COVID-19 on Foreign Investors: Evidence from the Second Round of a Global Pulse Survey." World Bank, Washington, DC.

Schady, N., A. Holla, A. A. Sabarwal, J. Silva, and A. Yi Chang. 2023. *Collapse and Recovery: How the COVID-19 Pandemic Eroded Human Capital and What to Do about It.* Washington, DC: World Bank.

Shabnam, N. 2014. "Natural Disasters and Economic Growth: A Review." *International Journal of Disaster Risk Science* 5 (2): 157-63.

Stern, N., and M. Romani. 2023. *The Global Growth Story of the 21st Century: Driven by Investment and Innovation in Green Technologies and Artificial Intelligence.* London: London School of Economics.

Ulku, H., and G. R. Zaourak. 2022. *Unleashing Central America's Growth Potential: Synthesis Report.* Washington, DC: World Bank.

Wilms, P., J. Swank, and J. de Haan. 2018. "Determinants of the Real Impact of Banking Crises: A Review and New Evidence." *North American Journal of Economics and Finance* 43 (January): 54-70.

World Bank. 2013. *World Development Report 2013: Jobs.* Washington, DC: World Bank.

World Bank. 2015. *Global Economic Prospects: Having Fiscal Space and Using It.* January. Washington, DC: World Bank.

World Bank. 2016. *World Development Report 2016: Digital Dividends.* Washington, DC: World Bank.

World Bank. 2017a. *Global Economic Prospects: Weak Investment in Uncertain Times.* January. Washington, DC: World Bank.

World Bank. 2017b. *World Development Report 2017: Governance and the Law.* Washington, DC: World Bank.

World Bank. 2018. *Learning to Realize Education's Promise.* Washington, DC: World Bank.

World Bank. 2019a. *Global Economic Prospects: Heightened Tensions, Subdued Investment.* June. Washington, DC: World Bank.

World Bank. 2019b. *World Development Report 2019: The Changing Nature of Work.* Washington, DC: World Bank.

World Bank. 2020. *World Development Report 2020: Trading for Development in the Age of Global Value Chains.* Washington, DC: World Bank.

World Bank. 2021. *Global Economic Prospects.* June. Washington, DC: World Bank.

World Bank. 2022. *Global Economic Prospects.* January. Washington, DC: World Bank.

World Bank. 2023. *Global Economic Prospects.* January. Washington, DC: World Bank.

World Economic Forum. 2022. "Carbon-Neutral Manufacturing Is Possible: Here's How." Davos Agenda 2022, January 12. https://weforum.org/agenda/2022/01/carbon-neutral-manufacturing-possible-net-zero

PART I
Potential Growth: An Economy's Speed Limit

With hindsight, it has become clear that there was in fact no coherent growth story for most emerging markets. Scratch the surface, and you found high growth rates driven not by productive transformation but by domestic demand, in turn fueled by temporary commodity booms and unsustainable levels of public or, more often, private borrowing.

Dani Rodrik, 2015
Ford Foundation Professor of International Political Economy,
Harvard Kennedy School

After enjoying years of enviable economic performance, emerging markets are coming under strain, with a marked divergence in growth among them. As some of these economies slow down, the goal of eradicating extreme poverty will become harder as it burrows in and becomes more concentrated in regions most affected by conflict.

Kaushik Basu, 2015
Carl Marks Professor of International Studies and Professor of Economics,
Cornell University,
and Former Chief Economist of the World Bank

If developing economies are to continue to converge with their advanced counterparts, they will need to deploy new technologies relatively efficiently, taking into account the role of labor-market skills and regulations. This will not be easy, but it is possible—and, indeed, necessary.

Kemal Derviş, 2018
Nonresident Distinguished Fellow,
Brookings Institution,
and Former Head of the United Nations Development Programme

CHAPTER 1

Potential Not Realized:
An International Database of Potential Growth

Potential growth—the rate of expansion an economy can sustain at full capacity and employment—critically drives a wide range of macroeconomic and development outcomes. To assess the evolution of potential growth in recent decades, this chapter compiles the most comprehensive database used to date in such research, covering the nine most commonly used measures of potential growth for up to 173 countries over 1981-2021. The chapter describes the database and some of the findings from it. All measures of global potential growth studied in the chapter consistently show steady declines over the past decade, with all the fundamental drivers of growth gradually losing momentum. The weakening of potential growth has been highly synchronous across countries: In 2011-21, potential growth was below its 2000-10 average in 96 percent of advanced economies and 57 percent of emerging market and developing economies. Adverse events, such as the global financial crisis and the coronavirus disease 2019 (COVID-19) pandemic, with their ensuing global recessions, have contributed to the trend decline. At the country level also, national recessions have left legacies of lower potential growth even five years after their onset, by about 1.4 percentage points on average. The persistent effect of recessions on potential growth has operated through weaker growth of investment, employment, and productivity.

Introduction

The global economy headed into the COVID-19 pandemic and the Russian Federation's invasion of Ukraine after a decade of slowing growth. The pandemic-induced global recession of 2020 further deepened this slowdown, and Russia's invasion of Ukraine in February 2022 has already left additional scars. These adverse shocks have not just reduced actual global output growth but have also dampened potential growth: the rate of increase of potential output, defined as the level of output an economy would sustain at full capacity utilization and full employment. Potential growth is a critical determinant of a wide range of macroeconomic and development outcomes, including sustained improvement in living standards and poverty reduction.

Potential growth is of fundamental importance to short- and long-run macroeconomic analysis and policy, but it is not directly observable. An extensive literature has employed three main methods for estimating growth in potential output, each of which has its advantages and disadvantages. Measures of potential growth based on production function estimates make it possible to study the contributions of the fundamental drivers of growth—namely, the growth of the factors of production and technical progress—but

Note: This chapter was prepared by Sinem Kilic Celik, M. Ayhan Kose, Franziska Ohnsorge, and Franz Ulrich Ruch.

involve assumptions that may be viewed as far-fetched. A second method uses economic analysts' long-term (five-year-ahead) forecasts for output growth, which may be assumed to incorporate their judgments. The third method obtains measures of potential growth from statistical filters of actual data on growth; it may be best at ensuring consistency between estimates of potential growth and output gaps, on the one hand, and indicators of domestic demand pressures, on the other.

This chapter introduces the most comprehensive international database for the nine most commonly used measures of potential growth, based on these three methods, for the largest available sample of countries over the period 1981-2021. This database and the analysis in this chapter also serve as the foundation for chapters 2 and 5, which examine past and prospective potential growth, globally and regionally, and policies to improve them. In addition, this chapter addresses the following questions.

- How has potential growth evolved in recent decades?

- How have recessions and other adverse developments affected potential growth?

- Through which channels have such developments affected potential growth?

The chapter makes the following major contributions to the literature.

- *Largest database of potential growth.* The chapter introduces the first comprehensive database of the nine most commonly used measures of potential growth for the largest available country sample—of up to 173 economies (37 advanced economies and 136 emerging market and developing economies [EMDEs])—over 1981-2021. These measures comprise one based on the production function approach; five based on the application of univariate filters (Hodrick-Prescott, Baxter-King, Christiano-Fitzgerald, Butterworth, and unobserved-components filters); one based on a multivariate Kalman filter; and two based on long-term growth forecasts. Previous studies have limited themselves to a single method of measuring potential growth, such as the production function approach (OECD 2014) or multivariate filters (ADB 2016; IMF 2015). This study builds on earlier work published before the pandemic that employed several measures of potential growth (Kilic Celik, Kose, and Ohnsorge 2020; World Bank 2018).

- *Broader assessment of the evolution of potential growth over time and across countries.* The chapter documents that all measures of potential growth show an internationally widespread decline in global potential growth in the decade before the pandemic. Earlier studies documented the decline for only a subset of measures (for example, Chalaux and Guillemette 2019; Kilic Celik, Kose, and Ohnsorge 2020).

- *Comprehensive analysis of the impact of recessions and other adverse events.* The chapter describes the first study to systematically compare the long-term damage to potential growth of short-term economic disruptions—such as recessions, banking crises, and epidemics—in a large set of countries. Thus far, only a few studies have estimated the effects of recessions on growth in potential output, and they were confined to a sample of member countries of the Organisation for Economic Co-operation and Development (OECD) and the production function approach (Furceri and Mourougane 2012; Mourougane 2017). This chapter broadens the earlier research by estimating the effects of recessions, banking crises, and epidemics in a large sample of advanced economies and EMDEs and for a wide range of measures of potential growth.

- *Study of channels through which adverse events affect potential growth.* The chapter estimates empirically, using a set of local-projections models, the channels through which short-term economic disruptions have dampened potential growth. Specifically, it estimates the effects of disruptions on the growth of the labor supply, of investment, and of total factor productivity (TFP) in a consistent framework. Previous studies have typically examined overall effects on growth or effects through individual channels.

The theoretical literature has analyzed, typically using dynamic stochastic general equilibrium models, several mechanisms through which short-term output disruptions (associated with recessions and other adverse events) may have longer-term effects. Weak aggregate demand during such disruptions may reduce the expected profitability of, and thus discourage, productivity-increasing research and development (Fatás 2000). It may similarly discourage investment in productivity-raising new technologies that would otherwise have improved productivity (Anzoategui et al. 2019). Investors who expect weak aggregate demand to persist will be reluctant, more broadly, to invest; reduced investment will tend to lower asset prices, which, through wealth effects, will further depress consumption (Caballero and Simsek 2017). If a financial crisis accompanies aggregate weakness in demand, financial market frictions can restrict firms' access to credit and start-up capital, further reducing investment and productivity growth.[1]

Short-run disruptions can also damage potential output through productivity losses due to resource misallocation (Dieppe, Kilic Celik, and Okou 2021; Furceri et al. 2021); productivity gains stemming from the exit of low-productivity firms may partly offset these losses (Bloom et al. 2020). Finally, high unemployment that accompanies weak aggregate demand tends to lead to human capital losses and reduced job search activity among the long-term unemployed (Blanchard and Summers 1987; Lockwood 1991).

Empirical estimates have documented that some of these mechanisms have indeed been at work during past recessions. An analysis of data for a large sample of countries during 1960-2018 found that financial crises, especially when accompanied by a rapid buildup of debt, were associated with persistent productivity losses (Dieppe, Kilic Celik, and Okou 2021). Among a large sample of firms in six EMDEs in Europe, firms in sectors that faced the largest adverse demand shocks during the 2009 global recession reduced

---

[1] For details of these empirical findings involving financial markets, see Claessens and Kose (2017), Queralto (2013), and Wilms, Swank, and de Haan (2018).

their capacities the most (Nguyen and Qian 2014). In a sample of 61 countries during 1954-2010, lower labor productivity growth followed banking crises, consistent with a loss of human capital during these crises (Oulton and Sebastia-Barriel 2016). Other studies have found that the return of actual output growth or levels to prerecession trends is nonlinear and dependent on the persistence, depth, and source of the recession and on whether financial crises accompanied it.[2] None of these studies, however, systematically examines the various channels through which short-term disruptions reduce potential growth.

The chapter reports the following key findings.

- *Trend decline in potential growth.* An internationally widespread decline in potential growth occurred in 2011-21, relative to 2000-10. All estimates of potential growth show this decline, globally and for the main country groups: advanced economies and EMDEs. Global potential growth, as estimated using the production function approach, fell to 2.6 percent a year during 2011-21 from 3.5 percent a year during 2000-10; advanced-economy potential growth fell to 1.4 percent a year during 2011-21, 0.8 percentage point below its 2000-10 average; and EMDE potential growth fell to 5.0 percent a year during 2011-21 from 6.0 percent a year during 2000-10. The weakening of potential growth was highly synchronized across countries: during 2011-21, potential growth was below its 2000-10 average in 96 percent of advanced economies and 57 percent of EMDEs. This widespread decline reflected a multitude of factors. All the fundamental drivers of growth faded in 2011-21: TFP growth slowed, investment weakened, and labor force growth declined.

- *Persistent impact of recessions on potential growth.* Recessions, even five years later, were associated, on average, with a decline of about 1.4 percentage points in potential growth. While the magnitude of the estimated decline in potential growth five years after a recession depended on the measure (with a range of 0.2-1.4 percentage points), it was always statistically significantly negative. The effect was somewhat stronger in EMDEs than in advanced economies: in EMDEs, potential growth was still, on average, 1.6 percentage points lower five years after the recession, whereas in advanced economies, it was only 1.3 percentage points lower.

- *Larger impact of recessions than other adverse events on potential growth.* Recessions tended to have somewhat more severe effects on potential growth than did other adverse events. Banking crises were associated with initially larger falls in potential growth (peaking at 1.8 percentage point after two years) as a result of a collapse in investment. However, these declines tended to unwind quickly, such that after five years, potential growth had fallen only 1.2 percentage points. Epidemics were associated with more modest, but still statistically significant, short- and medium-

---

[2] For a discussion of the impact of financial crises on growth, see Ball (2014); Claessens, Kose, and Terrones (2009, 2012); Furceri and Mourougane (2012); and Haltmeier (2012).

term declines in potential growth. These declines were more severe in EMDEs than in advanced economies, which may have been better able to limit the economic damage through fiscal and monetary stimulus.

- *Adverse effects through multiple channels.* Recessions affected potential growth through multiple channels. Four to five years after an average recession, the annual growth of investment, employment, and productivity remained significantly lower than in "normal" years (by 3 percentage points, 0.7 percentage point, and 0.7 percentage point, respectively). This contrasts with what took place in respect to banking crises, which tended to be associated mostly with lasting losses of productivity growth, and epidemics, which were mainly associated with lasting employment losses, possibly reflecting economic shifts caused by behavioral responses to epidemics.

- *Different features of estimates of potential growth.* The comprehensive database also allows comparisons across measures of potential growth. Forecast-based estimates tend to be systematically higher than other estimates, and estimates based on univariate filtering techniques systematically lower. Estimates based on filtering techniques tend to be the most volatile and to track actual growth most closely, as expected. Estimates based on the production function approach tend to be the most stable and the least correlated with actual growth, as they capture slow-moving drivers of potential growth.

The chapter proceeds as follows. The next section presents the database, then is followed by a section that describes movements in potential growth around the world in recent decades and a section that estimates the effects on potential growth of recessions. The chapter's penultimate section documents the channels through which these effects operate. The final section concludes.

Database

The literature has used three main methods to estimate potential growth, and several different measures can be derived using variants of these three methods. The comprehensive database developed here allows a comparison of the behaviors of such measures.

The database includes nine measures of potential growth for up to 173 countries over periods as long as 1981-2021. The baseline measure of annual potential growth, estimated using the production function approach, is available for up to 30 advanced economies and 64 EMDEs for 1998-2021 (table 1F.1; annex 1A). Six univariate and multivariate filter-based estimates of potential growth, which require quarterly data, are available for up to 37 advanced economies and 52 EMDEs for 1980Q1-2022Q1, with projections to 2024Q4 (table 1F.1; annexes 1B and 1C). Estimates of potential growth based on the *World Economic Outlook*, published by the International Monetary Fund (IMF), are available for up to 37 advanced economies and 136 EMDEs for 1990-2022 (annex 1D). Estimates of potential growth based on consensus forecasts are available for up to 34 advanced economies and 44 EMDEs for 1990-2022.

The database also includes projections for a subset of measures. For the production function approach, projections are available for 2022-32. Chapter 5 presents and analyzes these projections and the methodology on which they are based. For the filter-based estimates, forecasts are available up to 2024Q4.

This chapter and chapters 2 and 5 discuss aggregates for the global economy and for particular country groups. These aggregates are averages weighted by real gross domestic product (GDP) (at 2010-19 prices and market exchange rates) for a balanced sample of 30 advanced economies and 53 EMDEs for 2000-21, unless specified otherwise. The 53 EMDEs comprise 6 economies in East Asia and Pacific (EAP), 9 economies in Europe and Central Asia (ECA), 16 economies in Latin America and the Caribbean (LAC), 5 economies in the Middle East and North Africa (MNA), 3 economies in South Asia (SAR), and 14 economies in Sub-Saharan Africa (SSA). (The regions referred to here, and throughout the book, are as defined by the World Bank.) Data for about half of EMDEs (mainly in ECA and SSA) are not available before 1998. Hence, to ensure broad country coverage, the sample period is restricted to 2000-21 (and 2022-30 in chapter 5) when international averages are discussed. However, when the robustness of trends among different measures is discussed, the sample is restricted to those countries for which data are available for all measures.

Basic concepts

The literature has employed three main methods for estimating potential growth, sometimes with different objectives. Some have been used to analyze short-term movements in potential growth, while others have focused on long-term developments (Basu and Fernald 2009). Time-series filtering techniques, including univariate or multivariate filters, may be used to estimate movements in potential growth in the short term, while estimates growth in potential output over longer periods are usually based on structural models that include a production function or on long-term growth forecasts.

In the short term, when factors of production cannot be reallocated in response to shocks, potential growth may be viewed as the growth of output that can be sustained without putting pressure on given productive capacity and inflation (Okun 1962). In the short term, temporary disruptions and boosts to supply that may dissipate over the longer term can buffet growth in potential output. For example, a shift in the composition of demand may render part of the existing capital stock obsolete, effectively reducing potential output and its growth in the short term. However, over the longer term, firms would be expected to adjust to the new structure of demand, returning growth in potential output toward its previous path. The short-term measure is particularly relevant for demand management and monetary policy, since temporary supply constraints or upward demand shocks tend to reduce the effective slack in the economy, with implications for macroeconomic policy and the monetary policy interest rate. Central banks, in particular, need to focus on movements in potential growth in the short term as they gauge deviations of actual from potential output levels over the horizon of monetary policy transmission, about one to two years.

In the production function framework, growth in potential output is a function of growth in the factors of production: the capital stock and the labor force, along with current technological progress (Solow 1962). Growth in potential output in the long term thus depends on these fundamental drivers, an implicit assumption being that the factors of production are allocated to their most productive uses, regardless of temporary supply shocks. Finance and economy ministries often focus on potential growth over longer periods, aware that boosting it will promote fiscal sustainability over longer time horizons.

Measures of growth in potential output

The literature has largely focused on three methods of estimating potential growth: a production function method, time-series filters, and analysts' growth forecasts.

- *Production function method.* The production function approach represents potential output as a function of the fully utilized capital stock, fully employed labor force, and technology as measured by TFP. For analytical convenience, the production function is often assumed to have a particular form, known as Cobb-Douglas.[3] In this chapter, potential TFP growth is estimated as the predicted value of a parsimonious panel regression of five-year averages of trend TFP growth on lagged per capita income relative to the advanced-economy average (to proxy convergence-related productivity catch-up), education and demographic indicators, and trend investment (annex 1A). Potential labor supply is estimated as the population-weighted aggregate of predicted values of age- and gender-specific labor force participation rates from regressions on policy outcomes and cohort characteristics, business cycles, and country effects. The potential capital stock is assumed to match the actual capital stock.

- *Time-series filtering methods.* These methods employ univariate or multivariate filters. In this chapter, univariate filters involve estimates of trend output using only GDP data series (annex 1B). Multivariate filters use the empirical relationship between GDP and other variables (such as inflation, unemployment rates, commodity prices, or financial variables) to help distinguish short-run deviations of output from trends (annex 1C). The database in this chapter employs five univariate filters: the Hodrick-Prescott filter, the Baxter-King filter, the Christiano-Fitzgerald filter, the Butterworth filter, and a filter based on an unobserved-components model. An additional multivariate filter uses financial variables and commodity prices, a Phillips curve relationship, a Taylor rule, and Okun's law.

- *Growth forecasts.* This method is applied in this chapter using two sets of long-term (five-year-ahead) growth forecasts, from Consensus Economics and the IMF's *World Economic Outlook* database (annex 1D). These forecasts are based partly on models analysts use and partly on the analysts' judgment. Judgment can play an important

---

[3] Constant returns to scale and a constant elasticity of substitution between capital and labor characterize the Cobb-Douglas production function.

role during periods of major structural change, which models may not be well-equipped to capture.

Each approach comes with advantages and disadvantages (table 1F.2). Even in data-poor environments, univariate filters are straightforward to implement. Multivariate filters employ additional information that can ensure that the measure of potential output is better aligned with its determinants, as economic theory suggests. In particular, multivariate filter-based estimates can ensure that estimated output gaps in the short term are consistent with indicators of domestic demand pressures (such as inflation, unemployment, current account balances, and capacity utilization). All statistical filters, however, have drawbacks: in particular, they suffer from well-known "endpoint" problems that tend to lead to large revisions as new data become available. The approach employed here includes forecasts of real GDP growth to minimize this problem. Since they capture high-frequency movements, measures of potential growth based on filtering techniques correlate strongly with actual output growth and with each other.

The production function approach has the advantage of taking into account the fundamental drivers of output on the supply side—factor inputs and technology—that dominate in the long run. While estimates of potential growth based on this approach are often consistent with long-term growth averages, they correlate less closely with actual growth in the short term. Potential growth measured by the production function approach is also only weakly correlated with estimates of potential growth obtained from filtering techniques. The production function approach has a number of drawbacks, however. It assumes a particular functional form of the relationships among factor inputs, technology, and output. Its application relies on imperfect measures of, or proxies for, the growth of potential TFP, labor supply, and the capital stock. And it is unable to capture cyclical shocks to capacity and supply that may cause short-term fluctuations in potential output. Finally, the approach provides measures of *growth* in potential output, but derivation of *levels* of potential output would require additional steps to identify an "anchor level" in which the output gap is closed.

Long-term growth forecasts generally incorporate analysts' judgment and thus capture factors that cannot be econometrically modeled. As a result, in a way similar to estimates based on the production function approach, these forecasts are only weakly correlated with filter-based estimates of potential growth. However, in practice, forecasts can be sticky and, at times, difficult to interpret.

Comparison of different measures of potential growth

The estimated rates of potential growth resulting from the application of these methods differed in their levels and evolutions over time. This section briefly explores these differences.

First, differences among estimates of potential growth were wider for advanced economies than EMDEs (figures 1.1.A and 1.1.B). During 2000-21, potential growth estimated from forecasts was the highest among the nine measures in more than half the

FIGURE 1.1 Estimates of potential growth

By all measures, growth in potential output slowed in 2011-21 relative to 2000-10 in the global economy, in EMDEs, and in advanced economies. Filter-based measures are more volatile and less persistent. Forecasts are most often the highest estimates of potential growth.

A. Range of advanced-economy average annual potential growth across methodologies

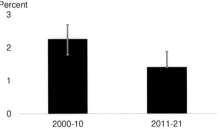

B. Range of EMDE average annual potential growth across methodologies

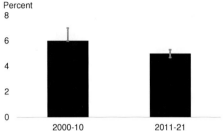

C. Methodologies generating highest and lowest estimates of potential growth

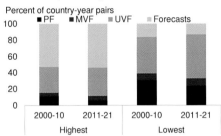

D. Uncertainty in regard to global potential growth

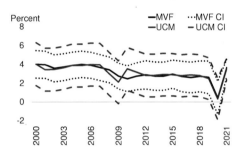

E. Standard deviation of estimates of potential growth, 2000-19

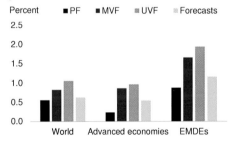

F. Persistence in estimates of potential growth, 2000-19

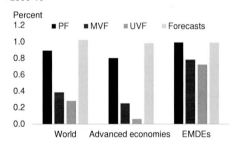

Source: World Bank.
Note: Aggregates refer to weighted averages (constant real gross domestic product [GDP] weights at average 2010-19 prices and exchange rates). "Forecasts" are five-year-ahead growth forecasts from the International Monetary Fund's *World Economic Outlook*. EMDEs = emerging market and developing economies; MVF = multivariate filter; PF = production function approach; UCM = unobserved-components model;
UVF = univariate filter.
A.B. Blue bars denote production function-based estimates. Orange whiskers indicate the range of the eight estimates considered.
C. Figure shows the share of country-year pairs during each period in which each methodology generates either the highest or the lowest estimate of potential growth. Only country-year pairs for which estimates from at least two methodologies are available are considered. "UVF" refers to any of four univariate filters (Christiano-Fitzgerald, Baxter-King, Hodrick-Prescott, or Butterworth). Unbalanced sample of 30 advanced economies and 25 EMDEs for 1998-2021.
D. "UCM CI" and "MVF CI" refer to 95 percent confidence bands for each methodology. Unbalanced sample of 30 advanced economies and 25 EMDEs for 2000-21.
E. Standard deviation of estimates of potential growth over 2000-19. "UVF" refers to the maximum standard deviation among the univariate filters. Unbalanced sample of 30 advanced economies and 40 EMDEs.
F. Coefficient estimates on lagged potential growth from an autoregressive process of order 1 regression of global, advanced-economy, and EMDE potential growth for 2000-19. "UVF" refers to the coefficient of the smallest estimate among the univariate filters. Unbalanced sample of 30 advanced economies and 25 EMDEs for 2000-21.

country-year pairs (figure 1.1.C). Univariate filters generally produced the lowest estimates. At the country level, the same pattern was found: forecast-based measures of potential growth tended to be the highest, and measures from univariate filters the lowest, especially over the past decade.

Second, multivariate filter-based estimates of potential growth had narrower confidence bands than those based on univariate filters (figure 1.1.D). This difference likely reflects the use of additional demand pressure indicators in multivariate filters that help identify the output gap more accurately. Confidence intervals cannot be computed for estimates based on the production function approach or analysts' forecasts.

Third, global, advanced-economy, and EMDE estimates of potential growth based on univariate and multivariate filters typically have the highest variances, while those based on the production function approach have the lowest (figure 1.1.E). At the country level, univariate filter estimates have the largest variance (in about 75 percent of cases).

Fourth, univariate filter-based estimates have the least persistence, especially those for advanced economies, while estimates from forecasts and the production function approach have the most persistence across all groups of countries (figure 1.1.F).[4] These findings are intuitively appealing, as filter-based estimates are designed to capture time-series variation, whereas the others rely on more persistent drivers of potential growth.

Fifth, estimates from different multivariate and univariate filters tend to be highly correlated, with a median within-country correlation coefficient above 85 percent (figure 1.2.A). However, they correlate only moderately with estimates from the production function approach and analysts' forecasts. Similarly, production function-based and forecast-based estimates correlate only moderately with each other, whereas estimates from the two sources of growth forecasts employed in this chapter are highly correlated with each other.

Finally, as expected, estimates of potential growth based on filters derived from the unobserved-components model most closely track actual growth, with an average correlation coefficient of 0.95 across the country sample, followed by estimates based on the multivariate filter and other univariate filters (figure 1.2.B). As expected given its construction from slow-moving variables, the production function approach deviates more from actual growth (with a correlation of 0.45 with actual growth). The correlation is even lower for forecast-based measures of potential growth, which tend to change only when forecasters modify their views about drivers of long-term growth.

Evolution of potential growth

This section first reviews the evolution of potential growth over the past two decades. It then focuses on potential growth during the last two global recessions, those of 2009 and 2020. While both subsections rely mostly on the production function-based

---

[4] The coefficient on lagged potential growth from a regression with one autoregressive term is taken to capture the degree of persistence here.

FIGURE 1.2 **Comparison of estimates of potential growth**

Filter-based estimates of potential growth are highly correlated with each other and with actual output growth. Forecast-based estimates tend to be less correlated with other estimates of potential growth and least correlated with actual growth.

A. Correlation of estimates of potential growth, 2000-21

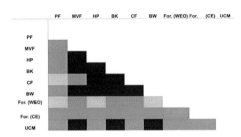

B. Correlation of estimates of potential growth with actual growth, 2000-20

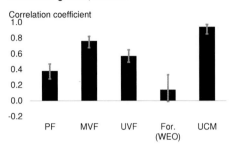

Source: World Bank.
Note: BK = Baxter-King filter; BW = Butterworth; CF = Christiano-Fitzgerald filter; For. = forecast; For. (CE) = five-year-ahead growth forecasts from Consensus Economics; For. (WEO) = five-year-ahead growth forecasts from the International Monetary Fund's World Economic Outlook database; HP = Hodrick-Prescott filter; MVF = multivariate filter; PF = production function approach; UCM = unobserved-components model; UVF = univariate filter.
A. Figure shows the within-country correlations during 2000-20 between different measures of potential growth. Red represents correlations greater than 80 percent, orange those between 60 and 80 percent, yellow those between 40 and 60 percent, and blue those between 20 and 40 percent. Unbalanced sample of 37 advanced economies and 63 EMDEs for 2000-21.
B. Blue bars show the median of within-country correlations during 2000-20 between different measures of potential growth and actual growth. Orange whiskers represent the 25th and 75th percentiles of within-country correlation during the same period. Unbalanced sample of 37 advanced economies and 95 EMDEs for 2000-20.

measures of potential growth, the findings are consistent with those from the other measures of potential growth.

Potential growth over time

Global potential growth, as estimated using the production function approach, fell to 2.6 percent a year over 2011-21 from 3.5 percent a year during 2000-10 (figure 1.3.A).[5] The weakening of potential growth was internationally widespread. Thus, during 2011-21, potential growth was below its 2000-10 average in 96 percent of advanced economies and 57 percent of EMDEs. Economies with potential growth below its 2000-10 average accounted for about 80 percent of global GDP in 2022 (figure 1.3.B). Estimates of per capita potential growth also show a trend decline over time, to 2.0 percent a year in 2011-21 from 2.7 percent a year during 2000-10 (figure 1.3.C). These estimates suggest a trend slowdown in global potential growth around the cyclical shocks that depressed actual growth below its elevated average in the early 2000s.

The finding of a decline in potential growth is robust with respect to the measure used, although the magnitude of the slowdown differs across the measures. To ensure

---

[5] Data for half the EMDEs (mainly those in ECA and SSA) are not available before 1998. Hence, to ensure broad country coverage, the sample period is restricted to 2000-21 for discussions of country groups. However, when robustness of trends among different measures is discussed, the sample is restricted to those countries for which data are available for all measures.

FIGURE 1.3 **Evolution of potential growth**

By all measures, potential growth slowed between 2000-10 and 2011-21 globally, in EMDEs, in advanced economies, and in most countries. It also slowed in per capita terms.

A. Potential growth

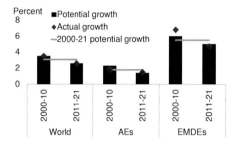

B. Share of economies and GDP with potential growth below 2000-10 average, 2011-21

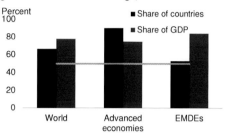

C. Per capita potential growth

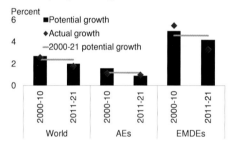

D. Global potential growth

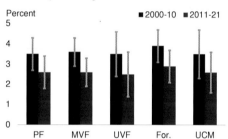

Sources: UN population statistics; World Bank.
Note: AEs = advanced economies; EMDEs = emerging market and developing economies; "For." = five-year-ahead growth forecasts from the International Monetary Fund's *World Economic Outlook*; GDP = gross domestic product; MVF = multivariate filter; PF = production function approach; UCM = unobserved-components model; UVF = univariate filter.
A.B.C. Based on potential growth derived using production function approach. GDP-weighted averages. Sample includes 30 advanced and 53 emerging market and developing economies.
B. Number of economies with potential growth in each period below its 2000-10 average and their share of global or group GDP. Horizontal line indicates 50 percent. Unbalanced sample of 30 advanced economies and 53 EMDEs for 2000-21.
D. Based on common sample of 30 advanced economies and 25 EMDEs for 2000-21 to ensure consistency in samples across methodologies. Orange whiskers indicate range implied by GDP-weighted average of country-specific standard deviations of estimates of potential growth for each approach.

comparability, a smaller sample of 30 advanced economies and 25 EMDEs for which all nine measures are available was employed. By all these measures, global potential growth slowed by 0.9-1 percentage point a year from its average in 2000-10, to 2.5-2.9 percent a year in 2011-21 (figure 1.3.D).

In *advanced economies,* the slowdown in potential growth set in before the global financial crisis. After a sharp decline during 2008-10—the period of the global financial crisis and the start of the euro area sovereign debt crisis—potential growth stabilized in 2011-21 as investment growth recovered. However, at 1.4 percent a year over 2011-21, potential growth in advanced economies was 0.8 percentage point below its 2000-10 average (figure 1.4.A). As in the broader set of advanced economies, potential growth in the Group of Seven economies (Canada, France, Germany, Italy, Japan, the United

FIGURE 1.4 Drivers of potential growth

The decline in potential growth between 2000-10 and 2011-21 reflected reduced contributions from growth in TFP, investment, and the labor force and occurred in all EMDE regions.

A. Contributions to potential growth

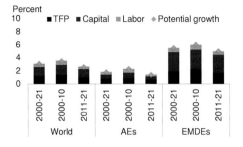

B. Contributions to potential growth

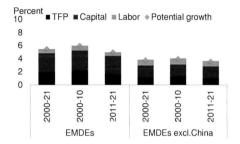

C. Potential growth in EMDE regions

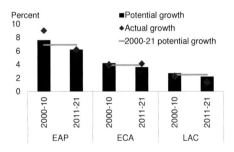

D. Potential growth in EMDE regions

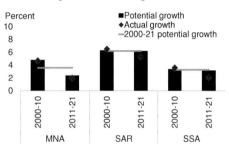

E. Share of economies with potential growth below 2000-10 average, 2011-21

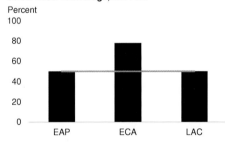

F. Share of economies with potential growth below 2000-10 average, 2011-21

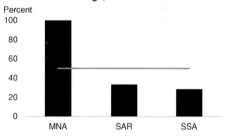

Source: World Bank.
Note: Averages, weighted by gross domestic product (GDP), of production function-based estimates of potential growth. AEs = advanced economies; EAP = East Asia and Pacific; ECA = Europe and Central Asia; EMDEs = emerging market and developing economies; excl. = excluding; LAC = Latin America and the Caribbean; MNA = Middle East and North Africa; SAR = South Asia; SSA = Sub-Saharan Africa; TFP = total factor productivity.
A.B. Sample of 30 advanced economies and 53 EMDEs.
E.F. Shares of GDP in each region accounted for by economies with potential growth in the period below its 2000-10 average; figure depicts a total of 53 EMDEs. Regional samples include the largest available coverage for each region. Sample includes 6 countries in EAP region, 9 in ECA, 16 in LAC, 5 in MNA, 3 in SAR, and 14 in SSA. All MNA countries had higher potential growth in 2000-10 than in 2011-21 (and than the full-period average) because of a commodities boom in the first decade of the 2000s that was followed by a commodity price plunge, political tensions, and conflict in the second decade of the 2000s.

Kingdom, and the United States) was 1.5 percent a year on average in 2011-21, 0.5 percentage point below its 2000-10 average.

EMDEs, by contrast, enjoyed a short-lived pre-global recession surge in potential growth in the 2000s that subsequently faded. In the wake of the global financial crisis and associated global recession, a surge in public investment underpinned EMDE potential growth, offsetting softening growth of both TFP and the labor supply. As EMDE policy stimulus was unwound and as investment growth plummeted in commodity-exporting EMDEs amid the oil price slide in 2014-16, EMDE potential growth slowed sharply in 2015-19. A sharp slowdown in investment growth during 2010-19 also depressed potential growth in China, whereas the slowdown was milder in other EMDEs, where investment growth remained more robust and demographics were more favorable (chapter 2). Overall, at 5.0 percent a year, EMDE potential growth during 2011-21 fell short of its average by 1.0 percentage point a year during 2000-10 (figure 1.4.B).

Chapter 2 assesses in detail the evolution of potential growth across various *EMDE regions* (that is, regions of EMDEs). In brief, potential growth fell furthest in those regions that had benefited from rapid convergence of per capita incomes in the early 2000s or included many commodity-exporting EMDEs (figures 1.4.C and 1.4.D). The slowdown in potential growth in 2011-21 relative to its 2000-10 average was sharpest in MNA, where investment growth plunged amid the oil price drop of 2014-16 and conflict and policy uncertainty persisted in parts of the region.

In EAP, potential growth in 2011-21 was lower by 1.4 percentage points a year than in 2000-10. This decline mostly reflected a slowdown in potential growth in China, partly as a result of policy efforts aimed at rebalancing growth away from investment toward more sustainable engines of growth; adding to this was slower growth of both TFP and the working-age population.

In ECA and LCA, potential growth in 2011-21 was lower by 0.5-0.6 percentage point a year than in 2000-10. The ECA region's previous two decades of rapid integration into European Union production networks, beginning in the 1990s, gradually diminished its potential for further catch-up productivity growth. The region also hosts several energy-exporting countries (including Russia) that suffered recessions or slowdowns in the wake of the 2014-16 slump in oil prices. In LAC, potential growth suffered from weakened productivity growth, partly as a result of adverse terms-of-trade shocks and bouts of policy uncertainty, as well as less favorable demographics.

Potential growth in SSA also declined somewhat (by 0.2 percentage point a year in 2011-21 relative to 2000-10). Favorable demographics and rapid capital accumulation, which accelerated as resource discoveries were developed into operating mines and oil fields and governments undertook large-scale investments in public infrastructure, only partly offset a sharp slowdown in TFP growth.

In 2011-21, potential growth in SAR remained broadly unchanged from that in 2000-10. Growth of the labor force benefited from a demographic dividend. The share of the population of working age rose by more than one-tenth between 2000 and 2021, reaching 67 percent in 2021. Capital and TFP also maintained their growth momentum in 2011-21. Growth in investment remained broadly robust over this period—faster than the EMDE average—and the investment-to-GDP ratio rose by 5 percentage points of GDP between 2000 and 2021, to more than 28 percent of GDP in 2021.

Potential growth during global recessions

The 2000-21 period spans two global recessions—the 2009 recession that was triggered by the global financial crisis and the 2020 recession that was caused by the COVID-19 pandemic. These recessions disrupted fixed-capital investment and caused widespread employment and output losses. In the case of the 2020 recession, disruptions of education systems caused by pandemic-induced reductions in social interaction also slowed down human capital accumulation.

By the production function-based measure of potential growth, global potential growth slowed by 1.2 and 1.3 percentage point from two years before the global recessions of 2009 and 2020, respectively, to the recession year itself (figure 1.5.A). The slowdowns in potential growth in EMDEs differed more between the two recessions (1.3 percentage points in 2007-09 and 1.7 percentage points in 2018-20) than the slowdowns in advanced economies (1.2 percentage points in 2007-09 and 1.1 percentage points in 2018-20; figures 1.5.B and 1.5.C). The considerably smaller slowdown in EMDEs in the 2009 global recession largely reflected investment-driven support for potential growth in China during the global financial crisis. In EMDEs excluding China, potential growth declined by 1.2 and 2.0 percentage points in the 2009 and 2020 recessions, respectively (figure 1.5.D).

In advanced economies, the slowdown in potential growth in the two global recessions reflected steep declines in investment and TFP growth, whereas in EMDEs it reflected mostly a decline in TFP growth (figures 1.6.A-1.6.D). In both country groups, slowing labor force growth also contributed. The steeper slowdown in potential growth in EMDEs in 2020 than in 2009 reflected the deeper collapse in investment, but also the pandemic-induced fall in potential labor force participation.

Although both global recessions resulted in a slowdown in potential growth, they differed in regard to the behavior of potential growth in the subsequent recoveries. A decade of investment weakness and reduced productivity growth followed the global financial crisis, leading to a failure of potential growth to return to prerecession rates. In contrast, the swiftest first-year output rebound of any global recession over the past eight decades followed the 2020 global recession (World Bank 2021a). Strong growth in investment, especially in advanced economies, and a productivity rebound accompanied this recovery in output, and together they lifted potential growth to prerecession rates globally, in advanced economies, and in EMDEs. However, the impact of this initial rebound in potential growth is likely to be temporary because of the persistent headwinds the fundamental drivers of potential growth are facing (see chapter 5).

FIGURE 1.5 Potential growth around the global recessions of 2009 and 2020

Potential growth fell in the global recessions of 2009 and 2020 in both advanced economies and EMDEs. The declines were particularly steep during the COVID-19-induced global recession of 2020.

A. World: Potential growth

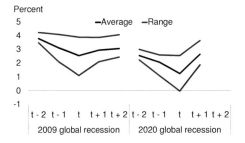

B. Advanced economies: Potential growth

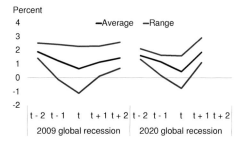

C. EMDEs: Potential growth

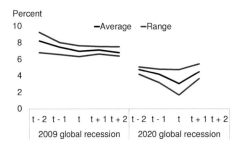

D. EMDEs excluding China: Potential growth

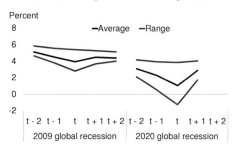

Sources: International Monetary Fund, *World Economic Outlook*; World Bank.
Note: "Average" is an unweighted average of seven measures of potential growth (excluding expectations). "Range" reflects the maximum and minimum. Figures show potential growth around global recessions in *t* = 2009 and *t* = 2020. Unbalanced sample of 30 advanced economies and 25 EMDEs for 2007-21. EMDEs = emerging market and developing economies.

These estimated movements in potential growth around global recessions were similar for almost all measures of potential growth, except those based on forecasts. Potential growth declined in the two recession years globally, in advanced economies, in EMDEs, and in EMDEs excluding China.[6] On average across the eight measures that showed declines in the two recessions, global potential growth slowed by about 1.3 percentage points from two years before the recession to the year of the recession.[7] The slowdown was larger in EMDEs (1.5 percentage points) than in advanced economies (1.2 percentage points). The recession year in both episodes generally saw the trough in potential growth according to all measures. The estimated decline in potential growth was smallest for production function-based measures and largest for measures obtained using univariate filters.

---

[6] For the COVID-19-induced global recession of 2020, this is broadly consistent with the findings of persistently lower potential output levels by Bodnár et al. (2020) for the euro area and Fernald and Li (2021) for the United States.

[7] Measures based on consensus forecasts for long-term growth are not covered here because they are based on a much smaller country sample.

FIGURE 1.6 Drivers of potential growth around the global recessions of 2009 and 2020

The decline in potential growth in the global recessions of 2009 and 2020 reflected falls in the contributions of growth in TFP and the supply of labor and, except in China in 2009, capital accumulation.

A. World: Contributions to potential growth

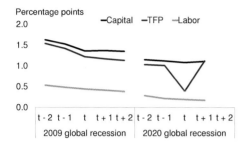

B. Advanced economies: Contributions to potential growth

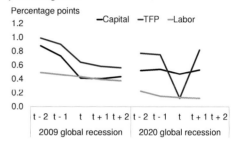

C. EMDEs: Contributions to potential growth

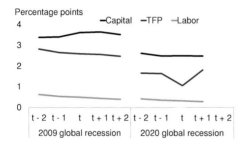

D. EMDEs excluding China: Contributions to potential growth

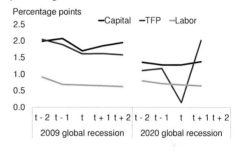

Sources: International Monetary Fund, *World Economic Outlook*; World Bank.
Note: Figures show the contributions of capital, total factor productivity (TFP), and labor to potential growth around *t* = 2009 and *t* = 2020. Unbalanced sample of 30 advanced economies and 25 EMDEs for 2007-21. EMDEs = emerging market and developing economies.

The long-term effects of short-term shocks on potential growth

The COVID-19-induced output collapse of 2020 renewed concerns about the impact of recessions on the level and growth of potential output. A number of studies have documented the lasting effects of country-specific recessions and financial crises on the level or growth of actual or potential output (Cerra and Saxena 2008; Furceri and Mourougane 2012; Mourougane 2017). However, these studies have mostly focused on OECD member countries using only production function-based estimates of potential growth.

This section broadens the scope of the earlier literature in three dimensions. First, it examines the effect of country-specific recessions on potential growth in a much larger sample of countries, including both advanced economies and EMDEs. Second, it employs all the measures of potential growth described earlier in the chapter to obtain a better understanding of the linkages between recessions and potential growth. Third, in

FIGURE 1.7 **Characteristics of recessions**

Most recessions at the country level have occurred during global recessions. Growth has slowed by about 8 percentage points between the year before the recession and its trough.

A. Share of countries with recessions

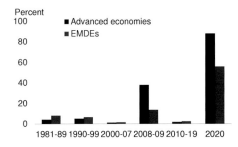

B. World: Actual growth during recessions

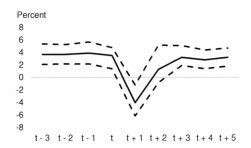

C. Advanced economies: Actual growth during recessions

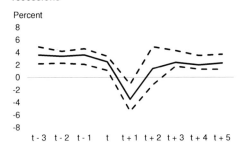

D. EMDEs: Actual growth during recessions

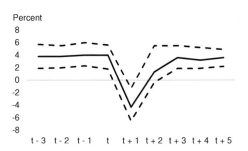

Source: World Bank.
Note: Recessions are defined as the period from the peak preceding a business cycle trough to the trough, with a trough defined as a year in which output growth is both negative and at least one standard deviation below its long-term average. Sample includes
91 recession events in 33 advanced economies and 190 recession events in 77 EMDEs during 1981-2020. EMDEs = emerging market and developing economies.
B. Unweighted averages of actual growth during recessions as defined in annex 1E. *t* denotes the peak year preceding the recession.

addition to recessions, it considers other adverse events, such as banking crises and epidemics, and compares their effects on potential growth.

Definition. A (country-specific) recession is defined as a period from a peak in output preceding a business cycle trough to the trough, with a trough defined as a year in which output growth is both negative and at least one standard deviation below its long-term (1995-2020) average (as in Huidrom, Kose, and Ohnsorge 2016). This definition yields up to 124 recessions in 37 advanced economies and up to 351 recessions in 101 EMDEs during 1980-2020.

Duration and amplitude of recessions. Almost half of such recessions at the country level occurred during global recession years (1975, 1982, 1991, 2009, and 2020; figure 1.7.A). Recessions at the country level, on average, lasted 1.5 years and were associated with a contraction in actual output of 4.0 percent, on average (figure 1.7.B). Advanced economies had, on average, somewhat less severe recessions than EMDEs (with drops of 3.5 percent and 4.3 percent, respectively; figures 1.7.C and 1.7.D). Recessions in the two country groups had similar durations, at 1.5 years.

Effects on potential growth: Methodology. A local-projections method is employed to estimate the evolution of potential growth following recessions (annex 1E). The model estimates the cumulative effect of recessions on potential growth, following Jordà (2005) and Teulings and Zubanov (2014). In impulse responses, the model estimates the effect of short-term shocks (the recession, banking crisis, or epidemic event) over a horizon h on potential growth while controlling for other determinants:

$$y_{i,t+h} - y_{i,t} = \alpha_h + \beta_h shock_{i,t} + \gamma_h \Delta y_{i,t-1} + fixed\ effects_i + \varepsilon_{i,t} ,$$

in which $y_{i,t}$ is potential growth. The model controls for country fixed effects to capture time-invariant cross-country differences. The variable $shock_{i,t}$ is a dummy variable for a recession event (or banking crisis or epidemic), the main variable of interest. Lagged potential growth $y_{i,t-1}$ controls for the history of potential growth.

Long-term effect of recessions. Even five years after recessions, potential growth as measured by the production function approach is estimated, on average, to have been lower by 1.4 percentage points than if a recession had not occurred (figure 1.8.A). Coefficient estimates for the recession dummy are statistically significantly negative for the first five years after a recession. The effect is estimated to have been somewhat stronger and more persistent in regard to EMDEs, with potential growth 1.6 percentage points lower five years after a recession, compared with 1.3 percentage points for advanced economies (figures 1.8.B and 1.8.C).

These results are broadly robust to the choice of measure for potential growth and definition of recessions. Four to five years after recessions, potential growth as measured by most methods other than the production function approach is estimated to have been lower by 0.2-1.3 percentage points than if a recession had not occurred (annex 1F.16).[8]

Recessions could alternatively be defined as years of negative output growth, regardless of the depth of the output decline. This alternative definition of events would yield 541 recessions events (151 events in 37 advanced economies and 390 events in 101 EMDEs), about 14 percent more than the baseline sample of 475 events.[9] Potential growth slowed statistically significantly following recessions defined in this way also.

Long-term effect of other adverse events. The effects of banking crises and epidemics on potential growth are also examined and compared with those of recessions (annex tables 1F.13 and 1F.14). The banking crises examined are those Laeven and Valencia

---

[8] The only exceptions are, for advanced economies, forecast-based estimates from the IMF's World Economic Outlook database and, for EMDEs, estimates using multivariate and Hodrick-Prescott filters. One possible reason for the unresponsiveness of some forecast-based measures might be that forecasters' perception of long-term growth is stickier for advanced economies than for EMDEs.

[9] By this alternative definition, the average recession is associated with an actual output contraction of 3.7 percent and lasts 1.6 years.

FIGURE 1.8 **Effects of recessions on potential growth**

Recessions have had a significant and long-lasting negative effect on potential growth, especially in EMDEs. Recessions have accompanied most banking crises and roughly half of epidemics.

A. World: Response of growth in potential output after recessions

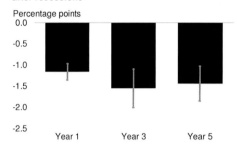

B. Advanced economies: Response of growth in potential output after recessions

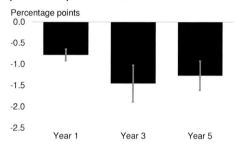

C. EMDEs: Response of growth in potential output after recessions

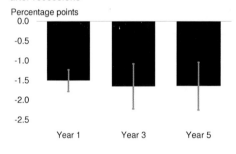

D. Share of adverse events associated with recessions

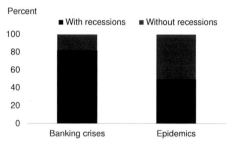

Source: World Bank.
Note: Recessions are defined as the period from the peak preceding a business cycle trough to the trough, with troughs defined as years in which output growth is both negative and one standard deviation below the long-term average. Banking crises are identified as in Laeven and Valencia (2020). Epidemics include Severe Acute Respiratory Syndrome (SARS) in 2003, swine flu in 2009, Middle East Respiratory Syndrome (MERS) in 2012, Ebola in 2014, and Zika in 2016. EMDEs = emerging market and developing economies.
A.-C. Blue bars are coefficient estimates from local-projections model. Orange whiskers indicate 90 percent confidence interval. Methodological details are in annex 1E. Sample includes unbalanced panel of 28 advanced economies 50 EMDEs for 1998-2020. "Year 1," "Year 3," and "Year 5" refer to the first, third, and fifth year following the recession.
D. Share of events associated with recessions is the share of events that coincide with a recession in a 3-year window, out of the total number of events. Sample includes unbalanced panel of 33 advanced economies and 98 EMDEs for 1981-2020.

(2020) identified: a sample of 25 banking crises in 32 advanced economies and 41 banking crises in 91 EMDEs during the period 1990-2021. During the year of an average banking crisis globally, actual output rose by 0.7 percent—well below the average annual global output growth during the sample period of 1990-2021 (3.5 percent) and even further below average annual output growth in EMDEs over this period (4.1 percent). The average crisis lasted less than one year.

Five recent epidemics are examined: Severe Acute Respiratory Syndrome (SARS) in 2003, swine flu in 2009, Middle East Respiratory Syndrome (MERS) in 2012, Ebola in 2014, and Zika in 2016. They affected 96 countries: 32 advanced economies and 64 EMDEs. On average, they were accompanied by close-to-zero output growth, compared with the average growth of 4.0 percent in these countries during the sample period outside these episodes.

Like recessions, both banking crises and epidemics reduced potential growth, but the time profiles of their effects differed from those of recessions. Banking crises tended to have stronger short-term impacts on potential growth than recessions but somewhat smaller long-term effects.[10] Overall, 81 percent of banking crises were associated with recessions within three years (figure 1.8.D). When estimates based on the production function approach are used, potential growth slowed more steeply in the first one to two years after banking crises than in the first one to two years after recessions, but the initial decline in potential growth after banking crises was subsequently partly reversed, whereas the slowing effect of recessions strengthened over time (figures 1.8.A and 1.9.A). Banking crises are estimated to have had even weaker long-term effects on other measures of potential growth than on measures based on the production function approach (annex 1E).[11] Banking crises had a stronger but shorter-lived effect in EMDEs than in advanced economies; five years after a banking crisis, the effect was no longer statistically significant in EMDEs but still significant in advanced economies (figures 1.9.B and 1.9.C). The fading effect of banking crises on potential growth may in part reflect the lack of a lasting impact on the growth of employment and investment, especially in EMDEs, as economic rebounds often followed the disruptions of banking crises.

The strong initial impact of banking crises on potential growth, as well as their declining and highly heterogeneous longer-term effects, are in line with estimates of actual output losses reported in the literature. Candelon, Carare, and Miao (2016) document significant growth slowdowns in the first year following banking crises that become more muted in subsequent years. Similarly, Dwyer, Devereux, and Baie (2013) document wide heterogeneity in growth impacts five years after banking crises.[12] In a comprehensive review of the literature, Claessens and Kose (2018) also find that the duration of a recession depends on the features of the financial stress that accompanies it. In particular, house price busts, especially when combined with credit crunches, can prolong recessions, whereas a rapid recovery in housing and asset markets can accelerate the broader economic recovery from financial stress.

Epidemics, too, had somewhat more modest, but still statistically significant, negative long-term effects on potential growth than did recessions—larger in EMDEs than in

---

[10] Results for currency crises and debt crises suggest limited and short-lived impacts that are statistically significant only in the year of the event (currency crises) or up to two years after the event (debt crises).

[11] The exercise is repeated for banking crises that were followed by recessions within a three-year window. There were 20 such events in the sample used here. The results indicate statistically significant impacts of recessions combined with banking crises, with somewhat larger short-term effects than, but similar long-term effects to, banking crises. The difference between the response of potential growth to banking crises with recessions and its response to banking crises without recessions is, however, not statistically significant.

[12] Even if banking crises have a had only a short-lived effect on output growth, they have had a persistent effect on output levels. Cerra and Saxena (2008) showed this for actual output levels five to ten years after financial crises; Ollivaud and Turner (2014) showed it for potential output levels three to seven years after the global financial crisis.

FIGURE 1.9 Effects of banking crises and epidemics on potential growth

Although banking crises and epidemics, like recessions, have lowered potential growth significantly, they have had a more modest longer-term effect in EMDEs than recessions.

A. Response of growth in potential output after banking crises

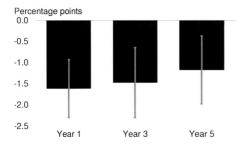

B. Response of growth in potential output in advanced economies five years later

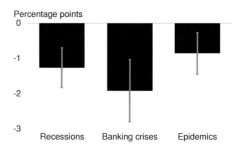

C. Response of growth in potential output in EMDEs five years later

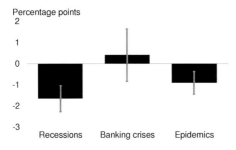

D. Response of growth in potential output after epidemics

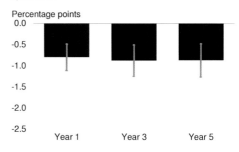

Source: World Bank.

Note: Blue bars are coefficient estimates from local-projections model. Orange whiskers indicate 90 percent confidence intervals. Annex 1E provides methodological details. Recessions are defined as the period from the peak preceding a business cycle trough to trough, with troughs defined as years in which output growth is both negative and one standard deviation below the long-term average. Banking crises are identified as in Laeven and Valencia (2012, 2018, 2020). Epidemics include Severe Acute Respiratory Syndrome (SARS) in 2003, swine flu in 2009, Middle East Respiratory Syndrome (MERS) in 2012, Ebola in 2014, and Zika in 2016. Sample includes unbalanced panel of 32 advanced economies and 97 EMDEs for 1981-2020. In panels A and D, "Year 1," "Year 3," and "Year 5" refer to the first, third, and fifth year following the crisis, respectively. EMDEs = emerging market and developing economies.

advanced economies (figures 1.9.B and 1.9.C). Based on the production function measure, potential growth five years after epidemics was lower by 0.9 percentage point than it would otherwise have been (compared with declines of 1.2 and 1.4 percentage points after banking crises and recessions, respectively). One reason for the more muted effect of epidemics than of recessions is their more subdued effect on productivity over the medium term. Experience since 2020, when the COVID-19 pandemic erupted, has shown how rapidly productivity can rebound when pandemic restrictions are lifted and disruptions are resolved.

How do short-term shocks affect potential growth?

The previous section established that recessions have been associated with significantly slower potential growth for several subsequent years. This section assesses three possible channels through which this process has unfolded: growth in employment, investment, and TFP. The literature provides ample evidence that as the production function approach suggests, all three of these channels are likely to have been important in weakening potential growth following recessions and other adverse events.

Effects of recessions

- *Employment and labor supply.* In a recession, unemployment generally rises significantly and remains elevated for a prolonged period. For example, in the sample of recessions examined here, unemployment remained higher by 1.8 percentage points on average, three years after the recession than would have been the case otherwise (annex 1E). Such a lasting effect is in line with other findings in the literature. In the United States, for example, an increase of 1 percentage point in state-level unemployment during the 2007-09 recession was associated with employment rates 0.3 percentage point lower in 2015 (Yagan 2019). Following recessions, lingering uncertainty about future sales prospects may discourage firms from hiring (Baker, Bloom, and Davis 2016; Bloom 2009, 2014). Financial constraints may force more indebted firms into greater job cuts in the event of demand drops (Giroud and Mueller 2017). Long spells of unemployment may discourage workers and erode the skills of the long-term unemployed (Ball 2009; Blanchard 1991; Blanchard and Summers 1987). Thus, the decrease in employment over a prolonged period after a recession tends to have adverse consequences for labor supply and potential output.

- *Investment and capital accumulation.* Gross fixed investment typically falls more sharply in response to economic downturns than do other components of GDP (Kydland and Prescott 1982). A recession can cause investors to reassess long-term growth prospects. A downgrade in growth forecasts can erode prospects of long-term returns on investment or risks around expected returns and, thus, discourage investment. Access to finance for investment may also become more restricted and discourage investment, especially for younger, more innovative, and riskier firms (Fort et al. 2013).[13] Reduced capital accumulation in a recession will directly reduce potential growth.

- *Total factor productivity.* A collapse in investment growth reduces potential growth not only directly, but also indirectly, by slowing the adoption of productivity-enhancing embodied technologies and the reallocation of resources toward more productive uses (Dieppe, Kilic Celik, and Okou 2021; Syverson 2011). Workers losing their jobs during recessions may enter permanently lower-skilled career paths (Huckfeldt 2022). Skills mismatches between job market entrants and job requirements are larger during recessions than expansions and tend to be long-lasting, suggesting persistent productivity losses from such mismatches (Liu, Salvanes, and Sørensen 2016). Recessions are also likely to be associated with

---

[13] Similar lasting impacts of investment weakness have been shown for banking crises (Wilms, Swank, and de Haan 2018).

reduced spending on research and development, with negative consequences for the growth of TFP.

All three channels were at work during the recessions considered in this study (annex 1E). Five years after the average recession, TFP growth is estimated to have been lower by 0.7 percentage point than it would have been without a recession and, in EMDEs, lower by 0.9 percentage point (figures 1.10.A and 1.11.A). Investment growth declined steeply in the first year of the average recession and remained significantly lower five years later—3 percentage points below what it would have been without a recession, both globally and in EMDEs (figures 1.10.B and 1.11.B).

The effect was somewhat shorter lived for employment. Four years after the average recession, employment growth was lower by about 0.7 percentage point than what it would have been otherwise. However, for EMDEs, this effect was no longer statistically significant by the fifth year (figures 1.10.C and 1.11.C). The absence of a longer-lasting employment response in EMDEs is in part likely to reflect the large, flexible informal economies that help these economies absorb shocks to labor markets.

Effects of banking crises and epidemics

Banking crises have tended to have short-lived effects on the growth of TFP, investment, and employment (figures 1.10.D-F and 1.11.A-F). Five years after the average banking crisis, neither investment growth nor employment growth were statistically significantly lower than otherwise; only TFP growth was still statistically significantly lower. Epidemics were associated, even five years later, with statistically significantly lower TFP growth, investment growth, and—in contrast to recessions and banking crises— potential growth in the supply of labor. Epidemics had a somewhat stronger effect on investment growth after five years, and a weaker effect on TFP growth, than did recessions (figures 1.10.D-F).

Banking crises had larger long-term adverse effects on TFP growth, investment growth, and employment growth in advanced economies than in EMDEs, possibly reflecting the larger role of finance in, and greater financial development of, advanced economies. Conversely, epidemics had larger long-term adverse effects on these variables in EMDEs than in advanced economies, in part perhaps because EMDE governments and central banks had less policy room to dampen the economic effects of epidemic disruptions (figures 1.11.A-F).

Conclusion

Potential growth, the growth an economy can generate at full employment and full capacity, is critical for a sustained increase in living standards. This chapter has introduced the most comprehensive international database of potential growth, including the nine most widely used measures of potential growth for 173 countries over 1981-2021. At the global level, all nine measures point to a steady decline in potential

FIGURE 1.10 **Effects of adverse events on growth of employment, TFP, and investment**

Recessions have been associated with immediate declines in the growth of both investment and employment, which have been reversed gradually over time. In contrast, declines in TFP growth have increased over time. Banking crises have been associated with particularly lasting losses in TFP growth and epidemics with losses in employment growth.

A. Response of potential TFP growth after recessions

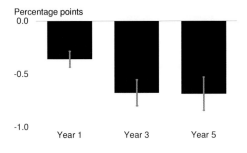

B. Response of investment growth after recessions

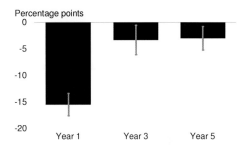

C. Response of employment growth after recessions

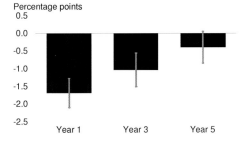

D. Response of employment growth five years later

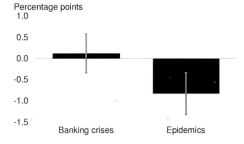

E. Response of potential TFP growth five years later

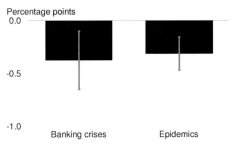

F. Response of investment growth five years later

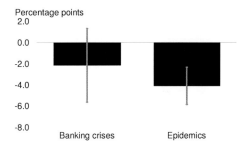

Source: World Bank.
Note: Blue bars are coefficient estimates from local-projections model. Orange whiskers indicate 90 percent confidence intervals. Recessions are defined as the period from the peak preceding a business cycle trough to the trough, with troughs defined as years in which output growth is both negative and one standard deviation below the long-term average. Banking crises are identified as in Laeven and Valencia (2020). Epidemics include Severe Acute Respiratory Syndrome (SARS) in 2003, swine flu in 2009, Middle East Respiratory Syndrome (MERS) in 2012, Ebola in 2014, and Zika in 2016. Sample includes unbalanced panel of 32 advanced economies and 97 EMDEs for 1981-2020. In panels A and D, "Year 1," "Year 3," and "Year 5" refer to the first, third, and fifth year following the recession, respectively. EMDEs = emerging market and developing economies; TFP = total factor productivity.

FIGURE 1.11 Effects of adverse events on growth of employment, TFP, and investment in advanced economies and EMDEs

Recessions have had similar long-term effects on TFP growth and investment growth in advanced economies and EMDEs, but larger effects on employment growth in advanced economies. Banking crises have had larger long-term adverse effects on TFP, investment, and employment growth in advanced economies than in EMDEs. Conversely, epidemics have had larger long-term adverse effects on TFP, investment, and employment growth in EMDEs than in advanced economies.

A. EMDEs: Response of potential TFP growth five years later

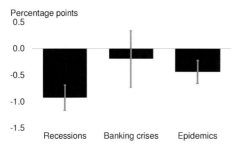

B. EMDEs: Response of investment growth five years later

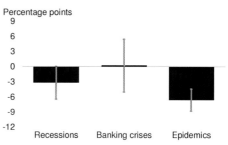

C. EMDEs: Response of employment growth five years later

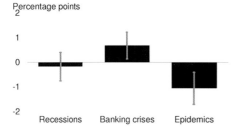

D. Advanced economies: Response of potential TFP growth five years later

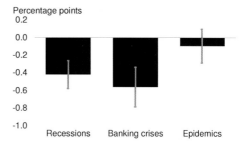

E. Advanced economies: Response of investment growth five years later

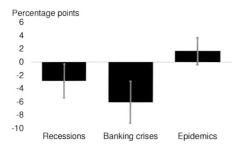

F. Advanced economies: Response of employment growth five years later

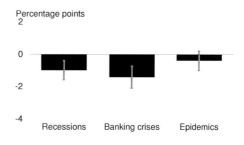

Source: World Bank.
Note: Blue bars are coefficient estimates from local-projections model. Orange whiskers indicate 90 percent confidence intervals. Recessions are defined as the period from the peak preceding a business cycle trough to the trough, with troughs defined as years in which output growth is both negative and one standard deviation below the long-term average. Banking crises are identified as in Laeven and Valencia (2012, 2018, 2020). Epidemics include Severe Acute Respiratory Syndrome (SARS) (2003), swine flu (2009), Middle East Respiratory Syndrome (MERS) (2012), Ebola (2014), and Zika (2016). Sample includes unbalanced panel of 32 advanced economies and 97 EMDEs for 1981-2020. EMDEs = emerging market and developing economies; TFP = total factor productivity.

growth in the past decade. This decline has been internationally widespread, with potential growth in 2011-21 falling below its 2000-10 average in 70 percent of countries. The decline in potential growth between 2000-10 and 2011-21 was almost as large in advanced economies (0.8 percentage point per year) as in EMDEs (1.0 percentage point per year).

The chapter has also presented an application of the new database by studying the effects of recessions and other adverse events on potential growth. Recessions, on average, have been followed, even five years later, by a drop of 1.4 percentage points in potential growth. The magnitude of this estimated decline varies somewhat among the possible measures of potential growth, but it is virtually always statistically significant. This lasting effect of recessions operates through the channels of reductions in investment growth, employment growth, and productivity growth. Four to five years after recessions, investment growth, productivity growth, and employment growth have remained statistically significantly lower. In addition, this chapter has compared the effects of recessions with those of other adverse events, such as banking crises and epidemics. The long-term effect of recessions has been somewhat deeper than that of banking crises and more broad-based than that of epidemics.

Understanding the behavior of potential growth is of fundamental importance to short- and long-run macroeconomic analyses and policy formulation. The new database will facilitate future research on a number of topics related to potential growth.

- *Role of human capital accumulation in driving potential growth.* To improve estimates of potential growth based on the production function approach, broader measures of human capital could be constructed, using information beyond the education enrollment and completion metrics and life expectancy data used in this chapter. The COVID-19 pandemic demonstrated the critical importance of a broader measure of human capital that takes into account such factors as morbidity and the quality of schooling (Angrist et al. 2021; World Bank 2018). The World Bank's *Human Capital Index* offers one such measure but is thus far available only for very few countries and years (World Bank 2021b). In addition, there is some evidence that increased human capital enhances growth more in the presence of better institutions (Ali, Egbetokun, and Memon 2018). Future specifications could take into account such interaction effects.

- *Effects of climate change-related weather events on potential growth.* There is growing evidence that climate change-related weather events are causing increasingly frequent and severe damage to output and that they have consequences for potential growth. Some of these consequences are associated with increased migration (Missirian and Schlenker 2017), shorter working hours in industries with widespread outdoor labor due to excessive heat (ILO 2019), falls in total factor productivity (Economides and Xepapadeas 2018), and increased economic volatility (Panton 2020). Overall, climate change has been shown to be associated with significant output losses (Cantelmo, Melina, and Papageorgiou 2019; Colacito, Hoffman, and Phan 2018; Kahn et al. 2019). Conversely, increased investment designed either to increase resilience to adverse climate events or to mitigate climate change could provide a boost to potential growth (IMF 2019). Chapter 5 explores some of these diverging forces. In any event, it will be essential to analyze the implications of climate change for potential growth.

- *Role of natural resources in the measurement of potential growth.* Particularly for countries that rely heavily on natural resources, taking into account natural resources as a factor of production whose depletion can reduce potential growth could improve production function-based estimates. In addition, research could take into account the adverse implications of natural resources for other factors of production and productivity. For example, natural resources affect the growth benefits of foreign direct investment (Hayat 2018) and of aggregate investment in general (Gylfason and Zoega 2006). The amount of available natural resources can also have adverse consequences for productivity through productivity-reducing rent-seeking behavior (Torvik 2002) and sectoral shifts (Stokke 2008).

- *Implications of emerging trends in drivers of growth.* Measures of TFP based on the production function approach could be refined to capture new developments. For example, energy transition could generate large sectoral shifts, with consequences for TFP growth and major investments (IMF 2021). The broadening use of digital technologies, the shift from trade in goods to trade in equipment services ("servitization"), and shifts in global value chains could change patterns of cross-country technology transfers and hence affect productivity growth and flows of foreign direct investment (chapters 6 and 7). Servitization and digitalization have been associated with productivity gains in affected firms and industries (Cette, Nevoux, and Py 2022; Gal et al. 2019). Conversely, concerns have been raised that friend-shoring or near-shoring of global value chains may be associated with productivity losses (Moran and Oldenski 2016; Quian, Liu, and Steenbergen 2022).

- *Better measures of output gaps.* Output gap estimates are important inputs into macroeconomic policy decisions, especially monetary ones. Hence, controlling for additional external factors could tailor multivariate filter-based estimates of potential growth to capture more closely the relationship between domestic inflation and domestic monetary policy. These external factors include global output gaps, global commodity price cycles, and global financial cycles. Estimates, especially those for EMDEs, could also be extended backward in time and systematically tested and adjusted for major structural breaks.

ANNEX 1A **Production function approach**

The production function approach assumes that a Cobb-Douglas production function with constant returns to scale can capture potential output (Solow 1957):[14]

$$Y_t = A_t K_t^{\alpha} L_t^{(1-\alpha)},$$

in which Y_t is potential output, A_t is potential TFP, K_t is the potential capital stock, L_t is potential employment, and α is the share of capital in output. To extend the sample employed in this chapter beyond 2019—the latest available data from the Penn World Table—TFP was recalculated as the Solow residual of output, employment (extended using data from Haver Analytics) and capital (extended using investment data from Haver Analytics and the perpetual inventory method; table 1F.3). Labor and capital shares are the within-country averages of those reported in the Penn World Table. The production function approach does not separately account for human capital, but human capital affects growth of TFP and the labor supply, as described later in this annex.

Fitted values from panel regression estimates proxy two of the three components of potential output: potential TFP and potential employment. The third component, the contribution of capital to potential growth, is assumed to be the same as the contribution of capital to actual growth, as shown in the Penn World Table (and extended using data from Haver Analytics). This approach yields an unbalanced panel data set for 30 advanced economies and 64 EMDEs for 1998-2021 (table 1F.4). The same approach, using appropriate assumptions, can be employed to project potential growth into the future. Chapter 5 details these assumptions and the approach for projections for 2022-32.

Capital stock data from Penn World Table 10.0 is used until the latest available year in the data set (2019 for most countries in the sample). For 2020-21, investment data are compiled from national statistical agencies and Haver Analytics, while the capital stock is estimated from investment data by means of the perpetual inventory method using historical average depreciation rates.[15]

Potential TFP growth is defined as the fitted value of a panel fixed-effects regression, for 33 advanced economies and 92 EMDEs for 1983-2020, of the Hodrick-Prescott-filtered trend of actual TFP growth (the Solow residual) on determinants of productivity. These determinants include GDP per capita relative to that in advanced economies, education (secondary school completion rate), the working-age share of the population, and the five-year moving average of real investment growth (as in Abiad, Leigh, and Mody 2007;

---

[14] The estimates of potential growth this approach produces may be biased if the assumption of constant returns to scale is not valid (Dribe et al. 2017). For a detailed discussion of drawbacks of growth accounting, see Dieppe and Kilic Celik (2021). That said, the approach is widely used for its conceptual simplicity and ease of interpretation.

[15] Implicitly, this approach does not account for the possibility that inefficient investment is written off during downturns. Hence, it may overstate the capital stock during downturns.

Bijsterbosch and Kolasa 2010; Feyrer 2007; Turner et al. 2016).[16] To allow for nonlinearities in the productivity dividends from education, schooling is interacted with a dummy for schooling in the bottom two-thirds across the sample. A dummy is included for commodity exporters during the period 2003-07. This dummy is intended to capture the impact of the exceptionally large commodity price boom that temporarily lifted commodity exporters' growth during this period. Potential TFP is thus:

$$\Delta tfp_{i,t} = \alpha_0 + \alpha_1 \ GDP \ per \ capita_{i,t} + \alpha_2 \ wap_{i,t}$$

$$+ \ \alpha_3 \ education_{i,t} + \alpha_4 \ education_{i,t} * D_{edu}$$

$$+ \ \alpha_5 \ D_{cebi,t} + \alpha_6 \ \Delta inv_{i,t} + \varepsilon_{i,t},$$

in which $\Delta tfp_{i,t}$ is the logarithmic first difference of trend TFP, *GDP per capita*$_{i,t}$ is GDP per capita in percent of advanced-economy per capita GDP, *wap*$_{i,t}$ is the working-age share of the population, *education*$_{i,t}$ is the percent share of the population who have completed secondary school, $\Delta inv_{i,t}$ is the five-year moving average of real investment growth, D_{edu} is a dummy variable taking the value of 1 if the secondary completion rate is in the bottom two-thirds of the distribution, and $D_{cebi,t}$ is a dummy variable for the period 2003-07 taking the value 1 if the country is a commodity exporter.[17]

The data are compiled using a wide range of sources: UN population statistics (for population growth and working-age share of the population), Barro and Lee (2013) (for secondary school completion), the World Bank's World Development Indicators (for secondary school completion and GDP per capita relative to that in advanced economies), and Haver Analytics (for investment).

The regression results are broadly in line with those in the previous literature (table 1F.5). TFP growth slows as per capita incomes converge toward advanced-economy levels (Barro and Sala-i-Martin 1997). A better-educated population and accelerated investment growth are associated with higher TFP growth. However, the impact of education diminishes as education levels rise toward advanced-economy levels (Benhabib and Spiegel 1994, 2005; Coe, Helpman, and Hoffmaister 1997; Kato 2016). As a result, the coefficient on secondary school completion rates is significant only for countries with completion rates below the top third.

---

[16] The results are robust to using GDP per capita instead of GDP per capita as a percentage of advanced-economy GDP per capita. GDP per capita relative to a frontier (advanced economies) is used here to proxy the catch-up effect highlighted in the literature on stochastic frontier analysis (Growiec et al. 2015).

[17] This approach is similar to those of Abiad, Leigh, and Mody (2007) and Bijsterbosch and Kolasa (2010). Abiad, Leigh and Mody (2007) estimate five-year nonoverlapping averages of TFP growth as a function of per capita GDP, schooling, population growth, trade openness, and a nonlinear function of current account deficits and foreign direct investment for a sample of 22 European countries for 1975-2004. Bijsterbosch and Kolasa (2010) estimate five-year nonoverlapping averages of labor productivity growth as a function of relative productivity levels (which here are proxied with relative per capita GDP), the share of high-skilled workers in employment, and investment as a percentage of value added for sectoral data for eight European countries for 1996-2005.

The results are broadly robust to a number of alternative specifications (tables 1F.5 and 1F.6). Two different methodologies are used to estimate trend TFP growth (a linear-quadratic trend and three-, five-, and seven-year moving averages) instead of the Hodrick-Prescott-filtered trend. The three- and seven-year rolling averages of investment growth are used. In most specifications, the coefficient estimates remain significant and retain their signs; however, the working-age population share becomes nonsignificant in some specifications. The inclusion of spending on research and development, which is available only for a much smaller sample, and urbanization also do not materially change the results.

Potential labor supply is defined as the product of the working-age population and the fitted value of age- and gender-specific regressions of labor force participation rates ($lfpr_{a,g,t}$) in percent on their structural determinants ($X_{a,g,t}$) and with cohort effects, fixed effects, and the state of the business cycle—defined as the deviation of the logarithm of real GDP from the Hodrick-Prescott-filtered trend—controlled for. The vector $X_{a,g,t}$ includes gender-specific education outcomes (secondary and tertiary completion rates as a percentage of the population over the age of 25 and enrollment rates as a percentage of population of the age group that officially corresponds to the level of education), age-specific fertility rates (births per woman), and life expectancy (in years). These are interacted with a dummy variable D_{emde} which takes the value of 1 for EMDEs. The vector $C_{a,g,t}$ includes all the control variables:[18]

$$lfpr_{a,g,t} = \alpha_{a,g} + \beta_{a,g}\,X_{a,g,t} + \gamma_{a,g}\,X_{a,g,t} * D_{emde} + \delta_{a,g}\,C_{a,g,t} + \varepsilon_{a,g,t}.$$

Data on the working-age population come from the UN Population Prospects Database. Data for age- and gender-specific labor force participation rates are available from Key Indicators of the Labour Market of the International Labour Organization's Population Statistics Database for 1990-2019, which is spliced with OECD Labour Force Statistics for 1960-2020 for 33 advanced economies and 16 EMDEs. This produces data for age- and gender-specific labor force participation rates for 1960-2020 for up to 38 advanced economies and 142 EMDEs.[19] Rates of completion of secondary and tertiary education are from Barro and Lee (2013) and the World Development Indicators; age-specific fertility rate and life expectancy are from the UN's World Population Projections database; gender-specific secondary and tertiary school enrollment rates are from the World Development Indicators. The regression sample includes up to 35 advanced economies and 133 EMDEs for 1987-2020.[20]

---

[18] This approach combines those by Fallick and Pingle (2007) and Goldin (1994). For the United States, Fallick and Pingle (2007) estimate labor force participation by age group and gender as a function of cohort and age fixed effects as well as business cycle fluctuations. Goldin (1994) models aggregate labor force participation rates as a function of country-level variables such as female schooling. The regression used here incorporates both cohort effects and country-level variables modeling human capital and other factors driving labor force participation.

[19] This is an unbalanced sample, because some of the exogenous variables are not available for the full period for all countries. However, the regression results are robust to restricting the sample to the balanced panel with fully available data.

[20] Since UN data for life expectancy are available only for five-year periods, historical life expectancy data from the World Development Indicators database is used. For projection years or missing data, UN Population Prospects data are spliced with data from World Development Indicators database.

The regression results are broadly in line with findings in the previous literature (table 1F.7).

First, among teenage and younger women, fertility rates are associated with higher labor force participation, as mothers are more likely to discontinue their education and participate in the labor force, especially in advanced economies (Azevedo, Lopez-Calva, and Perova 2012; Fletcher and Wolfe 2009; Herrera, Sahn, and Villa 2016). This effect is more muted in EMDEs, potentially reflecting an earlier average age of marriage, which tends to be associated with lower female labor force participation (United Nations 2012).

Second, for relevant age groups, educational attainment is associated with higher participation rates, except in the cases of young men and women aged 20-24. The positive correlation between completion rates and labor force participation may partly reflect higher compensation for more educated workers. For young men, higher tertiary educational attainment is associated with lower labor force participation. This might reflect the lack of demand for employment in sectors in which these workers, if educated, would expect to be employed, discouraging them from labor force participation (Klasen and Pieters 2013). However, for men aged 50-64 and all workers aged 65 years and older, education becomes a nonsignificant determinant of labor force participation (as in Fallick and Pingle 2007). Tertiary enrollment rates in all relevant age groups are associated with lower labor force participation rates, as students devote time to completing their degrees (Kinoshita and Guo 2015; Linacre 2007; Tansel 2002).

Third, life expectancy is one of the main determinants of participation for workers aged 50 and above (Fallick and Pingle 2007). For the younger ones among them, between the ages of 50-64, higher life expectancy is associated with higher labor force participation, possibly reflecting the need to accumulate savings for a longer retirement period or the positive association between better health among older workers and higher incomes (Haider and Loughran 2001). Among those aged 65 years or older, higher life expectancy is associated with higher labor force participation in advanced economies but does not significantly change participation in EMDEs. Life expectancy may be a weak proxy for a healthy old age in EMDEs with less-developed health care systems or in which differences in life expectancy might mostly reflect differences in infant mortality (Eggleston and Fuchs 2012).

Fourth, labor force participation is procyclical—albeit less so in EMDEs than in advanced economies—in most age groups until the age of 50. Labor force participation rises when real GDP is above its Hodrick-Prescott-filtered trend and declines when real GDP is below its Hodrick-Prescott-filtered trend.[21] As age increases, the sensitivity to cyclicality decreases, and participation eventually becomes countercyclical (Balakrishnan et al. 2015; Duval, Eris, and Furceri 2011). This may reflect greater ability of more

---

[21] In several instances, there were no statistically significant differences between advanced economies and EMDEs in the cyclicality of their labor force participation. Hence, the interactions were omitted from the regressions.

experienced workers to remain employed or return to employment after spells of unemployment during recessions (Elsby, Hobijn, and Şahin 2015; Shimer 2013). However, participation becomes procyclical again (although not statistically significantly so) for workers aged 65 and above as they become eligible to retire and may be readier to drop out of the labor force in a weaker economy. This result is broadly robust to defining the business cycle as deviations of real GDP from its 10-year moving average or from a linear-quadratic trend (tables 1F.8 and 1F.9).

ANNEX 1B **Univariate filters**

Univariate statistical filters decompose a series y_t into trend, cyclical, and noise components. Although they are all essentially weighted moving averages of the series y_t, they differ in their weights. In this chapter, the trend component is used as a proxy for potential output.

Five univariate filters are applied to estimate potential output: filters based on Hodrick and Prescott (1997), three band-pass filters (Baxter and King 1999; Butterworth 1930 and Gomez 2001; Christiano and Fitzgerald 2003), and a filter based on an unobserved-components model. The measures are estimated for 37 advanced economies and 52 EMDEs for 1980Q1-2022Q2 (table 1F.10). Forecasts from the *Global Economic Prospects* report provide data to 2024. A smaller sample is used in comparisons with other approaches, to ensure consistency of samples (tables 1F.11 and 1F.12).

Hodrick-Prescott filter

The Hodrick-Prescott filter minimizes deviations of a series y_t from its trend τ_t, assuming a degree of smoothness λ of the trend. It chooses the trend τ_t that minimizes

$$\sum_{t=1}^{T}(y_t-\tau_t)^2+\lambda\sum_{t=2}^{T-1}\left[(\tau_{t+1}-\tau_t)-(\tau_t-\tau_{t-1})\right]^2,$$

in which T is the sample size. A larger λ indicates a smoother trend. For $\lambda = 0$, the trend is equal to the actual series, and for $\lambda\to+\infty$ the trend is a linear time trend with a constant growth rate. Typically, the value of λ is set at 1,600 for quarterly data. The trend is estimated based on past values as well as projected values of the series y_t.

Band-pass filters

The three band-pass filters aim to isolate fluctuations in a time series that lie in a specific band of frequencies. They eliminate slow-moving components (trend) and very high-frequency components (noise) and define the intermediate components as the business cycle. Specifically, the three band-pass filters differ in their approximations of the optimal linear filter (also known as the "ideal" band-pass filter) to deal with finite time series.

The *Baxter and King filter* is a moving average of the data with symmetric weights on lags and leads. Therefore, it loses observations in the beginning and toward the end of the sample. It is particularly well suited when the raw series follows a near-independent and identically distributed process (Christiano and Fitzgerald 2003). Specifically, the cyclical component of the Baxter and King filter is given by

$$\hat{c}_t = b(L) y_t,$$

in which *b(L)* is the lag polynomial given by

$$b(L) = \sum_{j=-k}^{k} b_j^k L^j,$$

with $b_j^k = b_{-j}^k$. Note that *k* observations will be lost in both ends of the sample. The higher *k*, the closer the filter is to the ideal filter, but also the higher are the number of lost observations. The default business cycle frequencies used here (required for estimation) are between 1.5 and 8 years.

The *Christiano and Fitzgerald filter* is a one-sided moving average of the data with weights that minimize the distance between the approximated and the "ideal" filter. Since the filter is one sided, it does not lose observations toward the end of the sample. It is most suitable for random-walk series. The optimal cycle at time *t*, $\hat{c}_t$, is given by

$$\hat{c}_t = \sum_{j=-f}^{p} b_j^{p,f} y_{t-j},$$

in which $b_j^{p,f}$ are the optimal weights of the filter that solve

$$\underset{b_j^{p,f}}{\text{Min}}\, E\left[(\hat{c}_t - c_t)^2 \big| y \right],$$

and c_t is the filtered series under the "ideal" (infinite sample) band-pass filter. By default, the Christiano and Fitzgerald filter business cycle frequencies are set between 1.5 and 8 years.

The *Butterworth filter*—widely used in electrical engineering for signal extraction—isolates only low-frequency fluctuations, not high-frequency ones. Pollock (2000) proposes the use of this filter for macroeconomic time-series filtering as an alternative to traditional linear filters such as the Hodrick-Prescott filter. The low-pass Butterworth filter is characterized by two parameters, λ and *n*, and can be specified as

$$b(L) = \frac{\lambda(1+L)^n (1+L^{-1})^n}{(1+L)^n (1+L^{-1})^n + \lambda(1-L)^n (1-L^{-1})^n},$$

in which *L* is a lag operator, λ is the smoothness parameter and *n* is the degree of the filter.

Unobserved-components model

Most univariate filters can be nested into the unobserved-components model.[22] In contrast to other univariate filters, the unobserved-components model does not impose

---

[22] For example, if the trend and cyclical components are uncorrelated white noise, the unobserved-components model coincides with the Hodrick-Prescott filter if the noise-to-signal ratio matches the Hodrick-Prescott filter's smoothing parameter (Hamilton 2018).

specific parameter assumptions about the degree of smoothing, lead and lag windows, or business cycle frequencies. Instead, it relies on assumptions about the underlying process output gaps and potential growth follow and is estimated using the Kalman filter (Harvey 1990):

$$LY_t = L\bar{Y}_t + Y_{GAPt} \ , \tag{1B.1}$$

$$L\bar{Y}_t = L\bar{Y}_{t-1} + G_t + \varepsilon_{\bar{Y}_t} \ , \tag{1B.2}$$

$$G_t = (1-\tau) G_{ss} + \tau G_{t-1} + \varepsilon_{Gt} \ , \tag{1B.3}$$

$$Y_{GAPt} = \beta_1 Y_{GAPt-1} + \beta_2 Y_{GAPt-2} + \gamma_t Y_{GAP} \ , \tag{1B.4}$$

in which LY is the log of seasonally adjusted quarterly real GDP, $L\bar{Y}$ the log of potential output, Y_{GAP} the output gap, G_t growth in potential output, G_{ss} the steady-state level to which growth is assumed to converge over the long term, and ε_Y and ε_G are independently and identically distributed disturbances. Note that the shock ε_Y shifts the level of potential output, whereas ε_G is a shock to growth in potential output. Equation (1B.3) assumes that potential growth converges (at a speed of convergence τ) to its steady level G_{ss} after a shock. The output gap follows a commonly used second-order autoregressive process (equation 1B.4). The Kalman filter algorithm yields (posterior) time-varying variance-covariance matrices for the smoothed estimates of the unobserved state variables, potential growth, and the output gap. The standard deviation of potential growth is used to calculate the 95 percent confidence band around estimated potential growth.

ANNEX 1C Multivariate filters

The unobserved-components model can be expanded to include additional indicators of domestic demand pressures to help identify the output gap (Beneš et al. 2010). The most commonly used indicators are inflation and the unemployment rate. Specifically, the univariate model (equations 1B.1-1B.4) is further augmented with a Phillips curve relationship between inflation and output gaps (equation 1C.1), an Okun's law relationship between unemployment rates and output gaps (equations 1C.2-1C.5), a relationship between capacity utilization and output gaps (equations 1C.6-1C.9), and a set of equations describing the Taylor rule (equations 1C.10-1C.13).

Given the large variation in available data across economies, switches are employed to add selected equations to each country model based on the country's specific data set. If house prices or the unemployment rate data are not available for a specific country, the relevant equations would not be included. At minimum, all countries have output, inflation, and commodity price data.[23]

---

[23] Three economies—Lesotho, Namibia, and Tanzania—have only output, inflation, and commodity price data.

Model components

The *Phillips curve* relates inflation to the output gap, controlling for the impact of supply-side shocks such as import prices on domestic inflation:

$$\pi_t = \rho\,\pi_{t-1} + (1-\rho)\,\pi_{t+1} + \alpha_1 Y_{GAPt} + \lambda_1 \pi_{mt} + \varepsilon_\pi\,, \tag{1C.1}$$

in which π_t is annualized quarter-over-quarter inflation at time t, π_{mt} is import price inflation at time t, and Y_{GAPt} is the output gap at time t. Expectations are assumed to be an average of adaptive and rational expectations, weighted by ρ. Inflation expectations are linked to fixed-horizon forecasts of inflation from Consensus Economics where available.[24]

Okun's law relates the unemployment gap U_{GAPt} (defined as the difference between the actual unemployment rate U_t and the equilibrium, or natural, unemployment rate $\bar{U}_t$ in equation 1C.2) to the output gap (in equation 1C.3) as

$$U_{GAPt} = U_t - \bar{U}_t\,, \tag{1C.2}$$

$$U_{GAPt} = \gamma U_{GAPt-1} - \alpha_2 Y_{GAPt} + \varepsilon_{tUGAP}\,. \tag{1C.3}$$

Following Blagrave et al. (2015), the model specifies the equilibrium unemployment rate process in deviation from steady state. Equation (1C.4) specifies the process for U_t. It implies that following a shock, the nonaccelerating inflation rate of unemployment $\bar{U}_t$ converges back to its steady-state value U_{ss} according to the parameter τ_l and has a trend component G_U that has an autoregressive process (1C.5):

$$\bar{U}_t - U_{ss} = \tau_1(\bar{U}_{t-1} - U_{ss}) + G_{Ut} + \varepsilon_{Ut}\,, \tag{1C.4}$$

$$G_{Ut} = \tau_u G_{Ut-1} + \varepsilon_{Gt}\,. \tag{1C.5}$$

Since *capacity utilization* C_t is highly procyclical, it can help identify the cyclical component of output even when other indicators (such as, say, a stable unemployment gap during jobless recoveries or stable inflation in highly open economies) do not signal cyclical upturns. Equations (1C.6)-(1C.9) describe the relation between capacity utilization and output gaps and the exogenous process for capacity utilization, in which $\bar{C}_{ss}$ is the steady-state rate of capacity utilization; C_{GAPt} is the capacity utilization gap, defined as the difference between actual and noninflationary capacity utilization $\bar{C}_t$; and G_{Ct} is the growth of capacity utilization:

$$C_{GAPt} = q\,C_{GAPt-1} + \alpha_3 Y_{GAPt} + \varepsilon_{CGAPt} \tag{1C.6}$$

$$C_t = C_{GAPt} + \bar{C}_t \tag{1C.7}$$

$$\bar{C}_t - \bar{C}_{ss} = \tau_2(\bar{C}_{t-1} - \bar{C}_{ss}) + G_{Ct} + \varepsilon_{Ct} \tag{1C.8}$$

$$G_{Ct} = \tau_c G_{Ct-1} + \varepsilon_{Gt}\,. \tag{1C.9}$$

---

[24] Fixed-horizon forecasts transform the fixed-event forecasts (for example, for 2022 and 2023) provided by Consensus Economics into one-year-ahead forecasts (in other words, at a fixed horizon in the future). See Bordo and Siklos (2017) and Siklos (2013) for details.

A *Taylor rule* describes monetary policy in economies that use short-term policy interest rates as an instrument of monetary policy:

$$i_t = \tau_i i_{t-1} + (1-\tau_i)(r_t^* + \pi_t^* + \gamma_\pi(\pi_{t+4} - \pi_t^*) + \gamma_{YGAP}Y_{GAPt}) + \varepsilon_{it} , \quad (1C.10)$$

in which i_t is the nominal policy interest rate that responds to forecast inflation from its target (π_t^*) and the output gap. The ex ante real interest rate is defined using the Fisher equation as

$$r_t = i_t - \pi_{4t+1} , \quad (1C.11)$$

in which π_{4t+1} is the year-over-year change in consumer prices. The neutral real interest rate is modeled as in Laubach and Williams (2003):

$$r_t^* = cG_t + Z_t , \quad (1C.12)$$

$$Z_t = Z_{t-1} + \varepsilon_{Zt} . \quad (1C.13)$$

An *output gap* process closes the model. Inflation and unemployment might fail to capture all domestic demand pressures, such as credit or asset price growth or commodity price cycles.[25] This might lead to an underestimation of the output gap and an overestimation of potential output, especially at the peak of the cycle. Instead of assuming that the output gap process is exogenous, as in the traditional multivariate Kalman filter, the model includes three additional indicators in the output gap equation—house price, credit, and commodity price growth:

$$Y_{GAPt} = \beta_1 Y_{GAPt-1} + \beta_2 hpr_{t-1} + \beta_3 compr_{t-1} + \beta_4 cr_{t-1} + \beta_5(r_t - r_t^*) + \varepsilon_{YGAPt}, \quad (1C.14)$$

in which cr_t, hpr_t, and $compr_t$ are cyclical components of year-over-year growth in private sector credit deflated by consumer price inflation, quarterly seasonally adjusted house prices, and export-weighted real average commodity prices, respectively, and $r_t - r_t^*$ is the deviation of the real policy rate from its equilibrium level.

Estimation

The model uses the Kalman filter algorithm and Bayesian techniques on quarterly data covering 1980Q1-2022Q2 for up to 36 advanced economies and 52 EMDEs. A key parameter determining the shape of potential output is the variance of the output gap relative to innovations in potential growth. The variances of the innovations ε_{YGAPt} and ε_{Gt} are set such that their ratio equals the typically used smoothness parameter of the Hodrick-Prescott filter.

The prior for the elasticity of output gap with respect to commodity price β_3 (the central bank's response to deviations of inflation from target) and the coefficient on potential

[25] See Borio (2013, 2014) and Summers (2014) for advanced economies, Jesus et al. (2015) for Latin America and the Caribbean, and Kemp (2015) for South Africa. The cyclical component of copper prices helps explain mining sector output gaps in Chile (Blagrave and Santoro 2016).

growth in the neutral real interest rate follows a normal distribution in the case of commodity prices to allow for a potentially negative impact of commodity price increases in commodity importers. The prior distributions for all standard deviations are inverse gamma distributions. All other estimated priors follow a beta distribution.

The standard deviations of ε_{CGAPt} and ε_{UGAPt} are set as the ordinary least-squares standard errors of equations (1C.1) and (1C.5) based on Hodrick-Prescott-filtered data. Steady-state values of growth, unemployment, and capacity utilization are calibrated to the sample means of their corresponding Hodrick-Prescott-filtered series. Estimates of potential growth from the multivariate filter model and the unobserved-components model used in this chapter are based on $L\bar{Y}_t$ and include both level and growth shocks to potential growth.

As in the case of the unobserved-components model, the Kalman filter algorithm yields (posterior) time-varying variance-covariance matrices for the filtered estimates of all unobserved state variables, including potential growth. From this matrix, the standard deviation of potential growth is used to calculate the 95 percent confidence band around estimated potential growth.

Data

Based on the univariate and multivariate filters, output gaps and potential growth are estimated for up to 37 advanced economies and 52 EMDEs for as long a period as 1980Q1-2024Q4 (table 1F.10). A smaller sample is used in comparisons with other approaches, to ensure constant samples (tables 1F.11 and 1F.12). GDP, inflation, unemployment rates, growth in private sector credit, and capacity utilization rates are from Haver Analytics. House price growth is from the Bank for International Settlements, commodity prices are from the World Bank's Commodities Price Data ("Pink Sheet"), and export weights are from the UN Comtrade database. Country-specific output gaps are aggregated using real GDP weights at 2010-19 exchange rates and prices.

ANNEX 1D **Long-term growth expectations**

Expectations of output growth over long horizons capture forecasters' assessment of long-term sustainable growth, since they are stripped of unpredictable short-term shocks. Two sources of expectations are used in this chapter: the International Monetary Fund's World Economic Outlook (WEO) database, published twice a year, and mean GDP forecasts from Consensus Economics, published on a quarterly basis. Since the longest available forecast horizon is five years for the WEO, five-year-ahead forecasts are selected for both sources for consistency across these two measures. The WEO provides five-year-ahead forecasts for up to 173 economies (37 advanced economies, 136 EMDEs) for 1990-2021. Consensus forecasts are available for up to 78 economies (34 advanced economies and 44 EMDEs) for 1990-2022, and the database includes the April data.

ANNEX 1E **Local-projections estimation**

A local-projections estimation is used to explore the evolution of potential growth, employment growth, potential TFP growth, and investment growth following recessions, banking crises, and epidemics. The model estimates the cumulative impact of recessions, following Jordà (2005) and Teulings and Zubanov (2014).[26]

In impulse responses, the model estimates the effect of short-term shocks (a recession, banking crisis, or epidemic event) over a horizon h on potential growth while controlling for other determinants:

$$y_{i,t+h} - y_{i,t} = \alpha_h + \beta_h shock_{i,t} + \gamma_h \Delta y_{i,t-1} + fixedeffects_i + \varepsilon_{i,t} \ ,$$

in which $y_{i,t}$ is potential growth. The model controls for country fixed effects to capture time-invariant cross-country differences.[27] The variable $shock_{i,t}$ is a dummy variable for a recession event (or banking crisis or epidemic), the main variable of interest. Lagged potential growth $y_{i,t-1}$ controls for the history of potential growth.

For channels, the same specification is used, in which $y_{i,t}$ is employment growth, potential TFP growth, or investment growth. This model also controls for country fixed effects to capture time-invariant cross-country differences. Lagged potential growth $y_{i,t-1}$ controls for the history of employment growth, potential TFP growth, or investment growth. Banking crises are defined as in Laeven and Valencia (2018), and table 1F.13 lists the ones corresponding to the potential growth measures. Epidemics include Severe Acute Respiratory Syndrome (SARS) (2003), swine flu (2009), Middle East Respiratory Syndrome (MERS) (2012), Ebola (2014), and Zika (2016), and table 1F.14 lists affected countries.

Tables 1F.15-1F.18 show results for the impact of recessions, banking crises, and epidemics on alternative measures of potential growth. Tables 1F.19-1F.20 show results for the impact of recessions, banking crises, and epidemics on employment, total factor productivity, and investment growth.

---

[26] Plagborg-Møller and Wolf (2021) show that vector autoregression and local-projections method estimations yield the same impulse response functions, but Li, Plagborg-Møller and Wolf (2022) show that local-projections method estimators have larger variance (but lower bias), especially for the medium- and long-term horizons, than vector autoregression estimators.

[27] A dummy for time effects is not necessary, because the time variable t refers to the time since the start of the event and pertains to different years for different countries.

ANNEX 1F Tables

TABLE 1F.1 Methodology, time, and country coverage

Methodology	Time coverage*	Advanced economies	Emerging market and developing economies
Production function approach	1998-2032	**30** (AUS, AUT, BEL, CAN, CHE, CYP, DEU, DNK, ESP, EST, FIN, FRA, GBR, GRC, HKG, HRV, IRL, ISR, ITA, JPN, KOR, LTU, LVA, NLD, NOR, PRT, SVK, SVN, SWE, USA)	**64** (ALB, ARG, ARM, BDI, BEN, BGD, BGR, BOL, BRA, BRB, CAF, CHL, CHN, CMR, COL, CRI, DOM, ECU, EGY, GAB, GTM, HND, HUN, IDN, IND, IRN, IRQ, JAM, JOR, KAZ, KEN, KGZ, LAO, LSO, MAR, MDA, MEX, MNG, MOZ, MRT, MUS, MYS, NAM, NER, NIC, PAK, PER, PHL, POL, PRY, QAT, ROU, RWA, SDN, SEN, SRB, TGO, THA, TJK, TUN, TUR, URY, VNM, ZAF)
Multivariate filter	1981-2024	**37** (AUS, AUT, BEL, CAN, CHE, CYP, CZE, DEU, DNK, ESP, EST, FIN, FRA, GBR, GRC, HKG, HRV, IRL, ISL, ISR, ITA, JPN, KOR, LTU, LUX, LVA, MLT, NLD, NOR, NZL, PRT, SGP, SVK, SVN, SWE, TWN, USA)	**52** (ALB, ARG, AZE, BGR, BHR, BLZ, BOL, BRA, BWA, CHL, CHN, CMR, COL, CRI, DOM, ECU, EGY, GEO, GTM, HND, HUN, IDN, IND, IRN, JOR, KAZ, KEN, KWT, LSO, MAR, MEX, MKD, MNG, MYS, NAM, NGA, NIC, PAN, PER, PHL, POL, PRY, ROU, SAU, SLV, THA, TUN, TUR, TZA, URY, VNM, ZAF)
Univariate filters	1980Q1-2024Q4	**37** (AUS, AUT, BEL, CAN, CHE, CYP, CZE, DEU, DNK, ESP, EST, FIN, FRA, GBR, GRC, HKG, HRV, IRL, ISL, ISR, ITA, JPN, KOR, LTU, LUX, LVA, MLT, NLD, NOR, NZL, PRT, SGP, SVK, SVN, SWE, TWN, USA)	**52** (ALB, ARG, AZE, BGR, BHR, BLZ, BOL, BRA, BWA, CHL, CHN, CMR, COL, CRI, DOM, ECU, EGY, GEO, GTM, HND, HUN, IDN, IND, IRN, JOR, KAZ, KEN, KWT, LSO, MAR, MEX, MKD, MNG, MYS, NAM, NGA, NIC, PAN, PER, PHL, POL, PRY, ROU, SAU, SLV, THA, TUN, TUR, TZA, URY, VNM, ZAF)
WEO five-year-ahead expectations	1990-2022	**37** (AUS, AUT, BEL, CAN, CHE, CYP, CZE, DEU, DNK, ESP, EST, FIN, FRA, GBR, GRC, HKG, HRV, IRL, ISL, ISR, ITA, JPN, KOR, LTU, LUX, LVA, MLT, NLD, NOR, NZL, PRT, SGP, SVK, SVN, SWE, TWN, USA)	**136** (AFG, AGO, ALB, ARE, ARG, ARM, ATG, AZE, BDI, BEN, BFA, BGD, BGR, BHR, BHS, BIH, BLZ, BOL, BRA, BRB, BRN, BTN, BWA, CAF, CHL, CHN, CMR, COD, COG, COL, COM, CPV, CRI, DJI, DMA, DOM, DZA, ECU, EGY, ERI, ETH, FSM, GAB, GEO, GHA, GIN, GMB, GNB, GNQ, GRD, GTM, GUY, HND, HTI, HUN, IDN, IND, IRN, IRQ, JAM, JOR, KAZ, KEN, KGZ, KHM, KIR, KNA, KWT, LAO, LBN, LBR, LBY, LCA, LSO, MAR, MDA, MDG, MDV, MEX, MKD, MLI, MMR, MNG, MOZ, MRT, MUS, MWI, MYS, NAM, NER, NGA, NIC, NPL, OMN, PAK, PAN, PER, PHL, PNG, POL, PRY, QAT, ROU, RWA, SAU, SDN, SEN, SLB, SLV, SOM, SRB, SSD, STP, SUR, SWZ, SYC, SYR, TCD, TGO, THA, TJK, TLS, TON, TUN, TUR, TZA, UGA, URY, UZB, VCT, VNM, VUT, WSM, YEM, ZAF, ZMB)

Source: World Bank.
Note: Economy codes are available at https://www.iban.com/country-codes. WEO = *World Economic Outlook*.

TABLE 1F.2 **Methods for estimating potential growth**

Methodology	Advantages	Disadvantages
Production function approach	Produces estimates that help explain the movement of potential output in terms of its inputs. Low correlation with actual output growth.	Relies on proxies for potential growth in productivity and the supply of labor and capital accumulation that could be subject to measurement errors. Relies on assumption of specific functional form.
Time-series filters	Univariate filters are straightforward to implement, even in data-poor environments.	"Endpoint" problems can lead to large revisions as new data become available.[a]
	Multivariate filters produce output gaps that are consistent with indicators of domestic demand pressures (inflation, unemployment, current account deficits, capacity utilization).	Strong correlation with actual output growth, which could reflect short-term shocks to potential growth or, alternatively, be associated with cyclical movements.
Long-term growth expectations	In principle, incorporate judgment and thus capture factors that cannot be modeled during periods of high volatility.	In practice, tend to be sticky and, at times, in ways that are challenging to interpret.

Source: World Bank.

a. A filter developed by Hamilton (2018) avoids the endpoint problem but is highly volatile, especially during recessions. Since it retains much of the cyclical movement of output, it is not included in the database presented here.

TABLE 1F.3 **List of variables**

Variable	Units	Source	Sample
GDP in U.S. dollars	Millions of U.S. dollars, at market exchange rates	International Monetary Fund (IMF), World Economic Outlook database	194 countries, 1980-2021
Real GDP in local currency	Millions of local currency	Haver Analytics	93 countries, 1980Q2-2021Q4
GDP per capita	U.S. dollars at market exchange rates	IMF, World Economic Outlook database; UN population statistics	182 countries, 1980-2021
Population, by age and gender	Number	UN population statistics and projections	184 countries, 1950-2035
Labor force, by age and gender	Number	International Labour Organization, Key Indicators of the Labour Market database; Organisation for Economic Co-operation and Development, OECD Labour Force Statistics.	180 countries, 1960-2020
Investment growth	Percent	Haver Analytics	187 countries, 1961-2021
Secondary education completion rate	Percent of population in relevant age group that completed secondary education	Barro and Lee (2013); World Bank, World Development Indicators	179 countries, 1960-2020
Tertiary education completion rate	Percent of population in relevant age group that completed tertiary education	Barro and Lee (2013); World Bank, World Development Indicators	174 countries, 1960-2020
Secondary education enrollment rate	Percent of population in age group that enrolled in secondary education	World Bank, World Development Indicators	193 countries, 1970-2020
Tertiary education enrollment rate	Percent of population in age group that enrolled in tertiary education	World Bank, World Development Indicators	192 countries, 1970-2020
Life expectancy	Years	UN population statistics and projections	181 countries, 1985-2035
Fertility rate	Number of births per 1,000 women	UN population statistics and projections	175 countries, 1960-2095
Employment	Number	Penn World Table	181 countries, 1950-2019
Urban population	Share of total population	World Bank, World Development Indicators	194 countries, 1960-2020
R&D spending	Percent of GDP	World Bank, World Development Indicators	144 countries, 1996-2019
Consumer price inflation	Percent	Haver Analytics	93 countries, 1980Q1-2021Q4
Inflation expectations	Percent	Consensus Economics	74 countries, 1980Q1-2021Q4
Unemployment rate	Percent of labor force	Haver Analytics	66 countries, 1980Q1-2021Q4
Capacity utilization rate	Percent of capacity	Haver Analytics	31 countries, 1980Q1-2021Q4
Import price inflation	Percent	Haver Analytics	74 countries, 1980Q1-2021Q4
Private credit growth	Percentage points of GDP	Haver Analytics	57 countries, 1980Q1-2021Q4
Average commodity export price	Index	Federal Reserve Bank of St. Louis; UN Comtrade; World Bank	93 countries, 1980Q1-2021Q4
Monetary policy rates	Percent	Haver Analytics	80 countries, 1980Q1-2021Q4
House price growth	Percent	Bank for International Settlements	55 countries, 1980Q1-2021Q4

TABLE 1F.3 List of variables (*continued*)

Variable	Units	Source	Sample
WEO real GDP growth forecasts	Percent	IMF, World Economic Outlook database	175 countries, 1990-2021
Consensus real GDP growth forecasts	Percent	Consensus Economics	78 countries, 1990-2022

Source: World Bank.
Note: GDP = gross domestic product; R&D = research and development; WEO = *World Economic Outlook*.

TABLE 1F.4 Sample coverage for production function-based estimates of potential growth

Economy	Sample period	Economy	Sample period	Economy	Sample period
Australia	1998-2032	**Europe and Central Asia**		**Middle East and North Africa**	
Austria	1998-2032	Albania	1998-2032	Egypt, Arab Rep.	1998-2032
Belgium	1998-2032	Armenia	1998-2032	Iraq	2001-2019
Canada	1998-2032	Bulgaria	2000-2032	Iran, Islamic Rep.	1998-2032
Cyprus	1998-2032	Hungary	1998-2032	Jordan	1998-2032
Croatia	1998-2032	Kazakhstan	1998-2032	Morocco	1998-2032
Denmark	1998-2032	Kyrgyz Republic	2000-2032	Qatar	1998-2016
Estonia	1998-2032	Moldova	2013-2032	Tunisia	1998-2032
Finland	1998-2032	Poland	1998-2032		
France	1998-2032	Romania	1998-2032	**South Asia**	
Germany	1998-2032	Serbia	1998-2032	Bangladesh	1998-2032
Greece	1998-2032	Tajikistan	1998-2032	India	1998-2032
Hong Kong SAR, China	1998-2032	Turkey	1994-2030	Pakistan	1998-2032
Iceland	1998-2032				
Israel	1998-2032	**Latin America and Caribbean**		**Sub-Saharan Africa**	
Italy	1998-2032	Argentina	1998-2032	Benin	1998-2032
Japan	1998-2032	Barbados	1998-2016	Burundi	1998-2032
Korea	1998-2032	Bolivia	1998-2032	Cameroon	1998-2032
Latvia	1998-2032	Brazil	1998-2032	Central African Republic	1998-2019
Lithuania	2000-2032	Chile	1998-2032	Gabon	1998-2032
Netherlands	1998-2032	Colombia	1998-2032	Kenya	1998-2032
Norway	1998-2032	Costa Rica	1998-2032	Lesotho	1998-2032
Portugal	1998-2032	Dominican Republic	1998-2032	Mauritania	2000-2032
Slovak Republic	1998-2032	Ecuador	1998-2032	Mauritius	1998-2032
Slovenia	1998-2032	Guatemala	1998-2032	Mozambique	1998-2032
Spain	1998-2032	Honduras	1998-2032	Namibia	1998-2032
Sweden	1998-2032	Jamaica	1998-2032	Niger	1998-2032
Switzerland	1998-2032	Mexico	1998-2032	Rwanda	2000-2016
United Kingdom	1998-2032	Nicaragua	1998-2032	Senegal	1998-2032
United States	1998-2032	Paraguay	1998-2032	South Africa	1998-2032
		Peru	1998-2032	Sudan	1998-2019
East Asia and Pacific		Uruguay	1998-2032	Togo	1998-2032
China	1998-2032				
Indonesia	1998-2032				
Malaysia	1998-2032				
Mongolia	1998-2032				
Philippines	1998-2032				
Thailand	1998-2032				
Vietnam	2013-2021				

Source: World Bank.
Note: Chapter 5 details the methodology and assumptions underlying projections for 2022-32.

TABLE 1F.5 Regression results for total factor productivity

Dependent variable: TFP growth	Baseline H-P trend	3-year moving average	5-year moving average	7-year moving average	Linear-quadratic trend
GDP per capita rel. to that of advanced economies	-0.06***	-0.07***	-0.07***	-0.06***	-0.06***
	(0.000)	(0.001)	(0.002)	(0.002)	(0.001)
Working-age population	4.16˙	3.05	4.70	6.86**	3.13
	(0.100)	(0.326)	(0.143)	(0.044)	(0.321)
Secondary completion rate	0.003	0.003	0.010	0.009	-0.029***
	(0.701)	(0.807)	(0.375)	(0.397)	(0.002)
Secondary completion rate (bottom two-thirds)	0.009˙	0.012˙	0.009	0.004	0.004
	(0.061)	(0.068)	(0.142)	(0.466)	(0.464)
Investment growth (five-year moving average)	0.088***	0.178***	0.185***	0.169***	0.118***
	(0.000)	(0.000)	(0.000)	(0.000)	(0.000)
Commodity exporters credit boom dummy	0.592***	1.094***	0.778**	0.664**	1.001***
	(0.000)	(0.002)	(0.035)	(0.040)	(0.000)
Number of observations	706	694	692	687	706
Number of countries	125	125	125	125	125
Within R-squared	0.26	0.27	0.29	0.29	0.25

Source: World Bank.

Note: Estimations are based on standard errors clustered around countries. Annex 1.3 defines methodology. Sample includes unbalanced panel of 33 advanced economies 92 EMDEs for 1983-2020. *p*-statistics are shown in parentheses. GDP = gross domestic product; H-P = Hodrick-Prescott; rel. = relative; TFP = total factor productivity.

Significance level: * = 10 percent, ** = 5 percent, *** = 1 percent.

TABLE 1F.6 Regression results for total factor productivity

Dependent variable: TFP growth	H-P trend	H-P trend	H-P trend	H-P trend
GDP per capita relative to that of advanced economies	-0.06***	-0.06***	-0.06***	-0.05***
	(0.000)	(0.000)	(0.000)	(0.000)
Working-age population	5.96**	4.70	6.54**	6.13**
	(0.024)	(0.115)	(0.038)	(0.047)
Secondary completion rate	-0.002	-0.001	0.013	0.000
	(0.770)	(0.847)	(0.139)	(0.968)
Secondary completion rate (bottom two-thirds)	0.007	0.011**	0.012**	0.006
	(0.125)	(0.028)	(0.013)	(0.255)
Investment growth (three-year moving average)	0.009			
	(0.672)			
Investment growth (five-year moving average)			0.084***	0.111***
			(0.000)	(0.000)
Investment growth (seven-year moving average)		0.007		
		(0.763)		
Commodity exporters credit boom dummy	0.953***	0.924***	0.557***	0.902***
	(0.000)	(0.000)	(0.000)	(0.000)
Urban population			-0.066**	
			(0.031)	
R&D spending as percent of GDP				-0.092
				(0.752)
Number of observations	778	698	706	497
Number of countries	125	125	125	109
Within R-squared	0.15	0.15	0.28	0.34

Source: World Bank.
Note: Estimations are based on standard errors clustered around countries. Sample includes unbalanced panel of 33 advanced economies and 92 EMDEs for 1983-2020. *p*-statistics are shown in parentheses. GDP = gross domestic product; H-P = Hodrick-Prescott; R&D = research and development; TFP = total factor productivity.
Significance level: * = 10 percent, ** = 5 percent, *** = 1 percent.

TABLE 1F.7 Regression results for labor force participation rates, baseline

	15–19 years old		20–24 years old		25–49 years old		50–64 years old		65+ years old	
	Female	Male	Female	Male	Female	Male	Female	Male	Female	Male
Fertility	0.734*** (0.000)		0.057* (0.000)		0.000 (0.945)					
Secondary enrollment	0.197*** (0.000)	0.127*** (0.000)								
Tertiary enrollment			-0.114*** (0.000)	-0.180*** (0.000)						
Completion of secondary education			0.039 (0.249)	-0.023 (0.394)	0.235*** (0.000)	0.130*** (0.000)	0.406*** (0.000)	0.063 (0.221)		
Completion of tertiary education			0.158** (0.002)	-0.099* (0.045)	0.323*** (0.000)	0.313*** (0.000)	0.486** (0.003)	0.426** (0.002)		
Life expectancy							0.569*** (0.000)	-2.679** (0.003)	0.101*** (0.000)	0.227*** (0.000)
Cycle	16.14*** (0.000)	21.43*** (0.000)	1.04 (0.144)	11.54*** (0.000)	1.504 (0.182)	-0.591** (0.008)	0.590 (0.495)	-2.329** (0.008)	1.435 (0.394)	21.76 (0.399)
Cycle * Life Expectancy									-0.031 (0.216)	-0.192 (0.584)
Fertility * EMDE	-0.669*** (0.000)		-0.066** (0.006)							
Secondary Enrollment * EMDE	-0.337*** (0.000)									
Completion of Secondary Education * EMDE			-0.027 (0.495)	-0.038 (0.238)						
Completion of Tertiary Education * EMDE			-0.127 (0.056)	0.153* (0.000)						
Life Expectancy * EMDE									-0.143*** (0.000)	-0.608*** (0.000)
Secondary Enrollment * EMDE	-0.337*** (0.000)									
Completion of Secondary Education * EMDE			-0.027 (0.495)	-0.038 (0.238)						

TABLE 1F.7 Regression results for labor force participation rates, baseline (continued)

	15-19 years old		20-24 years old		25-49 years old		50-64 years old		65+ years old	
	Female	Male	Female	Male	Female	Male	Female	Male	Female	Male
Completion of Tertiary Education * EMDE			-0.127 (0.056)	0.153* (0.000)						
Life Expectancy * EMDE									-0.143*** (0.000)	-0.608*** (0.000)
Cycle * EMDE	-17.90*** (0.000)	-24.21*** (0.000)		-11.72*** (0.000)	-1.456* (0.038)					16.46 (0.526)
Cycle * Life Expectancy * EMDE										0.039 (0.912)
Coefficient of fertility in EMDEs	0.065*** (0.000)		-0.009 (0.234)							
Coefficient of secondary enrollment in EMDEs	-0.133*** (0.000)									
Coefficient of secondary education in EMDEs			-0.012 (0.570)	-0.058*** (0.000)						
Coefficient of tertiary education in EMDEs			0.031 (0.478)	-0.063 (0.189)						
Coefficient of cycle in EMDEs	-0.145** (0.008)	-2.78** (0.001)		-0.18 (0.801)	0.048** (0.009)					
Country fixed effects	Yes	Yes	Yes	Yes	Yes	Yes	Yes	Yes	Yes	Yes
Cohort fixed effects	No	No	No	No	No	No	Yes	Yes	Yes	Yes
County-cohort fixed effects	Yes	Yes	Yes	Yes	Yes	Yes	Yes	Yes	Yes	Yes
Age fixed effects	No	No	No	No	Yes	Yes	Yes	Yes	Yes	Yes
Number of observations	4,432	4,484	3,741	3,789	21,382	21,654	12,239	12,261	5,111	5,111
Number of countries	163	165	151	154	158	160	145	145	168	168
Adjusted R-squared	0.997	0.997	0.999	0.999	0.997	0.999	0.986	0.993	0.998	0.999

Sources: Barro and Lee (2013); International Labour Organization, Key Indicators of the Labour Market; Organisation for Economic Co-operation and Development, OECD Labour Force Statistics; UN, World Population Prospects; World Bank, World Development Indicators; and World Bank staff estimations.
Note: Business cycles are defined as deviation of real gross domestic product (GDP) from Hodrick-Prescott-filtered trend. Sample includes unbalanced panel of 35 advanced economies and 133 EMDEs for 1987-2020. *p*-statistics are shown in parentheses. EMDEs = emerging market and developing economies.
Significance level: * = 10 percent, ** = 5 percent, *** = 1 percent.

TABLE 1F.8 Regression results for labor force participation rates, robustness test: 10-year moving average

	15-19 years old		20-24 years old		25-49 years old		50-64 years old		65+ years old	
	Female	Male	Female	Male	Female	Male	Female	Male	Female	Male
Fertility	0.706***		0.076**		0.004**					
	(0.000)		(0.009)		(0.002)					
Secondary enrollment	0.202***	0.149***								
	(0.000)	(0.000)								
Tertiary enrollment			-0.112***	-0.171***						
			(0.000)	(0.000)						
Completion of secondary education			0.022	0.030	0.252***	0.149***	0.341***	-0.014		
			(0.540)	(0.296)	(0.000)	(0.000)	(0.000)	(0.786)		
Completion of tertiary education			0.167**	-0.070	0.354***	0.335***	0.570***	0.145		
			(0.002)	(0.166)	(0.000)	(0.000)	(0.000)	(0.265)		
Life expectancy							0.621***	1.127***	0.101***	0.227***
							(0.000)	(0.000)	(0.000)	(0.000)
Cycle	26.37***	34.46***	5.54***	19.59***	0.336	0.663	-2.63*	-0.789	1.74	51.62
	(0.000)	(0.000)	(0.000)	(0.000)	(0.832)	(0.077)	(0.042)	(0.566)	(0.826)	(0.127)
Cycle * Life Expectancy									-0.023	-0.594
									(0.574)	(0.193)
Fertility * EMDE	-0.664***		-0.067**							
	(0.000)		(0.005)							
Secondary Enrollment * EMDE	-0.332***									
	(0.000)									
Completion of Secondary Education * EMDE			-0.023	-0.057						
			(0.565)	(0.080)						
Completion of Tertiary Education * EMDE			-0.127	0.153*						
			(0.056)	(0.000)						
Life Expectancy * EMDE									-0.143***	-0.608***
									(0.000)	(0.000)
Cycle * EMDE	-17.83***	-23.82***		-11.46***	-2.51*				-17.04	
	(0.000)	(0.000)		(0.000)	(0.033)				(0.526)	
Cycle * Life Expectancy * EMDE									0.057	
									(0.876)	

TABLE 1F.8 Regression results for labor force participation rates, robustness test: 10-year moving average (continued)

	15-19 years old		20-24 years old		25-49 years old		50-64 years old		65+ years old	
	Female	Male	Female	Male	Female	Male	Female	Male	Female	Male
Coefficient of fertility in EMDEs	0.070***		-0.008							
	(0.000)		(0.251)							
Coefficient of secondary enrollment in EMDEs	-0.133***									
	(0.000)									
Coefficient of secondary education in EMDEs			-0.015	-0.046***						
			(0.470)	(0.000)						
Coefficient of tertiary education in EMDEs			-0.035	0.047						
			(0.450)	(0.322)						
Coefficient of cycle in EMDEs	-1.69*	-2.09*		0.220	-1.00**					
	(0.033)	(0.039)		(0.745)	(0.006)					
Country fixed effects	Yes	Yes	Yes	Yes	Yes	Yes	Yes	Yes	Yes	Yes
Cohort fixed effects	No	No	No	No	No	No	Yes	Yes	Yes	Yes
County-cohort fixed effects	Yes	Yes	Yes	Yes	Yes	Yes	Yes	Yes	Yes	Yes
Age fixed effects	No	No	No	No	Yes	Yes	Yes	Yes	Yes	Yes
Number of observations	3,807	3,807	3,631	3,630	20,588	20,583	11,751	11,773	4,207	4,207
Number of countries	138	138	138	138	138	138	138	138	138	138
Adjusted R-squared	0.997	0.996	0.999	0.999	0.997	0.999	0.986	0.993	0.998	0.999

Sources: Barro and Lee (2013); International Labour Organization, Key Indicators of the Labour Market; Organisation for Economic Co-operation and Development, OECD Labour Force Statistics; UN, World Population Prospects; World Bank, World Development Indicators; and World Bank staff estimations.
Note: Sample of countries is balanced across gender- and age-specific regressions. Business cycles are defined as deviation of real gross domestic product (GDP) from Hodrick-Prescott-filtered trend. Sample includes balanced panel of 34 advanced economies and 104 EMDEs for 1987-2020. p-statistics are shown in parentheses.
Significance level: * = 10 percent, ** = 5 percent, *** = 1 percent.

TABLE 1F.9 Regression results for labor force participation rates, robustness test: Linear-quadratic trend

	15-19 years old		20-24 years old		25-49 years old		50-64 years old		65+ years old	
	Female	Male	Female	Male	Female	Male	Female	Male	Female	Male
Fertility	0.697***		0.059*		0.000					
	(0.000)		(0.011)		(0.922)					
Secondary enrollment	0.202***	0.125***								
	(0.000)	(0.000)								
Tertiary enrollment			-0.113***	-0.180***						
			(0.000)	(0.000)						
Completion of secondary education			0.040	-0.013	0.236***	0.1340***	0.403***	0.064		
			(0.233)	(0.642)	(0.000)	(0.000)	(0.000)	(0.218)		
Completion of tertiary education			0.158**	-0.100*	0.321***	0.311***	0.490**	0.431**		
			(0.002)	(0.041)	(0.000)	(0.000)	(0.003)	(0.001)		
Life expectancy							0.571***	0.972***	0.101***	0.229***
							(0.000)	(0.000)	(0.000)	(0.000)
Cycle	15.11***	24.22***	0.281	12.72***	3.24**	0.156	-1.56	-2.12*	1.45	17.01
	(0.000)	(0.000)	(0.684)	(0.000)	(0.003)	(0.470)	(0.101)	(0.014)	(0.512)	(0.491)
Cycle * Life Expectancy									-0.027	-0.118
									(0.275)	(0.348)
Fertility * EMDE	-0.630***		-0.067**							
	(0.000)		(0.005)							
Secondary Enrollment * EMDE	-0.342***									
	(0.000)									
Completion of Secondary Education * EMDE			-0.029	-0.048						
			(0.482)	(0.133)						
Completion of Tertiary Education * EMDE			-0.126	0.155*						
			(0.058)	(0.014)						
Life Expectancy * EMDE									-0.145***	-0.620***
									(0.000)	(0.000)

TABLE 1F.9 Regression results for labor force participation rates, robustness test: Linear-quadratic trend (continued)

	15-19 years old		20-24 years old		25-49 years old		50-64 years old		65+ years old	
	Female	Male	Female	Male	Female	Male	Female	Male	Female	Male
Cycle * EMDE	-16.77***	-25.50***		-12.11***	-3.91**					-16.58
	(0.000)	(0.000)		(0.000)	(0.001)					(0.504)
Cycle * Life Expectancy * EMDE										0.073
										(0.829)
Coefficient of fertility in EMDEs	0.067***		-0.008							
	(0.000)		(0.285)							
Coefficient of secondary enrollment in EMDEs	-0.138***									
	(0.000)									
Coefficient of secondary education in EMDEs			0.011	-0.164***						
			(0.556)	(0.000)						
Coefficient of tertiary education in EMDEs			0.032	-0.083						
			(0.472)	(0.253)						
Coefficient of cycle in EMDEs	-1.66**	-1.28		0.35	-0.667*					
	(0.007)	(0.103)		(0.740)	(0.063)					
Country fixed effects	Yes	Yes	Yes	Yes	Yes	Yes	Yes	Yes	Yes	Yes
Cohort fixed effects	No	No	No	No	No	No	Yes	Yes	Yes	Yes
County-cohort fixed effects	Yes	Yes	Yes	Yes	Yes	Yes	Yes	Yes	Yes	Yes
Age fixed effects	No	No	No	No	Yes	Yes	Yes	Yes	Yes	Yes
Number of observations	4,428	4,480	3,741	3,789	21,382	21,654	12,239	12,261	5,107	5,107
Number of countries	163	165	151	154	158	160	145	145	168	168
Adjusted R-squared	0.997	0.997	0.999	0.999	0.997	0.999	0.986	0.993	0.998	0.999

Sources: Barro and Lee (2013); International Labour Organization, Key Indicators of the Labour Market; Organisation for Economic Co-operation and Development, OECD Labour Force Statistics; UN, World Population Prospects; World Bank, World Development Indicators; and World Bank staff estimations.

Note: Business cycles are defined as deviation of real gross domestic product (GDP) from linear-quadratic trend. Sample includes unbalanced panel of 35 advanced economies and 133 EMDEs for 1987-2020. p-statistics are shown in parentheses.

Significance level: * = 10 percent, ** = 5 percent, *** = 1 percent.

TABLE 1F.10 Coverage for univariate and multivariate filter-based estimates

Economy	Sample period	Economy	Sample period	Economy	Sample period
Australia	1981-2024	**East Asia and Pacific**		Paraguay	1994-2024
Austria	1995-2024	China	1992-2024	Peru	1998-2024
Belgium	1995-2024	Indonesia	2001-2024	Uruguay	1997-2024
Canada	1981-2024	Malaysia	2005-2024	**Middle East and North Africa**	
Croatia	2000-2024	Mongolia	2010-2024	Bahrain	2008-2024
Cyprus	1995-2024	Philippines	1998-2024	Egypt, Arab Rep.	2007-2024
Czech Rep.	1996-2024	Thailand	1993-2024	Iran, Islamic Rep.	2012-2024
Denmark	1991-2024	Vietnam	2008-2024	Jordan	1992-2024
Estonia	1995-2024	**Europe and Central Asia**		Kuwait	2010-2024
Finland	1981-2024	Albania	2008-2024	Morocco	1998-2024
France	1981-2024	Azerbaijan	2001-2024	Saudi Arabia	2010-2024
Germany	1981-2024	Bulgaria	2000-2024	Tunisia	2000-2024
Greece	1995-2024	Georgia	2003-2024	**South Asia**	
Hong Kong SAR, China	1990-2024	Hungary	1998-2024	India	1997-2024
Iceland	1995-2024	Kazakhstan	1996-2024	**Sub-Saharan Africa**	
Ireland	1995-2024	North Macedonia	2000-2024	Botswana	1994-2024
Israel	1995-2024	Poland	1996-2024	Cameroon	1999-2024
Italy	1981-2024	Romania	1995-2024	Kenya	2009-2024
Japan	1981-2024	Turkey	2001-2024	Lesotho	2007-2024
Korea	1981-2024	**Latin America and Caribbean**		Namibia	2000-2024
Latvia	1995-2024	Argentina	2004-2024	Nigeria	2010-2024
Lithuania	1995-2024	Belize	1994-2024	South Africa	1981-2024
Luxembourg	1995-2024	Bolivia	1990-2024	Tanzania	2010-2024
Malta	2000-2024	Brazil	1990-2024		
Netherlands	1981-2024	Chile	1996-2024		
New Zealand	1988-2024	Colombia	2000-2024		
Norway	1981-2024	Costa Rica	1991-2024		
Portugal	1995-2024	Dominican Republic	2007-2024		
Singapore	1981-2024	Ecuador	2001-2024		
Slovak Republic	1995-2024	El Salvador	1990-2024		
Slovenia	1995-2024	Guatemala	2001-2024		
Spain	1995-2024	Honduras	2000-2024		
Sweden	1981-2024	Mexico	2000-2024		
Switzerland	1981-2024	Nicaragua	2006-2024		
Taiwan	1982-2024	Panama	2007-2024		
United Kingdom	1981-2024				
United States	1981-2024				

Source: World Bank.
Note: Forecasts for 2022Q2-2024Q4 are based on the June 2022 *Global Economic Prospects* report.

TABLE 1F.11 Coverage for production function approach, filter-based, and expectations-based estimates: Advanced economies

Economy	Production function approach	Univariate and multivariate filters	WEO expectations
Australia	1998-2032	1981-2024	1990-2022
Austria	1998-2032	1995-2024	1990-2022
Belgium	1998-2032	1995-2024	1990-2022
Canada	1998-2032	1981-2024	1990-2022
Croatia	1998-2032	2000-2024	1994-2022
Cyprus	1998-2032	1995-2024	1990-2022
Denmark	1998-2032	1991-2024	1990-2022
Estonia	1998-2032	1995-2024	1993-2022
Finland	1998-2032	1981-2024	1990-2022
France	1998-2032	1981-2024	1990-2022
Germany	1998-2032	1981-2024	1990-2022
Greece	1998-2032	1995-2024	1990-2022
Hong Kong SAR, China	1998-2032	1990-2024	1990-2022
Ireland	1998-2032	1995-2024	1990-2022
Israel	1998-2032	1995-2024	1990-2022
Italy	1998-2032	1981-2024	1990-2022
Japan	1998-2032	1981-2024	1990-2022
Korea, Rep.	1998-2032	1981-2024	1990-2022
Latvia	1998-2032	1995-2024	1993-2022
Lithuania	2000-2032	1995-2024	1993-2022
Netherlands	1998-2032	1981-2024	1990-2022
Norway	1998-2032	1981-2024	1990-2022
Portugal	1998-2032	1995-2024	1990-2022
Slovak Republic	1998-2032	1995-2024	1994-2022
Slovenia	1998-2032	1995-2024	1994-2022
Spain	1998-2032	1995-2024	1990-2022
Sweden	1998-2032	1981-2024	1990-2022
Switzerland	1998-2032	1981-2024	1990-2022
United Kingdom	1998-2032	1981-2024	1990-2022
United States	1998-2032	1981-2024	1990-2022

Source: World Bank.
Note: Forecasts for filter-based estimates for 2022Q2-2024Q4 are based on the June 2022 *Global Economic Prospects* report. Forecasts for production function-based estimates are derived as described in chapter 5. Univariate filters: Hodrick-Prescott, Baxter-King, Christiano-Fitzgerald, Butterworth, and unobserved-components model. WEO = *World Economic Outlook*.

TABLE 1F.12 Coverage for production function approach, filter-based, and expectations-based estimates: Emerging market and developing economies

Economy	Production function approach	Univariate and multivariate filters	WEO expectations
Albania	1998-2032	2008-2024	1993-2021
Argentina	1998-2032	2004-2024	1990-2021
Bolivia	1998-2032	1990-2024	1990-2021
Brazil	1998-2032	1990-2024	1990-2021
Bulgaria	2000-2032	2000-2024	2000-2021
Cameroon	1998-2032	1999-2024	1990-2021
Chile	1998-2032	1996-2024	1990-2021
China	1998-2032	1992-2024	1990-2021
Colombia	1998-2032	2000-2024	1990-2021
Costa Rica	1998-2032	1991-2024	1990-2021
Dominican Republic	1998-2032	2007-2024	1990-2021
Ecuador	1998-2032	2001-2024	1990-2021
Egypt, Arab Rep.	1998-2032	2007-2024	1990-2021
Guatemala	1998-2032	2001-2024	1990-2021
Honduras	1998-2032	2000-2024	1990-2021
Hungary	1998-2032	1998-2024	1990-2021
India	1998-2032	1997-2024	1990-2021
Indonesia	1998-2032	2001-2024	1990-2021
Iran, Islamic Rep.	1998-2032	2012-2024	1990-2021
Jordan	1998-2032	1992-2024	1990-2021
Kazakhstan	1998-2032	1996-2024	1993-2021
Kenya	1998-2032	2009-2024	1990-2021
Lesotho	1998-2032	2007-2024	1990-2021
Malaysia	1998-2032	2005-2024	1990-2021
Mexico	1998-2032	2000-2024	1990-2021
Mongolia	1998-2032	2010-2024	1993-2021
Morocco	1998-2032	1998-2024	1990-2021
Namibia	1998-2032	2000-2024	1994-2021
Nicaragua	1998-2032	2006-2024	1990-2021
Paraguay	1998-2032	1994-2024	1990-2021
Peru	1998-2032	1998-2024	1990-2021
Philippines	1998-2032	1998-2024	1990-2021
Poland	1998-2032	1996-2024	1990-2021
Romania	1998-2032	1995-2024	1993-2021
South Africa	1998-2032	1981-2024	1990-2021
Thailand	1998-2032	1993-2024	1990-2021
Tunisia	1998-2032	2000-2024	1990-2021
Turkey	1998-2032	2001-2024	1990-2021
Uruguay	1998-2032	1997-2024	1990-2021
Vietnam	2013-2032	2008-2024	1990-2021

Source: World Bank.
Note: Includes only countries for which data are available from 2001. Forecasts for filter-based estimates for 2022Q2-2024Q4 are based on the June 2022 *Global Economic Prospects* report. Forecasts for production function-based estimates are derived as described in chapter 5. Univariate filters: Hodrick-Prescott, Baxter-King, Christiano-Fitzgerald, Butterworth, and unobserved-components model. WEO = *World Economic Outlook*.

TABLE 1F.13 List of banking crises

Regions	Countries
Advanced economies	AUT (2008), BEL (2008), CHE (2008), CYP (2011), CZE (1996), DEU (2008), DNK (2008), ESP (2008), FIN (1991), FRA (2008), GBR (2007), GRC (2008), HRV (1998), IRL (2008), ISL (2008), ITA (2008), JPN (1997), KOR (1997), LTU (1995), LUX (2008), LVA (1995), LVA (2008), NLD (2008), NOR (1991), PRT (2008), SVK (1998), SVN (2008), SWE (1991), SWE (2008), USA (2007)
Emerging market and developing economies	ALB (1994), ARG (1995), ARG (2001), ARM (1994), AZE (1995), BDI (1994), BFA (1990), BOL (1994), BRA (1990), BRA (1994), CAF (1995), CHN (1998), CMR (1995), COD (1991), COD (1994), COG (1992), COL (1998), CPV (1993), CRI (1994), DJI (1991), DOM (2003), DZA (1990), ECU (1998), GIN (1993), GNB (1995), GNB (2014), GUY (1993), HTI (1994), HUN (1991), HUN (2008), IDN (1997), IND (1993), JAM (1996), KAZ (2008), KEN (1992), KGZ (1995), LBN (1990), LBR (1991), MDA (2014), MEX (1994), MNG (2008), MYS (1997), NGA (1991), NGA (2009), NIC (1990), NIC (2000), PHL (1997), POL (1992), PRY (1995), ROU (1998), STP (1992), TCD (1992), TGO (1993), THA (1997), TUN (1991), TUR (2000), UGA (1994), URY (2002), VNM (1997), YEM (1996)

Sources: Laeven and Valencia (2018); World Bank.
Note: The list of banking crises corresponds to the sample of measures of potential growth. Economy codes are available at https://www.iban.com/country-codes.

TABLE 1F.14 List of economies affected by epidemics

Epidemics	Economies
SARS (2003)	CAN, CHN, FRA, MYS, PHL, SGP, THA, VNM, ZAF, HKG, TWN.
Swine flu (2009)	AFG, ALB, ARE, ARG, ARM, AUS, AZE, BGD, BGR, BHR, BHS, BIH, BLR, BMU, BOL, BRA, BRB, BRN, CAN, CHE, CHL, CHN, COL, CRI, CUB, CZE, DEU, DOM, DZA, ECU, EGY, ESP, EST, FRA, GBR, GEO, GHA, GRC, GTM, HND, HRV, HUN, IDN, IND, IRL, IRN, IRQ, ISL, ISR, ITA, JAM, JOR, JPN, KHM, KOR, KWT, LAO, LBN, LBY, LKA, LTU, LUX, LVA, MAR, MDA, MDG, MDV, MEX, MHL, MLT, MNE, MNG, MOZ, MUS, MYS, NAM, NGA, NIC, NLD, NOR, NPL, NZL, OMN, PAK, PAN, PER, PHL, POL, PRY, PYF, QAT, ROU, RUS, SAU, SDN, SGP, SLB, SLV, SRB, SUR, SVK, SVN, SWE, SYR, THA, TON, TUN, TUR, TZA, UKR, URY, USA, VNM, WSM, YEM, ZAF.
MERS (2012)	ARE, AUT, DEU, DZA, FRA, GBR, GRC, IRN, JOR, KOR, KWT, MYS, OMN, QAT, SAU, TUN, TUR, YEM.
Ebola (2014)	MLI, NGA, GIN, LBR, SLE.
Zika (2016)	BOL, BRA, COL, DOM, GLP, MTQ, PRI, SUR, USA.

Source: World Bank.
Note: Economy codes are available at https://www.iban.com/country-codes. MERS = Middle East Respiratory Syndrome; SARS = Severe Acute Respiratory Syndrome.

TABLE 1F.15 Impulse responses of potential growth to recessions

Definition of potential output	h	Recessions: Baseline definition			Recessions: Alternative definition		
		World	AEs	EMDEs	World	AEs	EMDEs
Production function approach	0	-0.042	0.066	-0.138	-0.046	0.042	-0.123
	1	-1.153***	-0.773***	-1.499***	-1.123***	-0.792***	-1.414***
	2	-1.573***	-1.407***	-1.738***	-1.432***	-1.402***	-1.454***
	3	-1.542***	-1.444***	-1.645***	-1.401***	-1.432***	-1.371***
	4	-1.521***	-1.421***	-1.639***	-1.348***	-1.386***	-1.308***
	5	-1.431***	-1.257***	-1.635***	-1.244***	-1.193***	-1.296***
Multivariate filter	0	-0.355***	-0.354***	-0.352***	-0.348***	-0.342***	-0.352***
	1	-2.082***	-1.782***	-2.465***	-2.014***	-1.709***	-2.419***
	2	-1.298***	-1.485***	-0.947***	-1.215***	-1.372***	-0.91***
	3	-0.734***	-1.033***	-0.192	-0.647***	-0.848***	-0.272
	4	-0.442*	-0.699**	0.06	-0.356*	-0.488**	-0.103
	5	-0.133	-0.215	0.025	-0.123	-0.143	-0.089
Expectations (WEO)	0	-0.058	-0.06	-0.057	-0.04	-0.037	-0.042
	1	-0.208**	0.055	-0.356***	0.08	0.128*	0.052
	2	-0.33**	-0.143	-0.425**	-0.036	-0.042	-0.032
	3	-0.315*	-0.144	-0.403	-0.282	-0.08	-0.395
	4	-0.251	-0.072	-0.348	-0.282**	-0.022	-0.433**
	5	-0.262*	-0.125	-0.336	-0.269**	-0.078	-0.378*
Unobserved-components model	0	-0.208***	-0.215***	-0.2***	-0.215***	-0.238***	-0.184***
	1	-1.83***	-1.605***	-2.102***	-1.794***	-1.597***	-2.037***
	2	-0.638***	-0.711***	-0.532***	-0.599***	-0.67***	-0.497***
	3	-0.279***	-0.256**	-0.316*	-0.275***	-0.217**	-0.362**
	4	-0.3***	-0.298**	-0.301**	-0.297***	-0.262**	-0.358***
	5	-0.198*	-0.143	-0.288***	-0.19**	-0.118	-0.314***

Source: World Bank.

Note: "Recessions: Baseline definition" refers to the period from the peak preceding a business cycle trough to the trough, with troughs defined as years of output growth that is both negative and one standard deviation below the long-term average (as in Huidrom, Kose, and Ohnsorge 2016). "Recessions: Alternative definition" refers to years of negative output growth only, regardless of the depth of the output decline. The column *h* refers to years after a recession occurred. Sample includes unbalanced panel of 33 advanced economies and 77 EMDEs for 1981-2020. AEs = advanced economies; EMDEs = emerging market and developing economies; WEO = *World Economic Outlook*.

Significance level: * = 10 percent, ** = 5 percent, *** = 1 percent.

TABLE 1F.16 Impulse responses of potential growth to recessions: Other measures

Definition of potential output	h	Recessions: Baseline definition			Recessions: Alternative definition		
		World	AEs	EMDEs	World	AEs	EMDEs
Expectations (CF)	0	0.004	0.04	-0.056	0.012	0.041	-0.04
	1	-0.084	-0.024	-0.189**	-0.087*	-0.058	-0.139*
	2	-0.157**	-0.127	-0.207*	-0.135**	-0.13	-0.145
	3	-0.114	-0.07	-0.171	-0.077	-0.083	-0.067
	4	-0.215**	-0.134*	-0.361	-0.241***	-0.224***	-0.272
	5	-0.19**	-0.187*	-0.203	-0.214**	-0.26**	-0.124
Hodrick-Prescott filter	0	-0.165***	-0.194***	-0.128***	-0.16***	-0.181***	-0.132***
	1	-0.212***	-0.337***	-0.046	-0.2***	-0.298***	-0.066
	2	-0.493***	-0.664***	-0.224	-0.412***	-0.512**	-0.264
	3	-0.32	-0.544*	0.056	-0.232	-0.35	-0.053
	4	-0.146	-0.321	0.17	-0.072	-0.132	0.006
	5	0.058	-0.047	0.249	0.089	0.089	0.055
Christiano-Fitzgerald filter	0	-0.691***	-0.575***	-0.8***	-0.673***	-0.524***	-0.826***
	1	-0.809***	-0.937***	-0.61***	-0.798***	-0.867***	-0.67***
	2	-1.299***	-1.572***	-0.795**	-1.193***	-1.304***	-0.956**
	3	-1.233***	-1.563***	-0.608	-1.061***	-1.215***	-0.749*
	4	-1.029***	-1.419***	-0.257	-0.887***	-1.062***	-0.548
	5	-0.685**	-0.833*	-0.406	-0.598**	-0.579	-0.666
Baxter-King filter	0	-2.161***	-1.983***	-2.388***	-2.113***	-1.932***	-2.351***
	1	-4.197***	-4.099***	-4.327***	-4.08***	-3.983***	-4.216***
	2	-3.413***	-3.607***	-3.071***	-3.132***	-3.295***	-2.843***
	3	-1.589***	-1.799***	-1.2**	-1.42***	-1.512***	-1.254**
	4	-1.469***	-1.614***	-1.166**	-1.303***	-1.281***	-1.353***
	5	-1.333***	-1.298***	-1.396***	-1.167***	-1.047***	-1.417***
Butterworth filter	0	-0.703***	-0.562***	-0.744***	-0.693***	-0.544***	-0.726***
	1	-1.507***	-1.27***	-1.672***	-1.461***	-1.212***	-1.626***
	2	-1.419***	-1.493***	-1.078***	-1.29***	-1.307***	-1.01***
	3	-1.103***	-1.017***	-1.05**	-0.979***	-0.813***	-1.044***
	4	-0.792***	-0.75**	-0.784*	-0.679***	-0.554**	-0.834**
	5	-0.443**	-0.433	-0.425	-0.378**	-0.293	-0.51*

Source: World Bank.

Note: "Recessions: Baseline definition" refers to the period from the peak preceding a business cycle trough to the trough, with troughs defined as years of output growth that is both negative and one standard deviation below the long-term average (as in Huidrom, Kose, and Ohnsorge 2016). "Recessions: Alternative definition" refers to years of negative output growth only, regardless of the depth of the output decline. The column *h* refers to years after a recession occurred. Sample includes unbalanced panel of 33 advanced economies and 77 EMDEs for 1981-2020. AEs = advanced economies; CF = Consensus Forecasts; EMDEs = emerging market and developing economies.

Significance level: * = 10 percent, ** = 5 percent, *** = 1 percent.

TABLE 1F.17 Impulse responses of potential growth to banking crises and epidemics

Definition of potential output	h	Banking crises			Epidemics		
		World	AEs	EMDEs	World	AEs	EMDEs
Production function approach	0	-0.574***	-0.538*	-0.763**	-0.731***	-0.846***	-0.68***
	1	-1.605***	-1.508**	-1.865***	-0.796***	-1.035***	-0.649***
	2	-1.75***	-1.979***	-1.402***	-0.77***	-0.911***	-0.655***
	3	-1.467***	-1.958***	-0.451	-0.872***	-1.057***	-0.77**
	4	-1.286***	-1.929***	0.031	-1.083***	-1.126***	-1.062***
	5	-1.169**	-1.908***	0.416	-0.866***	-0.849**	-0.895***
Multivariate filter	0	-0.349**	-0.406**	-0.209	-0.229**	-0.247	-0.214
	1	-0.746***	-0.981***	-0.119	-0.021	-0.198	0.12
	2	-0.724**	-1.25***	0.743	0.195	0.169	0.215
	3	-0.27	-0.81**	1.176**	0.305	0.531*	0.127
	4	0.127	-0.279	1.183*	0.232	0.63**	-0.081
	5	0.4	0.052	1.339*	0.335	0.874**	-0.121
Expectations (WEO)	0	-0.025	-0.044	-0.019	-0.421***	-0.173	-0.525***
	1	-0.08	0.065	-0.155	-0.334***	-0.287***	-0.358**
	2	0.028	-0.035	0.076	-0.313*	-0.176	-0.374
	3	0.276	0.088	0.394	-0.479***	-0.175	-0.609***
	4	0.174	0.141	0.199	-0.519***	-0.19	-0.661***
	5	0.142	0.071	0.199	-0.623***	-0.208	-0.808***
Unobserved-components model	0	-0.573***	-0.736***	-0.278	-0.664***	-0.792***	-0.564***
	1	-1.399***	-1.731***	-0.806**	0.139*	0.133	0.146
	2	-0.364**	-0.67***	0.18	0.075	0.083	0.066
	3	-0.133	-0.48***	0.488***	-0.075	-0.059	-0.085
	4	-0.356**	-0.796***	0.43**	-0.198	-0.028	-0.335*
	5	-0.299**	-0.553***	0.152	0.005	0.191	-0.156

Sources: Laeven and Valencia (2018); World Bank.
Note: Sample includes unbalanced panel of 33 advanced economies and 98 EMDEs for 1981-2020. The column *h* refers to years after a crisis occurred. AEs = advanced economies; EMDEs = emerging market and developing economies.
Significance level: * = 10 percent, ** = 5 percent, *** = 1 percent.

TABLE 1F.18 Impulse responses of potential growth to banking crises and epidemics: Other measures

Definition of potential output	h	Banking crises			Epidemics		
		World	AEs	EMDEs	World	AEs	EMDEs
Expectations (CF)	0	0.046	0.093**	-0.046	-0.081	-0.105	-0.062
	1	-0.33**	-0.144	-0.753***	-0.005	-0.148*	0.179
	2	-0.192	-0.163	-0.266	0.077	-0.082	0.275**
	3	-0.094	0.186	-0.632***	-0.056	-0.142**	0.027
	4	-0.212*	-0.102	-0.4	0.003	-0.063	0.082
	5	-0.285*	-0.161	-0.5	-0.104	-0.141	-0.039
Hodrick-Prescott filter	0	-0.132**	-0.229***	0.113	0.065**	0.163***	-0.01
	1	-0.177	-0.431***	0.456	0.297***	0.546***	0.104
	2	0.002	-0.39	0.979	0.499***	0.878***	0.199
	3	0.258	-0.224	1.453*	0.554***	1.037***	0.17
	4	0.497	-0.006	1.747*	0.509**	1.097***	0.042
	5	0.761*	0.299	1.913*	0.456*	1.146***	-0.124
Christiano-Fitzgerald filter	0	-0.485***	-0.53***	-0.253	-0.451***	-0.444***	-0.421***
	1	-1.034***	-1.365***	-0.005	-0.396***	-0.21	-0.513**
	2	-1.096***	-1.612***	0.338	0.032	0.284	-0.151
	3	-0.757	-1.481***	1.181	0.364	0.673**	0.12
	4	-0.344	-1.083**	1.512	0.214	0.57*	-0.086
	5	0.166	-0.501	1.825	0.604**	1.091***	0.174
Baxter-King filter	0	-2.288***	-2.64***	-1.31*	-0.666***	-0.739**	-0.614***
	1	-3.877***	-4.73***	-1.525	0.415	0.492	0.341
	2	-2.149***	-2.975***	0.125	0.677**	0.833**	0.539
	3	-0.921	-1.768***	1.427	0.173	0.428	-0.031
	4	-1.198**	-1.993***	1.001	0.02	0.407	-0.284
	5	-0.875*	-1.59***	1.114	0.249	0.88*	-0.269
Butterworth filter	0	-0.899***	-0.739***	-0.597	-0.45	0.03	-0.553*
	1	-1.382***	-1.429***	-0.515	0.196	0.665***	0.116
	2	-0.892**	-1.085***	0.249	0.295	0.876***	0.095
	3	-0.476	-0.745**	0.782	0.117	0.803***	-0.204
	4	-0.212	-0.619*	1.073	0.214	0.809***	-0.164
	5	0.117	-0.278	1.262	0.212	0.922**	-0.318

Sources: Laeven and Valencia (2018); World Bank.
Note: Sample includes unbalanced panel of 33 advanced economies and 98 EMDEs for 1981-2020. The column *h* refers to years after a crisis occurred. AEs = advanced economies; CF = Consensus Forecasts; EMDEs = emerging market and developing economies. Significance level: * = 10 percent, ** = 5 percent, *** = 1 percent.

TABLE 1F.19 Channels: Impulse responses of total factor productivity, investment, employment, and actual growth rates to recessions

Definition of potential output	h	Recessions: Baseline definition			Recessions: Alternative definition		
		World	AEs	EMDEs	World	AEs	EMDEs
Total factor productivity	0	-0.066**	-0.019	-0.108**	-0.064**	-0.041**	-0.087*
	1	-0.359***	-0.228***	-0.471***	-0.353***	-0.251***	-0.443***
	2	-0.626***	-0.476***	-0.743***	-0.577***	-0.495***	-0.64***
	3	-0.676***	-0.495***	-0.819***	-0.635***	-0.527***	-0.723***
	4	-0.759***	-0.497***	-0.985***	-0.69***	-0.519***	-0.842***
	5	-0.686***	-0.418***	-0.919***	-0.619***	-0.425***	-0.793***
Investment	0	-1.842**	-2.913***	-1.151	-2.469***	-3.515***	-1.7*
	1	-15.501***	-12.809***	-17.097***	-15.483***	-12.99***	-17.006***
	2	-7.689***	-10.231***	-6.265**	-7.37***	-9.332***	-6.151**
	3	-3.348**	-4.079**	-2.936	-2.963*	-3.696***	-2.484
	4	-2.947*	-2.897	-2.976	-1.814	-2.478*	-1.414
	5	-3.017**	-2.838*	-3.13	-3.601***	-2.588**	-4.216**
Employment	0	-0.432***	-0.309	-0.497**	-0.446***	-0.435***	-0.444**
	1	-1.691***	-2.898***	-1.247***	-1.723***	-2.845***	-1.248***
	2	-1.29***	-3.4***	-0.471	-1.331***	-3.13***	-0.549*
	3	-1.038***	-1.592***	-0.819**	-1.025***	-1.509***	-0.817**
	4	-0.717***	-1.046***	-0.586*	-0.631***	-0.964***	-0.482
	5	-0.398	-0.975***	-0.16	-0.393	-0.86***	-0.179
Unemployment	0	-0.039	-0.077	-0.017	-0.048	-0.055	-0.044
	1	1.326***	1.555***	1.21***	1.281***	1.588***	1.126***
	2	1.88***	3.424***	1.15***	1.78***	3.417***	1.048***
	3	1.786***	3.457***	1.002***	1.698***	3.515***	0.897***
	4	1.689***	3.257***	0.902***	1.577***	3.234***	0.803**
	5	1.656***	3.34***	0.811**	1.464***	3.112***	0.695**
Actual growth	0	0.019	-0.887***	0.419	-0.02	-0.986***	0.446
	1	-8.809***	-7.157***	-9.597***	-8.474***	-6.843***	-9.305***
	2	-4.992***	-4.506***	-5.197***	-4.649***	-3.94***	-4.979***
	3	-1.399**	-2.503**	-0.957	-1.337**	-2.112**	-0.988
	4	-2.349***	-2.539***	-2.28**	-2.095***	-2.012***	-2.144**
	5	-1.124**	-1.609**	-0.903	-0.886*	-1.209**	-0.719

Source: World Bank.

Note: "Recessions: Baseline definition" refers to the period from the peak preceding a business cycle trough to the trough, with troughs defined as years of output growth that is both negative and one standard deviation below the long-term average (as in Huidrom, Kose, and Ohnsorge 2016). "Recessions: Alternative definition" refers to years of negative output growth only, regardless of the depth of the output decline. Sample includes unbalanced panel of 32 advanced economies and 79 EMDEs for 1981-2020. The column *h* refers to years after a recession occurred. AEs = advanced economies; EMDEs = emerging market and developing economies.

Significance level: * = 10 percent, ** = 5 percent, *** = 1 percent.

TABLE 1F.20 Channels: Impulse responses of total factor productivity, investment, employment, and actual growth rates to banking crises and epidemics

Definition of potential output	h	Banking crises			Epidemics		
		World	AEs	EMDEs	World	AEs	EMDEs
Total factor productivity	0	-0.177***	-0.119***	-0.279**	-0.235***	-0.241***	-0.223***
	1	-0.559***	-0.419***	-0.771***	-0.276***	-0.307***	-0.248***
	2	-0.627***	-0.566***	-0.748***	-0.296***	-0.306***	-0.278***
	3	-0.562***	-0.619***	-0.531**	-0.394***	-0.389***	-0.388***
	4	-0.54***	-0.655***	-0.446	-0.524***	-0.358***	-0.606***
	5	-0.375**	-0.558***	-0.189	-0.315***	-0.093	-0.434***
Investment	0	-4.451*	4.119	4.576	-12.522***	-9.658***	-13.252***
	1	-14.031***	-16.744***	-12.31***	-3.487**	-1.575	-4.275**
	2	-1.649	-11.541***	4.509	-2.762*	2.696**	-4.803**
	3	3.182	-2.718	6.846*	-3.202***	0.203	-4.575***
	4	0.507	-6.409***	4.781*	-3.442**	-0.446	-4.772**
	5	-2.145	-6.08***	0.303	-4.085***	1.671	-6.537***
Employment	0	-0.223	-0.677*	-0.03	-1.662***	-2.784***	-1.167***
	1	-1.196***	-3.444***	-0.358	-0.951***	-1.419***	-0.764*
	2	-0.501	-2.528***	0.243	-0.866***	-0.584**	-1.009**
	3	-0.166	-1.511***	0.339	-0.574*	-0.897***	-0.44
	4	-0.198	-1.551***	0.316	-0.926***	-0.662*	-1.021**
	5	0.12	-1.403***	0.692**	-0.828***	-0.377	-1.039***
Unemployment	0	0.382**	0.473**	0.355	0.869***	1.881***	0.465***
	1	1.592***	2.81***	0.909***	1.063***	2.516***	0.497**
	2	1.891***	3.574***	0.928***	1.089***	2.402***	0.599**
	3	1.828***	3.822***	0.663**	1.151***	2.701***	0.592**
	4	2.1***	4.494***	0.694**	1.316***	2.841***	0.742***
	5	2.156***	4.684***	0.661**	1.033***	2.401***	0.51*
Actual growth	0	-0.629	-2.113**	0.026	-3.956***	-4.161***	-3.76***
	1	-2.026	-5.123***	-0.64	-0.362	0.903	-0.871
	2	0.967	-0.462	1.609	-0.128	0.491	-0.403
	3	1.809**	0.055	2.596**	-1.124***	-0.51	-1.379***
	4	1.859**	-1.334	3.292***	-1.137***	-0.287	-1.491***
	5	1.66*	-0.419	2.603**	-1.081***	0.183	-1.731***

Sources: Laeven and Valencia (2018); and World Bank.

Note: Sample includes unbalanced panel of 32 advanced economies and 100 EMDEs for 1981-2020. The column *h* refers to years after a recession occurred. AEs = advanced economies; EMDEs = emerging market and developing economies.

Significance level: * = 10 percent, ** = 5 percent, *** = 1 percent.

References

Abiad, A. G., D. Leigh, and A. Mody. 2007. "International Finance and Income Convergence: Europe Is Different." IMF Working Paper 07/64, International Monetary Fund, Washington, DC.

ADB (Asian Development Bank). 2016. *Asian Development Outlook 2016: Asia's Potential Growth.* Manila: Asian Development Bank.

Ali, M., A. Egbetokun, and M. H. Memon. 2018. "Human Capital, Social Capabilities and Economic Growth." *Economies* 6 (2): 1-18.

Angrist, N., S. Djankov, P. K. Goldberg, and H. A. Patrinos. 2021. "Measuring Human Capital Using Global Learning Data." *Nature* 592 (7854): 403-08.

Anzoategui, D., D. Comin, M. Gertler, and J. Martinez. 2019. "Endogenous Technology Adoption and R&D as Sources of Business Cycle Persistence." *American Economic Journal: Macroeconomics* 11 (3): 67-110.

Azevedo, J. P., L. F. Lopez-Calva, and E. Perova. 2012. "Is the Baby to Blame? An Inquiry into the Consequences of Early Childbearing." Policy Research Working Paper 6074, World Bank, Washington, DC.

Baker, S. R., N. Bloom, and S. J. Davis. 2016. "Measuring Economic Policy Uncertainty." *Quarterly Journal of Economics* 131 (4): 1593-636.

Balakrishnan, R., M. Dao, J. Solé, and J. Zook. 2015. "Recent U.S. Labor Force Dynamics: Reversible or Not?" IMF Working Paper 15/76, International Monetary Fund, Washington, DC.

Ball, L. M. 2009. "Hysteresis in Unemployment: Old and New Evidence." NBER Working Paper 14818, National Bureau of Economic Research, Cambridge, MA.

Ball, L. M. 2014. "Long-Term Damage from the Great Recession in OECD Countries." NBER Working Paper 20185, National Bureau of Economic Research, Cambridge, MA.

Barro, R. J., and J. W. Lee. 2013. "A New Data Set of Educational Attainment in the World, 1950-2010." *Journal of Development Economics* 104 (September): 184-98.

Barro, R. J., and X. Sala-i-Martin. 1997. "Technological Diffusion, Convergence, and Growth." *Journal of Economic Growth* 2 (1): 1-26.

Basu, K. 2015. Quoted in "Continuing Slowdown in Emerging Markets Heralds Lengthy Era of Weak Growth." Press Release 2016/207/DEC, World Bank, Washington, DC.

Basu, S., and J. G. Fernald. 2009. "What Do We Know (and Not Know) about Potential Output?" *Federal Reserve Bank of St Louis Review* 91 (4): 187-213.

Baxter, M., and R. King. 1999. "Measuring Business Cycles: Approximate Band-Pass Filters for Economic Time Series." *Review of Economics and Statistics* 81 (4): 575-93.

Beneš, J., K. Clinton, R. Garcia-Saltos, M. Johnson, D. Laxton, P. Manchev, and T. Matheson. 2010. "Estimating Potential Output with a Multivariate Filter." IMF Working Paper 10/285, International Monetary Fund, Washington, DC.

Benhabib, J., and M. M. Spiegel. 1994. "The Role of Human Capital in Economic Development: Evidence from Aggregate Cross-Country Data." *Journal of Monetary Economics* 34 (2): 143-73.

Benhabib, J., and M. M. Spiegel. 2005. "Human Capital and Technology Diffusion." In *Handbook of Economic Growth*, vol. 1, part A, edited by P. Aghion and S. N. Durlauf, 935-66. Amsterdam: Elsevier.

Bijsterbosch, M., and M. Kolasa. 2010. "FDI and Productivity Convergence in Central and Eastern Europe: An Industry-Level Investigation." *Review of World Economics* 145 (4): 689-712.

Blagrave, P., R. Garcia-Saltos, D. Laxton, and F. Zhang. 2015. "A Simple Multivariate Filter for Estimating Potential Output." IMF Working Paper 15/79, International Monetary Fund, Washington, DC.

Blagrave, P., and M. Santoro. 2016. "Estimating Potential Output in Chile: A Multivariate Filter for Mining and Non-Mining Sectors." IMF Working Paper 16/201, International Monetary Fund, Washington, DC.

Blanchard, O. J. 1991. "Wage Bargaining and Unemployment Persistence." NBER Working Paper 3664, National Bureau of Economic Research, Cambridge, MA.

Blanchard, O. J., and L. H. Summers. 1987. "Hysteresis in Unemployment." *European Economic Review* 31 (1-2): 288-95.

Bloom, N. 2009. "The Impact of Uncertainty Shocks." *Econometrica* 77 (3): 623-85.

Bloom, N. 2014. "Fluctuations in Uncertainty." *Journal of Economic Perspectives* 28 (2): 153-76.

Bloom, N., P. Bunn, P. Mizen, P. Smietanka, and G. Thwaites. 2020. "The Impact of Covid-19 on Productivity." NBER Working Paper 28233, National Bureau of Economic Research, Cambridge, MA.

Bodnár, K., J. Le Roux, P. Lopez-Garcia, and B. Szörfi. 2020. "The Impact of COVID-19 on Potential Output in the Euro Area." Economic Bulletin Articles 7, European Central Bank, Frankfurt.

Bordo, M. D., and P. L. Siklos. 2017. "Central Bank Credibility before and after the Crisis." *Open Economies Review* 28 (1): 19-45.

Borio, C. 2013. "The Great Financial Crisis: Setting Priorities for New Statistics." *Journal of Banking Regulation* 14 (3): 306-17.

Borio, C. 2014. "The Financial Cycle and Macroeconomics: What Have We Learnt?" *Journal of Banking & Finance* 45 (August): 182-98.

Butterworth, S. 1930. "On the Theory of Filter Amplifiers." *Experimental Wireless and the Wireless Engineer* 7: 536-41.

Caballero, R. J., and A. Simsek. 2017. "A Risk-Centric Model of Demand Recessions and Macroprudential Policy." NBER Working Paper 23614, National Bureau of Economic Research, Cambridge, MA.

Candelon, B., A. Carare, and K. Miao. 2016. "Revisiting the New Normal Hypothesis." *Journal of International Money and Finance* 66 (September): 5-31.

Cantelmo, A., G. Melina, and C. Papageorgiou. 2019. "Macroeconomic Outcomes in Disaster-Prone Countries." IMF Working Paper 19/217, International Monetary Fund, Washington, DC.

Cerra, V., and S. C. Saxena. 2008. "Growth Dynamics: The Myth of Economic Recovery." *American Economic Review* 98 (1): 439-57.

Cette, G., S. Nevoux, and L. Py. 2022. "The Impact of ICTs and Digitalization on Productivity and Labor Share: Evidence from French Firms." *Economics of Innovation and New Technology* 31(8): 669-92.

Chalaux, T., and Y. Guillemette. 2019. "The OECD Potential Output Estimation Methodology." OECD Economics Department Working Paper 1563, Organisation for Economic Co-operation and Development, Paris.

Christiano, L. J., and T. J. Fitzgerald. 2003. "The Band Pass Filter." *International Economic Review* 44 (2): 435-65.

Claessens, S., and M. A. Kose. 2017. "Macroeconomic Implications of Financial Imperfections: A Survey." BIS Working Paper 677, Bank for International Settlements, Basel.

Claessens, S., and M. A. Kose. 2018. "Frontiers of Macrofinancial Linkages." BIS Paper 95, Bank for International Settlements, Basel.

Claessens, S., M. A. Kose, and M. E. Terrones. 2009. "What Happens during Recessions, Crunches and Busts?" *Economic Policy* 24 (60): 653-700.

Claessens, S., M. A. Kose, and M. E. Terrones. 2012. "How Do Business and Financial Cycles Interact?" *Journal of International Economics* 87 (1): 178-90.

Coe, D. T., E. Helpman, and A. W. Hoffmaister. 1997. "North-South R&D Spillovers." *Economic Journal* 107 (440): 134-49.

Colacito, R., B. Hoffman, and T. Phan. 2018. "Temperature and Growth: A Panel Analysis of the United States." Working Paper 18-09, Federal Reserve Bank of Richmond, Richmond, VA.

Derviş, K. 2018. "The Future of Economic Convergence." *Project Syndicate,* February 12, 2018.

Dieppe, A., and S. Kilic Celik. 2021. "Productivity: Conceptual Considerations and Measurement Challenges." In *Global Productivity: Trends, Drivers, and Policies*, edited by A. Dieppe, 59-63. Washington, DC: World Bank.

Dieppe, A., S. Kilic Celik, and C. Okou. 2021. "What Happens to Productivity during Major Adverse Events?" In *Global Productivity: Trends, Drivers, and Policies*, edited by A. Dieppe, 141-97. Washington, DC: World Bank.

Dribe, M., M. Breschi, A. Gagnon, D. Gauvreau, H. A. Hanson, T. N. Maloney, S. Mazzoni, et al. 2017. "Socio-economic Status and Fertility Decline: Insights from Historical Transitions in Europe and North America." *Population Studies* 71 (1): 3-21.

Duval, R., M. Eris, and D. Furceri. 2011. "The Effects of Downturns on Labour Force Participation: Evidence and Causes." OECD Economics Department Working Paper 875, Organisation for Economic Co-operation and Development, Paris.

Dwyer, G. P., J. Devereux, and S. Baie. 2013. "Recessions, Growth and Banking Crises." *Journal of International Money and Finance* 38 (November): 18-40.

Economides, G., and A. Xepapadeas. 2018. "Monetary Policy under Climate Change." CESifo Working Paper 7021, Center for Economic Studies, Munich Society for the Promotion of Economic Research, Munich.

Eggleston, K. N., and V. R. Fuchs. 2012. "The New Demographic Transition: Most Gains in Life Expectancy Now Realized Late in Life." *Journal of Economic Perspectives* 26 (3): 137-56.

Elsby, M. W. L., B. Hobijn, and A. Şahin. 2015. "On the Importance of the Participation Margin for Labor Market Fluctuations." *Journal of Monetary Economics* 72 (C): 64-82.

Fallick, B., and J. Pingle. 2007. "A Cohort-Based Model for Labor Force Participation." Finance and Economics Discussion Series 2007-09, Board of Governors of the Federal Reserve System, Washington, DC.

Fatás, A. 2000. "Do Business Cycles Cast Long Shadows? Short-Run Persistence and Economic Growth." *Journal of Economic Growth* 5 (2): 147-62.

Fernald, J., and H. Li. 2021. "The Impact of COVID on Potential Output." Working Paper 2021-09, Federal Reserve Bank of San Francisco, San Francisco, CA.

Feyrer, J. 2007. "Demographics and Productivity." *Review of Economics and Statistics* 89 (1): 100-09.

Fletcher, J. M., and B. L. Wolfe. 2009. "Education and Labor Market Consequences of Teenage Childbearing: Evidence Using the Timing of Pregnancy Outcomes and Community Fixed Effects." *Journal of Human Resources* 44 (2): 303-25.

Fort, T., J. Haltiwanger, R. Jarmin, and J. Miranda. 2013. "How Firms Respond to Business Cycles: The Role of Firm Age and Firm Size." NBER Working Paper 19134, National Bureau of Economic Research, Cambridge, MA.

Furceri, D., S. Kilic Celik, J. T. Jalles, and K. Koloskova. 2021. "Recessions and Total Factor Productivity: Evidence from Sectoral Data." *Economic Modelling* 94 (January): 130-38.

Furceri, D., and A. Mourougane. 2012. "The Effect of Financial Crises on Potential Output: New Empirical Evidence from OECD Countries." *Journal of Macroeconomics* 34 (3): 822-32.

Gal, P., G. Nicoletti, C. von Rüden. and T. Renault. 2019. "Digitalization and Productivity: In Search of the Holy Grail—Firm-Level Empirical Evidence from European Countries." *International Productivity Monitor* 37: 39-71.

Giroud, X., and H. M. Mueller. 2017. "Firm Leverage, Consumer Demand, and Employment Losses During the Great Recession." *Quarterly Journal of Economics* 132(1): 271-316.

Goldin, C. 1994. "The U-Shaped Female Labor Force Function in Economic Development and Economic History." NBER Working Paper 4707, National Bureau of Economic Research, Cambridge, MA.

Gomez, V. 2001. "The Use of Butterworth Filters for Trend and Cycle Estimation in Economic Time Series." *Journal of Business and Economic Statistics* 19 (3): 365-73.

Growiec, J., A. Pajor, D. Pell, and A. Predki. 2015. "The Shape of Aggregate Production Functions: Evidence from Estimates of the World Technology Frontier." *Bank i Kredyt* 46 (4): 299-326.

Gylfason, T., and G. Zoega. 2006. "Natural Resources and Economic Growth: The Role of Investment." *World Economy* 29 (8): 1091-115.

Haider, S., and D. Loughran. 2001. "Elderly Labor Supply: Work or Play?" Center for Retirement Research Working Paper 2001-04, Center for Retirement, Boston College, Boston, MA.

Haltmeier, J. 2012. "Do Recessions Affect Potential Output?" International Finance Discussion Paper 1066, Board of Governors of the Federal Reserve System, Washington, DC.

Hamilton, J. D. 2018. "Why You Should Never Use the Hodrick-Prescott Filter." *Review of Economics and Statistics* 100 (5): 831-43.

Harvey, A. C. 1990. *Forecasting, Structural Time Series Models and the Kalman Filter.* Cambridge: Cambridge University Press.

Hayat, A. 2018. "FDI and Economic Growth: The Role of Natural Resources?" *Journal of Economic Studies* 45 (2): 283-95.

Herrera, C., D. E. Sahn, and K. M. Villa. 2016. "Teen Fertility and Labor Market Segmentation: Evidence from Madagascar." IZA Discussion Paper 10464, IZA Institute of Labor Economics, Bonn, Germany.

Hodrick, R. J., and E. C. Prescott. 1997. "Postwar U.S. Business Cycles: An Empirical Investigation." *Journal of Money, Credit and Banking* 29 (1): 1-16.

Huckfeldt, C. 2022. "Understanding the Scarring Effect of Recessions." *American Economic Review* 112 (4): 1273-310.

Huidrom, R., M. A. Kose, and F. Ohnsorge. 2016. "Challenges of Fiscal Policy in Emerging Market and Developing Economies." CAMA Working Paper 34/2016, Centre for Applied Macroeconomic Analysis, Australian National University, Sydney, Australia.

ILO (International Labour Organization). 2019. "Working on a Warmer Planet: The Impact of Heat Stress on Labor Productivity and Decent Work." International Labour Organization, Geneva.

IMF (International Monetary Fund). 2015. "Where Are We Headed? Perspectives on Potential Growth." In *World Economic Outlook,* April. Washington, DC: International Monetary Fund.

IMF (International Monetary Fund). 2019. "Eastern Caribbean Currency Union." IMF Selected Issues Paper, IMF Country Report 19/63, International Monetary Fund, Washington, DC.

IMF (International Monetary Fund). 2021. *Reaching Net Zero Emissions.* Washington, DC: International Monetary Fund.

Jesus, F., Sotocinal, N. R., and C. Bayudan-Dacuycuy. 2015. "The Impact of Financial Factors on the Output Gap and Estimates of Potential Output Growth." Asian Development Bank Economics Working Paper 457, Asian Development Bank, Manila.

Jordà, Ò. 2005. "Estimation and Inference of Impulse Responses by Local Projections." *American Economic Review* 95 (1): 161-82.

Kahn, M. E., K. Mohaddes, R. N. C. Ng, M. H. Pesaran, M. Raissi, and J.-C. Yang. 2019. "Long-Term Macroeconomic Effects of Climate Change: A Cross-Country Analysis." IMF Working Paper 19/215, International Monetary Fund, Washington, DC.

Kato, H. 2016. *An Empirical Analysis of Population and Technology Progress.* Tokyo: Springer.

Kemp, J. H. 2015. "Measuring Potential Output for the South African Economy: Embedding Information about the Financial Cycle." *South African Journal of Economics* 83 (4): 549-68.

Kilic Celik, S., M. A. Kose, and F. Ohnsorge. 2020. "Subdued Potential Growth: Sources and Remedies." In *Growth in a Time of Change: Global and Country Perspectives on a New Agenda*, edited by H.-Y. Kim and Z. Qureshi, 25-74. Washington, DC: Brookings Institution.

Kinoshita, Y., and F. Guo. 2015. "What Can Boost Labor Force Participation in Asia?" IMF Working Paper 56, International Monetary Fund, Washington, DC.

Klasen, S., and J. Pieters. 2013. "What Explains the Stagnation of Female Labor Force Participation in Urban India?" Discussion Papers 146, Courant Research Centre: Poverty, Equity and Growth, Göttingen, Germany.

Kydland, F. E., and E. C. Prescott. 1982. "Time to Build and Aggregate Fluctuations." *Econometrica* 50 (6): 1345-70.

Laeven, L., and F. Valencia. 2012. "Systemic Banking Crises Database: An Update." IMF Working Paper 12/163, International Monetary Fund, Washington, DC.

Laeven, L., and F. Valencia. 2018. "Systemic Banking Crises Revisited." IMF Working Paper 18/206, International Monetary Fund, Washington, DC.

Laeven, L., and F. Valencia. 2020. "Systemic Banking Crises Database II." *IMF Economic Review* 68 (2): 307-61.

Laubach, T., and J. C. Williams. 2003. "Measuring the Natural Rate of Interest." *Review of Economics and Statistics* 85 (4): 1063-70.

Li, D., M. Plagborg-Møller, and C. K. Wolf. 2022. "Local Projections vs. VARs: Lessons from Thousands of DGPs." NBER Working Paper 30207, National Bureau of Economic Research, Cambridge, MA.

Linacre, S. 2007. "Labour Force Participation: An International Comparison." *Australian Social Trends* 4102: 1-7.

Liu, K., K. G. Salvanes, and E. Ø. Sørensen. 2016. "Good Skills in Bad Times: Cyclical Skill Mismatch and the Long-Term Effects of Graduating in a Recession." *European Economic Review* 84: 3-17.

Lockwood, B. 1991. "Information Externalities in the Labour Market and the Duration of Unemployment." *Review of Economic Studies* 58 (4): 733-53.

Missirian, A., and W. Schlenker. 2017. "Asylum Applications Respond to Temperature Fluctuations." *Science* 358 (6370): 1610-14.

Moran, T. and L. Oldenski. 2016. "How Offshoring and Global Supply Chains Enhance the US Economy," Policy Brief 16-5, Peterson Institute for International Economics, Washington, DC.

Mourougane, A. 2017. "Crisis, Potential Output and Hysteresis." *International Economics* 149 (May): 1-14.

Nguyen, H., and R. Qian. 2014. "Demand Collapse of Credit Crunch to Firms? Evidence from World Bank's Financial Crisis Survey in Eastern Europe." *Journal of International Money and Finance* 47 (October): 125-44.

OECD (Organisation for Economic Co-operation and Development). 2014. "Growth Prospects and Fiscal Requirements over the Long Term." In *OECD Economic Outlook*, Vol. 2014, Issue 1. Paris: Organisation for Economic Co-operation and Development.

Okun, A. M. 1962. "Potential GNP and Its Measurement and Significance." In *Proceedings of the Business and Economics Statistics Section of the American Statistical Association*, 98-104.

Ollivaud, P., and D. Turner. 2014. "The Effect of the Global Financial Crisis on OECD Potential Output." *OECD Journal: Economic Studies:* 41-60.

Oulton, N., and M. Sebastia-Barriel. 2016. "Effects of Financial Crises on Productivity, Capital and Employment." *Review of Income and Wealth* 63 (s1): S90-S112.

Panton, A. J. 2020. "Climate Hysteresis and Monetary Policy." CAMA Working Paper 76/2020, Centre for Applied Macroeconomic Analysis, Australian National University, Sydney, Australia.

Plagborg-Møller, M., and C. K. Wolf. 2021. "Local Projections and VARs Estimate the Same Impulse Responses." *Econometrica* 89 (2): 955-80.

Pollock, D. S. G. 2000. "Trend Estimation and De-trending via Rational Square-Wave Filters." *Journal of Econometrics* 99 (2): 317-34.

Queralto, A. 2013. "A Model of Slow Recoveries from Financial Crises." International Finance Discussion Papers 1097, Board of Governors of the Federal Reserve System, Washington, DC.

Quian, C. Z., Y. Liu, and V. Steenbergen. 2022. "Global Value Chains in the Time of COVID-19." In *An Investment Perspective in Global Value Chains,* edited by C. Z. Quian, Y. Liu, and V. Steenbergen. Washington, DC: World Bank.

Rodrik, D. 2015. "Back to Fundamentals in Emerging Markets." *Project Syndicate,* August 13, 2015.

Shimer, R. 2013. "Job Search, Labor-Force Participation, and Wage Rigidities." In *Advances in Economics and Econometrics: Tenth World Congress,* edited by D. Acemoglu, M. Arellano, and E. Dekel. Cambridge: Cambridge University Press.

Siklos, P. L. 2013. "Sources of Disagreement in Inflation Forecasts: An International Empirical Investigation." *Journal of International Economics* 90 (1): 218-31.

Solow, R. M. 1957. "Technical Change and the Aggregate Production Function." *Review of Economics and Statistics* 39 (3): 312-20.

Solow, R. M. 1962. "Technical Progress, Capital Formation, and Economic Growth." *American Economic Review* 52 (2): 76-86.

Stokke, H. E. 2008. "Resource Boom, Productivity Growth and Real Exchange Rate Dynamics—A Dynamic General Equilibrium Analysis of South Africa." *Economic Modelling* 25 (1): 148-60.

Summers, L. H. 2014. "U.S. Economic Prospects: Secular Stagnation, Hysteresis, and the Zero Lower Bound." *Business Economics* 49 (2): 65-73.

Syverson, C. 2011. "What Determines Productivity?" *Journal of Economic Literature* 49 (2): 326-65.

Tansel, A. 2002. "Determinants of School Attainment of Boys and Girls in Turkey: Individual, Household and Community Factors." *Economics of Education Review* 21 (5): 455-70.

Teulings, C. N., and N. Zubanov. 2014. "Is Economic Recovery a Myth? Robust Estimation of Impulse Responses." *Journal of Applied Econometrics* 29 (3): 497-514.

Torvik, R. 2002. "Natural Resources, Rent Seeking and Welfare." *Journal of Development Economics* 67 (2): 455-70.

Turner, D., M. C. Cavalleri, Y. Guillemette, A. Kopoin, P. Ollivaud, and E. Rusticelli. 2016. "An Investigation into Improving the Real-Time Reliability of OECD Output Gap Estimates." Economics Department Working Paper 1294, Organisation for Economic Co-operation and Development, Paris.

United Nations. 2012. "World Population Monitoring. Adolescents and Youth." United Nations, New York.

Wilms, P., J. Swank, and J. de Haan. 2018. "Determinants of the Real Impact of Banking Crises: A Review and New Evidence." *North American Journal of Economics and Finance* 43 (January): 54-70.

World Bank. 2018. *Learning to Realize Education's Promise.* Washington, DC: World Bank.

World Bank. 2021a. *Global Economic Prospects.* June. Washington, DC: World Bank.

World Bank. 2021b. *The Human Capital Index 2020 Update: Human Capital in the Time of COVID-19.* Washington, DC: World Bank.

Yagan, D. 2019. "Employment Hysteresis from the Great Recession." *Journal of Political Economy* 127 (5): 2505-58.

CHAPTER 2

Regional Dimensions of Potential Growth: Hopes and Realities

Potential growth slowed in most emerging market and developing economy (EMDE) regions in the past decade. The steepest slowdown occurred in the Middle East and North Africa (MNA), followed by East Asia and Pacific (EAP), although potential growth in EAP remained one of the two highest among EMDE regions, the other being South Asia (SAR), where potential growth remained broadly unchanged. Projections of the fundamental drivers of growth suggest that, without reforms, potential growth in EMDEs will continue to weaken over the remainder of this decade. The slowdown will be most pronounced in EAP and Europe and Central Asia (ECA) because of slowing labor force growth and weak investment, and least pronounced in Sub-Saharan Africa (SSA), where multiple adverse shocks over the past decade are assumed to dissipate. Potential growth in Latin America and the Caribbean (LAC), MNA, and SAR is expected to be broadly steady as slowing population growth is offset by strengthening productivity. The projected declines in potential growth are not inevitable. Many EMDEs could lift potential growth by implementing reforms, with policy priorities varying across regions.

Introduction

The global economy suffered two major adverse shocks to start the 2020s: the coronavirus disease 2019 (COVID-19) pandemic and the Russian Federation's invasion of Ukraine. After a strong rebound in 2021 from the pandemic-induced recession of 2020, global growth in 2022 slowed precipitously (figure 2.1). The war in Ukraine has disrupted activity and trade, pent-up demand in the wake of COVID-19 lockdowns has faded, and macroeconomic policy support for demand is being withdrawn amid high inflation.

While the growth slowdown in EMDEs in 2022 was partly cyclical, it also reflected underlying structural weakness. Potential growth—the rate of increase of potential output, or the level of output an economy would sustain at full capacity utilization and full employment—slowed in the past decade (2011-21) relative to the preceding one in a wide swath of EMDEs and in almost all EMDE regions (chapter 1). If the drivers of current trends do not undergo major reversals, potential growth is expected to continue slowing down over the remainder of this decade.

Yet there have been wide differences in these trends, as well as in prospects for long-term growth, across EMDE regions and these have implications for regional policy priorities.

Note: This chapter was prepared by Sergiy Kasyanenko, Philip Kenworthy, Sinem Kilic Celik, Franz Ulrich Ruch, Ekaterine Vashakmadze, and Collette Wheeler.

FIGURE 2.1 Actual and potential growth in EMDEs

After recovering in 2021 from the pandemic-induced recession, global growth is expected to decline sharply in 2022-23, as the war in Ukraine disrupts activity and trade and as many countries withdraw policy support for demand amid high inflation. This cyclical slowdown is occurring amid a broad-based slowdown in potential growth, in both aggregate and per capita terms. The estimates of potential growth are robust to the estimation method used.

A. Actual GDP growth

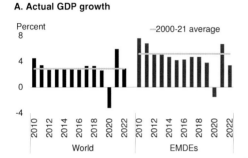

B. Potential GDP growth

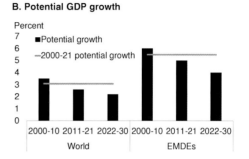

Sources: Haver Analytics; Penn World Table; UN, World Population Prospects; World Bank.
Note: EMDEs = emerging market and developing economies. Data for 2022-30 are forecasts.
A. Aggregate growth rates are calculated using gross domestic product (GDP) weights at average 2010-19 prices and market exchange rates.
B. Period averages of annual GDP-weighted averages. World sample includes up to 53 EMDEs and 30 advanced economies.

This chapter examines differences across the World Bank's six EMDE regions by addressing the following questions for each region.

- How have potential growth and its drivers evolved since the turn of the century?

- What are the prospects for potential growth?

- Which policies would lift potential growth?

Contributions. This chapter adds regional granularity to the analysis of global slowdown in potential growth in chapter 1 and does so in a consistent manner across EMDE regions. Drawing on a rich body of region-specific studies and using the comprehensive new database introduced in chapter 1, this chapter presents the first study to systematically analyze potential growth in all six EMDE regions in a consistent manner. Other major cross-country studies of potential growth have largely focused on advanced economies (Dabla-Norris et al. 2015; IMF 2015; OECD 2014) or Asian economies (ADB 2016). This chapter examines data for up to 6 EMDEs in EAP, 9 in ECA, 16 in LAC, 5 in MNA, 3 in SAR, and 14 in SSA over the past two decades (2000-21) and considers prospects for the remainder of this decade (2022-30).

Findings. The chapter documents a rich array of regional differences. First, the slowdown in potential growth in the past decade (2011-21) from the preceding decade (2000-10) was steepest in MNA, followed by EAP, although potential growth in EAP remained higher than that in all other regions except SAR. ECA and LAC experienced less pronounced slowdowns, but potential growth in LAC remained the lowest among all EMDE regions. In SAR, potential growth remained almost unchanged, at the highest rate among EMDE regions, and in SSA, potential growth weakened only moderately and remained one of the lowest among EMDE regions, at about half the average for SAR.

Second, EAP is expected to show the sharpest decline among EMDE regions in both aggregate and per capita potential growth during 2022-30—about 1.6 percentage points a year on average—with the slowdown mainly reflecting slower capital accumulation and growth in total factor productivity (TFP) in China. The second-largest decline in potential growth in 2022-30 is projected for ECA, resulting in part from fallout from the war in Ukraine, but also from continued weakness in labor force growth. In SSA, potential growth is projected to decline moderately, as strengthening TFP growth is expected to partially offset weakening investment and slowing population growth. Elsewhere, potential growth is projected to be broadly unchanged (in LAC and SAR) or even rise (in MNA) in 2022-30 as strengthening TFP growth offsets demographic headwinds to potential growth.

Third, particularly weak TFP growth in LAC, MNA, and SSA makes policy action to raise productivity growth especially important for these regions. There is also considerable room to strengthen flagging labor force growth in MNA and SAR, by encouraging female labor force participation, and in EAP and ECA, by raising labor force participation among older workers. LAC and SSA have particularly weak prospects for investment growth, and a wide range of measures are likely to be required to reignite it. Chapter 4 discusses such measures. A climate-related investment push could catalyze a boost to potential growth in all EMDE regions.

Regional potential growth in the rearview mirror

Potential growth weakened broadly across EMDEs in the past decade (2011-21) relative to the preceding one (2000-10). In the past decade, potential growth in EMDEs averaged 5 percent a year, 1.0 percentage point below its average in the preceding one.[1] Per capita potential growth also slowed. Potential growth slowed in more than half of EMDEs and in all but one EMDE region (SAR). This finding is robust to the approach employed to measure potential growth (figure 2.2).

Weakening potential growth is cause for worry. First, the slowdown in potential growth raises concerns about the prospects for per capita income growth, poverty reduction, and convergence of per capita incomes with those in advanced economies. In some EMDE regions, especially MNA, EAP, and ECA, per capita incomes converged significantly

---

[1] Unless otherwise noted, and in keeping with the long-term focus of this chapter, potential growth is estimated using the production function approach, which takes into account movements in labor supply and capital accumulation and provides estimates of total factor productivity growth based on various assumptions (for example, that factors of production are paid their marginal products). Chapter 1 provides detailed descriptions of the production function approach and alternative methods for measuring potential growth (including statistical filters and a growth expectations approach).

FIGURE 2.2 Potential growth in EMDE regions, 2000-10 and 2011-20

Potential growth was slower in the 2010s than the 2000s by virtually all estimation methods and in all EMDE regions except one—SAR—with the steepest slowdowns in MNA and EAP. Nevertheless, potential growth in EAP, along with SAR, remained higher than that in the other EMDE regions.

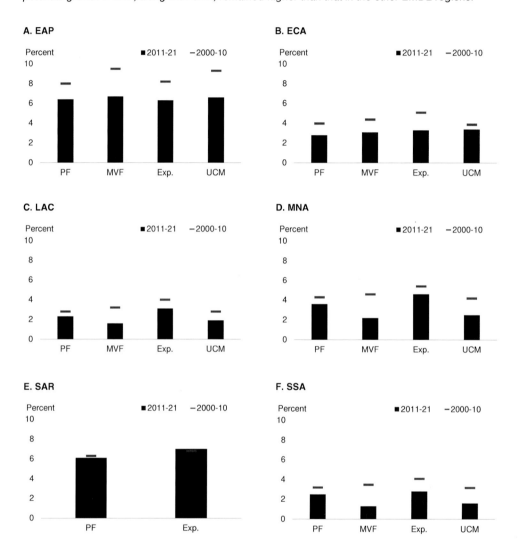

Sources: Haver Analytics; Penn World Table; UN, World Population Prospects; World Bank.
Note: Period averages of annual averages weighted by gross domestic product (GDP). Samples differ across measures, depending on data availability.

For SAR, insufficient data are available for filter-based estimates until 2010. The sample includes 28 economies; 3 in EAP (China, the Philippines, and Thailand), 5 in ECA (Bulgaria, Hungary, Kazakhstan, Poland, and Romania), 10 in LAC (Bolivia, Brazil, Chile, Colombia, Costa Rica, Honduras, Mexico, Paraguay, Peru, and Uruguay), 3 in MNA (Jordan, Morocco, and Tunisia), 4 in SAR (Bangladesh, India, Pakistan, and Sri Lanka), and 3 in SSA (Cameroon, Namibia, and South Africa). Because of the limited sample, MVF and UCM estimates are excluded from the SAR region. Note that quantitative estimates may differ from those presented in figure 2.3 because of sample differences. Figure 2.2 ensures sample consistency across measures; figure 2.3 ensures sample consistency across time. EAP = East Asia and Pacific; ECA = Europe and Central Asia; Exp. = estimates based on five-year-ahead *World Economic Outlook* growth forecasts; LAC = Latin America and the Caribbean; MNA = Middle East and North Africa; MVF = multivariate filter-based; PF= production function approach; SAR = South Asia; SSA = Sub-Saharan Africa; UCM = univariate filter-based (specifically, the Hodrick-Prescott filter).

more slowly with those in advanced economies in 2011-21 than in 2000-10. Declining potential growth is likely to impede the ability of EMDEs to meet their development goals, including poverty reduction.[2] Second, a weakening of potential growth erodes countries' ability to service their debt. This is a serious ongoing concern, with government debt relative to gross domestic product (GDP) at multidecade highs in all EMDE regions except SSA.

The weakening of potential growth in EMDEs in the past decade was broad-based, with all of its drivers—TFP growth, labor force growth, and capital accumulation—fading (chapter 1). Developments across regions nonetheless varied. The MNA region experienced the steepest decline in potential growth, at 2.4 percentage points per year. Capital accumulation plunged on account of the sharp drop in oil prices from mid-2014 to early 2016, policy uncertainty increased in some parts of the region, and conflicts in certain countries destroyed capital.

Potential growth fell almost 1.4 percentage points a year on average in EAP, although at about 6.2 percent a year, it remained higher there than in all other regions except SAR. The slowdown in EAP was largely due to developments in China—rebalancing of growth away from investment, together with slower growth of both TFP and the working-age population. Potential growth in the rest of the region strengthened by 0.6 percentage point a year, reflecting rebounds in capital accumulation following the downturn originating in the 1997-98 Asian financial crisis, amid generally supportive demographic trends.

In ECA, LAC, and SSA, potential growth fell more moderately in 2011-21, by 0.6, 0.5, and 0.2 percentage point a year, respectively, but from lower rates in 2000-10 than those in EAP and SAR. The decline in ECA reflected diminishing productivity catch-up with Western Europe following two decades of rapid integration into its production networks, labor markets, and institutions and a slowdown in labor force growth as working-age population growth slowed and, in some cases, turned negative. Potential growth in LAC remained the lowest among EMDE regions. In LAC, it was dampened by slowing labor force growth and a continued decline in TFP growth, as a series of shocks, including plunging commodity prices, debt distress, and bouts of political instability, hit the region. In SSA, a sharp slowdown in TFP growth more than offset buoyant labor force growth and rising capital accumulation. Investment in natural resource sectors and infrastructure supported capital accumulation in SSA.

In contrast to that in other EMDE regions, potential growth in SAR was virtually unchanged in 2011-21 and became, together with EAP, the strongest among EMDE regions. All drivers of growth remained broadly steady, with demographic trends remaining supportive and robust investment growth and solid TFP growth elsewhere offsetting investment weakness and lower TFP growth in India.

---

[2] Research suggests that two-thirds of cross-country differences in growth of the poorest households' income is attributable to differences in average income growth (Barro 2000; Dollar, Kleineberg, and Kraay 2016).

FIGURE 2.3 Contributions to potential growth in EMDE regions

Without reforms, potential growth in EMDEs will continue to weaken over the remainder of this decade. The slowdown will be most pronounced in EAP and ECA because of slowing labor force growth and weak investment. The slowdown is projected to be least pronounced in SSA, where the multiple adverse shocks over the past decade are assumed to dissipate. Potential growth in LAC, MNA, and SAR is expected to be broadly steady as a recovery in productivity as past shocks dissipate offsets slowing population growth.

A. Contributions to regional potential growth

B. Contributions to regional potential growth

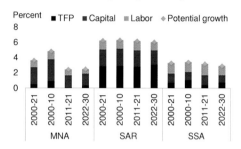

Sources: Haver Analytics; Penn World Table; UN, World Population Prospects; World Bank.
Note: Period averages of annual averages weighted by gross domestic product (GDP). Estimates are based on the production function approach. Sample includes 6 countries in EAP, 9 in ECA, 16 in LAC, 5 in MNA, 3 in SAR, and 14 in SSA. Note that quantitative estimates may differ from those presented in figure 2.2 because of sample differences. Figure 2.2 ensures sample consistency across measures; figure 2.3 ensures sample consistency across time. Data for 2022-30 are forecasts. EAP = East Asia and Pacific; ECA = Europe and Central Asia;
LAC = Latin America and the Caribbean; MNA = Middle East and North Africa; SAR = South Asia; SSA = Sub-Saharan Africa; TFP = total factor productivity.

Prospects for regional potential growth

In the absence of reforms, potential growth in EMDEs is projected to decline further in the remainder of the 2020s (figure 2.3). The pandemic-induced shock in 2020 is expected to have lasting effects on long-term growth across EMDEs, and the fallout from the war in Ukraine will exacerbate many of these effects. The adverse effects of these two shocks on human capital, investor confidence, fixed-capital formation, and supply chains will weigh on long-term growth prospects.

Current projections for the fundamental drivers of potential growth in EMDEs suggest that it will slow by a further 0.9 percentage point a year in the remainder of this decade (2022-30) to 4.0 percent a year (chapter 5).[3] The slowdown is expected to be broad-based, reflecting declining contributions from all the fundamental drivers of growth, but especially from capital accumulation, which accounts for more than half of the slowdown. Decelerating TFP growth and slowing growth in the supply of labor are each expected to account for one-quarter of the slowdown.

---

[3] Throughout this chapter, potential growth projections for 2022-30 are predicated on population size and composition in line with the medium-fertility scenario of UN population projections, trend improvements in education and health outcomes, and investment growth constant at its long-term average. Chapter 5 provides details.

Of the six EMDE regions, EAP is expected to experience the sharpest decline in potential growth during 2022-30: about 1.6 percentage points a year on average, primarily as a result of reduced capital accumulation and slower TFP growth, especially in China, whose policy efforts to rein in credit growth are expected to resume once economic activity recovers from pandemic disruptions. After a decade of resilience, potential growth elsewhere in the region is also expected to moderate somewhat (by 0.1 percentage point a year on average) as labor force growth eases.

In ECA and SSA, potential growth is projected to slow somewhat. A moderate pickup in TFP growth as the adverse shocks of the past decade subside is expected to offset only partly investment weakness and diminishing demographic dividends in the rest of the decade. In ECA, the slowdown in potential growth also reflects the fallout from the war in Ukraine, which will depress investment in the region for several years.

In LAC, MNA, and SAR, potential growth is projected to be broadly unchanged in 2022-30. SAR has benefited from demographic tailwinds over the past decade, but these are expected to fade in the remainder of the 2020s; a recovery in TFP growth, however, is expected to offset the fading tailwinds. Labor force growth is expected to continue declining in LAC, but modestly quicker TFP growth should counteract this too, assuming political and social stability do not deteriorate. In MNA, the effect of slowing working-age population growth is expected to outweigh the recovery in TFP growth as adverse shocks that have dampened TFP growth over the past decade (war, political uncertainty, and commodity price shocks) do not recur.

In per capita terms, between 2011-21 and 2022-30, potential growth is expected to slow fastest in EAP, while staying stable in ECA. In LAC, SAR, and SSA, potential growth is expected to inch up in per capita terms. In MNA potential growth in per capita terms is expected to strengthen by 0.5 percentage point between 2011-21 and 2022-30.

There is substantial uncertainty about prospects for potential growth, but on balance, risks to the baseline projections are tilted to the downside. The main downside risks are related to the possibility of a prolonged war in Ukraine or geopolitical tensions elsewhere and their impact on global trade, value chains, and commodity prices. A prolonged war or other geopolitical tensions that disrupt global markets and networks would weigh on both TFP growth and capital accumulation. In addition, a sharper-than-assumed tightening of global financial conditions, possibly in response to persistently high inflation, could trigger global financial stress and stall investment (chapter 1). Future epidemics could lead to further learning losses and thus hold back human capital accumulation, especially among the most vulnerable. This would deepen inequality within and across EMDEs (World Bank 2022h).

In some regions, specific factors could improve prospects for potential growth relative to the baseline forecasts. These include an acceleration of technological innovation after the pandemic (particularly in SAR), easing of constraints on the labor supply in countries hosting Ukrainian refugees (in ECA), and possibly higher global demand for inputs needed to achieve energy transition away from fossil fuels (particularly in LAC).

Regional reform priorities

The prospect of a further weakening of potential growth in EMDEs is unfortunate, but such a weakening is not inevitable. Reforms, especially those tailored to specific regions or countries, can lift potential growth. Reforms can target any of a range of shortcomings: unfilled investment needs, poor human capital accumulation (such as low school enrollment or completion rates and poor health indicators), weak labor force growth (such as increasingly challenging demographic conditions and low female labor force participation), and weak productivity (such as product and labor market distortions and high rates of informality).

Particularly weak TFP growth in LAC, MNA, and SSA makes policy action to raise productivity growth especially important for these regions. In LAC, such actions could include improvements in transport infrastructure, harmonization of regulatory standards to deepen regional and global trade, improved access to education for poor households, and measures to provide incentives for more research and development (R&D). In MNA, priorities include further efforts to diversify economies away from energy production, measures to reduce the role of the state and level the playing field for the private sector, and improvements in education. In SSA, priorities include measures to improve agricultural productivity; expand access to markets, finance, and inputs; strengthen education outcomes and the quality of schools; and improve business climates. Still-robust working-age population growth may provide SSA with an opportunity for higher potential growth—as long as job creation can keep pace with labor force growth to ensure productive employment.[4]

Even in the regions with the strongest TFP growth—EAP and SAR—measures to raise it further are available. In SAR, tackling high levels of informality, improving regional integration, and boosting participation in global value chains could all strengthen productivity growth. In EAP, spurring innovation and technology adaptation through higher spending on R&D and increased foreign direct investment, which can be an important source of technology transfer, could boost productivity growth. China and other upper-middle-income economies in the region could improve the effectiveness of R&D spending and take measures to raise productivity in the services sectors, by reducing barriers to competition.

MNA and SAR, in particular, have significant room to strengthen flagging labor force growth. Female labor force participation in these regions is about one-half the EMDE average, and measures to raise it to the EMDE average could boost potential growth in the remainder of the decade by 1.2 percentage points a year. In other regions, especially EAP and ECA, population aging will be a heavy drag on potential growth unless measures are taken to extend healthy lives and increase working opportunities for older people.

---

[4] To the extent that younger cohorts have greater labor force participation rates and are better educated than older cohorts, working-age population growth would also boost potential growth per capita.

LAC and SSA have particularly weak prospects for investment growth. Efforts to improve the stability of policy frameworks and the macroeconomy could generate important growth dividends in many economies, as could improvements to business climates and security.

In LAC, strengthening investment growth would require structural reforms to increase domestic saving, boost returns on private investment, and prioritize productive public investment over unproductive government spending. Such reforms could help upgrade infrastructure to raise international competitiveness and to improve adaptation to more frequent natural disasters.

In SSA, reforms to improve the efficiency of state-owned enterprises could free up capital for other firms to invest. Economic diversification to nonresource sectors and productivity increases in agriculture could also draw investment into these sectors. Additionally, greater openness to trade, technological readiness, security, and policy stability might improve investment prospects. Lowering nontariff trade barriers might help boost intra-African trade and, thus, increase market size and attract investment. Many SSA countries have large investment gaps, while limited fiscal space and high debt severely constrain spending on public investment. Joint efforts from national governments, international partners, and the private sector are needed to finance growth-enhancing investment projects, especially in infrastructure, health care, and education.

Mitigation and adaptation policies to limit carbon emissions and the impact of climate change are key to lifting potential growth in all EMDE regions. Incentives for green investment can raise capital accumulation and productivity growth while helping meet nationally determined contributions to climate change-related goals. Similarly, improving infrastructure (for example, installing better-draining systems for flood protection) and planning for extreme weather events (including higher temperatures) could reduce economic losses and preserve capital stocks and productivity (EAP and SSA; chapter 5).

The pandemic has also highlighted the dividends that boosting digital infrastructure investment can provide. Policies supporting automation and adoption of digital technologies can enhance productivity and potential growth (EAP, ECA, and SSA).

The remainder of this chapter discusses the recent evolution of, and prospects for, potential growth in each of the six EMDE regions. Each section examines the drivers of the region's potential growth and presents region-specific policy options for lifting it.

EAST ASIA
and PACIFIC

Growth in potential output in EAP declined in 2011-21 relative to 2000-10, in part on account of economic disruptions related to the COVID-19 pandemic. The weakening of potential growth in EAP was broad-based, with all drivers of potential growth fading. Prospects for the fundamental drivers of growth suggest that without policy reforms, the recent slowdown of potential growth in EAP will accelerate and broaden in the remainder of this decade. While policies may be able to stem or even reverse the projected slowing in the growth of factor inputs, policies to raise TFP growth offer a more promising way for many of the region's economies to mitigate the slowdown of potential growth and speed up the convergence of per capita incomes toward advanced-economy levels. Higher investment in infrastructure designed to improve disaster resilience and meet climate goals could provide an additional boost to potential growth.

Introduction

Since the 1997-98 Asian financial crisis, the EAP region has had output growth nearly twice that of the median EMDE (figure 2.4). However, the region's growth slowed between 2011 and 2021, with the slowdown reflecting both cyclical downturns and a weakening of the region's potential growth, most notably that in China, which accounts for 84 percent of the region's GDP. Elsewhere in the region, potential growth strengthened somewhat in 2011-21, particularly in Indonesia, Malaysia, and the Philippines, in part reflecting reforms implemented to rebuild economies devastated by the 1997-98 financial crisis.

The COVID-19 pandemic has caused major economic disruptions in the region, including a plunge in fixed-capital investment and a sharp decline in labor supply in 2020. The subsequent recovery has been uneven across EAP countries, and investment remains below prepandemic levels in many economies. The worst affected and the slowest to recover have been Myanmar and several Pacific Island countries. The pandemic is expected to have an enduring impact on business investment (because of lower revenues, increased costs, and heightened uncertainty), productivity, and labor markets. Weaker educational attainments, especially in countries that the shock most heavily affected (Cambodia, Myanmar, the Philippines, Thailand, and many Pacific Island economies), are expected to have a lasting effect on labor markets. Weaker human

---

Note: Estimates using the production function approach are available for China Indonesia, Mongolia, Malaysia, Philippines, and Thailand.

FIGURE 2.4 **EAP: Regional growth in actual and potential output**

Following the 1997-98 Asian financial crisis, output growth in EAP was nearly twice as high as in the median EMDE between 2000-21. However, the region's growth slowed in the latter half of this period, owing to both cyclical developments and a weakening of the region's rate of potential growth, which mainly reflected slowing potential growth in China. Elsewhere in the region, potential growth strengthened somewhat in 2011-21, in part on account of reform efforts.

A. GDP growth

B. Growth in potential output

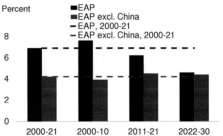

C. Contributions of potential growth and business cycle to actual growth

D. Estimates of potential growth

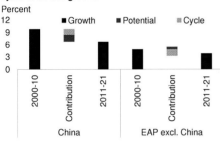
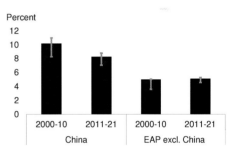

E. Regional potential growth by different estimates

F. China's potential growth by different estimates

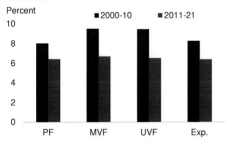
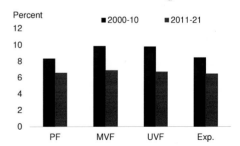

Sources: International Monetary Fund; Penn World Table; UN, World Population Prospects; World Bank, World Development Indicators database.

Note: Averages weighted by gross domestic product (GDP) (using average real U.S. dollar GDP at average 2010-19 prices and market exchange rates). Period averages. Data for 2022-23 and 2022-30 are forecasts. EAP = East Asia and Pacific; EMDE = emerging market and developing economy; excl. = excluding.

A. Horizontal lines show median GDP-weighted averages for the six EMDE regions; orange whiskers show minimum-maximum range.

B.C. Estimates of potential growth are based on production function approach. Sample includes six EAP economies (China, Indonesia, Malaysia, Mongolia, the Philippines, and Thailand).

C. Blue bars denote average actual growth over each 10-year period. Red bars denote contribution of potential growth to change in actual growth between the two 5-year periods; orange bars denote contribution of cyclical growth.

D. Orange whiskers show minimum-maximum range of estimates of potential growth in the four estimation methods. Chapter 1 provides details on the approaches. Sample includes three EAP economies (China, the Philippines, and Thailand). "EAP excl. China" includes Indonesia, Mongolia, the Philippines, and Thailand.

E.F. Expectations-based estimates ("Exp.") are potential growth proxied by five-year-ahead IMF *World Economic Outlook* growth forecasts. Chapter 1 provides details on the approaches. Sample includes three EAP economies (China, the Philippines, and Thailand). MVF = multivariate filter; PF = production function approach; UVF = univariate filter (Hodrick-Prescott filter).

and physical capital will weigh on medium- and long-term growth prospects in the region and exacerbate the current slowdown.

EAP faces several major challenges to inclusive and sustainable growth: slowing global growth and external demand; elevated and rising debt, exacerbated by tighter financing conditions; highly volatile commodity prices; and uncertainty related to the outlook for supply chains, trade, technology transfer, and investment amid the war in Ukraine and lingering geopolitical tensions. These negative developments are exacerbating the ongoing structural trends and further depressing regional investment and potential growth.

In the remainder of the current decade (2022-30), growth in potential output in EAP is projected to slow to 4.6 percent a year on average, from 6.2 percent a year in 2011-21. China's potential growth will continue to decelerate on diminishing returns to capital investment and slowing TFP growth. Potential growth in the rest of the region is also expected to decline somewhat as a result of slowing labor force growth.

Policy efforts in several areas could boost potential growth, support poverty reduction, and help several middle-income economies attain high-income status. While policies may be able to stem or even reverse the projected slowing of factor inputs, policies to raise productivity growth offer the most promising path for the region's economies to improve their growth performance and speed up the convergence of their per capita incomes to advanced-economy levels.

Lowering nontariff barriers and liberalizing trade in services would help the region take advantage of shifts in the global trade landscape and boost productivity and competitiveness. Allocating financial resources more efficiently would require strengthening prudential measures and supervision. In the field of energy, policies must address energy security issues through long-term sustainable development strategies (World Bank 2022e). Encouraging investment in renewables could improve long-term energy security and reduce emissions. More climate-resilient infrastructure could also help mitigate a possible climate change-related reduction in annual potential growth resulting from increasingly frequent extreme weather events that damage capital stocks and erode labor productivity.

Evolution and drivers of potential growth in EAP

At an average annual rate of 6.2 percent over 2011-21, growth in potential output in EAP was nearly twice as high as in the median EMDE, but it was still below its 7.6 percent average rate in 2000-10.[5] The slowdown in potential growth is mostly

---

[5] Estimates of potential growth can vary depending on the methodology used. However, other studies have obtained results similar to those described here, and the slowdown in China's potential growth, in particular, is clear and undisputed. For instance, Anand et al. (2014) report that China's potential GDP growth peaked around 2006-07 at 11 percent a year and had declined to below 8 percent by 2013. By contrast, potential growth in Association of Southeast Asian Nations countries (for example, Indonesia, Malaysia, the Philippines, Thailand, and Vietnam) has been stable or rising. The ADB (2016) reports a gradual decline in China's potential growth since 2008. Bai and Zhang (2017), Maliszewski and Zhang (2015), Nabar and N'Diaye (2013), and Perkins and Rawski (2008) also confirm the slowdown of potential growth in China.

attributable to China, where potential growth is estimated to have fallen from 8.3 percent a year in 2000-10 to 6.6 percent a year in 2011-21. Following efforts to prop up growth through credit-fueled investment, the Chinese government initiated policies in 2012 to make growth more sustainable and less dependent on investment and exports (World Bank 2017d). By 2019, China's growth had converged to its potential rate, but significant financial vulnerabilities that had accumulated remained unresolved (World Bank 2021d).

In EAP outside China, growth in potential output rose to 4.5 percent in 2011-21, higher by 0.6 percentage point than in 2000-10. Following the 1997-98 Asian financial crisis, Indonesia, Malaysia, the Philippines, and Thailand introduced policy reforms that helped investment growth rebound from its collapse during the crisis. In some countries, however, potential growth declined in 2011-21 compared with 2000-21, largely owing to unfavorable demographic trends and idiosyncratic factors. In Thailand, for example, potential growth weakened to about 3.2 percent a year in 2011-21 (from 3.5 percent in 2000-10), close to the lowest rate in Southeast Asia, as demographic dividends diminished and domestic uncertainty and frequent flooding weighed on TFP growth and capital accumulation (World Bank 2020h).

The pandemic disruptions of 2020-22 are expected to have lasting negative effects on economic growth across EAP through their adverse impact on human capital and fixed-capital formation. Following a significant contraction in 2020, investment in the region rebounded in 2021 but remained about 4 percentage points below its prepandemic trend; this gap is not expected to close over the remainder of the decade. Pandemic-related school closures, lost working hours and job skills, and especially large declines in earnings of those working in the informal sector—a significant proportion of the workforce in some economies in the region—also negatively affected actual and potential output in the region (World Bank 2020b). The collapse in activity, investment, and trade, as well as prolonged border closures, is also estimated to have dampened TFP growth.

Of the 1.4 percentage-point decline in EAP's annual rate of potential growth between 2000-10 and 2011-21, falling TFP growth is estimated to account for about three-fifths, with the remaining two-fifths attributable equally to slowing growth in the supply of labor and capital accumulation (figure 2.5). Developments in China, which experienced a broad-based slowdown in all drivers of potential growth, strongly influenced the shift in each of these drivers. The slowing in China's TFP growth may be attributed to several factors, including narrowing room for productivity catch-up, declining returns to investment and a misallocation of resources during a prolonged investment boom, and shifts of resources from manufacturing to services (Maliszewski and Zhang 2015; Nabar and N'Diaye 2013). Nevertheless, the contribution of TFP growth to growth in potential output in China in 2011-21 remained above the EMDE average (Anand et al. 2014; World Bank 2018a).

The reduced contribution of labor force growth to growth in potential output reflects a sharp slowdown in China's working-age population growth related to aging. Thus, the

FIGURE 2.5 **EAP: Drivers of growth in potential output**

The slowdown of EAP's growth in potential output in 2011-21 relative to 2000-10 is mostly attributable to China, where potential growth fell from 8.3 percent to 6.6 percent a year. Of the 1.4 percentage-point fall in EAP's annual potential growth, slower TFP growth accounts for three-fifths, with the remainder due to slower labor force growth and slower capital accumulation. China experienced a broad-based slowdown in all drivers. In the rest of the region, potential growth in 2011-21 continued to rely heavily on growth of factor inputs, especially fixed investment. In most EAP countries, TFP growth slowed or remained weak in the prepandemic decade.

A. Potential GDP growth

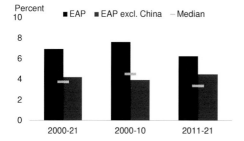

B. Contributions to potential GDP growth

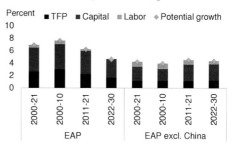

C. Investment growth

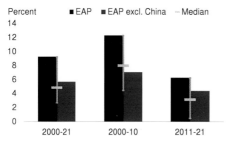

D. Potential TFP growth

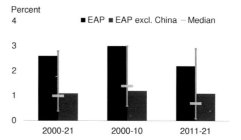

E. Secondary education attainment

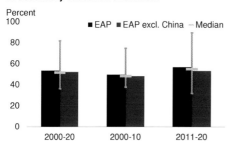

F. Working-age population growth

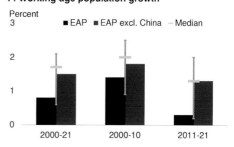

Sources: Haver Analytics; Penn World Table; UN Educational, Scientific, and Cultural Organization (UNESCO) Institute for Statistics; UN, World Population Prospects; World Bank, World Development Indicators database.

Note: Gross domestic product (GDP) weights are calculated using average real U.S. dollar GDP (at average 2010-19 prices and market exchange rates). Data for 2022-30 are forecasts. EAP = East Asia and Pacific; excl. = excluding; TFP = total factor productivity.

A.C.-F. Bars show period averages of annual GDP-weighted averages. Horizontal lines show median of GDP-weighted averages for the six EMDE regions. Orange whiskers show minimum-maximum ranges.

A.B. Estimates are based on production function approach. Sample includes 53 EMDEs, of which 6 economies are from EAP (China, Indonesia, Malaysia, Mongolia, the Philippines, and Thailand).

C.D. Sample includes China, Indonesia, Malaysia, Mongolia, the Philippines, and Thailand (for which estimates of potential growth are available for both investment growth and TFP growth measures for the period 2000-21).

E. Period averages of simple annual averages. Percentage of population aged 25 and above that completed at least lower secondary education. "EAP excl. China" includes Indonesia, Malaysia, Mongolia, the Philippines, and Thailand.

F. "Working-age population" refers to population aged 15-64. Sample includes six EAP economies.

contribution of labor force growth to China's growth in potential output fell from 0.5 percentage point to 0.2 percentage point between 2000-10 and 2011-21. Finally, the reduced contribution of capital accumulation to China's potential growth in 2011-21 reflects a moderation from the stimulus-driven investment peaks of 2010-12, which had produced overcapacity in some sectors. Nevertheless, China's investment-to-GDP ratio was still as high as 60 percent, on average, in 2011-21.

Aside from China, the rest of the region relied more heavily on growth in factor inputs, particularly capital, to drive growth in potential output during 2011-21. Notably, a larger contribution from capital accumulation outweighed a diminished contribution from slowing labor force growth. Although TFP growth remained subdued overall, it inched up in 2011-21 in the Philippines from its post-Asian financial crisis lows. In Mongolia, domestic policy setbacks and commodity price volatility weighed on total factor productivity growth and capital accumulation.

In the five decades to about 2010, a rapidly growing working-age population supported economic growth in EAP (IMF 2017c; World Bank 2015). Many economies in the region reaped a demographic dividend as the number of workers grew faster than the number of dependents. In the region as a whole, demographic trends have since become less favorable and are expected to deteriorate further over the next decade. The deceleration in working-age population growth has been especially stark in China and Thailand, on account of population aging (Bloom, Canning, and Fink 2011). Several economies in the region, however, are still enjoying a demographic dividend (Cambodia, Indonesia, the Lao People's Democratic Republic, Malaysia, Myanmar, Papua New Guinea, and the Philippines).

Several factors besides demographic developments have affected labor force growth in EAP. An increase in secondary school completion rates of 10 percentage points between 2000-10 and 2011-21, a rise in the tertiary enrollment rate of 14 percentage points in the same time frame, and improvements in health reflected in an extension of life expectancy by two years have boosted labor force participation rates (and productivity). China and Malaysia have made particularly large strides in improving life expectancy and education over the past two decades. Although female labor force participation rates increased in some countries between 2000-10 and 2011-21, they remain relatively low in several of the largest economies in the region (Indonesia and Malaysia).

Capital accumulation slowed in most EAP economies in the second half of 2011-21 owing to several factors. In some member economies of the Association of Southeast Asian Nations (ASEAN), such as Indonesia and the Philippines, supportive monetary policy spurred investment in the first decade after the global financial crisis, but its influence subsequently waned. In Malaysia, capital accumulation increased in the aftermath of the Asian financial crisis but later moderated, reflecting the worsening of terms of trade and heightened policy uncertainty. Despite the slowdown, the contribution of capital accumulation to potential growth in EAP remained larger than that in other EMDE regions, reflecting high domestic savings rates and generally sustained inflows of foreign direct investment (FDI). The region attracted half of global

FDI during 2011-21, with FDI representing more than 5 percent of GDP in one-third of EAP economies and playing an important role in the transfer of new technologies, development of human capital, integration into global markets, enterprise restructuring, and improved competitiveness (Moura and Forte 2010; World Bank 2017c). The region's relatively rapid capital accumulation has helped finance infrastructure upgrades. In the Philippines, for instance, improved macroeconomic policy management and the government's public-private partnership initiative have boosted infrastructure investment.

In most EAP countries, potential TFP growth slowed or remained relatively weak in 2011-21. The slowing has been attributed to both temporary and more persistent factors (Asian Productivity Organization 2016; World Bank 2018a). Temporary factors include heightened policy uncertainty (Myanmar) and investment weakness in several commodity-exporting economies severely affected by the 2014-16 plunge in commodity prices (Mongolia and Papua New Guinea). More persistent factors include a declining scope for closing the technology gap with advanced economies (China), maturing global value chains of some products (China and Malaysia), and slowing human capital accumulation in lower-income economies with limited fiscal space for education spending (Cambodia and Lao PDR). Slowing TFP growth due to slowing factor reallocation from agriculture to sectors with higher or faster productivity growth also has had persistent effects (China, Malaysia, and Thailand).

Rapid integration into global and regional supply chains in the wake of China's accession to the World Trade Organization in 2001 boosted productivity in the region, and especially China. More recently, however, the maturing of these supply chains has caused previously surging productivity growth to wane (Constantinescu, Mattoo, and Ruta 2017; Kummritz, Taglioni, and Winkler 2017). Among the factors constraining TFP growth in EAP are weak research and development spending (Indonesia, the Philippines, Thailand, and Vietnam), inadequate infrastructure (Indonesia and Thailand), low economic complexity (Indonesia, the Philippines, and Vietnam), and price distortions and stringent product market regulations (Malaysia and Thailand). Distortions of economic incentives leading to factor misallocation also appear to be holding back TFP growth in China and Vietnam (World Bank 2022e).

The COVID-19 pandemic has caused damage that is likely to be long-lasting to key drivers of EAP's potential growth. In addition to significantly disrupting economic activity, trade, and investment in 2020, the pandemic has left deep scars, including reduced physical and human capital and a retreat from global supply chains, which are likely to dampen potential growth for a prolonged period. Worsening health outcomes, food insecurity, job losses, and school closures have contributed to the erosion of human capital. COVID-19-related school disruptions have resulted in substantial learning losses in many EAP countries: It is estimated that students in EAP have lost an average of two-thirds of a year of learning, with significant variations across subregions. These learning losses have added to challenges that the region already faced prior to the pandemic, as a number of countries were already performing poorly on international learning assessments (Molato-Gayares et al. 2022; World Bank 2021g, 2021i).

Higher public and private indebtedness, weaker bank balance sheets, and increased uncertainty associated with the pandemic now threaten to limit public and private capital accumulation—the main driver of potential growth in much of EAP. Reduced investment, coupled with firm closures and losses of valuable intangible assets (like firm-worker relationships), have weighed on productivity. The disruption of trade and global value chains could also affect productivity by leading to a less efficient allocation of resources across sectors and firms and by dampening the diffusion of technology.

Prospects for potential growth in EAP

Potential GDP growth in EAP is projected to slow further to an average rate of 4.6 percent a year in 2022-30, down from 6.2 percent a year in 2011-21. China accounts for much of the projected slowdown, but slowing potential growth is expected to spread to the rest of the region as well. Part of the projected slowdown is due to the pandemic and the war in Ukraine, the effects of which are expected to be most severe and longest lasting in the countries that have suffered most from the collapse of global tourism and trade. Growth prospects have also deteriorated for countries that have recently suffered natural disasters, domestic policy uncertainty, and terms-of-trade shocks.

In terms of the production function framework, each of the three main drivers of growth in potential output are expected to contribute to the worsening outlook, with weaker capital accumulation accounting for most of the slowdown, followed by falling growth in TFP and the supply of labor. Capital accumulation is projected to slow most steeply in China, where policy efforts to rein in credit growth have recently resumed. In contrast, in the Philippines, investment is expected to pick up from depressed levels and boost growth in potential output. Heightened geopolitical tensions may weaken investment in the region through higher interest rates, reduced business confidence, and heightened uncertainty.

Maturing electronics technologies and the slowing expansion of global value chains are expected to dampen TFP growth further in EAP. Geopolitical tensions may also weaken gains from increasing international division of labor and diffusion of technology.

Demographic trends that are already slowing labor force growth are expected to continue, putting the region at risk of growing old before becoming rich (figure 2.6). China is expected to experience the largest decline in the share of working-age population. In contrast, for some countries, including Cambodia, Lao PDR, and Papua New Guinea, increases in working-age populations are expected, and these countries could continue to reap demographic dividends if they generate sufficient jobs.

Risks to the baseline projection for growth in potential output are predominantly on the downside. Downside risks include a worsening of the conflict between Russia and Ukraine, persistent geopolitical tensions, and associated trade disruptions. Worsening geopolitical tensions could further destabilize global economic activity and, in the longer term, cause global trade, investment, technology transfer, and financial networks to

FIGURE 2.6 **EAP: Potential growth—Baseline and reform scenarios**

Projections for the fundamental drivers of potential growth suggest that unless policy reforms are implemented, the recent slowdown in EAP will accelerate and broaden during 2022-30. Demographic trends are set to continue slowing potential growth. In a scenario in which each country in EAP repeats its largest 10-year improvements in investment growth, educational outcomes, life expectancy, and female labor force participation during 2000-21, potential growth could instead be raised, by 0.8 percentage point a year, by the end of this decade.

A. Baseline projection for growth in potential output

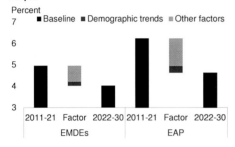

B. Natural disasters, 1980-2021

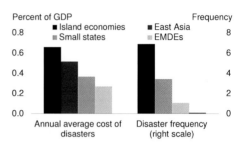

C. Working-age population

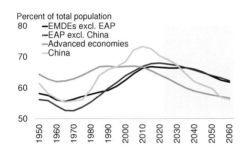

D. Per capita income when working-age population share was at its peak

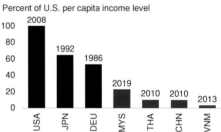

E. Reform scenarios

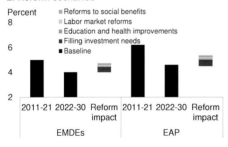

F. Climate change scenarios

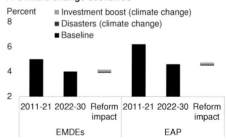

Sources: International Monetary Fund; Penn World Table; UN, World Population Prospects; World Bank.

Note: Shaded areas indicate forecast. Panel shows period averages, weighted using average real U.S. dollar gross domestic product (GDP) at average 2010-19 prices and market exchange rates. Data for 2022-30 are forecasts. EAP = East Asia and Pacific; EMDEs = emerging market and developing economies; excl. = excluding.

A. Estimates of potential growth are based on production function approach. Chapter 1 describes the methodology and chapter 5 the projections. "Other factors" include trend improvements in human capital and investment growth relative to its long-term average. Sample includes 53 EMDEs (6 from EAP).

B. "East Asia" includes 10 EMDEs in EAP; "Island economies" includes 13 EMDEs in EAP. "Disaster frequency" is calculated based on the annual average number of natural disasters between 1980 and 2021 per 10,000 square kilometers of land area.

C. "Working-age population" is defined as those aged 15 to 64.

D. Per capita income in the year that share of working-age population peaked (years shown above the bars). Red bars are EAP economies whose working-age population shares are expected to have peaked before 2020. CHN = China; DEU = Germany; JPN = Japan; MYS = Malaysia; THA = Thailand; USA = United States; VNM = Vietnam.

E.F. Estimates of potential growth are based on production function approach. Sample includes 53 EMDEs (6 from EAP: China, Indonesia, Malaysia, Mongolia, the Philippines, and Thailand). Chapter 1 describes methodology and chapter 5 reform scenarios.

fragment (World Bank 2022i). The drag on activity from persistent trade and supply disruptions and high commodity prices could also cause the global economy to become mired in stagflation, with inflationary pressures requiring substantially more monetary tightening than currently assumed.

Policy options to lift potential growth in EAP

The baseline projection for 2022-30 shows a further slowdown in growth in EAP's potential output, which will also result in a slower convergence of per capita incomes with those of advanced economies. However, this outcome can be avoided if countries in the region implement growth-enhancing reforms. To illustrate, in a scenario in which each country in EAP is assumed to repeat its largest 10-year improvements in investment growth, educational outcomes, life expectancy, and female labor force participation during 2000-21, it is estimated that potential growth could be raised by 0.8 percentage point a year by the end of this decade. More than half of this increase (approximately 0.5 percentage point a year) would come from the boost to investment growth.

The region faces the consequences of climate change, including more frequent and more severe droughts, flooding, coastal erosion, typhoons, and cyclones, as well as rising oceans. It is estimated that investment in climate change mitigation and adaptation could strengthen the region's resilience to climate change and boost annual potential growth by 0.1 percentage point by the end of this decade. Small island countries remain particularly vulnerable to risks of natural disasters, including weather-related events, losing on average about 1 percent of GDP a year to damage from such disasters (Scandurra et al. 2018). More climate-resilient infrastructure could also help mitigate a possible climate change-related reduction in annual potential growth resulting from increasingly frequent extreme weather events that damage capital stocks and erode labor productivity.

The EAP region, particularly China, is a major contributor to rising emissions of greenhouse gases: Its emissions of these gases tripled between 2000 and 2019, and they now account for nearly one-third of global emissions (World Bank 2021f). Early action by the region on climate change, therefore, has global as well as regional importance. A transition to less carbon-intensive growth requires fundamental and costly shifts in consumption and production patterns. Policy priorities include phasing out fossil fuel and energy subsidies; adjusting carbon prices; fostering green public investment in low-carbon and resilient infrastructure and innovation; and undertaking low-carbon policy reforms in key sectors, such as energy, transport, agriculture, land use, and urban planning. The increased viability of green technologies should allow EAP countries to cut carbon emissions and preserve energy security.

The reallocation of labor and other resources from agriculture to higher-productivity sectors, a process that has encouraged urbanization, has contributed in a major way to the rapid growth of the region's potential output in past decades. EAP has the potential for continued rapid urban development (Baker and Gadgil 2017). Although more than 450 million people moved to cities between 2000 and 2016, the share of people in EAP living in urban centers was only 57 percent in 2020, well below the advanced-economy average of 80 percent.[6] China had an urbanization rate in 2020 of 65 percent, with only 25 percent of the population living in urban agglomerations, compared with 45.3 percent in the United States. With a large share of the EAP workforce still engaged in agriculture, there is still scope for substantial productivity gains from resource reallocation, particularly in Cambodia, Indonesia, the Philippines, Thailand, Timor-Leste, and Vietnam. To promote further urbanization, possible measures include investing in infrastructure and social services, making land more accessible on a fair and transparent basis, encouraging facilities that support recent migrants, and coordinating urban services across municipal boundaries (see, for instance, ADB 2016; Bryson and Nelson 2016; Creehan 2015; and World Bank and PRC 2014).

At the same time, increasing productivity in agriculture requires renewed efforts to remove barriers and distortions that prevent a reallocation of productive resources across farms. Sustaining growth in agricultural productivity requires farmers to adapt to a steady stream of new farm practices and technologies, manage inputs more efficiently, adopt new crops and production systems, improve the quality of their products, and conserve natural resources.

Institutional reforms—such as better corporate governance, enhanced auditing and accounting standards, and stronger regulatory frameworks—could promote competition and productivity growth (Malaysia and Thailand). Improving the business climate would also help raise productivity in some economies (Cambodia, Fiji, Lao PDR, Myanmar, Papua New Guinea, Timor-Leste, and the small Pacific Islands). Cambodia, Lao PDR, Myanmar, and Papua New Guinea rank low on Transparency International's Corruption Perception Index and on other governance indicators. Enhanced transparency, strengthened accountability, and greater responsiveness of state institutions to the needs of the private sector would bolster investor confidence and invite productivity-enhancing investment (World Bank 2021g).

Several countries in the region continue to have sizable infrastructure investment needs (Vashakmadze et al. 2017). In some economies, better public infrastructure could foster connectivity and spur innovation. Financing such investment will depend on country circumstances: It may need to be accomplished by broadening the tax base (Cambodia, Indonesia, Lao PDR, Malaysia, Mongolia, Papua New Guinea, and the Philippines), increasing the efficiency of public investment (Indonesia, Lao PDR, and Vietnam; Dabla-Norris et al. 2012), rebalancing public expenditures toward investment, or promoting public-private cooperation (Cambodia and Pacific Island countries; World Bank 2022d). Developing and implementing rigorous and transparent processes for project selection, appraisal, and procurement could make public investment more efficient and improve the operation and maintenance of assets (Ollivaud, Guillemette, and Turner 2016). Enhancing the transparency and governance of state-owned enterprises could also help ease pressure on fiscal resources.

---

[6] Urbanization rates are particularly low in Papua New Guinea (13 percent), Cambodia (21 percent), and Myanmar and Vietnam (about 35 percent).

Over several decades, the region's openness to international trade has led to significant productivity gains (Eris and Ulasan 2013; Havrylyshyn 1990; Trejos and Barboza 2015). Increased domestic and international competition could strengthen incentives for productivity-enhancing technological innovation. However, in recent years, weaker growth in advanced economies, signs of weakened commitment to trade liberalization, and increased risks of protectionism have threatened prospects for further trade expansion. On the other hand, the movement of some production out of China and an incipient digital transformation are creating new opportunities for some economies in the region to expand their exports. Policy efforts in several key areas could help counter the risks and make the most of the opportunities.

Lowering nontariff barriers would further expand global and regional trade, help the region take advantage of shifts in the global trade landscape, and improve the international allocation of investment, thereby boosting productivity and competitiveness. Barriers to services trade remain elevated in many countries of the region (Indonesia, Malaysia, the Philippines, and Thailand; Beverelli, Fiorini, and Hoekman 2017; World Bank 2022n). Restrictions on foreign control and ownership of firms, discretionary licensing, and limits on the operations of foreign companies can all reduce trade in international services. In addition, foreign entry restrictions in some EAP countries curtail the provision of legal, accounting, engineering, and other professional services.

Participation in deep trade agreements such as those negotiated among members of the ASEAN economic community and the Regional Comprehensive Economic Partnership can catalyze domestic reforms as well as secure access to markets abroad. Such partnerships can also help boost the region's resilience, as they did during the global financial crisis in 2008-09, and support the development of small and medium-sized enterprises (Estrades et al. 2022). Growth-promoting domestic reforms may include policies that facilitate domestic labor mobility and the entry and exit of firms to allow reallocation of resources to more efficient enterprises.

The ASEAN-4 countries (Indonesia, Malaysia, Thailand, and the Philippines) have begun to strengthen the quality and flexibility of their domestic education systems. Many EAP countries, however, have long suffered from a learning crisis, with low levels of educational attainment partly due to the absence of policy initiatives. Extended school closures during the pandemic—with schools in the region closed for about 73 percent of instruction days between February 2020 and October 2021—led to substantial further learning losses, especially for the poor. These losses must be reversed to prevent lasting damage to student progression, human capital formation, and opportunities for productive work (Molato-Gayares et al. 2022). Reforms to improve education quality would also raise labor force skills and promote productivity growth (World Bank 2018a). Now that schools have reopened, measures to adjust school curricula and develop rapid catch-up periods can also mitigate learning losses. In the longer term, countries should seek to develop more resilient and inclusive education systems that can deliver learning in the event of future crises, including through remote learning. In addition, reforms that raise female secondary and tertiary enrollment and completion rates could increase female workforce participation rates.

Policies that spur innovation and adoption of technology could also boost the growth of TFP and potential output (Cirera and Maloney 2017). These policies include higher spending on R&D and promotion of inward FDI, which can be an important source of technology transfer. In China and other upper-middle-income economies in EAP, reducing barriers to competition could improve the effectiveness of R&D spending and raise productivity in the services sectors (Bai and Zhang 2017; World Bank and PRC 2012). Lower-middle-income countries may be able to capitalize on FDI inflows by strengthening their capacity to adopt new technologies, the diffusion of which could boost productivity across a broad range of firms (World Bank 2022d). However, building adoptive capacity may require enhancing managerial and technical skills and improving access to finance and digital infrastructure (Acemoglu and Restrepo 2017).

Growth in potential output in Europe and Central Asia is projected to slow to an annual average pace of 3.0 percent in 2022-30 from 3.6 percent in 2011-21. Investment has weakened against the backdrop of sustained geopolitical tensions and pronounced uncertainty, as has the growth of the labor force. The dual shocks of the COVID-19 pandemic and the war in Ukraine are expected to inflict substantial damage on the drivers of potential growth and exacerbate existing structural challenges. Given its limited fiscal space, the region needs structural reforms to help boost jobs and incomes, strengthen resilience to shocks, and promote sustainable growth over the next decade.

Introduction

Two destabilizing shocks in quick succession have hit emerging market and developing economies (EMDEs) in ECA hard. The COVID-19 pandemic induced a recession in 2020, reversing recent progress in raising living standards and leaving deep economic scars among vulnerable populations. Just as regional output was edging toward its prepandemic trend in early 2022, Russia invaded Ukraine. The invasion has since unraveled the region's economic recovery from the pandemic-induced recession, with its effects reverberating through commodity and financial markets, trade and migration links, business and consumer confidence, and weaker external demand from the euro area—ECA's largest trading partner (Guénette, Kenworthy, and Wheeler 2022; World Bank 2022g). Regional output is forecast to shrink by about 0.3 percent in 2022 and to barely grow in 2023 (figure 2.7.A; World Bank 2022i, forthcoming). As a result, the regional economy faces large output losses—particularly in Russia and Ukraine (figure 2.7.B).

In the past, downward revisions to long-term growth forecasts have often followed large negative shocks to economic activity—as was the experience for the region in the 2010s after the global financial crisis and European debt crisis, as well as after the 2014-16 oil price plunge for ECA's energy exporters (figure 2.7.C). Once again, the region is at risk of facing another decade of disappointing growth, as the pandemic and invasion of Ukraine inflict damage on the underlying drivers of long-term growth—especially labor productivity—by weakening investment, disrupting supply chains, hindering

Note: Estimates using the production function approach are available for Albania, Armenia, Bulgaria, Hungary, Kazakhstan, Kyrgyz Republic, Poland, Romania, and Türkiye.

FIGURE 2.7 **ECA: Output growth and potential growth**

As the ECA region emerged from the steep pandemic-induced recession of 2020, it appeared set to close the output gap that had resulted from that recession. The Russian Federation's invasion of Ukraine, however, has proven to be a major setback, and the gap has since widened. Scarring from the pandemic and war, combined with intensifying demographic pressures, is expected to dampen output growth over the remainder of this decade. Potential growth is projected to fall from 3.6 percent a year over 2011-21 to 3.0 percent a year over 2022-30.

A. GDP growth

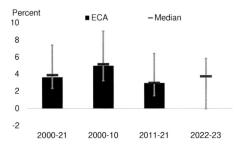

B. Deviation of output from prepandemic trend

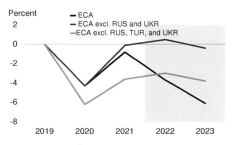

C. Contributions of potential growth and business cycle to actual growth

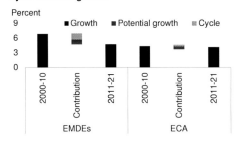

D. Contributions to potential growth: EMDEs and ECA

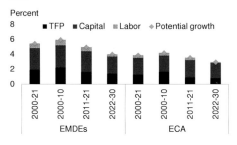

E. Contributions to potential growth: Central Asia and South Caucasus

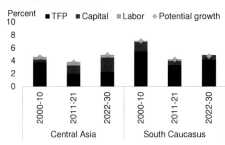

F. Contributions to potential growth: Central Europe and Western Balkans

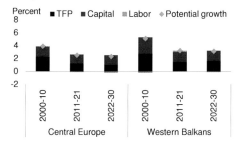

Sources: Penn World Table; World Bank.

Note: Shaded area indicates forecast. Gross domestic product (GDP) weights are calculated using average real U.S. dollar GDP (at average 2010-19 prices and market exchange rates). Data for 2022-30 are forecasts. ECA = Europe and Central Asia; EMDEs = emerging market and developing economies; RUS = Russian Federation; TFP = total factor productivity; TUR = Türkiye; UKR = Ukraine.

A. Bars show period averages of annual GDP-weighted averages. Horizontal lines denote the median region, with orange whiskers showing minimum-maximum ranges across regions.

B. Panel shows the percent deviation between the *Global Economic Prospects* report forecasts released in June 2022 (World Bank 2022i) and January 2020 (World Bank 2020d). For 2023, the January 2020 baseline is extended using projected growth for 2022.

C. Blue bars denote average actual growth over each 10-year period. Red bars denote contribution of potential growth to change in actual growth between the two 5-year periods; orange bars denote contribution of cyclical growth.

C.-F. Period averages of annual GDP-weighted averages. Estimates are based on production function approach. Sample includes 53 EMDEs, of which 9 are from ECA (Türkiye, 2 in Central Asia, 4 in Central Europe, 1 in South Caucasus, and 1 in Western Balkans). Russian Federation and Ukraine are excluded.

innovation, and scarring human capital through sustained education and job losses (Dieppe 2021; Dieppe, Kilic-Celik, and Okou 2021).

Against this backdrop, growth in potential output is projected to slow from an annual average pace of 3.6 percent per year over 2011-21 to 3 percent per year over 2022-30 (figure 2.7.D).[7] The projected slowdown is not broadly shared across ECA countries, however, as it largely reflects weaker growth in Türkiye and to a lesser extent Poland— the second- and third-largest economies in the region, respectively. Elsewhere in ECA, potential growth in the remainder of this decade is projected to be either stronger or broadly in line with its pace in 2011-21 (figure 2.7.E). In some Central European and Western Balkan economies, a pickup in growth is expected, driven by significant spending related to the European Union (EU) and associated reforms (figure 2.7.F). In particular, increased R&D spending could support digital and green agendas in ECA EU countries and encourage the acceleration of technological innovation and TFP.

The pandemic and invasion of Ukraine have amplified the region's longstanding structural challenges, which include deteriorating governance in some countries, lack of infrastructure in some cases in the eastern part of the region, and education systems that create skills mismatches in the labor market. With limited space for fiscal stimulus, structural reforms are needed to raise ECA economies to higher growth paths than the baseline projection, boost jobs and incomes, and strengthen resilience to shocks. These include reforms to the still-large state-owned enterprise sector, governance, and education systems, as well as efforts to achieve green and inclusive growth.

Evolution and drivers of potential growth in ECA

Even prior to the invasion of Ukraine, growth in potential output in ECA had fallen from 4.2 percent during 2000-10 to 3.6 percent in 2011-21. Robust growth, as rapid economic transformation supported capital accumulation, characterized the period before the global financial crisis. Relatively strong growth partly reflected the benefits of high commodity prices for the region's commodity exporters and sweeping reforms in several countries as part of the EU accession process (EBRD 2017).

Following rapid progress toward convergence of living standards with those of the EU over the 2000s, a series of shocks—the global financial crisis of 2008-09, the European debt crisis of 2010-12, the 2014-16 oil price plunge, the COVID-19 pandemic that erupted in 2020, and Russia's invasion of Ukraine in early 2022—have hit the region, and they have all dampened growth and investment drivers and prospects. In addition to these shocks, various domestic crises, including those related to social and political

---

[7] Given data limitations, estimates of potential growth and its drivers are available for nine ECA economies: Armenia, Albania, Bulgaria, Hungary, Kazakhstan, Kyrgyz Republic, Poland, Romania, and Türkiye. Central Europe is thus represented only by Bulgaria, Hungary, Poland, and Romania; Central Asia by Kazakhstan and the Kyrgyz Republic; the South Caucasus by Armenia; and the Western Balkans by Albania. For the purposes of this section, the 2000s are assumed to cover the period 2000-10, the 2010s the period 2011-21, and the 2020s the period 2022-30. The 2000s and 2010s are selected to ensure that the averages include both the global recession and its rebound. The 2020s are selected to cover projections.

unrest, have also weighed on growth prospects. As a result, per capita income growth fell from 3.8 percent per year over 2000-10 to 3.4 percent per year over 2011-21.

Capital accumulation has made the largest contribution to growth in potential output in ECA over the past two decades. Average private investment growth in the region fell to about 4.9 percent per year over 2011-21, down from 7 percent per year in 2000-10. Total investment fell from 8 percent per year over 2000-10 to 4.7 percent per year over 2011-21 (figure 2.8.B). Capital accumulation contributed 2.4 percentage points a year to potential growth, on average, during 2011-21, broadly in line with its levels in 2000-10. Private sector and investment growth continues to struggle on account of unskilled labor forces or skill mismatches, limited access to finance, and burdensome logistics and poor market integration in many ECA economies, particularly those in the eastern part of the region that are not tied to the EU accession process. Dividends from public investment in ECA have lagged those in the EU, with the lag in many cases reflecting institutional quality gaps, weak public procurement processes, and constraints to administration and absorption capacity.

For most of the 2010s, investment in several ECA economies—including Albania, Armenia, Bulgaria, and Romania—failed to regain ground lost in the wake of the global financial crisis and European debt crises. In the region's energy exporters, investment weakened alongside the sharp fall in oil prices over 2014-16. The rise in geopolitical tensions following Russia's annexation of Crimea in 2014 also triggered a broad decline in investor confidence. The maturing of global value chains—the expansion of which had driven productivity-enhancing investment in a major way—also likely played a role in slowing capital accumulation, given ECA's deep integration into global markets.

While demographic developments in some other EMDE regions has supported output growth over the past two decades, in many ECA economies a combination of aging populations, low birth rates, and emigration has weighed on growth. In several ECA economies, particularly those in Central Europe, the share of the elderly in the population has risen rapidly. In Poland, the increase in the share of the population aged 65 years or older exceeded 5 percentage points over the 2010s—well above the EU average of 3 percentage points (European Commission 2021). In many parts of the region, emigration added to the pressures arising from the natural drop in the population and the effect of population aging on labor force growth (Bossavie et al. 2022). As a result, growth in working-age populations and labor supplies slowed, and labor shortages in individual sectors were common (figures 2.8.C and 2.8.D). Demographic developments, however, have been uneven across ECA. Over the past two decades, the population has declined in half of the region's economies, while other economies, especially Türkiye and those in Central Asia, have reported population gains (and in some cases strong ones).

Demographic pressures in many ECA countries stem from low labor force participation, especially among those living in rural and underserved areas. Precarious employment and low-quality jobs have contributed to a high incidence of undeclared work in some ECA economies, including those in Central Europe, which tends to have lower levels of

FIGURE 2.8 ECA: Growth in potential output and its drivers

All drivers of potential growth are expected to weaken in Europe and Central Asia in the remainder of this decade. The Russian Federation's invasion of Ukraine and heightened policy uncertainty have hit private investment hard. Meanwhile, a projected further decline in the labor force, largely reflecting population aging, will be a drag on potential growth. Earlier gains from human capital accumulation are fading, with the quality of education in some economies deteriorating.

A. Potential GDP growth

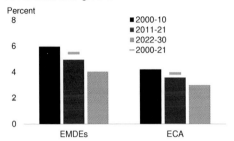

B. Investment growth

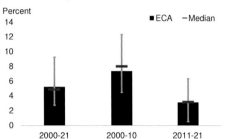

C. Labor force participation rate

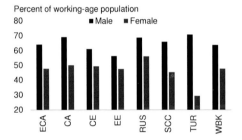

D. Working-age population growth

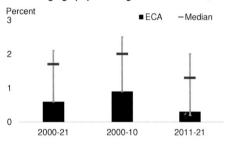

E. Share of population aged 30-34 years with tertiary education

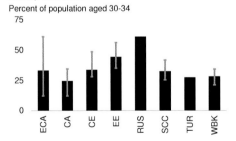

F. Quality-adjusted years of higher education

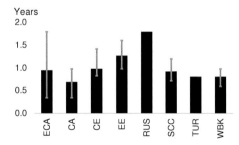

Sources: European Commission; Eurostat; Penn World Table; UN, World Population Prospects; World Bank, World Development Indicators database.

Note: Panel shows period averages, weighted using average real U.S. dollar gross domestic product (GDP) at average 2010-19 prices and market exchange rates. Data for 2022-30 are forecasts. CA = Central Asia; CE = Central Europe; ECA = Europe and Central Asia; EE = Eastern Europe; EMDEs = emerging market and developing economies; RUS = Russian Federation; SCC = South Caucasus; TUR = Türkiye;
WBK = Western Balkans.

A. Estimates are based on production function approach. Sample includes 53 EMDEs, of which 9 are from ECA (Türkiye, 2 in Central Asia, 4 in Central Europe, 1 in South Caucasus, and 1 in Western Balkans). Russian Federation and Ukraine are excluded.

B. Bars show averages. Orange whiskers show minimum-maximum, ranges. Sample includes 13 ECA economies, including Türkiye, Russian Federation, and Ukraine.

C. Panel shows share of population aged 15 and older by gender that is economically active. Averages are unweighted.

D. Bars show averages. Median marker and whiskers show median and minimum-maximum ranges for EMDE regions. "Working-age population" refers to population aged 15-64 years. Sample includes 22 ECA economies.

E.F. Aggregates are simple averages of country-level data, calculated as in World Bank (2020i).

informality than other parts of the region (El-Ganainy et al. 2021; Ohnsorge and Yu 2021). Women, especially migrant women, have had more limited employment opportunities than men with similar levels of tertiary education (Frattini and Solmone 2022). This has been most evident in Romania. As a result of these challenges, labor activity rates in many ECA countries have remained below those of EU peers. Because of these trends, the average contribution of labor force growth to growth in potential output in ECA remained modest, though stable, between 2000-10 and 2011-21.

The accumulation of human and physical capital has lost momentum in the last decade—weighing on potential TFP growth. Gains in both life expectancy and educational achievement have leveled off, with educational reform losing momentum after the large strides of the early 2000s (Patrinos 2022). Although ECA has had high school enrollment for decades, as well as the highest average number of years of education among EMDE regions for both males and females, its quality-adjusted years of education and scores on the Programme for International Student Assessment (PISA) trail the EU average in many cases, with some backsliding even in the decade prior to the pandemic (figure 2.8.E; World Bank 2020c). Levels of basic skills in reading, mathematics, and science in ECA, as measured by PISA scores, fell between 2006 and 2018, roughly to levels observed in 2000 (Patrinos 2022). Educational outcomes are low even in some ECA EU countries, such as Bulgaria, where almost half of teenagers lack basic reading, mathematics, and science skills (against one in five in the EU). In contrast, Poland's educational outcomes have been high, and its years of quality-adjusted education have been increasing, especially in the younger cohorts, which has likely contributed to faster catch-up with the EU than among ECA peers (World Bank 2022l).

While several factors seem likely to have contributed to the apparent fall in educational attainment in ECA, insufficient investment, especially in preprimary and primary education, has likely played a significant role. In ECA as a whole, government spending on education fell from 4.2 to 3.9 percent of GDP between 2009 and 2019. Widening income inequality among the families of students in the region may have also had an effect. In many ECA countries, socioeconomically advantaged students have considerably higher learning outcomes than disadvantaged students, who are often effectively segregated from high achievers (OECD 2021b).

Not only do educational challenges weigh on an inclusive recovery, however; they also hinder the private sector and dampen long-term growth prospects.[8] Mismatches between labor market needs and skills impose a significant constraint on growth in potential output in ECA. ECA countries rank above the EU average in skill mismatches, the gaps being particularly large for Albania and Bulgaria (IMF 2021b). Across ECA, skills of graduates from vocational and higher education are often poorly aligned with needs.

---

[8] Data from the World Bank Enterprise Surveys indicate that an inadequately educated workforce is one of the largest constraints on firms' ability to grow in Bulgaria, Poland, and Romania—especially in Bulgaria and Romania, where nearly a quarter of firms identify education as a constraint (World Bank 2022i).

One result is the high proportion of young people neither employed nor in education or training (NEETs). Most ECA countries had NEET rates above the EU average in 2021, and women in Bulgaria, Poland, and Romania had rates more than 10 percentage points higher than those for men. High NEET rates may reflect weak labor market policies and lower spending in ECA countries compared with those in the EU. Participation in training (based on survey data from recent years) has ranged from less than 2 percent of the population aged 25-64 years in Bulgaria to 6 percent in Hungary and Türkiye. This compares with an EU average of 11 percent (European Commission 2022).

Other major drivers of TFP growth also slowed in 2011-21. After a boost from reforms related to EU accession, governance reform efforts have slowed in many new member states and backtracked in others, weakening the business environment and likely hindering competition and innovation. Pervasive corruption and large informal sectors in some countries are major constraints on the ability of private firms to invest, innovate, and close productivity gaps with those in the remainder of the EU. In 2018, ECA countries continued to fall short of the EU average in the public institutions component of the World Economic Forum's Global Competitiveness Index, with already sizable gaps in ethics and corruption widening in some cases. The state's outsized footprint in the economy tends to magnify the adverse effects of such poor governance (figure 2.9.A-2.9.D). Even in ECA's EU countries, World Bank Enterprise Surveys data for 2019 indicate that institutional weakness hindered private sector activity: firms highlighted obstacles related to meeting with tax officials in Bulgaria and Romania and competition from informal firms in Bulgaria and Poland (figures 2.9.E and 2.9.F).

Another important driver of TFP growth is R&D spending, which promotes technological innovation (Hallward-Driemeier et al. 2020).[9] Average R&D spending in the region remained under 1 percent of GDP throughout the 2010s, whereas in the EU it had risen from about 2 percent in 2010 to 2.2 percent by 2018. Thus, a deteriorating business environment, weakening governance, and sluggish R&D investment have likely all tended to slow or constrain TFP growth in ECA in the past decade, with the average contribution of TFP growth to growth in potential output estimated to have declined from 1.7 percentage points in 2000-10 to less than 1 percentage point in 2011-21.

The COVID-19 pandemic and the Russian invasion of Ukraine are likely to have weakened ECA's potential growth through several channels. Increased uncertainty, including uncertainty about the longer-term international economic landscape and risks of deglobalization, and reduced investor confidence are likely to have dampened fixed investment.

The pandemic has also set back human capital formation. Schools in ECA were closed completely for nearly 65 days and partially for more than 75 days, on average, between

---

[9] Innovations typically result from a financially demanding research process that generates intellectual-property assets. These assets include patented inventions or ideas for the digital setting that are protected by copyright or otherwise (Pelikánová 2019).

FIGURE 2.9 **ECA: Drivers of growth in potential output**

Progress on reforms and the transition to a competitive market economy has stalled in many ECA countries. Inefficiencies of state-owned enterprises, stalled efforts to improve governance and reduce corruption, and delays in promoting private sector development weigh on potential growth.

A. EBRD state-owned enterprise activity and assets

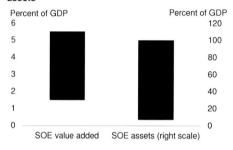

B. EBRD assessment of governance, 2021

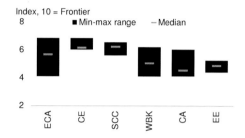

C. EBRD assessment of transition to a competitive market economy, 2021

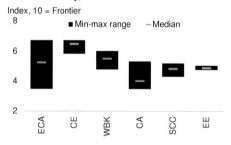

D. EBRD assessment of integration, 2021

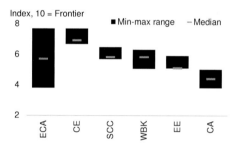

E. World Bank Enterprise Surveys: Share of firms that met with tax officials

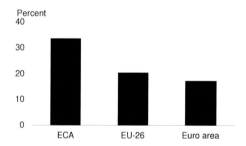

F. World Bank Enterprise Surveys: Share of firms that introduce process innovation and invest in R&D

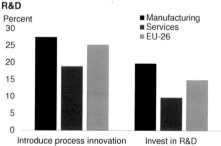

Sources: EBRD (2020, 2021); Sanja and Tabak (2020); World Bank; World Bank, Enterprise Surveys DataBank.
Note: CA = Central Asia; CE = Central Europe; EBRD = European Bank for Reconstruction and Development; ECA = Europe and Central Asia; EE = Eastern Europe; EU-26 = European Union member states excluding Germany; min-max = minimum-maximum; R&D = research and development; SCC = South Caucasus; SOE = state-owned enterprise; WBK = Western Balkans.
A. SOE data are 2014-16 averages, as presented in Sanja and Tabak (2020). Sample includes 25 of the 38 countries covered by the EBRD, of which 17 are ECA EMDEs.
B.-D. Data reflect the scores of transition qualities, which measure each economy's performance against that of comparator economies in EBRD regions, as presented in EBRD (2021). Scores range from 1 to 10, where 10 represents a synthetic frontier corresponding to the standards of a sustainable market economy.
E.F. Data for the EU-26 grouping and the euro area exclude Germany. Aggregates are calculated as averages. Data are for 2019.
E. Panel shows percent of firms that were visited or inspected by tax officials or were required to meet with them over the year preceding the survey.
F. "Introduce process innovation" data indicate the percent of firms that introduced any new or significantly improved process over the three years preceding the survey, including methods of manufacturing products or offering services; logistics, delivery, or distribution methods; or any supporting activities for processes. "Invest in R&D" data indicate the percent of firms over the fiscal year preceding the survey that invested in formal research and development activities.

March 2020 and September 2021 (Donnelly and Patrinos 2021; Patrinos 2022). Survey data point to a year's worth of learning losses among students in at least 11 ECA countries (Patrinos 2022). The adverse economic effects will become more pronounced as the cohort of current children enters the labor market. Poor and vulnerable populations and underserved regions have likely had larger education losses from the pandemic, partly owing to preexisting challenges that include uneven digital connectivity, low public expenditure on education, and inequitable learning opportunities and outcomes. On top of that, Russia's invasion of Ukraine has triggered an influx of displaced people from Ukraine—about half of which are children—to neighboring ECA countries, whom will require additional resources to meet their educational needs.

As have past crises, the pandemic triggered a rise in the share of young people who are neither employed nor in education or training. The recent increase raises concern that many of today's young people will remain out of the labor market for years to come, facing a higher likelihood of poverty and reducing actual and potential output in the countries where they live (European Commission 2022).

Prior to the invasion of Ukraine, ECA working hours had nearly returned to their pre-pandemic trend (ILO 2022b). The negative impacts of the pandemic on labor supply and markets has varied across ECA countries, partly owing to differing levels of government support for jobs and incomes, resulting in uneven shocks to country-level potential growth. In some economies, employment retention schemes partly mitigated job losses, resulting in 2020 employment rates that were largely unchanged from those in 2019. This pattern was observed, for example, in Hungary, Poland, and Romania, as well as in some Western Balkan economies, including North Macedonia and Serbia. In contrast, employment rates fell and unemployment rose sharply in 2020 in many countries in Eastern Europe, the South Caucasus, and Central Asia, where employment retention schemes were smaller or absent. In many of these countries, which tend to have high levels of informality, shifts from wage and salaried work to self-employment stemmed increases in unemployment somewhat (ILO 2022b).

The labor market recovery since 2020 has been similarly uneven across and within countries, as well as across sectors. In Türkiye, Poland, and Kazakhstan—ECA's second-, third-, and fourth-largest economies, respectively—employment has returned to pre-pandemic rates, and in the Central European economies, labor market slack has returned to or fallen below prepandemic levels.[10] In contrast, the recovery has been more sluggish in some economies in the South Caucasus and Central Asia. In some cases, labor market recoveries have been shallower than unemployment data suggest, because increases in people outside the labor force have offset employment losses—reflecting, for example, job seekers that have become discouraged from long spells of unemployment. High-frequency World Bank phone survey data indicate persistent financial concerns

---

[10] Labor market slack is measured by Eurostat and is defined as unemployed, inactive, unavailable, and underemployed people as a share of the labor force and potential additional labor force (that is, those inactive and unavailable).

among the poor and vulnerable, as pandemic-related job and income losses have disproportionately affected them, particularly in lagging regions within countries (World Bank 2022f).[11] As a result, the erosion of human capital from pandemic-induced unemployment has varied in ECA, which could lead to divergences in potential growth over the coming years.

The pandemic has highlighted not only the critical role of digital connectivity for the continuity of provision of public services and economic activity, but also the digital divide across income groups and geographic regions. Although access to broadband internet has expanded over the past decade in ECA, with almost all households having access by 2018, a large share of the population still lacks basic digital skills and does not use digital technologies. In 2021, less than half of Central and Eastern Europeans had basic digital skills. This has limited the use of the internet for e-commerce and interaction with public authorities to levels much lower than those in the rest of Europe.[12] Moreover, highly skilled and high-wage workers have found it much easier to work remotely than low-skilled workers. Thus, low-skilled workers experienced a significantly larger drop in employment, especially during the first wave of the pandemic, when policies on social interaction were at their most restrictive. Lack of access to digital devices during school closures also put disadvantaged students at higher risk of learning losses (World Bank 2021h). This underscores the fact that harnessing the potential benefits of the digital transition widely requires a broad range of complementary elements, including access to broadband, trust in the digital system, and a baseline of digital skills among the population.

Prospects for potential growth in ECA

Growth in potential output in ECA is projected to slow from an annual average pace of 3.6 percent per year over 2011-21 to 3.0 percent per year in 2022-30—compared with 4.2 percent per year in 2000-10. As a result, potential per capita growth is expected to slightly decelerate to 2.8 percent per year over 2022-30 from 2.9 percent per year in 2011-21. The projected slowdown reflects a continued deceleration of all the main drivers of growth, exacerbated by the effects of the pandemic and the war in Ukraine.

Potential growth is expected to depend increasingly on capital accumulation as its other drivers—growth of the labor force and TFP—weaken as a result of increasingly unfavorable demographic developments. Intensifying demographic pressures are expected to constrain labor force growth, whose contribution to potential growth is projected at less than 0.1 percentage point a year, on average, over 2022-30. Meanwhile, TFP growth is expected to remain relatively weak, at less than 1 percent a year, over the

---

[11] As measured by Eurostat's Nomenclature of Territorial Units for Statistics (NUTS) 2 and NUTS 3 regions, which comprise Bulgaria, Hungary, Montenegro, Poland, Serbia, Romania, and Türkiye.

[12] In 2021, ECA countries ranked among the lowest on the EU in the European Commission's Digital Economy and Society Index. Low rankings reflect weakness in digital connectivity (for example, in Bulgaria, where only 59 percent of households subscribe to broadband services, well below the EU average of 77 percent), in online delivery of public services (Bulgaria, Romania), and in digital skills (for example, in Bulgaria, Poland, and Romania; only 29 percent of Bulgarians aged 16 to 74 years have basic digital skills, compared with the EU average of 56 percent).

remainder of this decade. Capital accumulation may be constrained by slowing progress with reforms; lingering structural bottlenecks, including lack of digital skills; low R&D spending; and waning gains from earlier reforms, particularly in ECA's five EU member states, as they inch closer to convergence of living standards with those of the EU.[13] Thus, in the baseline projection, capital accumulation accounts for about 70 percent of growth in potential output in 2022-30.

The projected slowdown in growth in potential output in ECA is not evenly spread across countries. It largely reflects slowdowns in Türkiye and, to a lesser extent, Poland. In Türkiye, potential growth is projected to fall from 4.6 percent a year in 2011-21 to 3.4 percent a year in 2022-30, as the contribution of capital accumulation slows. Investment prospects have deteriorated sharply owing to a weakening of macroeconomic policy frameworks and macroeconomic stability, which has dented confidence and increased uncertainty. The earthquakes that hit Türkiye in February 2023 may result in increased investment over the next few years as reconstruction efforts get under way, but largely to replace capital stock that has been damaged or destroyed (chapter 4). Despite the possibility of temporary upticks in growth due to reconstruction, adverse events such as earthquakes can have large sustained negative effects on productivity in the longer run through dislocating labor, tightening credit conditions, disrupting value chains, and decreasing innovation. Beyond the impact of the earthquakes and heightened uncertainty around investment prospects, other structural headwinds are weighing on potential growth over the remainder of the decade, including low labor force participation and weak productivity growth (World Bank 2020i).

In Poland also, all drivers of potential growth are expected to weaken in the remainder of this decade. TFP gains from earlier reforms are expected to fade as the country continues to close its per capita income gap with the EU. The disbursement of NextGenerationEU funds has been delayed, dampening investment, compounding existing challenges in regard to the absorption of funds, and threatening a missed opportunity to boost TFP given that investments and reforms associated with these funds must be implemented by the end of 2026. The contribution from labor force growth is expected to become negative as the working-age population declines, though the immigration of Ukrainian workers could partly offset this—an upside risk to the baseline forecast.

Elsewhere in ECA, growth in potential output in 2022-30 is projected to be either stronger than, or close to, the growth rates of 2011-21. In some Central European and Western Balkan economies, sizable EU-related spending is expected to drive faster growth. Potential growth in these economies could be even stronger than projected in the baseline if the reforms associated with EU spending are successfully implemented (World Bank 2022k). In particular, national targets for increasing R&D spending could support digital and green agendas and help raise TFP growth above the baseline.

---

[13] This is especially true in the case of Poland, where output per capita in equivalent-purchasing-power terms was already about three-quarters of the EU average in 2019.

Although prospects for potential growth vary across the region, demographic headwinds are expected to intensify in each ECA economy as populations age and birth rates remain low (European Commission 2021). Consequently, the working-age shares of populations in ECA economies are expected either to continue increasing more slowly or to fall from peaks reached a decade ago or earlier; the shares of those retiring are expected to rise. Without policies to bolster labor force participation rates, improve job opportunities to discourage emigration, and better integrate immigrants, labor force growth will continue to fall and could become a drag on potential growth, with added fiscal challenges. Thus, the average contribution of labor force growth to potential growth in ECA is projected in the baseline to fall from 0.3 percentage point a year over 2011-21 to less than 0.1 percentage point a year over 2022-30. For 9 of the 13 countries for which data are available, labor force growth is expected to be a drag on potential growth. Even in the countries where this is not the case—Türkiye and the countries of Central Asia—it is expected to make a weaker contribution in 2022-30 than it did in 2011-21. Türkiye, in particular, suffers from low labor force participation: Its employment rate in 2019, at 54 percent, was nearly 20 percentage points below the EU average, reflecting, in particular, a large gap in female participation and employment (34 percent in Türkiye versus 67 percent in the EU).

The baseline projection is subject to many risks related to the possibilities of further pandemic outbreaks and a more prolonged or severe conflict in Ukraine than presently envisaged. Even after the pandemic and war recede, they may have lingering effects in increasing inequality by magnifying existing disparities and causing large human capital losses among people who are already disadvantaged. This could weaken potential growth, especially if large segments of the population are left behind.

There are also some upside risks to the projections. For countries neighboring Ukraine, the migration resulting from Russia's invasion could alleviate constraints on the labor supply. Some of Ukraine's neighbors in ECA, particularly Poland and Romania, have taken in large numbers of Ukrainian refugees. Unlike in some previous migration waves, however, roughly half of these migrants are children, and the share over the age of 64 years is also relatively high (UNHCR 2022). The inflows of Ukrainian refugees could boost the labor supply by about 1 million in Poland and over 60,000 in Romania, implying increases in growth in potential output of 0.4 and 0.1 percentage point a year, respectively, unless or until the migrants return (IMF 2022b; Strzelecki, Growiec, and Wyszyński 2020; World Bank 2022k). The EU's recently announced measures to provide services to forcibly displaced persons are supporting the integration of these new workers. The possible increase to potential growth could be even higher, since Ukrainian migrants, on average, have more years of schooling than the native populations in the receiving countries.

Policy options to lift potential growth in ECA

ECA faces formidable challenges in seeking convergence of its living standards with those in the EU, particularly given the prospect of weakened growth in potential output in the years ahead (Dieppe 2021). However, reforms that fill the region's remaining investment needs, including climate adaptation and resilience, bolstering human capital to address the pandemic's negative effects and deteriorating education outcomes, and mitigating demographic headwinds, could lift potential growth meaningfully. Reforms that address ECA's structural shortcomings related to the quality of governance and institutions and private sector development and increase investment in R&D and the digital transition could boost investment.

In a scenario that assumes each country repeats its largest 10-year increase on record in investment growth, education outcomes, life expectancy, and elderly and female labor force participation, it is estimated that growth in potential output could pick up from the baseline rate of 3.0 percent a year to 3.8 percent a year in 2022-30—faster than the 3.5 percent annual pace of 2011-21 (figure 2.10.A). Higher investment is expected to contribute three-quarters of the estimated 0.8 percentage-point boost to annual potential growth. Reforms to social benefits (assumed to raise labor force participation) account for another quarter. The remainder results from labor market reforms (also assumed to raise labor force participation) and education and health improvements. In a separate scenario in which investment is increased to tackle climate change, potential growth over 2022-30 would rise by 0.4 percentage point a year over the baseline, to 3.4 percent—only slightly lower than the average pace of 2011-21 (figure 2.10.B).[14]

Strong institutions and conducive business climates, a strong rule of law with secure and enforceable property rights and minimal expropriation risk, a stable and confidence-inspiring policy environment, and low costs of doing business encourage private investment and innovation. The same factors encourage participation in the formal sector, which tends to have higher levels of productivity than informal activity (World Bank 2018a, 2019b, 2021h). Stronger private-sector-driven growth in ECA will depend critically on structural reforms to make the region's economies more market based.

Given large gaps in the quality of governance between ECA's economies and their EU peers, reforms that strengthen institutions should be given priority. Action on this front would support TFP growth as well as investment (World Bank 2021h). A weak rule of law can result in an uneven playing field that puts the private sector at a disadvantage when competing against the state, while corruption can contribute to state capture of private sector activity. Failure to establish a strong rule of law and eliminate corruption will damage economic growth and increase fiscal risks, including those related to spillovers from impaired corporate balance sheets to public sector balance sheets, which, as history shows, can lead to large fiscal costs (Bova et al. 2016).

A related challenge are the large and still not entirely reformed state-owned enterprise sectors in many ECA countries. Indeed, the state's large footprint in many ECA economies has grown larger since 2020 because of the need for government support related to the pandemic and the war in Ukraine.[15] A larger state footprint, combined

---

[14] See chapter 5 for a detailed description of the assumptions.

[15] In the near to medium term, policy makers must carefully balance the need to support vulnerable populations, especially given the sharp increases in commodity prices, exacerbated by the war in Ukraine, with the need to shore up fiscal sustainability—a key requirement for government effectiveness. Over time, government involvement is likely to retreat as support is unwound.

FIGURE 2.10 **ECA: Growth in potential output**

A reform package targeting an aging workforce, female labor force participation, education, and investment could lift potential growth in ECA in 2022-30 above its 2011-21 average. Investment related to mitigating climate change alone could boost potential growth above its 2011-21 average. In some of ECA's European Union (EU) economies, substantial EU funding and associated reforms could double potential growth.

A. Potential growth under reform scenarios

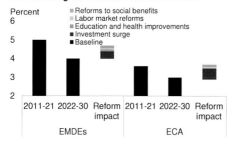

B. Climate change scenarios

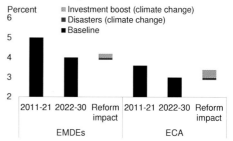

C. Share of firms reporting competition from informal firms as a constraint, 2019

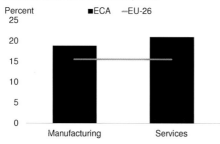

D. Poland: Ukrainian migrants and forcibly displaced people, through June 2022

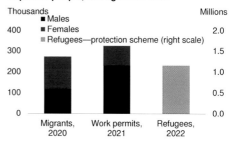

E. Impact on Central European potential growth from NGEU reforms and policy targets

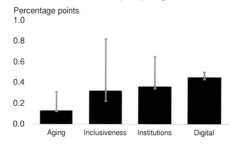

F. EBRD assessment of green transition, 2021

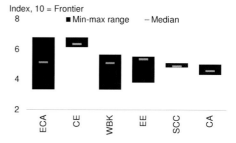

Sources: EBRD (2020, 2021); Haver Analytics; IMF; Oxford Economic Model; Penn World Table; UN High Commissioner for Refugees; UN, World Population Prospects; World Bank, Enterprise Surveys DataBank; World Bank, World Development Indicators database.
Note: Period averages of real averages weighted by gross domestic product (GDP). Data for 2022-30 are forecasts. CA = Central Asia; CE = Central Europe; ECA = Europe and Central Asia; EE = Eastern Europe; EMDEs = emerging market and developing economies; EU-26 = European Union member states excluding Germany; min-max = minimum-maximum; SCC = South Caucasus; WBK = Western Balkans.
A.B. Estimates of potential growth are based on production function approach. Sample includes 53 EMDEs. of which 9 are from ECA. Chapter 1 describes methodology and chapter 5 reform scenarios.
C. Panel shows percent of firms identifying practices of competitors in the informal sector as a major constraint. Data for the EU-26 country grouping and the euro area exclude Germany. Aggregates are calculated as averages.
D. "Refugees" indicates those registered for national protection schemes. Migrants indicate migrant stock in mid-2020.
E. Panel shows impact on potential output in Central Europe of NextGenerationEU (NGEU) reforms, as described in World Bank (2022k). Orange whiskers show min-max range. Sample includes Bulgaria, Poland, and Romania.
F. Panel shows scores for transition quality, which measures each economy's performance against that of comparator economies in European Bank for Reconstruction and Development (EBRD) regions, as presented in EBRD (2021). Scores range from 1 to 10 (10 = standards of a sustainable market economy).

with weak rule of law in many cases, increases the likelihood of an uneven playing field that puts the private sector at a disadvantage. Pervasive corruption and state capture likewise impose formidable constraints on the ability of private firms in ECA to invest and innovate. It is thus critical for ECA countries to strengthen institutional quality and ensure that the state promotes the efficient allocation of resources.

Among the most effective and ways of improving government efficiency, accountability, control of corruption, and delivery of services are digitalization and broader use of information technologies in the public sector (World Bank 2021i). Policies to enhance data transparency and security can also play an important role in strengthening institutions, including strengthening them by making governments more accountable, which in the long run should raise per capita incomes (Islam and Lederman 2020).

In the context of institutional reform, ECA governments have considerable scope to reform and even dismantle regulatory barriers to doing business and entrepreneurship. They should aim to ensure effective regulation that is conducive to the efficient working of competitive markets while addressing market failures (figure 2.10.C; Kilic Celik, Kose, and Ohnsorge 2020).

Lack of exposure to international competition—often the result of nontariff barriers and complex trade rules, as well as restrictive regulations governing product markets and services—remains a structural bottleneck to growth in the region, hindering the ability to raise exports as well as attract domestic and foreign investment. The Organisation for Economic Co-operation and Development's indicator of product market regulation shows conditions in ECA to be 30 percent more prohibitive than the EU average, with particular bottlenecks arising from high levels of public ownership and barriers to trade and investment (OECD 2022).

The invasion of Ukraine has put at risk decades of hard-won gains in regional trade and investment integration by fracturing critical trade routes, supply chains, and financial intermediation. This could result in less specialization, fewer economies of scale, less competition, and a slower spread of productivity-enhancing innovations.

Many ECA countries urgently need policies to tackle intensifying demographic pressures by raising labor force participation. These policies include measures that would help raise retirement ages toward EU levels and help align women's retirement ages with those for men. In most ECA countries, the average effective age for exiting the labor market remains below the EU average, with an earlier retirement age for women accounting for a large part of this gap. Over the next decade, average effective retirement ages are expected to increase in the EU to 65 years for men and women, but in most ECA countries they will remain below this level (European Commission 2021). In some cases, such as Poland, earlier reforms to increase the retirement age of women have been reversed, with current legislation in Poland setting retirement ages at 65 years for men and 60 years for women. But several economies (Bulgaria, Romania, and Türkiye) are planning pension reforms that will lift statutory retirement ages for men and women over the next decade or so.[16] These measures can be supplemented with others that increase the average effective age for exiting the labor market (Carone et al. 2016). For instance, broader labor market policies that are tailored to older workers, including measures that provide incentives for older workers to search for jobs, and support the retention of older workers, as well as increased investment in health care to promote healthier aging, can complement reforms to the age at which workers qualify for pension (Bodnár and Nerlich 2020).

Despite efforts to increase female labor force participation, women continue to make up a large share of the inactive population in both ECA and the EU.[17] Job training programs specifically for women, including vocational training, may boost female labor force participation. Such programs are especially urgent given low training participation in the region (Bandiera, Buehren, Burgess, et al. 2020).

Measures that support the integration of migrants from Ukraine could boost the labor force and consequently potential growth (figure 2.10.D; IMF 2022b; Strzelecki, Growiec, and Wyszyński 2020).

Active labor market policies, including measures that promote job search, training, and retraining, can address the skill-matching issues discussed earlier. Many of these policies should target lower-income and lower-skilled households, which are at highest risk for lost human potential. Digital infrastructure in schools needs urgent attention, while the rural-urban gap in education and challenges for inclusion (for example, for Roma in Romania) persist. Even Poland, which has the strongest learning outcomes among EU ECA countries, has significant regional disparities, with the share of 25- to 64-year-olds with tertiary education as low as 24 percent in some regions—less than half that in the Warsaw capital region (OECD 2021a). To address the harm the pandemic has caused and facilitate recovery of lost learning, potential measures could include high-quality school-based tutoring and enrichment programs targeting the most vulnerable students (Patrinos 2022).

For ECA's EU economies, the EU's National Recovery and Resilience Plans, funded by the largest financing package the EU has ever approved, provide a unique opportunity for a new wave of reforms to boost potential growth and accelerate its convergence with that in the EU (figure 2.10.E). These plans are intended to include policy measures and investments—including investments from NextGenerationEU, the EU's 800 billion euro program to support economic recovery from the COVID-19 pandemic. They aim to promote equitable recovery, indicating that some of the additional jobs could be created in lagging regions. If the additional jobs from these investments draw on the

---

[16] Increasing the female retirement age has been found to bolster female participation in such countries as Japan and Switzerland (Lalive and Staubli 2015).

[17] In Romania, women make up about three-quarters of the inactive population aged 25 to 59 years (among the highest shares in the EU), pointing to the need for further investment to expand access to child and elder care. The share of women in the inactive population aged 55 to 64 years is above the EU average in both Poland and Romania, partly reflecting lower legislated retirement ages and thus younger average effective exit ages.

inactive working-age population in lagging regions, the benefits could be substantial, with a 1 percent boost to the labor force by 2030 relative to the baseline projection.

Green transition will require policies to promote investment and structural change. An increase in green investment would likely boost potential growth, assuming cuts in other capital expenditures do not offset the increase. And if these investments involve technological innovation, thus lifting TFP, the boost to potential growth could be larger. The impact on growth of the green transition will depend on green fiscal and other complementary policies (World Bank 2022l). In Central Europe, green investments mapped out in the National Recovery and Resilience Plans are expected to lift potential growth over the next decade but will require private sector investment and participation to reach longer-term climate goals.[18] The EU's Economic and Investment Plan for the Western Balkans, aimed at fostering that region's integration with the EU, and convergence of its living standards with those in the EU, includes sizable funding for green transition—a key priority given that Western Balkan economies are among those in ECA farthest from the green transition frontier (figure 2.10.F).

The pandemic has highlighted the urgent need for reforms to promote the adoption of automation and digital technologies in ECA, given the wide digital gaps between the region and the EU and the region's persistent labor shortages. Policies to expand access to digital connectivity can raise productivity and potential output, including by helping to advance inclusion and catch up, institutional improvement, and green transition. Expanding broadband and mobile internet access would promote more equitable access for distance learning across income levels and facilitate remote working (Barrero et al. 2021; Morikawa 2021). In addition to its productivity-enhancing effects, wider internet access has been found to increase female labor force participation (Viollaz and Winkler 2020). ECA's EU countries should take full advantage of reforms funded through NextGenerationEU to foster the digital transition.

Policies to raise R&D spending have considerable potential in ECA, given that its levels are currently low and it is an important driver of TFP growth (Yuan et al. 2021). Raising R&D spending may be one of the most promising ways of speeding up the convergence of ECA's per capita incomes with those in the EU. Increasing R&D spending might improve digital connectivity and promote more inclusive growth. Smaller firms and lagging regions in ECA have much to gain from such innovation (Hallward-Driemeier et al. 2020).

---

[18] NextGenerationEU is expected to deliver a large boost to public investment, with the largest share of National Recovery and Resilience Plan spending allocated toward climate change-related investments (37 percent of such plans).

LATIN AMERICA
and the CARIBBEAN

The COVID-19 pandemic and the war in Ukraine have set back growth in LAC's potential output, exacerbating a trend that goes back two decades. Following a steep decline in 2020, investment largely recovered in 2021, but medium-term prospects for investment growth remain too modest for it to lift potential growth. This, together with sustained weakness in total factor productivity growth and slow growth of working-age populations, most notably in South America, suggests that growth in potential output will remain weak in the remainder of this decade. Reforms to boost labor force participation and improve education and health outcomes could help lift potential growth, but the most effective approach is likely to be addressing reforms that raise investment growth or boost productive efficiency. Investment in climate-related transition could also boost potential output growth in LAC.

Introduction

Prior to the pandemic-induced recession of 2020, output growth in LAC had already slowed sharply, from a high of 6.7 percent in 2010 to an annual average of less than 1 percent between 2015 and 2019, including a recession in 2016. This weakening of the region's growth was due to a combination of cyclical and structural factors, including lower global commodity prices and economic and political challenges in some of the region's largest economies. TFP growth slowed to a crawl in the prepandemic decade, turning negative in some years. Growth in potential output in LAC is also estimated to have declined in the 2010s and is the lowest among EMDE regions.

In 2020, LAC experienced the deepest pandemic-induced recession of any EMDE region, and several LAC countries were among those with the highest per capita death rates globally. Widespread disruptions to education and severe damage to public health set back human capital accumulation. Following a precipitous fall in 2020, investment largely recovered in 2021, but consensus forecasts suggest that investment growth will remain too low to lift growth in potential output significantly. The global supply shock from the war in Ukraine that began in February 2022 is also likely to reduce potential growth in LAC. The war's impacts on inflation and commodity markets have contributed to an extended period of macroeconomic instability, raising recession risks even as recovery from the 2020 recession remains incomplete (World Bank 2022b).

Note: Estimates using the production function approach are available for Argentina, Bolivia, Brazil, Chile, Colombia, Costa Rica, Dominican Republic, Ecuador, Guatemala, Honduras, Jamaica, Mexico, Nicaragua, Paraguay, Peru, and Uruguay.

Negative effects on investment due to tighter financial conditions are likely to outweigh any positive response to higher prices in regional commodity exporters.

The prospect of sustained weakness in TFP growth and deteriorating demographic conditions, most notably in South America, suggests that growth in potential output in the remainder of this decade will be roughly unchanged from its low levels in 2011-21. Policies to boost labor force participation and improve education and health outcomes could raise potential growth to some extent, but the most effective approach in LAC is likely to be reforms that increase investment growth or improve productive efficiency. Investment in climate-related transition could also boost growth in LAC, given the region's endowments of natural resources that are likely to be critical inputs to achieve such transition, such as lithium and copper.

Evolution and drivers of potential growth in LAC

During 2011-21, growth in potential output in LAC is estimated to have averaged about 2.2 percent a year, below the 2000-10 annual average of 2.7 percent (figure 2.11).[19] Shrinking contributions from the growth of TFP and labor account for the slowing of potential growth. The finding that potential growth declined is robust to the method of estimation.

Potential TFP growth in LAC, which has long been below that in other EMDE regions, slowed to virtually zero after peaking in 2007; potential TFP was essentially flat between 2015 and 2019. Weak investment growth, starting in the mid-2010s, held back the absorption of productivity-enhancing new technologies, with commodity-exporting economies struggling to adapt to falling commodity prices (OECD 2016). Worsening terms of trade, a consequence of the downturn in commodity prices, may also have dampened TFP growth in the region's commodity exporters by reducing spending on R&D and slowing innovation (Aslam et al. 2016). Evidence that improving terms of trade during 2001-07 explained more than one-quarter of average TFP growth in this period in Chile, Mexico, and Peru supports this hypothesis (Castillo and Rojas 2014). In keeping with anemic TFP growth and a severe cyclical downturn, per capita growth fell far below its estimated potential level of 1.2 percent per year during 2011-21, with actual per capita income growth registering only 0.4 percent per year.

Shortcomings in education and training have long dampened productivity growth in LAC. Although access to education has steadily risen in recent decades, the low quality of primary and secondary education, relative to international standards and that in countries with similar per capita incomes, has hindered productivity gains (OECD 2015; OECD, CAF, and ECLAC 2016; World Bank 2021a). Further, at the tertiary level, graduation rates are low, and quality appears to have suffered as demand has expanded rapidly (World Bank 2021e). Still-stringent labor and product market regulations and high levels of informality, as well as institutional weaknesses, reflected in

---

[19] For the period 2000-22, 20 LAC economies are included in the estimation, representing 99 percent of 2020 LAC GDP.

FIGURE 2.11 **LAC: Output growth and drivers of potential growth**

While much of the decline in output growth in Latin America and the Caribbean during the period 2011-21 was cyclical, drivers of potential growth also weakened markedly compared with those in 2000-10. Potential TFP growth slowed to near zero, while investment growth was anemic, in part reflecting much weaker terms of trade.

A. GDP growth

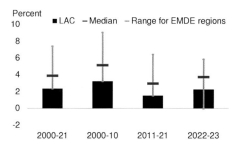

B. Potential GDP growth

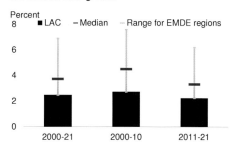

C. Potential growth by different measures

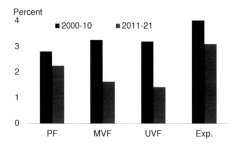

D. Potential TFP growth

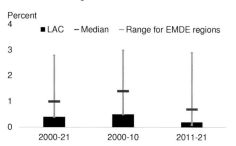

E. Investment growth and changes in terms of trade

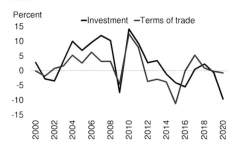

F. Investment growth

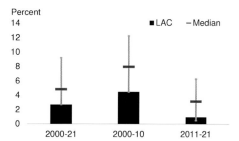

Sources: Haver Analytics; national statistical agencies; Penn World Table; UN, World Population Prospects; World Bank, World Development Indicators.

Note: Gross domestic product (GDP) weights are calculated using average real U.S. dollar GDP (at average 2010-19 prices and market exchange rates). Data for 2022-23 are forecasts. EMDEs = emerging market and developing economies; LAC = Latin America and the Caribbean; TFP = total factor productivity.

A.B.D.F. Bars show period averages of annual GDP-weighted averages. Horizontal lines show the median of GDP-weighted averages of the six EMDE regions; orange whiskers show minimum-maximum EMDE range (of which LAC is the minimum).

B. Estimates are based on production function approach.

C. Expectations-based estimates ("Exp.") are potential growth proxied by five-year-ahead IMF *World Economic Outlook* growth forecasts. Chapter 1 provides details on the approaches. Sample is a consistent set of 10 economies. MVF = multivariate filter; PF = production function approach; UVF = univariate filter (specifically, the Hodrick-Prescott filter).

D.F. Sample includes 53 EMDEs, of which 16 are LAC economies.

E. Panel shows investment-weighted average growth rates and GDP-weighted terms-of-trade changes. Sample includes 20 LAC economies.

such problems as elevated levels of wasteful government expenditure and corruption, further impede regional productivity growth (de Paulo, de Andrade Lima, and Tigre 2022; IDB 2018).

Numerous studies have documented that weak TFP growth has been the principal contributor to the region's low growth in potential output (Aravena, Friedman, and Hofman 2017; IMF 2017b; Loayza, Fajnzylber, and Calderón 2005; see also, for instance, Faal 2005 on Mexico and Ollivaud, Guillemette, and Turner 2016 on Chile). One study found that in the nearly half a century leading up to the financial crisis of 2008-09, relatively low TFP growth, rather than relatively weak capital accumulation or labor force growth, was the main factor contributing to the widening income gap between most LAC countries and the United States (Daude and Fernández-Arias 2010).[20]

The contribution of labor force growth to LAC's growth in potential output has declined substantially since the early 2000s, mainly owing to falling population growth. Growth of the working-age population fell to an average of 1.3 percent a year in 2011-21 from 1.8 percent a year in 2000-10 in spite of a marginal rise in the working-age share of the population. Labor's contribution to growth has declined even though female labor force participation has risen more than in other EMDE regions. It increased by approximately 10 percentage points between the mid-1990s and 2019, reaching nearly 60 percent.

The growth of fixed-capital investment in LAC over 2000-21 broadly followed the contours of movements in commodity prices and the region's terms of trade. Investment growth was weak in the early 2000s, stronger in the decade 2003-13 (except for the period of the global financial crisis), and weaker again in 2014-19, contracting by 1.3 percent a year on average. It then collapsed more than 11 percent in the 2020 recession, followed by a rebound in 2021 amid sharply rising commodity prices. In 2011-21, investment grew at an average rate of just 1 percent a year, well below the 2000-10 annual average of 4.5 percent. Although the deterioration in the region's terms of trade was a key factor underlying much of the investment decline prior to the pandemic, policy uncertainty and bouts of tightening financial conditions were also important (chapter 4; IMF 2015; World Bank 2016, 2017d). In some commodity-exporting countries, procyclical effects on fiscal revenues and public capital expenditures augmented the role of commodity price movements.

Among LAC's three subregions, the largest in economic size, South America, predominantly accounted for the slowing of potential growth between 2000-10 and 2011-21. About half of the countries in South America experienced a slowdown in potential growth during that period, including the largest two economies, Argentina and

---

[20] Another study applying growth accounting to data from 1820 onward found that over nearly 200 years, among nine LAC countries, only Chile narrowed the differential in per capita income between itself and the United States (Hofman and Valderrama 2020).

FIGURE 2.12 **LAC: Growth in potential output**

Slowing growth of the working population and potential TFP weakened growth in potential output in South America in 2011-21, relative to 2000-10. In Central America and Mexico, weaker potential growth in 2011-21 reflected demographics and capital accumulation. In the Caribbean, growth in potential output rose. Outsized pandemic-related school closures in LAC have damaged human capital accumulation.

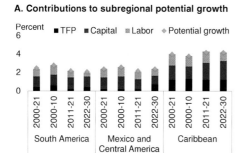

A. Contributions to subregional potential growth

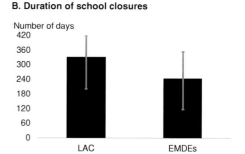

B. Duration of school closures

Sources: Hale et al. (2021); Haver Analytics; Penn World Table; UN, World Population Prospects; World Bank.
Note: Gross domestic product (GDP) weights are calculated using average real U.S. dollar GDP (at average 2010-19 prices and market exchange rates) for the period 2011-19. Data for 2022-30 are forecasts. EMDEs = emerging market and developing economies; LAC = Latin America and the Caribbean; TFP = total factor productivity.
A. Period averages of annual GDP-weighted averages. Estimates of potential growth are based on production function approach. South America includes nine economies (Argentina, Brazil, Bolivia, Chile, Colombia, Ecuador, Paraguay, Peru, and Uruguay), Mexico and Central America includes five economies (Costa Rica, Guatemala, Honduras, Mexico, and Nicaragua), and Caribbean includes two economies (Dominican Republic and Jamaica).
B. Simple averages. Orange whiskers are interquartile range. Sample includes 137 EMDEs (33 from LAC).

Brazil (figure 2.12). Although the contribution to potential growth from TFP in Mexico and Central America remained lower than that in other LAC subregions, at just 0.2 percentage point a year during 2011-21, this subregion avoided the slowdown in potential TFP growth that afflicted South America and other EMDEs. TFP growth contributed more to potential growth in the Caribbean than in the other subregions but still slowed between 2000-10 and 2011-21. Increasing contributions from labor force growth and capital accumulation offset this slowdown, however, so that the Caribbean was the only LAC subregion where potential growth increased in 2011-21, relative to 2000-10.

The pandemic-induced recession of 2020, which was deeper in LAC than in any other EMDE region, and its aftereffects, have eroded potential growth further. Although total investment largely recovered to its long-term trend in 2021, inward foreign direct investment (FDI) is estimated to have fallen more sharply in 2020 and not to have recovered to its prepandemic level in 2021 (UNCTAD 2022). This fall in inward FDI may imply less transfer of productivity-enhancing knowledge and technology (Bruhn, Calegario, and Mendonca 2020). Perhaps even more significant, LAC saw the longest school closures among EMDEs, holding back the development of human capital in young people. In March 2021, it was estimated that the number of secondary school children in LAC unable to read a basic text might have increased by more than 15 percent (World Bank 2021a). Such learning losses, if not remediated promptly, are likely to lower labor productivity and lifetime incomes for the current school-age generation (Werner, Komatsuzaki, and Pizzinelli 2021). To the extent that they compromise social mobility, such losses can also compound over generations (Hill and Narayan 2020).

Prospects for potential growth in LAC

In the rest of the 2020s, growth in potential output in LAC appears likely to stagnate at low levels, with no improvement in South America and a slight pickup in Mexico and Central America offset by a modest slowdown in the Caribbean. Labor force growth seems likely to continue to decline. Investment growth is expected to improve somewhat on average, but not markedly, and only after further near-term weakness. TFP is expected to regain some momentum from its near-zero growth rate in 2011-19, but only enough to offset the effects of slowing labor force growth. Thus, without significant policy action or a major productivity breakthrough, potential growth in LAC is expected to remain at 2.2 percent a year in 2022-30, identical to that during the period 2011-21 and the lowest rate among all EMDE regions (figure 2.13).[21]

Not only will a falling working-age population share (expected to soon peak) constrain the contribution of labor force growth to growth in potential output in 2022-30, but so will limited potential for additional gains in already-high female labor force participation rates. With the contribution from labor force growth shrinking, potential growth is expected to sustain itself, as a result of a slight increase in per capita potential growth in 2022-30, to 1.6 percent. A modest projected pickup in potential TFP growth, expected to contribute about 0.5 percentage point a year to potential growth, will underpin improved per capita potential growth. This estimate takes into account the past relationships in LAC between investment growth and TFP growth and between rising commodity prices and investment growth. However, no simple mapping can be assumed between commodity-related investment and productivity improvements, especially given the potential for expansion of exports of primary commodities to crowd out manufacturing and compromise the competitiveness of other sectors (Alvarado, Iniguez, and Ponce 2017).

The war in Ukraine is expected to have largely negative effects on growth in potential output in LAC (World Bank 2022c). It has already contributed to tighter financial conditions, through both confidence and monetary policy channels. By driving commodity prices higher, the war has further increased already-elevated inflation in LAC and advanced economies, contributing to larger interest rate increases as central banks sharply tightened rates to ensure inflation expectations remained anchored. Elevated geopolitical uncertainty brought on by the war has also soured global risk appetite, which is likely to curb investment in many EMDEs, including those in LAC. The combination of a sharp rise in global interest rates and faltering investor confidence

---

[21] For the period 2022-30, 16 LAC economies are included in estimations, representing 97 percent of 2020 LAC GDP.

FIGURE 2.13 **LAC: Prospects for potential growth**

Growth in potential output is expected to stagnate in Latin America and the Caribbean in 2022-30 as declines in the Caribbean and South America offset modest improvements in Central America and Mexico. Slowing labor force growth is the primary reason potential growth is not expected to improve, with per capita potential growth projected to increase marginally. In contrast to EMDEs as a whole, LAC economies are expected to see a small improvement in potential TFP growth.

A. Potential growth

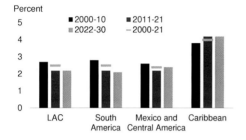

B. Potential growth per capita

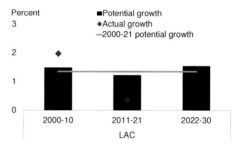

C. Working-age population in LAC

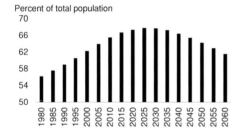

D. Contributions to potential growth

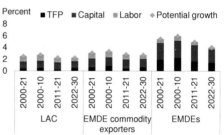

Sources: Haver Analytics; Penn World Table; UN, World Population Prospects; World Bank.
Note: Gross domestic product (GDP) weights are calculated using average real U.S. dollar GDP (at average 2010-19 prices and market exchange rates) for the period 2011-19. Data for 2022-30 are forecasts. EMDEs = emerging market and developing economies; LAC = Latin America and the Caribbean; TFP = total factor productivity.
A.D. Period averages of annual GDP-weighted averages. Estimates are based on production function approach.
A. LAC subregions are as in figure 2.12.
C. Projections are based on median fertility and mortality scenario, and medium international migration, per the definition of projection scenarios in the *World Population Prospects,* published by the United Nations Department of Economic and Social Affairs.
D. Sample includes 53 EMDEs, of which 16 are from LAC, and 30 commodity exporters.

could precipitate financial crises in some EMDEs, including vulnerable countries in LAC, possibly resulting in large permanent output losses (Kose et al. 2021). A sustained war and secular rise in geopolitical uncertainty could also further fracture global trade and financial networks, which could raise trade costs, shrink markets, and slow the dissemination of technological innovation (Guénette, Kenworthy, and Wheeler 2022).

However, the war could also have some partially offsetting effects that benefit potential growth in LAC. Concerns about the resilience of geographically dispersed manufacturing supply chains could bolster manufacturing investment in some LAC economies (so-called near-shoring). Heightened awareness of vulnerabilities related to dependence on fossil fuels and concentration of suppliers could also raise investment in the region's extractive industries. LAC is endowed with minerals and metals that are important inputs for electrification and the manufacture of renewable-energy technologies, demand for which could accelerate given heightened focus on energy security globally (World Bank 2022c). The region also offers potential alternative sources of oil and gas supply while the world is transitioning to clean energy. Capturing enduring productivity benefits from such resource-related tailwinds will likely depend on policy makers' harnessing increased commodity earnings to fund sustainable infrastructure and enact health, education, and governance reforms.

Policy options to lift potential growth in LAC

In a scenario in which each country in LAC repeats its largest 10-year improvements during 2000-21 in education outcomes, life expectancy, and female labor force participation, and labor force participation among older workers rises modestly as a result of reforms to social benefits, it is estimated that average annual growth in potential output in the region in 2022-30 could increase by about 0.2 percentage point (figure 2.14).

A sustained investment boom could offer greater benefits in regard to potential growth. Raising investment growth over 2022-30 by its largest previous 10-year increase (per country between 2000 and 2021) could increase potential growth by an average of about 0.3 percentage point a year, via capital accumulation and improved potential TFP growth. Structural reforms to increase domestic savings and boost returns to private investment (for example, via improvements in competitiveness, infrastructure, and the diffusion of new technologies), rather than a transitory rise in commodity prices, as was often the case in the past, would need to underpin an investment boom in order for it to be durable. Indeed, past analyses highlight the risks for LAC countries of conflating several years of higher commodity rents with improvements in potential output (Alberola et al. 2016).

An investment drive focused purely on meeting the climate change-linked elements of the region's infrastructure-related Sustainable Development Goals (SDGs) by 2030 could also materially benefit growth in potential output. It is estimated that investments to address climate change could raise LAC's annual potential growth by 0.1 percentage point. More climate-resilient infrastructure could also help mitigate a possible climate change-related reduction of 0.1 percentage point in annual potential growth resulting from increasingly frequent extreme weather events that damage capital stocks and erode labor productivity (OECD 2018). But the potential benefits of climate-smart investment go beyond mitigating bad outcomes. Many investments needed to help boost productivity directly can also aid climate change adaptation or mitigation. For example, more efficient irrigation systems would raise agricultural productivity as a first-order consequence but also increase the sector's climate resilience (World Bank 2022c). Increasing the contribution of renewables to the energy mix could also dampen an important source of volatility in the terms of trade of the region's energy importers, which could reduce the volatility of their growth. LAC may be the EMDE region best

FIGURE 2.14 **LAC: Policies to raise growth in potential output**

Improvements in education, health care, and female labor force participation, as well as reforms to social benefits, could boost potential growth in LAC. However, greater investment is likely to deliver the largest gains. Rigid labor markets and limited investment in innovation generally hamper LAC more than they do other EMDE regions. In the public sector, policy making could become more transparent, while cuts in unproductive spending could free up resources for investment.

A. Potential growth under reform scenarios

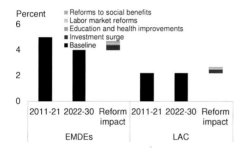

B. Effects of infrastructure investment and climate disasters on potential growth

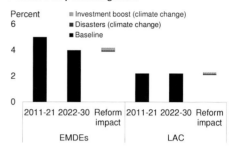

C. Labor market flexibility

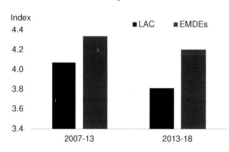

D. Government consumption

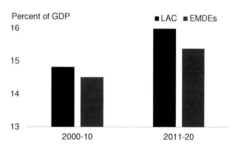

E. Research and development

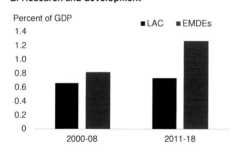

F. Transparency of policy making

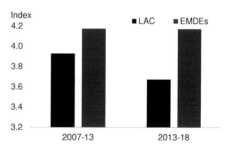

Sources: Haver Analytics; Penn World Table; UN, World Population Prospects; World Bank; World Economic Forum, Global Competitiveness Index.

Note: Gross domestic product (GDP) weights are calculated using average real U.S. dollar GDP (at average 2010-19 prices and market exchange rates). Data for 2022-30 are forecasts. EMDEs = emerging market and developing economies; LAC = Latin America and the Caribbean.

A.B. Period averages of annual GDP-weighted averages. Estimates of potential growth are based on production function approach. Sample includes 53 EMDEs (16 from LAC). Chapter 1 describes methodology and chapter 5 reform scenarios.

C.-F. Cross-period simple averages of annual GDP-weighted averages. Samples include, for panel C, 112 EMDEs (23 from LAC); for panel D, 53 EMDEs (11 from LAC); for panel E, 101 EMDEs (18 from LAC); for panel F, 112 EMDEs (23 from LAC).

positioned to rapidly achieve the infrastructure- and climate-related SDGs because its existing energy mix is comparatively green (largely on account of hydropower). This implies a smaller marginal investment requirement.

Most of the positive growth effects of the reforms assumed in the scenarios result from higher investment. Limited fiscal space, however, tends to constrain public investment in LAC (Vashakmadze et al. 2017). In such circumstances, curtailing unproductive public spending to increase space for productive investment or increasing the efficiency of public investment (for example, through additional use of public-private partnerships) could improve the quality of infrastructure, while avoiding potential distortions from increased taxation (IDB 2018). Improvements in transportation infrastructure could be especially effective in raising productivity in the region's urban environments, which show little evidence of positive agglomeration effects, in contrast to those in advanced economies. High and increasing costs from congestion in many of the region's largest cities may lie behind this apparent lack of returns to urban scale (Ferreyra and Roberts 2018). Meanwhile, improving telecommunications infrastructure, which is relatively cheap compared with meeting gaps in infrastructure investment in other sectors, could help accelerate the adoption of new information and communications technologies in ways that could both raise firm productivity and result in more inclusive growth (Brichetti et al. 2021; Dutz, Alemida, and Packard 2018).

Gains from the reforms assumed in the scenarios will vary among countries depending on the countries' specific characteristics and circumstances. Mexico and several other Central American economies, for instance, have rates of female labor force participation well below those for males. Measures to improve access to childcare and parental leave have been found to raise female labor force participation in LAC (Novta and Wong 2017). Moreover, since Central American economies have some of the highest child dependency ratios and worst education attainment records in LAC, this subregion would likely benefit significantly from investments in education and health care. In many countries in the region, as in other parts of the world, students from the poorest households have been found to be substantially less competent in reading and mathematics than those from the richest households (World Bank 2018a). The COVID-19 pandemic is likely to have further exacerbated these inequalities, given that learning losses have been acute among children from low-income families with less access to distance learning (World Bank 2022h). Improving skills absorption by poor students may therefore have outsized positive effects on future productivity, which could help mitigate some of the inequality-increasing consequences of pandemic-related learning losses.

Reforms in several areas beyond the scope of the scenario analysis could also boost growth in potential output by raising productivity growth. Labor markets in LAC have long been less flexible than those in other EMDE regions. Reforms to deregulate labor markets, including those regarding inflexible wage-setting processes, hiring and firing constraints, and aligning compensation with productivity, would likely pay productivity dividends. Improving educational quality could raise productivity generally; there is evidence of positive growth externalities from higher skill levels in Latin America (Ferreyra et al. 2017; Ferreyra and Roberts 2018). LAC has relatively high enrollment rates in tertiary education, which many countries in the region subsidize heavily, yet a larger proportion of firms in LAC cite skills shortages as their biggest obstacle than in the average EMDE. This may reflect the distribution of subjects studied (the relative paucity of science, technology, engineering, and mathematics majors), low graduation rates, and inadequate accountability in the university sector (World Bank 2021m). Beyond traditional education, active labor market policies to encourage the reskilling and reabsorption of workers could help mitigate a long-term trend in LAC of workers that are displaced out of high-productivity industries transitioning into lower-productivity work, thereby constraining overall labor productivity growth (Dieppe 2021).

Addressing the challenges associated with widespread informality could lift productivity (La Porta and Shleifer 2014; Ohnsorge and Yu 2021). Indeed, research has found that a drop of 1 percentage point in the informal share of the LAC economy has been associated with a 0.5 percentage-point narrowing of the gap in TFP between LAC and the United States (IDB 2013). Together with better-functioning labor markets, policy interventions that simplify business licensing and tax procedures and increase access to social security systems would also help reduce informality (Garcia-Saltos, Teodoru, and Zhang 2016; OECD 2017). At the same time, policy makers should be wary of tax and regulatory schemes that inadvertently encourage firms to stay small. Larger firms can, for example, face higher effective tax rates, which may discourage expansion. Meanwhile, schemes that favor smaller firms may result in excessive capital allocation to low-growth businesses. These factors may contribute to persistently low TFP growth (IDB 2018).

In addition, LAC has important opportunities to spur innovation, which underperforms that in other EMDE regions (World Economic Forum 2017). For example, policy-led efforts to ensure the education system encourages innovation: promote collaboration among firms, universities, and research institutes; and increase access to finance for innovation could all be beneficial (Vostroknutova et al. 2015). Creating incentives for firms to invest in internal research and development may boost productivity. Latin American firms that invest in R&D have been found to be better able to produce product innovations than those that do not, and firms that innovate are found to have significantly higher labor productivity (Crespi, Tacsir, and Vargas 2016). Creating incentives for R&D or funding more of it from government budgets may be a worthy use of scarce fiscal space given evidence of large paybacks and given that R&D spending in LAC is below EMDE averages and has fallen further behind in recent years (World Bank 2021m). It is also important to recognize the merits of scale regarding R&D investment. Multiple studies have documented that size is one of the best predictors of R&D spending by firms in the region (for example, Alvarez and Grazzi 2018).

There are further productivity gains to be made from deepening trade integration. Despite several extra- and intraregional trade agreements, LAC is less open to trade than most other EMDE regions (World Bank 2016). International linkages and integration into global value chains have been shown to increase firm productivity, but even the LAC economies most integrated into global value chains are not highly integrated by global standards (Dieppe 2021; Montalbano, Nenci, and Pietrobelli 2016; Steinwender and Shu 2018). LAC also has relatively low intraregional trade intensity, partly because of sparse regional road and rail networks and mediocre logistical services. Improved physical networks, streamlined customs procedures, and other domestic trade facilitation measures could substantially reduce trade costs (World Bank 2021h). Reduced trade costs for manufacturing and services firms could help foster greater export diversification in LAC, where exports of primary commodities tend to dominate. While greater diversification is not in itself a driver of productivity, it is likely to reduce output volatility, which is associated with stronger growth (Acharya and Raju 2020). Formal trade agreements could have greater impact through the inclusion of measures to harmonize regional standards and liberalize restrictions related to rules of origin (OECD, CAF, and ECLAC 2018). Increased trade integration could lift productivity across sectors in LAC by increasing competition and by providing opportunities for firms to specialize and take advantage of economies of scale. In the medium to long term, increased trade linkages could facilitate knowledge and technology transfer (Bown et al. 2017).

Many long-term productivity challenges in LAC can also be considered through the lens of low trust and related institutional weaknesses or poor governance. There is evidence that low trust feeds into institutional shortcomings and is associated with lower productivity and growth (Keefer and Scartascini 2022). Low trust in government may curtail the extent to which the public sector can effectively step in to correct market failures and address externalities. Weaknesses in judicial and legal processes may undermine the enforcement of contracts, discouraging investment, while high levels of violence in some countries in the region are an ongoing challenge for the building of stronger business environments. A lack of transparency in policy making may lead to perceptions that policy making is capricious or not geared to the public benefit. Entrenched social perceptions about trust and institutional integrity can take time to shift. Nonetheless, even modest additional commitments to increasing transparency and data availability could help to build trust in public authorities and public policy, while narrowing the scope for corruption and the erosion of institutional norms (Scartascini and Valle Luna 2020).

Growth in potential output in the Middle East and North Africa is estimated to have halved between the 2000s and 2010s owing to a broad-based slowing of capital accumulation, total factor productivity growth (in economies dominated by extractive sectors and large public sectors), and labor force growth. Potential growth in the region is projected to remain lackluster in the remainder of this decade, with a further decline in the contribution of labor force growth to growth in potential output offsetting an anemic improvement in total factor productivity growth. Reversing the slowdown in potential growth requires urgent reforms to kindle private-sector-led growth.

Introduction

GDP growth has been uneven over the past two decades in MNA. Growth was relatively rapid during the 2000s, supported by rising oil prices (figure 2.15). But it slowed in the 2010s, mainly owing to the effects of political turmoil, most notably the 2011 Arab Spring revolutions in the Arab Republic of Egypt, Libya, Tunisia, and the Republic of Yemen; military conflicts in Iraq and the Syrian Arab Republic; the broader war on the Islamic State of Iraq and al-Sham (ISIS); the collapse in oil prices in 2014-16; and effects of the COVID-19 pandemic at the end of the period (Ianchovichina 2017). In 2022, growth suffered further from Russia's invasion of Ukraine and its repercussions.

This section estimates growth in potential output for five countries in MNA, accounting for almost half of the region's GDP. The estimates indicate that potential growth in the region halved between the 2000s and 2010s, with the slowdown driven by broad-based decelerations in capital stock, in total factor productivity (in economies dominated by extractive sectors and large public sectors), and in working-age populations. The pandemic has further damaged these drivers. In 2020, the region's output contracted by 3.6 percent, mainly reflecting pandemic-related mobility restrictions on activity and a collapse in oil prices. The growth rebound in 2021 was insufficient to reverse the decline in output. Investment collapsed by more than 6 percent in 2020 and rebounded by only 5.3 percent in 2021. Human capital accumulation also suffered, with an average of about 8 percent of working hours lost in 2020-21, higher than the global average.

Note: Estimates using the production function approach are available for Egypt, the Islamic Republic of Iran, Jordan, Morocco, and Tunisia.

FIGURE 2.15 MNA: Output growth and drivers of potential growth

Output growth in the MNA region was markedly weaker in the past decade than in the preceding one, as political instability, a collapse in oil prices, low investment, conflict, and the pandemic all buffeted the region. These developments, along with a significant slowdown in growth of the working-age population, also affected potential growth. Political stability has remained below the average in emerging and developing economies and weaker among oil-importing economies since the 2011 Arab Spring.

A. GDP growth

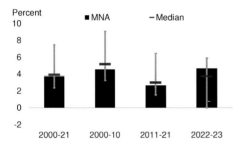

B. Contributions to growth in potential output

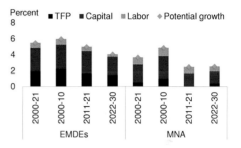

C. Working-age population growth

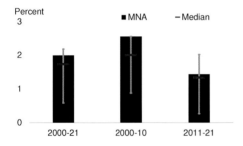

D. Political stability

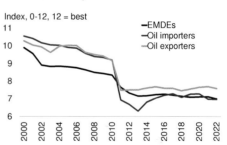

Sources: International Monetary Fund; Penn World Table; PRS Group; UN, World Population Prospects; World Bank.
Note: Gross domestic product (GDP) weights are calculated using average real U.S. dollar GDP (at average 2010-19 prices and market exchange rates). Data for 2022-23 and 2022-30 are forecasts. EMDEs = emerging market and developing economies; MNA = Middle East and North Africa; TFP = total factor productivity.
A.C. Bars show period averages of annual GDP-weighted averages. Horizontal lines show median GDP-weighted averages of the six EMDE regions; orange whiskers show maximum-minimum ranges.
B. Period averages of annual GDP-weighted averages. Estimates are based on the production function approach. Sample includes 53 EMDEs, of which 5 are from MNA.
C. Working-age population refers to population aged 15-64. Sample includes 53 EMDEs (5 from MNA).
D. Based on the government stability subindex of the *International Country Risk Guide*. Unweighted average for 10 MNA oil exporters, 6 MNA oil importers, and 102 EMDEs.

Growth in potential output in the region is projected to remain lackluster in the remainder of this decade, at 2.5 percent a year on average. An anemic improvement in TFP growth and stronger investment are expected to offset a reduction in the contribution of labor to potential growth. Fixed-capital accumulation is expected to account for almost two-thirds of growth in potential output, with investment growth projected to be significantly stronger than in the 2010s, when it was negative half of the time. Human capital accumulation is projected to slow owing to weaker growth in the working-age population.

Reversing the slowdown in potential growth since the 2000s requires urgent reforms to kindle private-sector-led growth and diversify economies. Most of the region's growth since the 1970s has relied on growth of employment rather than of productivity, as well as the expansion of public sectors (ILO 2022a). This has left the region with a multitude of structural challenges, including large gender gaps in the workforce and education attainment, limited economic diversification, excessive state involvement in activity, armed conflicts, weak governance, and macroeconomic instability. Policy action to address these challenges could significantly boost growth in both potential and actual output. Thus, reprioritizing public spending, ensuring a green transition while mitigating the effects of climate change, and enabling and providing incentives for the private sector could increase investment. Increasing access to education and work for women and the poor, improving worker skills, upgrading health systems, and reversing income losses caused by the pandemic could raise human capital accumulation.

Evolution and drivers of potential growth in MNA

Output growth in the MNA region declined sharply from an average of 4.5 percent a year in the 2000s to about 2.6 percent a year in the 2010s. Analysis suggests that the slowdown was largely the result of a decline in the region's rate of potential growth. Several approaches to estimating potential growth—through estimation of a production function and the use of filters or data for long-term (five-year-ahead) growth expectations to identify trends—indicate that potential growth in the 2010s was lower than that in the 2000s (figure 2.16). Based on the production function approach, potential growth is estimated to have slowed from 4.8 percent a year in the 2000s to 2.4 percent a year in the 2010s. On a per capita basis, the slowdown was even starker, from 3.4 percent in the 2000s to 0.8 percent in the 2010s. Although the literature on the subject is sparse, it supports this result, documenting a broad-based decline in potential growth since 2000 in the MNA region, in both oil exporters and oil importers. The literature also supports the finding that the decline has been more severe than that for EMDEs in aggregate (Alkhareif, Barnett, and Alsadoun 2017; IMF 2016, 2017a; Mitra et al. 2015).

The decline in potential growth in MNA in the past decade had several contributory factors, including high geopolitical tensions, volatile oil prices, limited economic diversification in many MNA countries, a predominant role of the state in many cases, and armed conflicts within the region. In terms of the production function framework, all major components of growth in potential output—labor force growth, capital accumulation, and TFP growth—slowed between the 2000s and 2010s, with more than half of the slowdown in potential growth attributable to slower growth of the capital stock. Investment growth slowed from an annual average of about 9 percent in the 2000s to less than 1 percent a year on average in the 2010s. Among oil exporters, the collapse in oil prices in 2014-16 depressed investment growth, while in several oil importers, increased political and economic uncertainty took its toll. Countries afflicted by conflict or fragility suffered the outright destruction of capital (World Bank 2017e).

FIGURE 2.16 **MNA: Growth in potential output**

After halving between 2000-10 and 2011-21, growth in potential output in the MNA region is expected to remain weak in the remainder of this decade. The slowdown in the past decade is a finding common to different methods of estimating potential growth. Real investment growth has been volatile and was negative in six of the years during 2009-21. Female labor force participation remains about one-fifth, significantly lower than in other emerging market and developing economy regions.

A. Growth in potential output

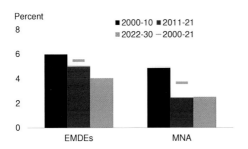

B. Growth in potential output by different estimates

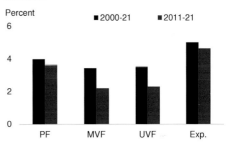

C. Investment growth

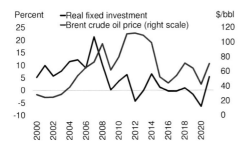

D. Female labor force participation

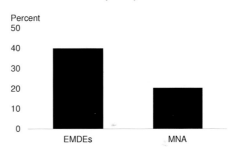

Sources: International Monetary Fund; Penn World Table; UN, World Population Prospects; World Bank.
Note: Gross domestic product (GDP) weights are calculated using average real U.S. dollar GDP (at average 2010-19 prices and market exchange rates). EMDEs = emerging market and developing economies; MNA = Middle East and North Africa.
A.B. Period averages of annual GDP-weighted averages.
A. Estimates are based on the production function approach. Sample includes 53 EMDEs, of which 5 are from the MNA region. Data for 2022-30 are forecasts.
B. Expectations-based estimates ("Exp.") are potential growth proxied by five-year-ahead IMF *World Economic Outlook* growth forecasts. Chapter 1 provides details on the approaches. Sample includes three economies (Jordan, Morocco, and Tunisia). MVF = multivariate filter; PF = production function approach; UVF = univariate filter (specifically, the Hodrick-Prescott filter).
C. Based on growth rate of real fixed investment and Brent crude oil price. bbl = barrel.
D. Based on female labor force as a percentage of total labor force. Sample includes 155 EMDEs (19 from MNA) from 2012 to 2021.

The second-largest contributor to the slowdown in growth in potential output in MNA was a decline in TFP growth, which turned close to zero in the 2010s. This decline widened the gap in productivity between the region and advanced economies (Dieppe 2021). One source of the decline in TFP growth was the weakening of investment growth. Prior to the 2009 Great Recession, capital accumulation in oil-exporting economies primarily supported productivity growth in MNA. But this ended with the collapse of oil prices in 2014-16. Other factors limiting TFP growth were the dominance of commodity production sectors, inefficient investment, weak competition due to the large role of the state, and armed conflicts.

In the past decade, the contribution of labor force growth to growth in potential output declined mainly because of a precipitous slowdown in population growth, particularly in the member countries of the Gulf Cooperation Council (GCC). Labor force participation rates also declined, particularly among oil importers. The region's female labor force participation rates, which are among the lowest in the world, also held back the contribution of labor force growth to potential growth. For example, women make up just under four-tenths, on average, of the populations of GCC economies and yet represent only about one-tenth of the labor force. Moreover, while educational attainment among both men and women improved in the past decade, the quality of education, as measured, for example, by primary school proficiency tests, remained lower than that in most other regions (World Bank 2018b).

The pandemic did further damage to the drivers of potential growth. Fixed investment in 2021 was more than 10 percent lower than was expected prior to the pandemic, with negative and long-lasting consequences for the growth of the capital stock. Higher long-term unemployment, disruptions to education, and a deterioration of health outcomes have also eroded human capital. Pandemic-related school closures since 2020 have averaged 48 weeks in MNA, above the global average of 38 weeks. This outsized damage to human capital accumulation is likely to have undermined poverty reduction efforts and impaired the lifetime earnings of many (Azevedo, Hasan, et al. 2021).

Prospects for potential growth in MNA

Over the 2020s, growth in potential output in MNA is expected to remain weak, at 2.5 percent a year, only marginally above its average annual rate in the 2010s of 2.4 percent. Per capita potential growth is expected to increase to 1.3 percent from 0.8 percent in the 2010s. This mainly reflects a tepid improvement in TFP growth, which is expected to offset a further projected decline in the contribution of labor force growth, in part as a result of projected changes in demographic structures. Population growth is expected to slow to 1.3 percent a year on average, down from growth of close to 3 percent a year on average in the two decades before the pandemic. The working-age share of the population is expected to rebound to its 2013 peak, after a decade of decline.

Recent progress in structural reforms, particularly in the GCC economies, is underpinning the outlook for potential growth. These reforms include increased participation of women in the workforce, improvements in the business climate, and diversification of the economies of commodity-dependent countries. Outside the GCC economies, however, reform momentum has remained lackluster.

In Saudi Arabia, increasing female labor force participation and reforms to the Kafala sponsorship program for expatriate workers have created a strong foundation for improving potential productivity growth, particularly by improving skill matchings and disseminating new knowledge. Female labor force participation increased from 18.7 percent in the second quarter of 2017 to 33.4 percent in the first quarter of 2022, with about 350,000 women having entered employment over this period. Investment should benefit from the 2021 National Investment Strategy, which aims to expand the role of the private sector and increase foreign direct investment. The government has also undertaken reforms to improve the regulation and supervision of financial institutions (such as the laws on the resolution of systemically important financial institutions and on strengthening anti-money laundering and combating the financing of terrorism) and the functioning and liquidity of debt and equity markets (IMF 2021d). Saudi Arabia has also introduced value-added taxes to promote the diversification of its economy and improve revenue mobilization—part of a broader GCC initiative, with implementation also in Bahrain, Oman, and the United Arab Emirates. Such broadening of the tax base can help ensure fiscal sustainability, make fiscal policy less procyclical, and increase funding for productivity-enhancing investments.

The United Arab Emirates has also taken steps to encourage greater inclusion of women in the workforce, strengthen working arrangements for expatriates, and improve the business climate more broadly. In the wake of reforms, female labor force participation rates increased by about 15 percentage points in the five years to 2020, reaching 66 percent. In the labor market, the government in 2021 passed a new labor law that standardizes employment contracts, caps working hours, and aligns weekends with those in key trading partners. To diversify its economy, it recently introduced a 9 percent corporate income tax and value-added tax. To attract further foreign investment, a new commercial law allows full foreign ownership of companies, while a simplified trademarks law improves protection for existing trademarks. The United Arab Emirates has made progress in diversifying its economy. For example, oil revenues fell from 69 percent of total government revenues to just 41 percent over the decade to 2020.

In Egypt, the implementation of macroeconomic stabilization policies and structural reforms since 2016 helped to raise potential growth by more than 1.3 percentage points in 2021 from its trough in 2014. Macroeconomic stabilization measures have included the liberalization of the exchange rate regime and devaluation of the pound, as well as fiscal measures to stabilize public debt, including the introduction of a value-added tax, reductions in energy subsidies, and actions to mobilize revenue and decrease expenditure. Structural reforms have targeted business licensing and insolvency and have also included labor market reforms focused on women and youth. In response to these measures, the unemployment rate has dropped to its lowest level in nearly two decades, with increasing labor force participation rates. More recently the private sector has benefited from legal reforms that allow it to participate in infrastructure, services, and public utility projects.

In the Islamic Republic of Iran, the 2022 budget announced efforts to cap subsidies on imports of basic goods, impose a tax on gasoline and petroleum, and sell state assets. Legal changes to the power of the central bank also assisted in achieving financial stability objectives. But further structural reforms are needed to address widespread inefficiencies, stabilize fiscal spending and lower inflation, and remove significant price distortions. Implicit subsidies, mainly in the energy sector, recently accounted for more than 45 percent of GDP (World Bank 2021j).

The projections of potential growth in MNA are highly uncertain. There are some upside risks to the baseline projections. The region's relatively low female labor force participation and exceptionally high share of youth in the population (people younger than 25 years account for one-third of the population) indicate a large pool of potential new entrants to the labor market and consumer base. This, in turn, could substantially increase returns to investment and innovation, but this increase will hinge on whether the private sector is sufficiently vibrant and able to draw on a well-educated workforce in flexible labor markets.

Risks to the baseline projections of potential growth, however, remain predominantly to the downside. While the war in Ukraine has provided a massive windfall to oil exporters, the longer-term benefits of this windfall depend on whether it is funneled into financing reforms and diversifying economies. For oil-importing economies in the region, the war in Ukraine may undermine longer-term growth prospects by raising the risk of social unrest and conflict, counteracting human capital gains through malnourishment and increased poverty, and increasing the likelihood of financial and balance of payments crises (Dieppe 2021; Hadzi-Vaskov, Pienknagura, and Ricci 2021; Kilic Celik, Kose, and Ohnsorge 2020; World Bank 2021h). More broadly, the pandemic could fragment global trade and investment networks, increase global uncertainty, and persistently increase borrowing costs, thereby limiting investment prospects. The pandemic remains an ongoing risk and could further destroy human capital and undermine investment if new variants appear that significantly disrupt activity and raise uncertainty.

Policy options to lift potential growth in MNA

The region faces multiple impediments to faster potential growth, including high dependence on the production and export of commodities, widespread poor governance and ongoing political instability, wide gender gaps in the labor market, large and less productive public sectors, fragility and conflict, prolonged crises in some economies and high debt and rising crisis risks in others, the repercussions of the COVID-19 pandemic, and climate change. A major challenge for the region is the deep-seated structural impediments to private-sector-led growth. These impediments need to be tackled to enable job creation and substantial improvements in living standards.

Reforms could yield significant gains. Cross-country experience indicates that reforms of education and health systems and labor markets can raise potential growth. A scenario analysis applied to the MNA region suggests that labor market policies to raise the female labor force participation rate in each country by the largest 10-year improvement in MNA during 2000-21 could lift average potential growth by 0.1 percentage point a year during the remainder of this decade. Similar steps to address gaps in investment could yield a further boost of 0.3 percentage point a year (figure 2.17). Reforms that are stronger than historical improvements in the region, which are modest by comparison with those in the average EMDE, could substantially increase the gains. Thus, raising female labor force participation to the EMDE average gradually over 2022-30—from 21 to 53 percent—would raise potential growth by 1.2 percentage points a year. While this

FIGURE 2.17 **MNA: Policies to raise potential growth**

The MNA region could more than double its prospective rate of potential growth by investing in climate adaptation and mitigation and in infrastructure, reforming labor markets and social benefits, and boosting education. Policies to address rising climate risks are vital on account of the rising number of climate events. Policies to diversify sources of growth in oil exporters could help reduce their heavy dependence on fossil fuels for government revenue and exports.

A. Potential growth and contributions

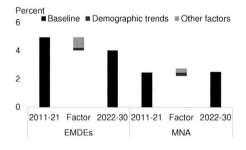

B. Reform scenarios

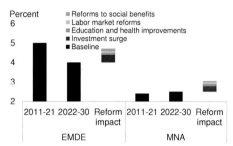

C. Climate change scenarios

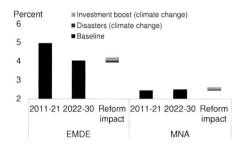

D. Female labor force participation scenarios

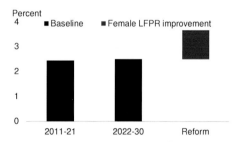

E. Share of oil revenue in total revenue in oil exporters

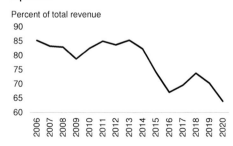

F. Climate risk

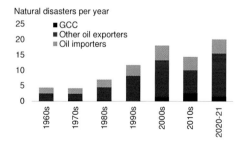

Sources: Centre for Research on the Epidemiology of Disaster, EM-DAT: The International Disaster Database; Haver Analytics; Penn World Table; UN, World Population Prospects; World Bank.
Note: Gross domestic product (GDP) weights are calculated using average real U.S. dollar GDP (at average 2010-19 prices and market exchange rates) for the period 2011-21. Data for 2022-30 are forecasts. EMDEs = emerging market and developing economies; LFPR = labor force participation rate; MNA = Middle East and North Africa.
A.-D. Period averages of annual GDP-weighted averages. Estimates are based on the production function approach. Chapter 1 describes methodology and chapter 5 reform scenarios.
A. Sample includes 53 EMDEs, of which 5 are from MNA. "Other factors" include trend improvements in human capital and stable investment growth relative to its long-term average.
B. Sample includes 53 EMDEs (5 from MNA).
E. Unweighted averages for seven MNA economies.
F. Includes data for 19 MNA economies. GCC = Gulf Cooperation Council.

would be a major spike in female labor force participation, the recent increases in Saudi Arabia, from 20 percent in 2017 to 35 percent in 2021, show that sizable increases are possible over the course of a few years. Furthermore, boosting investment in climate change adaption and mitigation in the region by 1.2 percent of GDP per year could raise potential growth by an additional 0.1 percentage point a year.

Improving governance could also raise the region's potential growth significantly. Weak governance in the region has been found to crowd out private investment and discourage private sector growth (Benhassine et al. 2009; Nabli 2007). Improved governance in the education sector, such as more structured measurement of results in training and educational programs, would enhance the matching of skills across workers and employers and could provide more and better-quality jobs in the private sector (Gatti et al. 2013). Perceptions of widespread corruption, which is a highly cited constraint on business activity in MNA in the World Bank's Enterprise Surveys, also reflect weak governance in the region. Corruption tends to discourage interactions between private firms and public authorities, and more corruption is associated with lower employment and productivity (EBRD, EIB, and World Bank 2016). Strengthening legal frameworks, including those in areas like corporate governance and bankruptcy resolution, can alleviate constraints on legitimate market transactions.

Economies in the region remain heavily reliant on the production and export of primary commodities. The diversification of agriculture-dependent economies (Morocco) and oil-dependent economies (GCC economies, the Islamic Republic of Iran, and Iraq) remains a top priority to increase economic stability and boost potential growth. Among the region's oil-exporting economies, oil revenue still accounted for about one-third of output, two-thirds of merchandise exports, and three-quarters of government revenue in 2019. With the world transitioning away from fossil fuels, the oil intensity of global output declined by about one-third in the two decades to 2019, and this trend will likely continue. Policies to promote diversification include measures to increase competition in product markets and avoid market concentration, measures that support the reallocation of economic resources to new activities, measures to lower trade costs and improve infrastructure and logistics, rationalization and reduction of energy subsidies, and liberalization of trade in services and foreign direct investment (Dieppe 2021; Kose and Ohnsorge 2020).

Armed conflict poses significant threats to the lives and livelihoods of the region's people and destroys human and physical capital. Breaking cycles of conflict can substantially improve growth prospects in fragile states. Close to half of conflicts globally, and one-third in MNA, are recurrences of past conflicts, often over similar issues (Jarland et al. 2020). Countries where there is conflict have some of the widest gender gaps in education, labor force participation, and political participation. In the region's fragile economies, the investment in reconstruction needed to maintain adequate provision of health, education, electricity, and water and sanitation services remains a high priority (World Bank 2017e). In countries hosting refugees, these policies need to be adapted to the structural changes that refugee crises have brought, such as through the adoption of more innovative financing mechanisms to fund higher demand for delivery of health services (World Bank 2017f). Addressing fragility by creating opportunities for women can also support medium- and long-term development in these economies (Bakken and Buhaug 2020; World Bank and GDC 2020).

The COVID-19 pandemic may leave lasting scars on productivity and potential growth in the region if governments do not address such consequences as human capital losses, increased debt, and health care burdens (Dieppe 2021; Kilic Celik, Kose, and Ohnsorge 2020). To minimize losses to human capital and productivity, countries could increase investment in health care systems, and in the field of education, increase investment in multiple ways of learning; improve the equity, adaptability, and resilience of education systems; increase surveillance and data collection to assess possible learning losses; and develop and implement policies to accelerate learning (UNESCO, UNICEF, and World Bank 2021; World Bank 2021l).

High levels of government debt constrain some economies' ability to reverse the past decade's slowdown in potential growth: Public debt in MNA oil importers in 2021 was more than 90 percent of GDP (World Bank 2021k). High debt can make it difficult to implement countercyclical policy, increase productive investment (including investment in human and physical capital), and boost private sector confidence. Policy reforms are needed to address high debt, mitigate its negative effects on economic activity, and reduce the likelihood of financial crises. These reforms include implementing sound and transparent debt management frameworks, ensuring that financial regulation and supervision promote sustainable debt accumulation in the public and private sectors, and progressing with governance reforms to minimize waste and corruption (Kose et al. 2021).

Climate change is likely to have devastating effects on lives and livelihoods in MNA, with natural disasters—including heat waves and floods—already more frequent in recent decades. Over time, rising temperatures will reduce agricultural yields and growing areas and exacerbate existing water scarcity. This could undermine food security, forcing migration, lowering labor productivity, and raising the likelihood of conflict. By one estimate, crop yields in the region could fall by up to 30 percent if temperatures were to rise by 1.5-2 degrees Celsius relative to preindustrial times and by almost 60 percent if they were to rise by 3-4 degrees (World Bank 2014).

Mitigation, adaptation, and a focus on a green and inclusive recovery in the post-pandemic world are key to ensuring sustainable future growth (Acerbi et al. 2021; IMF 2021c). Policies to limit climate change include repricing fossil fuels, for example through a carbon tax, to appropriately reflect costs to the environment. High energy subsidies in the region, accounting for 13 percent of government expenditure on average in 2021, could be rationalized, reduced, and replaced with targeted social spending to protect the vulnerable from the resulting price rises. Many economies in the region have adopted plans to adapt to climate change in order to protect human and physical capital (Kuwait, Oman, Saudi Arabia, and the United Arab Emirates), including integrated water management actions, sustainable agriculture practices, reduced desertification, and early warning systems for natural disasters (IMF 2021c).

Country-specific reform agendas are essential to improve potential growth in the region. In Saudi Arabia, codifying legal practices is an important step in strengthening the legal system. Rationalizing state involvement in the economy, for instance, by privatizing poorly performing state assets, could improve the allocation of capital and empower the private sector. This is particularly important in diversifying the country's economy away from fossil fuels. Labor market reforms should be considered to further increase the participation of women in the labor force. A law requiring the disclosure of assets, an effective anticorruption strategy, and the efficient implementation of Saudi Vision 2030 reforms could all improve governance.[22]

Effective implementation of the UAE 2050 Strategy, with appropriately sequenced and timed reforms, and the UAE Green Agenda 2030 could help reverse declines in potential growth. Reforms include commercializing nonstrategic government-related entities, investing in education and training in emerging fields that assist in diversifying the economy, and further aligning national and expatriate labor laws and public and private wages.

In Egypt, maintaining the gains from previous structural and macroeconomic reforms is not assured, with further reforms needed to address persistent fiscal and external vulnerabilities, as well as structural impediments to growth. To further promote macroeconomic stabilization, reforms could focus on improving the transparency of fiscal reporting and debt management, rationalizing the central bank's subsidized lending schemes, and improving liquidity management to enhance monetary policy transmission. On structural policies, reforms are needed to further strengthen revenue mobilization (including through limiting tax exemptions and reforming real estate taxes), increasing the role of the private sector by rationalizing state ownership, reducing tariffs and nontariff barriers, and enhancing the independence of regulatory authorities.

In the Islamic Republic of Iran, structural reforms are urgently needed to address widespread inefficiencies, the lack of fiscal sustainability, and price distortions. Further measures to raise government revenue—eliminating tax exemptions and improving tax compliance—and stabilize government expenditures are needed with a particular focus on subsidy reform. This would also assist in bringing down the high intensity of energy usage. Reforms to the monetary policy framework—a price stability mandate, greater central bank independence, rationalized lending operations, and stronger supervisory and resolution powers—could improve macroeconomic and financial sector stability.

---

[22] See Government of Saudi Arabia (2022) for more details on Saudi Vision 2030.

SOUTH ASIA

South Asia is the only EMDE region not to have suffered a decline in the growth rate of potential output in 2011-21 relative to the preceding decade. Its potential growth in the last decade was close to that of East Asia and Pacific but faster than that of other EMDE regions. It continued to be bolstered by an expanding working-age population, a high investment rate, and productivity-raising shifts of resources away from agriculture and informal activity. The pace of potential growth is expected to remain robust in the remainder of the 2020s and to be supported by all major drivers of growth. However, there is still scope to boost the region's potential growth significantly through product and labor market reforms. These reforms include measures to increase women's participation in economic activity, to accelerate investment in mitigating and adapting to climate change, and to expand investment in human capital.

Introduction

Economic activity in the SAR region rebounded strongly from the recession caused by the COVID-19 pandemic, expanding by 7.9 percent in 2021 after a drop of 4.5 percent in 2020. Output in the region is on track to grow by about 6.0 percent a year between 2022 and 2030, faster than the 2010s annual average of 5.5 percent and only moderately slower than growth in the 2000s (figure 2.18). This will make SAR the fastest-growing EMDE region in the remainder of this decade. SAR's robust growth performance and outlook reflect the region's high rate of potential growth as demographic trends expand the working-age population, the investment rate remains elevated, and productivity growth continues to benefit from the shift of resources away from agriculture and informal activity.

The COVID-19 pandemic massively disrupted the drivers of potential growth, and its impact on future potential growth is uncertain. The pandemic lowered investment in 2021 to about 9 percent below prepandemic projections, and this gap is expected to remain over much of the remainder of this decade, even with investment growing a little faster than its previous trend rate. The region was also affected by pandemic-related school closures, which were much more prevalent than the global average, as were lost working hours and job losses. In addition, the pandemic hit SAR's exceptionally large informal sector hard, and the job and income losses to its participants may have had long-lasting negative effects on their productivity.

Note: Estimates using the production function approach are available for Bangladesh, India, and Pakistan.

FIGURE 2.18 **SAR: Output growth and drivers of potential growth**

Output growth has remained robust in South Asia over the last two decades, and it is expected to be the fastest-growing emerging market and developing economy region in the remainder of this decade. Total factor productivity has contributed the most to maintaining robust potential growth. Investment growth has slowed from its breakneck pace in 2000-10. Secondary education attainment levels have improved but remain relatively poor.

A. GDP growth

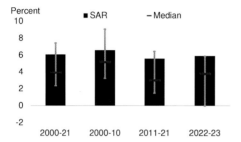

B. Contributions to potential growth

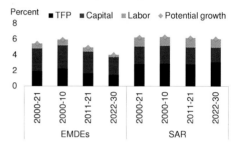

C. Investment growth

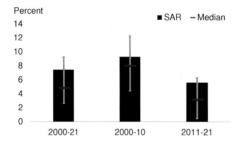

D. Potential TFP growth

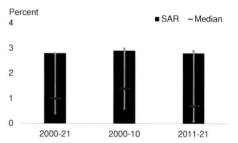

E. Secondary education attainment

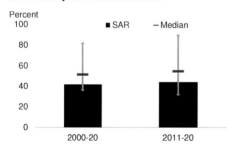

F. Working-age population growth

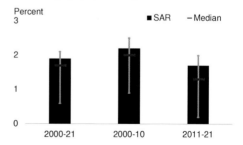

Sources: Haver Analytics; Penn World Table; UN, World Population Prospects; World Bank, World Development Indicators database.

Note: Gross domestic product (GDP) weights are calculated using average real U.S. dollar GDP (at average 2010-19 prices and market exchange rates). Data for 2022-23 and 2022-30 are forecasts. EMDEs = emerging market and developing economies; SAR = South Asia; TFP = total factor productivity.

A.C.-F. Bars show period averages of annual GDP-weighted averages. Horizontal lines show median of GDP-weighted averages for the six EMDE regions. Orange whiskers show maximum-minimum range.

B. Estimates are based on the production function approach. Sample includes 53 EMDEs, of which 3 are from SAR (Bangladesh, India, and Pakistan).

C.D. Sample includes three SAR economies (for which potential growth estimate is available for both investment growth and total factor productivity [TFP] growth measures for the period 2000-21).

E. Period averages of simple annual averages. Percentage of population aged 25 and above that completed at least lower secondary education. Sample for SAR includes Bangladesh, Pakistan, and Sri Lanka.

F. Working-age population refers to population aged 15-64. Sample includes three SAR economies.

With these and other factors taken into account, SAR's potential growth is projected in the baseline to slow only marginally to 6.1 percent a year on average in the 2020s, from 6.2 percent a year in the 2010s. This section estimates past and prospective potential growth for four commodity-importing countries in SAR, which together account for close to 90 percent of the region's output. The projection of sustained robust potential growth in the 2020s is based on projected contributions from all major drivers of growth. Investment growth is forecast to remain robust at above 6 percent a year, encouraged by the implementation of reforms that will also help generate productivity growth. Although population growth is expected to moderate, stabilization of the participation rate after two decades of decline, increases in the shares of working-age populations, and improvements in educational attainment will support labor force growth. However, the outlook is uncertain, and downside risks prevail, especially risks regarding the lasting impacts of the pandemic and the consequences of a more prolonged war in Ukraine than assumed in the baseline.

Achieving faster sustained growth in the region than projected in the baseline scenario will require addressing the structural factors that hinder growth. These factors include limited female participation in economic activity; high levels of informal economic activity, particularly in agriculture, which is characterized by low productivity; limited integration into global value chains; and lagging educational standards and attainment. Fewer than one-fourth of working-age women in SAR are in the labor force, although many more work in the informal economy; increasing female participation in the formal economy could significantly boost potential growth. Implementing other important reforms to enhance product and labor markets, accelerate investment in mitigating and adapting to climate change, and invest in human capital could also increase potential growth.

Evolution and drivers of potential growth in SAR

Growth in potential output in SAR in the 2010s was broadly stable from the 2000s, at an annual average of 6.2 percent (figure 2.19). On a per capita basis, potential growth accelerated from 4.7 percent to 5 percent as population growth slowed. Potential growth peaked in 2007 and has since slowed in line with declines in the growth of the capital stock and the labor force. The country-level estimates incorporated in the regional average are broadly consistent with those obtained in other studies for the region. In the case of India, estimates of potential growth since 2010 have been in the range of 6-8 percent a year (Bhoi and Behera 2017; Blagrave et al. 2015; Mishra 2013; Rodrik and Subramanian 2004).

Capital accumulation, labor force growth, and TFP growth are estimated to have made broadly stable contributions to growth in potential output in SAR over the past two decades. The largest contributor has been TFP growth, which was mostly unchanged between the 2000s and 2010s, with that lack of substantial change partly reflecting continued sectoral reallocation of resources from agriculture into manufacturing and services (Dieppe 2021). TFP growth in 2000-21 in SAR was more than one-half higher than that for EMDEs in aggregate, with the higher rate of TFP growth in SAR largely

FIGURE 2.19 **SAR: Growth in potential output**

Growth in potential output in South Asia is expected to remain robust in the remainder of this decade and avoid the precipitous slowdown that is expected in other emerging market and developing economy regions. Total factor productivity growth has remained robust in SAR as productivity-enhancing sectoral reallocation of resources from agriculture has continued. The pandemic, and especially its impact on education, will continue to weigh on potential growth.

A. Growth in potential output

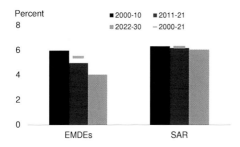

B. Growth in potential output by different estimates

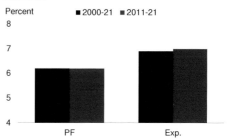

C. Within- and between-sector contributions to productivity growth

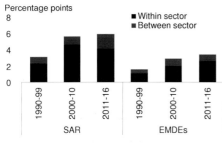

D. School closures

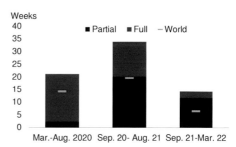

Sources: Asian Productivity Organization Productivity database; Groningen Growth Development Centre Productivity Level Database; International Labour Organization, ILOSTAT database; Organisation for Economic Co-operation and Development, STAN STructural ANalysis Database; Penn World Table; UN Educational, Scientific and Cultural Organization; UN, World Population Prospects; World Bank; World Bank, World Development Indicators database.

Note: Gross domestic product (GDP) weights are calculated using average real U.S. dollar GDP (at average 2010-19 prices and market exchange rates) for the period 2011-21. Data for 2022-30 are forecasts. EMDEs = emerging market and developing economies; SAR = South Asia.

A.B. Period averages of annual GDP-weighted averages.

A. Estimates are based on the production function approach. Sample includes 53 EMDEs, of which 3 are from SAR (Bangladesh, India, and Pakistan).

B. Expectations-based estimates ("Exp.") are potential growth proxied by five-year-ahead IMF *World Economic Outlook* growth forecasts. Chapter 1 provides details on the approaches. Expectations sample includes Afghanistan, Bangladesh, Bhutan, India, Maldives, Nepal, and Pakistan. PF = production function approach.

C. Productivity is defined as real GDP per worker (at 2010 market prices and exchange rates). Sample includes 3 EMDEs from SAR (India, Pakistan, and Sri Lanka) and 19 other EMDEs. Growth "within sector" effects show the contribution of the initial productivity growth rate of each sector weighted by real value added, with employment shares held fixed. Growth "between sector" effects show the contribution arising from changes in sectoral employment shares. Medians of country-specific contributions.

D. Unweighted averages. Data up to March 2022.

reflecting a greater contribution from sectoral reallocation. SAR's TFP growth also benefited from rising secondary schooling completion rates, although they increased more slowly (by about 15 percentage points) than that in all EMDEs between 2000 and 2021.

The second-largest contributor to SAR's growth in potential output in the past two decades has been capital accumulation, even though investment growth slowed from an average 9.3 percent a year in the 2000s to closer to 5.6 percent in the 2010s. There have also been significant country differences, with continued strong investment growth in Bangladesh (more than 8 percent a year over the last two decades), rising investment growth in Nepal, but slowing investment growth in India. Several factors have contributed to the slowdown in India's investment growth, including heightened regulatory and policy uncertainties, delayed project approvals and implementation, continued bottlenecks in the energy sector, and reform setbacks (Anand et al. 2014). Large corporate debt overhangs and nonperforming assets in the banking sector have weighed on credit and investment growth across the region.

The contribution of labor force growth to growth in potential output in SAR has remained strong over the last two decades, exceeding that in all other EMDE regions except SSA. The median labor force participation rate in SAR declined from 58 percent in 2000 to a trough of 56 percent in 2014 but has since increased marginally. Population growth slowed slightly between the 2000s and 2010s, averaging about 2 percent a year over the two decades. The region enjoyed a demographic dividend as the share of the working-age population continued to rise. Gains in education outcomes have been limited in the region. Secondary school completion rates in the region were about 40 percent in the 2010s. Moreover, the increase of 5 percentage points from the first decade of the 2000s was the second smallest increase among EMDE regions.

The COVID-19 pandemic disrupted life and undermined all three drivers of potential growth in the region. It led to a contraction of over 10 percent in fixed investment in 2020, with only a partial reversal in 2021. Investment in 2022 is expected to remain 5 percent below the prepandemic trend, and this gap is expected to endure over much of the remainder of this decade. Lower participation rates, disruptions to education, and a deterioration in health outcomes will have eroded human capital. Pandemic-related school closures averaged 70 weeks in South Asia through March 2022—much higher than the global average of 41 weeks—and kept nearly 400 million children out of school (UNESCO and UNICEF 2021). The damage to human capital accumulation could undermine the pace of poverty reduction, significantly impair the lifetime earnings of many, and reduce upward social mobility across generations (Azevedo, Rogers, et al. 2021; World Bank 2021o, 2022e). The pandemic also had adverse effects on the informally employed—predominantly low-skilled, rural, female, and young workers—who accounted for 59 percent of total employment in 2010-18 in the region, significantly higher than the rate in other EMDE regions (Ohnsorge and Yu 2021). The services sector suffered particularly severe income losses, given widespread informality and the limited ability of informal firms to access government support (Apedo-Amah et al. 2020; World Bank 2020g).

Prospects for potential growth in SAR

Growth in potential output in SAR is projected to average 6.1 percent a year between 2022-30, a slight slowdown from 6.2-6.3 percent a year in the 2000s and 2010s. This slowdown is less pronounced than that in other EMDE regions and leaves potential growth well above that in other regions. Per capita potential growth is expected to rise slightly, to 5.1 percent from 5.0 percent in the 2010s.

A projected recovery in TFP growth mainly underpins the forecast of continued solid growth in potential output in SAR through 2030. This recovery is partly due to the expected effects of assumed improvements in educational attainment, despite pandemic setbacks, as well as improvements in transport connectivity and agricultural productivity. Higher TFP growth is expected to largely offset a moderation in working-age population growth and a slightly smaller contribution from capital accumulation. Reform momentum in several economies is expected to help maintain the growth of TFP and potential output.

India, which accounts for about three-fourths of SAR output, has shifted the focus of government spending toward infrastructure investment, has consolidated labor regulations, is privatizing underperforming state-owned assets, and is modernizing and integrating the logistics sector. During 2019-20, it consolidated, rationalized, and simplified several labor laws that presented long-standing barriers to growth. These laws covered wages, social security, occupational health and safety, and industrial relations. The Make in India initiative, which began in late 2014, promotes investment, innovation, and the acquisition of skills to support workforce modernization. To boost international trade, the government has been modernizing and simplifying trade procedures through digitalization and infrastructure upgrades and liberalizing services trade policies by raising limits on foreign ownership (World Bank 2020e). The government has also taken steps to address the causes of past stress in the banking sector, including improving regulations and introducing a new bankruptcy law with a rule-based and time-bound resolution mechanism. The budget for 2021-22 created a "bad bank" to acquire and resolve legacy nonperforming assets, inject further capital into state banks, and increase foreign ownership in the insurance sector.

Other countries in the region have also taken action to promote more conducive environments for private sector activity. To improve macroeconomic stability, Pakistan has strengthened the functional and administrative autonomy of the central bank, prohibited government borrowing from the central bank, and established price stability as monetary policy's primary objective (World Bank 2022j). Nepal is planning reforms to improve governance and transparency, upgrade the tax system and improve spending efficiency, enhance public debt management, and strengthen financial regulation and supervision (IMF 2022a).

The baseline projection of SAR's potential growth is subject to significant uncertainty and risks, predominantly on the downside. The COVID-19 pandemic and the war in Ukraine are of particular concern, as these shocks have put significant pressure on policy buffers, increased fiscal and financial sector vulnerabilities, and thereby heightened risks of financial crises (Dieppe 2021; Kilic Celik, Kose, and Ohnsorge 2020). In Sri Lanka, the two shocks, together with existing domestic vulnerabilities, led to a balance of payments and sovereign debt crisis in mid-2022. While policies to resolve this crisis are now being implemented, with the support of the international community, losses to the country's potential growth are likely to be significant in the years ahead. Other economies in the region are at risk of similar crises given the size of potential shocks and elevated fiscal and financial vulnerabilities. The risk of a global recession has also risen because of the two shocks, and such a recession would damage the region's actual and potential growth. Future waves of the pandemic and the possibility of new variants could further disrupt education and employment and discourage investment, leading to further losses to potential growth. Meanwhile, the war in Ukraine has increased global uncertainty and could lead to a prolonged fragmentation of global trade and investment networks. Gains from further improvements in agriculture productivity, which explained two-thirds of agricultural output growth globally from 2001 to 2015, may also be at risk as a result of higher input costs and the fragmentation of trade and finance (Fuglie et al. 2020). Regarding upside risks to potential growth in SAR, the pandemic has accelerated technology adoption, which may promote future productivity gains (World Bank 2021n).

Policies to lift potential growth in SAR

Additional structural reforms in SAR could significantly boost the growth of productivity, employment, and potential output. In a scenario in which each country in SAR is assumed to repeat its largest 10-year improvements in investment growth, educational outcomes, life expectancy, and female labor force participation during 2000-21, it is estimated that SAR's rate of potential annual growth in the remainder of this decade would rise by 0.3 percentage point (figure 2.20). However, this underestimates the potential benefits of significant reforms. First, the region has made no progress in raising female labor force participation over the last two decades, from about 30 percent. If it were to raise this participation rate over the remainder of this decade to the EMDE average of 55 percent, it is estimated that potential growth would be higher by 1.2 percentage points. Second, investment in climate change adaption and mitigation of about 2.3 percent of GDP per year could boost potential growth by an additional 0.4 percentage point. While this scenario analysis indicates how reforms could raise SAR's potential growth in the years ahead, there are also other possible reforms to consider.

Labor productivity in SAR remains the lowest among all EMDE regions, in part reflecting high informality, the relatively large role of agriculture, and the region's limited integration into the global economy (Dieppe 2021). Policies to reduce informality include investing in human capital, increasing access to credit and public sector support, and improving the business environment (Ohnsorge and Yu 2021; World Bank 2020g). Informal employment is particularly high among young, low-skilled, female, and rural workers, and policies for educating and training these groups can help their transition to formal employment. Greater access to credit for informal workers can also encourage formalization, while expanding access to microfinance and

FIGURE 2.20 **SAR: Policies to raise growth in potential output**

South Asia can achieve even faster potential growth than projected in the decade ahead by investing in climate mitigation and adaptation and by improving its labor market and health outcomes. Agriculture remains a significant part of the economy, and policies to raise its productivity can have a significant impact on overall productivity. The frequency of extreme weather events has increased over time, and damage per event has risen.

A. Growth in potential output and contributions

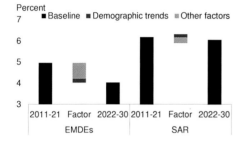

B. Reform scenarios

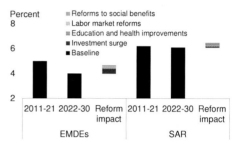

C. Climate change scenarios

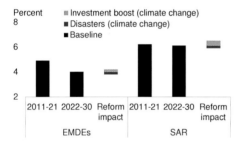

D. Female labor force scenarios

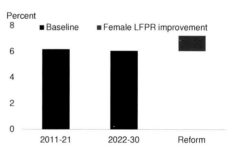

E. Share of agriculture sector in GDP and employment

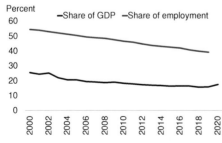

F. Climate risk

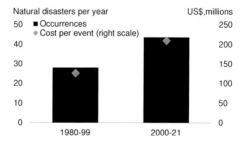

Sources: Centre for Research on the Epidemiology of Disaster, EM-DAT: The International Disaster Database; Penn World Table; UN, World Population Prospects; World Bank, World Development Indicators database.
Note: Gross domestic product (GDP) weights are calculated using average real U.S. dollar GDP (at average 2010-19 prices and market exchange rates) for the period 2011-21. Data for 2022-30 are forecasts. EMDEs = emerging market and developing economies; SAR = South Asia.
A.-D. Period averages of annual GDP-weighted averages. Estimates of potential growth are based on production function approach. Chapter 1 describes methodology and chapter 5 reform scenarios.
A. Sample includes 53 EMDEs, of which 3 are from SAR region. "Other factors" include trend improvements in human capital and stable investment growth relative to output growth.
B. Sample includes 53 EMDEs, of which 3 are from SAR region.
D. LFPR = labor force participation rate.
E. Sample includes eight SAR economies.
F. Based on data from 1980 to 2021. "Cost per event" in current 2021 US dollars.

other services has been shown to increase investment and productivity among informal enterprises (ILO 2016). Gaining access to high-quality public services can also provide incentives for informal firms to become formal. Enhanced monitoring and enforcement of tax and other regulations can also discourage informality. India introduced the Goods and Services Tax in 2017 partly to encourage formalization of activity.

Agriculture remains a large part of the economy in SAR, accounting for 18 percent of value added and 42 percent of employment. Despite a threefold increase in crop yields in the region over the last four decades, the average yield of cereal grains in SAR is still half that in East Asia (Fuglie et al. 2020). With two-thirds of the livelihoods of the extreme poor globally dependent on agriculture, and with many of those in SAR, increasing productivity in this sector is especially important and has a large potential impact on economy-wide productivity. Policies to increase agricultural productivity include increasing research spending on agriculture; measures to raise productivity on existing farms and promote the reallocation of resources to the most productive ones; measures to promote the adoption of new technologies; expansion of training for farmers in the best available techniques; development of financial products that meet the needs of farmers; and assisting in the transfer of excess labor from agriculture to other sectors (Fuglie et al. 2020).

Enhancing the region's integration into global value chains and promoting the diversification of its exports could also boost productivity growth and private sector investment. In other regions, international trade integration has been associated with faster economic growth, but SAR lags behind them in regional as well as global integration of trade and investment flows (Pathikonda and Farole 2017). Closing infrastructure gaps, removing regulatory and other impediments to business, and promoting a shift toward higher-value-added manufacturing could support closer trade and investment ties (Lopez-Acevedo and Robertson 2016). The region's exports remain highly concentrated in a narrow range of products, which are often of relatively poor quality and less complex than those of peers (Lian et al. 2021). Policies to promote diversification of exports could focus on raising research and development spending, investing in infrastructure (including infrastructure supporting digital technologies) and education, adopting new technologies, and increasing openness to trade.

SAR's business environment has significant room for improvement. In particular, reform priorities include improving government effectiveness and controlling corruption.

Additional steps to address vulnerabilities in corporate and banking sector balance sheets in the region could lift credit growth and the growth of investment and potential output. Banks' high ratios of nonperforming loans hold back the supply of credit. At the same time, high corporate debt hinders credit demand and investment, and parts of the corporate sector may require debt restructuring or even the exit of firms. Addressing the problem of so-called zombie firms—firms that are unable to cover interest payments from operating profits—could free up credit and resources for more productive uses (Banerjee and Hofmann 2022). In India, for example, 10 percent of nonfinancial firms, accounting for 10 percent of total bank credit, have been identified as zombies (Pattanaik, Muduli, and Jose 2022).

Greater investment in human capital might also help lift productivity, labor incomes, and potential output, by fostering shifts of resources to higher-value-added and more innovative sectors (Aturupane et al. 2014), among other things. Policies in this area include measures to raise the participation of women in the workforce, increase access to higher and better education, and invest in vocational training programs. Improving women's access to economic opportunities—still far more limited in SAR than in other EMDE regions—remains a significant source of gains in potential growth (Hsieh et al. 2019). Less than one-fourth of working-age women are in the labor force in SAR, compared with more than half in other EMDE regions (World Bank 2022m). Women's participation in the workforce can also bring complementary benefits, including improvements in the nutrition of children and associated increases in productivity.

Country-specific reform agendas are key to boosting potential growth in the region. For example, in Bangladesh, reforms could focus on strengthening trade competitiveness through tariff reform such as the implementation of the National Single Window and the Customs Modernization Strategic Action Plan (2019-22); increasing investment and FDI through full operationalization of new economic zones; increasing investment in climate adaptation; and addressing the pandemic's impact on the financial sector, by strengthening banks' relatively weak capital positions and exiting regulatory forbearance (World Bank 2022a), among other measures.

In India, potential growth could benefit from accelerated implementation of an already-ambitious reform agenda. Addressing the aftermath of financial sector distress could unlock significant growth. India has a less developed financial system than many of its peers, with a heavy state presence. To improve the sector's efficiency and depth, India could undertake reforms to further rationalize the role of public sector banks, ensure a level playing field in the banking sector, and promote the development of capital markets (World Bank 2020e). In regard to infrastructure, the reforms suggested by the Task Force on the National Infrastructure Pipeline should be implemented, including improving project preparation processes, enhancing the capacity and participation of the private sector, improving contract enforcement and dispute resolution, and improving sources of financing.

In Pakistan, priorities to raise potential growth include improving macroeconomic stability (avoiding destabilizing boom-bust cycles), increasing international competitiveness, and promoting equity and inclusion (World Bank 2020f, 2022j). Other policies beneficial to growth could include strengthening insolvency arrangements and creditor rights, improving the financial viability of the energy sector, and strengthening revenue mobilization and spending efficiency to better fund growth-promoting public investment.

The outlook for potential growth in SAR in the remainder of this decade and beyond is highly dependent on repercussions of the COVID-19 pandemic and climate change.

While both have highly uncertain impacts, those impacts will be almost entirely negative, and there are risks that they could be severely adverse. Policies to address these challenges are key to ensuring sustainable growth.

Regarding the COVID-19 pandemic, policies in SAR need to focus on mitigating its impact, including its impact on education and employment, as well as on improving resilience to future pandemics by investing in pandemic surveillance and the health sector. Pandemic-related closures kept more than 400 million children out of school in 2020-21 in the region, indicating an urgent need for countries to take measures to minimize education losses. SAR also has a large digital divide, with only 12 percent of school-aged children (3-17 years old) having access to the internet at home, well below the 33 percent of children globally (UNICEF and ITU 2020). Besides efforts to close the digital divide, countries should pursue education policies that develop information systems for large segments of the population, improve coordination across stakeholders to improve outcomes, and encourage innovation (World Bank 2018b). In the health sector, besides expanding current vaccination programs, countries could prepare for future waves of COVID-19 and future pandemics by investing in improving the procurement and distribution of vaccines; shifting resources and planning toward more preventative care for the vulnerable; creating more effective early warning systems; and promoting, through international cooperation, global solutions to this global problem through collective financing, mutual accountability, and strong multilateral systems (Global Preparedness Monitoring Board 2021; World Bank 2021o).

Climate change represents a significant threat to lives, livelihoods, and economic growth in the region, as in the rest of the world. Extreme weather events, including cyclones, floods, and droughts, have become more frequent in SAR, and the damage they cause has become more costly. The region is one of the most vulnerable to climate change-induced increases in poverty, disease, and child mortality, with half its population living in areas expected to become climate hot spots (Amarnath et al. 2017; Hallegatte et al. 2016; Jafino et al. 2020; Mani et al. 2018). Mitigation and adaptation are key to ensuring sustainable growth in the future (Agarwal et al. 2021; World Bank 2022j). The region, which accounted for about 9 percent of global emissions of greenhouse gases in 2018, can contribute to global mitigation efforts by providing incentives for use of renewable energy sources, rationalizing and reducing subsidies on fossil fuels, and appropriately pricing carbon emissions through carbon taxes (Friedlingstein et al. 2022). The introduction of carbon taxes would both lower pollution and increase fiscal revenues to fund productivity-enhancing investments, but care should be taken to minimize their impact on vulnerable households. Quickly formulating and effectively implementing comprehensive national adaptation plans could accelerate adaptation, which is also necessary given the already-changing climate. To date, only Sri Lanka has formulated and released such a plan.

Growth in potential output in Sub-Saharan Africa has been below the EMDE average since at least 2000. The effects of the COVID-19 pandemic and Russia's invasion of Ukraine have depressed growth in the region's potential output further, although not as much as in some other regions. This long period of anemic potential growth, with growth rates barely above the region's population growth, has resulted in stagnant growth in per capita potential output. Without economic reforms, potential growth in SSA is likely to weaken further over the rest of this decade, as growth in the supply of labor moderates and capital accumulation wanes, especially in South Africa.

Introduction

Over at least the past two decades, output growth in SSA has been consistently below the EMDE average. Although the region fared better during the 2008-09 global financial crisis than other EMDE regions, economic growth in many countries never returned to its 2000s average, as declining investment in extractive sectors, worsening security situations, rising public debt, and deepening poverty weighed on activity.[25] More than half of all SSA economies are expected to grow in 2022-24, but at a slower rate than in the 2010s, with that slower rate largely reflecting damage from the COVID-19 pandemic and the adverse effects of Russia's invasion of Ukraine on poverty and food security—two shocks that have further exacerbated underlying constraints on SSA's growth.

Growth in SSA's potential output has also been consistently below the EMDE average since at least 2000. The COVID-19 pandemic and Russia's invasion of Ukraine have depressed growth of the region's potential output further by adversely affecting fundamental drivers of potential growth, such as human and physical capital accumulation. In contrast to what took place in slowdowns in most other regions, potential growth in SSA in the 2010s slowed only slightly more than in the preceding decade, although it remained barely above the region's population growth.

Without significant progress in regard to reforms, actual and potential growth are likely to remain depressed across the region: It is projected that potential growth in SSA is

---

Note: Estimates using the production function approach are available for Benin, Burundi, Cameroon, Gabon, Kanya, Lesotho, Mauritania, Mauritius, Mozambique, Namibia, Niger, Senegal, South Africa, and Togo.

likely to fall below 3 percent a year over the 2020s, with a modest increase in TFP growth expected to only partly offset decelerating labor supply growth and slowing investment growth, especially in South Africa.

Weaker potential growth would delay the reversal of pandemic-inflicted losses in per capita incomes and hinder poverty reduction in SSA. The world's extreme poverty is increasingly concentrated in SSA: Nearly 60 percent of people living in extreme poverty live in the region (World Bank 2022h).[23] The COVID-19 pandemic reduced per capita incomes in SSA by nearly 5 percent in 2020, twice as much as in EMDEs more broadly, and caused widespread losses in learning and health outcomes (World Bank, UNESCO, and UNICEF 2021). Recent sharp cost-of-living increases caused by soaring food and fuel prices, largely resulting from the war in Ukraine, are pushing even more people into extreme poverty and acute food insecurity across the region. Boosting potential growth in SSA could substantially mitigate the damage arising from these developments.

The sharp deceleration of growth since 2019, triggered by the pandemic and steepened by Russia's invasion of Ukraine, increases the likelihood that SSA will miss achieving the SDGs. Investment has fallen across most sectors related to the SDGs, worsening constraints in industries that were already weak prior to the pandemic, such as power generation, agriculture, and health (UNCTAD 2021c). The SSA region also remains one of the most vulnerable to climate change-induced disruptions to development prospects (Rozenberg and Fay 2019).

This multitude of challenges confronting SSA underscores the urgency of structural reforms to boost potential growth, including reforms that spur private investment, skills development, and female labor force participation. There are substantial opportunities to boost potential growth through investment in SSA food systems and green and resilient infrastructure, with benefits magnified through productivity-enhancing technology transfers. Comprehensive reforms to strengthen health care, labor force participation, education, and social protection could similarly be transformative, unlocking the region's underutilized potential human capital.

Evolution and drivers of potential growth in SSA

Growth in potential output in SSA stood at 3.2 percent a year during the 2010s, only slightly below its average of 3.4 percent during the 2000s (figure 2.21). The experience of SSA contrasts with that of EMDEs as a whole, in which potential growth during the 2010s was a full percentage point slower than in the first decade of the 2000s.

The relative stability of growth in potential output in SSA reflects two largely offsetting factors: A sharp deceleration in TFP canceling out a boost from a significant increase in public investment and a rise in the working-age share of the population. TFP in SSA decelerated sharply in the 2010s, and especially in 2015-19. During the latter period,

---

[23] Extreme poverty is measured as the number of people living on less than $2.15 at 2017 prices.

FIGURE 2.21 **SSA: Economic growth and drivers of potential growth**

GDP growth in Sub-Saharan Africa has slowed sharply in the last decade as rising public debt, worsening security situations in some countries, and a drop in commodity prices has curtailed investment and economic activity. Growth in potential output in the region has been consistently below the EMDE average, partly as a result of weak investment growth in South Africa—the region's second-largest economy.

A. GDP growth

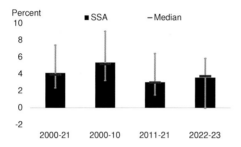

B. Contributions to potential GDP growth

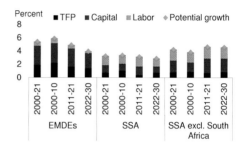

C. Investment growth

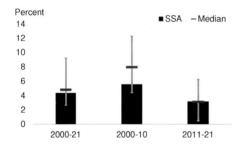

D. Potential TFP growth

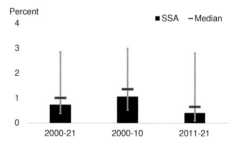

E. Secondary education attainment

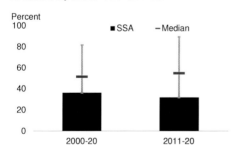

F. Working-age population growth

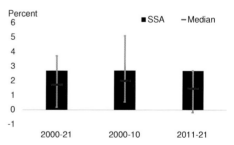

Sources: Penn World Table; UN, World Population Prospects; World Bank; World Bank, World Development Indicators database.
Note: Gross domestic product (GDP) weights are calculated using average real U.S. dollar GDP (at average 2010-19 prices and market exchange rates). Data for 2022-23 and 2022-30 are forecasts. EMDEs = emerging market and developing economies; excl. = excluding;
SSA = Sub-Saharan Africa; TFP = total factor productivity.
A.C.D.F. Bars show period averages of annual GDP-weighted averages. Horizontal lines show median of GDP-weighted averages for six EMDE regions; vertical lines denote range of regional averages.
B. Period averages of annual GDP-weighted averages. Estimates are based on production function approach. Sample includes 53 EMDEs (14 from SSA).
C. D. Sample includes 14 SSA economies (for which potential growth estimate is available for both investment growth and TFP growth measures for the period 2000-21).
E. Period averages of simple annual averages. Percentage of population aged 25 and above that completed at least lower secondary education.
F. Working-age population refers to population aged 15-64. Sample includes 14 SSA economies.

following the collapse of commodity prices and a decline in investment in extractive industries, potential TFP growth reached its slowest rate since 2000. This slowdown in TFP growth in SSA and other EMDE regions during the prepandemic decade has been attributed in part to a slowdown in convergence to the technological frontier. After a rapid catch-up in the 2000s, convergence has slowed amid weaker inflows of FDI and lagging capabilities to adopt frontier technologies (Kemp and Smit 2015; UNCTAD 2021b).[24]

More than many other EMDEs, the economies of SSA have continued to benefit from a young and growing labor force. The contribution of growth in the supply of labor to growth in potential output increased by about 0.2 percentage point a year between the 2000s and 2010s amid rapid expansion in working-age populations. If South Africa is excluded from the calculations, it increased slightly more, as rising labor force participation accompanied rapid population growth. This contrasts with what has taken place in other EMDE regions, where population aging has dampened growth in the supply of labor.

The weakening of SSA's potential growth in the past decade was mainly concentrated in South Africa, the region's second-largest economy. In fact, if South Africa is excluded from the calculations, potential growth in the region accelerated from 3.9 percent a year during the 2000s to 4.7 percent a year during the 2010s—not far below the EMDE average of 5.0 percent—largely on account of strong public investment. With South Africa again excluded, the contribution of capital stock growth to growth in potential output in SSA rose from 1.5 percentage points a year in the 2000s to 2.2 percentage points a year in the 2010s. Macroeconomic stimulus policies after the global financial crisis, initiatives promoting public investment in non-resource-intensive countries, and rising FDI inflows in metal exporters drove this increase. Efforts to improve the business environment supported private investment activity and investor confidence in many non-oil-producing countries (Devarajan and Kasekende 2011). Each year since 2012, SSA has been the EMDE region with the highest number of reforms to improve business climates (World Bank 2019a). However, in oil exporters, which account for almost 40 percent of SSA output, investment growth and FDI inflows fell substantially in the aftermath of the 2011-16 global commodity price plunge (World Bank 2017d).

Since 2019, the COVID-19 pandemic and Russia's invasion of Ukraine have substantially weakened all major drivers of potential growth in SSA, even more than in the rest of EMDEs. Economic activity in most SSA economies is more concentrated than in many other EMDEs in sectors directly hit by the pandemic. Remote work, which often allows a wide range of activities, is impossible in much of the region. And even in sectors in which it is possible, many countries lack the infrastructure needed for workers to switch to remote work during the COVID-19 lockdowns. Similarly, digital

---

[24] During the 2000s, potential TFP growth had strengthened because of improvements in health and education outcomes, as well as a decline in the share of the labor force engaged in agriculture and the associated reallocation of workers to higher-productivity sectors (Abdychev et al. 2018; McMillan and Harttgen 2014).

inequalities, lack of reliable internet service, and power access limited the feasibility of remote learning in many SSA countries. As a result, learning losses from school closures have been more severe than in other EMDE regions and have disproportionately affected vulnerable households, deepening the learning crisis in the region (Angrist et al. 2021).

Several other structural features of the region's economies have made SSA more vulnerable to slowdowns of potential growth. The sharp drop in commodity prices at the start of the pandemic severely reduced investment in extractive industries, particularly in oil-producing countries, compounding the adverse effect of delays in maintenance work due to mobility restrictions. The collapse of fiscal revenues and reorientation of government spending to pandemic relief measures took a major toll on public investment. Investment is expected to recover but could remain well below prepandemic trends.

In addition, SSA has the highest share of informality across all EMDE regions, with informal firms, especially those owned by women, hit particularly hard during COVID-19 lockdowns. Many informally employed workers, who were outside social protection nets, had to dispose of productive assets and deplete savings to cope with income losses and rising living costs, which further weakened their already-low productivity.

Russia's invasion of Ukraine has sharply increased the number of vulnerable people because of surging domestic inflation and spreading food and fuel shortages, especially in SSA countries with already-high levels of fragility. By increasing incidences of malnutrition and undernourishment, this increase in the number of vulnerable people is likely having a significant and lasting negative impact on human capital accumulation. In addition, because of deteriorating food affordability, many SSA governments are facing increased pressures to strengthen social protection and subsidize food and fuel at a time when fiscal space is already depleted. The resulting diversion of public funds from development projects, such as infrastructure investment, could delay progress toward other SDGs across the region. War-induced disruptions to global fertilizer and fuel supplies could also imperil sustained productivity growth in SSA agriculture, which already faces substantial risks due to the adverse impact of climate change (World Bank 2021b).

Prospects for potential growth in SSA

According to current baseline projections, growth in potential output in SSA will continue to drift lower, to below 3 percent a year on average in the 2020s, a modest increase in TFP growth only partly offsetting further slowdowns in capital accumulation and growth of the labor supply.[25] This would be a less steep slowdown than in the average EMDE, mainly because of relatively fast population growth. Nevertheless, potential growth at this rate would mean that potential GDP per capita in SSA would

---

[25] For a detailed description of the assumptions underlying this outlook, please see chapter 5.

rise by only 1.5 percent a year over the remainder of the 2020s, slowing the region's progress on poverty reduction and the reversal of pandemic-inflicted income losses.

South Africa, which faces both slowing labor force growth and slower capital accumulation, accounts for much of the weakness in the region's prospects for potential growth. With South Africa excluded from the calculations, potential growth in the region would remain broadly steady at 4.6 percent a year on average during the 2020s, exceeding EMDE average potential growth by more than a half percentage point. In per capita terms, however, it would still be weak, averaging 2.5 percent a year over the remainder of the 2020s, compared with 3.5 percent a year for EMDEs as a whole.

The underlying contribution of SSA's capital stock is projected to moderate to 1 percentage point a year in the 2020s. For 11 of the 13 SSA countries in this section's sample that export commodities, private investment in the resource sector is expected to continue growing in response to high commodity prices. Although financing costs are rising across the region as global financial conditions tighten, continued access to concessional financing will allow public investment to remain robust in some countries, supporting progress toward development goals. In contrast to that in the rest of the region, investment growth in South Africa is expected to recover only moderately during the next decade because of such structural impediments as high unemployment, weak infrastructure and institutions, slow progress in regard to reforms, elevated public debt, and deteriorating profitability of state-owned enterprises, especially in the power generation sector. If South Africa is excluded from the calculations, investment growth is expected to remain robust at about 5.9 percent a year.

This investment growth is also expected to support TFP growth across the region. In South Africa, a stronger record of innovation than in the broader region suggests that despite weaker investment growth in South Africa than in other SSA economies, the country's TFP growth may pick up in the reminder of the 2020s. South Africa is one of SSA's leaders in digital infrastructure and services and is therefore more prepared than the rest of the region to adopt frontier technologies in, for example, information technology and digital finance (figure 2.22; World Bank 2017g, 2019c). For SSA as a whole, the contribution of TFP growth to growth in potential output is expected to increase by about 0.3 percentage point a year. However, if South Africa is excluded from the calculations, the contribution is expected to increase by only 0.1 percentage point a year.

SSA is expected to experience a slower decline in fertility rates than other EMDE regions (Canning, Raja, and Yazbeck 2015). As a result, the youth dependency ratio (the population younger than 15 divided by the population aged 16-64) is projected to remain high, and the share of the working-age population is projected to continue to rise at a rate similar to that in the prepandemic decade—except in South Africa, where slowing labor force growth is expected to dampen potential growth.

There are substantial risks that potential growth in SSA could slow in the period ahead by more than projected. These risks include the emergence and spread of infectious

FIGURE 2.22 SSA: Obstacles to economic growth and reforms to accelerate potential growth

Many economies in Sub-Saharan Africa have weak capacity to adopt frontier technologies and tackle climate change, and heavy reliance on commodity exports increases exposures to commodity price shocks and makes growth and investment more volatile. Absent a renewed push to accelerate structural reforms that address these challenges, potential growth in SSA could remain weak over the next decade. Given SSA's sizable investment and infrastructure gaps, encouraging private investment, including projects that enhance the region's resilience to climate change and natural disasters, could deliver a large and sustainable boost to potential growth in the 2020s.

A. Networked Readiness Index

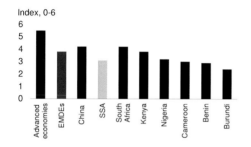

B. Climate change vulnerability and readiness index

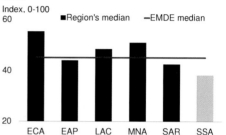

C. Potential GDP growth

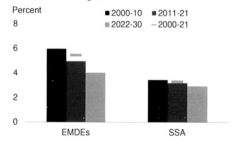

D. Per capita potential GDP growth

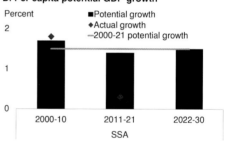

E. Reform scenarios

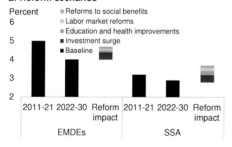

F. Climate change investment scenarios

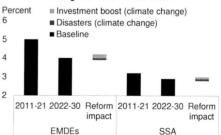

Sources: Notre Dame Global Adaptation Initiative; Penn World Table; Portulans Institute; UN, World Population Prospects; World Bank, World Development Indicators database; World Economic Forum.
Note: Estimates are based on production function approach. Data for 2022-30 are forecasts. ECA = Europe and Central Asia; EMDEs = emerging market and developing economies; EAP = East Asia and Pacific; LAC = Latin America and the Caribbean; MNA = Middle East and North Africa; SAR = South Asia; SSA = Sub-Saharan Africa.
A. The Portulans Institute's Network Readiness Index estimates preparedness to benefit from emerging technologies and capitalize on the opportunities presented by the digital transformation; higher values indicate better readiness. Group averages are unweighted.
B. Panel shows values for the Notre Dame Global Adaptation Initiative index, which reflects vulnerability to climate change and other global challenges, combined with readiness to improve resilience. A higher value indicates lower vulnerability, better readiness, or both. Sample includes 146 EMDEs; last observation is 2019.
D.-F. Sample includes 53 EMDEs (14 from SSA). Panel shows period averages, weighted using average real U.S. dollar gross domestic product (GDP) at average 2010-19 prices and market exchange rates.
E.F. Chapter 5 describes policy scenarios.

diseases, including new strains of COVID-19, which could further undermine improvements in health outcomes and disrupt the accumulation of human capital. SSA's high dependence on commodity exports—more than 90 percent of the region's economies are commodity exporters—leaves the region particularly vulnerable to commodity price swings and resulting volatility of growth. High levels of public debt and weak fiscal revenue mobilization could further constrain much-needed investment in some countries, especially if access to international financial markets and donor support remains restricted. Violence and insecurity amid rising poverty and income inequality could slow reforms, including ones that improve investment climates. Productivity in agriculture might decelerate substantially if costs of farming inputs remain elevated for an extended period and investment in green and resilient infrastructure fails to pick up. Insufficient access to agricultural inputs might lead to more low-productivity subsistence farming, rendering regional food systems even more vulnerable to shocks, especially in countries where climate change has already depressed productivity in farming.

Policy actions that promote sustained improvements in the fundamental drivers of potential growth, however, can mitigate many of these risks.

Policy options to lift potential growth in SSA

Meeting SSA's needs in regard to investment related to climate adaptation and resilience, boosting human capital, and increasing labor force participation could increase growth in the region's potential output. For example, in a scenario that assumes each country in SSA repeats its largest 10-year improvements in investment growth, educational outcomes, life expectancy, and female labor force participation during 2000-21, it is estimated that SSA's potential growth over the remainder of this decade could be boosted by about 0.8 percentage point a year, to an annual average of about 3.7 percent. Much of this boost would come from meeting investment needs, including those related to investment in climate change mitigation and adaptation projects (figure 2.22).[26]

A separate scenario representing increased investment in climate change adaptation and mitigation assumes that all SSA economies increase investment to limit climate change to 2 degrees Celsius and also become more resilient to its effects. The scenario is based on the World Bank's Country Climate and Development Reports. The additional capital spending includes, for example, investment in resilient infrastructure, flood prevention, and renewable power generation, and is estimated at about 1.2 percent of SSA GDP per year in the 2020s. The estimated boost to potential growth is 0.1 percentage point a year over this period.

Although public investment in SSA picked up in the mid-2000s and reached a peak of 5.8 percent of GDP in 2014, this rate was well below the average in other EMDE regions (World Bank 2017a). Partly as a result, SSA still has substantial infrastructure

---

[26] Please see chapter 5 for a detailed description of the assumptions.

investment needs. Furthermore, public investment fell sharply during the pandemic, reversing some of the progress in meeting these needs. Additional financing equivalent to 27-37 percent of SSA's 2022 GDP could be needed to return SSA to the prepandemic path for convergence of its incomes by the mid-2020s (IMF 2021a). The region's annual infrastructure investment needs, the largest among all EMDE regions, are estimated at more than 9 percent of regional GDP—nearly four times higher than estimates of the actual infrastructure spending in SSA (Fay et al. 2019; Rozenberg and Fay 2019). In all likelihood, a substantial boost in private as well as public sector investment is needed to cover infrastructure gaps and accelerate capital accumulation. If each country in the region repeated its best 10-year investment growth rate, the boost to potential growth in the 2020s is estimated at about 0.4 percentage point.

Increasing public investment could boost output in the short term, including by spurring private investment (World Bank 2017a). Many countries in the region have little fiscal space to raise public spending because of elevated public debt, weak revenue mobilization, and current pressures to boost social protection in response to the cost-of-living increases. There is, however, scope to reallocate resources from less productive spending programs and improve domestic revenue mobilization. Most countries in SSA have low ratios of tax revenues to GDP that could be increased through reforms, including broad-based consumption taxes, simplified tax design, and improved tax administration (Mabugu and Simbanegavi 2015). In many countries, reforms that improve business climates and promote economic diversification would also encourage private investment (including FDI) in nonresource sectors, broaden tax bases, and reduce vulnerabilities to fluctuations in commodity prices.

Rapid scaling up of infrastructure investment carries the risk that funds could be spent inefficiently. There is evidence that SSA has weaker institutions governing the life cycle of infrastructure projects than other EMDEs regions. This can lead to poor project selection, inadequate enforcement of procurement procedures, and failure to complete projects, limiting the success of large public investment projects (Dabla-Norris et al. 2012). Strengthening underlying institutional and governance capacities could play an important role in raising the efficiency of public investment in the region (Calderón, Cantú, and Chuhan-Pole 2018; Rajaram et al. 2014). Many SSA countries can greatly benefit from stronger institutions and reduced corruption. Structural reforms that address these issues would raise fiscal revenues and build the capacity to use public funds more efficiently. Improved governance would provide incentives for investment and job creation in the private sector, enhance developmental outcomes and support economic and social inclusion.

To meet infrastructure and investment needs, many countries in the region will need to boost private investment, particularly investment in green and climate change adaptation projects. Over the past few decades, SSA economies have made substantial progress in regard to reforms to improve the investment climate, including regulatory reforms. Nevertheless, considerable scope remains for simplifying regulations and administrative procedures related to starting a business, increasing the efficiency of the legal system, and reducing regulatory uncertainty. In addition, complementary reforms are needed to raise returns on private investment in many countries. These include increasing openness to trade, technological readiness, and policy stability. Reforms to improve security are urgently needed as well, especially in low-income countries (LICs). Persistently high levels of violence and insecurity, which are being exacerbated by social unrest caused by deteriorating living standards, could have a significant and lasting adverse impact on potential growth (Hadzi-Vaskov, Pienknagura, and Ricci 2021).

Further improvements in education and health outcomes could bolster potential growth by raising labor force participation rates, enhancing human capital accumulation, and boosting TFP growth. Although the region has achieved significant improvements in these areas, much more remains to be done. In half of the countries in the region, fewer than 50 percent of young people complete lower-secondary education, and fewer than 10 percent go on to higher education (World Bank 2017b). In addition, learning outcomes have been generally poor, and gender disparities have remained significant at the secondary and tertiary levels (Oleyere 2015). Completion rates adjusted for the quality of learning outcomes in Africa are some of the lowest in the world—for example, just 10 percent of lower secondary students in SSA achieve a minimum proficiency level in mathematics (UNESCO 2019). Priorities vary depending on country circumstances, but they center on investing in effective teaching, ensuring access to quality education for the poor, and closing gender gaps (World Bank 2017b).

Investment in health and education is especially urgent considering the scale of learning losses in SSA during the pandemic. School closures due to COVID-19 social restrictions are likely to have had a significant negative impact on long-term educational attainment across the region, as well as on the earning and employment prospects of new labor market entrants. In the aftermath of the 2015 Ebola outbreak, almost a fifth of girls in Sierra Leone never reenrolled in schools (Bandiera, Buehren, Goldstein, et al. 2020). One estimate suggests that a loss of one year of schooling because of COVID-19 school closures translates into as much as three years of learning losses in the long term (Angrist et al. 2021).

Major health indicators show SSA is lagging. Average life expectancy in the region was 62 years in 2020—well below the average of more than 70 years in other EMDE regions. Infectious diseases have disproportionate impacts on SSA. Building strong health systems, as well as setting up regional coordination mechanisms (to improve prevention, preparedness, and response to future pandemics), is critical for providing adequate health services.

Achieving the education and health improvements envisaged in the scenario analysis— that is, a rise in secondary school completion rates by 3.7 percentage points, tertiary completion rates by 0.4 percentage point, and life expectancy by three years—would raise potential growth by about 0.2 percentage point a year during 2020s.

The COVID-19 pandemic has also widened gender inequalities in SSA because women were employed disproportionately in the hardest-hit sectors, notably the informal economy. At about 64 percent, the labor force participation rate for women in SSA remains well below the 74 percent rate for men, indicating significant scope for increasing the number of women in the workforce. The prevalence of unpaid female labor and lack of affordable childcare, as well as gaps in educational attainment and restrictions on women's access to credit and rights to own and control assets, complicate raising female labor force participation in SSA (Seguino and Were 2015).

These challenges point to the need for policy and institutional frameworks to increase female labor force participation and promote female entrepreneurship. Reforms that remove obstacles to ownership rights, promote equal access to financial services, and expand the availability of childcare are critical for women's empowerment and gender equality (World Bank 2022o). If the female labor force participation rate were to increase by 2.5 percentage points, as the scenario analysis assumes, it would raise potential growth in the region by about 0.2 percentage point a year in the 2020s.

Reforms other than those the scenario analysis captures could pay significant dividends in terms of increased TFP (IMF 2022c). These reforms include diversification efforts to reduce reliance on the resource sector, stronger property rights to encourage productivity-enhancing investment, and greater transport connectivity to spur competition and within-region integration. For example, estimates suggest that the full implementation of the African Continental Free Trade Area could lift 30 million people from extreme poverty by 2035 through trade facilitation and the removal of tariff and nontariff barriers (World Bank 2020a). The region has substantial scope for raising productivity across many sectors and industries, including the formal sector, the agricultural sector, and the nonfarm informal sector, which could further boost the region's potential growth (Calderón 2021).

Many economies in SSA are striving to diversify away from exports of natural resources, especially by taking steps to increase the competitiveness of manufacturing, which suffers from poor business environments, lack of infrastructure, and high unit labor costs (Bhorat and Tarp 2016). Along with increased human capital and the removal of trade barriers, improvements in transport and energy infrastructure would increase the competitiveness of the region and facilitate its integration into global and regional value chains (Abreha et al. 2020; Allard et al. 2016). The African Continental Free Trade Area could be a strong catalyst for many intra-African productivity-boosting infrastructure projects, including the expansion of road networks, which would substantially reduce intraregional transportation costs, especially for landlocked countries (UNCTAD 2021a).

The COVID-19 pandemic has accelerated the adoption in SSA of digital technologies, which could significantly improve productivity across firms, both formal and informal, and sectors, especially agriculture (World Bank 2021c). More widespread digitalization would require additional sizable investment in infrastructure and skills, which governments could facilitate by promoting competition, eliminating barriers to entry, removing restrictive licensing in the telecommunications industry, and avoiding taxes and regulations that constrain the expansion of industries that provide services.

Across the region, the share of the labor force working in the low-productivity agricultural sector remains high. Many countries have substantial scope for raising agricultural productivity by, among other measures, improving land titles; promoting new farming techniques by, among other things, increasing access to credit; and providing the infrastructure needed to connect farms to markets (Fuglie et al. 2020). In Ethiopia, for instance, public investments in irrigation, transportation, and power have significantly increased agricultural productivity and incomes (Rodrik 2017). Improving productivity in agriculture, especially in LICs, is key to reducing food insecurity and extreme poverty across SSA.

TFP growth has accounted for about 60 percent of output growth in agriculture in EMDEs, and improvements in agricultural TFP have larger poverty-reducing effects than TFP growth in other sectors, especially in LICs where farming accounts for a big share of the economy (Fuglie et al. 2020; Ivanic and Martin 2018). Compared with that in other EMDE regions, agriculture represents a much larger share of output and employment in SSA, especially in the poorest countries. This larger share of agriculture in output and employment increases the need for policies that promote the diffusion and adaptation of new technologies in farming, including public spending on research and development in agriculture, targeting improvements in yields; eliminating barriers to the adoption of new technologies by private firms; and enforcing business-friendly sanitary and phytosanitary standards.

In many countries in SSA, increases in the share of the labor force employed in the informal sector have matched declines in the share engaged in agriculture (Ohnsorge and Yu 2021). Raising productivity in the informal sector is therefore an important policy objective. Fostering a supportive regulatory environment and promoting investment in basic infrastructure such as electricity, road networks, and information technology are key reforms that could make the informal sector more dynamic, encourage formalization, and increase the contribution of the resources currently employed in the informal sector to the region's long-run economic growth (Bhorat and Tarp 2016).

References

Abdychev, A., C. Alonso, E. Alper, D. Desruelle, S. Kothari, Y. Liu, M. Perinet, S. Rehman, A. Schimmelpfennig, and P. Sharma. 2018. *The Future of Work in Sub-Saharan Africa.* Washington, DC: International Monetary Fund.

Abreha, K., E. Lartey, T. Mengistae, S. Owusu, and A. Zeufack. 2020. "Africa in Manufacturing Global Value Chains: Cross-Country Patterns in the Dynamics of Linkages." Policy Research Working Paper 9439, World Bank, Washington, DC.

Acemoglu, D., and P. Restrepo. 2017. "Low-Skill and High-Skill Automation." Department of Economics Working Paper 17-12, Massachusetts Institute of Technology, Cambridge, MA.

Acerbi, M., M. Heger, H. Naber, and L. Sieghart. 2021. "Middle East and North Africa: Two Opportunities for Rebuilding after COVID-19 in Green and Inclusive Ways." *Arab Voices* (blog), November 22, 2021. https://blogs.worldbank.org/arabvoices/middle-east-north-africa-two-opportunities-rebuilding-after-covid-19-green-inclusive

Acharya, D., and Y. N. Raju. 2020. "Revisiting the Volatility-Growth Relationship: Some Cross-Country Evidence, 1978-2017." *Cogent Economics and Finance* 8 (1): 1826655.

ADB (Asian Development Bank). 2016. *Asian Development Outlook 2016: Asia's Potential Growth.* Manila: Asian Development Bank.

Agarwal, R., V. Balasundharam, P. Blagrave, R. Gudmundsson, and R. Mousa. 2021. "Climate Change in South Asia: Further Need for Mitigation and Adaptation," IMF Working Paper 21/217, International Monetary Fund, Washington, DC.

Alberola, E., R. Gondo, M. Lombardi, and D. Urbina. 2016. "Output Gaps and Policy Stabilization in Latin America: The Effect of Commodity and Capital Flow Cycles." BIS Working Paper 568, Bank for International Settlements, Basel.

Alkhareif, R. M., W. A. Barnett, and N. A. Alsadoun. 2017. "Estimating the Output Gap for Saudi Arabia." *International Journal of Economics and Finance*: 9 (3): 81-90.

Allard, C., J. I. Canales-Kriljenko, W. Chen, J. Gonzales-Garcia, E. Kitsios, and J. Trevino. 2016. "Trade Integration and Value Chains in Sub-Saharan Africa: In Pursuit of the Missing Link." Departmental Paper, International Monetary Fund, Washington, DC.

Alvarado, R., M. Iniguez, and P. Ponce. 2017. "Foreign Direct Investment and Economic Growth in Latin America." *Economic Analysis and Policy* 56 (December): 176-87.

Alvarez, R., and M. Grazzi. 2018. "Innovation and Entrepreneurship in Latin America. What Do We Know? What Would We Like to Know?" *Estudios de Economica* 45 (2): 157-71.

Amarnath, G., N. Alahacoon, V. Smakhtin, and P. Aggarwal. 2017. "Mapping Multiple Climate-Related Hazards in South Asia." IWMI Research Report 170, International Water Management Institute, Colombo, Sri Lanka.

Anand, R., M. K. C. Cheng, S. Rehman, and M. L. Zhang. 2014. "Potential Growth in Emerging Asia." IMF Working Paper 14/2, International Monetary Fund, Washington, DC.

Angrist, N., A. de Barros, R. Bhula, S. Chakera, C. Cummiskey, J. DeStefano, J. Floretta, M. Kaffenberger, B. Piper, and J. Stern. 2021. "Building Back Better to Avert a Learning Catastrophe: Estimating Learning Loss from Covid-19 School Shutdowns in Africa and Facilitating Short-Term and Long-Term Learning Recovery." *International Journal of Educational Development* 84 (July): 102397.

Apedo-Amah, M. C., B. Avdiu, X. Cirera, M. Cruz, E. Davies, A. Grover, L. Iacovone, et al. 2020. "Unmasking the Impact of COVID-19 on Businesses: Firm Level Evidence from Across the World." Policy Research Working Paper 9434, World Bank, Washington, DC.

Aravena, C., J. Friedman, and A. Hofman. 2017. "Sources of Productivity and Economic Growth in Latin America and the Caribbean, 1990-2013." *International Productivity Monitor* 33 (Fall): 51-76.

Asian Productivity Organization. 2016. *APO Productivity Databook*. Tokyo: Asian Productivity Organization.

Aslam, A., S. Beidas-Strom, R. Bems, O. Celasun, S. Kilic Celik, and Z. Kóczán. 2016. "Trading on Their Terms? Commodity Exporters in the Aftermath of the Commodity Boom." IMF Working Paper 16/127, International Monetary Fund, Washington, DC.

Aturupane, H., P. Glewwe, R. Ravina, U. Sonnadara, and S. Wisniewski. 2014. "An Assessment of the Impacts of Sri Lanka's Programme for School Improvement and School Report Card Programme on Students' Academic Progress." *Journal of Development Studies* 50 (12): 1647-69.

Azevedo, J. P., A. Hasan, D. Goldemberg, K. Geven, and S. A. Iqbal. 2021. "Simulating the Potential Impacts of COVID-19 School Closures on Schooling and Learning Outcomes: A Set of Global Estimates." *World Bank Research Observer* 36 (1): 1-40.

Azevedo, J. P., F. H. Rogers, S. E. Ahlgren, M. H. Cloutier, B. Chakroun, G. Chang, S. Mizunoya, N. J. Reuge, M. Brossard, and J. L. Bergmann. 2021. *The State of the Global Education Crisis: A Path to Recovery*. Washington, DC: World Bank Group.

Bai, C., and Q. Zhang. 2017. *A Research on China's Economic Growth Potential*. Abingdon, U.K.: Routledge.

Baker, J. L., and G. U. Gadgil. 2017. *East Asia and Pacific Cities: Expanding Opportunities for the Urban Poor*. Urban Development Series. Washington, DC: World Bank.

Bakken, I. V., and H. Buhaug. 2020. "Civil War and Female Empowerment." *Journal of Conflict Resolution* 65 (5): 982-1009.

Bandiera, O., N. Buehren, R. Burgess, M. Goldstein, S. Gulesci, I. Rasul, and M. Sulaiman. 2020. "Women's Empowerment in Action: Evidence from a Randomized Control Trial in Africa." *American Economic Journal: Applied Economics* 12 (1): 210-59.

Bandiera, O., N. Buehren, M. Goldstein, I. Rasul, and A. Smurra. 2020. "Do School Closures during an Epidemic Have Persistent Effects? Evidence from Sierra Leone in the Time of Ebola." Unpublished.

Banerjee, R., and B. Hofmann. 2022. "Corporate Zombies: Anatomy and Life Cycle." *Economic Policy* 37 (112): 757-803.

Barrero, J. M., N. Bloom, S. J. Davis, and B. H. Meyer. 2021. "COVID-19 Is a Persistent Reallocation Shock." *AEA Papers and Proceedings* 111 (May): 287-91.

Barro, R. 2000. "Inequality and Growth in a Panel of Countries." *Journal of Economic Growth* 5 (1): 5-32.

Benhassine, N., Y. Saadani Hassani, P. E. Keefer, A. H. Stone, and S. N. Wahba. 2009. *From Privilege to Competition: Unlocking Private-Led Growth in the Middle East and North Africa*. MENA Development Report. Washington, DC: World Bank Group.

Beverelli, C., M. Fiorini, and B. Hoekman. 2017. "Services Trade Policy and Manufacturing Productivity: The Role of Institutions." *Journal of International Economics* 104 (January): 166-82.

Bhoi, B. K., and H. K. Behera. 2017. "India's Potential Output Revisited." *Journal of Quantitative Economics* 15 (1): 101-20.

Bhorat, H., and F. Tarp, eds. 2016. *Africa's Lions: Growth Traps and Opportunities for Six African Economies*. Washington, DC: Brookings Institution Press.

Blagrave, P., M. R. Garcia-Saltos, M. D. Laxton, and F. Zhang. 2015. "A Simple Multivariate Filter for Estimating Potential Output." IMF Working Paper 15/79, International Monetary Fund, Washington, DC.

Bloom, D. E., D. Canning, and G. Fink. 2011. "Implications of Population Aging for Economic Growth." NBER Working Paper 16705, National Bureau of Economic Research, Cambridge, MA.

Bodnár, K., and C. Nerlich. 2020. "Drivers of Rising Labour Force Participation—The Role of Pension Reforms." *Economic Bulletin* no. 5. https://www.ecb.europa.eu/pub/economic-bulletin/html/eb202005.en.html#toc19

Bossavie, L., D. Garrote-Sánchez, M. Makovec, and Ç. Özden. 2022. *Skilled Migration: A Sign of Europe's Divide or Integration?* Washington, DC: World Bank.

Bova, M. E., M. Ruiz-Arranz, M. F. G. Toscani, and H. E. Ture. 2016. "The Fiscal Costs of Contingent Liabilities: A New Dataset." IMF Working Paper 16/14, International Monetary Fund, Washington, DC.

Bown, C., D. Lederman, S. Pienknagura, and R. Robertson. 2017. *Better Neighbors: Toward a Renewal of Integration in Latin America*. Washington, DC: World Bank.

Brichetti, J. P., L. Mastronardi, M. E. R. Amiassorho, T. Serebrisky, and B. Solis. 2021. *The Infrastructure Gap in Latin America and the Caribbean: Investment Needed through 2030 to Meet the Sustainable Development Goals*. Washington, DC: Inter-American Development Bank.

Bruhn, N. C. P., C. L. L. Calegario, and D. Mendonca. 2020. "Foreign Direct Investment in Developing Economies: A Study on the Productivity Spillover Effects in Latin America." *RAUSP Management Journal* 55 (1): 40-54.

Bryson, J. H., and E. Nelson. 2016. "Does China Face a Japanese-Like 'Lost Decade'?" Special Commentary, Wells Fargo.

Calderón, C. 2021. *Boosting Productivity in Sub-Saharan Africa: Policies and Institutions to Promote Efficiency*. Washington, DC: World Bank.

Calderón, C., C. Cantú, and P. Chuhan-Pole. 2018. "Infrastructure Development in Sub-Saharan Africa: A Scorecard." Policy Research Working Paper 8425, World Bank, Washington, DC.

Canning, D., S. Raja, and A. Yazbeck, eds. 2015. *Africa's Demographic Transition: Dividend or Disaster?* Washington, DC: World Bank.

Carone, G., P. Eckefeldt, L. Giamboni, V. Laine, and S. Pamies. 2016. "Pension Reforms in the EU since the Early 2000's: Achievements and Challenges Ahead." European Economy Discussion Paper 042, European Commission, Brussels. http://dx.doi.org/10.2139/ssrn.2964933

Castillo, P., and Y. Rojas. 2014. "Terms of Trade and Total Factor Productivity: Empirical Evidence from Latin American Emerging Markets." Working Paper 2014-012, Central Reserve Bank of Peru, Lima.

Cirera, X., and W. F. Maloney. 2017. *The Innovation Paradox: Developing-Country Capabilities and the Unrealized Promise of Technological Catch-Up*. Washington, DC: World Bank.

Constantinescu, C., A. Mattoo, and M. Ruta. 2017. "Trade Developments in 2016: Policy Uncertainty Weighs on World Trade." Global Trade Watch, World Bank, Washington, DC.

Creehan, S. 2015. "Why We Shouldn't Invoke Japan's 'Lost Decade' as China's Future." *Pacific Exchange Blog*, October 8, 2015. https://www.frbsf.org/banking/asia-program/pacific-exchange-blog/why-we-shouldnt-invoke-japans-lost-decade-as-chinas-future

Crespi, G., E. Tacsir, and F. Vargas. 2016. "Innovation Dynamics and Productivity: Evidence for Latin America." In *Firm Innovation and Productivity in Latin America and the Caribbean: The Engine of Economic Development*, edited by M. Grazzi and C. Pietrobelli. Washington, DC: Inter-American Development Bank.

Dabla-Norris, E., J. Brumby, A. Kyobe, Z. Mills, and C. Papageorgiou. 2012. "Investing in Public Investment: An Index of Public Investment Efficiency." *Journal of Economic Growth* 17 (3): 235-66.

Dabla-Norris, E., M. S. Guo, M. V. Haksar, M. Kim, M. K. Kochhar, K. Wiseman, and A. Zdzienicka. 2015. "The New Normal: A Sector-Level Perspective on Productivity Trends in Advanced Economies." IMF Staff Discussion Note 15/03, International Monetary Fund, Washington DC.

Daude, C., and E. Fernández-Arias. 2010. "On the Role of Productivity and Factor Accumulation in Economic Development in Latin America and the Caribbean." IDB Working Paper 155, Inter-American Development Bank. Washington, DC.

De Paulo, L. D., R. de Andrade Lima, and R. Tigre. 2022. "Corruption and Economic Growth in Latin America and the Caribbean." *Review of Development Economics* 26 (2): 756-73.

Devarajan, S., and L. A. Kasekende. 2011. "Africa and the Global Economic Crisis: Impacts, Policy Responses and Political Economy." *African Development Review* 23 (4): 421-38.

Dieppe, A., ed. 2021. *Global Productivity: Trends, Drivers, and Policies*. Washington, DC: World Bank.

Dieppe, A., S. Kilic Celik, and C. Okou. 2021. "Implications of Major Adverse Events on Productivity." Policy Research Working Paper 9411, World Bank, Washington, DC.

Dollar, D., T. Kleineberg, and A. Kraay. 2016. "Growth Is Still Good for the Poor." *European Economic Review* 81 (C): 68-85.

Donnelly, R., and H. A. Patrinos. 2021. "Learning Loss during Covid-19: An Early Systematic Review." *Prospects*. https://doi.org/10.1007/s11125-021-09582-6.

Dutz, A., R. Almeida, and T. Packard. 2018. *The Jobs of Tomorrow. Technology, Productivity, and Prosperity in Latin America and the Caribbean*. Washington, DC: World Bank.

EBRD (European Bank for Reconstruction and Development). 2017. *Transition Report 2017-18: Sustaining Growth*. London: European Bank for Reconstruction and Development.

EBRD (European Bank for Reconstruction and Development). 2020. "Economic Performance of State-Owned Enterprises in Emerging Economies: A Cross-Country Study." European Bank for Reconstruction and Development, London.

EBRD (European Bank for Reconstruction and Development). 2021. *Transition Report: 2021-22*. London: European Bank for Reconstruction and Development.

EBRD (European Bank for Reconstruction and Development), EIB (European Investment Bank), and World Bank. 2016. *What's Holding Back the Private Sector in MENA? Lessons from the Enterprise Survey*. London: European Bank for Reconstruction and Development.

El-Ganainy, A., E. Ernst, R. Merola, R. Rogerson, and M. Schindler. 2021. "Inclusivity in the Labor Market." IMF Working Paper 21/141, International Monetary Fund, Washington, DC.

Eris, M. N., and B. Ulasan. 2013. "Trade Openness and Economic Growth: Bayesian Model Averaging Estimate of Cross-Country Growth Regressions." *Economic Modelling* 33 (July): 867-83.

Estrades, P. C., M. Maliszewska, I. Osorio-Rodarte, S. E. Pereira, and M. Filipa. 2022. "Estimating the Economic and Distributional Impacts of the Regional Comprehensive Economic Partnership." Policy Research Working Paper 9939, World Bank, Washington, DC.

European Commission. 2021. *The 2021 Ageing Report: Economic and Budgetary Projections for the EU Member States (2019-2070).* Brussels: European Commission.

European Commission. 2022. "Report from the Commission to the European Parliament and the Council on the Implementation of the Recovery and Resilience Facility." European Commission, Brussels.

Faal, E. 2005. "GDP Growth, Potential Output, and Output Gaps in Mexico." IMF Working Paper 05/93, International Monetary Fund, Washington, DC.

Fay, M., H. Lee, M. Mastruzzi, S. Han, and C. Moonkyoung. 2019. "Hitting the Trillion Mark: A Look at How Much Countries Are Spending on Infrastructure." Policy Research Working Paper 8730, World Bank, Washington, DC.

Ferreyra, M. M., C. Avitabile, J. B. Álvarez, F. H. Paz, and S. Urzúa. 2017. *At a Crossroads: Higher Education in Latin America and the Caribbean.* Washington, DC: World Bank.

Ferreyra, M. M., and M. Roberts. 2018. *Raising the Bar for Productive Cities in Latin America and the Caribbean.* Washington, DC. World Bank.

Frattini, T., and I. Solmone. 2022. "The Labour Market Disadvantages for Immigrant Women." VoxEU.org, CEPR Policy Portal, March 30, 2022. https://cepr.org/voxeu/columns/labour-market-disadvantages-immigrant-women

Friedlingstein, P., M. W. Jones, M. O'Sullivan, R. M. Andrew, D. C. Bakker, J. Hauck, C. Le Quéré, et al. 2022. "Global Carbon Budget 2021." *Earth System Science Data* 14 (4): 1917-2005.

Fuglie, K., M. Gautam, A. Goyal, and W. F. Maloney. 2020. *Harvesting Prosperity: Technology and Productivity Growth in Agriculture.* Washington, DC: World Bank.

Garcia-Saltos, R., J. Teodoru, and F. Zhang. 2016. "Potential Output Growth Estimates for Central America and the Dominican Republic." IMF Working Paper 16/250, International Monetary Fund, Washington, DC.

Gatti, R., M. Morgandi, R. Grun, S. Brodmann, and D. Angel-Urdinola. 2013. *Jobs for Shared Prosperity: Time for Action in the Middle East and North Africa.* Washington, DC: World Bank.

Global Preparedness Monitoring Board. 2021. *From Worlds Apart to a World Prepared.* Geneva: World Health Organization.

Government of Saudi Arabia. 2022. *Vision 2030: Kingdom of Saudi Arabia.* https://www.vision2030.gov.sa/media/rc0b5oy1/saudi_vision203.pdf.

Guénette, J. D., P. G. Kenworthy, and C. M. Wheeler. 2022. "Implications of the War in Ukraine for the Global Economy." Equitable Growth, Finance, and Institutions Policy Note 3, World Bank, Washington, DC.

Hadzi-Vaskov, M., S. Pienknagura, and L. Ricci. 2021. "The Macroeconomic Impact of Social Unrest." CEPR Discussion Paper 16152, Center for Economic and Policy Research, Washington, DC.

Hale, T., N. Angrist, R. Goldszmidt, B. Kira, A. Petherick, T. Phillips, S. Webster, et al. 2021. "A Global Panel Database of Pandemic Policies (Oxford COVID-19 Government Response Tracker)." *Nature Human Behaviour* 5: 529-38.

Hallegatte, S., M. Bangalore, L. Bonzanigo, M. Faye, T. Kane, U. Narloch, J. Rozenberg, D. Treguer, and A. Vogt-Schlib. 2016. *Shock Waves: Managing the Impacts of Climate Change on Poverty.* Washington, DC: World Bank.

Hallward-Driemeier, M., G. Nayyar, W. Fengler, A. Aridi, and I. Gill. 2020. *Europe 4.0: Addressing the Digital Dilemma.* Washington, DC: World Bank.

Havrylyshyn, O. 1990. "Trade Policy and Productivity Gains in Developing Countries: A Survey of the Literature." *World Bank Research Observer* 5 (1): 1-24.

Hill, R. V., and A. Narayan. 2020. "COVID-19 and Inequality: A Review of the Evidence on Likely Impact and Policy Options." Working Paper 3, Centre for Disaster Protection, London.

Hofman, A., and P. Valderrama. 2020. "Long Run Growth Performance in Latin America—1820-2016." *Journal of Economic Surveys* 35 (3): 833-69.

Hsieh, C. T., E. Hurst, C. I. Jones, and P. J. Klenow. 2019. "The Allocation of Talent and US Economic Growth." *Econometrica* 87 (5): 1439-74.

Ianchovichina, E. 2017. *Eruptions of Popular Anger: The Economics of the Arab Spring and Its Aftermath.* MENA Development Report. Washington, DC: World Bank.

IDB (Inter-American Development Bank). 2013. *Rethinking Reforms: How Latin America and the Caribbean Can Escape Suppressed World Growth; A Mandate to Grow.* 2013 Latin America and the Caribbean Macroeconomic Report. Washington, DC: Inter-American Development Bank.

IDB (Inter-American Development Bank). 2018. *A Mandate to Grow.* 2018 Latin America and the Caribbean Macroeconomic Report. Washington, DC: Inter-American Development Bank.

ILO (International Labour Organization). 2016. "Role of Finance in Driving Formalization of Informal Enterprises." Thematic Policy Brief—Enterprise Formalization, International Labour Organization, Geneva.

ILO (International Labour Organization). 2022a. *Productivity Growth, Diversification and Structural Change in the Arab States.* Beirut: International Labour Organization.

ILO (International Labour Organization). 2022b. *World Employment and Social Outlook: Trends 2022.* Geneva: International Labour Organization.

IMF (International Monetary Fund). 2015. "Where Are We Headed? Perspectives on Potential Growth." In *World Economic Outlook: Uneven Growth—Short and Long-Term Factors.* April. Washington, DC: International Monetary Fund.

IMF (International Monetary Fund). 2016. "Saudi Arabia: Selected Issues." IMF Country Report 17/317, International Monetary Fund, Washington, DC.

IMF (International Monetary Fund). 2017a. "Arab Republic of Egypt: 2017 Article IV Consultation." Staff Report, International Monetary Fund, Washington, DC.

IMF (International Monetary Fund). 2017b. "Latin America: Stuck in Low Gear." In *Regional Economic Outlook Update: Western Hemisphere.* Washington, DC: International Monetary Fund.

IMF (International Monetary Fund). 2017c. "Preparing for Choppy Seas." In *Regional Economic Outlook: Asia and Pacific.* May. Washington, DC: International Monetary Fund.

IMF (International Monetary Fund). 2021a. "Background Note for International Financing Summit for Africa High-Level Event." International Monetary Fund, Washington, DC.

IMF (International Monetary Fund). 2021b. "Bulgaria: 2020 Article IV Consultation—Press Release; Staff Report; and Statement by the Executive Director for Bulgaria." IMF Country Report 21/27, International Monetary Fund, Washington, DC.

IMF (International Monetary Fund). 2021c. "Economic Prospects and Policy Challenges for the GCC Countries—2021." International Monetary Fund, Washington, DC.

IMF (International Monetary Fund). 2021d. "Saudi Arabia 2021 Article IV Consultation—Press Release and Staff Report." IMF Country Report 21/149, International Monetary Fund, Washington, DC.

IMF (International Monetary Fund). 2022a. "Nepal: Request for an Arrangement under the Extended Credit Facility." IMF Country Report 22/24, International Monetary Fund, Washington, DC.

IMF (International Monetary Fund). 2022b. "Republic of Poland: Selected Issues." IMF Country Report 22/59, International Monetary Fund, Washington, DC.

IMF (International Monetary Fund). 2022c. *Regional Economic Outlook: Sub-Saharan Africa—A New Shock and Little Room to Maneuver.* April. Washington, DC: International Monetary Fund.

Islam, A. M., and D. Lederman. 2020. "Data Transparency and Long-Run Growth." Policy Research Working Paper 9493, World Bank, Washington, DC.

Ivanic, M., and W. Martin. 2018. "Sectoral Productivity Growth and Poverty Reduction: National and Global Impacts." *World Development* 109 (September): 429-39.

Jafino, B., B. Walsh, J. Rozenberg, and S. Hallegatte. 2020. "Revised Estimates of the Impact of Climate Change on Extreme Poverty by 2030." Policy Research Working Paper 9417, World Bank, Washington, DC.

Jarland, J., H. M. Nygård, S. Gates, E. Hermansen, and V. B. Larsen. 2020. "How Should We Understand Patterns of Recurring Conflict?" Conflict Trends 3, Peace Research Institute, Oslo, Norway.

Keefer, P., and C. Scartascini. 2022. *Trust: The Key to Social Cohesion and Growth in Latin America and the Caribbean.* Washington, DC: Inter-American Development Bank.

Kemp, J., and B. Smit. 2015. "Estimating and Explaining Changes in Potential Growth in South Africa." Working Paper 14/2015, Department of Economics, Stellenbosch University, Stellenbosch, South Africa.

Kilic Celik, S., M. A. Kose, and F. Ohnsorge. 2020. "Subdued Potential Growth: Sources and Remedies." In *Growth in a Time of Change: Global and Country Perspectives on a New Agenda*, edited by H.-W. Kim and Z. Qureshi. Washington, DC: Brookings Institution.

Kose, M. A., P. Nagle, F. Ohnsorge, and N. Sugawara. 2021. *Global Waves of Debt: Causes and Consequences.* Washington, DC: World Bank.

Kose, M. A., and F. Ohnsorge, eds. 2020. *A Decade After the Global Recession: Lessons and Challenges for Emerging and Developing Economies.* Washington, DC: World Bank.

Kummritz, V., D. Taglioni, and D. Winkler. 2017. "Economic Upgrading through Global Value Chain Participation: Which Policies Increase the Value Added Gains?" Policy Research Working Paper 8007, World Bank, Washington, DC.

La Porta, R., and A. Shleifer. 2014. "Informality and Development." *Journal of Economic Perspectives* 28 (3): 109-26.

Lalive, S., and S. Staubli. 2015. "How Does Raising Women's Full Retirement Age Affect Labor Supply, Income, and Mortality?" NBER Working Paper 18660, National Bureau of Economic Research, Cambridge, MA.

Lian, W., F. Liu, K. Svirydzenka, and B. Zhu, 2021. "A Diversification Strategy for South Asia." IMF Working Paper 21/202, International Monetary Fund, Washington, DC.

Loayza, N., P. Fajnzylber, and C. Calderón. 2005. *Economic Growth in Latin America and the Caribbean: Sylized Facts, Explanations, and Forecasts.* Washington, DC: World Bank.

Lopez-Acevedo, G., and R. Robertson. 2016. *Stitches to Riches: Apparel Employment, Trade, and Economic Development in South Asia.* Washington, DC: World Bank.

Mabugu, R. E., and W. Simbanegavi. 2015. "Tax and Expenditure Reforms in Africa: An Overview." *Journal of African Economies* 24 (AERC Supplement 2): ii3-ii15.

Maliszewski, W., and L. Zhang. 2015. "China's Growth. Can Goldilocks Outgrow." IMF Working Paper 15/113, International Monetary Fund, Washington, DC.

Mani, M., S. Bandyopadhyay, S. Chonabayashi, A. Markandya, and T. Mosier. 2018. *South Asia's Hotspots: The Impact of Temperature and Precipitation Changes on Living Standards.* Washington, DC: World Bank.

McMillan, M. S., and K. Harttgen. 2014. "What Is Driving the African Growth Miracle?" NBER Working Paper 20077, National Bureau of Economic Research. Cambridge, MA.

Mishra, P. 2013. "Has India's Growth Story Withered?" *Economic and Political Weekly* 48 (15): 51-59.

Mitra, R., S. Hossain, and I. Hossain. 2015. "Aid and Per-Capita Economic Growth in Asia: A Panel Cointegration Test." *Economic Bulletin* 35 (3): 1693-99.

Molato-Gayares, R., A. Park, D. A. Raitzer, D. Suryadarma, M. Thomas, and P. Vandenberg. 2022. "How to Recover Learning Losses from COVID-19 School Closures in Asia and the Pacific." ADB Briefs 217, Asian Development Bank, Manila, Philippines.

Montalbano, P., S. Nenci, and C. Pietrobelli. 2016. "International Linkages, Value-Added Trade, and Firm Productivity in Latin America and the Caribbean." In *Firm Innovation and Productivity in Latin America and the Caribbean: The Engine of Economic Development*, edited by M. Grazzi and C. Pietrobelli, 285-316. Washington, DC: Inter-American Development Bank.

Morikawa, M. 2021. "The Productivity of Working from Home: Evidence from Japan." VoxEU.org, CEPR Policy Portal, March 12, 2021. https://voxeu.org/article/productivity-working-home-evidence-japan

Moura, R., and R. Forte. 2010. "The Effects of Foreign Direct Investment on the Host Country Economic Growth—Theory and Empirical Evidence." *Singapore Economic Review* 58 (3): 1-28.

Nabar, M. S., and P. N'Diaye. 2013. "Enhancing China's Medium-Term Growth Prospects: The Path to a High-Income Economy." IMF Working Paper 13/204, International Monetary Fund, Washington, DC.

Nabli, M. K. 2007. *Breaking the Barriers to Higher Economic Growth: Better Governance and Deeper Reforms in the Middle East and North Africa.* Washington, DC: World Bank.

Novta, N., and J. C. Wong. 2017. "Women at Work in Latin America and the Caribbean." IMF Working Paper 17/34, International Monetary Fund, Washington, DC.

OECD (Organisation for Economic Co-operation and Development). 2014. "Growth Prospects and Fiscal Requirements over the Long Term." In *OECD Economic Outlook.* Paris: Organisation for Economic Co-operation and Development.

OECD (Organisation for Economic Co-operation and Development). 2015. *Education at a Glance 2015: OECD Indicators.* Paris: Organisation for Economic Co-operation and Development.

OECD (Organisation for Economic Co-operation and Development). 2016. *Boosting Productivity and Inclusive Growth in Latin America.* Paris: Organisation for Economic Co-operation and Development.

OECD (Organisation for Economic Co-operation and Development). 2017. *OECD Economic Surveys: Mexico 2017.* Paris: Organisation for Economic Co-operation and Development.

OECD (Organisation for Economic Co-operation and Development). 2018. "Climate-Resilient Infrastructure." OECD Environment Policy Paper 14, Organisation for Economic Co-operation and Development, Paris.

OECD (Organisation for Economic Co-operation and Development). 2021a. *Education at a Glance 2021: OECD Indicators.* Paris: OECD Publishing.

OECD (Organisation for Economic Co-operation and Development). 2021b. *Education in Eastern Europe and Central Asia.* Paris: OECD Publishing.

OECD (Organisation for Economic Co-operation and Development). 2022. 2018 PMR database. Organisation for Economic Co-operation and Development, Paris.

OECD (Organisation for Economic Co-operation and Development), CAF (Corporación Andina de Fomento), and ECLAC (Economic Commission for Latin America and the Caribbean). 2016. *Latin American Economic Outlook 2017: Youth Skills and Entrepreneurship.* Paris: OECD Publishing.

OECD (Organisation for Economic Co-operation and Development), CAF (Corporación Andina de Fomento), and ECLAC (Economic Commission for Latin America and the Caribbean). 2018. *Latin American Economic Outlook 2018: Rethinking Institutions for Development.* Paris: OECD Publishing.

Ohnsorge, F., and S. Yu, eds. 2021. *The Long Shadow of Informality: Challenges and Policies.* Washington, DC: World Bank.

Oleyere, R. U. 2015. "School Enrollment, Attainment, and Returns to Education." In *The Oxford Handbook of Africa and Economics*, vol. 2, *Policies and Practices*, edited by C. Monga and J. Y. Lin. Oxford, UK: Oxford University Press.

Ollivaud, P., Y. Guillemette, and D. Turner. 2016. "Links between Weak Investment and the Slowdown in Productivity and Potential Output Growth across the OECD." Economics Department Working Paper 1304, Organisation for Economic Co-operation and Development, Paris.

Pathikonda, V., and T. Farole. 2017. "The Capabilities Driving Participation in Global Value Chains." *Journal of International Commerce, Economics and Policy* 8 (1): 1750006.

Patrinos, H. A. 2022. "Learning Recovery Plan for Countries in Europe and Central Asia." *Education for Global Development* (blog). May 5, 2022. https://blogs.worldbank.org/education/learning-recovery-plan-countries-europe-and-central-asia

Pattanaik, S., S. Muduli, and J. Jose. 2022. "Zombies and the Process of Creative Destruction." *RBI* [Reserve Bank of India] *Bulletin* (February), 53-66.

Pelikánová, R. M. 2019. "R&D Expenditure and Innovation in the EU and Selected Member States." *Journal of Entrepreneurship, Management and Innovation* 15 (1): 13-34.

Perkins, D. H., and T. G. Rawski. 2008. "Forecasting China's Economic Growth to 2025." In *China's Great Economic Transformation*, edited by L. Brandt and T. G. Rawski. Cambridge, U.K.: Cambridge University Press.

Rajaram, A., T. Minh Le, K. Kaiser, J. Kim, Jay-Hyung, and J. Frank. 2014. *The Power of Public Investment Management: Transforming Resources into Assets for Growth.* Directions in Development—Public Sector Governance. Washington, DC: World Bank.

Rodrik, D. 2017. "Growth without Industrialization?" *Project Syndicate.* https://www.project-syndicate.org/commentary/poor-economies-growing-without-industrializing-by-dani-rodrik-2017-10

Rodrik, D., and A. Subramanian. 2004. "Why India Can Grow at 7 per Cent a Year or More: Projections and Reflections." *Economic and Political Weekly* 39 (16): 1591-96.

Rozenberg, J., and M. Fay. 2019. *Beyond the Gap: How Countries Can Afford the Infrastructure They Need While Protecting the Planet.* Sustainable Infrastructure. Washington, DC: World Bank.

Sanja, B., and P. Tabak. 2020. "Economic Performance of State-Owned Enterprises in Emerging Economies: A Cross-Country Study." European Bank for Reconstruction and Development, London.

Scandurra, G., A. Romanoa, M. Ronghia, and A. Carforab. 2018. "On the Vulnerability of Small Island Developing States: A Dynamic Analysis." *Ecological Indicators* 84 (January): 382-92.

Scartascini, C., and J. Valle Luna. 2020. "The Elusive Quest for Growth in Latin America and the Caribbean: The Role of Trust." Policy Brief 341, Inter-American Development Bank, Washington, DC.

Seguino, S., and M. Were. 2015. "Gender, Economic Growth, and Development in Sub-Saharan Africa." In *The Oxford Handbook of Africa and Economics*, vol. 2, *Policies and Practices*, edited by C. Monga and J. Y. Lin. Oxford, U.K.: Oxford University Press.

Steinwender, C., and P. Shu. 2018. "The Impact of Trade Liberalization on Firm Productivity and Innovation." NBER Working Paper 24715, National Bureau of Economic Research, Cambridge, MA.

Strzelecki, P., J. Growiec, and R. Wyszyński. 2020. "The Contribution of Immigration from Ukraine to Economic Growth in Poland." NBP Working Paper 322, National Bank of Poland, Warsaw.

Trejos, S., and G. Barboza. 2015. "Dynamic Estimation of the Relationship between Trade Openness and Output Growth in Asia." *Journal of Asian Economics* 36 (February): 110-25.

UNCTAD (United Nations Conference on Trade and Development). 2021a. *Reaping the Potential Benefits of the African Continental Free Trade Area for Inclusive Growth.* New York: United Nations.

UNCTAD (United Nations Conference on Trade and Development). 2021b. *Technology and Innovation Report 2021: Catching Technological Waves Innovation with Equity.* New York: United Nations.

UNCTAD (United Nations Conference on Trade and Development). 2021c. *World Investment Report 2021: Investing in Sustainable Recovery.* New York: United Nations.

UNCTAD (United Nations Conference on Trade and Development). 2022. "Global FDI Rebounds Strongly in 2021, but Recovery Highly Uneven." Investment Trends Monitor 40, United Nations Conference on Trade and Development, Geneva.

UNESCO (United Nations Educational, Scientific and Cultural Organization). 2019. "Combining Data on Out-of-School Children, Completion and Learning to Offer a More Comprehensive View on SDG 4." Information Paper 61, UNESCO Institute for Statistics, Montreal, Canada.

UNESCO (United Nations Educational, Scientific and Cultural Organization) and UNICEF (United Nations International Children's Emergency Fund). 2021. *Situation Analysis on the Effects of and Responses to COVID-19 on the Education Sector in South Asia.* Sub-regional Report. October. Bangkok: UNICEF East Asia and Pacific Regional Office and UNESCO Bangkok Office.

UNESCO (United Nations Educational, Scientific and Cultural Organization), UNICEF (United Nations International Children's Emergency Fund), and World Bank. 2021. *COVID-19 Learning Losses: Rebuilding Quality Learning for All in the Middle East and North Africa.* Paris: UNESCO.

UNHCR (United Nations High Commissioner for Refugees). 2022. "Ukraine Situation." Flash Update 8, UNHCR Regional Bureau for Europe. https://data2.unhcr.org/en/documents/details/92011

UNICEF (United Nations International Children's Emergency Fund) and ITU (International Telecommunication Union). 2020. *How Many Children and Young People Have Internet Access at Home? Estimating Digital Connectivity during the COVID-19 Pandemic.* New York: United Nations International Children's Emergency Fund.

Vashakmadze, E., G. Kambou, D. Chen, B. Nandwa, Y. Okawa, and D. Vorisek. 2017. "Regional Dimensions of Recent Weakness in Investment: Drivers, Investment Needs and Policy Responses." Policy Research Working Paper 7991, World Bank, Washington, DC.

Viollaz, M., and H. Winkler. 2020. "Does the Internet Reduce Gender Gaps? The Case of Jordan." Policy Research Working Paper 9183, World Bank, Washington, DC.

Vostroknutova, E., A. Rodriguez, P. Saavedra, and J. Panzer. 2015. "Peru—Building on Success: Boosting Productivity for Faster Growth." Report 99400, World Bank, Washington, DC.

Werner, A., T. Komatsuzaki, and C. Pizzinelli. 2021. "Short-Term Shot and Long-Term Healing for Latin America and the Caribbean." *IMF Blog*, April 15, 2021. https://blogs.imf.org/2021/04/15/short-term-shot-and-long-term-healing-for-latin-america-and-the-caribbean

World Bank. 2014. *Turn Down the Heat: Confronting the New Climate Normal.* Washington, DC: World Bank.

World Bank. 2015. *Live Long and Prosper: Aging in East Asia and Pacific.* Washington, DC: World Bank.

World Bank. 2016. *Global Economic Prospects: Spillovers amid Weak Growth.* January. Washington, DC: World Bank.

World Bank. 2017a. *Africa's Pulse, No. 15.* April. Washington, DC: World Bank.

World Bank. 2017b. *Africa's Pulse, No. 16.* October. Washington, DC: World Bank.

World Bank. 2017c. *East Asia and Pacific Economic Update: Balance Act.* Washington, DC: World Bank.

World Bank. 2017d. *Global Economic Prospects: Weak Investment in Uncertain Times.* January. Washington, DC: World Bank.

World Bank. 2017e. *MENA Economic Monitor: The Economics of Post-conflict Reconstruction in MENA.* Washington, DC: World Bank.

World Bank. 2017f. *MENA Economic Monitor: Refugee Crisis in MENA: Meeting the Development Challenge.* Washington, DC: World Bank.

World Bank. 2017g. *South Africa Economic Update: Innovation for Productivity and Inclusiveness.* Washington, DC: World Bank.

World Bank. 2018a. *Global Economic Prospects: Broad-Based Upturn, but for How Long?* January. Washington, DC: World Bank.

World Bank. 2018b. *World Development Report: Learning to Realize Education's Promise.* Washington, DC: World Bank.

World Bank. 2019a. *Doing Business 2019. Training for Reform.* Washington, DC: World Bank.

World Bank. 2019b. *Global Economic Prospects.* January. Washington, DC: World Bank.

World Bank. 2019c. *South Africa Digital Economy Diagnostic.* Washington, DC: World Bank.

World Bank. 2020a. *The African Continental Free Trade Area: Economic and Distributional Effects.* Washington, DC: World Bank.

World Bank. 2020b. *East Asia and Pacific Economic Update: From Containment to Recovery.* Washington, DC: World Bank.

World Bank. 2020c. *Europe and Central Asia Economic Update: COVID-19 and Human Capital.* Fall. Washington, DC: World Bank.

World Bank. 2020d. *Global Economic Prospects.* January. Washington, DC: World Bank.

World Bank. 2020e. *India Development Update.* July. Washington, DC: World Bank.

World Bank. 2020f. *Islamic Republic of Pakistan: Leveling the Playing Field: Systematic Country Diagnostic.* Washington, DC: World Bank.

World Bank. 2020g. *South Asia Economic Focus: Beaten or Broken? Informality and COVID-19.* Fall. Washington, DC: World Bank.

World Bank. 2020h. *Thailand Economic Monitor: Productivity for Prosperity.* Washington, DC: World Bank Group.

World Bank. 2020i. *Turkey Economic Monitor.* Washington, DC: World Bank.

World Bank. 2021a. *Acting Now to Protect the Human Capital of Our Children: The Costs of and Response to COVID-19 Pandemic's Impact on the Education Sector in Latin America and the Caribbean.* Washington, DC: World Bank.

World Bank. 2021b. *Africa's Pulse, No. 24.* October. World Bank, Washington, DC.

World Bank. 2021c. *Africa's Pulse, No. 23.* April. Washington, DC: World Bank.

World Bank. 2021d. *China Economic Update: Rebalancing Act—From Recovery to High-Quality Growth.* Washington, DC: World Bank.

World Bank. 2021e. *COVID-19 Coronavirus Response: Latin America and the Caribbean—Tertiary Education.* Washington, DC: World Bank.

World Bank. 2021f. *East Asia and Pacific Economic Update: Long Covid.* Washington, DC: World Bank.

World Bank. 2021g. *East Asia and Pacific Economic Update: Uneven Recovery.* Washington, DC: World Bank.

World Bank. 2021h. *Global Economic Prospects.* January. Washington, DC: World Bank.

World Bank. 2021i. *Global Economic Prospects.* June. Washington, DC: World Bank.

World Bank. 2021j. *Iran Economic Monitor: Adapting to the New Normal—A Protracted Pandemic and Ongoing Sanctions.* October. Washington, DC: World Bank.

World Bank. 2021k. *Living with Debt: How Institutions Can Chart a Path to Recovery in the Middle East and North Africa.* Washington, DC: World Bank.

World Bank. 2021l. *Overconfident: How Economic and Health Fault Lines Left the Middle East and North Africa Ill-Prepared to Face COVID-19.* Washington, DC: World Bank.

World Bank. 2021m. *Recovering Growth: Rebuilding Dynamic Post-COVID 19 Economies and Fiscal Constraints*. Semiannual Report for Latin America and the Caribbean. Washington, DC: World Bank.

World Bank. 2021n. *South Asia Economic Focus: Shifting Gears: Digitization and Services-Led Development*. Fall. Washington, DC: World Bank.

World Bank. 2021o. *South Asia Economic Focus: South Asia Vaccinates.* April. World Bank, Washington, DC.

World Bank. 2022a. *Bangladesh Development Update: Recovery and Resilience amid Global Uncertainty*. April. Washington, DC: World Bank.

World Bank. 2022b. *Commodity Markets Outlook*. April. Washington, DC: World Bank.

World Bank. 2022c. *Consolidating the Recovery: Seizing Green Growth Opportunities*. Semiannual Report for Latin America and the Caribbean. Washington, DC: World Bank.

World Bank. 2022d. *East Asia and Pacific Economic Update: Braving the Storms*. Washington, DC: World Bank.

World Bank. 2022e. *East Asia and Pacific Economic Update: Reforms for Recovery*. Washington, DC: World Bank.

World Bank. 2022f. *EU Regular Economic Report 7*. Washington, DC: World Bank.

World Bank. 2022g. *Europe and Central Asia Economic Update: War in the Region*. Spring. Washington, DC: World Bank.

World Bank. 2022h. *Global Economic Prospects*. January. Washington, DC: World Bank.

World Bank. 2022i. *Global Economic Prospects*. June. Washington, DC: World Bank.

World Bank. 2022j. *Pakistan Development Update*. April. Washington, DC: World Bank.

World Bank. 2022k. "Part 2: Growth over the Next Decade." In *EU Regular Economic Report 8: Living up to Potential in the Wake of Adverse Shocks*. Washington, DC: World Bank.

World Bank. 2022l. "Poland Country Economic Memorandum—Green Growth." World Bank, Washington, DC.

World Bank. 2022m. *South Asia Economic Focus: Reshaping Norms—A New Way Forward*. April. Washington, DC: World Bank.

World Bank. 2022n. *Strengthening Services Trade in the Malaysian Economy*. Washington, DC.

World Bank. 2022o. *Women, Business and the Law 2022*. Washington, DC: World Bank.

World Bank. Forthcoming. Europe and Central Asia Economic Update. Washington, DC: World Bank.

World Bank and GDC (German Development Cooperation). 2020. *Building for Peace: Reconstruction for Security, Equity, and Sustainable Peace in MENA*. Washington, DC: World Bank.

World Bank and PRC (Development Research Center of the State Council of the People's Republic of China). 2012. *China 2030: Building a Modern, Harmonious, and Creative Society*. Washington, DC: World Bank.

World Bank and PRC (Development Research Center of the State Council, the People's Republic of China). 2014. *Urban China: Toward Efficient, Inclusive, and Sustainable Urbanization.* Washington, DC: World Bank.

World Bank, UNESCO (United Nations Educational, Scientific and Cultural Organization), and UNICEF (United Nations International Children's Emergency Fund). 2021. *The State of the Global Education Crisis: A Path to Recovery.* Washington, DC: World Bank.

World Economic Forum. 2017. *Global Economic Competitiveness Report 2017-2018.* Geneva: World Economic Forum.

Yuan, S., H. O. Musibau, S. Y. Genç, R. Shaheen, A. Ameen, and Z. Tan. 2021. "Digitalization of Economy Is the Key Factor behind Fourth Industrial Revolution: How G7 Countries Are Overcoming with the Financing Issues?" *Technological Forecasting and Social Change* 165: 120533.

PART II

Investment: Time for a Big Push

[…] forward-looking policies generally involve investment in human, social, or physical capital.

Ben Bernanke, 2017
2022 Nobel Laurate in Economics,
Distinguished Senior Fellow, Brookings Institution,
and Former Chairman of the U.S. Federal Reserve Bank

Much […] will depend on the assets we leave to those who come after us. Some assets take the form of physical capital, such as infrastructure, or human capital, including health and education. But it has become ever clearer that opportunities for future generations depend critically on natural capital (water, air, land, forests, biodiversity, and oceans), and social capital (public trust, strong institutions, and social cohesion).

Nicholas Stern, 2019
IG Patel Professor of Economics and Government,
London School of Economics,
and Former Chief Economist of the World Bank

Education does not just enable individuals to improve their lot in life; it enriches an economy's human capital, which is vital to prosperity and social progress.

Jong-Wha Lee, 2019
Dean of the College of Political Science and Economics,
Korea University,
and Former Chief Economist of the Asian Development Bank

CHAPTER 3
The Global Investment Slowdown: Challenges and Policies

Investment growth in emerging market and developing economies (EMDEs) is expected to remain below its average rate over the past two decades through the medium term. This subdued outlook follows a decade-long, geographically widespread slowdown in investment growth before the coronavirus disease 2019 (COVID-19) pandemic. An empirical analysis covering 2000-21 finds that periods of strong investment growth during this time frame were associated with strong growth in real output, robust growth in real credit, terms-of-trade improvements, growth in capital inflows, and spurts in reform of the investment climate. Each of these factors has been decreasingly supportive of investment growth since the 2007-09 global financial crisis. Weak investment growth is a concern because it dampens potential growth, is associated with weak trade, and makes achieving development and climate-related goals more difficult. Policies to boost investment growth need to be tailored to country circumstances but include comprehensive fiscal and structural reforms, repurposing of expenditure on inefficient subsidies among them. Given EMDEs' limited fiscal space, the international community will need to significantly increase international cooperation, official financing, and grants and leverage private sector financing for adequate investment to materialize.

Introduction

As the COVID-19 pandemic began in 2020, real investment growth had slowed in EMDEs over much of the previous decade, from nearly 11 percent in 2010 to 3.4 percent in 2019. In EMDEs excluding China, investment growth tumbled more sharply: from 9 percent in 2010 to a mere 0.9 percent in 2019. The slowdown during the 2010s occurred in all EMDE regions, in both commodity-importing and commodity-exporting economies, and in a large share of individual economies.

Advanced economies, by contrast, experienced more sluggish, but also more stable, investment growth, which hovered around its long-term average of 2 percent per year. Investment growth in advanced economies outpaced gross domestic product (GDP) growth during the 2000s and 2010s slightly, except for brief periods after the 2001 slowdown and 2009 recession. In contrast, in EMDEs, investment growth outpaced GDP growth by several percentage points in the 2000s but fell below output growth after 2013.

The pandemic triggered a severe investment contraction in EMDEs excluding China in 2020—a far deeper decline than in the 2009 global recession triggered by the global

---

Note: This chapter was prepared by Kersten Kevin Stamm and Dana Vorisek, with contributions from Hayley Pallan and Shu Yu.

FIGURE 3.1 Investment growth

EMDEs experienced a broad-based slowdown in investment growth in the period between the 2008-09 global financial crisis and the coronavirus disease 2019 (COVID-19) pandemic in 2020. The pandemic-induced investment contraction in EMDEs excluding China in 2020 was historically large and much sharper than that in advanced economies. The slowdown in investment growth in EMDEs during the 2010s reflected underlying trends in both commodity-exporting and commodity-importing economies and in the three largest EMDEs, especially China.

A. Investment growth

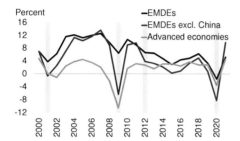

B. Investment growth relative to long-term average

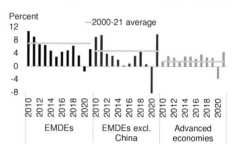

C. Contribution to EMDE investment growth, by commodity exporter status

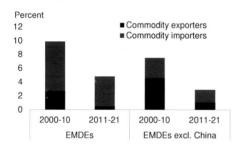

D. Contribution to EMDE investment growth, by country

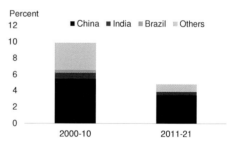

Sources: Haver Analytics; World Bank, World Development Indicators database.
Note: "Investment" refers to gross fixed-capital formation. Investment growth is calculated using countries' real annual investment in constant U.S. dollars as weights. Shaded areas indicate global recessions (in 2009 and 2020) and slowdowns (in 2001 and 2012).
A.B. Sample includes 69 EMDEs and 35 advanced economies. Last observation is 2021. EMDEs = emerging market and developing economies; excl. = excluding.
C.D. Bars show the percentage-point contribution of each country or country group to EMDE investment growth during the indicated years. Height of the bars is average EMDE investment growth during the indicated years. Sample includes 69 EMDEs.

financial crisis. EMDEs including China did not avoid an investment contraction in 2020, as they had in 2009 (figure 3.1.A). In advanced economies, however, investment shrank in 2020 by less than it had in 2009, buttressed by very large fiscal support packages and steep monetary loosening. After a sharp rebound in 2021, investment growth in EMDEs is projected to revert to a pace still below the average during the previous two decades. The medium-term investment growth outlook remains subdued and has been downgraded substantially, along with the GDP growth outlook. This is due to the effects of the Russian Federation's invasion of Ukraine on commodity markets and supply chains, as well as historically high debt-to-GDP ratios and the sharp tightening of financing conditions as monetary policy responds to rising inflation.

Slowing investment growth is a concern because investment is critical to sustaining long-term growth of potential output and per capita income. Capital accumulation raises labor productivity, the key driver of the long-term growth of real wages and household incomes, through capital deepening—equipping workers with more capital—and incorporation of productivity-enhancing technological advances.

Slowing investment growth has also held back progress toward meeting the Sustainable Development Goals (SDGs) and fulfilling commitments made under the Paris Agreement on climate change. Meeting these goals will require filling substantial unmet infrastructure needs, including growing needs for climate-resilient infrastructure and infrastructure that reduces net emissions of greenhouse gases. Given limited fiscal space in EMDEs, scaling up investment will require additional financing from the international community and the private sector.

Against this backdrop, this chapter addresses four questions:

- How has investment growth evolved over the past decade, and how does the performance of investment during the 2020 global recession compare with that during previous recessions?

- What are the key factors associated with investment growth?

- What are the implications of weak investment growth for development prospects?

- Which policies can help promote investment growth?

Contributions. The chapter makes several contributions to the literature on investment. It presents results of the first study to examine investment growth since the pandemic and Russia's invasion of Ukraine in a large sample of EMDEs. Additionally, since foreign direct investment (FDI) is a potentially critical source of technology spillovers and financing, this chapter reviews 62 studies since 1990 on the link between FDI, on the one hand, and output and aggregate domestic investment, on the other. The chapter also examines the likely medium- and long-term consequences of the damage to investment in EMDEs from the pandemic and the war in Ukraine, focusing on the effects on productivity, growth in potential output, trade, and the ability to achieve the SDGs and climate-related goals. Finally, the chapter provides recommendations regarding fiscal and structural policies to revive investment growth, including measures to promote private capital mobilization and capitalize on new opportunities created by the pandemic.

Previous studies analyzing investment in EMDEs have tended to be based on pre-global financial crisis data, confined to analysis of the global financial crisis, or focused on specific regions (Anand and Tulin 2014; Bahal, Raissi, and Tulin 2018; Caselli, Pagano, and Schivardi 2003; Cerra et al. 2016; Qureshi, Diaz-Sanchez, and Varoudakis 2015). Firm-level studies include Magud and Sosa (2015) and Li, Magud, and Valencia (2015). Banerjee, Kearns, and Lombardi (2015); IMF (2015); Leboeuf and Fay (2016); and

Ollivaud, Guillemette, and Turner (2016) have explored investment weakness in advanced economies. This study updates and extends two previous studies of investment trends and correlates in a large sample of EMDEs (World Bank 2017, 2019a).

Main findings. The chapter presents five main findings. *First*, compared with that during the years following the global financial crisis, the investment recovery following the COVID-19 pandemic is proceeding more slowly. The slow recovery partly reflects the wide-spread impact of the pandemic on investment: Investment contracted in nearly three-quarters of EMDEs during the pandemic. The effects of the pandemic and the war in Ukraine are expected to extend the prolonged and broad-based slowdown in investment growth in EMDEs during the 2010s. The slowdown occurred in all regions, in commodity-exporting and commodity-importing economies, and in growth of private and public investment.

Second, empirical analysis in the chapter finds that investment growth in EMDEs over the past two decades has been positively associated with output growth and, to a lesser degree, real credit growth and capital-flow-to-GDP ratios. Improvements in the terms of trade (for energy-exporting EMDEs) and spurts in reform of the investment climate have been associated with strengthening real investment growth. In contrast, in advanced economies, the most important correlate of investment growth over the same period has been output growth, and other factors have covaried less strongly with investment growth than in EMDEs.

Third, investment growth in EMDEs in 2022 remained about 5 percentage points below its 2000-21 average and nearly 0.5 percentage point in EMDEs excluding China. For all EMDEs, projected investment growth through 2024 will be insufficient to return investment to the level suggested by the prepandemic (2010-19) investment trend. Investment weakness of this type dampens long-term output growth and productivity, is associated with weak global trade growth, and makes meeting development and climate goals more challenging.

Fourth, a sustained improvement in investment growth in EMDEs will require the use of policy tools and international financial support, with appropriate prescriptions dependent on country circumstances. Macroeconomic policy can support investment in EMDEs in a variety of ways, preserving macroeconomic stability being just one of those ways. Even with constrained fiscal space, reallocating expenditures, freeing resources by moving away from distorting subsidies, improving the effectiveness of public investment, strengthening revenue collection, and engaging the private sector to cofinance infrastructure and other investment projects can boost spending on public investment. Structural policies will also play a key role in creating conditions conducive to attracting investment. Institutional reforms could address a range of impediments and inefficiencies, such as high business start-up costs, weak property rights, inefficient labor and product market policies, weak corporate governance, costly trade regulation, and shallow financial sectors. Setting appropriate, predictable rules governing investment, including investment in public-private partnerships, will also be important.

Fifth, a review of the literature since 1990 finds mixed evidence on the relationship between FDI and output growth but a mostly positive relationship between FDI and domestic investment. That said, several country characteristics, time period specifics, and features of FDI have influenced the relationships between FDI and output growth and FDI and investment. Greenfield investment in upstream and export-intensive, nonprimary sectors has tended to be more conducive to growth and investment. FDI has also tended to raise growth and investment more in countries with better institutions, more skilled labor forces, greater financial development, and higher trade openness.

Data and definitions. In this chapter, "investment" refers to real gross fixed-capital formation, including both private and public investment. "Gross fixed capital formation" includes produced tangible assets (for example, buildings, machinery, and equipment) and intangible assets (for example, computer software, mineral exploration, entertainment, and original writing or art) used for more than one year in the production of goods and services. Investment growth is calculated, using countries' real annual investment at average 2010-19 prices and constant 2019 U.S. dollars as weights, for 69 EMDEs and 35 advanced economies (table 3C.1). These economies have represented about 97 percent of global GDP since the mid-2000s. Investment cannot be decomposed into type of use, such as buildings, transport equipment, and information and communications technology equipment, because of limited comparable data for EMDEs. Lack of data availability also prevents a separate econometric exploration of private and public investment.

Trends and fluctuations in investment growth

After reaching historic highs in the lead-up to the global financial crisis, global investment growth slowed substantially in the 2010s, largely reflecting weakening investment growth in EMDEs, where this weakening was widespread. In each year between 2012 and 2020, investment growth was well below the pre-global financial crisis (2000-08) average in more than half of EMDEs. The slowdown during the 2010s occurred in both commodity-exporting and commodity-importing EMDEs, in all EMDE regions, and in each of the three largest EMDEs. This slowdown in EMDE investment growth in the decade before the pandemic happened alongside comparatively stable—albeit more sluggish—investment growth in advanced economies, occurred in most EMDEs, and involved slowdowns in both private and public components. Although investment growth in EMDEs remained above that in advanced economies, the difference in investment growth rates, especially in the second half of the decade, was much smaller than in the 2000s.

The investment contraction in EMDEs excluding China in 2020, the first year of the COVID-19 pandemic, was historically large and far deeper even than that during the global recession in 2009. The outlook for investment growth in EMDEs is weak and has been downgraded as a result of legacies of the pandemic and spillovers from the war in Ukraine, although the full effects of these events on investment remain unclear.

FIGURE 3.2 **Growth in private and public investment**

Growth in both private and public investment in EMDEs excluding China was weaker in the decade before the coronavirus disease 2019 (COVID-19) pandemic than during the years prior to the global financial crisis.

A. Growth in private investment

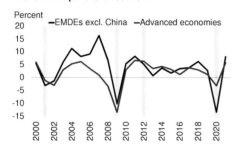

B. Growth in public investment

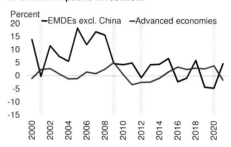

Sources: Haver Analytics; World Bank, World Development Indicators database.
Note: EMDEs = emerging market and developing economies; excl. = excluding.
A.B. Investment growth is calculated using countries' real annual investment in constant U.S. dollars as weights. Shaded areas indicate global recessions (in 2009 and 2020) and slowdowns (in 2001 and 2012). Sample includes 32 EMDEs excluding China and 11 advanced economies. Last observation is 2021.

Prepandemic slowdown

Several key features of investment growth in EMDEs during the prepandemic decade are evident. Investment growth in EMDEs fell from nearly 11 percent in 2010 to 3.4 percent in 2019. In EMDEs excluding China, investment growth tumbled more sharply: from 9 percent in 2010 to a mere 0.9 percent in 2019 (figures 3.1.A and 3.1.B). The slowdown during the 2010s occurred in both commodity-exporting and commodity-importing EMDEs and in all EMDE regions (figure 3.1.C; Vashakmadze et al. 2018). Slowing investment growth in China made a large contribution to the aggregate EMDE slowdown (figure 3.1.D). Private and public investment also grew at a slower pace in the 2010s than in the previous decade (figures 3.2.A and 3.2.B).

The slowdown in investment growth reflected both international and domestic factors. For commodity-exporting EMDEs, a steep drop in oil and metal prices between mid-2014 and early 2016 and the associated deterioration in the terms of trade were key factors.[1] In China, investment growth slowed following a domestic policy shift in 2010 toward more reliance on consumption and less reliance on investment and exports. Weak economic growth in advanced economies and high corporate leverage also generated investment-dampening spillovers to EMDEs during this period (Banerjee, Hofmann, and Mehrotra 2020).

A moderate uptick in EMDE investment growth in 2016-18 reflected, in part, a pickup in the growth of global manufacturing output and trade (World Bank 2019a). A

---

[1] Stocker et al. (2018); Vashakmadze et al. (2018); and World Bank (2017) discuss these issues. Several large commodity-exporting economies—including Brazil, the largest of these economies—experienced severe recessions during the commodity price collapse.

FIGURE 3.3 **Investment around global recessions**

Investment in EMDEs excluding China shrank by more than 8 percent in the pandemic-induced global recession of 2020, about 2 percentage points more than the drop during the global financial crisis. Because of the large number of EMDEs affected by the 2020 global recession, the investment recovery is proceeding more slowly than the recovery after the 2009 global recession.

A. Investment in EMDEs

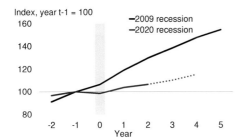

B. Investment growth in EMDEs excluding China

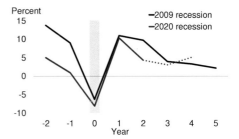

C. Investment in EMDEs excluding China

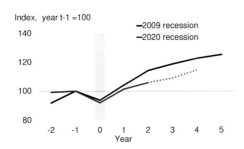

D. Share of EMDEs with an investment contraction

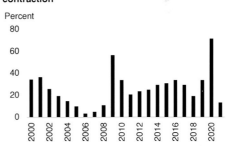

Sources: Haver Analytics; World Bank, World Development Indicators database.
Note: "Investment" refers to gross fixed-capital formation. Investment growth is calculated using countries' real annual investment in constant U.S. dollars as weights. EMDEs = emerging market and developing economies.
A.-C. On the *x*-axis, year 0 refers to the year of global recessions in 2009 and 2020. Dotted portions of lines are forecasts.
A.-D. Sample includes 69 EMDEs.

rebound in oil and metal prices in 2017-18, which encouraged capital expenditures in the commodity-dependent regions of Latin America and the Caribbean (LAC) and Sub-Saharan Africa (SSA), further supported the recovery. Public borrowing from China to finance infrastructure projects under the Belt and Road Initiative supported investment in countries in several regions, predominantly in East Asia and Pacific (EAP), Europe and Central Asia (ECA), and South Asia (SAR) (Council on Foreign Relations 2022; World Bank 2019a; chapter 4).

Collapse and rebound during the COVID-19 pandemic

The COVID-19 pandemic disrupted business operations and caused a spike in uncertainty. This resulted in a sharp contraction in aggregate investment in EMDEs, marking a departure from the previous global recession in 2009, when EMDEs avoided such a contraction (figure 3.3.A). EMDEs excluding China suffered an especially sharp investment contraction, of more than 8 percent—a deeper decline than in 2009. China

FIGURE 3.4 Median investment around domestic recessions and terms-of-trade shocks

The median decline in investment among EMDEs during the 2020 global recession was less severe than that in 2009 and within the range of declines in investment growth during domestic recessions. The median EMDE commodity exporter that experienced a terms-of-trade shock during the 2020 global recession saw a more severe investment contraction than in 2009, however, that contraction was below the range of investment declines during other terms-of-trade shocks.

A. Median investment in EMDEs around domestic recessions

B. Median investment in EMDE commodity exporters around domestic terms-of-trade shocks

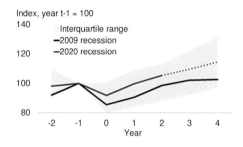
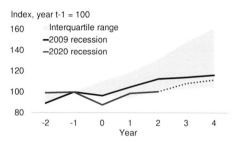

Sources: Haver Analytics; World Bank, World Development Indicators database.
Note: "Investment" refers to gross fixed-capital formation. Dotted portions of lines are forecasts. Sample includes the 69 EMDEs. EMDEs = emerging market and developing economies.
A. On the *x*-axis, year 0 refers to the year of national or global recession. Shaded area shows the interquartile range of investment for domestic recessions that occurred between 1979 and 2020, excluding the global recessions in 2009 and 2020.
B. On the *x*-axis, year 0 refers to the year of the trough in national terms of trade. Shaded area shows the interquartile range of investment for domestic troughs in the terms of trade that occurred between 1979 and 2020, excluding terms-of-trade shocks in 2009 and 2020. Data for 2009 and 2020 include only commodity-exporting EMDEs that also experienced a trough in the terms of trade in 2009 or 2020. Troughs in the terms of trade were identified using the Harding-Pagan method, adjusted for annual data.

was a notable exception, thanks to a large fiscal stimulus equivalent to about 6.5 percent of GDP (IMF 2021).

In EMDEs excluding China, investment shrank by about 2 percentage points more in 2020 than in the 2009 global recession, despite easier financial conditions and the provision of sizable fiscal stimulus in many large EMDEs (figures 3.3.B and 3.3.C). A key difference between the 2009 and 2020 decline in EMDE investment growth was the number of affected EMDEs. About 70 percent of EMDEs experienced an investment contraction in 2020, compared with 55 percent in 2009 (figure 3.3.D). Latin America and the Caribbean and South Asia had the sharpest investment contraction in 2020 among regions; output declined the most in these two regions as well (chapter 4). Yet while more EMDEs experienced a recession in 2020 than in 2009, in the median EMDE recession, investment declined less severely in 2020 than in 2009, and the subsequent rebound was more pronounced (figure 3.4.A). The terms-of-trade shock associated with the 2020 global recession, however, severely affected EMDE commodity exporters. The median EMDE commodity exporter saw a sharper decline in investment in 2020 than in 2009, with a shallower recovery (figure 3.4.B).

Investment in advanced economies also shrank in 2020, by 3.4 percent; however, this was far less than the 10.5 percent plunge in 2009. Massive fiscal and monetary stimulus dampened the investment contraction in 2020, unlike that in the aftermath of the 2009 financial crisis, and the disruptions in financial markets and in access to finance were much smaller. By the end of 2021, investment in advanced economies had already exceeded projections made just prior to the pandemic, in January 2020. Investment recovered more quickly in advanced economies after 2020 than after other global recessions during the past two decades.

Macroeconomic backdrop

Investment grew more slowly in EMDEs in the decade before the pandemic in the context of a worsening global macroeconomic environment. Slower output growth, lower commodity prices, lower and more volatile capital inflows to EMDEs, higher economic and geopolitical uncertainty, and a substantial buildup of public and private debt characterized the global economy in 2010-19, compared with that in 2002-07 (Kose and Ohnsorge 2020).

Weak activity. Investment tends to respond, and respond more than proportionately, to economic activity, a phenomenon dubbed the "accelerator effect" (Shapiro, Blanchard, and Lovell 1986). EMDE per capita output growth slowed sharply in the decade following the global financial crisis, from 7.5 percent in 2010 to 3.9 percent in 2019. There was a roughly parallel growth slowdown in EMDEs excluding China—from 5 percent in 2010 to 1.6 percent in 2019. To the extent that the slowing of growth in EMDEs was more structural than cyclical or transitory, sluggish investment growth can also be expected to persist (Didier et al. 2015; World Bank 2022d). The sources of the slowdown in output growth varied across EMDEs, but they included lower commodity prices, spillovers from weak growth in major economies, weakening productivity growth, tightening financial conditions, and a maturing of supply chains that slowed global trade growth. A decline of 1 percentage point in U.S. or euro area output growth has been found to reduce aggregate EMDE investment growth by more than 2 percentage points (World Bank 2017).

In China, growth slowed gradually as the economy rebalanced from investment- and export-driven growth in manufacturing to consumption-driven growth in services. This transition reduced commodity demand and prices, with adverse spillovers to commodity-exporting EMDEs (Huidrom et al. 2020; World Bank 2016a). A decline of 1 percentage point in China's output growth has been estimated to slow output growth in commodity-exporting EMDEs by about 1 percentage point after one year, with associated effects on investment growth (World Bank 2017).

In advanced economies, output growth in the decade after the global financial crisis was generally weaker than in the decade before, despite unprecedented monetary policy stimulus and easy financing conditions. A recession in 2012-13 followed the euro area crisis. Rising trade tensions, as well, hindered euro area growth prospects near the end of the decade (World Bank 2019b).

Adverse terms-of-trade shocks. Almost two-thirds of EMDEs rely on exports of energy, metal, or agricultural commodities. Most commodity prices (in U.S. dollar terms) fell sharply from their early-2011 peaks, with metal and energy prices plunging by

FIGURE 3.5 Commodity prices, terms of trade, and investment growth

The terms of trade of commodity exporters deteriorated between 2010 and 2019, with the deterioration reflecting steady declines in global prices of energy, metal, and agricultural commodities between 2011 and 2016. EMDEs with higher growth in their terms of trade experienced higher investment growth over 2000-21.

A. Commodity prices

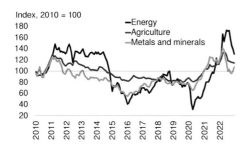

B. Investment growth in EMDEs with high and low growth in terms of trade, 2000-21

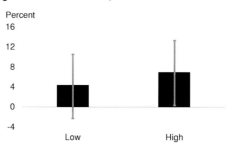

Sources: Haver Analytics; World Bank, World Development Indicators database.
Note: EMDEs = emerging market and developing economies.
A. Energy index includes crude oil (85 percent weight), coal, and natural gas. Agriculture index includes 21 agricultural commodities. Metals and minerals index includes the six metals traded on the London Metal Exchange (aluminum, copper, lead, nickel, tin, and zinc) plus iron ore. Prices indexes are calculated using commodity prices in nominal U.S. dollars. Last observation is December 2022.
B. Bars show group medians; vertical lines show interquartile ranges. "Low" and "high" indicate annual growth in the top and bottom third of the distribution, respectively. Difference in medians between "low" and "high" subsamples is significant at the 1 percent level. Sample includes 69 EMDEs.

more than 40 percent to troughs in 2016, followed by moderate recoveries in the following three years (figure 3.5.A). Surging U.S. oil production and a shift in Organization of the Petroleum Exporters policy in mid-2014 triggered an oil price plunge during 2014-16 that caused widespread disruptions in oil-exporting countries. By the end of 2019, energy prices were 21 percent below their 2010 levels, industrial metal prices 19 percent below, and agricultural commodity prices 13 percent below. As a result, the terms of trade of commodity exporters deteriorated by about 6 percent between 2011 and 2019 and those of oil exporters by 27 percent. EMDEs with lower growth in terms of trade experienced lower investment growth during 2000-21 (figure 3.5.B).

Rapid growth in private sector credit and debt overhang. After rising during most of the 2000s, annual growth of real credit to the private sector (from domestic and foreign financial institutions) in EMDEs began to retreat during the 2008-09 global financial crisis and subsequently slowed further, from 11.5 percent in 2011 to a trough of 4.8 percent in 2016, before stabilizing at about 6 percent in 2019-21 (figure 3.6.A). Credit grew highly unevenly, on average, in 2011-19 across EMDEs, however, with some countries experiencing credit surges despite overall downward trends. In contrast to what took place during the three decades before the global financial crisis, when investment surges accompanied 40 percent of credit booms or followed them within one or two years, credit booms since 2010 have been unusually "investment-less." Investment surges have accompanied or followed virtually none of the credit booms in

FIGURE 3.6 Credit growth, debt, and investment growth

Since 2011, weakening investment growth in EMDEs has been accompanied by slowing real credit growth to the private sector. EMDEs with slower credit growth experienced lower investment growth over 2000-21. Private sector debt has risen steadily, relative to GDP, in EMDEs over the past two decades. EMDEs with larger private-debt-to-GDP ratios experienced slower investment growth during 2000-21.

A. Private credit growth in EMDEs

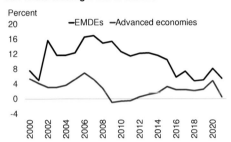

B. Private debt in EMDEs

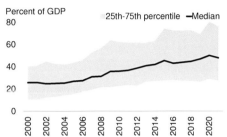

C. Investment growth in EMDEs with high and low credit growth, 2000-21

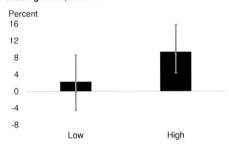

D. Investment growth in EMDEs with high and low private-debt-to-GDP ratios, 2000-21

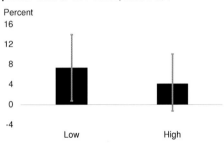

Sources: Bank for International Settlements; Haver Analytics; IMF, International Financial Statistics database; World Bank, World Development Indicators database.
Note: EMDEs = emerging market and developing economies; GDP = gross domestic product.
A. "Private credit" refers to real annual credit growth to the private sector. Lines show weighted averages using countries' real annual investment in constant U.S. dollars as weights. Sample includes 69 EMDEs and 35 advanced economies. Last observation is 2021.
B. "Private debt" refers to domestic credit to the private sector as a percent of GDP. Sample includes 71 EMDEs. Last observation is 2021.
C.D. Bars show group medians; vertical lines show interquartile ranges. "Low" and "high" indicate years when annual credit growth (panel C) and private-debt-to-GDP ratios (panel D) were in the bottom and top third of the distribution, respectively, during 2000-21. Difference in medians between "low" and "high" subsamples is significant at the 1 percent level.
C. Sample includes 69 EMDEs.
D. Sample includes 68 EMDEs.

EMDEs since the global financial crisis (box 3.1). In several EMDEs, rapid credit growth instead fueled above-average consumption growth.

Despite slowing credit growth since the global financial crisis, the ratio of outstanding credit to GDP has risen steadily (figure 3.6.B). In the median EMDE, private credit as a share of GDP rose by 20 percentage points of GDP from 2000 to 2021, and it rose by 27 percentage points in commodity-importing EMDEs. About four in ten EMDEs had private-credit-to-GDP ratios exceeding 60 percent in 2021, up from one in ten in 2000. High leverage can lead to financial stress, restrict future access to credit, and divert resources from productive investment (Banerjee and Duflo 2005; World Bank 2022i).

BOX 3.1 Investment-less credit booms

Credit to the private sector has at times risen sharply in some emerging market and developing economies (EMDEs). But these credit booms have been unusually "investment-less." Investment surges of the kind that were common in earlier episodes have accompanied virtually none of the credit booms in EMDEs since 2010. In 2020, private credit surged in 13 EMDEs, supporting private consumption during the pandemic, while investment fell notably below trend. Lower output growth once the credit booms have unwound has tended to follow the absence of investment surges during credit booms.

Introduction

Over the past decade, credit to the nonfinancial private sector from domestic and foreign lenders has risen rapidly in several EMDEs, while investment growth has slowed. In the past, credit booms have often financed rapid investment growth, with investment subsequently stalling. Against this background, this box addresses three questions:

• How has total investment, including both private and public investment, evolved during credit booms and deleveraging episodes in EMDEs?

• How often have investment booms accompanied credit booms?

• How has output growth evolved during credit booms and deleveraging episodes?

The results indicate that while investment often rose sharply in EMDEs during previous credit booms, this has not been the case for credit booms since 2010. In particular, investment surges accompanied none of the 2020 credit booms. This pattern is cause for concern because in the past, when investment surges did not accompany credit booms and those credit booms unwound, output growth has tended to slow more.

Data and definitions

Credit to the nonfinancial private sector consists of claims—including loans and debt securities—on households and nonfinancial corporations by the domestic financial system as well as external creditors. Annual credit data are available for 14 EMDEs for 1980-99 and 55 EMDEs for 2000-21. In this box, data for the broadest definition of credit are sourced from the Bank for International Settlements for 14 EMDEs from 1980 to 2021: Argentina, Brazil, China, Hungary, India, Indonesia, Malaysia, Mexico, Poland, the Russian Federation, Saudi Arabia, South Africa, Thailand, and Türkiye. For other EMDEs, in which credit from the domestic banking system remains the main source of credit

---

Note: This box was prepared by Shu Yu.

BOX 3.1 Investment-less credit booms (*continued*)

(Ohnsorge and Yu 2016), the box uses annual data on claims by banks on the private sector, sourced from the IMF's *International Financial Statistics*, to proxy credit to the nonfinancial private sector. This increases the sample by another 41 EMDEs, mainly from 2000 onward: Azerbaijan, Bahrain, Bangladesh, Bolivia, Botswana, Bulgaria, Chile, Colombia, Costa Rica, Côte d'Ivoire, Croatia, the Arab Republic of Egypt, Gabon, Georgia, Ghana, Guatemala, Honduras, Jamaica, Jordan, Kazakhstan, Kenya, Kuwait, Mauritius, Mongolia, Namibia, Nigeria, Oman, Pakistan, Panama, Paraguay, Peru, the Philippines, Qatar, Senegal, Serbia, Sri Lanka, Tunisia, Ukraine, Uruguay, República Bolivariana de Venezuela, and Zambia.

A credit boom is defined here as an episode during which the ratio of private sector credit to gross domestic product (GDP) is more than 1.65 standard deviations above its Hodrick-Prescott-filtered trend (that is, within the 90 percent confidence interval) in at least one year (Ohnsorge and Yu 2016; World Bank 2016b). An episode starts when the credit-to-GDP ratio first exceeds one standard deviation and ends when the ratio begins to fall. Conversely, a deleveraging episode is defined as an episode during which the ratio of private sector credit to GDP is more than 1.65 standard deviations below trend in at least one year. The deleveraging episode starts when the credit-to-GDP ratio first drops more than one standard deviation below trend and ends when the ratio begins to climb.

The box studies credit booms and deleveraging episodes within a seven-year event window that covers their peak or trough years ($t = 0$), the three prior years, and the three subsequent years. In the sample used here, there have been 65 credit booms and 32 deleveraging episodes in 55 EMDEs. A typical credit boom lasts about 2 years, while an average deleveraging episode lasts about 2.5 years.

Investment behavior during credit booms and deleveraging episodes

Credit booms have typically been associated with rising investment. During the median credit boom over the past two to three decades, real investment grew by 1 percentage point of GDP above its long-term (Hodrick-Prescott-filtered) trend until the peak of the credit boom (figure B3.1.1.A). In one-quarter of previous credit booms, the real-investment-to-GDP ratio dropped about 3.5 percentage points below its long-term (Hodrick-Prescott-filtered) trend during the two years after the peak. Investment swung sharply in the most pronounced credit boom and bust episodes. For example, during the Asian financial crisis of the late 1990s, investment contracted by an average of 35 percent in Indonesia, Malaysia, the Philippines, and Thailand in 1998 and expanded by 16 percent in 2000.

BOX 3.1 Investment-less credit booms (*continued*)

FIGURE B3.1.1 Investment and consumption growth during credit booms and deleveraging episodes

In the median credit boom in EMDEs, investment grew by about 1 percentage point of GDP more than its long-term trend until the credit boom peaked. Investment dropped below its long-term trend by about 1 percentage point of GDP before deleveraging episodes reached their troughs. Growth in private consumption increases slightly during a credit boom.

A. Investment around credit booms

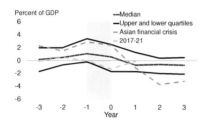

B. Investment around deleveraging episodes

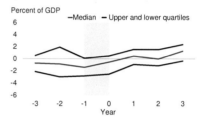

C. Consumption around credit booms

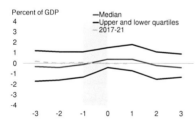

D. Consumption around deleveraging episodes

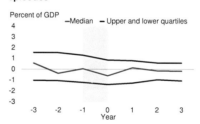

Sources: World Bank, World Development Indicators database.

Note: Red lines show sample medians of the cyclical component of investment in percent of GDP (derived using a Hodrick-Prescott filter); blue lines show the corresponding upper and lower quartiles. Shaded areas indicate credit booms. A credit boom is defined as an episode during which the cyclical component of the ratio of nonfinancial private sector credit to GDP (derived using a Hodrick-Prescott filter) is more than 1.65 standard deviations above trend in at least one year. The episode starts when the cyclical component first exceeds one standard deviation above trend. It ends in a peak year (year 0) when the ratio of nonfinancial private sector credit to GDP declines in the following year. A deleveraging episode is defined as an episode during which the cyclical component of the ratio of nonfinancial private sector credit to GDP (derived using a Hodrick-Prescott filter) is more than 1.65 standard deviations below trend in at least one year. The episode starts when the cyclical component first falls below one standard deviation. It ends in a trough year (year 0) when the ratio of nonfinancial private sector credit to GDP increases in the following year. To address the endpoint problem of a Hodrick-Prescott filter, the data set is expanded by setting the data for 2022-24 to be equal to the data in 2021 (2020 if data for 2021 are unavailable). The sample is for available data over 1980-2021 for 55 EMDEs. EMDEs = emerging market and developing economies; GDP = gross domestic product.

A. The orange dashed line is the median of the six EMDEs (China, Indonesia, Malaysia, Mongolia, the Philippines, and Thailand) that were affected by the 1997-98 Asian financial crisis (1997 is $t = 0$). The yellow dashed line for 2017-21 (where $t = 0$ for year 2020) shows the sample median for the corresponding period.

C. The yellow dashed line for 2017-21 (where $t = 0$ for year 2020) shows the sample median for the corresponding period.

BOX 3.1 Investment-less credit booms (*continued*)

Similarly, investment growth slowed during deleveraging episodes. Real investment dropped below its long-term trend by about 2 percentage points of GDP during the last three years of the median deleveraging episode (figure B3.1.1.B). After the trough of a typical deleveraging episode, real investment growth bounced back and, within three years, rose to near or slightly above its long-term trend.

Credit and investment booms together

Although investment growth tends to rise during credit booms, not all credit booms are associated with investment booms. For instance, Mendoza and Terrones (2012) document a coincidence between investment booms and credit booms in EMDEs between 1960 and 2010 of about 34 percent (26 percentage points lower than the coincidence in advanced economies). The moderate coincidence of credit booms and investment booms may reflect credit booms that mainly fueled consumption (Elekdag and Wu 2013; Mendoza and Terrones 2012). In one-quarter of past credit booms, consumption rose above its Hodrick-Prescott-filtered trend by 3 percentage points of GDP during the peak of the boom (figure B3.1.1.C). Consumption on average fell below trend by about 1 percentage point of GDP in the median deleveraging episode (figure B3.1.1.D).

Following former studies, this box defines an investment surge, in parallel with the way it defines credit booms, as an episode during which the investment-to-GDP ratio is at least one standard deviation higher (compared with 1.65 standard deviations higher for investment booms) than its Hodrick-Prescott-filtered trend. Similarly, an investment slowdown is defined as an episode in which the investment-to-GDP ratio is at least one standard deviation below its Hodrick-Prescott-filtered trend. [a]

Investment surges in advanced economies are found to have occurred more often with credit booms than in EMDEs, and the rise in investment was more rapid. In EMDEs, investment surges or booms around the peak year accompanied about one-third of credit booms (figure B3.1.2.A). More than 65 percent of investment surges that coincided with credit booms during the peak year qualified as investment booms in advanced economies, but only 56 percent of such investment surges turned out to be investment booms in EMDEs.

After the global financial crisis, the coincidence between credit booms and investment surges during the peak year of a credit boom dropped significantly (figure B3.1.2.B). Half of the EMDEs in a credit boom were also experiencing an investment surge in 2007, and two-thirds in 2008. However, from 2010 onward,

---

a. The results are similar when investment growth, instead of the investment-to-GDP ratio, is used.

BOX 3.1 Investment-less credit booms (*continued*)

FIGURE B3.1.2 Coincidence of investment surges and credit booms

Before the global financial crisis, investment surges or booms around the credit boom's peak accompanied about one-third of all credit booms in EMDEs. Investment surges or booms have accompanied only one-sixth of credit booms since 2010.

A. Investment surges during credit booms in EMDEs

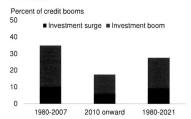

B. Investment surges during credit booms in EMDEs

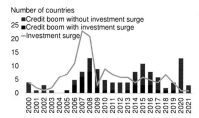

Sources: World Bank, World Development Indicators database.
Note: A credit boom is defined as in figure B3.1.1. An investment surge is defined as a year when the cyclical component of the investment-to-GDP ratio is more than one standard deviation (for an investment boom, more than 1.65 standard deviations) above the trend (derived using a Hodrick-Prescott filter). An investment slowdown is defined as a year when the cyclical component of the investment-to-GDP ratio is at least one standard deviation below the trend (derived using a Hodrick-Prescott filter). The sample is for available data over 1980-2021 for 55 EMDEs. EMDEs = emerging market and developing economies; GDP = gross domestic product.
A. Investment surges during the peak year ($t = 0$) or the following year ($t = 1$).

there were very few instances of simultaneous credit booms and investment surges, except in 2015. As the number of EMDEs in a credit boom increased from two in 2010 to seven in 2015, the number of EMDEs in investment surges dropped from nine to six.[b] In the years prior to the pandemic, the number of credit booms subsided, before rising again in 2020.

For the 13 countries experiencing credit booms in 2020 (Botswana, Brazil, Chile, Georgia, Honduras, Jamaica, Panama, Peru, the Philippines, Qatar, Saudi Arabia, Türkiye, and República Bolivariana de Venezuela), consumption as a share of GDP was about in line with the median during past credit boom episodes, while investment as a share of GDP was lower than in previous credit episodes (figure B3.1.1.A). Credit booms in 2020 seemed to support consumption during the pandemic rather than fueling investment surges as in some of the former credit booms (such as that during the 1997-98 Asian financial crisis).

---

b. The six countries are Ghana, Côte d'Ivoire, Namibia, Oman, Saudi Arabia, and Zambia. Data on investment growth do not support the identification of Saudi Arabia.

BOX 3.1 Investment-less credit booms (*continued*)

FIGURE B3.1.3 Output growth during credit booms and deleveraging episodes

In EMDEs during 1980-2021, output on average grew 2 percent above its trend during credit booms and fell 2 percent below its trend during deleveraging episodes. Output growth during credit booms tended to be stronger when accompanied by investment surges. During deleveraging episodes, declines were deeper when accompanied by investment slowdowns.

A. GDP during credit booms

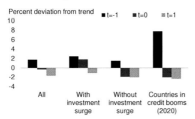

B. GDP during deleveraging episodes

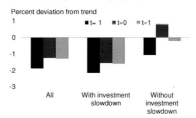

Sources: World Bank, World Development Indicators database.

Note: Credit booms and deleveraging episodes are defined as in figure B.3.1.1. Investment surges and slowdowns are defined as in figure B.3.1.2. The sample is for available data over 1980-2021 for 55 EMDEs. EMDEs = emerging market and developing economies; GDP = gross domestic product.

A. Bars show the group medians for cyclical components of GDP in percent deviation from its trend (derived using a Hodrick-Prescott filter) during all credit booms, credit booms with investment surges, credit booms without investment surges, and credit booms for four countries (China, Georgia, Jamaica, and Qatar) in 2020 over the three years around the peak year ($t = 0$).

B. Bars show group medians of the cyclical component of GDP in percent deviation from its trend (derived using a Hodrick-Prescott filter) during all deleveraging episodes, deleveraging episodes with investment slowdowns, and deleveraging episodes without investment slowdowns over the three years around the trough year ($t = 0$).

Output during credit booms and deleveraging episodes

In general, output has expanded during credit booms, but by less than investment (Mendoza and Terrones 2012). On average, over the whole sample period from 1980 to 2020, in the year before the median credit boom peaked, output increased by about 2.5 percent above trend in the median country in cases in which there was an investment surge. However, in cases in which there was no investment surge, output was slightly lower than trend (figure B3.1.3.A). As credit booms unwound from their peaks, output dropped below trend by about 1 percent over two years in the absence of investment surges. However, when there were investment surges, output was slightly above trend. That a credit boom without an investment surge disrupts output more than a credit boom with an investment surge may reflect the absence of a boost to potential output from capital accumulation that an investment surge could provide. In countries that experienced credit booms in 2020, output peaked at nearly 8 percent above trend in the year before the peak of the credit boom, much higher than in past credit booms, before falling to 2 percent below trend in the peak year of the credit boom.

BOX 3.1 Investment-less credit booms (*continued*)

During the median deleveraging episode, output fell by almost 2 percent below trend in the year prior to the trough and remained below trend until two years after the trough (figure B3.1.3.B). If an investment slowdown accompanied the deleveraging episode, output declined more sharply. In the median episode, it took three years for output to surpass its trend following the deleveraging trough.

Conclusion

Since 2010, numerous EMDEs have experienced periods of rapid growth in private sector credit. In contrast to what took place in many previous episodes, however, investment surges have not, in most cases, accompanied these credit surges. This was particularly the case during the 2020 global recession, when credit-to-GDP ratios surged in 13 EMDEs to support private consumption while investment fell far below trend. Output grew more in the lead-up to the most recent credit booms than in previous episodes, but less at the peak of the boom. During all credit boom episodes between 1980 and 2002, output suffered a larger downturn during the unwinding of the boom when credit booms occurred without investment surges.

EMDEs with lower credit growth and higher private-debt-to-GDP ratios experienced slower investment growth during 2000-21 (figures 3.6.C and 3.6.D).

Subdued and volatile capital inflows. While FDI inflows to EMDEs have risen substantially over time, their growth has slowed since 2010, partly on account of weak activity in advanced economies. Growth of non-FDI inflows has shown more resilience and volatility, reflecting investors' search for higher yields amid low interest rates in advanced economies, a shift from bank to nonbank flows, and increased interest from institutional investors (Cole et al. 2020; McQuade and Schmitz 2016). The global financial crisis led to a significant decrease in the average interest cost of outstanding government debt in advanced economies. In contrast, the average interest cost of outstanding government debt in EMDEs barely decreased, owing to persistently high risk premiums and increased reliance on international borrowing, particularly in foreign currency and on nonconcessional terms (United Nations Inter-Agency Task Force on Financing for Development 2022). Nevertheless, compared with the period leading up to the global financial crisis (2000-07), there were twice as many sudden stop events in EMDEs in the years prior to the COVID-19 pandemic (2011-19). During sudden stops, non-FDI inflows tend to decline much more sharply and for longer than FDI flows (Eichengreen, Gupta, and Masetti 2018).

The literature has produced mixed findings on the link between FDI and investment (box 3.2). Although there is evidence that FDI has a positive relationship with economic growth and investment, mainly in countries with well-developed financial markets, the literature has not found a consistent and significantly positive effect (Alfaro et al. 2004; OECD 2015). One possible explanation for the mixed evidence is that FDI crowds out domestic investment (Farla, de Crombrugghe, and Verspagen 2016).

Heightened uncertainty. Policy uncertainty increased in many EMDEs after the global financial crisis, owing to a variety of factors, including geopolitical tensions in Eastern Europe, security challenges and conflicts in the Middle East, and acute domestic political tensions in several EMDEs. While uncertainty clearly has negative effects on investment and output growth, the scale of those effects depends on the context. Studies have shown that the effects have been more pronounced in countries that have a lower tolerance for uncertainty or where uncertainty interacts with other constraints such as access to credit (Carrière-Swallow and Céspedes 2013; Hofstede 2001; Inklaar and Yang 2012).

Empirical analysis of investment growth

A panel regression analysis is used here to formalize the role of macroeconomic factors in driving investment weakness. Investment growth is estimated for 57 EMDEs covering 2000-21 as the dependent variable in a system generalized method of moments panel regression, similar to the approach in Nabar and Joyce (2009). Growth in real output, the terms of trade, and real private credit; the capital-flow-to-GDP ratio; and a dummy variable for large improvements in the investment climate proxy drivers of investment growth, such as the marginal return to capital and risk-adjusted cost of capital.

Correlates of EMDE investment growth

Real annual investment growth in EMDEs is found to be positively associated with real output growth, real credit growth, improvements in the terms of trade, increasing capital-flow-to-GDP ratios, and spurts in reform of the investment climate (annex 3A; tables 3C.2 and 3C.3). These results are consistent with those of other studies that find a wide number of the drivers of investment growth (G20 2016; IMF 2015; Libman, Montecino, and Razmi 2019). Other studies have also found corporate borrowing to be an important driver of investment growth (for example, Garcia-Escribano and Han 2015). The finding of positive links among institutional quality, financial development, and investment growth is also in line with previous work (Lim 2014). While reform spurts have a large and highly statistically significant coefficient, these events do not explain much of the variation in EMDE investment growth during 2000-21. On average, there were 0.8 investment profile reform spurts in the sample per year, and the majority of these occurred before 2010.

For advanced economies, which did not experience a slowdown in investment growth during the decade prior to the pandemic, output growth is the most important covariate of the explained yearly variation in investment growth during 2000-21. Other factors, such as real credit growth and the ratio of capital flows to GDP, are much less correlated

FIGURE 3.7 Estimated contribution of explanatory variables to predicted investment growth

The slowdown in investment growth in EMDEs in 2011-19 reflected, on average, declining output growth and real credit growth. In commodity importers, worsening real credit growth and several years of falling capital-flow-to-GDP ratios weighed on investment growth. In energy-exporting EMDEs, growth in terms of trade has been highly correlated with investment growth, as seen during the fall in commodity prices in 2015-16 and 2020 and the subsequent recoveries in 2017-18 and 2021.

A. Drivers of investment growth in EMDEs

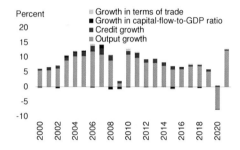

B. Drivers of investment growth in excess of GDP growth in EMDEs

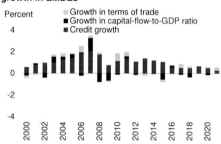

C. Drivers of investment growth in excess of GDP growth in EMDE commodity importers

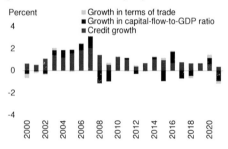

D. Drivers of investment growth in excess of GDP growth in EMDE energy exporters

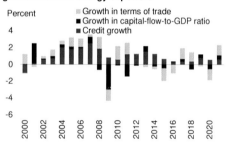

Source: World Bank.
Note: EMDEs = emerging market and developing economies; GDP = gross domestic product.
A.-D. Estimated impact of explanatory variables on investment growth in 57 EMDEs during 2000-21, based on the system generalized method of moments estimation presented in the chapter. Bars show the contribution of each explanatory variable to predicted investment growth (defined, for each variable, as the coefficient shown in the regression results in column (1) of table 3C.2 multiplied by the actual value of the variable). For presentational clarity, the figures show only the four explanatory variables with the largest contributions to predicted investment growth. Panels B, C, and D highlight the smaller but still significant contribution to investment growth after output growth is accounted for. Last observation is 2021.

with investment growth, while still significant.[2] Compared with that in EMDEs, investment growth in advanced economies is slightly more correlated with terms of trade and less correlated with capital flows and real credit growth.

Using the results of the main regression for EMDEs to predict the contribution of the explanatory variables to investment growth shows that between 2000 and 2021, investment growth in EMDEs was primarily correlated with real output growth, followed by real credit growth (figure 3.7.A). Declining capital-flow-to-GDP ratios

---

[2] At a significance level of 10 percent or better.

FIGURE 3.8 **Outlook for investment growth**

Investment growth in EMDEs is projected to be below its 2000-21 average rate in 2023 and 2024. The war in Ukraine adds to downside risks relating to the pandemic and could further hold back investment growth.

A. Investment growth: Short-term forecasts

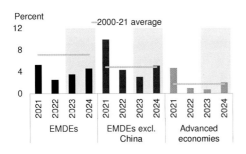

B. Investment growth: Short-term forecasts, by EMDE subgroup

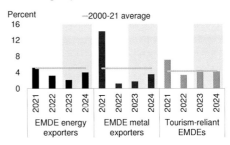

Sources: Haver Analytics; United Nations World Tourism Organization; World Bank, World Development Indicators database.
Note: "Investment" refers to gross fixed-capital formation. Gray shading indicates forecasts. EMDEs = emerging market and developing economies; excl. = excluding.
A.B. Investment growth is calculated using countries' real annual investment in constant U.S. dollars as weights. Sample includes 69 EMDEs and 35 advanced economies.
B. Sample includes 15 EMDE energy exporters, 9 EMDE metals exporters, and 14 tourism-reliant EMDEs.

contributed negatively to investment growth in commodity importers in multiple years after 2011, while energy-exporting EMDEs experienced particularly low credit growth after 2015 (figures 3.7.C and 3.7.D).

Terms of trade made a more volatile contribution and comoved strongly with investment growth in energy-exporting EMDEs, particularly during periods of falling or rising oil prices in 2015-16, 2017-18, 2020, and 2021 (Stocker et al. 2018). The negative shock to the terms of trade of energy-commodity exporters may be viewed as having lowered investment growth by reducing the expected return to capital in the exporting sector (Bleaney and Greenaway 2001). In contrast, improving terms of trade did not significantly offset the factors that slowed investment growth in commodity importers, in part because the improvement was less pronounced than the deterioration experienced by commodity exporters.

In 2020-21, the output growth collapse and rebound generated even larger swings in investment growth. In energy exporters, swings in the same direction in the terms of trade amplified the swings in investment growth. Low real credit growth did not compensate for the collapse in output in 2020 and then held back the recovery in 2021 in both commodity exporters and importers alike.

Investment prospects

After a robust rebound in 2021, investment growth is projected to average 3.5 percent per year in EMDEs, and 4.1 percent in EMDEs excluding China, in 2022-24, below the long-term (2000-21) average rates for both country groups (figure 3.8.A).

Commodity-exporting EMDEs are projected to have lower investment growth rates than tourism-reliant EMDEs (figure 3.8.B). Investment growth is projected to be below the individual-country trend of the past 20 years for about three-fifths of EMDEs in 2023 and 2024.

Following the global financial crisis, EMDEs excluding China returned to the investment level implied by the precrisis trend within two years (figure 3.9.A). China contributed materially to the recovery of investment in EMDEs, helping to raise investment above the level suggested by the precrisis trend by 2010 (figure 3.9.B). However, following the 2020 global recession, projected investment growth through 2024 in all EMDEs will be insufficient to return investment to the level suggested by the prepandemic trend from 2010 to 2019 (the period between the highly disruptive 2009 and 2020 global recessions). This is partly due to the weakness of investment recovery in China (figure 3.9.C). Investment in EMDEs excluding China is projected to return to its prepandemic trend by 2024, with the recovery after the global recession in 2020 taking two years longer than after the global financial crisis (figure 3.9.D).

The weak outlook for investment reflects several factors and may deteriorate further if the global economy tips into recession (Guénette, Kose, and Sugawara 2022). Uncertainties about the postpandemic economic landscape, the war in Ukraine, and elevated inflation and borrowing costs may discourage investment for some time. Tighter financial conditions are limiting the fiscal support governments can provide to stimulate public investment (World Bank 2023). At the same time, the legacy of high corporate debt, at the highest level in decades in EMDEs, may constrain investment growth after the pandemic (Caballero and Simsek 2020; Stiglitz 2020). In China, investment growth is projected to remain well below the average of the past two decades: Regulatory curbs on the property and financial sectors and continuing mobility restrictions related to the pandemic will both be restraining factors, in an environment of slower economic growth.

The globally synchronous nature of monetary (and fiscal) policy, while necessary to contain inflation and preserve creditworthiness, may compound the effects of tightening, creating potentially adverse consequences for investment. The empirical analysis in this chapter finds that slowing GDP growth and slowing credit growth are both associated with slower investment growth. Other empirical studies have found similar results. For example, in a study of a large sample of firms in 13 EMDEs, Borensztein and Ye (2018) find that while higher debt-service capacity is correlated with higher investment growth, when a firm's debt burden rises above a certain threshold, debt restrains investment.[3]

On the bright side, there is evidence that investment in digital technologies and sectoral reallocation has boosted productivity, at least in advanced economies, although it

---

[3] As described in annex 3A, the regression analysis in this chapter tested for nonlinear effects of credit growth and credit-to-GDP thresholds. The results were not significant at the aggregate country level.

FIGURE 3.9 **Investment compared with trend**

Following the global financial crisis, China contributed materially to the recovery of investment in EMDEs, helping to raise investment above the level suggested by the precrisis trend by 2010. After the coronavirus disease 2019 (COVID-19) pandemic, China is expected to be a source of weakness for EMDE investment. In EMDEs excluding China, investment is projected to return to levels suggested by the prepandemic trend by 2024. With China included, EMDE investment will not return to trend.

A. Investment in EMDEs excluding China compared with trend before global financial crisis

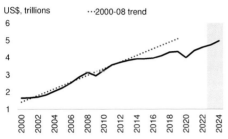

B. Investment in EMDEs compared with trend before global financial crisis

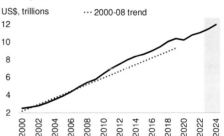

C. Investment in EMDEs excluding China compared with pre-COVID-19 trend

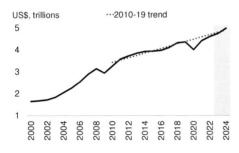

D. Investment in EMDEs compared with pre-COVID-19 trend

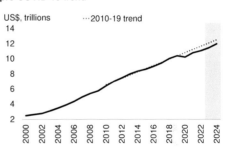

Sources: Haver Analytics; World Bank, World Development Indicators database.
Note: "Investment" refers to gross fixed-capital formation. Investment levels after 2022 are forecast. Trend lines are calculated using linear regression on investment levels during 2010-19 and 2000-08. Gray shading indicates forecasts. Sample includes 69 EMDEs. EMDEs = emerging market and developing economies.

remains to be seen how long-lasting these improvements will be (Criscuolo et al. 2021). Negative factors in major advanced economies appear to have outweighed these improvements' positive effects on total factor productivity (TFP) in the first year of the pandemic (Bloom et al. 2020).

Implications of weak investment growth

Weakening investment growth has lasting implications for global trade as well as for long-term output growth and EMDEs' ability to reach development and climate-related goals. The slowing of capital accumulation in EMDEs, and consequently of technological progress embedded in investment, implies slowing productivity growth and potential output, with adverse implications for EMDEs' ability to catch up with advanced-economy per capita incomes.

BOX 3.2 Macroeconomic implications of foreign direct investment in EMDEs

Inflows of foreign direct investment (FDI) to emerging market and developing economies (EMDEs) have trended downward since the turn of the century, raising concern about negative macroeconomic implications. With that in mind, this box reviews the literature on FDI. Covering research since 1990, a literature survey concludes that there are mixed results on the correlation between FDI and investment as well as that between FDI and growth in EMDEs. Although the literature lacks consensus, there is broad agreement that initial conditions in host countries can be important for linking FDI to domestic investment and growth.

Introduction

Inflows of FDI to EMDEs as a share of gross domestic product (GDP) have slowed over the past decade (figures B3.2.1.A and B3.2.1.B). The decline was broad-based, affecting commodity-exporting and commodity-importing EMDEs, and four of the six EMDE regions (figures B3.2.1.C and B3.2.1.D).

Several reasons have been proposed for the decline, including the maturation of global value chains and tightening FDI regulations.[a] In the 2010s, global value chain formation stagnated after two decades of rapid expansion (Qiang, Liu, and Steenbergen 2021). In addition, in the midst of the global financial crisis, a number of countries imposed restrictions on FDI after many years of FDI liberalization around the world (Sauvant 2009). During the coronavirus disease 2019 (COVID-19) pandemic, both advanced economies and EMDEs raised barriers to FDI, although EMDEs introduced an even larger number of measures to lower such barriers (figure B3.2.1.E). Over the past decade, barriers to FDI have generally been higher in EMDEs than in advanced economies, regardless of the sector receiving the FDI (figure B3.2.1.F). If geopolitical tensions intensify and lead to a further retrenchment in global value chains, it is possible that many EMDEs will face a prolonged period of FDI weakness.

Slowing FDI inflows, FDI restrictions, and frequent changes to them raise concerns about the effects on aggregate investment and output growth in these economies. Slowing FDI may also impede productivity-enhancing collateral benefits (Kose et al. 2009). With more FDI, countries may benefit from pressure for stable macroeconomic policies, financial development, and stronger institutions. However, the strength of the relationship between FDI and investment or growth remains a long-standing matter of debate, with mixed findings in the literature.

Note: This box was prepared by Hayley Pallan.

a. China-U.S. trade tensions since 2018 appear not to have led to a considerable decline in FDI in China yet, largely because of the presence of global value chains in capital-intensive industries (Blanchard et al. 2021).

BOX 3.2 Macroeconomic implications of foreign direct investment in EMDEs (*continued*)

FIGURE B3.2.1 **Trends in FDI since 2000**

FDI inflows as a share of GDP have declined in the past decade. The slowdown has been broad based, occurring in EMDEs and advanced economies, in commodity exporters and importers, and in most regions. FDI policies tend to be more restrictive in EMDEs than advanced economies. Since 2020, barriers to FDI have increased in both groups of countries, although FDI restrictions have simultaneously eased in EMDEs.

A. FDI inflows

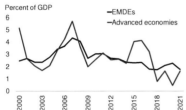

B. FDI inflows, by decade

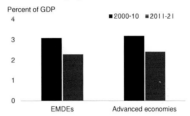

C. FDI inflows to EMDEs, by commodity-exporting status

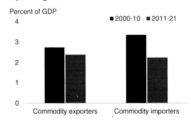

D. FDI inflows to EMDEs, by region

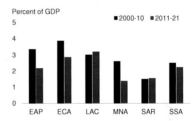

E. FDI barriers and easing measures, 2020-22

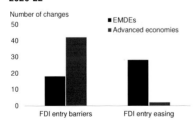

F. FDI Regulatory Restrictions Index, by sector, 2010-20

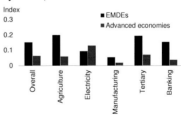

Sources: Organisation for Economic Co-operation and Development, FDI Regulatory Restrictiveness Index; United Nations Conference on Trade and Development; World Bank; World Bank FDI Entry and Screening Tracker.

Note: "FDI" is net FDI inflows as percent of GDP. EAP = East Asia and Pacific; ECA = Europe and Central Asia; EMDEs = emerging market and developing economies; FDI = foreign direct investment; GDP = gross domestic product; LAC = Latin America and the Caribbean; MNA = Middle East and North Africa; SAR = South Asia; SSA = Sub-Saharan Africa.

A. Last observation is 2021.

A.-D. Sample includes 36 advanced economies and 139 EMDEs. Bars show GDP-weighted annual averages of FDI during 2000-10 and 2011-21 (B-D).

E.F. Panel E shows number of barriers to entry of FDI and number of policies easing entry of FDI during 2020-22 for 24 advanced economies and 22 EMDEs. Bars in panel F show averages during 2010-20 for 32 advanced economies and 51 EMDEs. The indexes range from 0 (no restrictions) to 1 (complete restrictions).

BOX 3.2 Macroeconomic implications of foreign direct investment in EMDEs (*continued*)

FIGURE B3.2.2 Correlation of FDI, investment, and growth in EMDEs

Since the 1970s, FDI has had a positive correlation with both investment and growth in almost all decades. However, the strength of the correlation has been inconsistent over time.

A. Correlation between FDI and investment

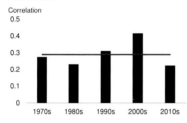

B. Correlation between FDI and growth

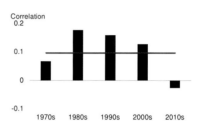

Source: World Bank.
Note: "FDI" is net FDI inflows as percent of GDP. EMDEs = emerging market and developing economies; FDI = foreign direct investment; GDP = gross domestic product.
A.B. Bars show the pooled correlation between FDI and gross fixed-capital formation (percent of GDP) or between FDI and growth in GDP per capita (percent). The red horizontal line shows the aggregate correlation for the period 1970-2020. All correlations are computed using a constant sample of 71 countries. All positive correlations are different from 0 with statistical significance.

Correlations between FDI inflows and investment and FDI inflows and output growth were weak, less than 0.3 and 0.1, respectively, during 1970-2020, with variation depending on the time period and country characteristics (figures B3.2.2 and B3.2.3). These correlations are somewhat lower in countries with better-developed financial systems, possibly because financial development affords greater consumption smoothing. And conversely, the correlations are somewhat larger in countries with high trade openness, better institutions, or a more skilled labor force, suggesting complementarities between these factors and FDI that can amplify growth dividends.

Against this backdrop, this box surveys prior empirical studies on FDI to address two questions:

- What is the link between FDI and investment?

- What is the link between FDI and output growth?

The box documents that the literature has found mixed evidence on the relationship between FDI and output growth but a mostly positive relationship between FDI and investment. FDI has tended to raise growth and investment

BOX 3.2 Macroeconomic implications of foreign direct investment in EMDEs (*continued*)

FIGURE B3.2.3 Correlation of FDI, investment, and growth in EMDEs by host country conditions

FDI has generally had stronger correlations with both investment and output growth in EMDEs with lower financial development, higher trade openness, better human capital, and stronger institutions.

A. Correlation, by financial development

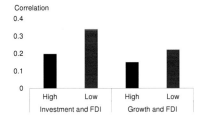

B. Correlation, by trade openness

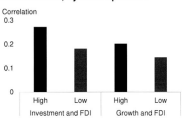

C. Correlation, by human capital

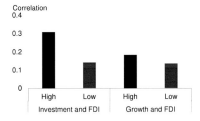

D. Correlation, by institutions

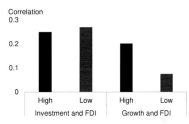

Sources: PRS Group, *International Country Risk Guide*; World Bank.
Note: "FDI" is net FDI inflows as percent of GDP. EMDEs = emerging market and developing economies; FDI = foreign direct investment; GDP = gross domestic product.
A.B. Bars show the pooled correlation between FDI and gross fixed-capital formation and between FDI and growth in GDP per capita for countries with high (greater than the 75th percentile; blue bars) and low (lower than the 25th percentile; red bars) levels of financial development or levels of trade openness. Financial development is measured as private credit as share of GDP. "Trade" refers to trade as a share of GDP. Differences between country groups are not statistically significant.
C.D. Bars show the pooled correlation between FDI and gross fixed-capital formation and between FDI and growth in GDP per capita for countries with high (blue bars) and low (red bars) levels of human capital or institutions. For human capital, "high" refers to pupil-to-teacher ratio less than the 25th percentile, and "low" refers to pupil-to-teacher ratio greater than the 75th percentile. For institutions, "high" refers to countries above the median, and "low" refers to countries below the median, of the Investment Profile Index in the PRS Group's *International Country Risk Guide*. Differences between country groups are not statistically significant.

more in countries with better institutions, more skilled labor forces, and greater financial development and openness and when FDI has been directed at manufacturing rather than the primary sector or services.

The remainder of the box reviews 62 studies of FDI, of which 25 pertain to investment and 37 to output growth, covering up to 150 countries and using data

BOX 3.2 Macroeconomic implications of foreign direct investment in EMDEs (*continued*)

for 1960-2018.[b] These studies have been selected based on two criteria: They include EMDEs in the empirical analysis, and they focus on the macroeconomic implications of FDI received in host economies. More than 80 percent of the studies are cross-country, and more than 65 percent of these cross-country studies use exclusively EMDE samples.

Findings of the literature on FDI and investment

The majority of the studies (60 percent) find a positive, statistically significant correlation between FDI and investment, sometimes called "crowding in" (figure B3.2.4.A; Ang 2009a; Kamaly 2014). This correlation is generally found regardless of whether the empirical analysis includes data prior to 1990. However, studies that include data after 2009 generally find mixed results.

Another 30 percent of studies on FDI and investment find mixed effects, and only 2 each find a negative effect or no effect. Mixed effects are recorded in the survey if a study finds a combination of positive, negative, or no effects. One of the studies finding no effect is based on subnational data for China; the other uses a predominantly Latin American and Caribbean country sample between the 1970s and 2000s. The two studies finding outright negative effects employ generalized method of moments techniques to avoid endogeneity or seek to identify long-run relationships, in contrast to other studies that rely mostly on ordinary least-squares regressions (Eregha 2012; Morrissey and Udomkerd-mongkol 2012).

The strength of the relationship between FDI and investment, which is mostly positive, depends on country characteristics, initial conditions, and types of FDI (figure B3.2.4.B). Initial conditions important for investment include financial development and institutions in the host economy.

- *Financial development.* The positive link between FDI inflows and domestic investment is stronger when countries have higher levels of financial development (Jude 2019). FDI may have served as a catalyst for economic activity when domestic firms have had access to sufficient financing to invest in expansions. On the other hand, low financial development may have hindered investment. In contrast, in the two decades after the collapse of the Soviet Union, financial development appears to have been associated with a weaker correlation between FDI and investment in Europe and Central Asia (Mileva 2008).

---

b. A separate strand of research on outward FDI finds that by investing abroad, home country firms may benefit from greater and more diversified growth opportunities (Arndt, Buch, and Schnitzer 2010; Desai, Fritz Foley, and Hines 2009; Hejazi and Pauly 2003; Herzer and Schrooten 2008).

BOX 3.2 Macroeconomic implications of foreign direct investment in EMDEs (*continued*)

FIGURE B3.2.4 Summary of empirical studies of FDI and investment in EMDEs

The literature mostly finds a positive relationship between FDI and investment, especially when using samples starting before the 1990s or ending prior to 2009. The strength of the relationship between FDI and investment depends on country characteristics and the features of FDI.

A. Findings on the relationship between FDI and investment

B. Studies on FDI and investment that account for initial conditions and type of FDI

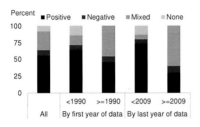

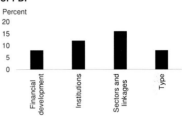

Sources: World Bank, based on 25 studies: Agosin and Machado (2005); Ahmed et al. (2015); Al-Sadig (2013); Amighini, McMillan, and Sanfilippo (2017); Ang (2009a); Arndt, Buch, and Schnitzer (2010); Ashraf and Herzer (2014); Borensztein, De Gregorio, and Lee (1998); Bosworth, Collins, and Reinhart (1999); Chen, Yao, and Malizard (2017); Eregha (2012); Ha, Holmes, and Tran (2022); Jude (2019); Kamaly (2014); Lautier and Moreaub (2012); Makki and Somwaru (2004); Mileva (2008); Mody and Murshid (2005); Morrissey and Udomkerdmongkol (2012); Ndikumana and Verick (2008); Nguyen (2021); Pels (2010); Tang, Selvanathan, and Selvanathan (2008); Wang (2013); and World Bank (2017).

Note: EMDEs = emerging market and developing economies; FDI = foreign direct investment.

A. First bar shows share of studies that find statistically significant positive, negative, mixed, or missing relationships between FDI and investment. Remaining sets of two bars show shares of studies if they are restricted based on the start date of their empirical analysis (before and after 1990) and the end date of their empirical analysis (before and after 2009).

B. Bars show the share of surveyed studies on FDI and investment that find a statistically significant role for specific initial conditions, as shown along the x-axis. "Sectors and linkages" refers to different effects of FDI on investment depending on the sector of FDI (that is, manufacturing or services). "Type" refers to different effects of FDI on investment depending on whether FDI is greenfield or mergers and acquisitions.

- *Institutions.* The positive relationship between FDI and investment is found to be stronger in countries with better institutions (as measured by the World Bank's Country Policy and Institutional Assessments) or competitiveness (Mody and Murshid 2005; Nguyen 2021). Political stability is shown to dampen the negative relationship between FDI and domestic investment (Morrissey and Udomkerdmongkol 2012).

- *Sectors and linkages.* FDI is associated with more investment when it occurs in the manufacturing sector, is directed to sectors that mainly source inputs domestically, or occurs in sectors that are export oriented (Amighini, McMillan, and Sanfilippo 2017; Ha, Holmes, and Tran 2022). These types of FDI may encourage investment through foreign firms purchasing domestic inputs, selling domestic firms cheaper inputs, or helping local firms integrate

BOX 3.2 Macroeconomic implications of foreign direct investment in EMDEs (*continued*)

into global value chains. FDI is associated with less investment when it is directed to sectors that mainly compete with domestic producers (Ha, Holmes, and Tran 2022). In such cases, investment would be lowered when foreign firms reduce demand for domestic inputs, as they are replaced by FDI inputs, resulting in less investment by local firms no longer in demand.

- *Type.* FDI can take the form of mergers and acquisitions or greenfield investment. Since mergers and acquisitions primarily involve a transfer of ownership, the net impact on domestic investment is unclear. In contrast, greenfield investment directly injects new capital into host countries and is associated with more domestic investment (Ashraf and Herzer 2014; Jude 2019). While greenfield FDI tends to create more investment overall, the effect is strongest in the long run (Jude 2019). Greenfield FDI includes capital-intensive start-up activities, and it takes time to observe their direct benefits and spillovers.

Findings of the literature on FDI and output growth

The evidence on the relationship between FDI and output growth has been mixed, with a positive relationship identified more often in samples starting after 1990 than in samples covering earlier years (figure B3.2.5.A).[c] Among those studies reviewed, only one used long-term cointegration methods for a pre-1990 sample; it identified a statistically significant negative relationship between FDI and output growth in 44 EMDEs between 1970 and 2005 (Herzer 2012). The broader mixed findings may reflect reverse causality running from growth to FDI, third factors driving both FDI and growth, or heterogeneity across time periods and country samples. Several studies have attempted to disentangle the direction of causality and control for a comprehensive set of other factors.

As in the literature on FDI and investment, the strength of the relationship between FDI and output growth depends on initial conditions in host countries and on types of FDI (figure B3.2.5.B). These initial conditions include country characteristics such as financial development, quality of institutions, human capital, and the extent of integration with the global economy.

- *Financial development.* The association between FDI and output growth is stronger in countries with more developed financial systems, in part because domestic firms in those countries are able to finance expansions that allow them to supply multinationals (Alfaro et al. 2004; Azman-Saini, Law, and Ahmadi 2010; Bengoa and Sanchez-Robles 2003; Hermes and Lensink

c. This is consistent with findings from a review of the literature before the global financial crisis (Kose et al. 2009).

BOX 3.2 Macroeconomic implications of foreign direct investment in EMDEs (*continued*)

FIGURE B3.2.5 Summary of empirical studies of FDI and growth in EMDEs

The literature mostly finds a mixed relationship between FDI and output growth, especially when using samples starting before the 1990s. The strength of the relationship between FDI and growth depends on country characteristics and the features of FDI.

A. Findings on the relationship between FDI and output growth

B. Studies on FDI and output growth that account for initial conditions and type of FDI

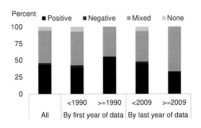
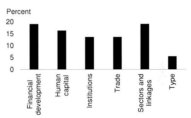

Sources: World Bank, based on 37 studies: Alfaro (2003); Alfaro and Charlton (2013); Alfaro et al. (2004); Alguacil, Cuadros, and Orts (2011); Ali and Asgher (2016); Ang (2009b); Aykut and Sayek (2007); Azman-Saini, Law, and Ahmad (2010); Balasubramanyam, Salisu, and Sapsford (1996); Benetrix, Pallan, and Panizza (2022); Bengoa and Sanchez-Robles (2003); Blanchard et al. (2016); Borensztein, De Gregorio, and Lee (1998); Busse and Groizard (2008); Carkovic and Levine (2005); Chakraborty and Nunnenkamp (2008); Choe (2003); Chowdhury and Mavrotas (2006); Cipollina et al. (2012); De Mello (1999); Driffield and Jones (2013); Gao (2004); Hansen and Rand (2006); Harms and Méon (2018); Hermes and Lensink (2003); Herzer (2012); Kohpaiboon (2003); Lee and Chang (2009); Luu (2016); Makki and Somwaru (2004); Mehic, Silajdzic, and Babic-Hodovic (2013); Nair-Reichert and Weinhold (2001); Osei and Kim (2020); Prasad, Rajan, and Subramanian (2007); Romer (1993); Wang (2009); and Wang and Wong (2011).
Note: EMDEs = emerging market and developing economies; FDI = foreign direct investment.
A. First bar shows share of studies that find statistically significant positive, negative, mixed, or missing relationships between FDI and growth. Remaining sets of two bars show shares of studies if they are restricted based on the start date of their empirical analysis (before and after 1990) and the end date of their empirical analysis (before and after 2009).
B. Bars show share of studies on FDI and growth that find a statistically significant role for specific initial conditions, as shown along the *x*-axis. "Sectors and linkages" refers to different effects of FDI on growth depending on the sector of FDI (that is, manufacturing or services). "Type" refers to different effects of FDI on growth depending on whether FDI is greenfield or mergers and acquisitions.

2003). Since the financial and capital account liberalizations of the 1990s, however, the link between financial development and growth has weakened (Benetrix, Pallan, and Panizza 2022). This weakening may reflect threshold effects in the rapid financial system growth that followed these liberalizations. For example, there appears to be a private-credit-to-GDP threshold above which FDI and growth no longer have a positive relationship, possibly because of an increased incidence of financial crises (Osei and Kim 2020).

- *Human capital.* FDI and output growth have a stronger positive link in countries with higher-skilled workforces, possibly because these countries are better equipped to absorb the productivity-enhancing new technology that

BOX 3.2 Macroeconomic implications of foreign direct investment in EMDEs (*continued*)

typically accompanies FDI (Bengoa and Sanchez-Robles 2003; Borensztein, De Gregorio, and Lee 1998; Romer 1993; Wang and Wong 2011). Since the 2000s, however, the amplifying role of human capital in the relationship between FDI and output growth appears to have diminished (Benetrix, Pallan, and Panizza 2022). [d]

- *Institutions.* Strong institutions, as measured by indexes of business regulation and freedom from government intervention, are associated with a stronger positive link between FDI and output growth or a dampened negative link (Alguacil, Cuadros, and Orts 2011; Driffield and Jones 2013; Herzer 2012). Conversely, excessive regulation is associated with a weaker link between FDI and output growth (Busse and Groizard 2008).

- *Trade.* Trade openness and global integration are associated with a stronger link between FDI and output growth (Balasubramanyam, Salisu, and Sapsford 1996; Kohpaiboon 2003; Makki and Somwaru 2004). However, in countries that rely heavily on primary sector exports, FDI and growth are found to be negatively correlated (Herzer 2012).

- *Sectors and linkages.* FDI in the manufacturing sector is found to be positively correlated with output growth, while FDI in other sectors has no significant correlation, or even a negative correlation (Ali and Asgher 2016; Aykut and Sayek 2007; Chakraborty and Nunnenkamp 2008; Wang 2009). FDI in high-tech, capital-intensive, and high-skill industries is associated with high output growth (Alfaro and Charlton 2013; Cipollina et al. 2012). Conversely, FDI in the primary sector, which tends to have few linkages to other domestic sectors, is not associated with greater output growth (Alfaro 2003).

- *Type.* Greenfield FDI is found to have a positive effect on output growth (Harms and Méon 2018), while mergers and acquisitions are associated with lower output growth (Luu 2016).

Conclusion

As summarized here, in a review of 62 studies, the literature has found mixed evidence on the relationship between FDI and output growth, but there is mostly a positive relationship between FDI and investment. That said, several country

d. These recent results may reflect the strong ties between global value chains and FDI (Adarov and Stehrer 2021; Qiang, Liu, and Steenbergen 2021). For example, Antràs (2020) explains that global value chains may lessen the prerequisites for a country to receive FDI because some segments of global value chains in developing countries require less skills than high-value-added segments.

BOX 3.2 Macroeconomic implications of foreign direct investment in EMDEs (*continued*)

characteristics, time period specifics, and features of FDI have influenced the relationships between FDI and output growth and FDI and investment. Greenfield investment in upstream and export-intensive, nonprimary sectors tends to be more conducive to growth and investment. FDI has also tended to raise growth and investment more in countries with better institutions, more skilled labor forces, greater financial development, and trade openness.

Policies can aim to encourage types of FDI or, more broadly, to improve the country-level conditions that make FDI enhance growth more. These policies include, for example, efforts to invest in education for a higher-skilled workforce capable of absorbing new technologies. Limiting trade restrictions can help countries attract, and benefit from, FDI related to global value chains, as EMDE country segments of global value chains typically produce inputs that are used in other parts of the production process or goods for sale elsewhere, which need to be exported to final consumers. Countries can also support financial development to attract FDI. In the long run, improving institutions and ensuring political stability can help generate growth- and investment-enhancing FDI inflows. Furthermore, investment promotion agencies have been found to have a positive effect on attracting FDI to targeted sectors (Harding and Javorcik 2011).

Slower global trade growth. Investment tends to be more import intensive than other components of demand, particularly through trade in capital goods. Weakening investment growth, therefore, contributed to the slowdown of trade before the pandemic (figures 3.10.A and 3.10.B; Bobasu et al. 2020; IMF 2016; World Bank 2015c). Capital goods imports by EMDEs tend to embody efficiency-enhancing technology transfers (Alfaro and Hammel 2007). Hence, the slowdown in such transfers may also have contributed to slowing EMDE productivity growth. A pullback in cross-border investment by multinational companies, which accounts for one-third of global trade, further accompanied the global investment weakness (Lakatos and Ohnsorge 2017). This slowdown occurred at the same time as, and may have been partly due to, the implementation by several countries of additional regulatory measures and nontariff barriers, such as restrictions on FDI and limitations on foreign purchases in public procurement (chapter 6).

Global trade also propagates a pickup or slowdown in investment growth across countries (chapter 6; Freund 2016). Trade can facilitate more efficient allocation of capital goods, in turn improving overall productivity and rates of return on capital, thus encouraging investment (Mutreja, Ravikumar, and Sposi 2014). For example, the marginal product of capital does not vary much between low- and high-income countries, and EMDEs with high relative prices of investment goods compared with consumption prices, will tend to have lower real investment rates (Caselli and Feyrer

FIGURE 3.10 **Slowdown in growth of investment and trade**

A downturn in the growth of imports accompanied the slowdown in investment growth in EMDEs after the global financial crisis. Both imports and investment fell below their 2000-10 trend, and the coronavirus disease 2019 (COVID-19) pandemic lowered them further.

A. EMDE investment and imports

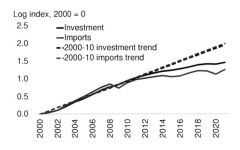

B. EMDE investment and import growth

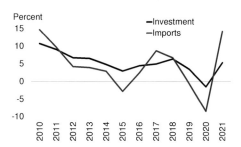

Sources: Haver Analytics; World Bank, World Development Indicators database.
Note: EMDEs = emerging market and developing economies. "Investment" refers to gross fixed-capital formation.
A. Levels of real gross fixed-capital formation and imports.
B. Aggregate investment growth is calculated using real annual investment in constant U.S. dollars as weights.

2007; Hsieh and Klenow 2003). Countries engaged in deepening trade integration have seen the prices of investment goods fall relative to the prices of consumption goods, especially between 2005 and 2011, thus boosting investment rates (Lian et al. 2019). Indeed, trade openness has been found to be positively correlated with capital accumulation (Alvarez 2017; Sposi, Yi, and Zhang 2019; Wacziarg and Welch 2008).

The deep global recession of 2020, together with pandemic-related lockdowns, led to a collapse of global trade in 2020. Continuing supply and shipping bottlenecks, weak demand, and continued pandemic-related mobility clampdowns in some countries hampered the subsequent recovery in trade. The war in Ukraine has further slowed global trade growth by disrupting commodity markets, logistics networks, and supply chains (Ruta 2022).

Slower growth in potential output. The prospect that investment growth will remain weak in the medium term raises fundamental concerns about the economic health of EMDEs and about meeting the infrastructure needs of expanding and urbanizing populations in many EMDEs. Before the COVID-19 pandemic, growth in potential output—the level of growth achievable at full capacity utilization and full employment—had already slowed in EMDEs (Kilic Celik, Kose, and Ohnsorge 2020; World Bank 2018). Projected low investment growth in the medium term will further weaken growth in potential output through 2030. This will result in capital accumulation contributing, on average, 0.6 percentage point a year less to EMDE potential growth in 2022-30 than in 2011-19. However, filling needs for investment in physical capital could partially offset the projected slowdown in potential growth during 2022-30 (chapter 1; figure 3.11.A; World Bank 2021a).

FIGURE 3.11 **Growth of investment, productivity, and potential output**

EMDEs with low investment growth also tend to have low TFP growth. Fluctuations in TFP growth in EMDEs between 2000 and 2020 mirror fluctuations in investment growth. Slowing investment and TFP growth have lowered potential growth in EMDEs, especially in commodity-importing EMDEs, among which China has an outsized weight.

A. Growth in potential output

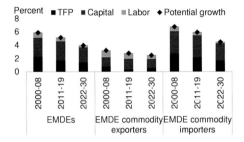

B. EMDE investment and total factor productivity

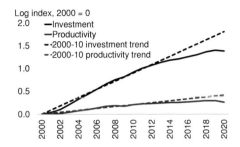

C. Investment and total factor productivity growth in EMDEs

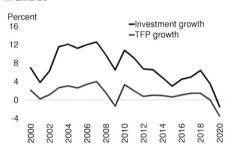

D. Total factor productivity growth in EMDEs with high and low investment growth, 2000-20

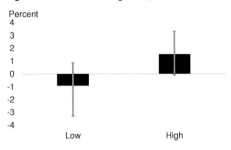

Sources: Dieppe (2021); Haver Analytics; International Labour Organization; Penn World Table; UN, World Population Prospects; World Bank.
Note: EMDEs = emerging market and developing economies; TFP = total factor productivity.
A. Growth in potential output is based on production function estimates. Sample includes 53 EMDEs.
B.C. Total factor productivity is derived from labor productivity (output per worker) by adjusting for human capital and capital deepening; see Dieppe (2021). "Investment" refers to gross fixed-capital formation. Investment growth and TFP growth are calculated using countries' real annual investment in constant U.S. dollars as weights. Sample includes 69 EMDEs.
D. Bars show group medians; vertical lines show interquartile ranges. "Low" and "high" indicate years when annual investment growth was in the bottom and top third of the distribution, respectively, during 2000-20. Difference in medians between "high" and "low" subsamples is significant at the 1 percent level. Sample includes 69 EMDEs.

Weaker investment growth leads to weaker growth in potential output by lowering TFP growth. In contrast, increased investment often involves the adoption of productivity-enhancing technologies, in the investment goods sector itself, among other places (Colecchia and Schreyer 2002; Hsieh and Klenow 2007; OECD 2016a). Weaker investment and TFP growth can also be a symptom of market distortions that subsidize investment by less productive firms (Restuccia and Rogerson 2008). Alongside slowing investment growth, TFP growth in EMDEs slowed in the decade prior to the pandemic to 1.2 percent per year in 2010-19, on average, from 2.3 percent per year in 2000-08 (figures 3.11.B and 3.11.C). EMDEs with low investment growth tend to also have low

TFP growth   (figure 3.11.D). TFP growth slowed in EMDEs despite evidence of somewhat faster cross-country absorption of technologies from countries at the productivity frontier (Comin and Ferrer 2013; Moelders 2016). Along with investment growth, TFP growth in EMDEs is projected to remain weak during the next decade (chapter 5). Slower labor productivity growth—the key driver of long-term growth in real wages and household incomes—would also reflect weak TFP growth (Blanchard and Katz 1999; Feldstein 2008).

The pandemic generated another major hit to productivity. If the impacts of the pandemic on the accumulation of physical and human capital and slowing TFP growth are taken into account, growth in potential output in EMDEs is estimated to drop to about 4 percent per year in 2022-30, from an estimated 5.1 percent per year in 2011-19 (chapter 5).

Slower progress toward the SDGs and climate goals. Achieving the SDGs and climate-related goals requires increasing investment in EMDEs. Raising infrastructure investment is especially important, following several years of subdued growth in public investment in infrastructure in EMDEs before the pandemic (Foster, Rana, and Gorgulu 2022; Vorisek and Yu 2020). Meeting commitments for reducing emissions of greenhouse gases, advancing the transition to clean energy, and capping the rise in temperature are expected to require an investment in infrastructure and other adaptations of several trillion U.S. dollars per year (table 3C.5; Black et al. 2022; IEA 2021a, 2021b; IPCC 2022; Songwe, Stern, and Bhattacharya 2022). For a partial set of EMDEs, building resilience to climate change and putting these economies on track to reduce emissions by 70 percent by 2050 is estimated to require investment of 1 to 10 percent of GDP annually between 2022-30, with higher investment needed in low-income countries (LICs) (figure 3.12.A; World Bank 2022a).[4] Similarly, LICs will need a much larger increase in spending (relative to GDP) to achieve the SDGs than will the average EMDE (Gaspar et al. 2019). Closing investment gaps will require substantial additional financing from the global community and the private sector.

Achieving the SDGs related to infrastructure (electricity, transport, water supply and sanitation) and infrastructure-related climate change preparation (flood protection, irrigation) in low- and middle-income countries will necessitate average investment of $1.5-$2.7 trillion per year (4.5-8.2 percent of these countries' combined annual GDP) during 2015-30. This investment will mostly be needed for transport and electricity (Rozenberg and Fay 2019), depending on policy choices and the quality and quantity of infrastructure services, with variance across regions (figure 3.12.B). The estimate of 4.5 percent of GDP anticipates investment in renewable energy; transport and land use planning that results in denser cities and less expensive, more reliable public transport and development of reliable railway systems for freight; and deployment of decentralized technologies such as minigrids and water purification systems in rural areas. Gaps in investment relative to the levels needed to reach the health-related SDGs also remain

---

[4] The range of 1-10 percent is for all countries with Country Climate and Development Reports as of late 2022.

FIGURE 3.12 Investment needs related to climate goals and the Sustainable Development Goals in EMDEs

Continued weak investment growth will make filling large investment gaps related to climate and development goals in EMDEs more challenging.

A. Additional investment needs for a resilient and low-carbon pathway, 2022-30

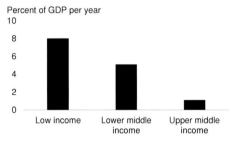

B. Average investment needs in infrastructure sectors related to SDGs, by region

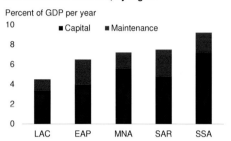

Sources: Rozenberg and Fay (2019); World Bank (2022a); World Bank.
Note: EAP = East Asia and Pacific; GDP = gross domestic product; LAC = Latin America and the Caribbean; MNA = Middle East and North Africa; SAR = South Asia; SDG = Sustainable Development Goal; SSA = Sub-Saharan Africa.
A. Bars show the annual needs for investment to build resilience to climate change and put countries on track to reduce emissions by 70 percent by 2050. Depending on availability, estimates include investment needs related to transport, energy, water, urban adaptations, industry, and landscape. In some World Bank Country Climate and Development Reports, especially those for low-income and lower-middle-income countries, estimated investments include development needs, especially those linked to closing the infrastructure gaps—such as solar minigrids to provide energy access—and cannot be considered entirely "additional" to preexisting financing needs.
B. Bars show average annual needs for spending on electricity, transport, water and sanitation, flood protection, and irrigation during 2015-30. Country sample includes low- and middle-income countries, as defined in the technical appendix of Rozenberg and Fay (2019).

substantial (Stenberg et al. 2017; UNCTAD 2014).[5] Likewise, investment in education is vital to achieving schooling-related SDGs, closing education achievement gaps created by the pandemic, and supporting long-term income growth (Barro 2013; Psacharopoulos et al. 2021).[6]

Investment in infrastructure has multiple potential benefits. For one, it appears to be inversely correlated with income inequality in EMDEs. Infrastructure investment can lower income inequality and poverty through direct channels, for example, by employing members of low-income households or providing services at lower cost and better quality, or indirect ones, for example, by lowering trade costs in stimulating economic growth.[7] Investment in climate-related resilience and adaptation, as well as

---

[5] Stenberg et al. (2017) estimate that meeting the health-related targets under SDG 3 in low- and middle-income countries would require about $370 billion (1.9 percent of GDP) in additional spending per year through 2030, mostly for health workers, infrastructure, and health equipment.

[6] Psacharopoulos et al. (2021) estimate that lifetime losses in incomes from school closures during the COVID-19 pandemic will amount to 0.8 percent of global GDP per year over the next 45 years. Barro (2013) finds that one additional year of male upper-level schooling can raise GDP growth by 1.2 percentage points per year. Jones (2003) theoretically shows how educational attainment can be interpreted as an investment rate.

[7] Calderón and Servén (2014) review multiple channels through which infrastructure investment affects the poor; Ferreira (1995) and Getachew (2010) discuss the role of public investment in infrastructure and Medeiros, Ribeiro, and do Amaral (2021) the role of infrastructure investment; and Maliszewska and van der Mensbrugghe (2019) examine the role of infrastructure investment in lowering trade costs and generating opportunities for the poor.

mitigation, is central to eliminating extreme poverty and achieving the SDGs. Such investment is perhaps most crucial in low-income and high-poverty countries, which are particularly vulnerable to the impact of climate change and increasingly frequent adverse weather events on agriculture, energy generation and usage, and water availability (World Bank 2022a). Green infrastructure and the adoption of environmentally sustainable technologies can support faster growth in the long term, while also mitigating climate change (OECD 2020; Strand and Toman 2010). Improving and expanding access to infrastructure can enhance productivity (Bizimana et al. 2021; Calderón, Moral-Benito, and Servén 2015; Perez-Sebastian and Steinbuks 2017). Public investment in infrastructure has also been found to create jobs, especially in LICs (Moszoro 2021).

Policies to promote investment growth

EMDEs have substantial investment needs—to bolster resilience to climate change, smooth the transition away from growth driven by natural resources, improve social conditions, and support long-term growth of output and per capita income. The urgent need to ramp up investment in EMDEs is clear. The challenges demand a multi-pronged strategy featuring a variety of fiscal and structural measures to boost growth in public and private investment, with the specific priorities differing according to country circumstances.

Fiscal and structural policy, especially over the medium and long term, can make a substantial dent in filling large investment needs in EMDEs. Multilateral institutions will also clearly need to assist EMDEs in financing their investment needs. Yet constrained fiscal space and the limited resources of multilateral development banks mean that the private capital mobilization has become vital to filling investment needs (Bhattacharya and Stern 2021; United Nations Inter-Agency Task Force on Financing for Development 2019; World Bank 2022f).

It is critical to design policies that can stimulate investment with lasting benefits while discouraging opportunistic behavior and to focus on high-quality investment projects (G20 2019). Successfully leveraging private sector capital to boost investment requires a set of policies to balance the risks, costs, and returns of investment projects, as well as overcoming common obstacles to private investment, such as poor business conditions, insufficient project pipelines, and underdeveloped domestic capital markets.

Two areas with strong growth potential are investment in digital capabilities and the transition to clean energy. The pandemic created new opportunities for the adoption of digital infrastructure in commerce and governance, while energy market volatility due to Russia's invasion of Ukraine and an increasingly urgent need to meet climate goals have made the development of clean, renewable, and affordable energy sources a priority.

The pandemic also underscored the need for investing in health and education. Healthier individuals are more productive, better at creating and adapting to new technologies, and inclined to invest more in education (Aghion, Howitt, and Murtin 2011). They also have a longer life expectancy and are likely to save more, which feeds back into investment (Zhang, Zhang, and Lee 2003). Investing in education is necessary not only to make up for the effect of lost schooling on future earnings, but also to explore how new approaches to learning and digitalization can reduce inequality in education in EMDEs, provided the appropriate underlying conditions, including the necessary infrastructure, are in place (Bashir et al. 2021; Muñoz-Najar et al. 2021; Wilichowski et al. 2021). In the long term, investment in education is needed to spur research and development and ultimately, innovation.

Fiscal policy

Countries can pay for public investment in infrastructure, education, and public health systems in several ways. First, they can raise funding through government borrowing, in particular through countercyclical fiscal stimulus programs during economic downturns, among other possible avenues. The extended low-interest-rate environment in the decade or more before 2022 offered an opportunity for many governments to borrow for investment projects, with limited risks to long-term fiscal sustainability (OECD 2016b). With debt burdens now at historically high levels and financing costs rising with global interest rates, however, EMDEs have limited capacity for expansionary fiscal policy financed through increased borrowing. Countries that are in or near debt distress can focus on fiscal sustainability in the short term to free fiscal resources for investment while taking care to protect spending on essential health, education and other social programs (Glassman, Keller, and Smitham 2023; World Bank 2022i).

Second, countries can increase revenues or cut other expenditures to finance increases in public investment. Strengthening tax administrations, broadening tax bases, or raising tax rates could increase revenues. Revenue-to-GDP ratios are particularly low in South Asia and Sub-Saharan Africa (World Bank 2015b, 2016b). Even without tax rate increases, efforts to remove exemptions, tighten tax administration, and broaden tax bases could yield revenue gains that increase resources to finance public investment projects. Measures that have proven successful in the past include the adoption of digital payments, taxpayer and property registration, and monitoring compliance (Okunogbe and Santoro 2021).

Less productive expenditures and those that are less clearly aligned with policy priorities could also be reallocated toward growth-enhancing investment. For example, eliminating distortive agriculture and fossil fuel subsidies would free sizable funds for investment in renewable energy, health, education, and targeted social safety net programs, even in fiscally constrained EMDEs (World Bank 2022c). Similarly, identifying inefficient spending on high-cost medicines and other health expenditures for which lower-cost alternatives are available could offer large gains in spending efficiency (Glassman, Keller, and Smitham 2023). For commodity-exporting economies, well-implemented fiscal rules and stabilization funds would allow governments to use windfall gains earned when commodity prices are high to smooth government investment and expenditures during economic downturns or when commodity prices are low. Procyclical fiscal policy in commodity-exporting countries has been found to worsen the depth of economic downturns (World Bank 2022d). Countercyclical fiscal rules need to also take into account spending on health, education, and aspects of social safety nets, which are often discretionary even in countries that have implemented fiscal rules (Glassman, Keller, and Smitham 2023).

Third, within an existing envelope of public spending on investment, it may be possible to improve spending efficiency and increase the benefits to growth (Buffie et al. 2012). For example, medium-term budget frameworks can improve spending predictability, while greater transparency of expenditures and independent spending evaluations can generate incentives to improve efficiency. Better coordination among different levels of government can reduce duplication and inconsistencies (Mandl, Dierx, and Ilzkovitz 2008; St. Aubyn et al. 2009). Limiting contractual and institutional risks related to public-private partnerships in infrastructure can reduce contingent liabilities, while careful monitoring of state-owned enterprises can limit the need to inject fiscal resources into these companies (Dappe et al. 2022; Dappe, Melecky, and Turkgulu 2022). Some countries also have capacity to improve budget execution of planned public investment (World Bank 2022b).

Engaging the private sector to cofinance infrastructure and other investment projects can limit the use of fiscal resources and diversify risks. EMDEs can also boost private capital mobilization through the use of syndicated loans, guarantees, and instruments for enhancing credit and managing disaster risk. Multilateral institutions have been engaged in offering all of these products to EMDEs in recent years, easing the challenges borrowers in these counties face when seeking financing from investors (World Bank 2022f, 2022h). Although private investors require adequate returns to compensate them for the risk they take on, they can improve the efficiency of infrastructure investment by contributing necessary skills and operational experience.

For EMDEs, boosting public investment can have large benefits in terms of output, because multipliers tend to be large (Izquierdo et al. 2019). Few studies estimate the fiscal multipliers for infrastructure investment in EMDEs, but the existing literature suggests that investment in green and digital infrastructure may have high multipliers (Vagliasindi and Gorgulu 2021). With the right conditions, public investment can boost private investment. Falling trade barriers and privatization efforts increase the likelihood public investment will have a positive effect on private investment, especially if the stock of infrastructure is low and access to credit is not constrained (Bahal, Raissi, and Tulin 2018; Erden and Holcombe 2005).

Fiscal policy can also support private investment indirectly. Prospects for growth of demand and output play a major role in private investment decisions. To the extent that a growth slowdown in EMDEs is cyclical, countercyclical fiscal stimulus can help raise private investment during and after a downturn, assuming there is policy space (Cerra, Hakamada, and Lama 2021; Huidrom, Kose, and Ohnsorge 2016). However, expansionary fiscal policy can also crowd out private investment, thereby hindering economic growth. If increased government borrowing, through the pressure it puts on

FIGURE 3.13 Investment growth around reform spurts and setbacks in EMDEs

In EMDEs, investment growth has increased around reform spurts. Reform setbacks have been associated with a significant decrease in investment growth.

A. Investment growth around reform spurts

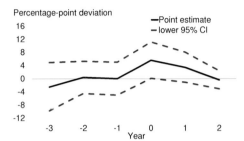

B. Investment growth around reform setbacks

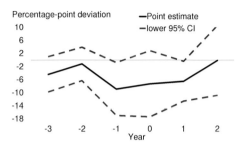

Sources: PRS Group, *International Country Risk Guide*; World Bank.
Note: Sample includes 60 EMDEs from 1984 to 2022. Annex 3B defines reform spurts and setbacks. Solid lines show the increase in investment growth around a reform spurt (panel A) or setback (panel B) at year = 0 relative to the countries not experiencing a reform spurt or setback. Dashed lines show the 95 percent confidence interval. EMDEs = emerging market and developing economies.

credit markets or through reactions of the central bank, leads to increases in interest rates and appreciation of the domestic currency, the cost of financing will increase and reduce a country's international competitiveness. For example, high levels of public investment in China after the global financial crisis initially boosted economic growth but also saddled cities with large amounts of public government debt (Huang, Pagano, and Panizza 2020). This increase in local public debt tightened financial conditions and lowered private investment by local manufacturing firms. Conversely, reducing fiscal deficits can, in some circumstances, boost private investment (Essl et al. 2019).

Monetary policy also has a role in supporting the growth of private investment, primarily by establishing an environment of low and stable inflation over the medium term, which will foster confidence in macroeconomic stability (World Bank 2022e). Monetary policy can also play a countercyclical role through its management of interest rates and credit growth. This can support investment growth when activity is weak and inflation is low, while also restraining investment when the economy is overheating.

Structural policy

Structural reforms of many types can reduce constraints to investment and ultimately boost investment growth. The empirical results in this chapter suggest that spurts in reform of the investment climate and higher real credit growth have been associated with stronger investment growth (annex 3A). This positive impact is also apparent in a panel regression of investment growth on large spurts and setbacks in investment climate reforms among 60 EMDEs during 1984-2022 (figure 3.13.A). Reform spurts are associated with significantly higher investment growth—by about 6 percentage points, on average. Reform setbacks have a more mixed impact (figure 3.13.B; annex 3B).

Reforms that improve the business and regulatory climate can enable investment that increases the willingness of investors to extend long-term financing to domestic firms, thus reducing rollover risks and, if financing is put toward infrastructure or research and development, yielding returns over decades. Business environment reforms can also amplify the positive effects of investment, such as less informality and more job creation.[8] Informal firms are both less productive and less capital intensive than formal firms (IMF 2019; Ohnsorge and Yu 2021). Structural reforms that encourage entry of informal firms into the formal sector can therefore raise investment and growth in potential output, particularly in countries where informal firms are prevalent. Reducing business start-up costs has been linked to higher profitability of incumbent firms and greater investment in information and communications technology. Stronger property rights can encourage business and real estate investment. Labor and product market reforms that increase firm profitability can encourage investment. In countries where access to finance is constrained, measures to promote financial deepening could boost investment, although risk indicators must be monitored to avoid financial instability (Kiyotaki and Moore 2005; Sahay et al. 2015).

Addressing climate change and building a resilient and reliable energy infrastructure requires structural reforms that encourage private investment participation and lower barriers of access for the private sector. Many EMDEs need governance and institutional reforms to improve and unify the often-fragmented regulatory and institutional environment, including regional cooperation in, for example, electricity trade. Unpredictable regulatory and policy risk is one reason capital costs two to three times more for solar energy producers in EMDEs (excluding China) than in advanced economies (IEA 2022).

EMDEs have made significant progress in establishing robust policy frameworks for renewable energy and energy efficiency since 2010, but the gap between their regulatory frameworks and those of advanced economies is still large, especially in the case of LICs (ESMAP 2020). Medium-term policy targets and development plans can lower the policy uncertainty holding back private investment (World Bank 2022i). For energy-importing EMDEs, Russia's invasion of Ukraine has underscored the energy security benefits of relying on a diversified mix of energy inputs, transitioning to clean sources of energy, and improving the energy efficiency of buildings and production processes (World Bank 2022g).

Setting appropriate, predictable rules relating to investment decisions can boost investment and help countries avoid potential pitfalls. Using firm-level data, Gutierrez and Philippon (2017) find that when firms invest less than would be expected based on their market performance, corporate governance and industry concentration explain two-thirds of this shortfall. Improvements in the planning and allocation of investment

---

[8] For the linkages between reform measures and investment growth, see Andrews, Criscuolo, and Gal (2015); Calcagnini, Ferrando, and Giombini (2015); Corcoran and Gillanders (2015); Field (2005); Munemo (2014); Reinikka and Svensson (2002); Schivardi and Viviano (2011); and Wacziarg and Welch (2008).

and in the implementation of public investment management systems, including reforms that resolve problems of asymmetric information and moral hazard, can enhance the benefits of infrastructure investment. This can be achieved, for example, through the establishment of a sound legal and institutional setting, robust appraisal systems, and effective procurement and monitoring systems (Gardner and Henry 2021; Kim, Fallov, and Groom 2020). For EMDEs in which public-private partnerships for infrastructure investment are common, a robust governance structure for such partnerships can limit fiscal risks and avoid opportunistic renegotiations (Dappe, Melecky, and Turkgulu 2022; Engel, Fischer, and Galetovic 2020). A robust regulatory framework for public-private partnerships is especially critical in LICs, where related reforms are lagging (World Bank 2020b).

Developing digital and technological infrastructure can be an important driver of investment growth. Policies to stimulate private and public investment include closing the gap in rural access to broadband networks, aligning regulations with international standards, implementing regulation that encourages competition, ensuring price affordability for consumers, and educating the workforce in skills relevant to information and communications technology (OECD and IDB 2016). Between 2003 and 2018, new high-speed undersea internet connections to Africa, in the presence of a reliable electricity supply, increased FDI flows into the technology and financial sectors of African countries and expanded the size of investment projects in those countries (Mensah and Traore 2022). In Nigeria, the expansion of mobile broadband internet led to an increase of consumption by covered households, lowered poverty rates, and raised labor market participation (Bahia et al. 2020). Multilateral institutions have a role to play in assisting EMDEs in developing a pipeline of projects of interest to investors.

In many EMDEs, underdeveloped and illiquid domestic financial markets limit investment, especially for small- and medium-sized firms (World Bank 2015a). Compared with those in advanced economies, banks extend less credit to the private sector as a share of GDP in EMDEs. This access gap to credit is largest for loans with long maturities (United Nations Inter-Agency Task Force on Financing for Development 2022). Development of domestic capital markets in EMDEs encompasses not only improving financial institutions, but also developing private markets for equity and debt. Policies to expand financial intermediation and access to credit include lowering information asymmetries (for example, on the creditworthiness of debtors), building the legal infrastructure for contract enforcement to lower collateral requirements, providing partial credit guarantees to intermediaries to mitigate specific risks and market failures, developing a digital infrastructure to lower market access costs for firms and small financial institutions, and establishing disclosure rules for asset allocation and investment decisions (United Nations Inter-Agency Task Force on Financing for Development 2022; World Bank 2022f).

Local currency equity and debt markets facilitate the entry of institutional investors, such as pension funds and private equity firms, which have a higher risk tolerance, and allow firms to access financing in EMDEs with less-developed financial intermediation infrastructures (United Nations Inter-Agency Task Force on Financing for Development 2022). Multilateral development banks can support development of these markets through the use of innovative products such as catastrophe bonds as well as blue and green bonds and provision of liquidity in local currency in the most illiquid capital markets, as well as assistance and advice to governments on building the necessary regulatory and institutional frameworks (World Bank 2015a, 2022f). Risk indicators must be monitored to avert financial instability as domestic capital markets are developed, however (Kiyotaki and Moore 2005; Sahay et al. 2015).

Trade-related reforms, such as simplifying border procedures, eliminating unnecessary duties, and improving trade-related transport infrastructure, could help increase trade flows, with associated benefits for investment (chapter 6; Breton, Ferrantino, and Maliszewska 2022). Lowering uncertainty related to at-the-border trade costs and committing to current or reduced tariff levels, as well as lowering other nontariff barriers, will decrease trade costs and encourage investment. High-quality and well-maintained infrastructure, such as ports and airports, should accompany these reforms (World Bank 2021b). In some EMDEs, lower barriers to cross-border trade finance would help close trade finance gaps and support trade growth (IFC and WTO 2022).

Membership in trade and integration agreements, such as the African Continental Free Trade Area, solidifies reforms, which should benefit a country's investment climate, particularly if such agreements boost integration into global value chains and help lower the cost of tradable investment goods (machinery and equipment), for which EMDEs still face significantly higher costs than advanced economies (Lian et al. 2019). These reforms should include standardization of inspection and labeling requirements, which add significant costs to trade even if tariffs are low (Moïsé and Le Bris 2013). Lower trade barriers can integrate participating economies into regional and global value chains, while investment, intellectual-property rights, and competition protocols aim to increase cross-border investments (Echandi, Maliszewska, and Steenbergen 2022; World Bank 2020a).

In the long term, many commodity-exporting EMDEs need to diversify their economies so that terms-of-trade shocks are less likely to have an impact on investment decisions. They can accomplish such diversification by, for instance, moving production up the value chain or building infrastructure that promotes the growth of activity outside the natural resource sector. EMDEs will also increasingly need to develop policies to offset the investment-dampening effects of population aging (Aksoy et al. 2019; Zhang, Zhang, and Lee 2003).

Conclusion

Investment growth slowed during the decade prior to the pandemic. On an aggregate level, investment collapsed more in EMDEs in 2020 (including or excluding China) than in the global recession in 2009, and the return to the prerecession trend is expected to take longer. The slowdown of investment growth in EMDEs during the decade prior to the pandemic and the subdued prospects for investment growth in the medium term can be observed, to varying degrees, in all EMDE regions. Chapter 4 explores investment trends and policies needed to boost investment in each of the six EMDE regions.

The empirical analysis in this chapter finds that strong growth in real output, robust growth in real credit, improvements in terms of trade, growth in capital inflows as a share of GDP, and spurts in reform of the investment environment are associated with strengthening real investment growth. For advanced economies, where investment growth was much lower than in EMDEs during the 2010s but also more stable, output growth is found to be the most important correlate of investment growth during 2000-21.

At a time when investment growth is projected to be sluggish in most EMDEs, fiscal space for expansion of public investment is limited, and borrowing conditions are much tighter than during the long period of easy credit in the decade prior to the pandemic. Policy makers will need to identify innovative ways to fill unmet investment needs. Meeting climate goals and SDG targets and supporting long-term growth requires sound fiscal policies, including debt sustainability, as well as targeted investment and reforms.

The sequencing and implementation of these reforms should reflect country-specific circumstances. For example, in countries under acute fiscal stress, the priority may be improving spending efficiency in public investment. In countries with anemic private investment, the priority may be business climate reforms, including robust competition policy, to foster private investment. In countries with large foreign direct investment, the priority may be to improve human capital to ensure that such foreign direct investment enhances growth.

Needed fiscal policies will include those increasing spending efficiency, implementing countercyclical fiscal rules, and strengthening tax administration and revenue collection. Additional financing from the international community and the private sector will need to complement fiscal policy to boost investment. Structural reforms such as lowering tariffs and nontariff barriers to trade, improving the business climate, and putting in place predictable rules such as governance structures that enable public-private partnerships will be needed to crowd in private investment. Public and private investment can both play important roles in boosting long-term growth prospects by supporting productive sectors or expanding infrastructure (including digital, transportation, and electricity infrastructure), improving health sector outcomes, and improving and expanding education. The impact of school closures during the pandemic makes the need for investment in education particularly significant.

Future research on investment could focus on several areas. One is to identify the policies most likely to boost growth in public and private investment and thereby the growth of output and per capita incomes. Promising research questions relate to the relative effectiveness of various institutional reforms in raising investment growth, as well as the quantitative benefits of investments in infrastructure and information and communications technology (Libman, Montecino, and Razmi 2019; Mensah and

Traore 2022). Public investment in infrastructure has been found to stimulate structural transformation and productivity (Perez-Sebastian and Steinbuks 2017).

Human development is strongly correlated with income per capita and economic growth. Countries with higher income levels tend to have not only a larger share of workers in the formal sector, where wages are typically higher than in the informal sector, but also a larger share of jobs that provide health care benefits, job stability, and good working conditions (Hovhannisyan et al. 2022). These job quality attributes improve access to health care, allow households to send their children to school, and minimize their chance of experiencing catastrophic expenditures. Yet within countries, there is often large heterogeneity in the quality of jobs across sectors of the economy (ILO 2008, 2013; OECD 2015). Identifying sectors and structural reforms that increase investment opportunities with the highest likelihood of providing good-quality jobs will help close education and health gaps to achieve the SDGs.

Another underdeveloped area of research is understanding the role of intangible investment (for example, intellectual property) in driving growth and productivity. Related questions will become increasingly important as EMDEs transition to knowledge- and technology-based economies. Data limitations, however, especially in regard to EMDEs, are hindering progress (Crouzet et al. 2022). The international community could support national statistical agencies in EMDEs in improving their capacity to measure and collect data on intangible investment.

ANNEX 3A Determinants of investment growth: Empirical framework

Framework. Investment decisions are based on the expected marginal return of capital and the risk-adjusted cost of financing the investment. While public investment decisions may also involve other considerations, private investment accounts for the majority of investment in emerging market and developing economies (EMDEs), about three-quarters of total gross fixed-capital formation.

Therefore, investment is modeled in this chapter as the level of investment I chosen such that the marginal return on capital (MPK) equals the cost of capital, which is the sum of the risk-adjusted real interest rate r and the rate of depreciation of capital δ, absent binding constraints:

$$MPK = r + \delta.$$

As a result, I also depends on the determinants of the marginal product of capital—especially total factor productivity TFP and the existing stock of capital K. Since investment decisions are about the expected future returns to capital, the cost of capital also includes a risk premium π:

$$I = I(TFP, K, r, \pi, \delta).$$

A higher cost of capital—whether due to higher risk premiums or higher risk-free real interest rates—would reduce investment, whereas higher productivity, lower depreciation, or a low capital stock would raise it.

To proxy these factors, the regression includes growth in real output, terms of trade, and real credit; change in capital flows as a percent of gross domestic product (GDP); and a dummy for spurts in investment reform. As exports are included in GDP, output growth also captures trade growth beyond its impact through terms of trade.

Data sources. Real investment growth is calculated from real gross fixed-capital formation taken primarily from Haver Analytics and, for countries or years not available in Haver Analytics, from the World Bank's World Development Indicators or *Global Economic Prospects* for 2021. Real output growth is taken from the *Global Economic Prospects*. Real credit growth to the private sector and the credit-to-GDP ratio in the robustness section are taken from the Bank for International Settlements and supplemented with data from the International Monetary Fund's *International Financial Statistics*. Credit growth proxies both depth of the financial sector as well as the cost of financing investment, since data on comparable financing costs for a sufficiently large number of countries over the past two decades is not available. Terms of trade are from the World Development Indicators and, for 2021, from the *Global Economic Prospects*. Capital flows are calculated using data on the sum of foreign direct investment, portfolio flows, and changes in external bank liabilities from the *International Financial Statistics*. Missing data for all three flow variables are imputed by taking the average of the values for adjacent years. This imputation is limited to at most two consecutive missing observations per economy. Reform spurts are calculated using the Investment Profile

Index taken from the PRS Group's *International Country Risk Guide*. Reform spurts are defined as a two-year increase in the index above two times the standard deviation of the country-specific index. The data set includes a panel of 57 EMDEs and 31 advanced economies and covers the period from 1999 to 2021. The regression starts in 2000 and allows for lagged variables.

Methodology. The analysis estimates the correlates of investment growth in 57 EMDEs for the period 2000-21 in a system generalized method of moments framework, with the third to sixth lag used to instrument the differenced equation and second lags for the level equation. Generalized method of moments instruments of this type are used for growth in output, real credit, capital flows, and terms of trade. The econometric framework is similar to that of Nabar and Joyce (2009). However, the focus in this chapter is on investment growth—a critical component of overall output growth (ultimately, the source of rising living standards)—rather than changes in the investment-to-GDP ratio, which would capture only changes in investment growth relative to output growth. Use of investment growth is in line with recent studies on advanced economies and individual EMDEs.[9] Table 3C.2 shows the results. The sample is unweighted to avoid a small number of EMDEs dominating the results (China and India, for example, account for a large share of total EMDE investment). Lastly, the terms-of-trade, real-credit-growth, and capital-flow variables exclude the top and bottom 1 percent of observations in the entire sample to deal with outliers. Standard errors are clustered at the country level.

Robustness. Table 3C.3 details a range of robustness checks. The regressions are robust to using ordinary least squares with fixed effects instead of system generalized method of moments (to account for the initial level of capital, for example). Further, when capital flows are divided into their components, the change in flows of foreign direct investment is not significant, but the changes in portfolio and bank flows are. The credit-to-GDP ratio is not significant once China is excluded from the sample, and credit growth does not exhibit nonlinear behavior. The regression is also robust to adding advanced economies to the sample (excluding Ireland, Malta, and Singapore, as these countries are large outliers in regard to capital flows). Further robustness checks in the system generalized method of moments specification include controlling for various institutional-quality variables from the *International Country Risk Guide* and time fixed effects, as well as the relative price of capital from Penn World Table 10. These additional variables are not significant, while the main results are generally robust. Only the coefficient on terms of trade becomes nonsignificant when global trend variables are included. The subsamples of commodity-importing EMDEs and commodity-exporting EMDEs are too small to generate significant results.

---

[9] Banerjee, Kearns, and Lombardi (2015); Barkbu et al. (2015); Bussière, Ferrara, and Milovich (2016); and Kothari, Lewellen, and Warner (2015) cover advanced economies. Anand and Tulin (2014) covers India.

ANNEX 3B **Investment growth and reforms**

Values in figure 3.13 are based on a panel data regression in which the dependent variable is real investment growth. A spurt (setback) is defined as a two-year increase (decrease) above (below) two times the country-specific standard deviation of the Investment Profile Index, a component of the *International Country Risk Guide,* published by the PRS Group. The sample spans 60 EMDEs over 1984-2022. Overall, there are 44 reform spurt events and 10 reform setback events.

In the regression, t denotes the end of a two-year spurt and s the end of a two-year setback. The coefficients are dummy variables for spurts and setbacks over the $[t-3, t+2]$ or $[s-3, s+2]$ window around these episodes (table 3C.4). In figure 3.13, "reform" at time t refers to the two-year change from $t-2$ to t. All coefficients show the investment growth differential of economies during an episode compared with those that experienced neither improvements nor setbacks. All estimates include time fixed effects to control for global common shocks and country fixed effects to control for time-invariant heterogeneity at the country level.

ANNEX 3C Tables

TABLE 3C.1 Economies in the investment sample

Emerging market and developing economies (EMDEs)			Advanced economies
East Asia and Pacific	**Latin America and the Caribbean**	**South Asia**	Australia
Cambodia *		India *	Austria
China *	Argentina	Nepal *	Belgium
Indonesia	Belize	Sri Lanka *	Canada
Malaysia *	Bolivia		Croatia
Mongolia	Brazil		Cyprus
Philippines *	Chile	**Sub-Saharan Africa**	Czech Republic
Thailand *	Colombia	Benin	Denmark
Vietnam *	Costa Rica	Botswana	Estonia
	Dominican Republic *	Burkina Faso	Finland
	Ecuador	Côte d'Ivoire	France
Europe and Central Asia	El Salvador *	Equatorial Guinea	Germany
Albania *	Guatemala	Ghana	Greece
Armenia	Honduras	Kenya	Hong Kong SAR, China
Belarus *	Jamaica *	Mali	Iceland
Bulgaria *	Mexico *	Mauritius *	Ireland
Hungary *	Nicaragua	Mozambique	Israel
North Macedonia *	Panama *	Namibia	Italy
Poland *	Paraguay	Niger	Japan
Romania *	Peru	Nigeria	Korea, Rep.
Russian Federation	Uruguay	Rwanda	Latvia
Türkiye *		Senegal	Lithuania
Ukraine		South Africa	Malta
	Middle East and North Africa	Tanzania	Netherlands
		Togo	New Zealand
	Algeria	Uganda	Norway
	Bahrain		Portugal
	Iran, Islamic Rep.		Singapore
	Kuwait		Slovak Republic
	Lebanon *		Slovenia
	Morocco *		Spain
	Oman		Sweden
	Saudi Arabia		Switzerland
	United Arab Emirates		United Kingdom
			United States

Source: World Bank.

Note: * indicates emerging market and developing economy (EMDE) commodity importers. Each EMDE is classified as a commodity importer or commodity exporter. An economy is defined as a commodity exporter when, on average in 2017-19, either (1) total commodity exports accounted for 30 percent or more of its total exports or (2) exports of any single commodity accounted for 20 percent or more of its total exports. Economies for which these thresholds were met as a result of reexports are excluded. When data are not available, judgment has been used. This taxonomy results in the classification of some well-diversified economies as importers, even if they are exporters of certain commodities (for example, Mexico).

TABLE 3C.2 **Correlates of investment growth**

Dependent variable: Real investment growth (percent)	(1) EMDEs	(2) Advanced economies
Real GDP growth (percent)	1.807***	1.699***
	(13.66)	(16.85)
Real credit growth (percent)	0.132***	0.060**
	(3.22)	(2.25)
Growth in terms of trade (percent)	0.095*	0.127***
	(1.95)	(3.07)
Spurt in reform of investment climate	6.970*	0.638
	(1.78)	(0.31)
Change in capital flows (percent of GDP)	0.218**	0.060***
	(2.15)	(3.42)
Constant	-2.854***	-1.231***
	(-5.30)	(-5.95)
Number of observations	1,024	625
Number of economies	57	31

Source: World Bank.

Note: Table presents results of a panel system generalized method of moments regression for 57 emerging market and developing economies (EMDEs) and 31 advanced economies during 2000-21. Column (1) shows results for the baseline regression for EMDEs. Column (2) shows results for the regression for advanced economies (excluding Ireland, Malta, and Singapore, as these countries are large outliers for capital flows). Real gross domestic product (GDP) growth, real credit growth, and growth in terms of trade, as well as changes in capital flows, are treated as endogenous. Standard errors are clustered at the country level. *t*-statistics are in parentheses. ***$p < 0.01$, **$p < 0.05$, *$p < 0.1$.

TABLE 3C.3 Correlates of robustness of investment growth

Dependent variable: Real investment growth (percent)	(1) EMDEs excl. China	(2) Split capital flows	(3) Credit-to-GDP ratio excl. China	(4) Real credit growth squared	(5) Nominal credit growth	(6) Global
Real GDP growth (percent)	1.839***	1.840***	1.979***	1.855***	1.854***	1.743***
	(14.04)	(12.73)	(17.58)	(14.06)	(13.85)	(19.29)
Real credit growth (percent)	0.132***	0.148***		0.102		0.102***
	(3.28)	(3.32)		(1.60)		(3.16)
Growth in terms of trade (percent)	0.084*	0.092*	0.116**	0.084*	0.086*	0.091*
	(1.75)	(1.78)	(2.25)	(1.87)	(1.75)	(1.85)
Spurt in reform of investment climate	7.834*	3.165*	8.173**	6.384*	7.701*	4.375*
	(1.87)	(1.83)	(2.01)	(1.82)	(1.99)	(1.80)
Change in capital flows (percent of GDP)	0.219**		0.195**	0.226**	0.203**	0.132***
	(2.16)		(2.05)	(2.14)	(2.17)	(3.55)
Change in FDI flows (percent of GDP)		0.102				
		(0.91)				
Change in portfolio flows (percent of GDP)		0.343**				
		(2.60)				
Change in net liabilities of financial corporations (percent of GDP)		0.076***				
		(2.90)				
Change in credit-to-GDP ratio (percent of GDP)			0.123			
			(1.38)			
Real credit growth squared				-0.000		
				(-0.20)		
Nominal credit growth					0.089**	
					(2.32)	
Constant	-2.861***	-3.049***	-2.509***	-2.719***	-3.221***	-2.056***
	(-5.34)	(-5.79)	(-4.72)	(-5.46)	(-5.23)	(-6.15)
Number of observations	1,002	948	1,022	1,024	1,037	1,649
Number of economies	56	57	56	57	57	88

Source: World Bank.

Note: Table presents results of a panel regression for 56-57 emerging market and developing economies (EMDEs) and 31 advanced economies during 2000-21. Number of economies varies based on data availability. Columns (1) to (5) show results of variations of the system generalized method of moments regression in column (1) of table 3C.2. Column (1) excludes China from the sample. Column (2) separates capital flows into the three components. Column (3) replaces real credit growth with the change in the credit-to-GDP ratio, excluding China. Column (4) tests for nonlinearity of real credit growth. Column (5) replaces real credit growth with nominal credit growth. Column (6) estimates the baseline for a global sample of 31 advanced economies (the sample excludes Ireland, Malta, and Singapore, as these economies are large outliers for capital flows) and 57 EMDEs. All additional control variables in columns (1) to (5) are assumed to be endogenous. Standard errors are clustered at the country level. *t*-statistics are in parentheses. FDI = foreign direct investment; GDP = gross domestic product.
***$p < 0.01$, **$p < 0.05$, *$p < 0.1$.

TABLE 3C.4 Investment growth around spurts and setbacks in reform of the investment climate

Dependent variable: Real investment growth (percent)	
$t-3$	-2.460
	(3.752)
$t-2$	0.385
	(2.501)
$t-1$	0.014
	(2.550)
Period t of reform spurt	5.577**
	(2.815)
$t+1$	3.417
	(2.320)
$t+2$	-0.393
	(1.403)
$s-3$	-4.395
	(2.772)
$s-2$	-1.163
	(2.592)
$s-1$	-8.891**
	(4.129)
Period s of reform setback	-7.323
	(5.137)
$s+1$	-6.490**
	(3.108)
$s+2$	-0.098
	(5.438)
Number of observations	1,854

Source: World Bank.
Note: The regression includes time and country fixed effects. t indicates the period of a significant reform spurt and s the period of a significant reform setback, as defined in annex 3B. Robust standard errors are in parentheses.
***$p < 0.01$, **$p < 0.05$, *$p < 0.1$.

TABLE 3C.5 Estimates of climate-related investment needs

Author(s) and year	Climate target	Concept (total vs. additional need)	Investment need or gap (nominal amount)	Investment need or gap (percent of GDP)	Time coverage	Country coverage	Sectors or adaptations covered	Methodology
Black et al. (2022)	Cap temperature increase at 2 degrees Celsius (°C)	Total need	$0.5 trillion per year	0.4 percent of GDP per year or 0.7 percent for high-income countries and 0.3 percent for low-income countries	2021-30	Global	"Cleaner technologies"	Computable general equilibrium (CGE) and a sector-based "assessment tool"
Citi (2022)	Net-zero emissions	Total need	$2.6 trillion per year during 2021-25; $3.8 trillion per year during 2026-30	2.6 percent of GDP per year during 2021-25; 3.3 percent of GDP during 2026-30	2021-30	Global		International Energy Agency (IEA) Net Zero Emissions by 2050 Scenario modeling by United Nations Framework Convention on Climate Change Race to Zero Campaign with support from Vivid Economics, Citi Global Perspectives & Solutions
Hallegatte et al. (2018)	Implicitly, the nationally determined contributions (NDCs) under the Paris Agreement	Total need	$115 billion per year	0.1 percent of GDP per year	2020-30	Global		Accounting exercise: Global estimate is derived based on per capita costs of adaptation for 50 countries for which NDC data are available, with the assumption that NDCs reflect actual needs
IEA (2021b)	Investment needed to limit global warming to 1.5°C	Total and additional need	Total need of $4 trillion (2020 dollars) per year; additional need (gap) of about $3 trillion (2020 dollars) per year	Total need of 4 percent of GDP per year; additional need (gap) of 3 percent of GDP	2020-30	Global	Clean electricity; decarbonization in buildings, industry, transport; low-emission fuel production	IEA World Energy Model simulations
IEA (2022)	World on track for net-zero emissions (consistent with 1.5°C) by 2050	Total need	$4.8 trillion (2021 dollars) per year	4 percent of GDP per year	2021-30	Global	Fuels, electricity, infrastructure, end-use adaptations (efficiency, electrification, renewables)	IEA GEC Model

TABLE 3C.5 Estimates of climate-related investment needs (*continued*)

Author(s) and year	Climate target	Concept (total vs. additional need)	Investment need or gap (nominal amount)	Investment need or gap (percent of GDP)	Time coverage	Country coverage	Sectors or adaptations covered	Methodology
IPCC (2018)	Investment needed to limit global warming to 1.5°C	Total need	$2.4 trillion per year (2010 dollars)	2.5 percent of GDP per year	2016-35	Global		Multimodel framework with multiple simulations
IPCC (2022)	Limit global warming to 1.5°C or 2°C	Total need	$2.3 trillion (2015 dollars) per year to meet the 1.5° C goal; $1.7 trillion (2015 dollars) per year to meet the 2°C goal	1.2 percent of GDP per year	2023-52	Global		Multimodel framework with multiple simulations
IRENA (2022)	Limit global warming to 1.5°C	Total need	$5.7 trillion per year	5.3 percent of GDP per year	2021-30	Global	Infrastructure, energy	International Renewable Energy Agency macroeconometric model
McCollum et al. (2018)	Implementation of NDCs by all countries by 2030	Additional need	$130 billion (2015 dollars) per year	0.1 percent of GDP per year	2015-30	Global	Energy	Six energy and integrated assessment models: AIM/ CGE, IMAGE, MESSAGEix-GLOBIOM, POLES, REMIND-MAgPIE, and WITCH-GLOBIOM
	2°C target	Additional need	$320 billion (2015 dollars) per year	0.4 percent of GDP per year	2015-30	Global	Energy	Six energy and integrated assessment models: AIM/ CGE, IMAGE, MESSAGEix-GLOBIOM, POLES, REMIND-MAgPIE, and WITCH-GLOBIOM
	1.5°C target	Additional need	$480 billion (2015 dollars) per year	0.5 percent of GDP per year	2015-30	Global	Energy	Six energy and integrated assessment models: AIM/ CGE, IMAGE, MESSAGEix-GLOBIOM, POLES, REMIND-MAgPIE, and WITCH-GLOBIOM

TABLE 3C.5 Estimates of climate-related investment needs (*continued*)

Author(s) and year	Climate target	Concept (total vs. additional need)	Investment need or gap (nominal amount)	Investment need or gap (percent of GDP)	Time coverage	Country coverage	Sectors or adaptations covered	Methodology
McKinsey Global Institute (2022)	Transition to net-zero emissions by 2050	Total and additional need	Total need of $9.2 trillion per year; additional need (gap) of $3.5 trillion per year	Total need of 6.8 percent of GDP per year; additional need (gap) of 2.6 percent of GDP per year	2021-50	Global	Infrastructure, energy	Net-zero emissions 2050 scenario defined by the Network for Greening the Financial System (NGFS) and the NGFS current policies scenario as a counterfactual in the REMIND-MAgPIE model
OECD (2017)	66 percent probability of staying below 2°C temperature increase	Total need	$6.9 trillion (2015 dollars) per year	7.5 percent of GDP per year	2016-30	Global	Energy supply and demand, transport, water and sanitation, telecommunications	
Paulson Institute, The Nature Conservancy, and Cornell Atkinson Center for Sustainability (2020)	Halt decline in biodiversity by 2030	Total and additional need	Total need of $722-$967 billion per year; additional need (gap, or "biodiversity financing gap") of $598-$824 billion per year	Total need of 0.7-1.0 percent of GDP per year; additional need (gap) of 0.6-0.8 percent of GDP per year	2019-30	Global	Biodiversity	Accounting exercise
Rockefeller Foundation and Boston Consulting Group (2022)	Net-zero emissions	Total need	$3.4 trillion per year during 2020-25; $4.1 trillion per year during 2026-30	3.7 percent of GDP per year during 2020-25; 3.8 percent of GDP per year during 2026-30	2020-30	Global		Extrapolations based on IEA net-zero emissions scenario
UNEP (2022)	Limit temperature increase to 1.5°C or 2°C	Total need	$11 trillion ($379 billion per year) for 1.5°C scenario; $9.5 trillion ($328 billion per year) for 2°C scenario		2022-50	Global		MAgPIE version 4.1, developed by Vivid Economics, and off-model analysis

TABLE 3C.5 Estimates of climate-related investment needs (*continued*)

Author(s) and year	Climate target	Concept (total vs. additional need)	Investment need or gap (nominal amount)	Investment need or gap (percent of GDP)	Time coverage	Country coverage	Sectors or adaptations covered	Methodology
Baarsch et al. (2015)	Limit temperature increase to 2°C	Total need	$0.2 trillion (2012 dollars) per year	0.7 percent of GDP per year	Through 2030	Middle- and low-income countries, excluding China	Adaptation and resilience	Integrated assessment model (Regional Dynamic Integrated Model of Climate and the Economy, AD-RICE2012)
	Limit temperature increase to 2°C	Total need	$0.5 trillion (2012 dollars) per year	0.6 percent of GDP per year	Through 2050	Middle- and low-income countries, excluding China	Adaptation and resilience	Integrated assessment model (AD-RICE2012)
IEA (2021a)	Net-zero emissions by 2050	Total need	$1.4 trillion per year	2.1 percent of GDP per year	2026-30	EMDEs, excluding China	Electricity, end-use energy efficiency (buildings, transport), and renewables	Scenario analysis (methodology unclear)
Markandya and González-Eguino (2019)	High-damage and low-damage scenarios	Total need	$29-$411 billion by 2030 (lower and upper bounds reflect low-damage/high-discount-rate and high-damage/low-discount-rate scenarios)	0.1-1.3 percent of GDP per year	Through 2030	Developing countries		Integrated assessment model
	High-damage and low-damage scenarios	Total need	$71 billion-$1.09 trillion by 2050 (lower and upper bounds reflect low-damage/high-discount-rate and high-damage/low-discount-rate scenarios)	0.1-1.5 percent of GDP per year	Through 2050	Developing countries		Integrated assessment model

TABLE 3C.5 Estimates of climate-related investment needs (*continued*)

Author(s) and year	Climate target	Concept (total vs. additional need)	Investment need or gap (nominal amount)	Investment need or gap (percent of GDP)	Time coverage	Country coverage	Sectors or adaptations covered	Methodology
Narain, Margulis, and Essam (2011)	Adaptation to limit temperature increase to 2°C	Total need	$70-$98 billion per year (2005 US$)	0.2-0.3 percent of GDP per year	2010-50	Developing countries	Infrastructure, coastal zones, water supply, agriculture, fisheries, forests and ecosystems, human health, extreme weather	Modeling exercises, including some CGE exercises
Rozenberg and Fay (2019)	Limit temperature increase to 2°C and fill investment needs	Total need	$640 billion-$2.7 trillion per year (2015 dollars)	2.0-8.2 percent of GDP per year	2015-30	Developing countries	Energy, transport, water and sanitation, irrigation, flood protection	Accounting exercises benchmarked against goals, CGE models
World Bank (2022a)	Resilient and low-carbon pathway			Need of 8 percent of GDP in low-income countries; 5.1 percent of GDP in lower-middle-income countries; 1.1 percent of GDP in upper-middle-income countries	2022-30	24 developing countries	Infrastructure, transport, energy/electricity, water and sanitation, urban, landscape, and industry	Scenario analysis

Source: World Bank.

Note: AIM/CGE = Asia-Pacific Integrated Model/Computable General Equilibrium; GDP = gross domestic product; GLOBIOM = Global Biosphere Management Model; IMAGE = Integrated Model to Assess the Global Environment; MAgPIE = Model of Agricultural Production and Its Impact on the Environment; MESSAGEix = Model for Energy Supply Strategy Alternatives and Their General Environmental Impact; POLES = Prospective Outlook on Long-Term Energy Systems; REMIND = Regional Model of Investments and Development; WITCH = World Induced Technical Change Hybrid.

References

Adarov, A., and R. Stehrer. 2021. "Implications of Foreign Direct Investment, Capital Formation and Its Structure for Global Value Chains." *World Economy* 44 (11): 3246-99.

Aghion, P., P. Howitt, and F. Murtin. 2011. "The Relationship between Health and Growth: When Lucas Meets Nelson-Phelps." *Review of Economics and Institutions* 2 (1): 1-24.

Agosin, M. R., and R. Machado. 2005. "Foreign Investment in Developing Countries: Does It Crowd In Domestic Investment?" *Oxford Development Studies* 33 (2): 149-62.

Ahmed, K. T., G. M. Ghani, N. Mohamad, and A. M. Derus. 2015. "Does Inward FDI Crowd-Out Domestic Investment? Evidence from Uganda." *Procedia-Social and Behavioral Sciences* 172: 419-26.

Aksoy, Y., H. S. Basso, R. P. Smith, and T. Grasl. 2019. "Demographic Structure and Macroeconomic Trends." *American Economic Journal: Macroeconomics* 11 (1): 193-222.

Al-Sadig, A. 2013. "The Effects of Foreign Direct Investment on Private Domestic Investment: Evidence from Developing Countries." *Empirical Economics* 44 (3): 1267-75.

Alfaro, L. 2003. "Foreign Direct Investment and Growth: Does the Sector Matter?" Unpublished manuscript, Harvard Business School, Cambridge, MA.

Alfaro, L., A. Chanda, S. Kalemli-Ozcan, and S. Sayek. 2004. "FDI and Economic Growth: The Role of Local Financial Markets." *Journal of International Economics* 64 (1): 89-112.

Alfaro, L., and A. Charlton. 2013. "Growth and the Quality of Foreign Direct Investment." In *The Industrial Policy Revolution I: The Role of Government Beyond Ideology*, edited by J. E. Stiglitz and J. Y. Lin, 162-204. London: Palgrave Macmillan.

Alfaro, L., and E. Hammel. 2007. "Capital Flows and Capital Goods." *Journal of International Economics* 72 (1): 128-50.

Alguacil, M., A. Cuadros, and V. Orts. 2011. "Inward FDI and Growth: The Role of Macroeconomic and Institutional Environment." *Journal of Policy Modeling* 33 (3): 481-96.

Ali, H., and M. T. Asgher. 2016. "The Role of the Sectoral Composition of Foreign Direct Investment on Economic Growth: A Policy Proposal for CPEC and Regional Partners." In *The Pakistan Development Review—Papers and Proceedings: The 32nd Conference of the Pakistan Society of Development Economists, December 13-15, 2016, Islamabad*, 89-103. Islamabad: Pakistan Institute of Development Economics.

Alvarez, F. 2017. "Capital Accumulation and International Trade." *Journal of Monetary Economics* 91 (C): 1-18.

Amighini, A. A., M. S. McMillan, and M. Sanfilippo. 2017. "FDI and Capital Formation in Developing Economies: New Evidence from Industry-Level Data." NBER Working Paper 23049, National Bureau of Economic Research, Cambridge, MA.

Anand, R., and V. Tulin. 2014. "Disentangling India's Investment Slowdown." Working Paper 14/47, International Monetary Fund, Washington, DC.

Andrews, D., C. Criscuolo, and P. N. Gal. 2015. "Frontier Firms, Technology Diffusion and Public Policy: Micro Evidence from OECD Countries." Productivity Working Paper 2015-02, Organisation for Economic Co-operation and Development, Paris.

Ang, J. B. 2009a. "Do Public Investment and FDI Crowd In or Crowd Out Private Domestic Investment in Malaysia?" *Applied Economics* 41 (7): 913-19.

Ang, J. B. 2009b. "Financial Development and the FDI-Growth Nexus: The Malaysian Experience." *Applied Economics* 41 (13): 1595-601.

Antràs, P. 2020. "Conceptual Aspects of Global Value Chains." *World Bank Economic Review* 34 (3): 551-74.

Arndt, C., C. M. Buch, and M. E. Schnitzer. 2010. "FDI and Domestic Investment: An Industry-Level View." *The BE Journal of Economic Analysis & Policy* 10 (1): 1-20.

Ashraf, A., and D. Herzer. 2014. "The Effects of Greenfield Investment and M&As on Domestic Investment in Developing Countries." *Applied Economics Letters* 21 (14): 997-1000.

Aykut, D., and S. Sayek. 2007. "The Role of the Sectoral Composition of Foreign Direct Investment on Growth." In *Do Multinationals Feed Local Development and Growth?,* edited by L. Piscitello and G. D. Santangelo, 35-59. Cambridge, MA: Elsevier.

Azman-Saini, W. N. W., S. H. Law, and A. H. Ahmad. 2010. "FDI and Economic Growth: New Evidence on the Role of Financial Markets." *Economics Letters* 107 (2): 211-13.

Baarsch, F., T. Lissner, C.-F. Schleussner, J. Grenadillos, K. de Bruin, M. Perrette, M. Schaeffer, and B. Hare. 2015. "Impacts of Low Aggregate INDCs Ambition: Technical Summary." Climate Analytics gGmbH, Berlin.

Bahal, G., M. Raissi, and V. Tulin. 2018. "Crowding-Out or Crowding-In? Public and Private Investment in India." *World Development* 109 (September): 323-33.

Bahia, K., P. Castells, G. Cruz, T. Masaki, X. Pedros, T. Pfutze, C. Rodriguez-Castelan, and H. Winkler. 2020. "The Welfare Effects of Mobile Broadband: Evidence from Nigeria." Policy Research Working Paper 9230, World Bank, Washington, DC.

Balasubramanyam, V. N., M. Salisu, and D. Sapsford. 1996. "Foreign Direct Investment and Growth in EP and IS Countries." *Economic Journal* 106 (434): 92-105.

Banerjee, A. V., and E. Duflo. 2005. "Growth Theory through the Lens of Development Economics." In *Handbook of Economic Growth*, vol. 1A, edited by P. Aghion and S. Durlauf, 473-552. Amsterdam: Elsevier.

Banerjee, R., B. Hofmann, and A. Mehrotra. 2020. "Corporate Investment and the Exchange Rate: The Financial Channel." BOFIT Discussion Papers 6/2020, Bank of Finland, Helsinki.

Banerjee, R., J. Kearns, and M. Lombardi. 2015. "(Why) Is Investment Weak?" *BIS Quarterly Review* (March): 67-82.

Barkbu, B., S. P. Berkmen, P. Lukyantsau, S. Saksonovs, and H. Schoelermann. 2015. "Investment in the Euro Area: Why Has It Been Weak?" IMF Working Paper 15/32, International Monetary Fund, Washington, DC.

Barro, R. J. 2013. "Health and Economic Growth." *Annals of Economics and Finance* 14 (2): 329-66.

Bashir, S., C. J. Dahlman, N. Kanehira, and K. Tilmes. 2021. *The Converging Technology Revolution and Human Capital: Potential and Implications for South Asia*. Washington, DC: World Bank.

Benetrix, A., H. Pallan, and U. Panizza. 2022. "The Elusive Link between FDI and Economic Growth." LTI Working Papers, Collegio Carlo Alberto, Torino, Italy.

Bengoa, M., and B. Sanchez-Robles. 2003. "Foreign Direct Investment, Economic Freedom and Growth: New Evidence from Latin America." *European Journal of Political Economy* 19 (3): 529-45.

Bernanke, B. 2017. "When Growth Is Not Enough." Remarks prepared for delivery on June 26, 2017, at the European Central Bank Forum on Central Banking at Sintra, Portugal.

Bhattacharya, A., and N. Stern. 2021. "Beyond the $100 Billion: Financing a Sustainable and Resilient Future." Policy Note, Grantham Research Institute on Climate Change and the Environment, London School of Economics and Political Science, London.

Bizimana, O., L. Jaramillo, S. Thomas, and J. Yoo. 2021. "Scaling Up Quality Infrastructure Investment." IMF Working Paper 21/117, International Monetary Fund, Washington, DC.

Black, S., J. Chateau, F. Jaumotte, I. W. H. Parry, G. Schwerhoff, S. D. Thube, and K. Zhunussova. 2022. "Getting on Track to Net Zero: Accelerating a Global Just Transition in This Decade." Staff Climate Note 2022/010, International Monetary Fund, Washington, DC.

Blanchard, E. J., A. U. Santos-Paulino, C. Trentini, and E. Milet. 2021. "Implications of Rising Trade Tensions for FDI Projects." *Transnational Corporations Journal* 28 (2): 161-83.

Blanchard, O. J., and L. Katz. 1999. "Wage Dynamics: Reconciling Theory and Evidence." NBER Working Paper 6924, National Bureau of Economic Research, Cambridge, MA.

Blanchard, O. J., J. D. Ostry, A. R. Ghosh, and M. Chamon. 2016. "Capital Flows: Expansionary or Contractionary?" *American Economic Review* 106 (5): 565-69.

Bleaney, M., and D. Greenaway. 2001. "The Impact of Terms of Trade and Real Exchange Rate Volatility on Investment and Growth in Sub-Saharan Africa." *Journal of Development Economics* 65 (2): 491-500.

Bloom, N., P. Bunn, P. Mizen, P. Smietanka, and G. Thwaites. 2020. "The Impact of Covid-19 on Productivity." NBER Working Paper 28233, National Bureau of Economic Research, Cambridge, MA.

Bobasu, A., A. Geis, L. Quaglietti, and M. Ricci. 2020. "Tracking Global Economic Uncertainty: Implications for Global Investment and Trade." ECB Economic Bulletin 1/2020, European Central Bank, Frankfurt.

Borensztein, E., J. De Gregorio, and J. W. Lee. 1998. "How Does Foreign Direct Investment Affect Economic Growth?" *Journal of International Economics* 45 (1): 115-35.

Borensztein, E., and L. S. Ye. 2018. "Corporate Debt Overhang and Investment: Firm-Level Evidence." Policy Research Working Paper 8553, World Bank, Washington, DC.

Bosworth, B. P., S. M. Collins, and C. M. Reinhart. 1999. "Capital Flows to Developing Economies: Implications for Saving and Investment." *Brookings Papers on Economic Activity* (1): 143-80.

Breton, P., M. J. Ferrantino, and M. Maliszewska. *Reshaping Global Value Chains in Light of COVID-19*. Washington, DC: World Bank.

Buffie, E. F., A. Berg, C. Pattillo, R. Portillo, and L.-F. Zanna. 2012. "Public Investment, Growth, and Debt Sustainability: Putting Together the Pieces." IMF Working Paper 12/144, International Monetary Fund, Washington, DC.

Busse, M., and J. L. Groizard. 2008. "Foreign Direct Investment, Regulations and Growth." *World Economy* 31 (7): 861-86.

Bussière, M., L. Ferrara, and J. Milovich. 2016. "Explaining the Recent Slump in Investment: The Role of Expected Demand and Uncertainty." *IMF Research Bulletin* 17 (1): 1-3.

Caballero, R. J., and A. Simsek. 2020. "Asset Prices and Aggregate Demand in a 'Covid-19' Shock: A Model of Endogenous Risk Intolerance and LSAPs." NBER Working Paper 27044, National Bureau of Economic Research, Cambridge, MA.

Calcagnini, G., A. Ferrando, and G. Giombini. 2015. "Multiple Market Imperfections, Firm Profitability and Investment." *European Journal of Law and Economics* 40 (1): 95-120.

Calderón, C., E. Moral-Benito, and L. Servén. 2015. "Is Infrastructure Capital Productive? A Dynamic Heterogeneous Approach." *Journal of Applied Econometrics* 30 (20): 177-98.

Calderón, C., and L. Servén. 2014. "Infrastructure, Growth, and Inequality: An Overview." Policy Research Working Paper 7034, World Bank, Washington, DC.

Carkovic, M., and R. Levine. 2005. "Does Foreign Direct Investment Accelerate Economic Growth." In *Does Foreign Direct Investment Promote Growth?*, edited by T. H. Moran, E. M. Graham, and M. Blomström, 195-220. New York: Columbia University Press.

Carrière-Swallow, Y., and L. F. Céspedes. 2013. "The Impact of Uncertainty Shocks in Emerging Economies." *Journal of International Economics* 90 (2): 316-25.

Caselli, F., and J. Feyrer. 2007. "The Marginal Product of Capital." *Quarterly Journal of Economics* 122 (2): 535-68.

Caselli, F., P. Pagano, and F. Schivardi. 2003. "Uncertainty and the Slowdown in Capital Accumulation in Europe." *Applied Economics* 35 (1): 79-89.

Cerra, V., A. Cuevas, C. Goes, I. Karpowicz, T. Matheson, I. Samake, and S. Vtyurina. 2016. "Highways to Heaven: Infrastructure Determinants and Trends in Latin America and the Caribbean." IMF Working Paper 16/185, International Monetary Fund, Washington, DC.

Cerra, V., M. Hakamada, and R. Lama. 2021. "Financial Crises, Investment Slumps, and Slow Recoveries." IMF Working Paper 21/170, International Monetary Fund, Washington, DC.

Chakraborty, C., and P. Nunnenkamp. 2008. "Economic Reforms, FDI, and Economic Growth in India: A Sector Level Analysis." *World Development* 36 (7): 1192-212.

Chen, G. S., Y. Yao, and J. Malizard. 2017. "Does Foreign Direct Investment Crowd In or Crowd Out Private Domestic Investment in China? The Effect of Entry Mode." *Economic Modelling* 61 (February): 409-19.

Choe, J. I. 2003. "Do Foreign Direct Investment and Gross Domestic Investment Promote Economic Growth?" *Review of Development Economics* 7 (1): 44-57.

Chowdhury, A., and G. Mavrotas. 2006. "FDI and Growth: What Causes What?" *World Economy* 29 (1): 9-19.

Cipollina, M., G. Giovannetti, F. Pietrovito, and A. F. Pozzolo. 2012. "FDI and Growth: What Cross-Country Industry Data Say." *World Economy* 35 (11): 1599-629.

Citi. 2022. "Climate Finance: Mobilizing the Public and Private Sector to Ensure a Just Energy Transition." *Sustainability Series*, November 4, 2022. https://www.citivelocity.com/citigps/climate-finance.

Cole, S., M. Melecky, F. Moelders, and T. Reed. 2020. "Long-Run Returns to Impact Investing in Emerging Markets and Developing Economies." NBER Working Paper 27870, National Bureau of Economic Research, Cambridge, MA.

Colecchia, A., and P. Schreyer. 2002. "ICT Investment and Economic Growth in the 1990s: Is the United States a Unique Case? A Comparative Study of Nine OECD Countries." *Review of Economics Dynamics* 5 (2): 408-42.

Comin, D., and M. M. Ferrer. 2013. "If Technology Has Arrived Everywhere, Why Has Income Diverged?" NBER Working Paper 19010, National Bureau of Economic Research, Cambridge, MA.

Corcoran, A., and R. Gillanders. 2015. "Foreign Direct Investment and the Ease of Doing Business." *Review of World Economics* 151 (1): 103-26.

Council on Foreign Relations. 2022. "Belt and Road Tracker." https://www.cfr.org/article/belt-and-road-tracker

Criscuolo, C., P. Gal, T. Leidecker, F. Losma, and G. Nicoletti. 2021. "The Role of Telework for Productivity during and Post-COVID-19: Results from an OECD Survey among Managers and Workers." Organisation for Economic Co-operation and Development, Paris.

Crouzet, N., J. C. Eberly, A. L. Eisfeldt, and D. Papanikolaou. 2022. "The Economics of Intangible Capital." *Journal of Economic Perspectives* 36 (3): 29-52.

Dappe, M. H., M. Melecky, and B. Turkgulu. 2022. "Fiscal Risks from Early Termination of Public-Private Partnerships in Infrastructure." Policy Research Working Paper 9972, World Bank, Washington, DC.

Dappe, M. H., A. Musacchio, C. Pan, Y. V. Semikolenova, B. Turkgulu, and J. Barboza. 2022. "Smoke and Mirrors: Infrastructure State-Owned Enterprises and Fiscal Risks." Policy Research Working Paper 9970, World Bank, Washington, DC.

De Mello, L. R. 1999. "Foreign Direct Investment-Led Growth: Evidence from Time Series and Panel Data." *Oxford Economic Papers* 51 (1): 133-51.

Desai, M. A., C. Fritz Foley, and J. R. Hines. 2009. "Domestic Effects of the Foreign Activities of US Multinationals." *American Economic Journal: Economic Policy* 1 (1): 181-203.

Didier, T., M. A. Kose, F. Ohnsorge, and L. S. Ye. 2015. "Slowdown in Emerging Markets: Rough Patch or Prolonged Weakness?" Policy Research Note 15/04, World Bank, Washington, DC.

Dieppe, A, ed. 2021. *Global Productivity: Trends, Drivers, and Policies.* Washington, DC: World Bank.

Driffield, N., and C. Jones. 2013. "Impact of FDI, ODA and Migrant Remittances on Economic Growth in Developing Countries: A Systems Approach." *European Journal of Development Research* 25 (2): 173-96.

Echandi, R., M. Maliszewska, and V. Steenbergen. 2022. *Making the Most of the African Continental Free Trade Area.* Washington, DC: World Bank.

Eichengreen, B., P. Gupta, and O. Masetti. 2018. "Are Capital Flows Fickle? Increasingly? And Does the Answer Still Depend on Type?" *Asian Economic Papers* 17 (1): 22-41.

Elekdag, S., and Y. Wu. 2013. "Rapid Credit Growth in Emerging Markets: Boon or Boom-Bust?" *Emerging Markets Finance and Trade* 49 (5): 45-62.

Engel, E., R. Fischer, and A. Galetovic. 2020. "When and How to Use Public-Private Partnerships in Infrastructure: Lessons from the International Experience." NBER Working Paper 26766, National Bureau of Economic Research, Cambridge, MA.

Erden, L., and R. G. Holcombe. 2005. "The Effects of Public Investment on Private Investment in Developing Countries." *Public Finance Review* 33 (5): 575-602.

Eregha, P. B. 2012. "The Dynamic Linkages between Foreign Direct Investment and Domestic Investment in ECOWAS Countries: A Panel Cointegration Analysis." *African Development Review* 24 (3): 208-20.

ESMAP (Energy Sector Management Assistance Program). 2020. "RISE 2020: Sustaining the Momentum." Washington, DC: World Bank.

Essl, S., S. K. Celik, P. Kirby, and A. Proite. 2019. "Debt in Low-Income Countries." Policy Research Working Paper 8794, World Bank, Washington, DC.

Farla, K., D. de Crombrugghe, and B. Verspagen. 2016. "Institutions, Foreign Direct Investment and Domestic Investment: Crowding Out or Crowding In?" *World Development* 88 (December): 1-9.

Feldstein, M. 2008. "Did Wages Reflect Growth in Productivity?" NBER Working Paper 13953, National Bureau of Economic Research, Cambridge, MA.

Ferreira, F. H. G. 1995. "Wealth Distribution Dynamics with Public-Private Capital Complementarity." Discussion Paper TE/95/286, London School of Economics and Political Science, London.

Field, E. 2005. "Property Rights and Investment in Urban Slums." *Journal of the European Economic Association* 3 (2-3): 279-90.

Foster, V., A. Rana, and N. Gorgulu. 2022. "Understanding Public Spending Trends for Infrastructure in Developing Countries." Policy Research Working Paper 9903, World Bank, Washington, DC.

Freund, C. 2016. "The Global Trade Slowdown and Secular Stagnation." *Trade and Investment Policy Watch* (blog), April 20, 2016. https://www.piie.com/blogs/trade-and-investment-policy-watch/global-trade-slowdown-and-secular-stagnation

G20 (Group of Twenty). 2016. "Developments in Investment and Policy Challenges." Paper for G-20, June. Organisation for Economic Co-operation and Development, Paris.

G20 (Group of Twenty). 2019. "G20 Principles for Quality Infrastructure Investment." Annex 6.1. G20 Finance and Central Bank Meeting, June 2019, Fukuoka, Japan.

Gao, T. 2004. "FDI, Openness and Income." *Journal of International Trade & Economic Development* 13 (3): 305-23.

Garcia-Escribano, M., and F. Han. 2015. "Credit Expansion in Emerging Markets: Propellor of Growth?" Working Paper 15/212, International Monetary Fund, Washington, DC.

Gardner, C., and P. B. Henry. 2021. "The Global Infrastructure Gap: Potential, Perils, and a Framework for Distinction." Working Paper, New York University, New York.

Gaspar, V., D. Amaglobali, M. Garcia-Escribano, D. Prady, and M. Soto. 2019. "Fiscal Policy and Development: Human, Social, and Physical Investments for the SDGs." Staff Discussion Note 2019/003, International Monetary Fund, Washington, DC.

Getachew, Y. Y. 2010. "Public Capital and Distributional Dynamics in a Two-Sector Growth Model." *Journal of Macroeconomics* 32 (2): 606-16.

Glassman, A, J. M. Keller, and E. Smitham. 2023. "The Future of Global Health Spending amidst Multiple Crises." CGD Note, Center for Global Development, Washington, DC.

Guénette, J. D., M. A. Kose, and N. Sugawara. 2022. "Is a Global Recession Imminent?" EFI Policy Note 4, World Bank, Washington, DC.

Gutierrez, G., and T. Philippon. 2017. "Investmentless Growth: An Empirical Investigation." *Brookings Papers on Economic Activity* (Fall): 89-169.

Ha, V., M. J. Holmes, and T. Q. Tran. 2022. "Does Foreign Investment Crowd in Domestic Investment? Evidence from Vietnam." *International Economics* 171 (2): 18-29.

Hallegatte, S., C. Brandon, R. Damania, Y. Lang, J. Roome, J. Rozenberg, and A. Tall. 2018. "The Economics (and Obstacles to) Aligning Development and Climate Change Adaptation: A World Bank Contribution to the Global Commission on Adaptation." Discussion Paper, Global Commission on Adaptation, Rotterdam, Netherlands.

Hansen, H., and J. Rand. 2006. "On the Causal Links between FDI and Growth in Developing Countries." *World Economy* 29 (1): 1-41.

Harding, T., and B. S. Javorcik. 2011. "Roll Out the Red Carpet and They Will Come: Investment Promotion and FDI Inflows." *Economic Journal* 121 (557): 1445-76.

Harms, P., and P.-G. Méon. 2018. "Good and Useless FDI: The Growth Effects of Greenfield Investment and Mergers and Acquisitions." *Review of International Economics* 26 (1): 37-59.

Hejazi, W., and P. Pauly. 2003. "Motivations for FDI and Domestic Capital Formation." *Journal of International Business Studies* 34 (3): 282-89.

Hermes, N., and R. Lensink. 2003. "Foreign Direct Investment, Financial Development and Economic Growth." *Journal of Development Studies* 40 (1): 142-63.

Herzer, D. 2012. "How Does Foreign Direct Investment Really Affect Developing Countries' Growth?" *Review of International Economics* 20 (2): 396-414.

Herzer, D., and M. Schrooten. 2008. "Outward FDI and Domestic Investment in Two Industrialized Countries." *Economics Letters* 99 (1): 139-43.

Hofstede, G. H. 2001. *Culture's Consequences: Comparing Values, Behaviors, Institutions, and Organizations across Nations.* Thousand Oaks, CA: Sage.

Hovhannisyan, S., V. Montalva-Talledo, T. Remick, C. Rodríguez-Castelán, and K. Stamm. 2022. "Global Job Quality: Evidence from Wage Employment across Developing Countries." Policy Research Working Paper 10134, World Bank, Washington, DC.

Hsieh, C.-T., and P. Klenow. 2007. "Relative Prices and Relative Prosperity." *American Economic Review* 97 (3): 562-85.

Huang, Y., M. Pagano, and U. Panizza. 2020. "Local Crowding-Out in China." *Journal of Finance* 75 (6): 2855-98.

Huidrom, R., M. A. Kose, H. Matsuoka, and F. Ohnsorge. 2020. "How Important Are Spillovers from Major Emerging Markets?" *International Finance* 23 (1): 47-63.

Huidrom, R., M. A. Kose, and F. Ohnsorge. 2016. "A Ride in Rough Waters." *Finance & Development* 53 (3): 1-4.

IEA (International Energy Agency). 2021a. "Financing Clean Energy Transitions in Emerging and Developing Economies." International Energy Agency, Paris.

IEA (International Energy Agency). 2021b. "Net Zero by 2050: A Roadmap for the Global Energy Sector." International Energy Agency, Paris.

IEA (International Energy Agency). 2022. "World Energy Outlook 2022." International Energy Agency, Paris.

IFC (International Finance Corporation) and WTO (World Trade Organization). 2022. "Trade Finance in West Africa." Geneva: World Trade Organization and Washington, DC: International Finance Corporation.

ILO (International Labour Organization). 2008. *Measurement of Decent Work.* Geneva: International Labour Organization.

ILO (International Labour Organization). 2013. *Decent Work Indicators: Guidelines for Producers and Users of Statistical and Legal Framework Indicators.* 2nd ed. Geneva: International Labour Organization.

IMF (International Monetary Fund). 2015. "Private Investment: What's the Holdup?" Chapter 4 in *World Economic Outlook*, April. Washington, DC: International Monetary Fund.

IMF (International Monetary Fund). 2016. "Global Trade: What's Behind the Slowdown?" Chapter 2 in *World Economic Outlook*, October. Washington, DC: International Monetary Fund.

IMF (International Monetary Fund). 2019. "Reigniting Growth in Low-Income and Emerging Market Economies: What Role Can Structural Reforms Play?" Chapter 3 in *World Economic Outlook*, October. Washington, DC: International Monetary Fund.

IMF (International Monetary Fund). 2021. "Fiscal Monitor Database of Country Fiscal Measures in Response to the COVID-19 Pandemic." International Monetary Fund, Washington, DC.

Inklaar, R., and J. Yang. 2012. "The Impact of Financial Crises and Tolerance for Uncertainty." *Journal of Development Economics* 97 (2): 466-80.

IPCC (Intergovernmental Panel on Climate Change). 2018. "Summary for Policymakers." In *Global Warming of 1.5°C: An IPCC Special Report on the Impacts of Global Warming of 1.5°C Above Pre-industrial Levels and Related Global GHG Emission Pathways, in the Context of Strengthening the Global Response to the Threat of Climate Change, Sustainable Development, and Efforts to Eradicate Poverty.* Geneva: Intergovernmental Panel on Climate Change.

IPCC (Intergovernmental Panel on Climate Change). 2022. *Climate Change 2022: Mitigation of Climate Change.* IPCC Sixth Assessment Report. Cambridge: Cambridge University Press.

IRENA (International Renewable Energy Agency). 2022. *World Energy Transitions Outlook 2022: 1.5° Pathway.* Abu Dhabi: International Renewable Energy Agency.

Izquierdo, A., R. Lama, J. P. Medina, J. Puig, D. Riera-Crichton, C. Vegh, and G. Vuletin. 2019. "Is the Public Investment Multiplier Higher in Developing Countries? An Empirical Exploration." IMF Working Paper 19/289, International Monetary Fund, Washington, DC.

Jones, C. 2003. "Human Capital, Ideas, and Economic Growth." In *Finance, Research, Education, and Growth*, edited by L. Paganetto and E. Phelps. London: Palgrave McMillan.

Jude, C. 2019. "Does FDI Crowd Out Domestic Investment in Transition Countries?" *Economics of Transition and Institutional Change* 27 (1): 163-200.

Kamaly, A. 2014. "Does FDI Crowd In or Out Domestic Investment? New Evidence from Emerging Economies." *Modern Economy* 5 (4): 391-400.

Kilic Celik, S., M. A. Kose, and F. Ohnsorge. 2020. "Subdued Potential Growth: Sources and Remedies." In *Growth in a Time of Change: Global and Country Perspectives on a New Agenda*, edited by H.-W. Kim and Z. Qureshi, 25-73. Washington, DC: Brookings Institution.

Kim, J.-H., J. A. Fallov, and S. Groom. 2020. *Public Investment Management Reference Guide.* Washington, DC: World Bank.

Kiyotaki, N., and J. Moore 2005. "Financial Deepening." *Journal of the European Economic Association* 3 (2/3): 701-13.

Kohpaiboon, A. 2003. "Foreign Trade Regimes and the FDI-Growth Nexus: A Case Study of Thailand." *Journal of Development Studies* 40 (2): 55-69.

Kose, M. A., and F. Ohnsorge, eds. 2020. *A Decade after the Global Recession: Lessons and Challenges for Emerging and Developing Economies.* Washington, DC: World Bank.

Kose, M. A., E. Prasad, K. Rogoff, and S.-J. Wei. 2009. "Financial Globalization: A Reappraisal." *IMF Staff Papers* 56 (1): 8-62.

Kothari, S. P., J. Lewellen, and J. B. Warner. 2015. "The Behavior of Aggregate Corporate Investment." MIT Sloan Research Paper 5112-14, Massachusetts Institute of Technology, Cambridge.

Lakatos, C., and F. Ohnsorge 2017. "Arm's-Length Trade: A Source of Post-crisis Trade Weakness." Policy Research Working Paper 8144, World Bank, Washington, DC.

Lautier, M., and F. Moreaub. 2012. "Domestic Investment and FDI in Developing Countries: The Missing Link." *Journal of Economic Development* 37 (3): 1-23.

Leboeuf, M., and B. Fay. 2016. "What Is Behind the Weakness in Global Investment?" Staff Discussion Paper 5, Bank of Canada, Ottawa.

Lee, C. C., and C. P. Chang. 2009. "FDI, Financial Development, and Economic Growth: International Evidence." *Journal of Applied Economics* 12 (2): 249-71.

Lee, J.-W. 2019. "Lessons of East Asia's Human-Capital Development." *Project Syndicate,* January 29, 2019.

Li, D., N. Magud, and F. Valencia. 2015. "Corporate Investment in Emerging Markets: Financing vs. Real Options Channel." IMF Working Paper 15/285, International Monetary Fund, Washington, DC.

Lian, W., N. Novta, E. Pugacheva, Y. Timmer, and P. Topalova. 2019. "The Price of Capital Goods: A Driver of Investment under Threat." IMF Working Paper 19/134, International Monetary Fund, Washington, DC.

Libman, E., J. A. Montecino, and A. Razmi. 2019. "Sustained Investment Surges." *Oxford Economic Papers* 71 (4): 1071-95.

Lim, J. J. 2014. "Institutional and Structural Determinants of Investment Worldwide." *Journal of Macroeconomics* 41 (September): 160-77.

Luu, H. 2016. "Greenfield Investments, Cross-Border M&As, and Economic Growth in Emerging Countries." *Economics and Business Letter* 5 (3): 87-94.

Magud, N., and S. Sosa. 2015. "Investment in Emerging Markets: We Are Not in Kansas Anymore . . . Or Are We?" IMF Working Paper 15/77, International Monetary Fund, Washington, DC.

Makki, S. S., and A. Somwaru. 2004. "Impact of Foreign Direct Investment and Trade on Economic Growth: Evidence from Developing Countries." *American Journal of Agricultural Economics* 86 (3): 795-801.

Maliszewska, M., and D. van der Mensbrugghe. 2019. "The Belt and Road Initiative: Economic, Poverty and Environmental Impacts." Policy Research Working Paper 8814, World Bank, Washington, DC.

Mandl, U., A. Dierx, and F. Ilzkovitz. 2008. "The Effectiveness and Efficiency of Public Spending." Economic Papers 301, European Commission, Brussels.

Markandya, A., and M. González-Eguino. 2019. "Integrated Assessment for Identifying Climate Finance Needs for Loss and Damage: A Critical Review." In *Loss and Damage from Climate Change: Concepts, Methods and Policy Options*, edited by R. Mechler, L. M. Bouwer, T. Schinko, S. Surminski, and J. Linnerooth-Bayer, 343-62. Cham, Switzerland: Springer.

McCollum, D. L., W. Zhou, C. Bertram, H.-S. de Boer, V. Bosetti, S. Busch, J. Després, et al. 2018. "Energy Investment Needs for Fulfilling the Paris Agreement and Achieving the Sustainable Development Goals." *Nature Energy* 3 (7): 589-99.

McKinsey Global Institute. 2022. "The Net-Zero Transition: What It Would Cost, What It Would Bring." McKinsey Global Institute.

McQuade, P., and M. Schmitz. 2016. "The Great Moderation in International Capital Flows: A Global Phenomenon?" ECB Working Paper 1952, European Central Bank, Frankfurt.

Medeiros, V., R. S. M. Ribeiro, and P. V. M. d. Amaral. 2021. "Infrastructure and Household Poverty in Brazil: A Regional Approach Using Multilevel Models." *World Development* 137: 105118.

Mehic, E., S. Silajdzic, and V. Babic-Hodovic. 2013. "The Impact of FDI on Economic Growth: Some Evidence from Southeast Europe." *Emerging Markets Finance and Trade* 49 (1): 5-20.

Mendoza, E., and M. E. Terrones. 2012. "An Anatomy of Credit Booms and Their Demise." *Journal Economia Chilena* 15 (2): 4-32.

Mensah, J., and N. Traore. 2022. "Infrastructure Quality and FDI Inflows: Evidence from the Arrival of High-Speed Internet in Africa." Policy Research Working Paper 9946, World Bank, Washington, DC.

Mileva, E. 2008. "The Impact of Capital Flows on Domestic Investment in Transition Economies." ECB Working Paper 871, European Central Bank, Frankfurt.

Mody, A., and A. P. Murshid. 2005. "Growing Up with Capital Flows." *Journal of International Economics* 65 (1): 249-66.

Moelders, F. 2016. "Global Productivity Slowdown and the Role of Technology Adoption in Emerging Markets." International Finance Corporation, Washington, DC.

Moïsé, E., and F. Le Bris. 2013. "Trade Costs—What Have We Learned?: A Synthesis Report." OECD Trade Policy Papers 150, Organisation for Economic Co-operation and Development, Paris.

Morrissey, O., and M. Udomkerdmongkol. 2012. "Governance, Private Investment and Foreign Direct Investment in Developing Countries." *World Development* 40 (3): 437-45.

Moszoro, M. 2021. "The Direct Employment Impact of Public Investment." IMF Working Paper 21/131, International Monetary Fund, Washington, DC.

Munemo, J. 2014. "Business Start-Up Regulations and the Complementarity between Foreign and Domestic Investment." *Review of World Economics* 150 (4): 745-61.

Muñoz-Najar, A., A. Gilberto, A. Hasan, C. Cobo, J. P. Azevedo, and M. Akmal. 2021. *Remote Learning during COVID-19: Lessons from Today, Principles for Tomorrow.* Washington, DC: World Bank.

Mutreja, P., B. Ravikumar, and M. J. Sposi. 2014. "Capital Goods Trade and Economic Development." Working Paper 2014-012B, Federal Reserve Bank of St. Louis, St. Louis, MO.

Nabar, N., and J. Joyce. 2009. "Sudden Stops, Banking Crises, and Investment Collapses." *Journal of Development Economics* 90 (2): 163-89.

Nair-Reichert, U., and D. Weinhold. 2001. "Causality Tests for Cross-Country Panels: A New Look at FDI and Economic Growth in Developing Countries." *Oxford Bulletin of Economics and Statistics* 63 (2): 153-71.

Narain, U., S. Margulis, and T. Essam. 2011. "Estimating Costs of Adaptation to Climate Change." *Climate Policy* 11 (3): 1001-19.

Ndikumana, L., and S. Verick. 2008. "The Linkages between FDI and Domestic Investment: Unravelling the Developmental Impact of Foreign Investment in Sub-Saharan Africa." *Development Policy Review* 26 (6): 713-26.

Nguyen, V. B. 2021. "The Relationship between FDI Inflows and Private Investment in Vietnam: Does Institutional Environment Matter?" *International Journal of Finance & Economics* 26 (1): 1151-62.

OECD (Organisation for Economic Co-operation and Development). 2015. "Lifting Investment for Higher Sustainable Growth." In *OECD Economic Outlook*, 205-79. Paris: Organisation for Economic Co-operation and Development.

OECD (Organisation for Economic Co-operation and Development). 2016a. *Compendium of Productivity Indicators 2016*. Paris: Organisation for Economic Co-operation and Development.

OECD (Organisation for Economic Co-operation and Development). 2016b. "Using the Fiscal Levers to Escape the Low-Growth Trap." In *OECD Economic Outlook*, Chapter 2. Paris: Organisation for Economic Co-operation and Development.

OECD (Organisation for Economic Co-operation and Development). 2017. *Investing in Climate, Investing in Growth*. Paris: Organisation for Economic Co-operation and Development.

OECD (Organisation for Economic Co-operation and Development). 2020. "Building Back Better: A Sustainable, Resilient Recovery after COVID-19." OECD Policy Responses to Coronavirus (COVID-19), OECD, Paris.

OECD (Organisation for Economic Co-operation and Development) and IDB (Inter-American Development Bank). 2016. "Broadband Policies for Latin America and the Caribbean: A Digital Economy Toolkit." Organisation for Economic Co-operation and Development, Paris.

Ohnsorge, F., and S. Yu. 2016. "Recent Credit Surge in Historical Context." Policy Research Working Paper 7704, World Bank, Washington, DC.

Ohnsorge, F., and S. Yu, eds. 2021. *The Long Shadow of Informality: Challenges and Policies*. Washington, DC: World Bank.

Okunogbe, O. M., and F. Santoro. 2021. "The Promise and Limitations of Information Technology for Tax Mobilization." Policy Research Working Paper 9848, World Bank, Washington, DC.

Ollivaud, P., Y. Guillemette, and D. Turner. 2016. "Links between Weak Investment and the Slowdown in Productivity and Potential Output Growth across the OECD." OECD Economics Department Working Papers 1304, Organisation for Economic Co-Operation and Development, Paris.

Osei, M. J., and J. Kim. 2020. "Foreign Direct Investment and Economic Growth: Is More Financial Development Better?" *Economic Modelling* 93 (December): 154-61.

Paulson Institute, Nature Conservancy, and Cornell Atkinson Center for Sustainability. 2020. "Financing Nature: Closing the Global Biodiversity Financing Gap." Paulson Institute, Chicago.

Pels, B. 2010. "Capital Inflows and Investment." IIIS Discussion Paper 330, Institute for International Integration Studies, Trinity College Dublin, Dublin, Ireland.

Perez-Sebastian, F., and J. Steinbuks. 2017. "Public Infrastructure and Structural Transformation." Policy Research Working Paper 8285, World Bank, Washington, DC.

Prasad, E. S., R. G. Rajan, and A. Subramanian. 2007. "Foreign Capital and Economic Growth." *Brookings Papers on Economic Activity* 2007 (2): 153-230.

Psacharopoulos, G., V. Collis, H. A. Patrinos, and E. Vegas. 2021. "The COVID-19 Cost of School Closures in Earnings and Income across the World." *Comparative Education Review* 65 (2): 271-87.

Qiang, C. Z., Y. Liu, and V. Steenbergen. 2021. *An Investment Perspective on Global Value Chains*. Washington, DC: World Bank.

Qureshi, Z., J. L. Diaz-Sanchez, and A. Varoudakis. 2015. "The Post-crisis Growth Slowdown in Emerging Economies and the Role of Structural Reforms." *Global Journal of Emerging Market Economies* 7 (2): 179-200.

Reinikka, R., and J. Svensson. 2002. "Coping with Poor Public Capital." *Journal of Development Economics* 69 (1): 51-69.

Restuccia, D., and R. Rogerson. 2008. "Policy Distortions and Aggregate Productivity with Heterogeneous Establishments." *Review of Economic Dynamics* 11 (4): 707-20.

Rockefeller Foundation and Boston Consulting Group. 2022. "Climate Finance Funding Flows and Opportunities: What Gets Measured Gets Financed." New York: The Rockefeller Organization.

Romer, P. 1993. "Idea Gaps and Object Gaps in Economic Development." *Journal of Monetary Economics* 32 (3): 543-73.

Rozenberg, J., and M. Fay, eds. 2019. *Beyond the Gap: How Countries Can Afford the Infrastructure They Need While Protecting the Planet.* Washington, DC: World Bank.

Ruta, M., ed. 2022. *The Impact of the War in Ukraine on Global Trade and Investment.* Trade, Investment, and Competitiveness: Equitable Growth, Finance and Institutions Insight. Washington, DC: World Bank.

Sahay, R., M. Čihák, P. N'Diaye, A. Barajas, R. Bi, D. Ayala, Y Gao, et al. 2015. "Rethinking Financial Deepening: Stability and Growth in Emerging Markets." IMF Staff Discussion Note 15/08, International Monetary Fund, Washington, DC.

Sauvant, K. P. 2009. "FDI Protectionism Is On the Rise." Policy Research Working Paper 5052, World Bank, Washington, DC.

Schivardi, F., and E. Viviano. 2011. "Entry Barriers in Retail Trade." *Economic Journal* 121 (551): 145-70.

Shapiro, M. D., O. J. Blanchard, and M. C. Lovell. 1986. "Investment, Output, and the Cost of Capital." *Brookings Papers on Economic Activity* 1986 (1): 111-64.

Songwe, V., N. Stern, and A. Bhattacharya. 2022. "Finance for Climate Action: Scaling Up Investment for Climate and Development." Grantham Research Institute on Climate Change and the Environment, London School of Economics and Political Science, London.

Sposi, M., M. Yi, and J. Zhang. 2019. "Trade Integration, Global Value Chains and Capital Accumulation." NBER Working Paper 28087, National Bureau of Economic Research, Cambridge, MA.

St. Aubyn, M., A. Pina, F. Garcia, and J. Pais. 2009. "Study on the Efficiency and Effectiveness of Public Spending on Tertiary Education." Economic Papers 390, European Commission, Brussels.

Stenberg, K., O. Hanssen, T. Edejer, M. Bertram, C. Brindley. A. Meshreky, J. E. Rosen, et al. 2017. "Financing Transformative Health Systems towards Achievement of the Health Sustainable Development Goals: A Model for Projected Resource Needs in 67 Low-Income and Middle-Income Countries." *Lancet Global Health* 5: e875-87.

Stern, N. 2019. "Sustainability's Moment of Truth." *Project Syndicate,* October 4, 2019.

Stiglitz, J. E. 2020. "The Pandemic Economic Crisis, Precautionary Behavior, and Mobility Constraints: An Application of the Dynamic Disequilibrium Model with Randomness." NBER Working Paper 27992, National Bureau of Economic Research, Cambridge, MA.

Stocker, M., J. Baffes, M. Some, D. Vorisek, and C. Wheeler. 2018. "The 2014-16 Oil Price Collapse in Retrospect: Sources and Implications." Policy Research Working Paper 8419, World Bank, Washington, DC.

Strand, J., and M. Toman. 2010. "Green Stimulus, Economic Recovery, and Long-Term Sustainable Development." Policy Research Working Paper 5163, World Bank, Washington, DC.

Tang, S., E. A. Selvanathan, and S. Selvanathan. 2008. "Foreign Direct Investment, Domestic Investment and Economic Growth in China: A Time Series Analysis." *World Economy* 31(10): 1292-309.

UNCTAD (United Nations Conference on Trade and Development). 2014. *World Investment Report 2014: Investment in SDGs; An Action Plan.* New York: United Nations.

UNEP (United Nations Environment Programme). 2022. *State of Finance for Nature: Time to Act; Doubling Investment by 2025 and Eliminating Nature-Negative Finance Flows.* Nairobi: United Nations Environment Programme.

United Nations Inter-Agency Task Force on Financing for Development. 2019. *Financing for Sustainable Development Report 2019.* New York: United Nations.

United Nations Inter-Agency Task Force on Financing for Development. 2022. *Financing for Sustainable Development Report 2022.* New York: United Nations.

Vagliasindi, M., and N. Gorgulu. 2021. "What Have We Learned about the Effectiveness of Infrastructure Investment as a Fiscal Stimulus?" Policy Research Working Paper 9796, World Bank, Washington, DC.

Vashakmadze, E., G. Kambou, D. Chen, B. Nandwa, Y. Okawa, and D. Vorisek. 2018. "Regional Dimensions of Recent Weakness in Investment: Drivers, Investment Needs and Policy Responses." *Journal of Infrastructure, Policy and Development* 2 (1): 37-66.

Vorisek, D., and S. Yu. 2020. "Understanding the Cost of Achieving the Sustainable Development Goals." Policy Research Working Paper 9146, World Bank, Washington, DC.

Wacziarg, R., and K. H. Welch. 2008. "Trade Liberalization and Growth: New Evidence." *World Bank Economic Review* 22 (2): 187-231.

Wang, J. 2013. "The Economic Impact of Special Economic Zones: Evidence from Chinese Municipalities." *Journal of Development Economics* 101 (1): 133-47.

Wang, M. 2009. "Manufacturing FDI and Economic Growth: Evidence from Asian Economies." *Applied Economics* 41 (8): 991-1002.

Wang, M., and M. C. Wong. 2011. "FDI, Education, and Economic Growth: Quality Matters." *Atlantic Economic Journal* 39 (2): 103-15.

Wilichowski, T., C. Cobo, A. Patil, and M. Quota. 2021. "How to Enhance Teacher Professional Development through Technology: Takeaways from Innovations across the Globe." *Education for Global Development* (blog), September 23, 2021. https://blogs.worldbank.org/education/how-enhance-teacher-professional-development-through-technology-takeaways-innovations

World Bank. 2015a. "From Billions to Trillions: Transforming Development Finance." Development Committee Paper, World Bank, Washington, DC.

World Bank. 2015b. *Global Economic Prospects: Having Fiscal Space and Using It.* January. Washington, DC: World Bank.

World Bank. 2015c. *Global Financial Development Report 2015/2016: Long-Term Finance.* Washington, DC: World Bank.

World Bank. 2016a. *Global Economic Prospects: Spillovers amid Weak Growth.* January. Washington, DC: World Bank.

World Bank. 2016b. "Investment Reality Check." *South Asia Economic Focus.* Fall. Washington, DC: World Bank.

World Bank. 2017. *Global Economic Prospects: Weak Investment in Uncertain Times.* January. Washington, DC: World Bank.

World Bank. 2018. *Global Economic Prospects: Broad-Based Upturn, but for How Long?* January. Washington, DC: World Bank.

World Bank. 2019a. *Global Economic Prospects: Darkening Skies.* January. Washington, DC: World Bank.

World Bank. 2019b. *Global Economic Prospects: Heightened Tensions, Subdued Investment.* June. Washington, DC: World Bank.

World Bank. 2020a. *The African Continental Free Trade Area: Economic and Distributional Effects.* Washington, DC: World Bank.

World Bank. 2020b. "Benchmarking Infrastructure Development 2020: Assessing Regulatory Quality to Prepare, Procure and Manage PPPs and Traditional Public Investment in Infrastructure Projects." World Bank, Washington, DC.

World Bank. 2021a. *Global Economic Prospects.* January. Washington, DC: World Bank.

World Bank. 2021b. *Global Economic Prospects.* June. Washington, DC: World Bank.

World Bank. 2022a. "Climate and Development: An Agenda for Action—Emerging Insights from World Bank Group 2021-22 Country Climate and Development Reports." World Bank, Washington, DC.

World Bank. 2022b. "Coping with Shocks: Migration and the Road to Resilience." *South Asia Economic Focus.* October. Washington, DC: World Bank.

World Bank. 2022c. "The Food and Energy Crisis—Weathering the Storm." Development Committee Paper, World Bank, Washington, DC.

World Bank. 2022d. *Global Economic Prospects.* January. Washington, DC: World Bank.

World Bank. 2022e. *Global Economic Prospects.* June. Washington, DC: World Bank.

World Bank. 2022f. "Update on World Bank Group Efforts to Facilitate Private Capital Investments." World Bank, Washington, DC.

World Bank 2022g. "Vietnam Country Climate and Development Report." World Bank, Washington, DC.

World Bank. 2022h. "World Bank Approaches to Mobilize Private Capital for Development: An Independent Evaluation." Independent Evaluation Group, World Bank, Washington, DC.

World Bank. 2022i. *World Development Report 2022: Finance for an Equitable Recovery.* Washington, DC: World Bank.

World Bank. 2023. *Global Economic Prospects.* January. Washington, DC: World Bank.

Zhang, J., J. Zhang, and R. Lee. 2003. "Rising Longevity, Education, Savings, and Growth." *Journal of Development Economics* 70 (February): 83-101.

CHAPTER 4

Regional Dimensions of Investment:
Moving in the Right Direction?

Investment growth slowed in the past decade in all emerging market and developing economy (EMDE) regions, but most sharply in East Asia and Pacific (EAP) and the Middle East and North Africa (MNA). Meanwhile, pressing investment needs remain. All regions need to boost infrastructure investment and investment in mitigating and adapting to climate change and reversing pandemic-related learning losses. In other areas, investment needs vary by region. They include accommodating high and rising urbanization (EAP, Latin America and the Caribbean [LAC], and South Asia [SAR]); boosting productivity, especially in sectors that employ large proportions of the population (for example, agriculture in Sub-Saharan Africa [SSA]); rebuilding after conflict (Europe and Central Asia [ECA], MNA, and SSA); improving trade linkages (LAC); and preparing for future public health crises. Across all EMDE regions, policy priorities include strengthening the efficiency of public investment, boosting private investment (especially in ECA, LAC, and MNA), and expanding the availability of finance for investment (especially in LAC and SSA).

Introduction

Investment in human capital and high-quality infrastructure has multiple benefits. It supports the provision of basic services to households and market access for firms, helps the integration of domestic and international markets, and promotes advances in labor productivity and per capita incomes through capital deepening and technical progress. Investment in infrastructure can also support climate change mitigation and adaptation.

Investment growth was slower in the past decade (2011-21) than in the preceding one (2000-10) in all six EMDE regions.[1] In all EMDE regions except EAP, investment fell in 2020 amid the outbreak of the coronavirus disease 2019 (COVID-19) pandemic and rebounded in 2021. In 2022, investment growth performance was mixed, and several regions now have a mediocre outlook for investment growth. This puts the spotlight on policies that could help meet the large and diverse investment needs across regions.

This chapter explores cross-regional differences by addressing three questions:

• How has investment growth evolved in the past two decades in each EMDE region?

Note: This chapter was prepared by Sergiy Kasyanenko, Philip Kenworthy, Franz Ulrich Ruch, Ekaterine Vashakmadze, Dana Vorisek, and Collette Wheeler.

[1] Throughout this chapter, unless otherwise specified, "investment" is, for the sake of brevity, understood to indicate investment levels and refers to real gross fixed-capital formation (public and private combined). "Investment growth" is measured as the annual percent change in real investment. Annual investment growth rates for country groups are weighted by average 2010-19 investment levels.

- What are the current and prospective investment needs in each EMDE region?

- Which policies could help countries address their investment needs in each EMDE region?

Contributions. This chapter adds regional granularity to the analysis of global investment growth in chapter 3 and does so consistently across the EMDE regions. It draws on a rich body of regional studies that have examined the constraints on investment growth and possible policy solutions.

Findings. The chapter identifies several patterns in investment growth among the six EMDE regions: EAP, ECA, LAC, MNA, SAR, and SSA. First, investment growth slowed in the past decade in all regions, but most sharply in EAP and MNA. In EAP, a policy shift in China aimed at reducing reliance on credit-fueled investment and mitigating risks to financial stability was largely responsible for the slowdown. In MNA, an oil price slide in 2014-16, armed conflicts, and persistent policy uncertainty contributed to the slowdown.

Second, investment growth is projected to remain well below its 2000-21 average in the near term in EAP, ECA, LAC, and SAR but to be close to its two-decade average in MNA and SSA. Consensus long-term (five-year-ahead) forecasts for investment growth have been downgraded repeatedly. Annual investment growth in the 2020s is now forecast to be lower than in the 2010s in all regions except in LAC and SAR, where adverse shocks that depressed investment growth in the 2010s are not expected to recur.

Third, all regions have large needs to invest in physical and human capital, whether to mitigate and adapt to climate change and reverse pandemic-related learning losses (all regions); improve very low levels of infrastructure development (SAR and SSA); accommodate rising levels of urbanization (EAP, LAC, and SAR); support productivity growth, particularly in sectors that employ large proportions of the population (for example, agriculture in SSA); rebuild following conflicts (ECA, MNA and SSA); improve trade linkages (LAC); or prepare for future public health crises.

Fourth, a range of policies are needed to lift investment. Priorities include strengthening the efficiency of public investment (especially in SAR and SSA), boosting private investment (particularly in LAC and MNA), and expanding the availability of financing for investment (all regions).

Investment trends

The decade 2000-10 saw double-digit, or near double-digit, average annual investment growth in EAP, ECA, MNA, and SAR. In the subsequent decade, 2011-21, investment growth decreased sharply in all regions, although the magnitude and causes of the decline varied across regions. Commodity price movements, domestic policies, uncertainty stemming from domestic conditions, and spillovers from key trading partners all played a role (Vashakmadze et al. 2018).

The sharpest slowdowns occurred in MNA and EAP, where investment growth averaged nearly 8 and 6 percentage points per year less, respectively, in 2011-21 than in 2000-10 (figure 4.1). In MNA, the oil price plunge of 2014-16, several armed conflicts, and persistent political uncertainty in some countries marked the decade 2011-21. Investment growth was negative in four of the six years of 2016-21. In EAP, the slowdown mostly reflected a policy shift in China aimed at reducing reliance for economic growth on credit-fueled investment and at managing risks to financial stability. Elsewhere in the region, investment growth weakened in commodity exporters, such as Indonesia, following commodity price declines in the middle of the decade, and in Thailand owing to policy uncertainty.

In three other regions—ECA, LAC, and SAR—average investment growth in 2011-21 was slower by more than 3 percentage points per year than in 2000-10. In ECA, investment was buffeted by spillovers from the euro area debt crisis, a domestic financial crisis in the Russian Federation, a middecade plunge in commodity prices, conflict in Eastern Europe and associated sanctions, and financial stress in Türkiye. In SAR, the slowdown, which mostly occurred in the first half of the decade, reflected excess manufacturing capacity in the face of sluggish external demand, financial sector stress, and uncertainties related to government policy. In LAC, slower investment growth in the 2010s mirrored a broader weakening of gross domestic product (GDP) growth, with severe recessions in the region's largest economies. SSA experienced the mildest slowdown in investment growth among the six regions in the 2010s, with strong growth in public investment limiting the overall investment slowdown to less than 2 percentage points a year.

Changes in the regional composition of aggregate EMDE investment and average EMDE investment growth accompanied the slowdown in investment growth in EMDEs in 2011-21. Most notably, despite slower investment growth in EAP in 2011-21, EAP's share of aggregate EMDE investment rose from half to more than three-fifths compared with that in 2000-10, while its share of EMDE investment growth jumped from about three-fifths to more than three-quarters (figure 4.2).

Investment growth is projected to remain well below its 2000-21 average in the near term in EAP, ECA, LAC, and SAR, but it is expected to be close to its two-decade average in MNA and SSA. Consensus long-term (five-year-ahead) forecasts for investment growth have been downgraded repeatedly. Annual average investment growth in 2022-30 is now forecast to be lower than in 2011-21 in all regions except in LAC and SAR, where adverse shocks that depressed investment growth in the 2010s are not expected to recur.

Medium- and long-term prospects for EMDE investment growth have deteriorated over the past decade. Five-year-ahead consensus forecasts have declined for all EMDE regions

FIGURE 4.1 **Average investment growth, by EMDE region**

Investment growth was slower in 2011-21 than in 2000-10 in all EMDE regions and declined in 2020 in every region except East Asia and Pacific. After rebounding in 2021, investment growth is projected to be below long-term averages in 2022-23 in some regions.

A. EAP investment growth

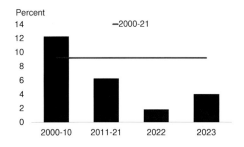

B. ECA investment growth

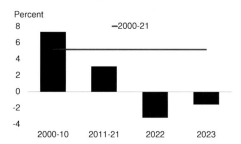

C. LAC investment growth

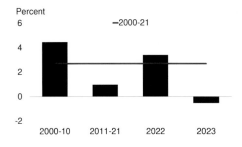

D. MNA investment growth

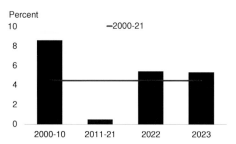

E. SAR investment growth

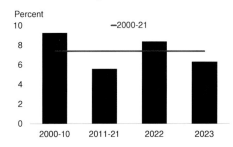

F. SSA investment growth

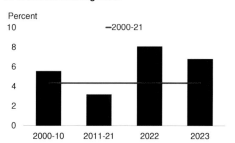

Sources: Haver Analytics; World Bank, World Development Indicators database; World Bank.
Note: EAP = East Asia and Pacific; ECA = Europe and Central Asia; EMDEs = emerging market and developing economies; LAC = Latin America and the Caribbean; MNA = Middle East and North Africa; SAR = South Asia; SSA = Sub-Saharan Africa.
A.-F. Investment growth rates are estimates for 2022 and forecasts for 2023. Regional investment growth rates are calculated using real annual fixed investment in constant U.S. dollars as weights. Growth rates for 2000-10, 2011-21, and 2000-21 are geometric averages of rates of regional annual investment growth. Sample includes 11 EAP, 13 ECA, 20 LAC, 11 MNA, 5 SAR, and 38 SSA economies.

FIGURE 4.2 **Regional contributions to EMDE investment and investment growth**

East Asia and Pacific accounted for the majority of EMDE investment and investment growth in the 2010s.

A. Share of EMDE investment

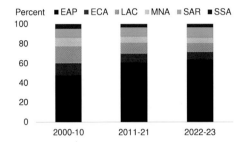

B. Contribution to EMDE investment growth

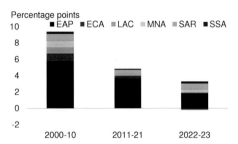

Sources: Haver Analytics; World Bank, World Development Indicators database; World Bank.
Note: EAP = East Asia and Pacific; ECA = Europe and Central Asia; EMDEs = emerging market and developing economies; LAC = Latin America and the Caribbean; MNA = Middle East and North Africa; SAR = South Asia; SSA = Sub-Saharan Africa. 2022-23 data are forecasts.
A.B. Investment growth rates are estimates for 2022 and forecasts for 2023. Regional investment growth rates are calculated using real annual fixed investment in constant U.S. dollars as weights. Shares for 2000-10, 2011-21, and 2022-23 are simple averages of regional annual investment growth. Sample includes 11 EAP, 13 ECA, 20 LAC, 11 MNA, 5 SAR, and 38 SSA economies.

for which data are available, and the 10-year-ahead projections are well below the actual growth rates of the 2010s (figure 4.3).

Investment needs

All EMDE regions continue to have substantial investment needs, reflecting several major challenges and policy priorities. All regions will need to invest heavily in infrastructure, whether to mitigate and adapt to climate change (all regions); reverse pandemic-related learning losses (all regions); improve very low levels of infrastructure development (SAR and SSA); accommodate high and rising levels of urbanization (EAP, LAC, and SAR); support productivity growth, particularly in sectors that employ large proportions of the population (for example, agriculture in SSA); rebuild following armed conflicts (ECA and MNA); improve trade linkages (LAC); or prepare for future public health crises (all regions). All regions will also need to address a likely widening of investment gaps during the pandemic, as governments redirected public spending to high-priority social safety nets and health care, even as the regions prepare their health and education systems for future crises.

Basic infrastructure. Despite some remarkable successes, providing essential public services (water, sanitation, electricity, and transport), which support health and safety and enable participation in economic activity, remains a challenge in many EMDEs, especially in SSA, but also in parts of other regions. About 775 million people worldwide lack access to clean water, 1.7 billion people do not have adequate sanitation, 2.4 billion people still cook their food with solid fuels (such as wood), and 1 billion people live more than two kilometers from an all-weather road.

FIGURE 4.3 Regional prospects for investment growth

Private sector forecasts of investment growth in all EMDE regions have declined over the past decade, with the sharpest downgrades in East Asia and Pacific and South Asia. Investment growth during the 2020s is projected to be well below the rates of the 2010s.

A. Five-year-ahead forecasts for investment growth

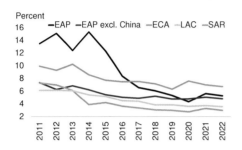

B. Actual and forecast investment growth

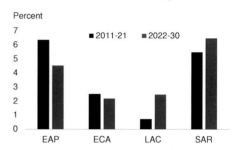

Sources: Consensus Economics; World Bank.
Note: EAP = East Asia and Pacific; ECA = Europe and Central Asia; EMDEs = emerging market and developing economies; excl. = excluding; LAC = Latin America and the Caribbean; SAR = South Asia.
A. Panel shows the five-year-ahead forecasts for investment growth as of the year shown on the x-axis. Sample includes data for six economies in EAP (China, Indonesia, Malaysia, the Philippines, Thailand, and Vietnam), seven in ECA (Bulgaria, Croatia, Hungary, Poland, Romania, Russian Federation, and Ukraine), six in LAC (Argentina, Brazil, Chile, Colombia, Mexico, and Peru) and one in SAR (India).
B. Geometric mean of actual investment growth in 2011-21 and of current-year to eight-year-ahead consensus forecasts for investment growth for 2022-30, as of September 2022. Includes six economies each in EAP, ECA, and LAC and one economy in SAR.

Climate change mitigation and adaptation. In large EMDEs with globally significant emissions of greenhouse gases, investment in climate-smart infrastructure and technologies by both public and private sectors is an urgent priority, and that investment will ideally be combined with other actions such as measures to improve energy efficiency. In smaller EMDEs, adaptation to climate change necessitates investment in new and retrofitted infrastructure, the maintenance of which will also require resources.

For EAP (for example, Vietnam), the World Bank recently estimated additional financing needs for adaptation measures at 4.5-5.4 percent of GDP per year (World Bank 2022k). Small island states in EAP and LAC have particularly large needs for investment to strengthen their resilience to the rising frequency of severe weather events and to address challenges from rising sea levels.

SAR and SSA are particularly vulnerable to climate-induced increases in poverty, disease, child mortality, and food prices. Half of SAR's population lives in areas expected to become climate hot spots and agriculture is a critical source of employment in those areas (Amarnath et al. 2017; Hallegatte et al. 2016; Jafino et al. 2020; Mani et al. 2018). Fragile states in SSA are particularly at risk because their governments often lack the institutional capacity needed to respond effectively to climate challenges (Maino and Emrullahu 2022).

Rebuilding following conflict. The war following Russia's invasion of Ukraine in early 2022 has dramatically expanded investment needs in ECA. Preliminary assessments for recovery and reconstruction needs in Ukraine across social, productive, and infrastructure sectors total $349 billion—more than 1.5 times the country's 2021 GDP (World Bank 2022j). The conflict has also dramatically worsened near-term prospects for investment in Belarus and Russia, in part because of international sanctions. MNA has a continued need to replace private and public capital destroyed during wars in Iraq, the Syrian Arab Republic, and the Republic of Yemen. Gobat and Kostial (2016) estimated the cost of rebuilding damaged or destroyed infrastructure in Syria to be in the range of $100-200 billion—more than 10 times the country's 2015 GDP. Iraq too faces large infrastructure investment needs, increased by conflict. It has been estimated that the country would need some $200 billion in 2018 prices to restore "hard" infrastructure to pre-ISIS levels, almost equal to its 2018 GDP (Gunter 2018). In the Republic of Yemen, recovery and reconstruction costs are estimated at $20-25 billion cumulatively over a five-year period, equivalent to 1.1-1.3 times the country's 2020 GDP (World Bank 2020g).

Education and health investment. Beyond investment in infrastructure and physical capital, the COVID-19 pandemic has underscored the need to invest in health and education. This is especially urgent in SSA, as it remains well behind other regions in human capital development. However, it is also essential in ECA, LAC, and MNA to ensure that education systems provide the skills needed for productive employment.

LAC spends more as a proportion of GDP on education and health care than any other EMDE region, but outcomes suggest that these investments could yield greater value. Educational attainment is highly unequal across income levels, and the region on average attains only mediocre Programme for International Student Assessment (PISA) scores.

In ECA, despite above-average levels of education, learning outcomes, as measured by PISA scores, have deteriorated over the past decade in some economies. There have also been substantial learning losses from the pandemic. With regard to health care, since 2000 such measures as the proportion of the population covered for essential services and maternal mortality rates have improved more slowly in ECA than in other regions.

MNA has the lowest share of human capital in total wealth among EMDE regions. It also has the lowest returns to education, reflecting in part low-quality education (Lange, Wodon, and Carey 2018; Montenegro and Patrinos 2014). With regard to health care, the fact that in 2021, the region shared with SAR the highest prevalence of diabetes among EMDE regions, at 12.1 percent of the adult population, indicates the level of inadequacies.

SAR also suffers from poor health care and health outcomes. Apart from the high prevalence of diabetes, SAR has the lowest number of hospital beds per capita among EMDE regions, and among the most burdensome out-of-pocket health care expenses. These issues result largely from low public health spending; at only 2 percent of GDP, it is well below those in all other EMDE regions. Urgent investment is required in health care to help address these challenges. Taxation that would bring health benefits, such as sugar taxes, has been suggested as one funding option to meet growing needs and help address morbidity (Kurowski et al. 2021). SAR also faces significant air pollution that imposes heavy health costs, and mitigation of that will require major investment.

SSA has especially urgent needs for investment in health and education considering the scale of human capital losses caused by the pandemic. The region remains one of the most vulnerable to public health risks, with many of its countries remaining ill-equipped to respond effectively to outbreaks of infectious diseases. Meanwhile, the region's educational outcomes are among the poorest in the world. Thus, just 10 percent of lower secondary students achieve minimum proficiency in mathematics, reflecting the lack of access to quality schooling, especially for the poor (UNESCO 2019).

Transport infrastructure. SSA has large transport infrastructure needs, especially to reap the full potential of the African Continental Free Trade Agreement (chapter 6). In many SSA countries, only a small proportion of the road network is paved, and railway development is broadly inadequate, often because of damage from wars or natural disasters or poor maintenance. In SAR also, the quantity and quality of transport infrastructure fall well behind those in most other regions, contributing to the region's lack of global integration. Transport infrastructure upgrades are also needed in EAP, ECA, and LAC to deepen the integration of remote parts of some countries and strengthen the resilience of regional value chains. EAP, LAC, and SAR need infrastructure investment, combined with effective land use regulation, to accommodate high and rising urbanization. The annual cost of traffic congestion is already estimated to be more than 1 percent of GDP in several major cities in LAC (Buenos Aires, São Paulo, Montevideo, and Santiago; Calatayud et al. 2021).

Digital connectivity. In EAP, on account of the presence of many small remote island states, and in ECA, where digitization falls well behind that in its main trading partners, increased public sector investment in digital connectivity infrastructure is needed— particularly high-speed fiber-optic lines ("the middle mile") and drop lines that allow individual homes to be connected ("the last mile"). The focus needs to be on reducing the digital divide by expanding international connectivity and local broadband service to remote islands and communities (chapter 7). The resilience of digital infrastructure to climate events and natural disasters also needs to be improved.

Policies to boost investment

Given current mediocre prospects for investment growth and the wide array of challenges that EMDEs face, policies to stimulate investment remain a priority. Although specific policy choices depend on national and regional circumstances, multi-pronged strategies are generally needed to boost growth in both public and private investment. The World Bank and other multilateral development institutions can help EMDEs design and implement these strategies.

Improving the efficiency of public investment. Increasing the efficiency of public investment is a priority for all EMDE regions, especially in lower-middle-income and low-income economies, on account of their limited resources. The efficiency of public investment in SSA and SAR consistently lags behind that in other EMDE regions, while in ECA it substantially trails that of European Union (EU) peers. This low efficiency partly reflects weaknesses in public investment management, including poor project selection, weak enforcement of procurement procedures, and poor monitoring of project execution. Improvements in these areas are often key. Effective use of medium-term budgeting frameworks can help improve spending efficiency, by improving the predictability and transparency of spending, as can the introduction of independent spending evaluations. Better coordination between various levels of government can help reduce duplication and inconsistencies. Rules that protect capital expenditures during periods of fiscal consolidation can also improve public investment efficiency.

Creating more fiscal space. Additional domestic tax revenues could provide needed space for public investment in priority areas. SAR and SSA have particularly low revenue-to-GDP ratios. Improved revenue collection, enhanced tax administration, a broader tax base, higher tax rates, or reduced exemptions could yield additional revenues. For example, new tax reform legislation in Indonesia is expected to raise revenue by 1.2 percent of GDP in the medium term. Shifting expenditures away from items that do not promote economic growth or other policy objectives could also boost productive public investment. Periodic public expenditure reviews that assess all expenditures against policy objectives could identify expenditure priorities. For some large countries in LAC, this might require reforms to reduce budget rigidities (Herrera and Olaberria 2020).

Promoting private investment. Empirical studies show that increases in public investment tend to raise private investment, but that this crowding-in effect may be temporary (Kose et al. 2017). A favorable business environment—including stable macroeconomic conditions, predictable policies and regulations, robust competition, and limited barriers to entry and exit—is an important precondition for vigorous growth in private investment anywhere. In LAC, tax reforms could encourage investment (Acosta-Ormaechea, Pienknagura, and Pizzinelli 2022). Greater mobilization of domestic saving (LAC), broader access to formal financial services (SSA), and stronger banking systems (EAP and SAR) could increase funding for private investment. By increasing market size, regional integration can provide incentives for private investment (ECA, LAC, SAR, and SSA). Other EMDE regions have successfully applied public-private partnerships, which are less common in MNA and SSA than elsewhere, to numerous sectors, although the need for autonomous regulatory agencies to oversee the private agents is clear. Since the effective use of high-productivity technologies often requires complementary skilled human capital, better-quality education and health systems typically foster private investment.

The remainder of the chapter is presented in six sections, one on each of the six EMDE regions. Each section examines the evolution of investment growth since 2000 and the region-specific underlying factors. Regional investment needs and policy options are also reviewed.

EAST ASIA
and PACIFIC

After several decades of strong growth, investment in East Asia and Pacific (EAP) slowed significantly in 2011-21 mainly on account of China. Investment growth fell sharply in 2020, during the COVID-19 pandemic outbreak, but remained positive, unlike in other EMDE regions. It rebounded in 2021-22 thanks to pandemic-related stimulus spending. Investment in China is expected to resume its structural deceleration when policy support is withdrawn. In the region excluding China, investment growth, which was negative in 2020, is expected to continue its recovery in 2022-23, but at rates that will be insufficient to prevent a further widening of the gap between investment and its prepandemic trend. The prospect of weak investment growth in EAP over the medium term raises concerns about growth in the region's potential output. Given the importance of investment in generating productivity and per capita income gains, it is important that the region reduce impediments to productive investment growth, including financial impediments.

Introduction

East Asia and Pacific accounted for 60 percent of EMDE investment during 2011-21. Investment growth in EAP slowed from 11.6 percent a year, on average, in 2000-08 to 6.4 percent a year in 2011-21. China, which represented 85 percent of EAP GDP and 90 percent of EAP investment in 2000-21, was the main contributor to this slowdown. In China, investment growth almost halved from 12.3 percent a year in 2000-08 to 6.6 percent a year in 2011-21. However, the decline in investment growth was not limited to China: in the region excluding China, investment growth also moderated, from 7.8 percent a year in 2000-08 to 4.7 percent a year in 2011-21.

In China, the slowdown in investment growth was policy-led and aimed at reducing the reliance of GDP growth on credit-fueled investment and at managing risks to financial stability. In the region excluding China, the moderation of investment growth, which started in the early 2010s, initially reflected the worsening terms of trade of large commodity exporters, including Indonesia and Malaysia, and increased policy uncertainty in Thailand. Investment growth in the region weakened further in 2018, partly reflecting increased global policy uncertainty related to the escalation in trade tensions between China and the United States. In 2020, investment growth fell sharply during the COVID-19 pandemic outbreak, turning negative in the region excluding China.

Investment growth rebounded in much of the region in 2021 and was robust in 2022. Nevertheless, in the region excluding China, where investment contracted by

7.6 percent in 2020, investment was still below its prepandemic level in mid-2022. In 2022-23, investment growth is expected to rise above its 2011-21 average rate, but not sufficiently to prevent a further widening of the gap between investment and its pre-pandemic trend. In China, after a couple of years of stimulus-fueled growth, investment is expected to resume its structural deceleration when policy support is withdrawn.

The prospect for weak investment growth in EAP over the medium term raises concerns about the effects on EAP's growth in potential output—the growth rate that can be sustained at full employment and capacity utilization. The sustained weakening of investment growth during the 2010s, together with declining total factor productivity (TFP) growth, has already contributed to a slowdown in labor productivity growth in EAP and, as a result, slower convergence toward per capita income levels in advanced economies (Dieppe 2020). The COVID-19 pandemic could have a prolonged adverse effect on investment in EAP that the fallout from the war in Ukraine and heightened geopolitical tensions could compound.

Despite several decades of rapid investment growth, investment needs in the region remain significant. Given the importance of investment in generating growth of productivity and per capita income, it is important that the region reduce impediments to productive investment, including those related to financing. For many EAP countries, boosting well-targeted public investment can have particularly large benefits due to high multipliers (Izquierdo, Pessino, and Vuletin 2018). At the same time, improving business climates and reducing policy uncertainty are essential to supporting private investment.

Several possibilities could improve the regional investment outlook. The recovery from the pandemic might trigger a productivity-enhancing investment surge. A boost could materialize through renewed investment in digital technologies in sectors such as manufacturing, finance, and education or through the onshoring of production of some essential products (Dieppe 2020). A pickup in investment would also create opportunities to shift infrastructure spending toward more resilient and environmentally sustainable options, in turn raising productivity and supporting progress toward the Sustainable Development Goals (Hallegatte and Hammer 2020).

Evolution of regional investment

Investment growth in EAP declined from 11.6 percent a year on average in 2000-08 to 6.4 percent a year in 2011-21. But it has remained higher than average investment growth in all EMDEs (figure 4.4). Investment slowed in a particularly pronounced way in China, where it dropped from a peak of 24.1 percent in 2009 to below 5 percent in 2019. This slowdown was policy-led and aimed at reducing reliance on credit-fueled investment for GDP growth and at managing risks to financial stability. It was achieved largely through tighter macroprudential regulations and stricter oversight of shadow banking.

In the region excluding China, the moderation of investment growth initially reflected the worsening of terms of trade in large commodity-exporting economies like Indonesia

FIGURE 4.4 **EAP: Investment growth**

Investment growth in EAP stabilized in 2021-22 after a decline in the preceding decade that largely reflected a policy-induced slowdown in China. In the rest of the region, following a decline in 2020, investment rebounded in 2021 and is expected to continue growing strongly in 2022-23. Foreign direct investment in the EAP region remains buoyant, and monetary policy is still accommodative, despite recent interest rate hikes.

A. Investment growth

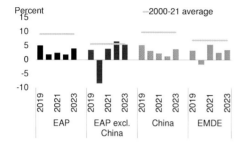

B. Investment growth from four quarters earlier

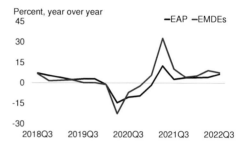

C. Foreign direct investment inflows

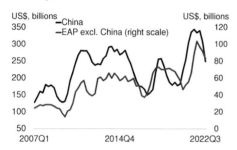

D. Monetary policy interest rates

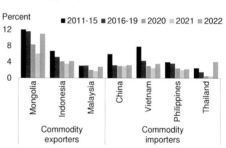

Sources: Haver Analytics; International Monetary Fund; United Nations Conference on Trade and Development; World Bank, World Development Indicators database; World Bank.
Note: EAP = East Asia and Pacific; EMDEs = emerging market and developing economies; excl. = excluding.
A. Averages weighted by gross domestic product (GDP). Data for 2023 are forecasts.
B. Includes 68 EMDEs, of which 7 are in EAP.
C. "EAP excl. China" includes Indonesia, Cambodia, Lao PDR, Malaysia, Mongolia, the Philippines, Thailand, and Vietnam.
D. Policy rates are the average of end-of-period data. Last observation is September 2022.

and Malaysia during 2014-16 (Vashakmadze et al. 2018; World Bank 2017). In this period, virtually all EAP economies recorded investment growth below long-term averages, with the lower investment growth mainly reflecting weak private investment. Tight monetary, fiscal, and prudential policies designed to contain rapid credit growth also limited investment growth in these countries. In smaller, more heavily commodity-dependent economies, including Mongolia and Papua New Guinea, investment contracted in the mid-2010s as foreign direct investment (FDI) in mining sector projects declined and countries tightened domestic macroeconomic policies sharply in response to balance of payments stress. Among the region's commodity-importing countries, investment weakness during the mid-2010s reflected policy uncertainty in the Philippines and Thailand, including delays in investment project approvals.

Investment growth in the region weakened further in early 2019, with the weakening partly reflecting increased global policy uncertainty amid the escalation in trade tensions between China and the United States. A short period of investment normalization in late 2019, supported by a stabilization of commodity prices and benign global financial conditions, was followed by a sharp weakening of investment growth at the onset of the pandemic in 2020. In EAP as a whole, investment growth in 2020 slowed to 3.2 percent. In China, stimulus policies moderated the weakening of investment growth, bringing it down to 4.4 percent. But in the rest of EAP, investment shrank by 7.6 percent. This decline, which occurred despite benign financial conditions, contrasts with the resilience of investment in the region excluding China during the 2009 global recession, when investment continued growing. However, investment in the region contracted less severely in 2020 than in 1999, after the Asian financial crisis, when investment in the region excluding China fell by almost 10 percent. The contraction in 2020 was sharpest in Malaysia, Mongolia, and the Philippines, where GDP also declined the most. Outside China, the decline in investment in 2020 was smallest in Vietnam, where a large fiscal stimulus program and resilient FDI inflows supported activity.

Investment growth rebounded in much of the region in 2021, led by stimulus-fueled public investment. However, private investment remained subdued, reflecting weak business confidence. In the region excluding China, investment growth is expected to accelerate in 2022 and 2023 before returning to its 2011-21 trend rate as policy support is unwound. Public investment is expected to play a smaller role in the near term. After the substantial fiscal stimulus of 2020, governments in the region have become more focused on safeguarding fiscal sustainability and containing debt-service costs. In China, investment is expected to resume its policy-guided deceleration once policy support begins to be withdrawn.

Uncertainty about the postpandemic economic landscape and the viability of existing production structures, as well as tightening financing conditions, will limit the growth of private investment. In 2020, investment contracted in about four-fifths of EAP economies. Investment rebounded in about two-thirds of EAP countries in 2021, but investment growth remained below its long-term average in almost all these cases, and investment declined further in the remaining one-third of countries (figure 4.5). Medium-term (five-year-ahead) private sector forecasts suggest continued weakness in investment growth, while sizable investment needs remain.

Regional investment needs

Infrastructure. Income and demographic shifts, urbanization, and climate change are the main forces driving investment needs in the region (figure 4.6). Rapid urbanization, large-scale migration, and population aging place heavy strains on urban infrastructure. In many East Asian countries, about one-third of the population lives in substandard housing. Meeting the growing demands that result from these trends while mitigating and adapting to climate change requires countries to strike a balance between economic growth and environmental protection. Estimates of the costs of the needed investment

FIGURE 4.5 **EAP: Investment growth slowdown and investment needs**

In 2020, investment fell in about four-fifths of EAP economies. In 2021, investment rebounded in about two-thirds of these economies, as the region began to recover from the downturn induced by coronavirus disease 2019 (COVID-19), but fell further in one-third. Medium-term private sector forecasts suggest continued weakness in investment growth in almost all EAP economies, despite sizable investment needs, especially in regard to infrastructure.

A. Share of countries with weak or negative investment growth

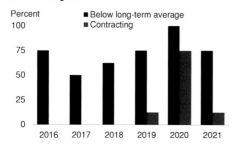

B. Contributions to investment growth

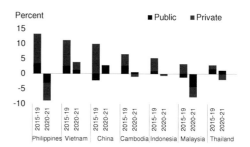

C. Five-year-ahead forecasts for investment growth

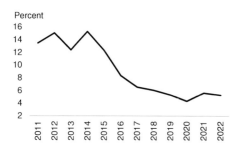

D. Infrastructure investment needs

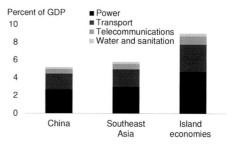

Sources: Bhattacharyay (2012); Haver Analytics; Inderst (2016); International Monetary Fund, Investment and Capital Stock data set; Rozenberg and Fay (2019); World Bank.
Note: EAP = East Asia and Pacific.
A. Share of countries in EAP region with investment growth below the region's long-term (2000-19) average or negative investment growth ("contracting").
B. Weighted averages of growth rates of gross fixed-capital formation in the public and private sectors, respectively, in constant 2005 U.S. dollars. The sample includes nine EAP economies.
C. Five-year-ahead Consensus Economics forecasts made in the year denoted. Weighted averages.
D. Climate-adjusted estimated infrastructure investment needs.

vary widely (ADB 2017; ESCAP 2022; Hansen 2022; OECD 2019a), but EAP countries clearly need to invest more than 5 percent of their GDPs over the next decade to meet the infrastructure needs of their growing economies (ADB 2017).

The largest costs would involve upgrades to power and transport infrastructure, investment in telecommunications, and real estate development. The region has significant disparities, including those within countries, in the density and quality of transport networks, electricity provision, housing, water, and sanitation. The within-country gaps are largest in China, primarily because of its size; Indonesia; and the lower-income economies among member countries of the Association of Southeast Asian Nations (ASEAN) (figure 4.5). But other EAP economies, including Malaysia, the

FIGURE 4.6 EAP: Infrastructure, environment, health, and education indicators

Despite significant progress, many EAP economies face challenges in regard to providing adequate transport networks, power and water supplies, and other utilities. At the same time, environmental problems confronting the region threaten to undermine economic growth and regional stability. Many EAP economies have made great progress toward education and human development goals, including those related to child survival, nutrition, and education, but some still face significant shortfalls with respect to education and other human resources.

A. Ranking of overall infrastructure
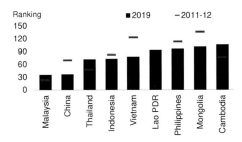

B. Quality of trade and transport-related infrastructure
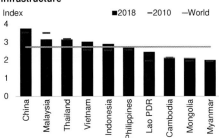

C. Share of urban population living in slums
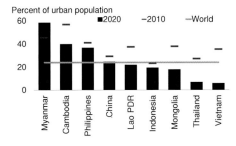

D. Environmental performance
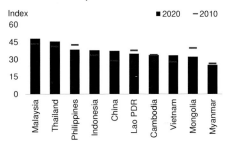

E. Under-five mortality rate
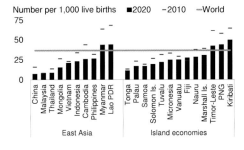

F. Ranking of capacity to retain or attract talent
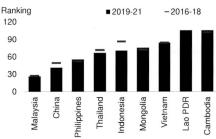

Sources: Lanvin and Monteiro (2021); Wolf et al. (2022); World Bank, World Development Indicators database; World Economic Forum.
Note: EAP = East Asia and Pacific.
A. World Economic Forum ranking of 140 countries according to the quality of their infrastructure. 1= best, 140 = worst.
B. Logistic Performance Index surveys conducted by the World Bank and Finland's Turku School of Economics. 1 = extremely underdeveloped by international standards, 7 = well developed and efficient by international standards.
D. The Environmental Performance Index is constructed by calculating and aggregating 20 indicators that reflect national-level environmental data, including data on child mortality, wastewater treatment, access to drinking water, access to sanitation, and air pollution (average exposure to particulate matter with diameters of 2.5 micrometers or less [PM2.5]). These indicators use a "proximity-to-target" methodology, which assesses how close a particular country is to an identified policy target. Scores are then converted to a scale of 0 to 100, with 0 being the farthest from the target (worst observed value) and 100 being closest to the target (best observed value).
E. Probability of dying between birth and five years of age, per 1,000 live births. Latest data are for 2020. Is. = Islands; PNG = Papua New Guinea.
F. Ranking on Global Talent Competitiveness Index conducted by Lanvin and Monteiro (2021). 1 = best, 134 = worst.

Philippines, and Thailand, also have substantial needs in the areas of upgrading and maintenance of infrastructure.

Despite some remarkable successes, providing adequate transport networks, power and water supplies, and other utilities remains a challenge across much of the region. Extensive construction activities are under way, with transport, especially rail, accounting for the largest share. The primary goal of these efforts is better integration of the region's transport networks and support for urbanization.

China's highway network more than doubled in size between 2010 and 2021, and the share of high-speed railways grew from 33 to 50 percent of total railway kilometers. However, transport density in China still falls far short of that in advanced economies. Infrastructure needs vary considerably across Chinese regions and range from establishing new high-speed railways to installing basic municipal infrastructure and pollution-reducing (or pollution-reversing) technologies.

Lack of adequate infrastructure is the main cause of Indonesia's reduced but still-high logistics costs (about 15 percent of companies' total expenditure), including high transport costs. Middle-income ASEAN countries, such as Malaysia and Thailand, are still investing heavily in rail and other public transport systems. In Malaysia, projects like the expansion of the public transport system in Kuala Lumpur and airport and port upgrades are expected to proceed through 2030, with a significant share of investment going toward renewable energy and green infrastructure. The Philippines ranks particularly low in regard to transport and trade-related infrastructure. Although the Philippines rose two places in the World Economic Forum's 2022 global infrastructure rankings to 57th place, this remains the country's lowest-ranked competitiveness factor. By contrast, the Philippines ranks quite high on measures of health and education infrastructure and the quality of its seaports and airports. In Cambodia and the Lao People's Democratic Republic, investment in basic road infrastructure is a priority.

Education and health care. The region has made great progress in human development outcomes, including child survival, nutrition, and education, but still faces serious shortfalls in the area of human resources.

- *Health care.* EMDEs in EAP reduced their child mortality rates by an average of one-fourth between 2010 and 2020. However, Kiribati, Lao PDR, Myanmar, Papua New Guinea, and Timor-Leste still have child mortality rates well above global averages. The region has historically faced a high incidence of infectious diseases, some of which have spread globally (for example, Severe Acute Respiratory Syndrome, pandemic influenza, and COVID-19; Lee and Pang 2015). Rates of noncommunicable diseases are expected to rise, and infectious diseases are expected to remain a risk associated with high population mobility and environmental degradation (Anbumozhi and Intal 2015). Adjusting to these trends will require public investment in basic infrastructure, education, health, and environmental protection.

- *Education.* Although enrollment in primary education in the region is almost universal, there are deficiencies in student retention (Cambodia, Lao PDR, and

Myanmar), quality of education (Cambodia, Lao PDR, Malaysia, Thailand, and Vietnam), and literacy rates (Cambodia, Lao PDR, Papua New Guinea, and Timor-Leste). Extended school closures during the pandemic led to substantial further learning losses, especially for the poor (chapter 2).

Environmental challenges. Many countries in the region face environmental problems that threaten to undermine not only economic growth and stability, but also living standards, lives, and livelihoods. The main challenges include water management, deforestation and land degradation, air pollution, and climate change. According to the Verisk Maplecroft Global Risk Analytics Dataset, which ranks the world's 576 largest urban centers on their exposure to a range of environmental and climate-related threats, 99 of the world's 100 riskiest cities are in Asia, including 37 in China, where air and water pollution presents a growing health risk. The worst-performing city in the ranking, Jakarta, also suffers from severe air pollution, but added to this are perennial threats from seismic activity and flooding. These have prompted the government of Indonesia to initiate relocating the capital.

Regional policy priorities

Improving spending efficiency. In the wake of the COVID-19 pandemic, EAP countries have been struggling to reconcile spending on relief, recovery, and growth with shrinking fiscal space. With economic recoveries now under way, countries could better target fiscal policy support (World Bank 2021e). More efficient and better targeted support for households and firms, rather than universal transfers and price regulations, would create space for investment in infrastructure for trade, energy, and technology diffusion (World Bank 2022b). When curtailing spending or raising taxes is difficult in the short term, countries can commit to future fiscal restraint and efficiency-enhancing reforms. Committing to fiscal rules and future revenue and expenditure reforms would help reconcile future spending needs with tightening budget constraints amid growing debt. Countries could also improve public investment management, which is key for increasing social rates of return. In the longer term, additional domestic tax revenues could help create space for needed public investment. Efforts to remove exemptions, improve tax administration capacity, and broaden tax bases could help generate budgetary resources. For example, new tax reform legislation in Indonesia is expected to raise revenue by 1.2 percent of GDP per year in the medium term.

Private sector participation can help improve efficiency and at the same time provide funding. Developing countries in Asia with relatively low income levels face major challenges in implementing public-private partnerships (Cambodia and Myanmar), especially in the context of infrastructure development. Among these challenges are governance issues, institutional structure and capacity constraints, weak public-private partnership laws and policies, and weak country and sovereign risk ratings. Several reforms could help these countries realize the potential benefits of public-private partnerships. Governments could centralize agencies that coordinate national infrastructure, in cooperation with the private sector and multilateral agencies. Multilateral development banks could work with the private sector to provide assurances in regard to quality and governance. A global "code of conduct" with a clear set of standards for businesses covering a regulatory framework, transparency principles, and a system for dispute resolution could enhance confidence in the private sector as a good partner.

Encouraging private investment. Confidence in the business environment is central to encouraging private investment (World Bank 2017). Measures to improve the environment could include cutting red tape where there are unnecessary regulations, clarifying laws and regulations, allowing greater market access to foreign companies, opening more investment areas to private enterprise (especially in services sectors), and cutting financing costs. Reforms to deepen capital markets and strengthen banking systems (for example, through faster and more effective insolvency procedures) can encourage private financing. (International Monetary Fund [IMF] country rankings for financial development in the region range widely, from 14th for Thailand to 170th for the Solomon Islands.) Measures and assistance to encourage diffusion of technology could support such reforms. Increased domestic and international competition could strengthen incentives for productivity-enhancing technological innovation, which improved access to finance and digital infrastructure could also promote. Eliminating domestic distortions, such as fossil fuel subsidies and local-content requirements, could encourage investment in and adoption of green technologies.

Focusing on developing skills that are in demand in labor markets. Primary and secondary education must focus on education quality, on learning outcomes, and on building effective and accountable educational systems. Higher education, vocational education, and job training can become more effective if institutions are given the right incentives to meet labor market demand. Efforts to help match job openings and the skills of prospective workers will also pay dividends, as will investments in "EdTech" (World Bank 2021d). The region's countries must reverse the substantial learning losses resulting from the extended school closures during the pandemic to prevent lasting damage to student progress, human capital formation, and opportunities for productive work (chapter 2).

Focusing on preventative health care. In the area of health care, additional investment should favor less costly preventative care rather than hospital care. However, this will entail reforms to insurance regimes.

Addressing environmental challenges. Policy makers can use a number of instruments in this area: phasing out fossil fuel and energy subsidies; aligning carbon prices with environmental policy goals, including emissions targets; raising public investment in low-carbon innovation and infrastructure; and undertaking low-carbon policy reforms in key sectors, such as energy, transport, agriculture, land use, and urban planning. Most countries have recently increased fuel subsidies as a temporary crisis measure aimed at moderating increases in fuel prices. This runs counter to the efforts in major EAP countries in the last few years to reduce such subsidies (China and Indonesia). Production of fossil fuels such as coal is also being revived. These actions should not be allowed to compromise the achievement of emission reduction commitments or perpetuate dependence on imported fossil fuels and the region's vulnerability to future energy price shocks.

The costs associated with moving toward a low-carbon economy need to be equitably distributed. Countries can feed the revenues generated by carbon pricing, for example, back into their economies to help subsidize abatement costs, alleviate negative social impacts, or cut taxes (World Bank 2021e). To garner support for a low-carbon economy, policy makers must emphasize its widespread benefits and adopt a holistic approach to support implementation. They need to encourage stakeholder participation; commit to scientific and technological research; emphasize long-term planning; implement reforms to align resource and utility pricing with costs, including externalities; improve governance and general institutional capacity; and strengthen regionally coordinated approaches and international support.

Investment growth in EAP is unlikely to revert to the high rates of the first decade of the 2000s, given the structural slowdown in China. But investment needs in the region remain substantial, and governments and multilateral agencies will continue to be important providers of funding. Such funding should be directed toward projects with the highest social returns. Close coordination of local, regional, and global initiatives will be needed to help reduce duplication and inconsistencies in public investment projects.

EUROPE and
CENTRAL ASIA

Investment growth in Europe and Central Asia weakened from an average annual rate of 7.3 percent in 2000-10 to 3.1 percent a year in 2011-21. The slowdown resulted from overlapping crises and structural headwinds. Current and prospective investment needs are sizable across ECA. They are within reach in the EU member states, while Ukraine will face enormous reconstruction challenges. More broadly, increased investment is needed to support the green and digital transitions, improve social protection, foster private sector development, and close the gaps in living standards between ECA and the EU.

Introduction

Europe and Central Asia accounted for less than 10 percent of EMDE investment in 2011-21—down from 12.2 percent in 2000-10 (figures 4.7.A-4.7.D).[2] The decline in ECA's share of EMDE investment reflected a steep fall in investment growth in the region, from an average annual rate of 7.3 percent in 2000-10 to 3.1 percent over 2011-21. Compared with 2000-10, average annual investment growth during 2011-21 was lower by more than 6 percentage points in almost half of ECA's economies.

The slowdown in investment growth over the past two decades has reflected several adverse shocks, including the global financial crisis of 2007-09, Russia's domestic financial crisis of 2008-09, the European debt crisis of 2009-11, conflicts in Eastern Europe, the 2014-16 oil price plunge for ECA's energy exporters, the COVID-19 pandemic, and intense financial pressures in Türkiye—the region's second-largest economy after Russia. In addition, structural pressures have weighed on ECA investment, including those related to maturing global value chains and stalled economic reform progress in some countries.

ECA investment fell in 2019—mostly on account of a decline in Türkiye amid weak investor sentiment and high policy uncertainty. It contracted a further 1.4 percent in 2020 with the onset of the COVID-19 pandemic. Investment rebounded by 5.6 percent in 2021, but Russia's invasion of Ukraine in February 2022 reversed the recovery. Investment in ECA is estimated to have shrunk by 3.2 percent in 2022 and is forecast to contract 1.6 percent in 2023—the sharpest fall projected for any EMDE region in 2023. In contrast to 2020, when the contraction in investment was widespread across ECA,

---

[2] Data are available for the following ECA economies: Albania, Armenia, Bulgaria, Belarus, Georgia, Hungary, North Macedonia, Moldova, Poland, Romania, Russia, Türkiye, and Ukraine.

FIGURE 4.7 ECA: Investment growth and needs

ECA suffered a sharp slowdown in output and investment growth in 2011-21, owing to several adverse shocks and structural changes. The recovery in 2021 that followed the pandemic-induced collapse in 2020 was short-lived because of the Russian Federation's invasion of Ukraine. ECA has sizable investment needs, especially those related to reconstruction in Ukraine.

A. Investment growth in ECA

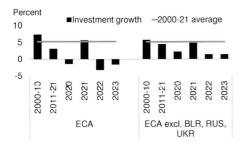

B. Investment growth in the Russian Federation and Türkiye

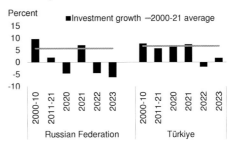

C. Investment growth in Central Europe and the Western Balkans

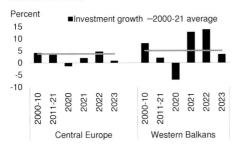

D. Investment growth in Central Europe and the Western Balkans

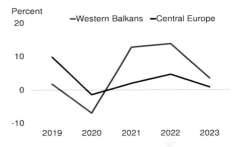

E. Estimated annual infrastructure investment to halve gap with euro area by 2030

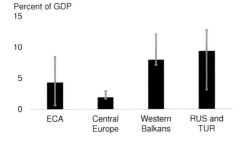

F. Estimated reconstruction costs in Ukraine versus post-World War II Marshall Plan for Europe

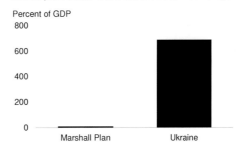

Sources: Board of Governors of the Federal Reserve; European Investment Bank; Global Infrastructure Hub; Government of Ukraine; International Monetary Fund; Kyiv School of Economics; Three Seas Initiative; U.S. Bureau of Economic Analysis; World Bank.
Note: BLR = Belarus; CE = Central Europe; ECA = Europe and Central Asia; excl. = excluding; GDP = gross domestic product; RUS = Russian Federation; TUR = Türkiye; UKR = Ukraine. Data for 2023 are forecasts.
A.C.D. Sample includes 13 ECA countries (panel A), 2 Western Balkan and 4 Central European economies (panels C and D).
E. Estimates of infrastructure investment needed to halve the infrastructure gap between each region and the euro area by 2030. Estimates for ECA are from the Global Infrastructure Hub, IMF (2020), Rozenberg and Fay (2019), and the Three Seas Initiative. Central Europe, the Western Balkans, and the Russian Federation and Türkiye are as estimated by IMF (2020). Bars show median, and orange whiskers show minimum and maximum range.
F. Reconstruction costs are converted into real 2015 U.S. dollars using the U.S. Bureau of Economic Analysis GDP deflator series. Ukraine costs are based on July 2022 estimates by the European Investment Bank, Kyiv School of Economics, and Government of Ukraine. Under the Marshall Plan, the U.S. provided about $13.3 billion in aid, or close to $1.1 trillion in real 2015 U.S. dollars, with 16 economies signing up for assistance.

Belarus, Russia, and Ukraine account for most of the fall in 2022, reflecting the war and the impact of international sanctions. With those three countries excluded, investment growth in ECA is projected to recover to 1.4 percent in both 2022 and 2023.

ECA has sizable current and prospective investment needs to support the green and digital transitions, improve social protection, foster private sector development, and close ECA's gaps with the European Union in living standards, although these gaps vary widely across ECA (figure 4.7.E). Over the remainder of this decade, the EU plans to step up lending and grants to Central Europe and the Western Balkans, partly meeting investment needs in these subregions. Eventually, Ukraine's immense reconstruction needs will require funding, including from the international donor community (figure 4.7.F). In contrast, the international sanctions imposed in response to the invasion of Ukraine are currently curbing the ability to narrow investment gaps in Belarus and Russia, leaving both economies with limited external financing options. The invasion will also make filling sizable investment needs more difficult in neighboring ECA economies. In the economies of the South Caucasus and Central Asia, which are closely linked to Russia, weaker economic growth in Russia will likely dent investment prospects, through reduced inflows of foreign direct investment, among other avenues.

Across ECA's economies, recent headwinds—including pandemic-related increases in government debt, negative spillovers from Russia's invasion of Ukraine, and tightening global and domestic financing conditions, as well as lingering structural issues—mean that efforts to strengthen the growth of investment, public or private, face severe challenges. Reforms are needed to confront the shocks from the pandemic and the invasion, to address long-standing structural challenges, and to set the stage for sustained recovery.

Evolution of regional investment

In 2011-21, ECA experienced the second-sharpest slowdown in investment growth, relative to the preceding decade, among EMDE regions. Investment growth fell from an average annual rate of 7.3 percent in 2000-10 to 3.1 percent a year in 2011-21, with the pace of growth in the second decade weaker in most ECA economies. Weakening investment growth in large part reflected the effects of several adverse shocks, including the global financial crisis (2007-09), Russia's domestic financial crisis (2008-09), spillovers from the European debt crisis (2009-11), Russia's annexation of Crimea in 2014 and associated sanctions, the 2014-16 oil price plunge, the COVID-19 pandemic, and financial stress in Türkiye. As a result, investment had not recovered to the levels observed prior to the global financial crisis in 90 percent of the ECA sample by 2019. Related to the weakening of investment growth, net FDI inflows fell from nearly 5.5 percent of GDP in 2007 to 1.8 percent of GDP in 2018-19.

In the aftermath of the European debt crisis of 2009-11, prospects for economic growth weakened significantly in the EU, ECA's largest trading partner.[3] The associated

---

[3] Ten-year-ahead GDP growth forecasts for the EU produced by Consensus Economics fell from 1.9 percent in 2007 to 1.2 percent in 2019.

weakening of prospective growth in demand for ECA's exports and in financial flows from the EU to ECA reduced prospective returns on investment in ECA and increased financing costs. As ECA countries rely heavily on financial flows from the EU (including for FDI), there were significant negative spillovers from deteriorating EU growth prospects to ECA investment (figure 4.8.A).[4] Just as investment growth was starting to firm up after 2016, the external environment deteriorated again, as a spike in policy uncertainty around the United Kingdom's exit from the EU weighed on trade growth and investor confidence in Europe. An escalation in trade tensions between China and the United States also dampened ECA's trade and investment prospects, as several economies in the region are deeply integrated into global markets and trade, especially supply chains for automobiles.

For most of the decade preceding the pandemic, declines in private investment persisted following the global financial crisis as ECA economies experienced multiple adverse shocks in quick succession. Investment financing became difficult to obtain from domestic banking sectors that were still healing from the crisis and earlier credit booms. Even by 2019, private investment had not recovered to 2008 levels in six ECA economies (Albania, Armenia, Belarus, Bulgaria, Ukraine, and Romania).[5] Central Europe and the Western Balkans made only weak recoveries between 2011 and 2016, in the aftermath of the European debt crisis, with the weakness reflecting disrupted financial intermediation and impaired banking systems and corporate sectors and accompanied by sharp increases in ratios of nonperforming loans (Bykova and Pindyuk 2019). Large amounts of foreign-currency-denominated debt amplified the damage to the banking sector (EBRD 2015). Following several years of rapid credit growth, Türkiye faced severe financial market pressures in 2018-19, prompting banking and corporate sector deleveraging, a deterioration in consumer and business confidence, and heightened policy uncertainty. As a result, private investment in Türkiye contracted in 2018 and 2019, the two years prior to the pandemic.

Long-term consensus forecasts for growth in private investment in Central Asia, Eastern Europe, and the South Caucasus also declined in the years leading up to the pandemic amid escalating geopolitical tensions and armed conflict (Eastern Europe and the South Caucasus) and sharp terms-of-trade shocks from falling commodity prices (Central Asia, Eastern Europe, and the South Caucasus; figures 4.8.B and 4.8.C). In the region's energy exporters, private investment weakened alongside the sharp fall in oil prices in 2014-16. A steep rise in geopolitical tensions following Russia's annexation of Crimea in 2014 also triggered a decline in investor confidence, with private investment in Eastern Europe contracting by double-digit percentages in both 2014 and 2015. The oil price plunge, combined with international sanctions that heavily restricted access to external finance in Russia, caused private investment in Russia to shrink in 2014-15. FDI

---

[4] Data are available for the following ECA economies: Albania, Armenia, Azerbaijan, Belarus, Bosnia and Herzegovina, Bulgaria, Georgia, Hungary, Kazakhstan, Kosovo, Kyrgyz Republic, Moldova, Montenegro, North Macedonia, Poland, Romania, Russia, Serbia, Tajikistan, Türkiye, and Ukraine.

[5] For five other ECA economies—Bosnia and Herzegovina, Hungary, Montenegro, Russia, and Serbia—private investment reached 2008 levels between 2016 and 2018.

FIGURE 4.8 **ECA: Investment prospects**

The Russian Federation's invasion of Ukraine has reversed the 2021 investment recovery in ECA and exacerbated the economic slowdown in the EU, ECA's largest trading partner. Long-standing structural issues, including stalled improvements in governance, are also weighing on investment.

A. Foreign direct investment liabilities, by source, 2019-20

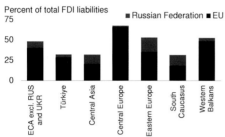

B. Political risk in 15 ECA countries and policy uncertainty in Poland and the Russian Federation

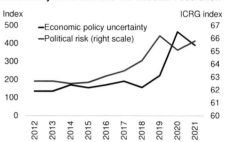

C. Investment growth, 2010-21, and 2022 forecasts for 2022-27

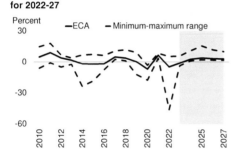

D. "Well-governed transition" indicator (EBRD assessment)

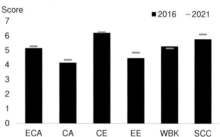

E. ECA countries' dependence on imports from the Russian Federation

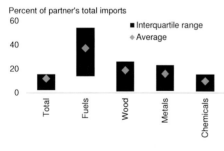

F. Deviation of investment from prepandemic projections

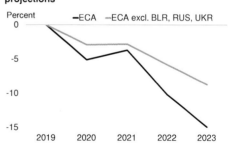

Sources: Baker, Bloom, and Davis (2016); Consensus Economics; European Bank for Reconstruction and Development (EBRD); Haver Analytics; International Monetary Fund; national sources; PRS Group, *International Country Risk Guide* (ICRG); Winkler, Wuester, and Knight (2022); World Bank.

Note: BLR = Belarus; CA = Central Asia; CE = Central Europe; ECA = Europe and Central Asia; EE = Eastern Europe; EU = European Union; excl. = excluding; FDI = foreign direct investment; GDP = gross domestic product; RUS = Russian Federation; SCC = South Caucasus; UKR = Ukraine; WBK = Western Balkans.

A. Unweighted 2019-20 averages.

B. Unweighted averages. Higher values indicate greater political stability risk and/or economic policy uncertainty. Political stability risk includes 15 ECA economies, as measured by the ICRG. Economic policy uncertainty for ECA is an average of values for Poland and the Russian Federation, as measured by national sources and Baker, Bloom, and Davis (2016).

C. Data prior to 2022 reflect actual investment growth. Shaded areas are based on the January 2023 Consensus Forecasts survey. Sample includes seven ECA countries. Solid line uses 2019 real U.S. GDP weights. Dashed lines show the minimum and maximum range.

D. The EBRD's "well-governed transition" indicator measures the quality of institutions and the processes that they support. Scores range from 1 to 10, with 10 representing a synthetic frontier corresponding to the standards of a sustainable market economy.

F. Lines show the percent deviation of the latest projections from forecasts released in the January 2020 edition of the *Global Economic Prospects* report (World Bank 2020c). For 2023, the January 2020 baseline is extended using projected growth for 2022.

inflows to Russia fell by more than three-quarters immediately following the imposition of international sanctions in 2014 and remained nearly 45 percent lower in subsequent years (UNCTAD 2022). Throughout the remainder of the decade, investment growth in Russia was tepid, reflecting subdued extractive investment, steep capital outflows, and persistent FDI losses. As a result, private investment in 2019 was lower than that in 2014. Neighboring countries suffered from spillover effects, including weaker trade, remittances, and FDI.

Public investment, accounting for about a quarter of total investment in ECA, was also constrained prior to the pandemic, as many governments faced falls in commodity revenues amid the sustained decline in commodity prices over 2011-16. Over the decade, most ECA countries implemented significant fiscal consolidations, with structural deficits narrowing or turning into surpluses in about two-thirds of the ECA economies for which there are data. In the region's energy exporters, fiscal adjustment needs grew in the second half of the decade. To ensure fiscal sustainability, these countries had to realign spending with lower revenues. The need for fiscal consolidation, in the wake of the European debt crisis, added to the woes of ECA's EU members (Central Europe) and candidate partners (Western Balkans). In Central Europe, fiscal consolidation over the 2010s proceeded gradually in Poland—ECA's third-largest economy—and eased somewhat in the other economies in the second half of the decade, especially in Romania. The absorption of sizable EU structural funds in the second half of the decade helped to ease fiscal constraints and bolster public investment.

Structural factors also played a role in the slowdown of investment growth in 2011-21. Weak governance and shortcomings in the transition to market-based economies presented challenges to effectively implementing public investment, strengthening spending efficiency, and supporting growth in private investment (figure 4.8.D). ECA's investment growth weakened alongside stalling progress with reforms and a weakening of other drivers of economic growth. After a reform boost from the EU accession process, governance reform efforts slowed in many of the new member states in Central Europe, while reform progress sputtered in some candidate economies in the Western Balkans. In some ECA countries, reform progress backtracked, weakening the business environment. In some cases, pervasive corruption and large informal sectors continue to be formidable constraints on the ability of private firms to invest, innovate, and close the productivity gap with the EU. Deterioration of the business environment, combined with shortcomings in the transition to market-based economies and weaker governance, are all likely to have contributed to slowing investment growth. Structural change at the global level also likely played a role, as global value chains—a major driver of productivity-enhancing investment and technology transfer—appeared to mature (Lakatos and Ohnsorge 2017).

Following a decade of weak growth, ECA investment fell by 1.4 percent in 2020, the first year of the COVID-19 pandemic. Of the five EMDE regions where investment declined in 2020—it continued to grow in East Asia and Pacific—ECA experienced the shallowest contraction, partly thanks to large fiscal support packages, with buoyant public investment offsetting sharp falls in private investment. The shallowness of the contraction also reflected positive output and investment growth in Türkiye, as financial pressures in that country abated somewhat from 2018-19. For many ECA economies, however, investment plunged in 2020 amid substantial portfolio outflows, with private investment falling by double-digit percentages in some economies in the South Caucasus and Western Balkans. FDI inflows collapsed more severely in ECA than in other EMDE regions in 2020, falling to a near 20-year low as large energy exporters, especially Russia, grappled with declines in extractive investment (UNCTAD 2021).

Following the pandemic-induced recession in 2020, ECA investment grew by 5.6 percent in 2021—a slightly stronger growth rate than the 2000-21 average of 5.2 percent, and one that was strong enough to bring investment in the year to within 4 percent of its pre-pandemic projection. This improvement was not region-wide, however, amid rising borrowing costs and elevated political tensions and policy uncertainty, with investment contracting in 2021 in Belarus, Bulgaria, Georgia, Kyrgyz Republic, and Montenegro (World Bank 2022e). As a result, investment in 2021 was at least 10 percent below pre-pandemic projections in some economies in Central Europe, Eastern Europe, the South Caucasus, and the Western Balkans.

Russia's invasion of Ukraine in February 2022 halted the economic recovery. The ensuing war has had far-reaching consequences for investment in ECA and regional supply chains, given many countries' economic linkages with Russia and Ukraine (figure 4.8.E). The invasion has caused a fresh plunge in investor confidence, as well as capital outflows, tighter financing conditions, higher inflation, and currency depreciations. The war has also dampened regional trade and investment by weighing on external demand from the euro area, as well as Russia. FDI inflows, which recovered to some extent in 2021 in many ECA economies, have become more muted and are likely to remain so (UNCTAD 2022). Although FDI inflows are largely from the EU, some countries in Central Asia, Eastern Europe, and the South Caucasus have relied heavily on Russia as a financing source.[6]

Russia's invasion of Ukraine has thus hit investment through multiple channels. Regional value chains have been interrupted, as many ECA economies depend heavily on both Russia and Ukraine for imports of key commodities and intermediate goods (Winkler, Wuester, and Knight 2022). The war has also pushed up inflation, prompting policy rate hikes in advanced economies and in most of ECA's economies and driving global and domestic borrowing costs higher. Moreover, limited fiscal space, which was narrowed by policies to support activity during the pandemic and the resulting increases in government debt, has made it more difficult to take countercyclical policy action and maintain public investment plans.

As a result of the invasion and associated sanctions, investment in ECA is estimated to have contracted by 3.2 percent in 2022 and projected to continue shrinking at 1.6

---

[6] Russia accounts for about one-third of FDI inflows into Armenia and Belarus and about one-fifth of FDI inflows into the Kyrgyz Republic and Moldova.

percent in 2023. While the contraction in 2022 was only about one-fifth as steep as that during the global financial crisis, it was far steeper than the pandemic-induced contraction of 2020. Unlike what happened in 2020, when the fall in investment was region-wide, Belarus, Russia, and Ukraine accounted for most of the contraction in 2022. Investment growth in ECA excluding these three countries is estimated to have remained positive in 2022, at 1.4 percent, and is projected to remain at that pace in 2023. In 2023, investment is projected to be nearly 15 percent below prepandemic projections in ECA and nearly 9 percent below these projections in ECA excluding Belarus, Russia, and Ukraine (figure 4.8.F). Regional investment is expected to pick up beyond 2023, owing to reconstruction efforts in Türkiye following two devastating earthquakes in February 2023.

Regional investment needs

Even before the COVID-19 pandemic, Russia's invasion of Ukraine, and the 2023 earthquakes in Türkiye, meeting ECA's sizable investment needs was expected to be a challenge, as prospects for investment growth trailed those in other EMDE regions amid heightened policy uncertainty and elevated geopolitical tensions. Public and private debt issuance in ECA also slowed from 2012-13 peaks in the decade prior to the pandemic, despite wide investment gaps (figure 4.9.A).

The pandemic, as a well as the war, is likely to have widened investment gaps in ECA by further eroding medium- to long-term investment prospects. The European Commission (2020a) estimated the gap in investment in Central Europe—which generally has lower investment needs than the rest of ECA—to have widened from about 4 percent of GDP in 2019 to 6 percent of GDP in 2020-21, with needs related to the green and digital transitions excluded. In Belarus and Russia—which are under international sanctions related to the invasion of Ukraine—investment in 2022 is estimated to have been at least 10 percent below prepandemic projections and, in Russia, by nearly 18 percent in 2023 (World Bank 2022e). Under the assumption that international sanctions remain, investment gaps in these countries are likely to remain wide, with investment increasingly relying on the public sector.

In Türkiye, the earthquakes in early February 2023 have affected about 13.5 million people—or more than 15 percent of Türkiye's 2021 population—with natural gas and electricity cut off in many areas and hundreds of buildings destroyed, based on early needs assessments. Natural disaster experience from other ECA countries suggests the economic cost and investment needs could become sizable for Türkiye. In Croatia, the two earthquakes in 2020 (which, although devastating, were smaller in magnitude and resulted in less than 10 deaths, in sharp contrast to what took place in Türkiye) inflicted economic losses of 8.7 percent of 2019 GDP.

Infrastructure. Gaps in infrastructure between ECA and the euro area remain large, including those in relation to roads, railways, air transport, power generation capacity, internet, and fixed and mobile telephone density. Closing half of these gaps by 2030

FIGURE 4.9 **ECA: Financing needs and constraints**

Tighter financing conditions could weigh on debt issuance in ECA. In many ECA economies, inefficiencies in public spending and weak absorption capacity are holding back dividends from public investment, which could stall the catching up of per capita incomes with those in the EU. Incomplete reforms to state-owned enterprises, a growing state footprint, and weak rule of law weigh on private investment.

A. Bond issuance and yield spreads

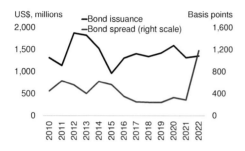

B. Efficiency gaps in public investment in infrastructure

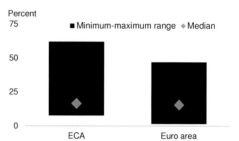

C. GDP per capita relative to EU-27

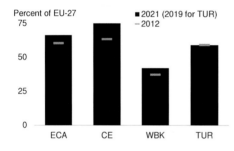

D. Cumulative absorption rates, 2014-20 EU spending program

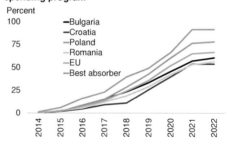

E. Planned EU investments in transport and green projects in the Western Balkans

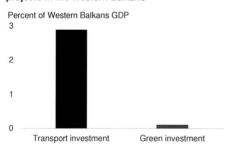

F. State-owned enterprise activity and assets, 2014-16

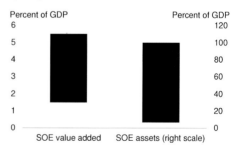

Sources: Bartlett, Bonomi, and Uvalic (2022); Dealogic; EBRD (2020); Eurostat; IMF (2021a); World Bank.
Note: CE = Central Europe; ECA = Europe and Central Asia; EU = European Union; GDP = gross domestic product; SOE = state-owned enterprise; TUR = Türkiye; WBK = Western Balkans.
A. Unweighted average for an unbalanced sample of 16 ECA economies for bond issuance and 11 ECA economies for bond spread.
B. An "efficiency gap" is the percent difference between a country's spending efficiency and that of the best performers. Higher values indicate greater inefficiency. Infrastructure spending efficiency is calculated using the volume and quality of infrastructure as the output and public capital stock and GDP per capita as the input, as estimated in IMF (2021a). Orange diamonds indicate medians, and bars show the minimum-maximum range. Sample size includes 15 economies in ECA and 16 in the euro area.
C. GDP per capita at current market prices in percent of the 27 European Union member states (EU-27) total per capita (based on purchasing-power standards). Aggregates are calculated using real U.S. dollar GDP at average 2010-19 prices and market exchange rates. Sample size includes 8 ECA economies.
D. Rates of absorption of EU funds reflect total net payments divided by planned EU spending for the 2014-20 EU spending program. "Best absorber" indicates the EU-27 country that achieved the highest rate of absorption of EU funds.
E. Investments in transport and green projects in percent of Western Balkans GDP.

would require infrastructure investment of between 3.0 and 8.5 percent of GDP a year (IMF 2020).[7] Infrastructure investment to meet the Sustainable Development Goals and limit climate change to 2 degrees Celsius would cost, on average, 4.2 percent of GDP a year in ECA (Rozenberg and Fay 2019).

Such estimates for ECA as a whole mask considerable variation across subregions. In the Western Balkans and Eastern Europe excluding Ukraine, halving infrastructure gaps with the euro area by 2030 could cost 7-12 percent of GDP per year—4-9 percent of GDP per year more than current investment levels (IMF 2020). In contrast, in Central Europe, the investment needed to close half the gap is 3 percent of GDP a year or less, given the larger initial infrastructure stock (IMF 2020).

ECA's sizable investment gaps are related partly to shortcomings in the efficiency of public investment in infrastructure relative to that of its EU peers (figure 4.9.B). In Bulgaria, for instance, the same public investment outcomes could have been achieved with considerably less investment spending (less by about 2 percent of GDP) if the efficiency of public investment and quality of infrastructure were closer to those of its peers (IMF 2022a).

Education. Although average years of education in ECA are among the highest of the EMDE regions, there is significant scope for increased investment, beyond gross fixed investment, to improve basic and tertiary education in ways that would raise labor productivity (World Bank 2020b). PISA scores and learning-adjusted years of schooling suggest that the ECA subregions and countries that most need improvements in the quality of basic education are Central Asia (Kazakhstan, the Kyrgyz Republic, Tajikistan, and Uzbekistan); the South Caucasus (Azerbaijan and Georgia); the Western Balkans (Albania, Bosnia and Herzegovina, Kosovo, Montenegro, and North Macedonia); Moldova; and, in Eastern Europe, Bulgaria and Romania. The latter two are among the EU countries that invest the least in education, including public expenditures on teachers and training, education infrastructure, digital learning, and equity and inclusion. Early childhood education is also important. On average, children who attend preschool stay in school nearly a year longer and are more likely to eventually be employed in high-skill jobs. High-quality interventions in the early years have a high benefit-to-cost ratio and can deliver annual returns of about 13 percent on investment (García et al. 2016).

In some economies in ECA, particularly Central Asia, inadequate investment in human capital has left parts of the workforce poorly equipped for rapid technological change (Flabbi and Gatti 2018). Low educational attainment among the workforce and inadequate skills have often been cited as constraints on doing business, job creation,

---

[7] This estimate is for total investment rather than additional investment needed over current investment. The sample includes ECA countries classified as EMDEs or advanced economies: Albania, Belarus, Bosnia and Herzegovina, Bulgaria, Croatia, the Czech Republic, Estonia, Hungary, Kosovo, Latvia, Lithuania, Moldova, Montenegro, North Macedonia, Poland, Romania, Russia, Serbia, the Slovak Republic, Slovenia, Türkiye, and Ukraine.

and innovation in ECA (Brancatelli, Marguerie, and Brodmann 2020; World Bank 2019c). An aging workforce, a declining working-age share in the total population, and high emigration rates among young and skilled workers in ECA highlight the need for education, training, and retraining to help workers adapt to new job requirements and technologies (Aiyar, Ebeke, and Shao 2016; Hallward-Driemeier and Nayyar 2018). Access to retraining programs, particularly for workers in sectors that have been hit the hardest—whether as a result of the pandemic or automation—can play an important role in facilitating workers' reemployment.

The COVID-19 pandemic underscored the critical need for investment in digital skills and technology to ensure educational continuity, as well as for resources to upgrade information and communications technology infrastructure to support virtual learning, particularly for more vulnerable households. Digital approaches to remote learning that were developed during the pandemic can be leveraged to broaden access to affordable education across EMDEs, including in ECA (Li and Lalani 2020). There is wide divergence in internet access, with some EU members having rates similar to those in euro area countries, while Central Asia lags even the EMDE average.

Digitalization. Investment in accelerating the digital transformation could support faster growth of productivity and output in ECA, while also strengthening economic resilience in times of crisis (Hallward-Driemeier et al. 2020; ITU 2020). During the pandemic, more than 50 percent of small and medium-sized enterprises surveyed by the Organisation for Economic Co-operation and Development (OECD) increased their use of digital tools to ensure business continuity in the wake of reduced mobility (OECD 2021b). Preliminary evidence also suggests that innovation and digitalization may have helped promote firm survival (Muzi et al. 2021).

Although ECA fares well relative to other EMDE regions on digital connectivity, weak investment in recent years has led to large infrastructure gaps in telecommunications, limiting the capacity for further regional integration (IMF 2014). Moreover, outdated technologies, lagging innovation, misallocation of labor to inefficient sectors, and market rigidities have weighed on productivity and contributed to divergences in TFP across countries and firms (Bahar and Santos 2018; Hallward-Driemeier et al. 2020; Syverson 2011). While the number of individuals using the internet in countries in Central Europe is on par with that in the rest of the EU, it is below the global average in several of ECA's poorest EMDEs, hindering their ability to close the distance to the TFP frontier (Burunciuc 2021; UN 2020). The digital divide also extends to firms, with small and medium-sized enterprises trailing larger companies in digital connectivity and adoption, particularly in high-speed broadband and e-commerce tools, which makes narrowing productivity gaps with larger companies even more challenging (Hallward-Driemeier et al. 2020; OECD 2021b).

For many ECA countries, improving digital infrastructure and expanding access to high-quality digital connectivity will require boosting investment in communications infrastructure (Hallward-Driemeier et al. 2020). Liberalized telecommunications, coupled with regulatory independence, effective control of monopoly power, and efficient taxation of digital services, can catalyze private sector investment to lower the cost of access to digital services and increase use of the internet, with positive spillovers to the rest of the economy (Arezki et al. 2021; Rodríguez-Castelán et al. 2021). Public investment can also play a role in supporting the digital transformation for firms, particularly finance-constrained small and medium-sized enterprises, by reducing cost barriers and accelerating digitalization.

Regional policy priorities

For ECA's EU economies, private and public investment will benefit from the phasing in of projects financed by EU funds. The EU's National Recovery and Resilience Plans, which are supported by the largest funding package ever approved by the EU, provide a unique opportunity to promote economic recovery as well as green and digital infrastructure and to help close investment and income gaps with more advanced EU members. In all, NextGenerationEU funds to support the plans amount to 9.3 percent of 2021 GDP in Bulgaria, 11.0 percent in Croatia, 6.3 percent in Poland, and 12.1 percent in Romania—much larger shares than the EU average of 5.6 percent. Since the passage of the plans, private investment prospects have also improved. In Bulgaria—the EU's poorest economy, in which output per capita is only about 55 percent of the EU average—private sector forecasts for long-term (10-year-ahead) investment growth almost doubled, from 1.6 percent in January 2020 to 3.0 percent in July 2022 (figure 4.9.C). Even in Poland—where output per capita is about three-quarters of the EU average—long-term forecasts for investment growth rose from 1.9 percent in January 2020 to 3.1 percent in July 2022. Across EU and partner economies, however, low absorption of funds because of inadequate administrative capacity and governance could temper the boost to investment (figure 4.9.D).

Western Balkan countries are also expected to be large recipients of EU funding over the remainder of the decade, which should help to counter headwinds to investment growth in these economies. The EU's Economic and Investment Plan for the Western Balkans aims at fostering integration of the Western Balkans with the EU and convergence of living standards in the Western Balkans with those in the EU, with financing over the next decade totaling more than 25 percent of Western Balkans GDP. The EU investments also include sizable funding for the green and digital transitions—a key priority given that Western Balkan economies are among those in ECA farthest from the green transition frontier and experiencing the highest levels of air pollution in Europe (Bartlett, Bonomi, and Uvalic 2022; European Fund for the Balkans 2021; OECD 2021a; Regional Cooperation Council 2018; UNEP 2019). The investments are largely in transport systems, which have long lacked sufficient investment, particularly in regard to logistics and maintenance (figure 4.9.E; European Commission 2021a, 2021b). Modernizing and improving transportation will promote climate goals, as currently less than half of railway networks in the Western Balkans are electrified, and most are powered by fossil fuels (European Commission 2020b).

In Ukraine, the focus will eventually turn to recovery and reconstruction. The World Bank (2022j) estimates that at least $349 billion (1.5 times 2021 GDP) will be needed, based on damage incurred as of June 1, 2022. Other estimates put total reconstruction costs in the range of $750 billion to $1.1 trillion, with infrastructure costs at about $190 billion (Arons 2022; Kyiv School of Economics 2022; Government of Ukraine 2022). Within about one month of Russia's invasion, infrastructure damage alone had already exceeded Ukraine's 2022 budget. Given these major reconstruction and investment needs, Ukraine's recovery will be contingent on substantial external financing on concessional terms. Domestic reforms that strengthen institutional quality and transparency, address structural bottlenecks, and ensure that the financial sector is able to bolster private-sector-led growth could usefully accompany reconstruction efforts.

More broadly, several steps can be taken to improve the climate for private investment in ECA. A supportive environment would include stable policy frameworks, which reduce uncertainty for businesses, and an effective regulatory environment, in which environmental standards are effectively enforced and strong competition is ensured through control of monopoly power (Ambec et al. 2013). Reforms that could promote private sector investment include the removal of distortions and restrictions on competition—including nontransparent investment regulations, cumbersome tax compliance rules, and more favorable treatment for state-owned enterprises—as well as better targeting of policy support measures.

Lack of exposure to international competition—partly because of nontariff barriers and complex trade rules—as well as restrictive regulations governing product markets and services remain structural bottlenecks to domestic and foreign investment in the region (Shepotylo and Vakhitov 2015; World Bank 2016f). Low innovation rates—which partly stem from weak competition, inadequate control of corruption, and the dominance of state-owned enterprises—continue to dampen the business environment and hinder investment in the region, particularly in the absence of progress in regard to other reforms (figure 4.9.F; EBRD 2018, 2019).

Structural reforms that help to close investment gaps and promote FDI inflows and greater participation in global value chains, by boosting private sector development and transition to competitive and inclusive markets, could help increase productivity in the region, particularly in the economies outside the EU (EBRD 2014, 2018; Gould 2018; World Bank 2019b). Greater economic integration and regional coordination could also help spur innovation and competition and help unleash the region's growth potential (Kunzel et al. 2019). The pace of future growth will largely depend on the successful implementation of structural reforms to improve the business environment, achieve debt sustainability, and restructure state-owned enterprises (Belarus, Kyrgyz Republic, Moldova, Ukraine, and Uzbekistan; EBRD 2017; Funke, Isakova, and Ivanyna 2017).

Improvements in public investment, including those that result from better prioritizing public expenditures and enhancing the appraisal and review of public investment projects, need to complement measures to improve the climate for public investment. Even in ECA's EU member states, public investment efficiency can be as much as 2 percent of GDP lower than in other EU countries. Sound policies with respect to infrastructure investment and improvements in governance, education, and public health might help countries become more integrated into global and regional value chains.

LATIN AMERICA
and the CARIBBEAN

Over 2000-21, investment growth in Latin America and the Caribbean averaged 2.7 percent a year but was volatile, as commodity price swings and financial cycles buffeted investment. LAC had the lowest average investment-to-GDP ratio among EMDE regions, with a falling ratio of public investment to GDP, despite substantial unmet needs—shown, for example, in mediocre logistics networks and high levels of urban congestion. The region spends proportionally more on human capital formation—education and health care—than its peers but does not seem to have derived commensurate value, suggesting room for improved efficiency. Many policies could help raise physical and human capital investment and improve outcomes in terms of output and welfare. More public spending could be allocated to investment, and the region could upgrade its capacity for project preparation and delivery. On the private investment side, it could improve regulatory and competition frameworks and consider investment-friendly reforms. The region could harness significant green investment dividends from renewable energy and related electrification, but transitioning sustainably and equitably will be crucial. More fundamentally, without achieving higher domestic savings, LAC is unlikely to consistently reach the levels of investment needed to narrow substantially the income gap with advanced economies.

Introduction

Latin America and the Caribbean accounted for about 13 percent of EMDE investment during 2000-21. Investment growth over the period was volatile. Following subdued growth in the early 2000s, investment surged in the period up to 2011 (with a temporary interruption in 2009 because of the global financial crisis), followed by a long fallow period from 2012 to 2020 when annual investment growth was never above 3.5 percent and negative in five of the nine years.

Throughout the period, investment growth and commodity price changes, the major driver of changes in the terms of trade in LAC, comoved closely. Indeed, the marked decline in investment growth from 2010-16 was concentrated in South American commodity exporters such as Brazil, Chile, and Peru, while investment in Central America and the Caribbean was more resilient. Global financial conditions, and U.S. monetary policy in particular, are also important determinants of investment cycles in LAC. Following a strong rebound from the pandemic trough of 2020, investment is forecast to once again underperform in 2023 and 2024. Much of this expected weakness reflects the lagged effects of sharp and synchronous monetary tightening in both LAC and advanced economies in 2022.

LAC has sizable prospective investment needs, especially in regard to the provision of infrastructure and other public goods like health care and education. Investment in LAC also offers potential sources of commodity inputs crucial to a global green transition, but it is likely to reap a long-term green investment dividend only with conducive policy frameworks in place and only if policy makers can successfully leverage commodity windfalls to raise living standards. More broadly, consistently higher investment growth will be required if potential output, labor productivity, and real per capita incomes are to grow faster in LAC countries (chapter 2).

Evolution of regional investment

During 2000-21, annual average investment growth in LAC was 2.7 percent, significantly lower than the average for all EMDEs of 7 percent. The investment-to-GDP ratio averaged 19 percent in LAC in 2000-21, the lowest allocation to investment of any EMDE region and well below the aggregate EMDE average of 28 percent. From the start to the end of the period, LAC's contribution to total EMDE investment declined from close to one-quarter in 2000 to less than one-tenth by the early 2020s. The public sector has shown particularly marked and pronounced weakness in investment since 2015, with that weakness reflecting fiscal constraints alongside the growth of spending related to government consumption. Indeed, in 2014, the stock of public capital per capita in LAC fell below the EMDE average, while the stock of private capital per capita remained at roughly twice the EMDE level (figure 4.10).

Fluctuations in LAC investment growth over the past two decades have broadly paralleled those in GDP growth. Regional investment grew healthily before the global financial crisis, as Argentina and Mexico emerged from recessions in 2003 and growth in Brazil picked up sharply from 2004 to 2008. Output and investment resumed steady expansions after the interruption of 2009 but faltered after 2011, and particularly in 2014-16, as commodity prices declined and the region's countries began to withdraw monetary accommodation. By 2015-16, Brazil was in a deep recession, with consecutive years of double-digit negative investment growth. More years of anemic regional growth of output and investment followed, as Argentina slipped back into economic crisis and growth remained weak in Brazil while slowing markedly in other sizable regional economies like Chile and Colombia. While the sharpest slowdowns occurred in some of LAC's largest economies, the weakness of investment growth in the late 2010s was widespread. Between 2016 and 2019, investment growth was consistently below its long-run regional average in more than half of the countries in LAC, and in 2016 and 2019 the proportion approached 70 percent.

The onset of the COVID-19 pandemic, immediately following the stagnation of the late 2010s, precipitated a collapse in investment by double-digit percentages in LAC in 2020 as lockdowns hit global demand and sent commodity prices plummeting. The decline was short-lived, however. In 2021, investment surged, underpinned by accommodative global financial conditions, a rapid recovery in commodity prices, and extensive fiscal stimulus by governments across the region. In Argentina and Brazil, investment-to-GDP

FIGURE 4.10 **LAC: Investment growth**

From 2014 to 2020, investment growth in LAC was below its post-2000 average. Weakening investment growth has been widespread across economies in the region and particularly pronounced in the public sector. Public capital stock per person in LAC fell below the level for EMDEs in aggregate in the late 2010s.

A. Investment growth

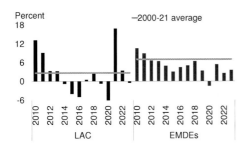

B. Countries with investment growth below its long-term average

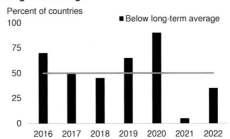

C. Five-year-ahead forecasts for investment growth

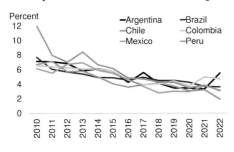

D. Public and private capital stocks per capita

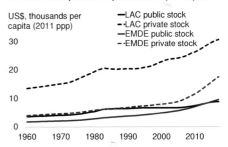

E. Investment growth by sector

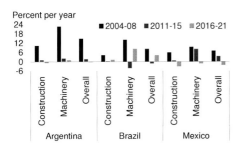

F. Growth in public and private investment

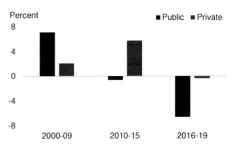

Sources: Consensus Economics; Haver Analytics; Instituto de Pesquisa Econômica Aplicada; International Monetary Fund; national sources; World Bank.
Note: EMDEs = emerging market and developing economies; LAC = Latin America and the Caribbean; ppp = purchasing-power parity.
A. Average growth rates are weighted by investment levels. Includes 98 EMDEs, of which 20 are in LAC.
B. Economy coverage is the same as for panel A.
C. Five-year-ahead consensus forecasts for investment growth.
E. For Argentina, 2004 is excluded. For Brazil, construction and machinery investment are derived using indicators of gross fixed-capital formation from the Instituto de Pesquisa Econômica Aplicada as proxies.
F. Annual average growth rates of real gross fixed-capital formation in specified time periods, weighted by private and public investment levels. Sample includes 19 EMDEs in LAC. Private investment includes investment through public-private partnerships.

ratios increased by nearly 3 and 2 percentage points, respectively. Prospects for 2023 look substantially weaker, however. With central banks in LAC undertaking some of the sharpest monetary tightening cycles globally, elevated interest rates are likely to dampen investment. Moreover, the decline in commodity prices from mid-2022 and the weak outlook for global growth indicate a likely weakening in the region's terms of trade. Historically, such weakening has been associated with slower investment growth.

Commodities remain the dominant category of exports from LAC, especially South America, and commodity price movements have been a key driver of investment growth fluctuations in the region (figure 4.11). The relationship between commodity price movements and investment growth in South America operates through multiple channels. Rising commodity prices, as seen in the mid-2000s, provide direct incentives for a supply response through higher investment in commodity production and auxiliary industries, which shows up most clearly in machinery investment. Regional terms of trade also improve, effectively transferring income to LAC from commodity importers, generally through real currency appreciation, among other mechanisms. Increased incomes and wealth feed broader increases in demand, to which investment also responds. Increasing fiscal revenues, which result from the prevalence of state-owned enterprises in key extractive sectors as well as the broader rise in economic activity, encourage increases in public investment (World Bank 2016a). Easier credit conditions strengthen these effects, reinforcing the cyclical alignment of credit and investment growth. When commodity prices subsequently reverse, as they did after 2012, the same channels operate in reverse. Monetary policy may also have exacerbated the volatility of investment, as underestimation of the cyclical components of growth may have led to underestimated positive output gaps during booms and therefore insufficiently restrictive policy (Ablerola et al. 2016).

External financial conditions, most notably in the United States, have had important spillovers onto investment in LAC (Araujo et al. 2016). The gradual tightening of U.S. monetary policy in 2015, coupled with falling commodity prices, saw South American currencies depreciate rapidly against the dollar, in some cases by as much as 30 percent. Concerns about the effects of depreciation on inflation led central banks, notably that in Brazil, to tighten policy despite weak demand, thus dampening investment. A spell of tighter financial conditions in the United States in 2016 further contributed to a period of tight financial conditions in Latin America that did not abate until 2017, when investment growth in the region again turned positive.

Beyond cyclical factors, low domestic saving and tax policies in LAC may have acted as structural headwinds to investment. Compared with OECD countries, LAC countries rely more on corporate income taxes, potentially generating disincentives to investment (Acosta-Ormaechea, Pienknagura, and Pizzinelli 2022). LAC countries also tend to have materially higher corporate taxes than other EMDEs. The average effective corporate tax rate in large LAC economies between 2017 and 2019 was about 29 percent, compared with the 23 percent average for all EMDEs.

FIGURE 4.11 **LAC: Correlates of investment growth**

Investment growth in LAC has been closely correlated with movements in commodity prices, which have buffeted regional growth. Financial and credit conditions have amplified the cycles. Corporation tax frameworks may represent a structural headwind to investment in LAC.

A. Investment growth and commodity price movements

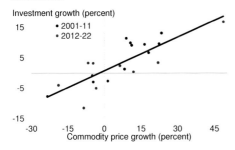

B. Growth of investment and credit

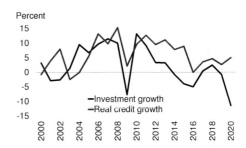

C. GDP growth

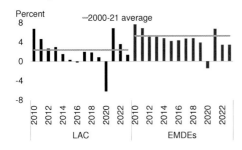

D. Corporation tax and investment growth in LAC

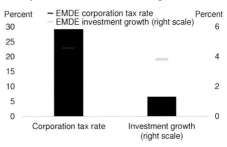

Sources: Haver Analytics; International Monetary Fund; Organisation for Economic Co-operation and Development; World Bank.
Note: EMDEs = emerging market and developing economies; GDP = gross domestic product; LAC = Latin America and the Caribbean.
A. "Commodity price growth" is a simple average of annual changes in the prices, in U.S. dollars, of energy, metals (excluding precious metals), and agricultural commodities.
B. Last observation is 2020. Investment-weighted average growth rates.
C. GDP-weighted average growth rates.
D. "Corporation tax rate" is the average effective corporation tax rate from 2017 through 2019. "Investment growth" is the average annual investment growth from 2017 through 2021. Sample includes 27 EMDEs (horizontal lines), with 7 from LAC (vertical bars).

Regional investment needs

Investment needs in the region remain significant, encompassing both gross fixed-capital formation for services like transportation and digital connectivity and, beyond gross fixed-capital formation, regarding investment in human capital formation through improved health care and education. Low-quality infrastructure, reflecting historically low investment, weighs on regional productivity and economic growth. Thus, infrastructure bottlenecks may be a key factor limiting agglomeration-related productivity gains that might otherwise be expected to accrue from the region's high levels of urbanization (Gómez-Lobo et al. 2022). High degrees of inequality in income and wealth between and within countries contributes to highly variable performance on health and education indicators. Even the region's richer countries have pockets of significant need, despite higher spending on human development than in other EMDEs (World Bank 2022d). LAC economies could benefit substantially from a global green transition, but realizing this potential benefit will require greater investment in enabling industries, backed by conducive policy frameworks. More generally, only higher investment growth, including in the private sector, can likely achieve the increase in labor productivity needed to raise living standards across LAC.

Infrastructure. Surveys indicate that mediocre infrastructure is a key constraint holding back LAC's development. In 2017, the average economy in LAC ranked 79th out of 136 countries on infrastructure quality, marginally better than the EMDE average but well below the averages for EAP, ECA, and MNA (World Economic Forum 2018). It has been estimated that meeting the infrastructure-related Sustainable Development Goals will require infrastructure investment in LAC of at least 4.5 percent of GDP annually (figure 4.12; World Bank 2019a). Based on extrapolations from data from 2008-15, roughly 70 percent of such needed infrastructure investment (more than 3 percent of GDP annually) is likely to be publicly funded. However, in the years leading up to the pandemic, public investment in infrastructure in LAC countries was about 1 percent of GDP, suggesting a sizable public investment gap (Infralatam, n.d.; Serebrisky et al. 2018). Past estimates of the gap in infrastructure investment in LAC are in the range of 3 to 4 percent of GDP (Brichetti et al. 2021; Kohli and Basil 2011).

Inadequate infrastructure provision is likely to be a key contributor to high levels of urban congestion. This is an important challenge, because LAC is projected to be the most urbanized EMDE region by 2050. Rising congestion costs may offset otherwise beneficial returns to scale in urban environments, representing one potential cause of an apparent lack of agglomeration benefits in productivity growth in LAC cities (Gómez-Lobo et al. 2022). The annual cost of traffic congestion alone is estimated to be worth more than 1 percent of production in Buenos Aires, São Paulo, Montevideo, and Santiago (Calatayud et al. 2021).

Improvements to telecommunications infrastructure can also boost connectivity and productivity, by facilitating expanded services trade, among other ways. LAC has greater mobile and broadband connectivity, on average, than other EMDE regions but lags substantially behind advanced economies. The need for a rapid switch to remote learning and work during the pandemic highlighted how digital connectivity can enhance social and economic resilience to crises (Bai et al. 2021; Strusani and Houngbonon 2020).

Recent country-level studies highlight the need for several countries in LAC to upgrade port infrastructure and transport connectivity in underserved potential export corridors (Argentina, Mexico, and the member countries of the Organization of Eastern Caribbean States; World Bank 2018a, 2018c, 2019d). Such investments should help reduce trade costs and facilitate diversification of trade in respect to products and partners.

FIGURE 4.12 **LAC: Investment needs**

Inadequate infrastructure impedes connectivity and productivity growth. Despite higher spending than in other EMDE regions, unequal access to education and health care holds back human capital formation in LAC. A global green transition promises opportunities, but higher levels of investment will be needed to realize them.

A. Annual infrastructure investment needs

B. Projected urban population share in 2050

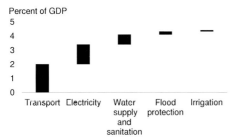
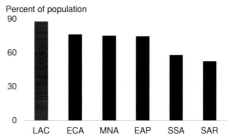

C. Fixed investment and health and education spending

D. Broadband and mobile connectivity

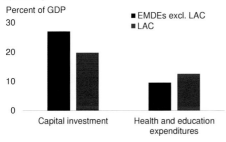
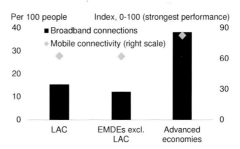

E. Selected health and education indicators

F. Proportion of global commodity reserves in LAC

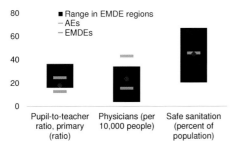
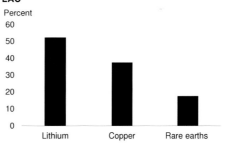

Sources: GSMA, Mobile Connectivity Index; Rozenberg and Fay (2019); UN Population Division; USGS (2022a, 2022c, 2022f); World Bank.

Note: AEs = advanced economies; EAP = East Asia and Pacific; ECA = Europe and Central Asia; EMDEs = emerging and developing economies; excl. = excluding; GDP = gross domestic product; LAC = Latin America and the Caribbean; MNA = Middle East and North Africa; SAR = South Asia; SSA = Sub-Saharan Africa.

A. Bars depict investment needs in LAC according to the "preferred investment scenario" ("ambitious goals, high efficiency") from Rozenberg and Fay (2019).

B. Projections by the United Nations Population Division.

C. Capital investment is gross fixed-capital formation. Health spending is current health expenditure. Education spending is general government expenditure on education. Values are a weighted average for LAC from 2015 to 2019 and an average of weighted averages for other regions from 2015 to 2019.

D. All values are population-weighted averages. "Broadband connections" shows 2020 values. "Mobile connectivity" is the 2021 average of Infrastructure and Affordability enabler scores within the GSMA's Mobile Connectivity Index.

E. AE, EMDE, and LAC values are simple averages of the latest available data across countries, excluding years before 2017. Sample includes 26 AEs and 109 EMDEs (23 in LAC) for pupil-teacher ratios; 31 AEs and 99 EMDEs (29 in LAC) for physicians; 36 AEs and 80 EMDEs (11 in LAC) for safe sanitation. "Safe sanitation" means facilities not shared with other households and with safe disposal.

F. Values are LAC proportions of total world reserves in 2022. "Lithium" includes Argentina, Brazil, and Chile. "Copper" includes Chile, Mexico, and Peru. "Rare earths" includes Brazil. Data availability limitations may result in slight underestimates.

Education. Beyond gross fixed-capital formation, LAC spends a significantly higher proportion of its GDP on education—about 5 percent—than any other EMDE region. However, LAC performs only moderately better than EMDE averages on measures of education quality, including pupil-teacher ratios and the proportion of trained teachers in primary education. This suggests there is scope to derive better value from education expenditures. On educational attainment, PISA scores in Chile, Colombia, Costa Rica, and Mexico register in the bottom quartile of those for OECD member countries, while most other LAC countries participating in PISA fall within the lower half of the rankings for countries that are not OECD members (OECD 2019b). Educational attainment in LAC mirrors the region's high income inequality; the richest 20 percent of pupils are five times more likely than the poorest 20 percent to complete upper secondary education (UNESCO 2020).

Against this backdrop, the COVID-19 pandemic set back educational progress across LAC, with the poorest households worst affected. LAC had some of the longest school closures in the world, and early evidence suggests significant learning losses, concentrated among younger and socioeconomically disadvantaged children, as a result (World Bank 2022i). The digital divide was a key driver of the disparities: Only about 40 percent of primary schools and 60 percent of secondary schools in LAC had access to the internet for educational purposes (World Bank 2021a). Given the increasing importance of digital skills, further government efforts to universalize connectivity in schools could boost lifetime earnings and enhance social mobility. More generally, the remediation of pandemic-related learning losses and assurance of more equitable educational access are likely to require more effective, and in rural and low-income areas greater, investment in education. Specific needs identified in recent World Bank country reports include improved teacher training and professional development (Argentina and Ecuador), expanded and enhanced early childhood education (Bolivia and El Salvador), and a greater focus on ensuring that education systems develop the skills employers are seeking (the Dominican Republic, Mexico, and Paraguay; World Bank 2018a, 2018b, 2018c, 2018f, 2019d, 2021i, 2022b).

Health care. LAC had higher health spending as a proportion of output, at about 8 percent of GDP in 2015-19, than any other EMDE region, with per capita health spending higher only in ECA. Above-average spending has some clear beneficial outcomes: Life expectancy in LAC compares favorably to that in other EMDE regions, the region has about twice the number of physicians per capita of the average EMDE, and vaccination rates are generally high. Nonetheless, improvement has been slow in important areas. In 2017, ECA, EAP, and MNA all had lower maternal mortality rates, which have fallen only slowly in LAC since 2000. Similarly, while LAC had the highest proportion, among EMDE regions, of the population covered for essential health services in 2000, it has since shown the slowest improvement on this metric, and EAP and ECA have overtaken it. The COVID-19 pandemic laid bare shortcomings in regional health care systems, with LAC suffering a disproportionate death toll, likely reflecting inequitable health care access (Schwalb et al. 2022). The region also continues to lag in aspects of public health infrastructure; the proportion of the population with access to well-managed sanitation services is below the EMDE average.

Investing in improved public health infrastructure and services for low-income groups is likely to be a cost-effective way to improve health outcomes and boost human capital. Recent studies of countries including Bolivia, Ecuador, El Salvador, and Paraguay suggest that improving sanitation in rural and low-income communities should be a priority (World Bank 2018c, 2018f, 2021i, 2022c). Investments that raise the efficiency of health care provision could also free up resources for other sectors. This is likely to be important in coming decades, given low productivity growth and growing demand in the health care sector and the increasing prevalence of noncommunicable diseases. Indeed, model-based estimates indicate that per capita health spending in LAC is set to grow faster than GDP at least up to 2050 (Rao et al. 2022). The region can meet its future health care demands at lower cost by investing in primary care facilities and triage capacity (including telemedicine), preventative public health interventions, and better information and data systems—all of which would lessen the burdens on governments and households (Savedoff et al. 2022).

Green transition. LAC economies could benefit substantially from the global transition toward greener forms of energy and broader emissions reduction. The region is endowed with a large proportion of the known reserves of several minerals and metals needed for electrifying transport and scaling up renewable-energy technologies. For example, LAC has roughly half of the world's lithium reserves (mainly in Argentina, Brazil, and Chile, though Bolivia has the largest known lithium resources in the world), more than a third of its copper reserves (Chile, Mexico, and Peru), and more than a fifth of its rare-earth reserves (Brazil), as well as significant amounts of nickel, manganese, and graphite (USGS 2022a, 2022b, 2022c, 2022d, 2022e, 2022f). However, the efficient extraction and processing of green minerals will require large-scale capital investment and improved technological methods to ensure sustainability. Chile is the only country in LAC that currently exports substantial amounts of lithium, and there are significant concerns that using water in the extraction of lithium from brine has the potential to strain water supplies (IEA 2022). In addition to sustainably expanding extractive capacity, which could further entrench LAC's dominance in exports of primary commodities, several governments in the region have ambitions to foster domestic green industries down the value chain, including electric vehicle and battery manufacturing. Evidence suggests that these plans may be more likely to succeed if public policy assumes a role in nurturing such industries, as the auto sector tends otherwise to innovate incrementally on existing production techniques (Aghion et al. 2016). However, successfully implementing such plans would likely require substantial upgrades to regional research and development, development of complex manufacturing capacity, and significant upskilling of workforces.

Regional policy priorities

While policy priorities differ among countries, across LAC there is a clear need for improved infrastructure and for more equitable access to quality education and health care. Given limited fiscal space, increasing public spending will be challenging, and policy makers may need to focus on reprioritizing and improving the efficiency of expenditures within existing budgets. At the same time, increasing the growth of output and productivity in the region's private sector will require stronger growth of business investment, beyond that focused on primary commodity extraction. This in turn will require more supportive environments for private enterprise.

Public investment. Estimates of infrastructure gaps in LAC indicate that the region underinvests in infrastructure, including that involved in the provision of transport, energy, telecommunications, and water. While some such services can be provided primarily by the private sector, LAC economies will likely need to materially increase public investment in infrastructure to reach the 2030 infrastructure-related Sustainable Development Goals. In some cases, public borrowing could fund projects that offer very high economic returns, but otherwise countries in LAC have limited fiscal space, particularly in the aftermath of the COVID-19 pandemic and prior years of weak growth. The first recourse for raising productive investment in public infrastructure could therefore be reprioritizing existing public expenditure away from unproductive uses. Public budgeting reviews could identify wasteful spending—estimated by one analysis to be as high as 4.4 percent of regional GDP (Izquierdo, Pessino, and Vuletin 2018). Some countries (Argentina, Bolivia, and Brazil) may need to institute reforms to reduce budget rigidities (Herrera and Olaberria 2020). Governments could also consider implementing fiscal rules that favor investment spending over consumption, though they would need to manage potential sustainability risks from poor-quality investment (Blanco et al. 2020). Measures that broaden the tax base, limit distortive tax expenditures, and improve tax compliance can help policy makers seeking to fund investment through raising additional revenues avert negative impacts on growth. Governments could also consider increasing consumption taxes on goods such as alcohol, tobacco, and sugar, which could raise revenue while helping combat chronic illnesses that are bad for both general welfare and the public purse (Estevão and Essl 2022).

Even absent broader fiscal reforms, LAC has substantial scope for improving infrastructure by raising the efficacy of public investment. One study estimated that by operating at the efficient frontier, LAC could double its output in infrastructure services with the same inputs (Suárez-Alemán, Serebrisky, and Perelman 2019). The region could derive substantial efficiency gains, for example, from improvements in project selection, planning, management, and procurement (Fay et al. 2017). In some cases, additional use of public-private partnerships may improve risk allocation in the financing of infrastructure projects, smooth budget outlays, and augment state capacity in project delivery and maintenance (Garcia-Kilroy and Rudolph 2017). Policy makers could also consider establishing functionally independent advisory commissions (such as those in place in New Zealand and the United Kingdom) to aid in planning infrastructure expenditures and establishing priorities among them.

Private investment. To improve incentives for private investment, LAC countries could reform taxation frameworks to reduce the relatively high dependence on corporate income taxes. In this context, broadly applicable reforms such as increased investment expensing are likely to provide more effective and efficient incentives than complex special tax regimes (Acosta-Ormaechea, Pienknagura, and Pizzinelli 2022). Countries could use carbon taxes to provide incentives for green investment and research (Aghion et al. 2016). Regulatory environments in LAC could be improved by, among other things, ensuring that regulators have technocratic governance and that regulatory frameworks are transparent. Processes should follow international best practices regarding, for example, policy consultations, impact assessments, and ex post evaluations (Querbach and Arndt 2017). Competition frameworks could be enhanced to reduce monopoly power, encourage innovation, and foster a level playing field among private firms as well as between private firms and state-owned enterprises. Upgrading the skills of the population through more effective utilization of education spending would increase the attractiveness of LAC as a destination for private investment. Policy makers could, for example, increase focus on educational attainment among students from low-income households while seeking efficiency improvements and better matching between skills that are in demand and subjects studied in higher education (Ferreyra et al. 2017). Combating corruption and reducing violence and social unrest would also bolster investor confidence (Keefer and Scartascini 2022).

Raising domestic saving. LAC has lower domestic saving rates than other EMDE regions, even after the influence of such factors as financial depth, demographics, and macroeconomic and political stability is accounted for (Becerra, Cavallo, and Noy 2015). Given historical long-term correlations between investment and domestic saving, it is unlikely that investment rates in LAC can durably increase without higher saving (Apergis and Tsoumas 2009). Policy makers therefore face a tension between increasing public investment and supporting higher national saving through government saving, sharpening the rationale for funding new investment out of existing fiscal envelopes. Evidence that public investment crowds out private investment in LAC is ambiguous, but mitigating this potential risk calls for governments to focus on investments that can raise total factor productivity, thereby increasing returns on private capital and creating incentives for private investment (Fernández, Imrohoroglu, and Tamayo 2017; Ramirez and Nazmi 2003; Santiago et al. 2020). Measures to increase financial access, trust in the banking system, and financial literacy (through early financial education, for example) could help raise household saving rates (Cavallo and Serebrisky 2016). In the absence of higher domestic savings, LAC will have to continue relying heavily on foreign savings to support growth of the region's capital stock—an approach that may have contributed to low investment-to-output ratios over the last 20 years.

MIDDLE EAST and NORTH AFRICA

Investment growth has been anemic in the Middle East and North Africa in recent years. It was negative in 6 of the 11 years from 2011-21. Periods of declining oil prices, armed conflicts, political upheaval, and weak governance have constrained investment. Investment needs, while varying substantially between the wealthier countries of the Gulf Cooperation Council and countries marred by fragility and violence, remain generally sizable, especially in the transport and energy sectors. The COVID-19 pandemic and climate change call for immediate investment to prevent losses to lives and livelihoods. Policies to encourage investment include rationalizing the role of the state in economic activity, creating incentives for the private sector to invest, and diversifying fossil-fuel-reliant economies so that they are better positioned for the future.

Introduction

The Middle East and North Africa accounted for 6 percent of investment in EMDEs during 2011-21. Over the past two decades (2000-21), investment growth collapsed momentously in the region, from an average of 8.6 percent a year in 2000-10 to 0.5 percent a year in 2011-21. Foreign direct investment inflows halved over the two decades and were the lowest among EMDE regions in the 2010s, at 1 percent of GDP. In 2022, investment growth is estimated to have been 5.4 percent, just above the 1990-2021 annual average of 5.0 percent (figure 4.13).

The precipitous slowdown in investment in the past decade reflected violence and conflict, the impacts of the COVID-19 pandemic, the effects on oil exporters of a large drop in oil prices in the middle of the decade, and macroeconomic and political instability in many net oil importers. The oil price collapse in 2014-16 led to a significant slowdown in investment growth among oil exporters, from about 9.1 percent a year in 2000-10 to 0.3 percent a year in 2011-21. Oil importers in the region also saw a steep slowdown in average annual investment growth between the two decades, from 6.6 percent to 1.6 percent.

The pandemic led to a 6.5 percent decline in investment in the region in 2020, with the drop in oil-importing countries three times greater than that in oil exporters. The rebound in 2021 was tepid, with investment growth of 5.3 percent. Consequently, investment in 2021 remained about 12 percent below prepandemic projections, and even further below projections in oil importers than in oil exporters. Over 2022-24,

FIGURE 4.13 **MNA: Investment growth and correlates**

Investment growth in the Middle East and North Africa slowed in the last decade and was negative more than half the time. The slowdown reflects a severe deterioration in the terms of trade in oil exporters, armed conflict and its spillovers, and political uncertainty in several oil importers. The pandemic has led to a persistent gap between actual investment and prepandemic forecasts.

A. Investment growth

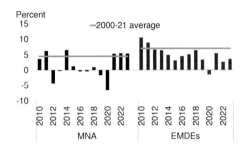

B. Economies with below-average or negative investment growth

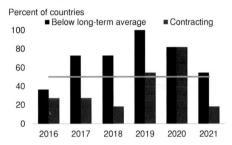

C. Investment

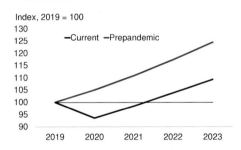

D. Composition of investment growth

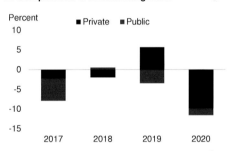

E. Terms of trade

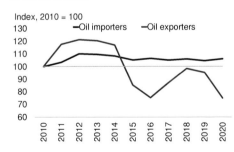

F. Political stability

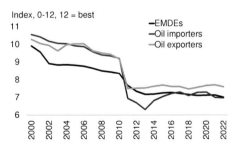

Sources: Haver Analytics; PRS Group, *International Country Risk Guide*; World Bank.
Note: EMDEs = emerging market and developing economies; MNA = Middle East and North Africa.
A. Averages weighted by investment levels. Sample includes 98 EMDEs and 11 from MNA.
B. Economy coverage is the same as for panel A. Share of countries in MNA region with investment growth below the long-term (2000-21) average or negative investment growth ("Contracting"). Orange line indicates 50 percent.
C. Investment level based on data and projections in the January 2020 and January 2023 *Global Economic Prospects* reports. Data for 2023 are forecasts.
D. Based on data from Bahrain, the Arab Republic of Egypt, the Islamic Republic of Iran, and Saudi Arabia. In Egypt, nominal investment is deflated using the gross capital formation deflator.
E. World Bank's net barter terms-of-trade indexes. Investment-weighted averages. Oil exporters include Algeria, Kuwait, Oman, Saudi Arabia, and the United Arab Emirates. Oil importers include Egypt, Jordan, Lebanon, Morocco, and Tunisia.
F. Based on the Government Stability subindex of the *International Country Risk Guide*. Unweighted average for 102 EMDEs, including 10 MNA oil exporters and 6 MNA oil importers.

growth in investment in MNA is expected to approximately match the region's longer-run (2000-21) average rate, with investment failing to catch up with its prepandemic trend.

Investment needs remain significant in MNA—especially among oil importers and economies suffering from fragility and conflict—including needs for investment in infrastructure and climate change adaptation and mitigation, as well as investment to address the legacy of the pandemic. But infrastructure needs vary widely across the region, from countries with some of the highest scores in the world for infrastructure quality—the United Arab Emirates is ranked fourth globally—to ones with some of the lowest (Lebanon and the Republic of Yemen). The region also needs to invest in preparing for a warmer and more volatile climate and a decarbonized future. A focus on green economic growth—promoting clean energy and ecofriendly investment—would yield greater economic returns by creating more jobs and averting environmental degradation. To meet the region's investment needs, its governments can implement policies that decrease the size of the state, support new industries in diversifying production and exports, provide appropriate incentives for the private sector through improvements in governance and investor protections, and efficiently price fossil fuels.

Evolution of regional investment

Over the last two decades, armed conflicts in several countries, far-reaching political changes, the oil price plunge of 2014-16, and lately the pandemic and war in Ukraine have weighed down economic activity and investor sentiment in MNA. As growth prospects dimmed, especially among oil-exporting countries, investment growth slowed sharply, from an annual average of 8.6 percent in 2000-10 to 0.5 percent a year in 2011-21. Foreign direct investment inflows halved to 1 percent of GDP on average during 2011-20, the lowest rate among EMDE regions. Investment contracted in four of the six years from 2016 to 2021. At the height of the COVID-19 pandemic, in 2020, investment declined by 6.5 percent, before rebounding by 5.3 percent on average in 2021-22. Investment in 2022 is expected to remain about 12 percent below its prepandemic projections and below prepandemic forecasts in four-fifths of the region's economies. While investment slowed for different reasons in the past decade in oil importers and exporters—the former battling external factors and the latter domestic policy uncertainty—the outcome has been anemic investment growth in both groups.

Investment in oil-exporting MNA economies

Investment growth in oil-exporting MNA economies—in which oil and gas account, on average, for four-tenths of output and most of fiscal revenues and goods exports—has evolved broadly in line with oil prices, which collapsed in 2014 and remained below averages for the 2010s until late 2021. The war in Ukraine raised oil prices again in 2022. While investment rebounded strongly in the first half of 2022, the future path of investment in the oil sector is unclear, given longer-term trends away from fossil fuels and high volatility and uncertainty in the oil market.

When the steep oil price decline began in mid-2014, governments in the region's oil-exporting economies initially responded with fiscal stimulus, often in the form of public investment. As a result, investment growth rose by more than 7 percentage points in 2014 to 7.4 percent. But the collapse in oil prices proved enduring and led to sustained oil revenue losses. The resulting fiscal constraints contributed to declines in investment over 2015-19 averaging 1.5 percent a year, with investment contracting in three of the four largest oil exporters: the Islamic Republic of Iran, Saudi Arabia, and the United Arab Emirates. The average terms of trade of oil exporters only recently returned to pre-2014 levels.[8]

The COVID-19 pandemic further depressed investment in these economies as they were hit by simultaneous shocks both to oil sectors and, because of mobility restrictions, to non-oil economic activity. In Saudi Arabia, investment collapsed by 10.4 percent in 2020, compared with the 4.5 percent average decline among oil exporters as a whole.

Growth averaging 5.8 percent across 2021 and 2022 followed the fall in investment in 2020. Investment in 2022 is estimated to have surpassed its 2019 level but to have remained 4 percent below prepandemic projections.

Investment in oil-importing MNA economies

Among oil-importing countries, investment contracted by 14 percent in 2020 following a decade of weak growth stemming from political tensions that began with the Arab Spring in 2011, spillovers from the euro area financial crisis of 2010-11, and domestic macroeconomic instability. During the 2010s, the only year of strong growth was 2016, when the Arab Republic of Egypt and Morocco, the two largest economies in the region that are net importers of oil, both ramped up infrastructure investment.

Since 2017, the public sector in Egypt has aggressively expanded investment, including investment in education and training. Gross capital formation grew by 36 percent between 2017 and 2020. Public investment has increased as part of a structural reform agenda, only partially completed, aimed at restoring the country's macroeconomic stability and promoting sustainable economic growth. Reforms have included the introduction of a more flexible exchange rate; fiscal reforms, including reductions in energy subsidies and improvements in public financial management; improvements to the monetary policy framework; a new law to streamline customs and reduce nontariff barriers; a new banking law; and increased freedom for the private sector to participate in more sectors of the economy (IMF 2021a). These reforms aimed partly at improving the environment for private investment. Increased public investment as part of a response to the pandemic partly offset a sharp decline in private investment in 2020.

Investment growth of 2.9 percent in oil importers in 2021 was anemic given the 14 percent COVID-induced collapse in 2020. It was also too little to lift investment above its 2019 level, which the region's oil importers are expected to surpass only in 2023.

---

[8] Panel regression estimates suggest that the resulting terms-of-trade shock accounted for nearly all of the slowdown in investment growth during the initial oil price decline in 2014.

Investment in 2022 is now estimated to have been almost 30 percent below prepandemic forecasts.

Regional investment needs

MNA needs to ramp up investment in infrastructure, which could support the economic recovery from the pandemic (figure 4.14). Investment outlays would likely yield the greatest benefits if directed at addressing the consequences of the pandemic, meeting infrastructure needs, diversifying economies, and mitigating and adapting to climate change. A main focus on green economic growth—promoting clean energy and ecofriendly investment—could yield the largest economic returns, by creating more jobs and averting environmental degradation (Batini et al. 2021). Environmental degradation of skies (air pollution) and seas (plastics) costs the region 2 percent of GDP a year on average (Heger et al. 2022). Upgrading infrastructure can also save lives and livelihoods, with an estimated 5.5 percent of GDP lost annually in the region as a result of poor roads and related accidents (Um 2020). Just as the region's challenges are diverse and complex, so are its needs for investment in infrastructure, education, health, and green technology.

Responding to the pandemic. The COVID-19 pandemic has highlighted inadequacies in the health and education sectors in MNA, and the urgent need to invest in them. Most MNA economies were ill-prepared for the pandemic, with public officials overconfident about health system capabilities (World Bank 2021g). Even prior to the pandemic, achieving universal health care coverage would have required countries globally to increase spending on primary health care by at least 1 percent of GDP (WHO 2019). Despite significant progress in MNA over the last two decades toward achieving universal health care—meaning access to health services, when and where needed, without financial hardship—the region still lags behind other EMDE regions and advanced economies in this regard. In some of the region's economies, public spending on health care, per capita, is among the lowest in the world, resulting in limited access and large out-of-pocket expenses for citizens. Insufficient investment in health services, particularly in non-Gulf Cooperation Council economies means inadequate numbers of health care workers, insufficient hospital beds per capita, and limited ability to provide essential health services.

Scores on the World Bank's Human Capital Index have risen over the past decade in almost 80 percent of MNA economies, with much of this gain coming from educational improvements.[9] Nonetheless, a child born in MNA in 2020 was expected to achieve only 56 percent of his or her potential productivity on average, according to the index. The pandemic has reversed some of the gains to education, with pandemic-related school closures averaging 48 weeks in 2020-21 in MNA, above the global average of 38 weeks. The resulting outsized damage to human capital accumulation could significantly

---

[9] The Human Capital Index measures the amount of human capital (that is, the level of productivity) a child born in a given year could expect to attain by the age of 18, based on the risks to health and education that child is expected to face.

FIGURE 4.14 **MNA: Infrastructure, health, and education indicators**

MNA has high needs for investment in infrastructure, especially in regard to electricity and transport. While MNA performs well relative to other EMDE regions on basic health measures, its education indicators remain generally below EMDE averages.

A. Infrastructure investment needs

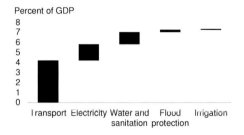

B. Quality of infrastructure

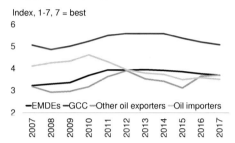

C. Universal health coverage

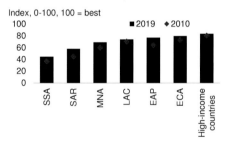

D. Health spending below EMDE median

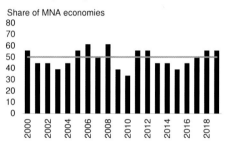

E. Selected human capital indicators

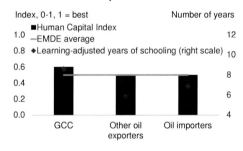

F. Infrastructure investment needs

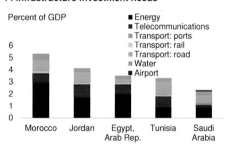

Sources: Group of Twenty (G20), Global Infrastructure Outlook; Rozenberg and Fay (2019); World Bank; World Economic Forum, Global Competitiveness Index; World Health Organization.

Note: EAP = East Asia and Pacific; ECA = Europe and Central Asia; EMDEs = emerging market and developing economies; GCC = Gulf Cooperation Council; GDP = gross domestic product; LAC = Latin America and the Caribbean; MNA = Middle East and North Africa; SAR = South Asia; SSA = Sub-Saharan Africa.

A. Investment needs in a "preferred investment scenario" as defined in Rozenberg and Fay (2019).

B. Unweighted averages of survey data from the World Economic Forum's Global Competitiveness Index. Data were collected using the question: "How would you assess general infrastructure (for example, transport, telephony, energy) in your country? (1 = extremely underdeveloped—among the worst in the world; 7 = extensive and efficient—among the best in the world)." Oil importers include the Arab Republic of Egypt, Jordan, Lebanon, Morocco, and Tunisia. Non-GCC oil exporters include Algeria, the Islamic Republic of Iran, Libya, and the Republic of Yemen. GCC countries include Bahrain, Kuwait, Oman, Qatar, Saudi Arabia, and the United Arab Emirates.

C. Unweighted averages. Based on the World Health Organization's Universal Health Coverage (UHC) Service Coverage Index.

D. Based on domestic general government health expenditure as a percentage of GDP. Sample includes 152 EMDEs (18 from MNA). Orange line indicates 50 percent.

E. Unweighted averages. Sample includes 138 EMDEs (16 from MNA).

F. Based on the G20's Global Infrastructure Outlook.

impair the lifetime earnings of many (Azevedo et al. 2021). Returns to education in MNA are also the lowest of any EMDE region, reflecting in part the low quality of education (Montenegro and Patrinos 2014). Anemic economic growth and job creation in the region have also contributed to high rates of youth unemployment, and the lack of work experience for many is a further setback for human capital (Kheyfets et al. 2019).

Responding to climate change. MNA has already been feeling the effects of climate change, with natural disasters, including heat waves and floods, becoming more frequent (IMF 2022b; World Bank 2014). Rising risks to lives and livelihoods highlight the urgent need to invest in climate change mitigation and adaptation and to ensure that the recovery from the pandemic is green and inclusive (Acerbi et al. 2021; IMF 2022b). Risks are particularly acute among economies dependent on agriculture: Rising temperatures are expected to reduce growing areas and crop yields and exacerbate water scarcity, which will undermine food security, force migration, lower labor productivity, and raise the likelihood of conflict. In Morocco, for example, where droughts are already a major source of macroeconomic vulnerability, a continuation of recent trends could result in a rationing of water to various sectors of the economy that could decrease GDP by up to 6.5 percent by 2050 (with new infrastructure and improved efficiency only partly offsetting the decline) and prompt the migration of up to 1.9 million people, or 5.4 percent of the population (World Bank 2022f). For the region, crop yields could decline by up to 30 percent if temperatures were to rise by 1.5-2 degrees Celsius relative to preindustrial times (World Bank 2014).

Taking into account the indirect costs of action needed for climate resilience increases estimates of the costs of adapting to climate change. These estimates are also dependent on assumptions about the climate outlook and therefore vary widely. The World Bank (2014) estimated the cost to the region at about 7.3 percent of GDP on average per year from 2015 to 2030. The IMF has estimated individual-country costs to be as low as 0.1 percent of GDP in Bahrain, Jordan, and Saudi Arabia, but as high as 2 percent of GDP in Iraq over the next 10 years.[10] Given the abundance of sunshine (radiant energy), much of the region can benefit from a shift to solar energy, the costs of which have decreased rapidly (IMF 2022b). Current generation capacity from renewables is only about one-tenth of total installed energy generation capacity in MNA (Um 2020).

Broader infrastructure needs. Investment needs in the region go beyond addressing climate change and the repercussions of the pandemic. Infrastructure needs are also important, although they vary widely across MNA. Infrastructure spending can create the foundation for strong private-sector-led growth and provide citizens with access to opportunities. Infrastructure investment in the region averaged 3 percent of GDP over the last decade, with that investment financed mainly by the public sector (Um 2020). This rate of investment will not be enough to meet infrastructure needs in the coming

---

[10] These estimates cover only adaptation to floods, storms, and rises in sea levels and do not address rising temperatures or droughts, an important risk for the region.

decade. If all MNA economies increased spending on roads by 1 percent of GDP per year, the share of the rural populations within reach of a primary or secondary road would still increase to only about one-half by 2030. Estimates suggest that infrastructure investment of about 7 percent of GDP will be needed to meet the Sustainable Development Goals by 2030 (figure 4.14.A). Increased investment in infrastructure could also help improve labor market conditions in MNA. Estache et al. (2013) estimated that each $1 billion of infrastructure investment has the potential to generate 110,000 infrastructure-related jobs, on average, in oil-importing MNA countries.

The region's oil-importing countries and its oil-exporting countries that are not members of the Gulf Cooperation Council show significant underinvestment in transport (roads, in particular) and electricity. According to the Group of Twenty's Global Infrastructure Outlook, Egypt will need to spend an average of 5.2 percent of GDP per year over the next decade to meet infrastructure needs, mainly in energy and telecommunications (Oxford Economics and Global Infrastructure Hub 2017). Egypt's energy sector could benefit from expanding and diversifying energy supply, a shift toward renewable sources, and the modernization of the oil and gas sector (World Bank 2018d).

Over 2001-17, Morocco had one of the highest investment rates globally, with that rate varying between 25 and 38 percent of GDP. Most of this represented public sector investment in infrastructure. In the latest available (2017) survey, the country ranked 42nd in quality of infrastructure, having risen more than 20 spots in a decade. Despite this achievement, Morocco's infrastructure investment needs remain large owing to growth in demand for infrastructure services arising from population growth and urbanization (World Bank 2020d). Over the next decade the country will need average infrastructure investment of 6.2 percent of GDP annually, mainly in the energy and transport sectors (Oxford Economics and Global Infrastructure Hub 2017).

Lebanon faces significant infrastructure deficiencies, including a dysfunctional electricity sector, water shortages, and inadequate waste and wastewater management (Harake and Kostopoulos 2018; Le Borgne and Jacobs 2016). The port explosion in Beirut in 2020 and the country's ongoing economic crisis have highlighted the need for infrastructure investment. The explosion is estimated to have caused damage equivalent to 15-19 percent of the country's 2020 GDP (World Bank, European Union, and United Nations 2020). Large numbers of Syrian refugees in Lebanon (and Jordan) have added to strains on the provision of public goods.

Countries involved in armed conflict are at risk of large-scale destruction of physical capital. In Syria, the war that began in 2011 has devastated the country's economy: in 2019, income per capita was no higher than in the early 1990s (World Bank 2022h). The cost of rebuilding infrastructure damaged or destroyed by the conflict has been estimated to be in the range of $100-200 billion in 2015 prices, the lower bound being about 10 times the country's 2015 GDP (Gobat and Kostial 2016). Iraq also faces large infrastructure investment needs, increased by conflict. It has been estimated that some

$200 billion in 2018 prices would be needed to restore "hard" infrastructure to levels prevailing before the Islamic State of Iraq and Syria became an active force in the country, an amount almost equal to Iraq's 2018 GDP (Gunter 2018). In the Republic of Yemen, recovery and reconstruction costs are estimated at $20-25 billion, equivalent to 1.1-1.3 times the country's 2020 GDP (World Bank 2020g).

Member countries of the Gulf Cooperation Council also have infrastructure needs, predominantly in regard to electricity generation, although the pandemic has highlighted the need to invest also in digital infrastructure. Saudi Arabia's infrastructure investment needs over the next decade are estimated at 2.8 percent of GDP, mainly in the areas of energy and road transport. With higher income levels, these countries' plans for public spending on infrastructure in the medium term generally track with their needs.

Regional policy priorities

Policy priorities differ across the region. In most of MNA, policy priorities include addressing low-quality education, reducing youth unemployment, improving governance, and decreasing the state's economic footprint. In agriculture-dependent economies and those with large populations along coastlines, adaptation to climate change is a priority. In economies that have faced conflict, a priority is to restore essential services and infrastructure. Among oil-dependent economies, priorities include diversification of production and exports and empowering the private sector.

Increasing public and private investment. Across the region, the scaling back of subsidies since 2014 has created some space for increased public spending on investment in infrastructure, health, and education, but more is needed (Parry, Black, and Vernon 2021). Several policies can raise the volume and efficiency of public and private investment. Countries with insufficient fiscal space to raise public investment to meet their needs could focus on creating incentives for private sector investment and increasing the efficiency of existing public spending. Improving the business climate by reforming governance and regulatory frameworks and enhancing investor protection could promote private sector investment, as could increased use of public-private partnerships (as has been undertaken, for example, in Morocco; EBRD 2015). In 2010-21, MNA accounted for only 2 percent of EMDEs' infrastructure projects with private participation. Public-private partnerships can improve the efficiency of investment, facilitate technology and skills transfer, and reduce the burden on public budgets (OECD 2019c).

Increasing the role of the private sector in economic activity is vital for most MNA economies. In some oil importers, the electricity sector would benefit from additional privatization (Lebanon) or a larger private sector contribution to electricity generation (Egypt). Egypt has helpfully amended laws to allow the private sector to participate in projects involving infrastructure, public services, and public utilities. Improved security conditions in the region are also essential for a sustained pickup in private investment.

Economies with large external and domestic imbalances should also make restoring macroeconomic stability a priority. Fiscal crises in several economies, which originated in poor economic management, were largely responsible for the weakening of investment growth among oil importers over the past decade. To promote macroeconomic stability, countries could act to improve monetary policy frameworks, introduce fiscal rules to decrease the procyclicality of government spending, implement measures to improve debt management, and undertake rigorous reviews of public spending to promote more productive outcomes.

Addressing education weaknesses. The region has the lowest share of human capital in total wealth globally, and returns to education are also the lowest of any EMDE region, reflecting in part low-quality education (Lange, Wodon, and Carey 2018; Montenegro and Patrinos 2014; World Bank 2018e). Policies to address weak educational outcomes include updating stagnant education systems to meet the needs of the twenty-first century—by adopting suitable technology, modernizing teaching methods, introducing vocational training for teachers, increasing learning assessments, and promoting the education of girls.

Addressing health care issues. Subnational governments responsible for providing health care services need predictable transfers from national governments. Effective spending reviews are also needed to reprioritize spending and accurately model the impact of spending choices on human capital outcomes. Prohealth taxation (for example, sugar taxes) could raise funding to meet growing needs and help reduce morbidity (Kurowski et al. 2021). In 2021, the region had the second-highest prevalence of diabetes among EMDE regions, only slightly behind that of SAR at 12.3 percent of the adult population.

Climate policies. Environmental degradation in the region remains a concern, with low environmental standards, subsidies that promote pollution, and a lack of comprehensive management plans, including plans for managing waste and coastal assets (Heger et al. 2022). Green initiatives, such as rationalizing energy subsidies and introducing carbon taxes, can help address these problems while also improving fiscal positions. Egypt was the first country in the region to issue a green bond, in 2020, to unlock finance for climate-smart projects. If adopted more broadly, bonds of this type could unlock significant sustainable finance. Empowering the broader public with information could be an important catalyst for change. Thus, governments could improve access to data on localized pollution, climate risk, and vulnerability to improve decision-making and investment design (World Bank 2021f).

Over 2000-21, investment in the South Asia region grew at the strong average rate of close to 8 percent a year, and the region's infrastructure gaps narrowed. But since 2020, the COVID-19 pandemic and war in Ukraine have dented investment growth in the region. The demands of a rapidly growing population, often-weak education standards, poor health care coverage, and high vulnerability to climate change indicate the need for a resumption of sustained, rapid investment growth. Given limited fiscal space in the region's economies to increase public investment, policies that provide incentives for private sector investment, increase social as well as private returns to investment, and promote greener growth would make filling these investment needs easier.

Introduction

South Asia accounted for 8 percent of EMDE investment, on average, over 2011-21. Investment grew by 7.4 percent annually, on average, in 2000-21, which was above the EMDE average.

Rapid investment growth in the early 2000s was followed by two periods of weakness in the 2010s that reflected weak output growth, excess manufacturing capacity in the face of sluggish external demand, and policy uncertainty in several countries. Then, in 2020, investment fell by about 10 percent as measures to restrict the spread of COVID-19 and reduced in-person interaction led to a collapse in economic activity and increased policy uncertainty. Fiscal support boosted public investment, but not by enough to offset the drop in investment in the private sector. In 2021, investment rebounded by 15 percent as the rollout of vaccines and a surge in goods demand boosted activity. Investment growth slowed from about 9 percent a year, on average, in 2000-10 to just over half that rate in 2011-21. Much of that slowdown was due to the private sector, which accounted for four-fifths of total investment in the region on average during 2000-21. Investment growth declined most steeply in India over the two decades ending in 2021, while in Nepal investment growth increased.

The rebound of investment growth in SAR in 2021 continued in 2022, at a rate of 8.4 percent. Nevertheless, investment in 2022 remained 7 percent below prepandemic projections. The outlook for investment growth in SAR is highly uncertain, with significant downside risks due to soaring inflation, rapid increases in interest rates, several economies in crisis, and rising risks of a global recession.

SAR had large investment needs before the pandemic, and they have only increased since. They include addressing poor health care coverage; raising still-low rates of school completion and improving poor-quality education; addressing mounting infrastructure needs to increase the integration of the region's economies into the global economy and to provide for the region's population—which accounts for a quarter of the world's population; addressing shortcomings highlighted and damage done by the pandemic; and adjusting to, and contributing to the alleviation of, climate change. Governments can help directly by increasing public investment, but limited fiscal space may make this challenging. They have other options, however, including increasing the efficiency of public investment, mobilizing private sector funds by boosting public-private partnerships, and improving the general business climate to promote private investment. Infrastructure investment can play an important role in improving the environment for business, raising labor productivity, and improving household incomes, as the recent launch of rapid transit systems in Pakistan and broader productivity gains made in the region have underscored (Bizimana et al. 2021; Mehar 2020).

Evolution of regional investment

Despite the strong average pace of investment growth in the region in the two decades to 2021, there have been two recent periods of weakness. The more recent one, related to the COVID-19 pandemic, resulted in a contraction in fixed investment by about 10 percent in 2020. Despite the strong rebound of 2021-22, investment in 2022 remained 7 percent below what it was forecast to be before the pandemic (figure 4.15). Nepal and Sri Lanka had particularly large investment shortfalls in 2022 with respect to prepandemic projections.

The earlier period of weak investment growth, in 2012-14, reflected a slowing of SAR's consumption-driven expansion. Investment growth slowed sharply from 13 percent in 2010 and remained weak in the following few years; it was barely 3 percent in 2014. The slowdown reflected weakening growth in India (which accounts for more than three-quarters of the region's total investment), only partially offset by pickups in Bhutan, Nepal, and Pakistan.

In India, structural bottlenecks, including unreliable power, poor road and rail networks, and arduous administrative requirements on business, have presented barriers to investment over the past decade, along with banking sector weaknesses that have constrained investment finance. A recent government investment drive recognizes the need to accelerate infrastructure development and remove impediments to private-sector-led growth. Investment growth in India slowed from an annual average of 10.5 percent in 2000-10 to 5.7 percent in 2011-21. In fiscal year (FY) 2013/14, private investment, which accounted for nine-tenths of total investment in the country, stagnated as global financial conditions tightened rapidly and capital outflows accelerated. Subsequent years saw continued muted investment growth relative to the preceding decade. The slowdown has been attributed to a range of factors, including excess capacity in manufacturing following the 2009 global recession, policy uncertainty, and reforms implemented by the Reserve Bank of India to address financial sector

FIGURE 4.15 **SAR: Investment growth and correlates**

Despite two periods of significant weakness, investment growth was higher in South Asia than in emerging market and developing economies as a whole over the last two decades. In recent years, most economies in the region have seen investment growth below long-term averages, in spite of improving terms of trade and political stability. The level of investment remains below the prepandemic trend as coronavirus disease 2019 (COVID-19) and the war in Ukraine undermine growth. The private sector drives most of the growth in investment in the region.

A. Investment growth

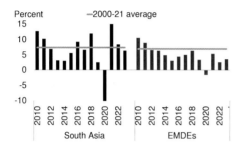

B. Share of SAR countries with weak investment growth

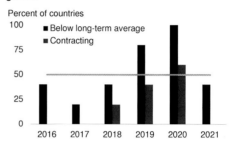

C. Investment

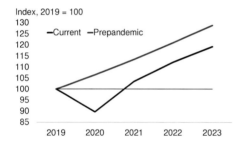

D. Contribution to investment growth

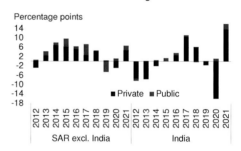

E. Terms of trade

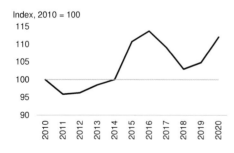

F. Political stability

Sources: Haver Analytics; PRS Group, *International Country Risk Guide*; Ministry of Finance of Sri Lanka; Reserve Bank of India; World Bank.

Note: EMDEs = emerging market and developing economies; excl. = excluding; SAR = South Asia.

A. Weighted averages. Sample includes 98 EMDEs and 5 from SAR.

B. Share of SAR economies with investment growth below its long-term average or negative. Long-term averages are country-specific and refer to available data over 2000-21.

C. Based on projections in the January 2020 and January 2023 *Global Economic Prospects* reports. Data for 2023 are forecasts.

D. "SAR excl. India" is weighted average for Bangladesh, Nepal, and Pakistan.

E. Investment-weighted averages.

F. Investment-weighted average scores on the *International Country Risk Guide*'s Political Risk Index. An increase denotes greater political stability.

weaknesses, particularly among state-owned banks (Tokuoka 2012; World Bank 2016e). Stress in the financial sector came to the fore again a few years later and slowed private fixed investment abruptly in FY2019/20.

COVID-19 led to a 10.4 percent contraction in fixed investment in India in FY2020/21, but a robust recovery followed, assisted by the government's investment drive. Thus in FY2021/22, investment rebounded by 15.8 percent, making the country's shortfall with respect to the prepandemic trend among the smallest in SAR. The FY2022/23 budget is expected to expand public investment by one-third and also includes an incentive program to boost private investment. By boosting public investment during years of private sector weakness (2013-16, 2020) the government played an important counter-cyclical role.

Bangladesh, the region's second-largest economy, experienced robust investment growth in 2000-21 at an annual average rate of 8.3 percent, without any slowing trend—unlike India. This robust growth reflects strong underlying GDP growth, fed partly by rapid urbanization; a rapidly growing, export-oriented ready-made garment sector; a high domestic saving rate; and high public investment. In fact, Bangladesh's public-investment-to-GDP ratio, at 6.5 percent of GDP in 2011-20, was double India's. Also, COVID-19 had a limited economic impact in Bangladesh: Investment slowed rather than contracted, growing by 4 percent in the fiscal year that ended in June 2020, with a rapid expansion of infrastructure-related public investment offsetting stagnating private investment. In the three fiscal years that ended in June 2022, public investment grew by 45 percent.

In Pakistan, investment has been subject to pronounced boom-bust cycles over the past two decades, with growth averaging only 3.1 percent a year in 2000-21, among the lowest average growth rates in SAR. In 2011-21, investment growth peaked in FY2014/15 at close to 16 percent and remained high for several years. The FY2014/15 surge mainly reflected the China-Pakistan Economic Corridor infrastructure project and the construction of a gas pipeline to Pakistan from the Islamic Republic of Iran. The former project is part of China's Belt and Road Initiative and consists of a network of highways, railways, and pipelines to connect western China to the Arabian Sea through the Gwadar Port in Pakistan. Largely reflecting the impact of the pandemic, investment contracted by 17 percent in the two fiscal years that ended in June 2020, and the recovery since then has been anemic. Government estimates for FY2021/22 suggest that investment was still 11 percent below its FY2014/15 peak. Severe flooding in 2022 is forecast to set fixed investment back even further in the next two years.

In Sri Lanka, investment growth averaged about 5 percent a year in 2000-21, with rising external debt partly financing expanding infrastructure investment. A balance of payments crisis erupted in the country in mid-2022, and with international reserves down to a quarter of their prepandemic (end-of-2019) level, the country abandoned its exchange rate peg and ceased external debt repayments. With the currency depreciating rapidly, inflation surged. Recurring electricity blackouts and an inability to import sufficient essentials, including food and energy, added to the country's challenges. Debt restructuring will be necessary to start the process of fiscal rehabilitation and macroeconomic stabilization. The crisis has significantly impaired the outlook for investment, which is expected in 2023 to fall back to levels last seen over a decade ago.

Regional investment needs

South Asia is the second most densely populated region in the world, behind East Asia and Pacific, with large and pressing infrastructure investment needs (figure 4.16). Progress in meeting these needs can promote inclusive, sustainable economic growth and private sector activity. The effects of the COVID-19 pandemic, the food and energy security concerns that have arisen from the war in Ukraine, and the challenges of climate change have increased investment needs. There is an interplay between recovery from the pandemic and action on climate change. Investments aimed at promoting economic recovery from the pandemic and preparing for future pandemics can be aligned with better climate outcomes and help to decouple future growth from fossil fuels. This is particularly important given the region's high emissions intensity and susceptibility to extreme weather events.

Responding to the pandemic. The pandemic has cost lives, raised morbidity, and reduced educational opportunities for millions of children. Reversing many of the pandemic's effects will require a robust investment response. For example, Benedek et al. (2021) estimate that because of the pandemic, average additional (public and private) spending of 2.5 percent of GDP a year through 2030 is needed to meet several Sustainable Development Goals.

Pandemic-related school closures in SAR averaged 70 weeks through March 2022—much higher than the global average of 41 weeks—and kept nearly 400 million children out of school for significant periods (UNESCO and UNICEF 2021). The loss in educational opportunities is likely to undermine poverty reduction, significantly impair the lifetime earnings of those affected, and reduce social mobility across generations (UNESCO, UNICEF, and World Bank 2021; World Bank 2021j, 2022h). The pandemic had an especially severe impact on the informally employed, who accounted for 59 percent of the region's total employment, on average, in 2010-18, significantly more than in other EMDE regions (Ohnsorge and Yu 2021). Income losses were severe, given widespread informality in the services sector and the limited ability of informal firms to access government support (Apedo-Amah et al. 2020; World Bank 2020e). South Asia's informal labor force consists predominantly of low-skilled, rural, female, or young workers.

The education crisis caused by the pandemic calls for an urgent response to ensure that learning environments are safe and learners marginalized by the pandemic are identified and enabled to catch up. To achieve these objectives, investment could focus on providing adequate infrastructure to ensure access to clean water, sanitation, and hygiene facilities; improving communication and information sharing between health and education authorities; and establishing infrastructure, including that pertaining to

FIGURE 4.16 **SAR: Investment needs**

Despite improvements since 2010, SAR still has sizable investment needs in the areas of public infrastructure (energy, transport) and human capital development. Years of schooling in South Asia are about half of what advanced economies achieve. Agriculture in the region is vulnerable to climate change and remains a significant part of economic activity and employment. Increasing research and development spending in agriculture could reverse the region's expected productivity losses from the changing climate.

A. Quality of infrastructure

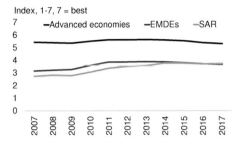

B. Infrastructure investment needs

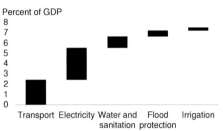

C. Public health expenditure

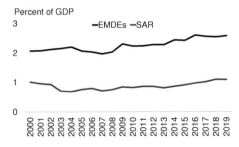

D. Human capital indicators

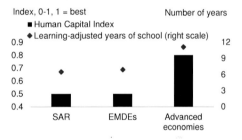

E. Agriculture output

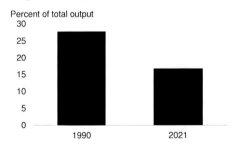

F. Agriculture research spending

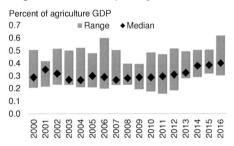

Sources: Agricultural Science and Technology Indicators; Haver Analytics; Rozenberg and Fay (2019); World Bank; World Health Organization.
Note: EMDEs = emerging market and developing economies; GDP = gross domestic product; SAR = South Asia.
B. Based on the "preferred investment scenario" in Rozenberg and Fay (2019).
C. Sample includes 152 EMDEs and 8 from SAR.
D. Sample includes 138 EMDEs (7 from SAR) and 35 advanced economies
F. Based on data for Bangladesh, India, Nepal, Pakistan, and Sri Lanka. "Range" reflects minimum and maximum values.

data and technology, to identify, target, and empower marginalized learners (UNESCO and UNICEF 2021; Van Cappelle, Chopra, and Ackers 2021; Van Cappelle et al. 2021).

By late 2022, the pandemic had officially led to over 600,000 deaths in SAR, about one-tenth of COVID-19 deaths globally. The pandemic undermined people's ability to work, study, and care for families and stretched health care capacity. The region entered the pandemic with underfunded health care systems: The median public-health-expenditure-to-income ratio was less than half the average for all EMDEs, and there were only 0.6 hospital beds per 1,000 people, the lowest rate of all EMDE regions. Along with these challenges, medical and personal protective equipment and testing and tracing infrastructure remain inadequate. While many countries in SAR had emergency response plans in place before the pandemic, many of these plans were designed to address natural disasters. Investing in adequate preparedness, both in respect to fixed investment and beyond, for future pandemics remains vital.

Addressing climate change. The region is one of the most vulnerable to climate change-induced increases in poverty, disease, child mortality, and food prices, with half its population living in areas expected to become climate hot spots (Amarnath et al. 2017; Hallegatte et al. 2016; Jafino et al. 2020; Mani et al. 2018). Projected losses from climate change for SAR economies are above the global average—as high as 18 percent of GDP per capita for Bhutan (Kahn et al. 2021). Elevated vulnerability, combined with continuing high global emissions of greenhouse gases, makes investing in mitigation and adaptation key to ensuring long-term sustainable growth (Agarwal et al. 2021; World Bank 2022g).[11] The International Finance Corporation (2017) identified $3.4 trillion in "climate-smart" investment opportunities in SAR from 2018 to 2030, including opportunities for investment in energy-efficient buildings, electric vehicles, and green transport infrastructure.

While the investment needed to achieve climate goals can be difficult to quantify precisely, the areas of investment needs are clear. Rising temperatures and increasingly erratic rainfall will exacerbate food and water shortages, lower agricultural productivity, and increase food price volatility. Agriculture is the sector most vulnerable to climate change, and it accounts for 40 percent of employment and 20 percent of output in SAR. To counter the climate risks to the sector, the region could focus on investing in more efficient growing methods, shifting to climate-smart agriculture to reduce water use and emissions of greenhouse gases, and increasing spending on agricultural research and development (Fuglie et al. 2020). In addition, forest restoration can act as a carbon sink to help offset emissions and create jobs, and countries in the region could adjust such policies as water and energy subsidies and grain price guarantees to improve resource allocation.

---

[11] South Asia accounted for about 9 percent of emissions of global greenhouse gases in 2018 (Friedlingstein et al. 2022).

Air pollution from burning fossil fuels remains a significant cause of climate change and is estimated to have contributed to more than 1 million premature deaths in SAR in 2018 (Myllyvirta 2020). Fossil fuels also form a large part of the region's import bill. Greater investment in renewable energy sources would reduce air pollution and result in lower public health burdens, increased energy security, and reduced dependence on energy imports.

SAR's rapid rate of urbanization—the second fastest among EMDE regions, into cities that are among the most exposed to climate risk—calls for investment in climate change adaptation. This includes improvements in land use and zoning policies, investment in resilient transport and building infrastructure, enhanced delivery of service, and improved disaster preparedness.

Infrastructure investment needs. Despite significant progress in expanding infrastructure in many SAR economies, both the quality and quantity of infrastructure in the region are still lower than in other EMDE regions (Bizimana et al. 2021). SAR is also one of the least economically integrated regions in the world, with inadequate transport and power infrastructure partly to blame (ADB 2009; World Bank 2016d). Rozenberg and Fay (2019) estimate that South Asia will need an average annual investment of 7.5 percent of GDP to meet infrastructure-related Sustainable Development Goals by 2030: the second-highest rate among EMDE regions. The Asian Development Bank (2017) has estimated that this rises to 8.8 percent of GDP if climate needs are included.

In India, the 2020 National Infrastructure Pipeline Task Force identified plans for investments amounting to the equivalent of about half of the country's FY2021 GDP on infrastructure projects between FY2019 and FY2025. The investments are in roads, railways, air and seaports, energy, and other infrastructure. Investment in the power sector is needed to meet growing energy demands, with total installed capacity expected to increase by two-thirds by 2025. Investment is also needed to shift energy production to renewable sources, improve access, and increase the efficiency of the sector. Electricity distribution loss is 19 percent in India, more than double the global average.

Bangladesh's infrastructure requires various improvements. Poor logistics currently hinder investment and international trade (World Bank 2021c). The World Bank (2021c) has estimated that logistic costs add 5-48 percent to production costs across sectors owing to congestion, poor reliability, poor quality, and widespread informality. While investment in the power sector has effectively met capacity needs over the last decade, further investment will help connect households to energy providers, diversify sources of power, and meet future needs (Government of Bangladesh 2020). The Government of Bangladesh (2020) has estimated that to meet demand for electricity through 2030, the country will need investment equivalent to 15 percent of FY2022 GDP in the coming years. In the transport sector, the road network remains inadequate, although investment in other modes of transport could reduce need in this area. Bangladesh's Eighth Five Year Plan estimates that to achieve its goals, the country must increase investment by 5 percent of GDP between FY2020 and FY2025, mainly in the private sector and through foreign direct investment.

Investment in human capital. Investment needs in health and education go beyond addressing the damage inflicted by the pandemic. Many countries in the region perform poorly on achieving universal health coverage. The region suffers from too few health care professionals, low spending on public health—only 2 percent of GDP, below the rate in all other EMDE regions—and shortages of health care equipment (World Bank 2021j). The lack of adequate health care, together with high poverty levels and inadequate nutrition, means that about one-third of children in the region are stunted and 4 percent do not live past the age of five. In education, learning gaps remain wide, indicating a need for additional resources to empower teachers, address geographic inequalities, and facilitate adoption of new methods of teaching. Thus, countries in the region generally fall short in enabling citizens to meet their productive potential. A child born in SAR is expected to attain only 48 percent of his or her productive potential, the second-worst performance among EMDE regions. Sizable additional outlays for human capital investment could alleviate poverty and increase the productive potential of millions of citizens (Estache and Garsous 2012; Romer 2016).

Regional policy priorities

The region's limited fiscal space will make it challenging to meet investment needs. Doing so will require reforms that reduce long-standing obstacles to the growth of productivity and investment, as well as more efficient spending. A targeted, multipronged policy strategy is needed that encourages investment by increasing returns on capital and by expanding sources of financing (Henckel and McKibbin 2017; Nataraj 2007).

Public investment promoting private investment. Under the right conditions, public investment can crowd in private investment (World Bank 2016e).[12] For example, private firms may be able to reap the benefits of scale if public infrastructure facilitates market access (Calderón, Moral-Benito, and Servéna 2010). Literature on India appears to suggest a positive crowding-in effect (Bahal, Raissi, and Tulin 2015; Jesintha and Sathanapriya 2011; World Bank 2006).

Efficiency of public investment. On average, countries lose about one-third of public investment expenditures through inefficiencies, and the rate is highest among Asian economies (Baum, Mogues, and Verdier 2020). One way to boost the efficiency of public investment would be to reform weak public investment management practices (Vu, Bizimana, and Nozaki 2020). Reforms could include improving project appraisal (with better technical, economic, and financial analysis) and project selection (by centralizing project review and increasing transparency), increasing maintenance funding throughout projects' life, and creating up-to-date and efficient registries to monitor public assets.

Financing. The region can expand public and private investment in several ways to help meet investment needs (ADB 2009, 2012, 2022; Andres, Biller, and Dappe 2014;

---

[12] Public investment could also crowd out private investment, as seen in Pakistan (World Bank 2016b).

Dobbs et al. 2013). *First*, public-private partnerships may offer gains in efficiency and cost-effectiveness (for example, by containing increases in public debt), raise economic growth, and at the same time alleviate fiscal pressures (Anadon and Surana 2015; Bizimana et al. 2021; Lee et al. 2018; Nataraj 2007). Such partnerships can draw private funding and expertise into socially desirable projects that the private sector would not undertake alone because of low private rates of return. The provision of water services and sanitation projects are good examples. Between 2010 and 2021, one-fifth of EMDE infrastructure projects with private participation were in South Asia.

Second, the region can better mobilize domestic savings, both by increasing access to the financial system (for example, by encouraging pension funds) and by broadening and raising government revenue collection. Goods and services taxes implemented in India in 2017, for example, doubled India's tax base in four years. Other tax reforms could increase tax revenue by 3-4 percentage points of GDP and thus provide additional funding for investment (ADB 2022).

Third, the region can increase the lending capacity of its banks through action to strengthen their balance sheets and improve the efficiency of capital allocation by increasing the commercial orientation of banks, through privatization and governance reforms, among other methods.

Fourth, countries in the region can increase the commercial orientation of state-owned enterprises, through better regulation, privatization, or concessions to private investors, and thereby raise efficiency and increase investment.

Fifth, the region's countries can reduce asset-liability mismatches in government accounts by tapping capital markets (for example, by issuing infrastructure bonds) rather than relying on bank lending for infrastructure-related projects.

Finally, the region can encourage FDI in infrastructure by removing regulatory obstacles to conducting business in restricted sectors (Kirkpatrick, Parker, and Zhang 2006; World Bank 2000). With FDI inflows in SAR averaging only 1.5 percent of GDP in 2000-21, tied with the Middle East and North Africa for the lowest rate among EMDE regions, there is scope to encourage further FDI inflows.

Reforms to foster an enabling environment for private investment. SAR's business climate ranks just ahead of that in Sub-Saharan Africa, but behind those in other EMDE regions (Lopez-Acevedo, Medvedev, and Palmade 2016; World Bank 2016c). In Bangladesh, India, and Pakistan, entry and administrative barriers have hampered investment in construction, finance, retail and wholesale trade, telecommunications, and health care. In India, the burden of regulatory compliance, delays in utility connections, difficulties in obtaining permits to start and operate a business, high taxes, and rigid labor markets raise the cost of doing business and discourage investment (Pachouri and Sharma 2016; Shirke and Srija 2014). Additionally, investors in India cite restrictive labor laws as one of the factors that limit employment opportunities for women and discourage the adoption of new technologies, thereby reducing productivity in manufacturing. During 2019-20, India consolidated, rationalized, and simplified several labor laws.

Reforms that promote international competitiveness and reduce barriers to international trade can encourage investment in export-oriented and import-competing sectors (Alfaro and Chari 2014). More generally, reforms to reduce regulations that are unnecessarily cumbersome (for example, those in certain aspects of land acquisition and environmental impact assessments) and to strengthen public-private partnership legislation (for example, consistent regulations and transparent bidding procedures) can foster investment. Strengthening processes for managing public investment, integrating infrastructure projects into budget cycles, and curbing corruption in infrastructure projects will not only improve the quality of infrastructure, but also increase the efficiency of government spending (Ali 2009; KPMG 2015). In several countries in the region, stalled reforms on land acquisition, including those in relation to compensation and environmental clearances, remain an impediment to infrastructure-related private investment.

Reforms to enhance the efficiency of the region's labor markets—encouraging greater female labor market participation, facilitating hiring and redundancy procedures, promoting training and retraining, and reducing taxes on low-paid workers—would increase the mobility and flexibility of the workforce (Shirke and Srija 2014). Should profits and household incomes subsequently rise, businesses will have incentives to expand operations.

Regional integration. Trade within the SAR region is less than a third of its potential, limiting inflows of FDI as well as gains from trade (Kathuria, Yatawara, and Zhu 2021). Security challenges and geopolitical tensions remain obstacles to a more conducive investment climate, especially for cross-border projects that could increase regional economic integration (Dash, Nafaraj, and Sahoo 2014). To create an environment more conducive to higher investment, the region could relax restrictive and opaque regimes governing outward FDI. Decreasing dispute resolution times would also help, as would rationalizing land ownership and sector-specific restrictions. Economies in the region could also facilitate and promote inward FDI by improving cross-border networks and information sharing. This might lift intraregional inward FDI, which currently makes up less than 1 percent of total inward FDI. Finally, digitalization, streamlining border and customs procedures, investing in ports and connectivity, and promoting regional trade agreements could help bring down trade costs, which average the equivalent of 134 percent tariffs in SAR and are the highest among EMDE regions (Ohnsorge, Quaglietti, and Rastogi 2021).

SUB-SAHARAN
AFRICA

Many countries in Sub-Saharan Africa experienced a sharp deceleration in investment following the commodity price collapse of 2014-16. The COVID-19 shock, which caused a significant decline in investment in 2020, halted the rebound that took place in 2018-19. The subsequent recovery has been tepid. SSA countries have some of the largest investment needs among EMDEs. The region needs to close infrastructure gaps, reverse the damage inflicted by the pandemic and the repercussions of the war in Ukraine, reduce vulnerabilities to climate change, and enhance food security. But without meaningful reforms and stronger international support, stronger investment growth will remain very challenging amid increasing public debt and tightening access to external financing.

Introduction

Sub-Saharan Africa accounted for about 3 percent of EMDE investment during 2011-21, with average annual investment growth of 3.3 percent. Following the commodity price collapse of 2014-16, SSA suffered the sharpest slowdown in investment growth among EMDE regions, from an average of 5.9 percent a year in 2011-14 to a decline of 0.3 percent a year in 2015-17, well below the region's long-term (2000-21) average annual growth rate of 4.6 percent. Investment growth picked up to 6.3 percent a year during 2018-19, before the COVID-19 pandemic brought it to a halt. This triggered a 5.8 percent drop in investment in the region in 2020, much larger than the 1.5 percent decline in EMDEs as a whole. The subsequent recovery has been tepid.

Weakness in South Africa and the region's oil exporters, especially Angola and, to a lesser extent, Nigeria, accounts for much of the slowdown in investment growth in SSA since 2014. Even by late 2021, investment in Nigeria and South Africa, the region's two largest economies, was 3 percent and 20 percent lower, respectively, than in 2014. Investment declined in South Africa every year between 2016 and 2020 against the backdrop of a major deterioration in the country's economic performance. In 2011, South Africa accounted for almost a quarter of all investment spending in SSA; by 2020, its share had fallen to about 16 percent. Elsewhere in SSA, investment growth slowed in commodity-dependent economies in the wake of the declines in commodity prices in 2014-16. For the region as a whole, slowdowns in investment growth reflected not only a sharp deterioration in the terms of trade, but also domestic political tensions and fiscal consolidation in several countries to stabilize public-debt-to-GDP ratios. Such increased fiscal stringency was a necessary reaction to the prior buildup of vulnerabilities during the rapid growth of the early 2010s. These included, in particular, rising public debt and widening current account deficits that in part reflected debt-financed surges in public investment.

Since 2020, a rapid buildup of government debt because of the COVID-19 pandemic, renewed fiscal pressures arising from weaker revenue growth and the repercussions of Russia's invasion of Ukraine, and the tightening of global financing conditions have constrained public investment in the region. Although investment is expected to grow at a rate close to its long-term trend in 2022-23, it will be insufficient to meet the region's investment needs, which are the largest among EMDE regions and are estimated to be roughly four times recent infrastructure spending. SSA needs a substantial acceleration in investment, not only in infrastructure, but also in agriculture, health and education, and social protection. An acceleration in investment would also reinvigorate economic growth and reverse pandemic-induced increases in poverty and inequality. Given fiscal constraints, it has become urgent to mobilize alternative sources of funding, including those from the domestic private sector and the international community. Private sector participation in infrastructure projects in the region is growing but remains limited.

To boost both public and private investment, SSA governments need to take action on a wide range of policies. These include efforts to improve tax collection to generate revenue for public investment, improve spending efficiency, enhance frameworks for public-private partnerships to encourage more private sector involvement in infrastructure projects, strengthen the governance and efficiency of state-owned enterprises, advance efforts to deepen regional integration to open opportunities for growth-enhancing intraregional infrastructure projects, and improve the business environment to encourage private enterprise and growth in private investment.

Evolution of regional investment

Extractive industries—minerals, metals, oil, and gas—play an important role in many resource-intensive economies in SSA. The resulting exposure to fluctuations in the global prices of these commodities, combined with the lumpiness of the large capital outlays intrinsic to the exploration-to-production cycles in extractive industries, makes economic growth and investment particularly volatile across the region, especially in SSA's less diversified economies. Foreign direct investment inflows into the region tend to be procyclical and concentrated in extractive sectors, with limited technology transfers or growth spillovers to nonresource sectors. Extractive industries are also a major source of fiscal revenues for many SSA governments, which often struggle to collect tax revenue from nonresource sectors. Surges in public investment, often financed by debt during periods of booming commodity prices, tend to fizzle out quickly when external conditions deteriorate.

For SSA as a whole, investment growth averaged 3.3 percent a year in 2011-21—almost half of its annual average in 2000-08 (figure 4.17.A). Rapid growth in public investment cooled after 2014, and private investment decelerated sharply. For example, investment growth in Ethiopia averaged almost 28 percent a year in 2008-14, driven by exceptionally rapid public investment in infrastructure (World Bank 2015). However,

FIGURE 4.17 **SSA: Slowdown in investment growth**

Investment growth in SSA slowed sharply after 2014 as commodity prices slipped. After a recovery in 2018-19, it turned negative in 2020 during the coronavirus disease 2019 (COVID-19) pandemic. Generally weak investment growth since 2014 reflects a deterioration in terms of trade among commodity exporters, sharply slower GDP growth in SSA's two largest economies, diminished fiscal space, declining external financing, and rising policy uncertainty and insecurity in some countries.

A. Investment growth

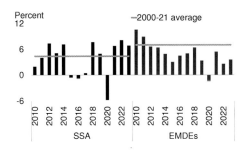

B. Share of SSA EMDEs with weak investment growth

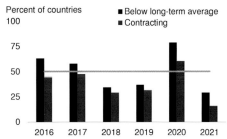

C. Gross foreign direct investment inflows to SSA, excluding South Africa

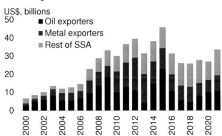

D. General government debt in SSA

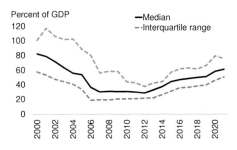

E. Chinese loans to SSA economies

F. International bond issuance by SSA governments

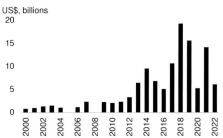

Sources: Boston University Global Development Policy Center; Dealogic; Haver Analytics; International Monetary Fund; United Nations Conference on Trade and Development; World Bank.
Note: EMDEs = emerging market and developing economies; GDP = gross domestic product; SSA = Sub-Saharan Africa.
A. Weighted averages. Includes 98 EMDEs, of which 38 are in SSA.
B. The orange line indicates 50 percent.
D. Median values. Dashed lines indicate interquartile range.
E. Commitments for loans to SSA governments and state-owned enterprises from Chinese commercial banks, government entities, companies, and other financing sources.
F. Last observation is July 2022.

investment growth slowed sharply, to just 9.3 percent, in 2015-21, because of elevated public sector debt, an unfavorable external environment, and rising insecurity. Severe economic slowdowns in the region's two largest economies, Nigeria and South Africa, had adverse spillovers on investment across the region as well. In 2021, investment growth was below its 2000-21 average in almost half of SSA countries and negative in about 16 percent of countries (figure 4.17.B).

Investment fell by 0.7 percent per year, on average, in South Africa in 2011-21, compared with average annual growth of more than 9 percent in 2000-08. This decline reflected a sharp deterioration in the country's economic fundamentals stemming from the lack of policies to tackle underlying structural constraints, including substantial inefficiencies in state-owned enterprises, high unemployment, and the energy crisis triggered by worsening power cuts. Investment by state-owned enterprises has played a major role in South Africa, representing almost 45 percent of all public sector capital expenditure in 2014-20, although this share has declined over time. Much of the recent weakness in public spending on investment can be attributed to Eskom. The latter, a public utility supplying electricity, accounts for about a half of all capital expenditure by state-owned enterprises in South Africa and has had significant governance and profitability problems (Statistics South Africa 2021).

Among oil exporters, investment growth also slowed significantly after 2014 in Angola, Chad, and Nigeria and turned negative in Equatorial Guinea, where oil production fell by nearly 60 percent from 2014 to 2021. Combinations of weak business environments, new capital and foreign exchange controls (Angola and Nigeria), austerity measures to offset falling commodity revenues (Angola, Chad, and Nigeria), and deteriorating security situations (Chad and Nigeria) exacerbated the effects of the sharp decline in oil prices in the mid-2010s. Together, these weighed heavily on investor sentiment. Falling capital spending in the SSA oil sector also reflected a secular decline in oil production because of aging oil fields and increasing production costs. Pandemic-related stoppages, supply chain problems, and maintenance delays further depressed investment in 2020 (Cherif and Matsumoto 2021). Fiscal space also diminished considerably for many of the region's oil producers, with sharp declines in tax revenues from the oil sector, which constrained public investment. Even so, some countries (Cameroon and Gabon) continued large infrastructure investment programs, boosting investment growth despite declining oil industry investment.

Similar to what took place in SSA oil exporters, investment growth in other commodity-exporting countries slowed sharply in 2015-17. Rapidly rising economic imbalances, including increasing private and public sector indebtedness and widening current account deficits, had accompanied strong economic growth during 2011-14. Pressures arising from these imbalances contributed to a broad-based slowdown in investment growth when commodity prices fell during 2015-17. Other contributory factors included a weak economic recovery in the European Union, slowing growth in China, tightening global financial conditions, and a weakening of SSA currencies. China, the United States, and the EU are the region's main sources of foreign investment, which cooled appreciably over the period and accelerated the decline in capital spending. Namibia, which relies on exports of such commodities as gold, copper, and uranium, illustrates these trends. In the early 2010s, investment in Namibia accelerated amid a boom in mining and expansionary fiscal policy. But investment declined in every year between 2015 and 2021 as the government pursued fiscal consolidation to stabilize its debt-to-GDP ratio and as the growth of credit to the private sector slowed sharply (IMF 2019). As a result, investment in Namibia fell from about 36 percent of GDP in 2014 to just 14 percent of GDP in 2021.

Weakening FDI inflows to the region also held back private investment in SSA. FDI inflows to SSA excluding South Africa increased from 1.8 percent of GDP on average in 1990-99 to almost 3.0 percent of GDP in 2000-15. However, they fell back to 2.1 percent of GDP in 2016-20 as commodity prices declined. After falling sharply in 2020, FDI inflows recovered somewhat in 2021 on higher commodity prices and muted global risk aversion, but in relation to GDP, they remained at their lowest level in almost two decades. In U.S. dollar terms, FDI inflows to SSA excluding South Africa in 2021 were still nearly 30 percent lower than in 2015 (figure 4.17.C).

In addition to the unfavorable external environment, the slowdown in investment growth after 2014 also reflected weakening domestic macroeconomic fundamentals and policies and uncertainties related to poor institutional and legal frameworks in some countries. Deteriorating fiscal and external current account positions across the region limited the ability of policy makers in some countries to implement countercyclical policies to support economic activity. In parallel, rising vulnerabilities weighed on capital inflows. Large current account deficits coupled with declining capital inflows put pressure on exchange rates. In several commodity exporters, increases in inflation, in some cases reflecting deep currency depreciations, prompted central banks to tighten policy, making it more costly for firms to invest.

Many countries in the region, particularly those with resource-rich economies, have failed to implement basic reforms to improve the business environment and rule of law. Uncertainty about the enforcement of contracts and property rights and the direction of policies has added to weak capacity for investment planning and execution. These factors have played a significant role in depressing investment across the region.

On the fiscal side, debt-financed public spending on investment failed to sustain investment growth momentum when commodity prices collapsed. In the early 2010s, a favorable external environment, increased financial market access, and growing bilateral lending by China encouraged many SSA governments to scale up public investment to help close large infrastructure gaps. The resulting public investment booms temporarily supported growth in many countries but also resulted in sharp increases in public debt. Indeed, after declining significantly following the IMF and World Bank's Heavily Indebted Poor Countries initiative and the IMF's Multilateral Debt Relief Initiative, public debt in SSA began to rise again in 2013 (figure 4.17.D). As countries shifted toward nonconcessional borrowing, debt-servicing costs rose and currencies depreciated; in some countries, official development assistance declined (Agou et al. 2019).

The COVID-19 pandemic subsequently saw public debt-to-GDP ratios again rise sharply across the region, with many governments making current spending a priority over public investment. General government gross debt in SSA increased by more than 10 percentage points of GDP, on average, reaching 72 percent of GDP in 2020, well above the 64 percent of GDP recorded in other EMDEs. Surging food, fertilizer, and fuel prices, partly owing to Russia's invasion of Ukraine, have heightened fiscal pressures in many countries, constraining the ability of governments to increase public investment. More recently, rising global borrowing costs, coupled with a drop in bilateral lending from China, have tightened access to external finance, posing further headwinds to investment (figure 4.17.E). Indeed, in 2022, international bond issuance by SSA countries fell by more than 60 percent (figure 4.17.F). Although this mirrors the overall trend of weak EMDE bond issuance, SSA had the second-steepest decline among EMDE regions, after the Middle East and North Africa.

Regional investment needs

SSA's strategic priority objectives—to reinvigorate economic growth and reduce poverty—will require investments in agriculture, infrastructure, health and education, and social protection (World Bank 2022g). The COVID-19 pandemic has dealt a serious blow to SSA's progress in the areas of poverty reduction and convergence of its incomes with those in advanced economies, hitting the region's low-income countries particularly hard. Additional financing equivalent to 27-37 percent of SSA's 2022 GDP may be needed by 2025 for SSA to return to its prepandemic path toward convergence of its incomes with those in advanced economies (IMF 2021b).

In *agriculture*, which provides a livelihood for almost two-thirds of SSA's population, investment in both physical capital and technology is needed to raise labor productivity. Increasing investment in agricultural research and development is essential not only for boosting growth in the region, but also for accelerating the transformation of farming in SSA toward more productive and resilient food systems (Fuglie et al. 2020). Infrastructure investment is also needed to support growth in agricultural productivity and export diversification. This includes investment to build or improve irrigation, road, and storage infrastructure and to develop higher value chains in agriculture.

Infrastructure investment more broadly is a key driver of growth in SSA, where it has accounted for more than half of the improvements in economic growth in the last decade (AfDB 2020). Several countries in the region have made progress in improving their infrastructure. Ethiopia and Tanzania, for example, have increased public spending on large infrastructure projects and improved the quality of their existing infrastructure assets, which contributed to their strong prepandemic growth performance.

Across the region, advances in *infrastructure for information and communications technology and connectivity,* primarily reflecting an unprecedented increase in mobile phone subscriptions, have helped move millions of households out of extreme poverty, particularly in rural areas (Bahia et al. 2020; World Bank 2021b).

By contrast, progress in regard to *power infrastructure* in the region has been far more limited, with power shortages and blackouts continuing to constrain economic activity across the region, especially in South Africa. Only about one-half of households have access to electricity in SSA, compared with more than 90 percent worldwide. Deterioration in the quantity and quality of power infrastructure has increased the need for investment in renewable energy. This has the potential to improve access to electricity while addressing climate change challenges.

Transport infrastructure development in the region has also been limited. In many SSA countries, only a small proportion of the road network is paved, and railway development is broadly inadequate. Higher-quality transportation infrastructure will be key to boosting intra-Africa trade, fostering the development of regional supply chains, and enhancing SSA's integration into the global economy. The African Continental Free Trade Agreement could catalyze the modernization of SSA transportation networks and facilitate cross-country cooperation on large intraregional transportation projects. For example, implementation of the agreement could increase demand for intra-Africa freight by more than a quarter, which would require substantial improvement to road and rail connectivity in SSA (UNECA 2022).

The region's annual infrastructure investment needs are estimated at more than 9 percent of GDP—the highest level among all EMDE regions and nearly four times estimated current infrastructure spending in SSA (figure 4.18.A; Fay et al. 2019; Rozenberg and Fay 2019). The gap between needed and actual investment reflects insufficient funding for new projects, limited private sector participation, and inefficient spending on the operation and maintenance of infrastructure assets.

Many of the region's economies rely on official external funding sources—multilateral and bilateral—to help finance investment in infrastructure. Official development finance, led by the World Bank and the African Development Bank, has increased appreciably and is supporting transport and water and sanitation investments in a number of countries in SSA. China has also emerged as a major bilateral source of infrastructure finance, increasingly so in the energy sector, particularly in hydropower-related projects.

Private sector participation in infrastructure investment has also increased recently following a large decline in the mid-2010s. Private participation accounted for nearly one-fourth of infrastructure funding commitments in 2020, compared with just 3 percent on average in 2016-17, with a large share of the investments going to the telecommunications, energy, and transport sectors (ICA 2022).

However, despite improved access to infrastructure financing in the late 2010s, bolstered by increased private sector participation, substantial infrastructure financing gaps remain (ICA 2018). The pandemic has widened these gaps further, while rising global fiscal pressures have decreased multilateral and bilateral lending to SSA. Lending from China has also weakened substantially on growing concerns about mounting public debt and increasing credit risks in SSA.

FIGURE 4.18 **SSA: Investment needs**

Sub-Saharan Africa has relatively high investment needs across a wide range of sectors. Despite some progress in improving infrastructure in the region, SSA continues to lag behind other EMDE regions, especially in energy and transport. It also lags in human capital accumulation.

A. Annual SSA infrastructure spending needs

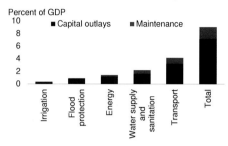

B. Logistics Performance Index

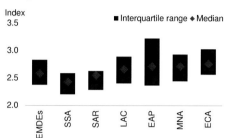

C. Selected health care indicators

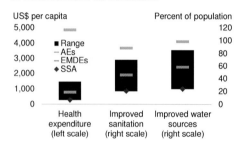

D. Selected education indicators

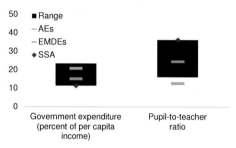

Sources: Haver Analytics; International Monetary Fund; Rozenberg and Fay (2019); World Bank.
Note: AEs = advanced economies; EAP = East Asia and Pacific; ECA = Europe and Central Asia; EMDEs = emerging market and developing economies; GDP = gross domestic product; LAC = Latin America and the Caribbean; MNA = Middle East and North Africa; SAR = South Asia; SSA = Sub-Saharan Africa.
A. Average annual cost of investment over the period 2015-30 in Rozenberg and Fay's (2019) "preferred scenario."
B. The World Bank's Logistics Performance Index measures the performance of trade logistics and is a weighted average of country scores on six key dimensions: customs performance, infrastructure quality, ease of arranging shipments, logistics services quality, consignments tracking and tracing, and timeliness of shipments. A higher value indicates better performance; for example, the index score for Germany, the top performer, is 4.2.
C. Blue bars denote range of unweighted regional averages across EMDE regions. Health expenditure is per capita in purchasing-power parity terms and reflects unweighted averages for 199 EMDEs (47 in SSA) and 34 advanced economies. "Improved sanitation" refers to the percentage of the population with access to improved sanitation facilities and is unweighted averages for 150 EMDEs (47 in SSA) and 33 advanced economies. "Improved water sources" refers to the percentage of the population with access to improved water sources and is unweighted averages for 148 EMDEs (47 in SSA) and 34 advanced economies. Latest data available during 2011-15.
D. Blue bars denote the range of unweighted regional averages across EMDE regions. Government expenditure is per primary student (in percent of per capita income) and reflects unweighted averages for 87 EMDEs (29 in SSA) and 32 advanced economies. "Pupil-to-teacher ratio" is in primary education (on a headcount basis) and is unweighted averages for 165 EMDEs (44 in SSA) and 31 advanced economies. Latest data available during 2011-15.

Across the region, investments are needed to raise the quality of *education and skills*, improve the *health* of populations, and expand access to basic public services, notably sanitation. Despite recent progress, SSA is behind other regions in human capital accumulation, partly because of insufficient spending on investment in education and health (figure 4.18.C and 4.18.D).

Finally, the COVID-19 pandemic has illustrated the importance of *social safety nets* as an effective tool for responding to crises. Investments in social protection could improve economic resilience, reduce poverty, and decrease income inequality across the region. Many SSA governments have achieved some progress in building more responsive, efficient, and inclusive social safety nets. However, population coverage remains low, partly because of the high prevalence of informality, leaving many vulnerable populations exposed to income and consumption shocks, such as those experienced during the recent surge in food and fuel prices.

Regional policy priorities

The COVID-19 pandemic and recent deterioration in the growth outlook for many SSA economies have created formidable challenges to the aim of strengthening the growth of investment, and particularly to the financing of infrastructure investment, in the region. In 2020, many countries diverted already-limited public resources from infrastructure projects to emergency spending on health and support for demand. Lockdowns, travel restrictions, supply chain disruptions, and higher input costs resulted in delays in project preparation and implementation. Since 2021, tightening global financing conditions and investment rating downgrades have raised borrowing costs and complicated access to international financial markets. As a result, funding commitments for infrastructure investment in SSA, after exceeding $100 billion in 2018 for the first time, have declined, leaving many untapped opportunities such as those in regard to renewable energy, climate resilience, digitalization, and agriculture, among others.

On a positive note, innovative solutions for financing infrastructure investment that mitigate key risk factors have been spreading rapidly in SSA. Tools such as blended finance, cofinancing between private investors and development finance institutions, public-private partnerships, and climate finance instruments are being deployed in countries across the region (AfDB 2022).

Nevertheless, financing investment projects in SSA remains challenging. Private investment has become more significant in a broad range of countries, albeit mainly in information and communications technology. Despite the rising importance of private finance (with private funding commitments for infrastructure investment having reached $19 billion in 2020, their highest ever level) and external finance, public sector budgets remain the primary source of funding for infrastructure investment in the region, accounting for more than 41 percent of all infrastructure spending commitments in 2020 (ICA 2022). Countries across the region finance about 65 percent of their infrastructure expenditures using domestic resources. In many of these countries, the fiscal space created by debt relief for heavily indebted poor countries, together with high commodity prices, facilitated these expenditures in the early 2010s. Other countries took advantage of improved access to markets and low interest rates to issue Eurobonds to finance infrastructure in the late 2010s. However, fiscal space has since diminished substantially across the region, both because of the rapid public debt buildup during the COVID-19 pandemic and more recently because of tightening global financing conditions and budgetary pressures to offset surging living costs, especially in low-income countries.

The capacity of countries in the region to use resources effectively for infrastructure investment remains a critical issue as well. The efficiency of public investment in SSA lags that in other EMDEs, reflecting poor project selection; weak enforcement of procurement procedures; failure to complete long-term projects with greater impact; inadequate frameworks for infrastructure policy; and weak capacity to assess key technical, financial, and fiscal risks associated with large-scale projects. These shortcomings point to a need to increase the capacity to scale up investment in public infrastructure.

SSA's infrastructure development faces major geographic and physical challenges, reflecting the region's low population density, low urbanization, large number of landlocked countries, and substantial vulnerability to climate change (Rigaud et al. 2018). Also, the region's sizable number of small countries have difficulty exploiting economies of scale. Adding to the challenges are inadequate trade logistics, which lag those in other EMDE regions. That said, large gains may still be possible through deeper regional integration of transportation and customs infrastructure, including simplification and standardization of regulations and procedures.

Reforms in several policy areas can help address investment needs and ensure sustainable financing:

- *Sustaining public investment.* Domestic fiscal resources—tax and nontax revenues—are likely to remain the dominant source of financing for infrastructure investment. However, the median ratio of tax revenues to GDP is just 12 percent in SSA, compared with 17 percent in other EMDEs. Enhancing domestic revenue mobilization would provide the most sustainable way of financing infrastructure investment. This would require improving tax collection as well as cost recovery. Without enhanced fiscal revenues, scaling up public spending on investment will entail challenging trade-offs to maintain debt sustainability, especially given that in many SSA countries public debt has increased over the past decade and that access to international borrowing has recently tightened substantially.

- *Encouraging greater private sector participation in infrastructure investment.* In 2021, commitments to investment in infrastructure with private participation stood at just 0.3 percent of GDP in SSA compared with almost 0.5 percent of GDP in Europe and Central Asia and Latin America and the Caribbean (World Bank 2021h). Considering SSA's substantial infrastructure gaps, many countries need to expand the pipeline of projects that can attract private investors. Innovative funding and deal structures that employ novel guarantees and risk-sharing mechanisms can be developed. Blended-finance instruments can leverage private sector development financing. Public-private partnerships are a tested strategy that can be applied to numerous sectors. However, SSA has one of the lowest average scores across many dimensions of preparation and management of, and enabling laws and regulations for, public-private partnerships (World Bank 2018g). The terms of public-private partnerships need to be monitored carefully to ensure such partnerships deliver competitive returns and to prevent abuse of market power in circumstances in which natural monopolies are the best way to deliver infrastructure services. Governments can establish autonomous regulatory agencies to oversee private agents accordingly.

- *Strengthening public investment management systems.* Increased capacity in public financial management is critical for scaling up infrastructure investment. Countries can strengthen technical capacity for project selection and appraisal and enhance the monitoring of project execution to minimize inefficiencies and overspending. The fiscal implications of public investment projects, including   public private partnerships, are often not adequately addressed. Fiscal expenditure frameworks need to incorporate contingent liabilities linked to public investments. Failure to do so could raise concerns about the sustainability of public debt. Operation and maintenance expenditures for existing infrastructure can be fully integrated into a medium-term expenditure framework to ensure adequate budgetary resources. Credible long-term national infrastructure strategies can provide signals that increase financing and supply chain capacity, improving delivery prospects. Regrettably, in some countries, policy uncertainties still lead to the selection of low-impact infrastructure projects because of short political cycles.

- *Promoting regional integration of infrastructure.* A regional approach to the provision of infrastructure services is needed to help overcome the region's geographic and physical challenges, which poor transport infrastructure and nontariff barriers to trade often amplify (Gammadigbe 2021). Such an approach will require fostering effective regional institutions, setting shared regional investment priorities, harmonizing regulatory frameworks and administrative procedures, and facilitating cross-border infrastructure projects (Coulibaly, Kassa, and Zeufack 2022; World Bank 2020f). Further reductions in barriers to intraregional trade—both tariff and nontariff, as is intended by the establishment of the African Continental Free Trade Area—can help facilitate intra-Africa trade and provide incentives for stronger cooperation on large intra-SSA infrastructure projects (World Bank 2020a).

References

Ablerola, E., R. Gondo, M. Lombardi, and D. Urbina. 2016. "Output Gaps and Policy Stabilisation in Latin America: The Effect of Commodity and Capital Flow Cycles." BIS Working Paper 568, Bank for International Settlements, Basel, Switzerland.

Acerbi, M., M. Heger, H. Naber, and L. Sieghart. 2021. "Middle East and North Africa: Two Opportunities for Rebuilding after COVID-19 in Green and Inclusive Ways." *Arab Voices* (blog), November 22, 2021. https://blogs.worldbank.org/arabvoices/middle-east-north-africa-two-opportunities-rebuilding-after-covid-19-green-inclusive

Acosta-Ormaechea, S., S. Pienknagura, and C. Pizzinelli. 2022. "Tax Policy for Inclusive Growth in Latin America and the Caribbean." IMF Working Paper 22/8, International Monetary Fund, Washington, DC.

ADB (Asian Development Bank). 2009. *Infrastructure for a Seamless Asia*. Manila, Philippines: Asian Development Bank.

ADB (Asian Development Bank). 2012. *Infrastructure for Supporting Inclusive Growth and Poverty Reduction in Asia*. Manila, Philippines: Asian Development Bank.

ADB (Asian Development Bank). 2017. *Meeting Asia's Infrastructure Needs*. Manila, Philippines: Asian Development Bank.

ADB (Asian Development Bank). 2022. "Mobilizing Taxes for Development." In *Asian Development Outlook 2022: Mobilizing Taxes for Development*. April. Manila, Philippines: Asian Development Bank.

AfDB (African Development Bank). 2020. "The Africa Infrastructure Development Index (AIDI) 2020." Economic Brief, July 2020, African Development Bank, Abidjan, Côte d'Ivoire.

AfDB (African Development Bank). 2022. *African Economic Outlook 2022: Supporting Climate Resilience and a Just Energy Transition in Africa*. Abidjan, Côte d'Ivoire: African Development Bank.

Agarwal, R., V. Balasundharam, P. Blagrave, R. Gudmundsson, and R. Mousa. 2021. "Climate Change in South Asia: Further Need for Mitigation and Adaptation." IMF Working Paper 21/217, International Monetary Fund, Washington, DC.

Aghion, P., A. Dechezleprêtre, D. Hémous, R. Martin, and J. Van Reenen. 2016. "Carbon Taxes, Path Dependency, and Directed Technical Change: Evidence from the Auto Industry." *Journal of Political Economy* 124 (1): 1-51.

Agou, G., C. Amo-Yartey, S. Mo Choi, D. Desruelle, C. Gicquel, T. Lessard, G. Melina, et al. 2019. "Sustainable Development, Sustainable Debt." Conference Paper, International Monetary Fund, Washington, DC.

Aiyar, S., C. Ebeke, and X. Shao. 2016. "The Impact of Workforce Aging on European Productivity." IMF Working Paper 16/238, International Monetary Fund, Washington, DC.

Alfaro, L., and A. Chari. 2014. "Deregulation, Misallocation, and Size: Evidence from India." *Journal of Law and Economics* 57 (4): 897-936.

Ali, A. 2009. "Effects of Corruption on FDI Inflows." *Cato Journal* 29 (2): 267-94.

Amarnath, G., N. Alahacoon, V. Smakhtin, and P. Aggarwal. 2017. "Mapping Multiple Climate-Related Hazards in South Asia." IWMI Research Report 170, International Water Management Institute, Colombo, Sri Lanka.

Ambec, S., M. A. Cohen, S. Elgie, and P. Lanoie. 2013. "The Porter Hypothesis at 20: Can Environmental Regulation Enhance Innovation and Competitiveness?" *Review of Environmental Economics and Policy* 7 (1): 2-22.

Anadon, D. L., and K. Surana. 2015. "Public Policy and Financial Resource Mobilization for Wind Energy in Developing Countries: A Comparison of Approaches and Outcomes in China and India." *Global Environmental Change* 35 (November): 340-59.

Anbumozhi, V., and P. Intal, Jr. 2015. "Can Thinking Green and Sustainability Be an Economic Opportunity for ASEAN?" ERIA Discussion Paper 2015-66, Economic Research Institute for ASEAN and East Asia, Jakarta, Indonesia.

Andres, L., D. Biller, and M. H. Dappe. 2014. "Infrastructure Gap in South Asia." Policy Research Working Paper 7032, World Bank, Washington, DC.

Apedo Amah, M. C., B. Avdiu, X. Cirera, M. Cruz, E. Davies, A. Grover, L. Iacovone, et al. 2020. "Unmasking the Impact of COVID-19 on Businesses." Policy Research Working Paper 9434, World Bank, Washington, DC.

Apergis, N., and C. Tsoumas. 2009. "A Survey of the Feldstein-Horioka Puzzle: What Has Been Done and Where We Stand." *Research in Economics* 63 (2): 64-76.

Araujo, J. T., E. Vostroknutova, M. Brueckner, K. M. Wacker, and M. Clavijo. 2016. *Beyond Commodities: The Growth Challenge of Latin America and the Caribbean.* Washington, DC: World Bank.

Arezki, R., V. Dequiedt, R. Y. Fan, and C. M. Rossotto. 2021. "Liberalization, Technology Adoption, and Stock Returns: Evidence from Telecom." Policy Research Working Paper 9561, World Bank, Washington, DC.

Arons, S. 2022. "Ukraine Reconstruction May Cost $1.1 Trillion, EIB Head Says." Bloomberg, June 22, 2020. https://www.bloomberg.com/news/articles/2022-06-21/ukraine-reconstruction-may-cost-1-1 -trillion-eib-head-says

Azevedo, J. P., A. Hasan, D. Goldemberg, K. Geven, and S. A. Iqbal. 2021. "Simulating the Potential Impacts of COVID-19 School Closures on Schooling and Learning Outcomes: A Set of Global Estimates." *World Bank Research Observer* 36 (1): 1-40.

Bahal, G., M. Raissi, and V. Tulin. 2015. "Crowding-Out or Crowding-In? Public and Private Investment in India." IMF Working Paper 15/264, International Monetary Fund, Washington, DC.

Bahar, D., and M. A. Santos. 2018. "One More Resource Curse: Dutch Disease and Export Concentration." *Journal of Development Economics* 132 (1): 102-14.

Bahia, K., P. Castells, G. Cruz, T. Masaki, X. Pedrós, T. Pfutze, C. Rodríguez-Castelán, and H. Winkler. 2020. "The Welfare Effects of Mobile Broadband Internet: Evidence from Nigeria." Policy Research Working Paper 9230, World Bank, Washington, DC.

Bai, J., E. Brynjolfsson, W. Jin, S. Steffen, and C. Wan. 2021. "Digital Resilience: How Work-from-Home Feasibility Affects Firm Performance." NBER Working Paper 28588, National Bureau of Economic Research, Cambridge, MA.

Baker, S. R., N. Bloom, and S. J. Davis. 2016. "Measuring Economic Policy Uncertainty." *Quarterly Journal of Economics* 131 (4): 1593-636.

Bartlett, W., M. Bonomi, and M. Uvalic. 2022. "The Economic and Investment Plan for the Western Balkans: Assessing the Possible Economic, Social and Environmental Impact of the Proposed Flagship Projects." European Parliament, Brussels.

Batini, N., G. Melina, M. di Serio, and M. Fragetta. 2021. "Building Back Better: How Big Are Green Spending Multipliers?" IMF Working Paper 21/087, International Monetary Fund, Washington, DC.

Baum, A., T. Mogues, and G. Verdier. 2020. "Getting the Most from Public Investment." In *Well Spent: How Strong Infrastructure Governance Can End Waste in Public Investment*, edited by G. Schwartz, M. Fouad, T. S. Hansen, and G. Verdier, 30-49. Washington, DC: World Bank.

Becerra, O., E. A. Cavallo, and I. Noy. 2015. "The Mystery of Saving in Latin America." IDB Working Paper 615, Inter-American Development Bank, Washington, DC.

Benedek, M. D., M. E. R. Gemayel, M. A. S. Senhadji, and A. F. Tieman. 2021. "A Post-pandemic Assessment of the Sustainable Development Goals." IMF Staff Discussion Note 2021/003, International Monetary Fund, Washington, DC.

Bhattacharyay, B. N. 2012. "Estimating Demand for Infrastructure 2010-2020." In *Infrastructure for Asian Connectivity*, edited by B. N. Bhattacharyay, M. Kawai, and R. Nag. Cheltenham, U.K., and Northampton, MA: Elgar.

Bizimana, O., L. Jaramillo, S. Thomas, and J. Yoo. 2021. "Scaling Up Infrastructure Investment in South Asia." IMF Working Paper 21/117, International Monetary Fund, Washington, DC.

Blanco, F., P. Saavedra, F. Koehler-Geib, and E. Skrok. 2020. *Fiscal Rules and Economic Size in Latin America and the Caribbean.* Washington, DC: World Bank.

Brancatelli, C., A. Marguerie, and S. Brodmann. 2020. "Job Creation and Demand for Skills in Kosovo: What Can We Learn from Job Portal Data?" Policy Research Working Paper 9266, World Bank, Washington, DC.

Brichetti, J. P., L. Mastronardi, M. E. R. Amiassorho, T. Serebrisky, and B. Solís. 2021. *The Infrastructure Gap in Latin America and the Caribbean: Investment Needed through 2030 to Meet the Sustainable Development Goals.* Washington, DC: Inter-American Development Bank.

Burunciuc, L. 2021. "How Central Asia Can Ensure It Doesn't Miss Out on a Digital Future." *Eurasian Perspectives* (blog), June 21, 2021. https://blogs.worldbank.org/europeandcentralasia/how-central-asia-can-ensure-it-doesnt-miss-out-digital-future

Bykova, A., and O. Pindyuk. 2019. "Non-performing Loans in Central and Southeast Europe." Policy Notes and Reports 32, Vienna Institute for International Economic Studies, Vienna, Austria.

Calatayud, A., S. S. González, F. Bedoya-Maya, F. Giraldez, and J. M. Márquez. 2021. *Urban Road Congestion in Latin America and the Caribbean: Characteristics, Costs, and Mitigation.* Washington, DC: Inter-American Development Bank.

Calderón, C., E. Moral-Benito, and L. Servén. 2011. "Is Infrastructure Capital Productive? A Dynamic Heterogeneous Approach." Policy Research Working Paper 5682, World Bank, Washington, DC.

Cavallo, E., and T. Serebrisky. 2016. *Saving for Development: How Latin America and the Caribbean Can Save More and Better.* Washington, DC: Inter-American Development Bank.

Cherif, R., and A. Matsumoto. 2021. "Sub-Saharan African Oil Exporters: The Future of Oil and the Imperative of Diversification." Special Series on COVID-19, International Monetary Fund, Washington, DC.

Coulibaly, S., W. Kassa, and A. G. Zeufack, eds. 2022. *Africa in the New Trade Environment: Market Access in Troubled Times.* Washington, DC: World Bank.

Dash, P. K., G. Nafaraj, and P. Sahoo. 2014. *Foreign Direct Investment in South Asia: Policy, Impact, Determinants and Challenges.* New Delhi: Springer.

Dieppe, A., ed. 2020. *Global Productivity: Trends, Drivers, and Policies*. Washington, DC: World Bank.

Dobbs, R., H. Pohl, D.-Y. Lin, J. Mischke, N. Garemo, J. Hexter, S. Matzinger, R. Palter, and R. Nanavatty. 2013. *Infrastructure Productivity: How to Save $1 Trillion a Year*. McKinsey Global Institute.

EBRD (European Bank for Reconstruction and Development). 2014. *Transition Report 2014: Innovation in Transition*. London: European Bank for Reconstruction and Development.

EBRD (European Bank for Reconstruction and Development). 2015. *Transition Report 2015-16*. London: European Bank for Reconstruction and Development.

EBRD (European Bank for Reconstruction and Development). 2017. *Transition Report 2017-18: Sustaining Growth*. London: European Bank for Reconstruction and Development.

EBRD (European Bank for Reconstruction and Development). 2018. "The Western Balkans in Transition: Diagnosing the Constraints on the Path to a Sustainable Market Economy." Background paper for the Western Balkans Investment Summit, European Bank for Reconstruction and Development, London, February 26.

EBRD (European Bank for Reconstruction and Development). 2019. *Transition Report 2019-20: Better Governance, Better Economies*. London: European Bank for Reconstruction and Development.

EBRD (European Bank for Reconstruction and Development). 2020. *Economic Performance of State-Owned Enterprises in Emerging Economies*. London: European Bank for Reconstruction and Development.

ESCAP (Economic and Social Commission for Asia and the Pacific). 2022. *Economic and Social Survey of Asia and the Pacific 2022: Economic Policies for an Inclusive Recovery and Development*. Bangkok, Thailand: United Nations.

Estache, A., and G. Garsous. 2012. "The Scope for an Impact of Infrastructure Investments on Jobs in Developing Countries." IFC Economics Note 4, International Finance Corporation, Washington, DC.

Estache, A., E. Ianchovichina, R. Bacon, and I. Salamon. 2013. *Infrastructure and Employment Creation in the Middle East and North Africa*. Washington, DC: World Bank.

Estevão, M., and S. Essl. 2022. "When the Debt Crises Hit, Don't Simply Blame the Pandemic." *Voices* (blog), June 28, 2022. https://blogs.worldbank.org/voices/when-debt-crises-hit-dont-simply-blame-pandemic

European Commission. 2020a. "Europe's Moment: Repair and Prepare for the Next Generation." Commission Staff Working Document, European Commission, Brussels.

European Commission. 2020b. "Guidelines for the Implementation of the Green Agenda for the Western Balkans." Commission Staff Working Document 223, European Commission, Brussels.

European Commission. 2021a. "Economic Reform Programme of Albania (2021-2023)." Commission Staff Working Document 89, European Commission, Brussels.

European Commission. 2021b. "Economic Reform Programme of Bosnia and Herzegovina (2021-2023)." Commission Staff Working Document 91, European Commission, Brussels.

European Fund for the Balkans. 2021. "Balkans United for Clean Air." Background Knowledge series, April. European Fund for the Balkans, Belgrade, Serbia.

Fay, M., L. A. Andres, C. Fox, U. Narloch, S. Straub, and M. Slawson. 2017. *Rethinking Infrastructure in Latin America and the Caribbean: Spending Better to Achieve More*. Washington, DC: World Bank.

Fay, M., H. I. Lee, M. Mastruzzi, S. Han, and C. Moonkyoung. 2019. "Hitting the Trillion Mark: A Look at How Much Countries Are Spending on Infrastructure." Policy Research Working Paper 8730, World Bank, Washington, DC.

Fernández, A., A. Imrohoroglu, and C. E. Tamayo. 2017. "Saving Rates in Latin America: A Neoclassical Perspective." IDB Working Paper 842, Inter-American Development Bank, Washington, DC.

Ferreyra, M., C. Avitabile, J. Alvarez, F. Paz, and S. Urzua. 2017. *At a Crossroads: Higher Education in Latin America and the Caribbean.* Washington, DC: World Bank.

Flabbi, L., and R. Gatti. 2018. "A Primer on Human Capital." Policy Research Working Paper 8309, World Bank, Washington, DC.

Friedlingstein, P., M. W. Jones, M. O'Sullivan, R. M. Andrew, D. C. E. Bakker, J. Hauck, C. Le Quéré, et al. 2022. "Global Carbon Budget 2021." *Earth System Science Data* 14 (4): 1917-2022.

Fuglie, K. M., A. Gautam, A. Goyal, and W. F. Maloney. 2020. *Harvesting Prosperity: Technology and Productivity Growth in Agriculture.* Washington, DC: World Bank.

Funke, N., A. Isakova, and M. Ivanyna. 2017. "Identifying Structural Reform Gaps in Emerging Europe, the Caucasus, and Central Asia." IMF Working Paper 17/82, International Monetary Fund, Washington, DC.

Gammadigbe, V. 2021. "Is Regional Trade Integration a Growth and Convergence Engine in Africa?" IMF Working Paper 21/19, International Monetary Fund, Washington, DC.

García, J. L., J. J. Heckman, D. E. Leaf, and M. J. Prados. 2016. "The Life-Cycle Benefits of an Influential Early Childhood Program." NBER Working Paper 22993, National Bureau of Economic Research, Cambridge, MA.

Garcia-Kilroy, C., and H. P. Rudolph. 2017. *Private Financing of Public Infrastructure through PPPs in Latin America and the Caribbean.* Washington, DC: World Bank.

Gobat, J., and M. K. Kostial. 2016. *Syria's Conflict Economy.* Washington, DC: International Monetary Fund.

Gómez-Lobo, A., S. S. González, V. G. Mejia, and A. Calatayud. 2022. "Agglomeration and Congestion in Latin America." IDB Working Paper 01324, Inter-American Development Bank, Washington, DC.

Gould, D. 2018. *Critical Connections: Promoting Economic Growth and Resilience in Europe and Central Asia. Europe and Central Asia Studies.* Washington, DC: World Bank.

Government of Bangladesh. 2020. *8th Five Year Plan July 2020-June 2025: Promoting Prosperity and Fostering Inclusiveness.* Dhaka, Bangladesh: Bangladesh Planning Commission.

Government of Ukraine. 2022. "Ukraine Recovery Conference." URC 2022, Lugano, Switzerland, July 4-5.

Gunter, F. R. 2018. "Rebuilding Iraq's Public Works Infrastructure Following the Defeat of ISIS." Foreign Policy Research Institute, Philadelphia, PA.

Hallegatte, S., M. Bangalore, L. Bonzanigo, M. Faye, T. Kane, U. Narloch, J. Rozenberg, D. Treguer, and A. Vogt-Schlib. 2016. *Shock Waves: Managing the Impacts of Climate Change on Poverty.* Washington, DC: World Bank.

Hallegatte, S., and S. Hammer. 2020. "Thinking ahead: For a Sustainable Recovery from COVID-19 (Coronavirus)." *Development and a Changing Climate* (blog), March 30, 2020. https://blogs.worldbank.org/climatechange/thinking-ahead-sustainable-recovery-covid-19-coronavirus

Hallward-Driemeier, M., and G. Nayyar. 2018. *Trouble in the Making? The Future of Manufacturing-Led Development.* Washington, DC: World Bank.

Hallward-Driemeier, M., G. Nayyar, W. Fengler, A. Aridi, and G. Indermit. 2020. *Europe 4.0: Addressing the Digital Dilemma.* Washington, DC: World Bank.

Hansen, T. 2022. "News from the Global Infrastructure Initiative: February 2022." McKinsey Global Institute.

Harake, W., and C. Kostopoulos. 2018. *Strategic Assessment: A Capital Investment Plan for Lebanon; Investment Opportunities and Reforms.* Washington, DC: World Bank.

Heger, M. P., L. Vashold, A. Palacios, M. Alahmadi, M. Bromhead, and M. Acerbi. 2022. *Blue Skies, Blue Seas: Air Pollution, Marine Plastics, and Coastal Erosion in the Middle East and North Africa.* MENA Development Report. Washington, DC: World Bank.

Henckel, T., and W. J. McKibbin. 2017. "The Economics of Infrastructure in a Globalized World: Issues, Lessons and Future Challenges." *Journal of Infrastructure, Policy and Development* 1(2): 254-72.

Herrera, S., and E. Olaberria. 2020. *Budget Rigidity in Latin America and the Caribbean: Causes, Consequences, and Policy Implications.* Washington, DC: World Bank.

ICA (Infrastructure Consortium for Africa). 2018. *Infrastructure Financing Trends in Africa—2018.* Abidjan, Côte d'Ivoire: Infrastructure Consortium for Africa.

ICA (Infrastructure Consortium for Africa). 2022. *Key Achievements in the Financing of African Infrastructure in 2019-2020.* Abidjan, Côte d'Ivoire: Infrastructure Consortium for Africa. https://www.icafrica.org/en/topics-programmes/key-achievements-in-the-financing-of-african-infrastructure-in-2019-2020

IEA (International Energy Agency). 2022. *The Role of Critical Minerals in Clean Energy Transitions.* World Energy Outlook Special Report. Paris: International Energy Agency.

IFC (International Finance Corporation). 2017. *Climate Investment Opportunities in South Asia: An IFC Analysis.* Washington, DC: International Finance Corporation.

IMF (International Monetary Fund). 2014. *The Caucasus and Central Asia: Transitioning to Emerging Markets.* Washington, DC: International Monetary Fund.

IMF (International Monetary Fund). 2019. "Namibia: Article IV Consultation Staff Report." International Monetary Fund, Washington, DC.

IMF (International Monetary Fund). 2020. "Infrastructure in Central, Eastern, and Southeastern Europe: Benchmarking, Macroeconomic Impact, and Policy Issues." International Monetary Fund, Washington, DC.

IMF (International Monetary Fund). 2021a. "Arab Republic of Egypt: 2021 Article IV Consultation—Press Release and Staff Report." IMF Country Report 21/163, International Monetary Fund, Washington, DC.

IMF (International Monetary Fund). 2021b. "Background Note for International Financing Summit for Africa High-Level Event." International Monetary Fund, Washington, DC.

IMF (International Monetary Fund). 2022a. "2022 Article IV Consultation—Press Release and Staff Report for Bulgaria." IMF Country Report 22/190, International Monetary Fund, Washington, DC.

IMF (International Monetary Fund). 2022b. *Feeling the Heat: Adapting to Climate Change in the Middle East and Central Asia.* Washington, DC: International Monetary Fund.

Inderst, G. 2016. "Infrastructure Investment, Private Finance, and Institutional Investors: Asia from a Global Perspective." Working Paper 555, Asian Development Bank Institute, Tokyo.

Infralatam (database). n.d. Development Bank for Latin America, Inter-American Development Bank, and Economic Commission for Latin America and the Caribbean, accessed July 1, 2022. http://infralatam.info/en/home

ITU (International Telecommunication Union). 2020. "Economic Impact of COVID-19 on Digital Infrastructure." GSR-20 Discussion Paper, International Telecommunication Union, Geneva.

Izquierdo, A., C. Pessino, and G. Vuletin, eds. 2018. *Better Spending for Better Lives: How Latin America and the Caribbean Can Do More with Less.* Washington, DC: Inter-American Development Bank.

Jafino, B., B. Walsh, J. Rozenberg, and S. Hallegatte. 2020. "Revised Estimates of the Impact of Climate Change on Extreme Poverty by 2030." Policy Research Working Paper 9417, World Bank, Washington, DC.

Jesintha, P., and M. Sathanapriya. 2011. "Public Private Partnership in India." *Journal of Management and Science* 1 (1): 61-68.

Kahn, M. E., K. Mohaddes, R. N. Ng, M. H. Pesaran, M. Raissi, and J. C. Yang. 2021. "Long-Term Macroeconomic Effects of Climate Change: A Cross-Country Analysis." *Energy Economics* 104 (December): 105624.

Kathuria, S., R. A. Yatawara, and X. Zhu. 2021. *Regional Investment Pioneers in South Asia: The Payoff of Knowing Your Neighbors.* Washington, DC: World Bank.

Keefer, P., and C. Scartascini. 2022. *Trust: The Key to Social Cohesion and Growth in Latin America and the Caribbean.* Washington, DC: Inter-American Development Bank.

Kheyfets, I., E. Sedmik, M. Audah, L. Gregory, and C. Krafft. 2019. "A New Lens on Education in MENA." In *Expectations and Aspirations: A New Framework for Education in the Middle East and North Africa*, edited by S. El Tayeb El-Kogali and C. Krafft, 67-84. Washington, DC: World Bank.

Kirkpatrick, C., D. Parker, and Y. Zhang. 2006. "Foreign Investment in Infrastructure in Developing Countries: Does Regulation Make a Difference?" *Transnational Corporations* 15 (1): 143-72.

Kohli, H. A., and P. Basil. 2011. "Requirements for Infrastructure Investment in Latin America under Alternate Growth Scenarios: 2011-2040." *Global Journal of Emerging Market Economies* 3 (1): 59-110.

Kose, M. A., F. Ohnsorge, L. S. Ye, and E. Islamaj. 2017. "Weakness in Investment Growth: Causes, Implications and Policy Responses." Policy Research Working Paper 7990, World Bank, Washington, DC.

KPMG. 2015. "Anti-bribery and Corruption: Rising to the Challenge in the Age of Globalization." KPMG International, Amstelveen, Netherlands. https://assets.kpmg/content/dam/kpmg/pdf/2015/09/anti-bribery-and-corruption-survey-2015-KPMG.pdf

Kunzel, P., P. de Imus, E. Gemayel, R. Herrala, A. Kireyev, and F. Talishli. 2019. "Opening Up in the Caucasus and Central Asia: Policy Frameworks to Support Regional and Global Integration." IMF Departmental Paper 18/07, International Monetary Fund, Washington, DC.

Kurowski, C., D. B. Evans, A. Tandon, P. H.-V. Eozenou, M. Schmidt, A. Irwin, J. S. Cain, E. S. Pambudi, and I. Postolovska. 2021. "From Double Shock to Double Recovery: Implications and

Options for Health Financing in the Time of COVID-19." Health, Nutrition, and Population Discussion Paper, World Bank, Washington, DC.

Kyiv School of Economics. 2022. "Damage Caused to Ukraine's Infrastructure during the War Increased to $113.5 Bln, Minimum Recovery Needs for Destroyed Assets Is Almost $200 Bln." Kyiv School of Economics, Kyiv, Ukraine. https://kse.ua/about-the-school/news/damage-caused-to-ukraine-s-infrastructure-during-the-war-increased-to-113-5-bln-minimum-recovery-needs-for-destroyed-assets-is-almost-200-bln/

Lakatos, C., and F. Ohnsorge. 2017. "Arm's-Length Trade: A Source of Post-crisis Trade Weakness." Policy Research Working Paper 8144, World Bank, Washington, DC.

Lange, G.-M., Q. Wodon, and K. Carey. 2018. *The Changing Wealth of Nations 2018: Building a Sustainable Future.* Washington, DC: World Bank.

Lanvin, B., and F. Monteiro, eds. 2021. *The Global Talent Competitiveness Index 2021: Talent Competitiveness in Times of COVID.* Fontainebleau, France: INSEAD.

Le Borgne, E., and T. Jacobs. 2016. "Lebanon: Promoting Poverty Reduction and Shared Prosperity." Systematic Country Diagnostic, World Bank, Washington, DC.

Lee, K., and T. Pang. 2015. "Asia and the Pacific: Health Policy Challenges of a Region in Transition." *Asia & the Pacific Policy Studies* 2 (2): 211-13.

Lee, M., X. Han, R. E. Gaspar, and E. Alano. 2018. "Deriving Macroeconomic Benefits from Public-Private Partnerships in Developing Asia." ADB Working Paper 551, Asian Development Bank, Manila, Philippines.

Li, C., and F. Lalani. 2020. "The COVID-19 Pandemic Has Changed Education Forever. This Is How." WEforum.org, April 29, 2020. https://www.weforum.org/agenda/2020/04/coronavirus-education-global-covid19-online-digital-learning/

Lopez-Acevedo, G., D. Medvedev, and V. Palmade, eds. 2016. *South Asia's Turn: Policies to Boost Competitiveness and Create the Next Export Powerhouse.* Washington, DC: World Bank.

Maino, R., and D. Emrullahu. 2022. "Climate Change in Sub-Saharan Africa Fragile States: Evidence from Panel Estimations." IMF Working Paper 22/54, International Monetary Fund, Washington, DC.

Mani, M., S. Bandyopadhyay, S. Chonabayashi, A. Markandya, and T. Mosier. 2018. *South Asia's Hotspots: The Impact of Temperature and Precipitation Changes on Living Standards.* Washington, DC: World Bank.

Mehar, M. A. 2020. "Infrastructure Development and Public-Private Partnership: Measuring Impacts of Urban Transport Infrastructure in Pakistan." ADBI Working Paper 1149, Asian Development Bank Institute, Tokyo.

Montenegro, C. E., and H. A. Patrinos. 2014. "Comparable Estimates of Returns to Schooling around the World." Policy Research Working Paper 7020, World Bank, Washington, DC.

Muzi, S., F. Jolevski, K. Ueda, and D. Viganola. 2021. "Productivity and Firm Exit during the COVID-19 Crisis: Cross-Country Evidence." Policy Research Working Paper 9671, World Bank, Washington, DC.

Myllyvirta, L. 2020. *Quantifying the Economic Costs of Air Pollution from Fossil Fuels.* Helsinki, Finland: Centre for Research on Energy and Clean Air.

Nataraj, G. 2007. "Infrastructure Challenges in South Asia: The Role of Public-Private Partnerships." ADBI Discussion Paper 80, Asia Development Bank Institute, Tokyo.

OECD (Organisation for Economic Co-operation and Development). 2019a. *Investment Policy Review of Southeast Asia.* Paris: Organisation for Economic Co-operation and Development.

OECD (Organisation for Economic Co-operation and Development). 2019b. "PISA 2018 Results: Combined Executive Summaries; Volumes I, II & III." Organisation for Economic Co-operation and Development, Paris.

OECD (Organization for Economic Co-operation and Development). 2019c. *Public-Private Partnerships in the Middle East and North Africa: A Handbook for Policy Makers.* Paris: Organization for Economic Co-operation and Development.

OECD (Organisation for Economic Co-operation and Development). 2021a. *Multi-dimensional Review of the Western Balkans: Assessing Opportunities and Constraints.* Paris: Organisation for Economic Co-operation and Development.

OECD (Organisation for Economic Co-operation and Development). 2021b. *SME and Entrepreneurship Outlook 2021.* Paris: Organization for Economic Co-operation and Development.

Ohnsorge, F., L. Quaglietti, and C. Rastogi. 2021. "High Trade Costs: Causes and Remedies." In *Global Economic Prospects.* June. Washington, DC: World Bank.

Ohnsorge, F., and S. Yu, eds. 2021. *The Long Shadow of Informality: Challenges and Policies.* Washington, DC: World Bank.

Oxford Economics and Global Infrastructure Hub. 2017. *Global Infrastructure Outlook: Infrastructure Investment Needs; 50 Countries, 7 Sectors to 2040.* https://www.oxfordeconomics.com/resource/global-infrastructure-outlook

Pachouri, A., and S. Sharma. 2016. "Barriers to Innovation in Indian Small and Medium-Sized Enterprises." ADB Economics Working Paper 588, Asian Development Bank, Manila, Phillipines.

Parry, I., S. Black, and N. Vernon. 2021. "Still Not Getting Energy Prices Right: A Global and Country Update of Fossil Fuel Subsidies." IMF Working Paper 21/236, International Monetary Fund, Washington, DC.

Querbach, T., and C. Arndt. 2017. "Regulatory Policy In Latin America: An Analysis of the State of Play." OECD Regulatory Policy Working Paper 7, Organisation for Economic Co-operation and Development, Paris.

Ramirez, M. D., and N. Nazmi. 2003. "Public Investment and Economic Growth in Latin America: An Empirical Test." *Review of Development Economics* 7 (1): 115-26.

Rao, K. D., A. I. V. Ortiz, T. Roberton, A. L. Hernandez, and C. Noonan. 2022. "Future Health Spending in Latin America and the Caribbean: Health Expenditure Projections & Scenario Analysis." IDB Technical Note 2457, Inter-American Development Bank, Washington, DC.

Regional Cooperation Council. 2018. "Study on Climate Change in the Western Balkans Region." Regional Cooperation Council, Sarajevo, Bosnia and Herzegovina.

Rigaud, K., K. de Sherbinin, B. Jones, J. Bergmann, V. Clement, K. Ober, J. Schewe, et al. 2018. *Groundswell: Preparing for Internal Climate Migration.* Washington, DC: World Bank.

Rodríguez-Castelán, C., R. Granguillhome Ochoa, S. Lach, and T. Masaki. 2021. "Mobile Internet Adoption in West Africa." Policy Research Working Paper 9560, World Bank, Washington, DC.

Romer, P. 2016. "To End Poverty, Give Everyone the Chance to Learn." Speech at "End Poverty Day," Dhaka, Bangladesh, October 17.

Rozenberg, J., and M. Fay. 2019. *Beyond the Gap: How Countries Can Afford the Infrastructure They Need While Protecting the Planet.* Sustainable Infrastructure Series. Washington, DC: World Bank.

Santiago, R., M. Koengkan, J. A. Fuinhas, and A. C. Marques. 2020. "The Relationship between Public Capital Stock, Private Capital Stock and Economic Growth in the Latin American and Caribbean Countries." *International Review of Economics* 67 (3): 293-317.

Savedoff, W., P. Bernal, M. Distrutti, L. Goyoneche, and C. Bernal. 2022. "Going Beyond Normal Challenges for Health and Healthcare in Latin America and the Caribbean Exposed by Covid-19." IDB Technical Note 2471, Inter-American Development Bank, Washington, DC.

Schwalb, A., E. Armyra, M. Méndez-Aranda, and C. Ugarte-Gil. 2022. "COVID-19 in Latin America and the Caribbean: Two Years of the Pandemic." *Journal of Internal Medicine* 292 (3): 409-27.

Serebrisky, T., A. Suárez-Alemán, C. Pastor, and A. Wohlhueter. 2018. "Lifting the Veil on Infrastructure Investment Data in Latin America and the Caribbean." IDB Technical Note 1366, Inter-American Development Bank, Washington, DC.

Shepotylo, O., and V. Vakhitov. 2015. "Services Liberalization and Productivity of Manufacturing Firms: Evidence from Ukraine." *Economics of Transition* 23 (1): 1-44.

Shirke, S.V., and A. Srija. 2014. "An Analysis of the Informal Labor Market in India." *Economy Matters.* October. Confederation of Indian Industry, New Delhi, India.

Statistics South Africa. 2021. "Capital Expenditure by the Public Sector for 2020." Statistical Release P9101, Statistics South Africa, Pretoria, South Africa.

Strusani, D., and G. V. Houngbonon. 2020. "What COVID-19 Means for Digital Infrastructure in Emerging Markets." EM Compass Note 83, International Finance Corporation, Washington, DC.

Suárez-Alemán, A., T. Serebrisky, and S. Perelman. 2019. "Benchmarking Economic Infrastructure Efficiency: How Does the Latin America and Caribbean Region Compare?" *Utilities Policy* 58 (June): 1-15.

Syverson, C. 2011. "What Determines Productivity?" *Journal of Economic Literature* 49 (2): 326-65.

Tokuoka, K. 2012. "Does the Business Environment Affect Corporate Investment in India?" IMF Working Paper 12/70, International Monetary Fund, Washington, DC.

Um, P. N. 2020. "Building Forward Better in MENA: How Infrastructure Investments Can Create Jobs." *Arab Voices* (blog), November 4, 2020. https://blogs.worldbank.org/arabvoices/building-forward-better-mena-how-infrastructure-investments-can-create-jobs

UN (United Nations). 2020. *E-Government Survey 2020: Digital Government in the Decade of Action for Sustainable Development.* New York: United Nations.

UNCTAD (United Nations Conference on Trade and Development). 2021. *World Investment Report 2021: Investing in Sustainable Recovery.* New York: United Nations.

UNCTAD (United Nations Conference on Trade and Development). 2022. *World Investment Report 2022: International Tax Reforms and Sustainable Investment.* New York: United Nations.

UNECA (United Nations Economic Commission for Africa). 2022. *Implications of the African Continental Free Trade Area for Demand for Transport Infrastructure and Services.* Addis Ababa, Ethiopia: United Nations.

UNEP (United Nations Environment Programme). 2019. "Air Pollution and Human Health: The Case of Western Balkans." United Nations Environment Programme, Nairobi, Kenya.

UNESCO (United Nations Educational, Scientific and Cultural Organization). 2019. "Combining Data on Out-of-School Children, Completion and Learning to Offer a More Comprehensive View on SDG 4." Information Paper 61, UNESCO Institute for Statistics, Montreal, Canada.

UNESCO (United Nations Educational, Scientific and Cultural Organization). 2020. "Latin America and the Caribbean: Inclusion and Education; All Means All." Global Education Monitoring Report, United Nations Educational, Scientific and Cultural Organization, Paris.

UNESCO (United Nations Educational, Scientific and Cultural Organization) and UNICEF (United Nations Children's Fund). 2021. *Situation Analysis on the Effects of and Responses to COVID-19 on the Education Sector in South Asia: Sub-regional Report.* October.

UNESCO (United Nations Educational, Scientific and Cultural Organization), UNICEF (United Nations Children's Fund), and World Bank. 2021. *The State of the Global Education Crisis: A Path to Recovery.* Washington, DC: World Bank.

USGS (United States Geological Survey). 2022a. "Copper: Mineral Commodity Summaries." United States Geological Survey, Washington, DC.

USGS (United States Geological Survey). 2022b. "Graphite: Mineral Commodity Summaries." United States Geological Survey, Washington, DC.

USGS (United States Geological Survey). 2022c. "Lithium: Mineral Commodity Summaries." United States Geological Survey, Washington, DC.

USGS (United States Geological Survey). 2022d. "Manganese: Mineral Commodity Summaries." United States Geological Survey, Washington, DC.

USGS (United States Geological Survey). 2022e. "Nickel: Mineral Commodity Summaries." United States Geological Survey, Washington, DC.

USGS (United States Geological Survey). 2022f. "Rare Earths: Mineral Commodity Summaries." United States Geological Survey, Washington, DC.

Van Cappelle, F., V. Chopra, and J. Ackers. 2021. "Education for All, Learning for Some: Inequities in Learning Continuity in India, Pakistan & Sri Lanka." 16th UKFIET Oxford Conference on International Education and Development, University of Oxford, Oxford, U.K.

Van Cappelle, F., V. Chopra, J. Ackers, and P. Gochyyev. 2021. "An Analysis of the Reach and Effectiveness of Distance Learning in India during School Closures Due to COVID-19." *International Journal of Educational Development* 85 (September): 102439.

Vashakmadze, E., G. Kambou, D. Chen, B. Nandwa, Y. Okawa, and D. Vorisek. 2018. "Regional Dimensions of Recent Weakness in Investment: Drivers, Investment Needs and Policy Responses." *Journal of Infrastructure, Policy and Development* 2 (1): 37-66.

Vu, H., O. Bizimana, and M. Nozaki. 2020. "Boosting Infrastructure in Emerging Asia." In *Well Spent: How Strong Infrastructure Governance Can End Waste in Public Investment*, edited by G. Schwartz, M. Fouad, T. S. Hansen, and G. Verdier. Washington, DC: International Monetary Fund.

WHO (World Health Organization). 2019. "Primary Health Care on the Road to Universal Health Coverage: 2019 Monitoring Report." Conference edition, World Health Organization, Geneva.

Winkler, D., L. Wuester, and D. Knight. 2022. "The Effects of Russia's Global Value-Chain Participation." In *The Impact of the War in Ukraine on Global Trade and Investment*, edited by M. Ruta, 57-69. Washington, DC: World Bank.

Wolf, M. J., J. W. Emerson, D. C. Esty, A. de Sherbinin, Z. A. Wendling, et al. 2022. *2022 Environmental Performance Index.* New Haven, CT: Yale Center for Environmental Law & Policy.

World Bank. 2000. *Attracting Foreign Direct Investment in Infrastructure: Why Is It So Difficult?* Washington, DC: World Bank.

World Bank. 2006. *India: Building Capacity for Public-Private Partnerships.* Washington, DC: World Bank.

World Bank. 2014. *Turn Down the Heat: Confronting the New Climate Normal.* Washington, DC: World Bank.

World Bank. 2015. *Ethiopia's Great Run: The Growth Acceleration and How to Pace It.* Washington, DC: World Bank.

World Bank. 2016a. *The Commodity Cycle in Latin America: Mirages and Dilemmas.* Latin American and the Caribbean Semiannual Report. Washington, DC: World Bank.

World Bank. 2016b. *Commodity Markets Outlook: OPEC in Historical Context.* October. Washington, DC: World Bank.

World Bank. 2016c. *Doing Business 2016: Measuring Regulatory Quality and Efficiency.* Washington, DC: World Bank.

World Bank. 2016d. *Global Economic Prospects: Spillovers amid Weak Growth.* January. Washington, DC: World Bank.

World Bank. 2016e. *South Asia Economic Focus: Investment Reality Check.* Washington, DC: World Bank.

World Bank. 2016f. *World Development Report 2016: Digital Dividends.* Washington, DC: World Bank.

World Bank. 2017. *Global Economic Prospects: Weak Investment in Uncertain Times.* January. Washington, DC: World Bank.

World Bank. 2018a. *Argentina: Escaping Crises, Sustaining Growth, Sharing Prosperity.* Systematic Country Diagnostic. Washington, DC: World Bank.

World Bank. 2018b. *Dominican Republic: Systematic Country Diagnostic.* Washington, DC: World Bank.

World Bank. 2018c. *Ecuador: Systematic Country Diagnostic.* Washington, DC: Washington, DC.

World Bank. 2018d. *Egypt: Enabling Private Investment and Commercial Financing in Infrastructure,* vol. 2. Washington, DC: World Bank.

World Bank. 2018e. "Expectations and Aspirations: A New Framework for Education in the Middle East and North Africa; Overview." World Bank, Washington, DC.

World Bank. 2018f. *Paraguay: Systematic Country Diagnostic.* Washington, DC: World Bank.

World Bank. 2018g. *Procuring Infrastructure Public-Private Partnerships Report 2018: Assessing Government Capability to Prepare, Procure, and Manage PPPs.* Washington, DC: World Bank.

World Bank. 2019a. *Beyond the Gap: How Countries Can Afford the Infrastructure They Need While Protecting the Planet.* Sustainable Infrastructure Series. Washington, DC: World Bank.

World Bank. 2019b. *Europe and Central Asia Economic Update: Migration and Brain Drain.* October. Washington, DC: World Bank.

World Bank. 2019c. *Global Economic Prospects: Heightened Tensions, Subdued Investment.* June. Washington, DC: World Bank.

World Bank. 2019d. *Mexico: Systematic Country Diagnostic.* Washington, DC: World Bank.

World Bank. 2020a. *The African Continental Free Trade Area: Economic and Distributional Effects.* Washington, DC: World Bank.

World Bank. 2020b. *Europe and Central Asia Economic Update: COVID-19 and Human Capital.* Fall. Washington, DC: World Bank.

World Bank. 2020c. *Global Economic Prospects.* January. Washington, DC: World Bank.

World Bank. 2020d. *Morocco Infrastructure Review.* Washington, DC: World Bank.

World Bank. 2020e. *South Asia Economic Focus: Beaten or Broken? Informality and COVID-19.* Fall. Washington, DC: World Bank.

World Bank. 2020f. *Supporting Africa's Recovery and Transformation: Regional Integration and Cooperation Assistance Strategy—Update for the Period FY21-FY23.* Washington, DC: World Bank.

World Bank. 2020g. *Yemen Dynamic Needs Assessment: Phase 3.* Washington, DC: World Bank.

World Bank. 2021a. *Acting Now to Protect the Human Capital of Our Children: The Costs of and Response to Covid-19 Pandemic's Impact on the Education Sector in Latin America and the Caribbean.* Washington, DC: World Bank.

World Bank. 2021b. *Africa's Pulse: COVID-19 and the Future of Work in Africa; Emerging Trends in Digital Technology Adoption.* April. Washington, DC: World Bank.

World Bank. 2021c. *Bangladesh Systematic County Diagnostic: 2021 Update.* Washington, DC: World Bank.

World Bank. 2021d. *East Asia and the Pacific Economic Update: Long Covid.* October. Washington, DC: World Bank.

World Bank. 2021e. *East Asia and the Pacific Economic Update: Uneven Recovery.* April. Washington, DC: World Bank.

World Bank. 2021f. *Enabling Private Investment in Climate Adaptation and Resilience: Current Status, Barriers to Investment and Blueprint for Action.* Washington, DC: World Bank.

World Bank. 2021g. *MENA Economic Update: Overconfident; How Economic and Health Fault Lines Left the Middle East and North Africa Ill-Prepared to Face COVID-19.* October. Washington, DC: World Bank.

World Bank. 2021h. *Private Participation in Infrastructure (PPI): 2021 Annual Report.* Washington, DC: World Bank.

World Bank. 2021i. *Rebalancing Inclusive and Sustainable Growth to Continue Reducing Poverty in Bolivia.* Systematic Country Diagnostic Update. Washington, DC: World Bank.

World Bank. 2021j. *South Asia Economic Focus: South Asia Vaccinates.* April. Washington, DC: World Bank.

World Bank. 2022a. *Africa's Pulse: Boosting Resilience: Future of Social Protection in Africa.* April. Washington, DC: World Bank.

World Bank. 2022b. *East Asia and the Pacific Economic Update: Braving the Storms.* October. Washington, DC: World Bank.

World Bank. 2022c. *El Salvador: Addressing Vulnerabilities to Sustain Poverty Reduction and Inclusive Growth*. Systematic Country Diagnostic Update. Washington, DC: World Bank.

World Bank. 2022d. *Global Economic Prospects*. January. Washington, DC: World Bank.

World Bank. 2022e. *Global Economic Prospects*. June. Washington, DC: World Bank.

World Bank. 2022f. *Morocco Country Climate and Development Report*. CCDR Series. Washington, DC: World Bank.

World Bank 2022g. *South Asia Economic Focus: Reshaping Norms; A New Way Forward*. April. Washington, DC: World Bank.

World Bank. 2022h. *Syria Economic Monitor: Lost Generation of Syrians*. Washington, DC: World Bank.

World Bank. 2022i. *Two Years After: Saving a Generation*. Washington, DC: World Bank.

World Bank. 2022j. "Ukraine Rapid Damage and Needs Assessment." World Bank, Washington, DC.

World Bank. 2022k. *Vietnam: Country Climate and Development Report*. CCDR Series. Washington, DC: World Bank.

World Bank, European Union, and United Nations. 2020. *Beirut Rapid Damage and Needs Assessment*. August. Washington, DC: World Bank.

World Economic Forum. 2018. *Global Competitiveness Report*. Geneva: World Economic Forum.

PART III

Policies: Recognition, Formulation, and Implementation

Structural reforms, deregulations … are very important in the long term and they will have significant impact for growth potential, but by nature they take time.

Haruhiko Kuroda, 2015
Governor of the Bank of Japan

From globalization to artificial intelligence, powerful forces are driving structural change in developed and developing economies alike.

Michael Spence, 2023
2001 Nobel Laurate in Economics,
William R. Berkley Professor in Economics and Business,
New York University

… though many experts fear that protectionism is undermining globalization, threatening to impede global economic growth, slower growth in global trade may be inevitable, and trade liberalization is decreasingly important.

Adair Turner, 2014
Chair, Energy Transitions Commission,
and Former Chairman of the U.K. Financial Services Authority

CHAPTER 5
Prospects for Potential Growth: Risks, Rewards, and Policies

Growth in potential output around the world slowed over the past two decades. This slowdown is expected to continue in the remainder of the 2020s: Global potential growth is projected to average 2.2 percent per year in 2022-30, 0.4 percentage point below its 2011-21 average. Emerging market and developing economies (EMDEs) will face an even steeper slowdown, of about 1.0 percentage point, to 4.0 percent per year on average during 2022-30. The slowdown will be widespread, affecting most EMDEs and countries accounting for 70 percent of global gross domestic product (GDP). Global potential growth over the remainder of this decade could be even slower than projected in the baseline scenario—by another 0.2- 0.9 percentage point a year—if investment growth, improvements in health and education outcomes, or developments in labor markets disappoint or if adverse events related, for example, to climate change materialize. A menu of policy options is available to help reverse the trend of weakening economic growth, including policies to enhance physical and human capital accumulation; to encourage labor force participation among women and older adults; to improve the efficiency of public spending; and to mitigate and adapt to climate change, including policies related to infrastructure investment to facilitate the green transition.

Introduction

Over the period 2011-21, global growth in potential output declined 0.9 percentage point per year below its 2000-10 average, to 2.6 percent a year on average (chapter 1). The weakening of growth was widespread, occurring in both advanced economies and emerging market and developing economies. The trend decline raises concerns about the underlying strength of the recovery from the pandemic over the next several years. In addition, climate change is expected to increase the frequency of natural disasters, which could additionally weaken global potential growth unless policy action is taken.

Potential output refers to the output an economy would sustain at full capacity utilization and full employment. As discussed in chapter 1, the growth rate of potential output critically determines a wide range of macroeconomic and development outcomes, including sustained improvements in living standards and poverty reduction.[1] In some EMDEs, especially commodity-exporting economies in Europe and Central Asia (ECA)

Note: This chapter was prepared by Sinem Kilic Celik, M. Ayhan Kose, and Franziska Ohnsorge.

[1] Research suggests that differences in average income growth account for two-thirds of cross-country differences in income growth among the poorest households (Barro 2000; Dollar, Kleineberg, and Kraay 2013). Sustained growth can also help reduce inequality, by raising the demand for agricultural output, which helps poor land holders (Christiaensen, Demery, and Kuhl 2011; Pham and Riedel 2019; Ravallion and Datt 2002), and by expanding urbanization, which disproportionately lifts wages for poorer workers (d'Costa and Overman 2014; Gould 2007; Yankow 2006), among other avenues.

and the Middle East and North Africa (MNA), the slowdown in potential growth could set back convergence of per capita incomes with those of advanced economies by more than a decade (figure 5.1). The possibility that the trend decline in potential growth will continue is a major concern in regard to prospects for growth and income convergence in EMDEs and presents a formidable challenge with respect to the international community's ability to meet its broader development goals.

This chapter addresses the following questions:

- What are the prospects for growth in potential output?

- What are the main risks that could lower potential growth?

- What policy options are available to lift potential growth?

To help answer these questions, this chapter employs estimates of potential growth in a large sample of countries from the comprehensive database presented in chapter 1. For clarity, and in keeping with a longer-term focus, the chapter uses the production function approach, whereas other measures of potential growth often incorporate short-term impacts of supply shocks.

Contributions. This chapter makes at least three contributions to the literature on potential growth.

- *Prospects for potential growth.* The chapter presents the first comprehensive set of projections of growth in potential output for the largest sample of countries for which data are available: 83 countries (30 advanced economies and 53 EMDEs) accounting for 95 percent of global GDP. The use of estimates of potential growth based on the production function approach permits a detailed analysis of the structural drivers of potential growth, which in broad terms are total factor productivity (TFP) growth, growth in the supply of labor, and growth in human and physical capital.[2] Since data for many EMDEs before 1998 are inadequate for application of the production function approach, the sample period begins in 2000. This exercise is also conducted at the regional level, with the results presented in chapter 2.

- *Climate change and potential growth.* The chapter analyzes the possible impacts of climate disasters, which are expected to become more frequent because of climate change. It also examines the possible effects investment to alleviate the effects of

---

[2] Much of the previous literature has focused on examining past trends, but not prospects (ADB 2016; Dabla-Norris et al. 2015; IMF 2015b; OECD 2014a). For European countries and member countries of the Organisation for Economic Co-operation and Development (OECD), respectively, the European Commission (2021) and the OECD (2014b) have prepared long-term growth forecasts based on production function approaches. For individual EMDEs or EMDE regions, the World Bank (2018b, 2019b, 2020a, 2021b, 2021c, 2022) has estimated prospects for potential growth. Other studies have used a statistical approach to assess long-term growth prospects for a handful of countries (for example, Modis 2013).

FIGURE 5.1 **Global output growth and relative per capita incomes**

Notwithstanding the strong rebound from the pandemic-induced global recession of 2020, projections for growth's fundamental drivers suggest that global potential growth will slow further in 2022-30 from its rate in 2011-21.

A. Growth in actual output

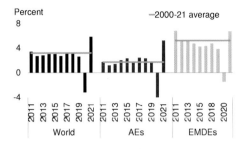

B. Growth in potential output

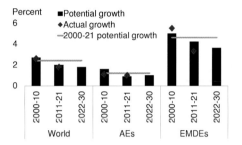

C. Per capita income in EMDEs as a percentage of that in advanced economies

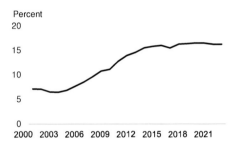

D. Per capita income as a percentage of that in advanced economies, 2022

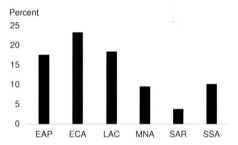

Sources: Penn World Table; World Bank.
Note: AEs = advanced economies; EAP = East Asia and Pacific; ECA = Europe and Central Asia; EMDEs = emerging market and developing economies; GDP = gross domestic product; LAC = Latin America and the Caribbean; MNA = Middle East and North Africa; SAR = South Asia; SSA = Sub-Saharan Africa.
A. Sample of 181 countries.
B.-D. Based on production function approach. GDP-weighted averages for a sample of 30 advanced economies and 53 EMDEs.
C. Per capita income differential between EMDEs and advanced economies is defined as the ratio of the GDP-weighted average percentage of GDP per capita in EMDEs to the GDP-weighted average percentage of GDP per capita in advanced economies.

climate change could have on potential growth. Several studies—reviewed in Shabnam (2014), Klomp and Valckx (2014), and Botzen, Deschenes, and Sanders (2019)—have found mixed evidence regarding both short-term and long-term impacts of natural disasters on incomes and output growth, with possibly larger and more lasting impacts in low-income countries. Broadly consistently with this literature, this chapter documents small, but statistically significant, damage to short-term growth, which dissipates quickly. The chapter goes on to estimate the impact investment to mitigate or reduce the damage from climate change could have on potential growth, drawing on the estimated investment needs presented in chapter 3.

- *Policies to promote potential growth.* The chapter explores, in a consistent framework, policy options to lift growth in potential output. A large literature has considered the impact of different policies and institutional settings on growth, including human capital improvements (World Bank 2018c), governance improvements (World Bank 2017c), trade and integration into global value chains (World Bank 2020b), new technologies (World Bank 2016, 2019a), and labor market changes (World Bank 2013). In contrast to these and other earlier studies, this chapter discusses growth-enhancing policy options in a way that is directly derived from the empirical framework provided by the production function approach, which is used to link policy options to their impacts on growth prospects.[3]

Findings. The chapter presents several findings.

- *Weaker prospects for potential growth.* The baseline scenario projects the slowdown in potential growth in the past two decades, described in chapter 1, will extend into the remainder of this decade. Trends in the fundamental drivers of growth suggest that global growth in potential output will slow further, by 0.4 percentage point a year on average, to 2.2 percent a year during 2022-30. Just under half of this slowdown will be due to demographic factors, including slowing working-age population growth and declining labor force participation as populations age. EMDE potential growth is projected to weaken considerably more, by about 1.0 percentage point a year, to 4.0 percent a year during 2022-30. In advanced economies, potential growth is expected to slow by 0.2 percentage point a year, to 1.2 percent a year, on average, during 2022-30. The slowdown will be internationally widespread: Most EMDEs, as well as economies accounting for almost 70 percent of global GDP, are projected to experience a slowdown in potential growth between 2011-21 and 2022-30. Among EMDE regions, the slowdown will be most pronounced in East Asia and the Pacific (EAP) and ECA because of slowing labor supply, investment, and TFP growth, and least pronounced in Sub-Saharan Africa (SSA), where the multiple adverse shocks of the past decade are assumed to dissipate (chapter 2). Potential growth in Latin America and the Caribbean (LAC), MNA, and South Asia (SAR) is expected to be broadly steady, with strengthening productivity growth offsetting slowing population growth. Global potential growth over the remainder of this decade could be even slower than projected in this baseline scenario—by another 0.2-0.9 percentage point a year—if investment growth, improvements in health and education outcomes, or developments in labor markets disappoint or if adverse events materialize.

- *Sizable impact of climate change on growth in potential output.* Natural disasters, which are expected to increase in frequency because of climate change, could reduce potential growth below the baseline projection. Over the past two decades, the average natural disaster has lowered potential growth in the affected country by 0.1 percentage point in the year of the disaster. However, increased infrastructure

---

[3] Several studies have investigated the link between the growth of output or productivity and structural reforms, focusing on the near-term benefits (Prati, Onorato, and Papageorgiou 2013) or productivity effects (Adler et al. 2017; Dabla-Norris, Ho, and Kyobe 2015). In some of these studies, the sample has consisted mostly of advanced economies (Banerji et al. 2017; de Haan and Wiese 2022; IMF 2015b, 2016a).

investment to alleviate the effects of climate change could more than offset this damage. For example, the literature review in chapter 3 summarizes estimates of climate-related investment needs averaging 2.3 percentage points of GDP per year; for EMDEs, this is equivalent to about one-third of the investment boost if they repeated their best 10-year investment performance. Such additional investment over the remainder of this decade could raise global potential growth by 0.1 percentage point a year and EMDE potential growth by 0.3 percentage point.

- *Policies supporting potential growth.* A number of policies could help reverse the projected further weakening of global potential growth and return it to its 2011-21 average rate. Reforms associated with higher investment in physical capital, enhanced human capital, and faster growth in the supply of labor could raise potential growth by 0.7 percentage point a year in 2022-30, both globally and in EMDEs. This increase would offset the 0.4 percentage-point decline in global potential growth between 2011-21 and 2022-30 projected in the baseline scenario and most of the 1.0 percentage-point slowdown projected for EMDEs. The policy options considered here could raise potential growth even more in EAP, ECA, and SSA, where large investment needs remain or where countries have strong track records of boosting investment.

Building on the analysis in chapter 1, the next section examines prospects for potential growth and is followed by a section discussing risks to prospects for potential growth, including those from climate change. The chapter's penultimate section reviews a wide range of policy options to raise potential growth. The final section provides a summary and suggests avenues for future research.

Prospects for potential growth

Factors weighing on potential growth over the last decade are likely to persist in the remainder of the current decade. This chapter estimates prospects for potential growth for a sample of 30 advanced economies and 53 EMDEs, unless otherwise specified (table 5.1). Demographic trends are expected to remain unfavorable, weighing on potential growth even while trend improvements in human capital investment and female labor force participation are expected to continue. Although growth of fixed investment is expected to pick up slightly in advanced economies from its prepandemic rates, it is unlikely to return to the rates seen in 2000-10, and in EMDEs it is expected to remain weak. Short of possible surges in productivity growth not assumed in the projections— which could occur as a result of technological breakthroughs or the exit of unproductive firms following the disruptions of the pandemic—these trends imply an outlook of mediocre potential growth.[4]

---

[4] Some studies dealing with individual advanced economies have suggested that the pandemic could have raised aggregate productivity through exit of unproductive firms (Kozeniauskas, Moreira, and Santos 2022; Van den bosch and Vanormelingen 2023).

Design of the baseline projections

The baseline projections presented here apply the production function approach to assumed paths for capital, population, and education and health outcomes. Projections for population-related variables (including age and gender structures of the population, fertility, and life expectancy) are based on UN population projections under assumptions of median fertility, normal mortality, and trend migration. Cohort effects are assumed to remain at their 2021 levels.[5]

Projections assume that education and health outcomes follow their long-term average trends. For example, gender-specific secondary and tertiary *enrollment* rates are assumed to continue rising through the forecast period at the average rates of the past two decades. Economy-wide averages are calculated as the population-weighted averages of these gender-specific rates. Similarly, gender-specific and age-specific secondary and tertiary education *completion* rates are assumed to rise at the average rates over the past two decades. Again, economy-wide averages are calculated as the population-weighted averages of these gender- and age-specific rates. These trends in education and health outcomes drive the projected growth of both TFP and labor supply.

Investment growth in the forecast period, 2022-30, is assumed to match the October 2022 consensus forecasts for each economy for which they are available. For economies for which consensus forecasts are unavailable, investment growth in 2022 is assumed to equal economy-specific long-term average investment growth, while for 2023-30, it is assumed for each economy to be the same as the average for the group—advanced economies or EMDEs—to which that economy belongs.

Evolution of drivers of global potential growth

In the baseline projections, the contributions to growth in potential output of its broad, fundamental drivers—capital accumulation and growth in the supply of labor and TFP—weaken further, except for the contribution of capital accumulation in advanced economies (figure 5.2). In the Group of Seven (G7), the seven largest advanced economies (Canada, France, Germany, Italy, Japan, the United Kingdom, and the United States), capital accumulation is expected to tick up over the remainder of the decade as major government investment plans get under way. In other advanced economies, capital accumulation is expected to remain stable and somewhat higher than in G7 countries.

Globally, faster capital accumulation in advanced economies is expected to offset slower capital accumulation in EMDEs, especially in China. In China, the policy-promoted shift away from investment-driven growth is assumed to continue. In EMDEs other than China, the pace of capital accumulation is projected to remain broadly steady.

---

[5] Cohort effects refer to systematically different labor market participation rates among different cohorts of workers over their life cycles (Balleer, Gomez-Salvador, and Turunen 2014; Kudlyak 2013).

FIGURE 5.2 **Contributions to potential growth**

All drivers of potential growth (except investment in G7 countries and TFP growth in EMDEs other than China) point to slower potential growth over 2022-30 than in 2011-21.

A. Contributions to potential growth

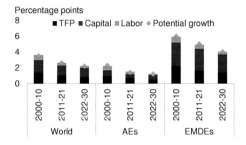

B. Contributions to potential growth in EMDEs

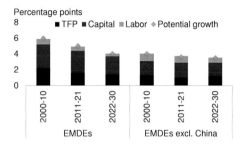

C. Contributions to potential growth in G7 and EM7

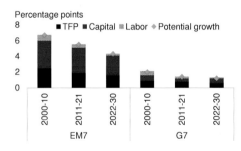

D. Contributions to potential growth in EMDE commodity exporters and non-commodity exporters

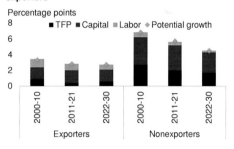

Sources: Penn World Table; World Bank.
Note: AEs = advanced economies; EMDEs = emerging market and developing economies; EM7 = seven largest emerging markets; excl. = excluding; G7 = Group of Seven; GDP = gross domestic product; TFP = total factor productivity. Based on production function approach, figure presents GDP-weighted arithmetic averages for a sample of 30 advanced economies and 53 EMDEs. "G7" is the GDP-weighted arithmetic average of values for Canada, France, Germany, Italy, Japan, the United Kingdom, and the United States. "EM7" is the GDP-weighted arithmetic average of values for Brazil, China, India, Indonesia, Mexico, and Türkiye. Data for 2022-30 are projections.

Subdued investment growth in China and reduced room for catch-up productivity growth in EMDEs as per capita income differentials narrow will sap EMDE productivity growth (figure 5.3). EMDEs excluding China start the period 2022-30 with per capita incomes averaging 14 percent of those in advanced economies, about 1 percentage point higher than in 2009. On the other hand, recoveries in TFP growth are assumed for those EMDEs, especially in LAC and SSA, that were hardest hit by adverse shocks, such as debt crises or natural disasters, in the past decade. These shocks reduced TFP growth to nil or even negative rates but, as they dissipate, TFP growth should recover. On balance, EMDE potential TFP growth is projected to be lower by about 0.2 percentage point per year over 2022-30 than over 2011-21.

Even if education and health outcomes continue to improve in line with their long-term trends, as assumed, slowing working-age population growth combined with withdrawal

FIGURE 5.3 **Total factor productivity growth**

Subdued investment, along with a slowdown in catch-up productivity growth in EMDEs as per capita income differentials narrow, is expected to sap productivity growth in 2022-30. Especially in LAC, SAR, and SSA, however, the effects of natural disasters and financial crises that weighed on productivity during 2011-21 are assumed to dissipate.

A. Average TFP growth

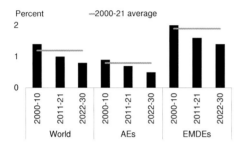

B. Share of economies and GDP with TFP growth below the average for the previous decade

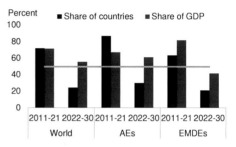

C. Per capita income as a percentage of that in advanced economies in 2000, 2009, and 2021

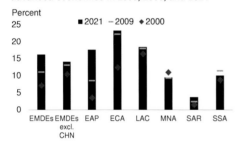

D. Average number of climate disasters and financial crises per year

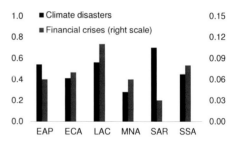

Sources: Centre for Research on the Epidemiology of Disaster, EM-DAT: The International Disaster Database; Penn World Table; World Bank.
Note: AEs = advanced economies; EAP = East Asia and Pacific; ECA = Europe and Central Asia; EMDEs = emerging market and developing economies; excl. = excluding; GDP = gross domestic product; LAC = Latin America and the Caribbean; MNA = Middle East and North Africa; SAR = South Asia; SSA = Sub-Saharan Africa; TFP = total factor productivity.
A. GDP-weighted arithmetic average of total factor productivity growth. Includes 30 advanced economies and 53 EMDEs.
B. Number of economies among 30 advanced economies and 53 EMDEs with lower growth of total factor productivity than the average for the previous decade.
C. GDP-weighted average of GDP per capita differential with advanced economies between 2009 and 2021, in percent of per capita incomes in advanced economies.
D. Simple average of number of climate disasters (1980-2018) and financial crises (1980-2018) per year in each region.

from the labor market among older cohorts of workers could reduce both global and EMDE potential growth by another 0.2 percentage point a year on average in 2022-30 relative to 2011-21 (figure 5.4).

Global prospects for potential growth

Absent unexpectedly favorable or adverse developments—such as significant productivity breakthroughs or natural disasters related to climate change—the baseline projects global potential growth in 2022-30 to weaken by 0.4 percentage point a year

FIGURE 5.4 **Demographics**

Aging populations combined with withdrawal from the labor market by older cohorts of workers could reduce global potential growth. That said, in advanced economies, migration could dampen the slowdown in potential growth by supporting labor force growth.

A. Impact on growth in per capita GDP of 1 percentage-point increase in share of working-age population

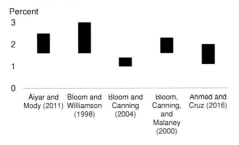

B. Working-age population

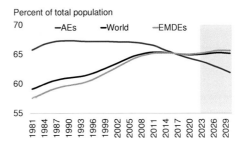

C. Working-age population

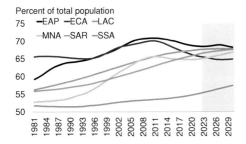

D. Potential growth and demographic trends

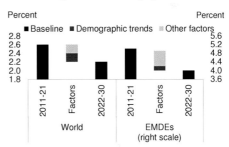

Sources: UN (2022); World Bank.
Note: AEs = advanced economies; EAP = East Asia and Pacific; ECA = Europe and Central Asia; EMDEs = emerging market and developing economies; GDP = gross domestic product; LAC = Latin America and the Caribbean; MNA = Middle East and North Africa; SAR = South Asia; SSA = Sub-Saharan Africa.
A. The sample for each study differs. Aiyar and Mody (2011): Indian states,1961-2001; Bloom and Williamson (1998): 78 countries, 1965-90; Bloom and Canning (2004): more than 70 countries, 1965-95; Bloom, Canning, and Malaney (2000): 70 countries, 1965-90; Ahmed and Cruz (2016): 160 countries, 1960-2010. Bars show range of estimates.
B.C. Population-weighted averages. The working-age population is defined as people aged 15-64 years.
D. GDP-weighted arithmetic averages derived using production function-based potential growth. "Other factors" reflects declining population growth, convergence-related productivity growth, policy changes, cohort effects, and a slowdown in investment growth relative to output growth. "Factors" reflects the percentage-point changes between the averages for 2011-21 and 2022-30.

relative to that in 2011-21, to 2.2 percent a year (figure 5.5). Potential growth is projected to slow in almost one-half of economies globally and more than one-third of advanced economies, accounting, respectively, for 70 percent of global GDP and 66 percent of advanced-economy GDP. More than one-half of the sample's EMDEs, accounting for 77 percent of EMDE output, are expected to experience slower potential growth in the remainder of the current decade than they did in 2011-21. Potential growth is projected to increase in, among others, smaller metal and energy commodity exporters, which are expected to benefit from increased investment growth.

FIGURE 5.5 Evolution of potential growth

The slowdown in global potential growth projected for 2022-30 in the baseline scenario cuts across the global economy, advanced economies, and EMDEs.

A. Potential growth

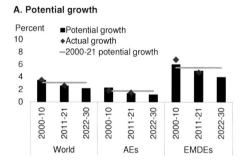

B. Potential growth

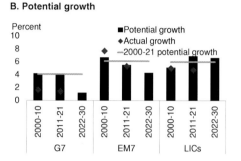

C. Potential growth of per capita output

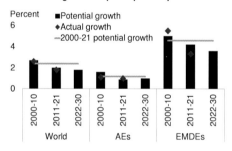

D. Potential growth of per capita output

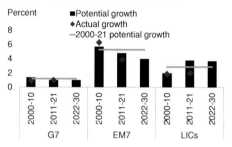

Sources: Penn World Table; World Bank.
Note: GDP-weighted averages based on potential growth derived using production function approach. Data for 2022-30 are projections. AEs = advanced economies; EM7 = seven largest emerging markets (Brazil, China, India, Indonesia, Mexico, and Türkiye); EMDEs = emerging market and developing economies; GDP = gross domestic product; G7 = Group of Seven (Canada, France, Germany, Italy, Japan, the United Kingdom, and the United States); LICs = low-income countries (four).
A.C. Sample includes 30 advanced and 53 emerging market and developing economies.

Growth in potential output in advanced economies is expected to slow by 0.2 percentage point to 1.2 percent a year in 2022-30. A slight pickup in the pace of capital accumulation is expected to partly offset further weakening of both TFP growth and, because of population aging, growth in the supply of labor. The same applies to the G7 countries, where potential growth is also expected to be 0.2 percentage point per year slower in 2022-30 than in 2011-21.

EMDE potential growth is projected to slow by about 1.0 percentage point a year in 2022-30, relative to 2011-21, to 4.0 percent a year. This slowdown mostly reflects demographic developments across most EMDEs and weaker capital accumulation, especially in China, as China's policy-guided decline in investment growth continues. In other EMDEs, capital accumulation is expected to slow only modestly. While China will account for 0.8 percentage point of the 1.0 percentage-point decline in EMDE potential growth, slower growth is projected for most of the EMDEs in the sample, with significant slowdowns expected for some other large EMDEs. These slowdowns could generate adverse spillovers to other EMDEs that the production function approach does not explicitly account for.[6]

Regional prospects for potential growth

Growth in potential output is expected to be slower in 2022-30 than in 2011-21 in three of the six EMDE regions and slower than in 2000-10 in all regions (figure 5.6; chapter 2). Working-age shares of the population are expected to shrink in EAP, ECA, and LAC and to rise in MNA, SAR, and SSA, but with a shift toward older cohorts with weaker labor market attachment in the latter group.

In *EAP*, potential growth is expected to slow as policies in China continue to shift growth away from investment toward more sustainable engines and the growth of the region's working-age population and TFP slows. China's potential growth is expected to slow to just under 5 percent per year on average in 2022-30, well below the average in excess of 7 percent in 2000-21 and within the range of recent long-term growth forecasts.[7] Elsewhere in EAP, potential growth is expected to decline only marginally between 2011-21 and 2022-30 and remain more than 4 percent a year.

In *ECA*, demographic trends and an expected further decline in investment growth are projected to shave off 0.6 percentage point a year from growth in potential output between 2011-21 and 2022-30.

In *SSA*, a modest pickup in TFP growth reflecting accelerated per capita income catch-up after the setbacks caused by multiple adverse shocks over the past decade, including the coronavirus disease 2019 (COVID-19) pandemic, is expected to partly offset slower growth of the labor supply and slower capital accumulation in 2022-30. The projected decline in potential growth in SSA is therefore milder than that in EAP and ECA. South Africa and, in particular, population aging and weak investment growth in that country mainly account for the decline: Elsewhere in SSA potential growth is expected to remain broadly steady, at 4.6 percent a year.

Potential growth in *LAC, MNA,* and *SAR* in 2022-30 is expected to change little, at the relatively weak rates of just above 2 percent per year in LAC and MNA and at a robust pace of more than 6 percent a year in SAR. TFP growth in LAC and MNA is expected to pick up, with the boost reflecting recoveries from the effects of the currency and debt crises of the past decade in some countries and modestly stronger investment growth in others, but diminishing demographic dividends are expected to offset this boost. The contribution of capital accumulation to potential growth in LAC and MNA is expected

---

[6] For example, a 1 percentage-point decline in growth in the seven largest EMDEs has been estimated to slow growth in other EMDEs by 0.9 percentage point a year over the following three years. A similar-sized decline in G7 growth could have a one-half to three times larger impact than a slowdown in the seven largest EMDEs (Huidrom et al. 2020).

[7] October 2022 consensus forecasts are for GDP growth of 4.1 percent per year in China on average over 2022-30. Rajah and Leng (2022) project growth will slow to the range of 2-3 percent by 2030; the World Economic Forum (2021) forecasts growth of about 5 percent on average over 2022-30.

FIGURE 5.6 Regional growth in potential output

Among EMDE regions, EAP and ECA are expected to experience the most pronounced slowdown in growth of potential output in 2022-30, with rapid population aging affecting both regions and the policy-guided slowdown in investment growth in China a key factor in EAP. In contrast, demographic dividends and catch-up productivity growth are expected to support potential growth in SAR and SSA.

A. Potential growth in EMDE regions

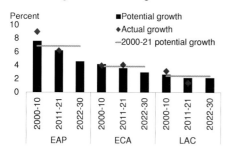

B. Potential growth in EMDE regions

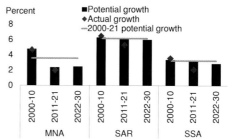

C. Share of countries with potential growth below the average for the previous decade in EMDE regions and the share of regional GDP they represent

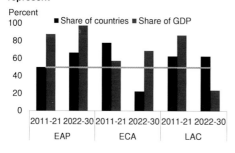

D. Share of countries with potential growth below the average for the previous decade in EMDE regions and the share of regional GDP they represent

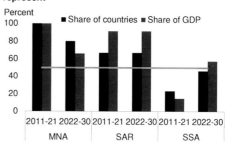

E. Contributions to regional potential growth

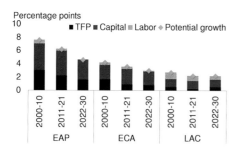

F. Contributions to regional potential growth

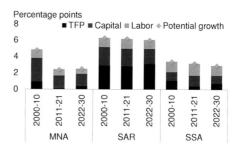

Sources: Penn World Table; World Bank.
Note: EAP = East Asia and Pacific; ECA = Europe and Central Asia; EMDEs = emerging market and developing economies; GDP = gross domestic product; LAC = Latin America and the Caribbean; MNA = Middle East and North Africa; SAR = South Asia; and SSA = Sub-Saharan Africa; TFP = total factor productivity.
A.B.E.F. GDP-weighted arithmetic averages using estimates of potential growth based on production function approach.
C.D. Number of economies and their share of the region's GDP. Sample includes 61 EMDEs. Data for 2022-30 are projections.

to be broadly unchanged, assuming no major intensification of geopolitical risks and uncertainty. In SAR, a pickup in TFP growth related to expected gains in educational attainment and agricultural productivity as well as still-robust growth of investment is expected largely to offset a slowdown in growth of the supply of labor.

Risks to prospects for potential growth: Downside scenario

Several adverse developments could deepen the slowdown in potential growth projected in the baseline scenario. The forecasts for investment growth underlying the baseline scenario could turn out to be overly optimistic. Natural disasters could increase in frequency and cause repeated shocks to output and productivity. A global recession in the near term could cause lasting setbacks to potential growth, in line with historical experience. Finally, policy-induced improvements in such areas as education, health care, and female labor force participation could disappoint. This section examines the implications of each of these downside risks in turn.

If any one of these risks materializes, potential growth could turn out lower than projected in the baseline, by 0.2-0.9 percentage point per year globally and 0.1-0.7 percentage point per year in EMDEs. This would be in keeping with the record of past long-term growth forecasts, which have had a significant optimism bias (Ho and Mauro 2016; Juhn and Loungani 2002; World Bank 2018a).

Investment disappointments

The baseline scenario assumes that investment growth over 2022-30 will match the one- to nine-year-ahead consensus forecasts in October 2022. However, during 2010-22, consensus forecasts overestimated global investment growth over the subsequent 10 years, on average, by 2.4 percentage points per year (figure 5.7).[8] For EMDEs, consensus forecasts in this period overestimated investment growth, on average, by 1.4 percentage points per year, with average forecast errors for ECA and LAC more than twice as large as those for EAP and SAR. Some of the forecast overoptimism reflected a failure to anticipate the global recessions of 2009 and 2020. But even with these two global recessions and their subsequent rebounds excluded, consensus forecasts in 2010-22 overpredicted global investment growth, on average, by 1.0 percentage point per year and EMDE investment growth by 1.4 percentage points per year over the subsequent 10-year period.

To take account of the possibility of forecast optimism in the baseline scenario for 2022-30, a risk scenario is constructed here in which investment growth in every year of the forecast period is reduced from the baseline, for each respective forecast horizon, by the average forecast bias in 2010-22. In this scenario, growth in potential output in 2022-30 is 0.1 percentage point a year lower in EMDEs and 0.3 percentage point a year lower globally than in the baseline.

---

[8] Working-age population growth forecasts have also been shown to be biased (Keilman 2001).

FIGURE 5.7 **Risks to prospects for potential growth**

Consensus forecasts have systematically overpredicted investment growth since 2000. If current forecasts for 2022-30 again turn out to be overly optimistic, potential growth could be lower than projected in the baseline scenario. If trend policy improvements assumed in the baseline do not materialize or if there are more frequent natural disasters or a global recession, potential growth could also be lower.

A. Forecast errors in global, advanced-economy, and EMDE investment growth

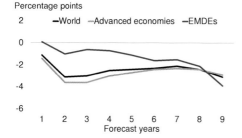

B. Errors in forecasts of investment growth for EMDE regions

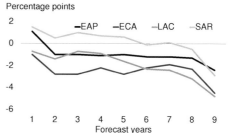

C. Global potential growth, adjusted for risks

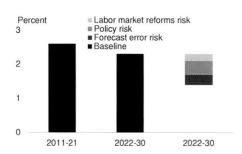

D. Deviation from baseline scenario for EMDE potential growth, adjusted for risks

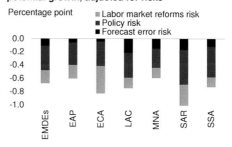

E. Potential growth with more frequent natural disasters

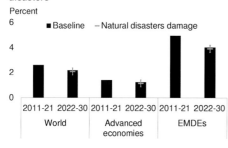

F. Potential growth after a global recession in 2023

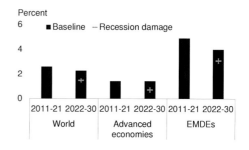

Sources: Consensus Economics; Haver Analytics; World Bank.

Note: EAP = East Asia and Pacific; ECA = Europe and Central Asia; EMDEs = emerging market and developing economies; GDP = gross domestic product; LAC = Latin America and the Caribbean; MNA = Middle East and North Africa; SAR = South Asia; SSA = Sub-Saharan Africa.

A.B. Data for 34 countries, of which 13 are EMDEs (3 in EAP [Indonesia, Malaysia, Thailand], 3 in ECA [Hungary, Poland, Romania], 6 in LAC [Argentina, Brazil, Chile, Colombia, Mexico, Peru], 1 in SAR [India]), since 2000. GDP-weighted averages (at 2010-19 exchange rates and prices). Forecast error is the difference between actual and forecast investment growth; a negative error indicates overoptimism.

C.D. GDP-weighted arithmetic averages. Baseline scenario assumes that investment growth will match consensus forecasts for 1- to 9-year-ahead investment growth for 2022-30. Correction for forecast error risk assumes that investment growth will fall by the country-specific average historical forecast error over 1- to 9-year horizons; correction for policy risk assumes that health and education outcomes will repeat the smallest increase on record over any 10-year period; correction for labor market reforms risk assumes that female labor force participation rate will repeat the smallest increase on record over any 10-year period.

E. Impact of natural disasters assumes that the number of climate disasters in 2022-30 will increase as much as it rose between 2000-10 and 2011-21 for each country, that is, from once every two years to twice every three years, on average.

F. Recession impact based on estimated impact of recessions in annex table 1F.15.

E.F. Orange whiskers display one standard deviation of the impact of climate disasters (panel E) and recessions (panel F).

Climate disasters

Climate change has become an increasingly urgent policy challenge as the frequency and impact of adverse climate events have increased (IPCC 2022). On average over 2000-18, the number of climate disasters—droughts, floods, and storms—per year increased by more than two-thirds over that in the previous two decades (1980-99). Among EMDE regions, storms disrupted economic activity most severely in 2000-18 in EAP and LAC, which have many particularly vulnerable small island states. In LAC, floods also caused notable disruptions of activity in mining and agriculture. Droughts had their most severe effects in ECA and SSA.

The effects of climate disasters on TFP growth estimated by Dieppe, Kilic Celik, and Okou (2020) are used here to construct a scenario representing an increased frequency of climate disasters relative to the baseline. The estimates were derived from a sample of 2,812 climate disasters over 1950-2018, of which 43 percent were floods, 30 percent storms, and 9 percent droughts, in 35 advanced economies and 89 EMDEs. Almost half of the disasters occurred in three EMDE regions: 292 in 8 EAP countries, 479 in 28 SSA countries, and 636 in 20 LAC countries. Each climate disaster is estimated to have reduced TFP growth, on average, by 0.1 percentage point in the year of the disaster.

These disasters had widely varying impacts over the medium term, depending on the speed and magnitude of reconstruction efforts. For example, three years after a climate disaster, TFP growth in countries affected was anywhere between 0 and 10 percent lower than in countries and years without disasters (Dieppe, Kilic Celik, and Okou 2020). Some countries, however, especially small states, have suffered much larger damages than the average effect suggests. The average small state has suffered losses and damages from climate-related disasters of 5 percent of GDP per year, on average (World Bank 2023). These losses have not occurred in a predictable pattern. Instead, it has not been uncommon for damages from a single climate-related disaster to cost a substantial portion of a country's GDP, or even multiples of GDP in extreme cases.

The climate change scenario depicted here assumes that the number of climate disasters in 2022-30 will increase over that in 2011-21 in each country by the same amount as the increase between 2000-10 and 2011-21. On average, this means two disasters every three years in 2022-30, up from one every two years in 2011-21. The negative effect of the greater frequency of disasters on each country's TFP growth is then estimated by multiplying the assumed increase in the number of disasters per year by the average impact of each disaster on TFP growth, as estimated by Dieppe, Kilic Celik, and Okou (2020).[9] In this scenario, both global and EMDE potential growth over 2022-30 would be lower by almost 0.1 percentage point a year than in 2011-21.

---

[9] Natural disasters have implications for output, productivity, and investment. The immediate effect might be damage to existing capital stock, followed by a rapid investment rebound in reconstruction. They tend to have a negligible net effect, as a whole, in the year in which they occur. In contrast, output rebounds tend to be more muted than investment rebounds, such that there are measurable output and TFP losses on an annual basis.

Recessions

With global output growth slowing sharply in 2022-23 amid tightening global financial conditions, there are risks of a global recession and of financial crises in EMDEs in the near term (World Bank 2023). In the past, slowing global growth and rising global financing costs have been associated with a significantly higher probability of currency crises and sovereign debt crises in EMDEs (Koh et al. 2020).

Recessions and financial crises have also been associated with lasting reductions in growth in potential output. Chapter 1 shows that national recessions in the period examined have typically been associated with reductions of about 1.4 percentage points in potential growth even after five years.[10] Based on chapter 1's econometric estimates of the effect over different forecast horizons, recessions in EMDEs in 2023 could lower potential growth over 2022-30 by 0.7-0.9 percentage point per year globally, in EMDEs, and in advanced economies.

Disappointing policies

The baseline scenario in this chapter assumes that education and health outcomes will continue to improve in 2022-30 in line with their country-specific long-term trends. However, improvements in such outcomes slowed over the 2010s (Dieppe 2020). An alternative scenario therefore assumes that such improvements continue, not at their historical average pace, but at the slowest 10-year pace for every country.

Hence, instead of assuming that secondary school completion rates in EMDEs improve, on average, by 12.3 percentage points between 2011-21 and 2022-30, as in the baseline scenario, the alternative scenario assumes that they improve by only 3.4 percentage points. Similarly, in the alternative scenario, tertiary completion rates in EMDEs improve by only 1.4 percentage point in 2022-30 compared with 2011-21, instead of the 4.2 percentage points in the baseline scenario. In advanced economies, secondary and tertiary school completion rates are expected to improve by 10 and 7.2 percentage points, respectively, in the baseline scenario, whereas they would pick up only about half as much in the alternative scenario.

The alternative, less optimistic, assumptions for education and health outcomes make a significant difference in regard to projected growth in the labor supply and TFP over 2022-30. Smaller improvements in life expectancy and education outcomes would discourage labor market participation among older and prime-age workers while encouraging participation of younger workers less markedly. They would also moderately dampen TFP growth. As a result, potential growth in both advanced economies and EMDEs could be slower by 0.4 percentage point than in the baseline scenario.

---

[10] See chapter 1 for a review of the related literature.

Policies to lift potential growth: Upside scenarios

This section uses the production function framework to construct upside scenarios driven by the implementation of policies that improve prospects for potential growth. Potential growth in each upside scenario, in which improved policies generate faster growth of physical or human capital, labor supply, or TFP, is compared with the baseline projections described earlier in the chapter.

Design of an upside scenario

The general approach used in the construction of each upside scenario is to assume, for each economy over the course of 2022-30, for a particular policy-related variable, a repetition of its best 10-year improvement during 2000-21, up to reasonable ceilings (figure 5.8). The potential growth dividend estimated in each scenario therefore depends on each country's track record as well as its room for improvement. The estimates do not take into account possible nonlinearities in reform impacts or possible synergies between different reform measures, so they may be lower bounds of reform impacts.

Investment growth in each economy is assumed to rise over the course of 2022-30 by the most that it increased in that economy in any 10-year period during 2000-21. Such an investment surge would not only boost potential growth but also help countries address needs for investment to adapt to, and mitigate, climate change.

Indicators of educational outcomes—secondary and tertiary enrollment and completion rates—are assumed to rise in each country by the largest improvement that country has experienced in any 10-year period during 2000-21, except that enrollment rates are capped at 100 percent and completion rates are capped at the highest levels observed in advanced economies in 2019, the latest available data point. Life expectancy is assumed to rise in each country by the largest increase in that country in any 10-year period during 2000-21, but not above the median advanced-economy life expectancy in 2019.

For each age group in each country, the female labor force participation rate is assumed to rise by the largest increase in that country over any 10-year period during 2000-21, but not to exceed the male labor force participation rate in the same age group. Separately, a reform to social benefits with labor market implications is modeled. For each gender and each country, labor force participation rates for workers in age groups 55-59, 60-64, and 65 years or older are assumed to rise to the participation rates of age groups that are five years younger, that is, those of age groups 50-54, 55-59, and 60-64 years, respectively. The increase is assumed to occur gradually over 20 years for each gender in each country.

Raising the growth rate and efficiency of physical capital

Scaled-up fixed investment can raise growth in potential output both directly, through the contribution of capital accumulation, and indirectly, by boosting TFP growth, since

FIGURE 5.8 **Policies to strengthen drivers of potential growth**

A major policy effort, on a par with previous achievements, could reverse the weakening of the drivers of potential growth projected in the baseline.

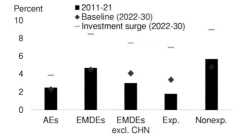

A. Investment growth

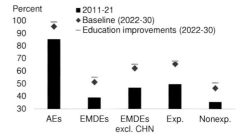

B. Secondary schooling completion

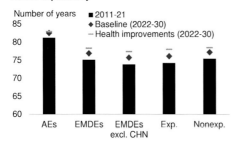

C. Life expectancy

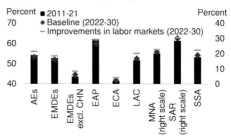

D. Female labor force participation

Sources: Penn World Table; World Bank.

Note: AEs = advanced economies; CHN = China; EAP = East Asia and Pacific; ECA = Europe and Central Asia; EMDEs = emerging market and developing economies; excl. = excluding; Exp. = commodity exporters; LAC = Latin America and the Caribbean; MNA = Middle East and North Africa; Nonexp. = commodity importers; SAR = South Asia; SSA = Sub-Saharan Africa.

A. "Baseline" investment growth assumes investment forecasts from Consensus Economics are realized, and "Investment surge" assumes best 10-year improvement record for each country is repeated.

B. "Baseline" secondary school completion rate assumes trend improvements in education are realized, and "Education improvements" assumes best 10-year improvement record for each country is repeated.

C. "Baseline" life expectancy assumes trend improvements in education are realized, and "Health improvements" assumes best 10-year improvement record for each country is repeated.

D. "Baseline" female labor force participation (LFP) assumes the predicted value for female LFP based on the trend improvements in determinants of the LFPs is realized, and "Improvements in labor markets" assumes best 10-year improvement record in female LFP for each country is repeated.

TFP-enhancing technological progress tends to be embodied in new investment. More efficient investment spending can also raise potential output.

Scaling up investment

UNCTAD (2014) has estimated that achieving the Sustainable Development Goals will require raising global investment needs by up to 3 percent of global GDP. All EMDEs and EMDE regions have sizable investment needs (chapters 3 and 4) that could be filled through either public or private investment or combinations of both, including public-private partnerships. Policies that increase public investment and promote private investment can be effective in supporting aggregate demand and activity in the short term as well as in raising growth in potential output in the longer term (Calderón and Servén 2010a, 2010b, 2014; World Bank 2017b).

Although the rapid increase in public debt over the past decade has constrained fiscal space in most EMDEs, there generally remains scope to shift government expenditures toward productive, growth-promoting public investment and away from less productive spending such as subsidies (World Bank 2017a). In many EMDEs, government revenue ratios relative to GDP remain low, indicating that they could be raised, by expanding tax bases and improving the quality of tax administration, among other measures (World Bank 2015).

In addition, policies can support growth-enhancing private investment. Innovation-promoting investment tends to be low in EMDE firms, partly because of limited availability of complementary inputs such as trained engineers and effective organization techniques (Cirera and Maloney 2017). Policies to expand the supply of complementary inputs and improve management skills could therefore promote private investment, as could improved protection of intellectual-property rights.

If, over the remainder of this decade, each economy raised its investment growth rate by as much as that economy's largest increase over any 10-year interval in 2000-21, investment would rise by 5.2 percentage points of GDP globally and by 7.4 percentage points of GDP in EMDEs over the course of 2022-30.[11] Such an investment boost would raise global potential growth during 2022-30 by 0.3 percentage point per year above its 2011-21 average, almost reversing the 0.4 percentage-point slowdown from 2011-21 in the baseline scenario (figure 5.9). EMDE potential growth would rise by 0.4 percentage point a year, reversing almost half of the slowdown from 2011-21 in the baseline.[12] Over the course of 2022-30, these higher growth rates would cumulate to increase potential output in 2030 by 3.3 percent globally and 3.5 percent in EMDEs relative to the baseline.

A package to adapt to, and mitigate, climate change could be part of such an investment push. Rozenberg and Fay (2019) estimate that to limit climate change to 2 degrees Celsius and stay on track to achieve infrastructure-related Sustainable Development Goals, EMDEs need to raise infrastructure investment by 1.1-3.5 percent of GDP per year just to meet flood protection goals and climate goals in the area of renewable power generation. They would need most of this increase to improve renewable-energy supply

---

[11] Since the investment surge is assumed to cumulate gradually over the period 2022-30, annual average investment growth over 2022-30 (shown in figure 5.8) increases less than the cumulative increase over the whole period.

[12] This impact lies within the range of other estimates. For example, Dinlersoz and Fu (2022) have estimated that China's expansion of infrastructure investment by 16 percentage points of GDP between 2002 and 2016 (about three times the magnitude in the scenario discussed in this chapter) raised output growth by 0.8-2.3 percentage points per year. The lower bound of this range is broadly in line with the estimate derived in this chapter. That said, cross-country estimates yield somewhat larger impacts. For example, estimates by Abiad, Debuque-Gonzales, and Sy (2018) suggest that an increase of 5 percentage points of GDP in infrastructure investment in almost 100 EMDEs during 1960-2017 was associated with output that was up to 6 percentage points higher after seven years, or 0.9 percentage point higher per year on average.

FIGURE 5.9 **Effect of policies on growth in potential output**

A repeat of past major reform efforts could prevent the projected slowdown in potential growth globally and in most EMDE regions.

A. Global potential growth in reform scenarios

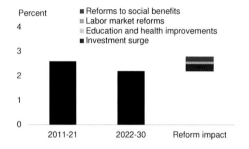

B. EMDE potential growth in reform scenarios

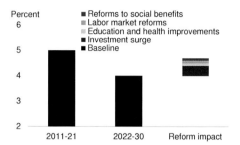

C. EMDE potential growth in reform scenarios

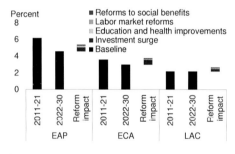

D. EMDE potential growth in reform scenarios

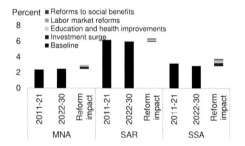

Source: World Bank estimates.
Note: EAP = East Asia and Pacific; ECA = Europe and Central Asia; EMDE = emerging market and developing economy; GDP = gross domestic product; LAC = Latin America and the Caribbean; MNA = Middle East and North Africa; SAR = South Asia; SSA = Sub-Saharan Africa.
A.-D. GDP-weighted arithmetic averages. Scenarios assume a repeat, in each country, of each country's best 10-year improvement.

and energy efficiency, to adopt appropriate standards of coastal protection for cities, and to address increased risks from river floods.

Estimates of investment needs related to climate change have spanned a wide range, as discussed in chapter 3. The World Bank's Country Climate and Development Reports for 13 countries (Argentina, China, Arab Republic of Egypt, Ghana, Iraq, Jordan, Kazakhstan, Morocco, Peru, the Philippines, South Africa, Türkiye, and Vietnam) have estimated these countries' additional needs for investment in these areas. The average of these 13 estimates is 2.3 percent of GDP per year—an estimate that is also approximately the average found in the broader literature review shown in chapter 3. Region-specific climate needs are assumed to be distributed across the six EMDE regions based on the regional distribution in Rozenberg and Fay (2019). An investment boost of this magnitude could raise global potential growth by 0.1 percentage point, EMDE potential growth by 0.2 percentage point, and potential growth in advanced economies by 0.1 percentage point (figure 5.10).

FIGURE 5.10 Effects of climate-related investment on potential growth

A major investment boost to mitigate and adapt to climate change could lift potential growth, especially if efforts to improve infrastructure spending efficiency accompanied it.

A. EMDEs: Potential growth in climate-related investment scenarios

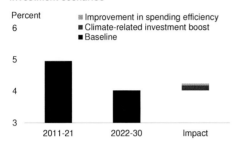

B. EMDEs excluding China: Potential growth in climate-related investment scenarios

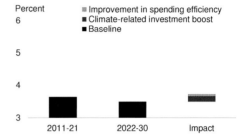

C. EMDEs: Potential growth in climate-related investment scenarios

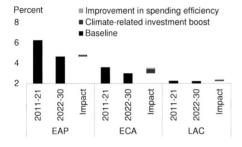

D. EMDEs: Potential growth in climate-related investment scenarios

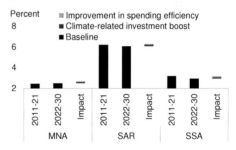

Source: World Bank estimates.
Note: EAP = East Asia and Pacific; ECA = Europe and Central Asia; GDP = gross domestic product; LAC = Latin America and the Caribbean; MNA = Middle East and North Africa; SAR = South Asia; SSA = Sub-Saharan Africa.
A.-D. GDP-weighted arithmetic averages. "Climate-related investment boost" assumes an increase in average annual investment between 2011-21 and 2022-30 of 2.3 percentage points of GDP, in line with the average of the values in the World Bank's Country Climate and Development Reports for 13 countries (Argentina; China; Egypt, Arab Rep.; Ghana; Iraq; Jordan; Kazakhstan; Morocco; Peru; the Philippines; South Africa; Türkiye; and Vietnam). The regional differences are in line with Rozenberg and Fay (2019). "Improvement in spending efficiency" assumes that each quartile of spending efficiency moves two quartiles among emerging market and developing economies (EMDEs).

Improving spending efficiency

Implicit in these scenarios, as well as the baseline scenario, is the premise that any additional investment will be used productively. In the context of EMDEs, particularly, there is evidence that absorptive capacity can limit the success of rapidly scaling up public investment, although less so in lower-income and capital-scarce countries (Presbitero 2016). One study of a large number of road construction projects in almost 100 EMDEs during 1984-2008 found significantly higher unit costs when a project was undertaken during a major scaling up of public investment (Gurara et al. 2021). Another found longer delays in projects undertaken while public investment was being scaled up (Espinoza and Presbitero 2021). It has also been found that investment tends to yield the greatest growth dividends when it eases bottlenecks to growth (Romp and de Haan 2007).

Without complementary policies, investment in climate-related infrastructure, in particular, may benefit potential output less than estimated earlier in this section. The energy transition is likely to require major structural transformation. Government policies that delay or deter reallocation of labor and capital toward green sectors may slow this transformation, reduce the productivity gains from investment, and thus lower its growth dividends. Likewise, a failure to implement such complementary reforms as metering and the enforcement of appropriate payment for energy use could dampen incentives to take up and make the best use of new climate-related investment.

To get a sense of the potential gains from improved investment efficiency, a scenario is estimated here that assumes that the efficiency of investment is improved as follows. Countries are ranked in quartiles based on recent spending efficiency as estimated by Herrera and Ouedraogo (2018). The scenario assumes that countries in the first quartile, with the lowest investment efficiency, raise investment efficiency to the level of those in third quartile; that countries in the second quartile raise investment efficiency to the level of those in the fourth quartile; and that all other countries raise investment efficiency to the level exhibited by the country with the highest spending efficiency. The effect of increased investment on TFP is then scaled up by the increase in spending efficiency.[13] The improvement in spending efficiency is applied only to the climate-related investment boost of 2.3 percentage points of GDP. If the assumed improvement in the efficiency of investment accompanied the climate investment boost, it is estimated that growth in potential output in EMDEs would be raised by an additional 0.1 percentage point per year on average during 2022-30. The impact would vary across countries, with a range from 0 to 0.3 percentage point depending on the initial level of spending efficiency and the magnitude of additional investment needs.

Raising human capital

In the framework used here, human capital has two dimensions: educational attainment and health outcomes (proxied by life expectancy). Policies to enhance human capital can increase not only labor supply, but also TFP. A better-educated and healthier workforce is more securely attached to the labor market and more productive. A better-educated workforce may also be better able to adjust to technological disruptions that reduce employment and wages for workers in certain sectors or with certain skills (Acemoglu and Restrepo 2017a).[14]

Education policies

While secondary school enrollment rates in the average EMDE are near advanced-economy levels, tertiary enrollment rates (46 percent) and secondary and tertiary

---

[13] Implicitly, the baseline exercise captures the "effectiveness" of investment associated with the average spending efficiency.

[14] Such technical disruptions may not have a clear-cut impact on output. For example, in aging societies, technological change that makes certain jobs redundant may relieve pressures from a shrinking labor supply (Acemoglu and Restrepo 2017b, 2017c). But automation may also expand labor demand by creating new tasks for which labor has a comparative advantage (Acemoglu and Restrepo 2016).

completion rates (39 and 8 percent, respectively) in 2011-21 were, on average, less than two-thirds of advanced-economy averages. This indicates the scope for expanding access to education in EMDEs, but increasing the quality of education is also critical to improve education outcomes (World Bank 2018c).

Policies to improve education outcomes are especially important at the current juncture, as school closures caused by the pandemic have resulted in lasting damage to the human capital of a generation of students (Azevedo et al. 2021; Mizunoya et al. 2021; UNICEF 2022). The development of metrics to assess progress toward learning goals is a prerequisite for effective policy actions to improve educational outcomes (World Bank 2018c). At the national level, such actions generally include policies to improve teacher training, increase teacher accountability, and enhance teachers' performance incentives (Evans and Popova 2016).[15] At the student level, policies include efforts to tailor teaching methods to the requirements of students (Kremer, Brannen, and Glennerster 2013), grants to encourage disadvantaged students to attend schools (Glewwe and Maralidharan 2015), and better early childhood nutrition and cognitive development to improve students' capacity to learn (Tsimpo Nkengne, Etang Ndip, and Wodon 2017).

In a stylized policy scenario presented here, education-related policy indicators— secondary and tertiary enrollment and completion rates—are assumed to rise over the course of 2022-30 in each country by as much as their largest improvement in that country in any 10-year period during 2000-21. This means that EMDEs, on average, would raise secondary school completion rates by almost 4 percentage points and secondary and tertiary enrollment rates by 12 and 5 percentage points, respectively, on average, in the remainder of this decade. In EMDEs that have made particularly large strides in improving education outcomes but still have ample room for further improvements, such as those in SAR, secondary school completion rates could rise as much as 20 percentage points in 2022-30, of which 6 percentage points would be due to such reforms. Advanced economies also have room for improvement, especially in higher level of education: tertiary enrollment rates would rise by 11 percentage points, on average, during the next decade, compared with the baseline scenario.

Rapid technological change and greater needs for interdisciplinary skills may also require new strategies for lifetime education and retraining that increase workers' mobility and adaptability throughout their careers. For example, analysis of job postings suggests that a growing number of jobs across a range of industries require soft skills as well as those related to communications and artificial intelligence (Liu and Lyu 2021; Squicciarini and Nachtigall 2021). Hence, an ability to acquire new skill sets may be a critical competency for workers for meeting the demands of future labor markets (OECD 2018).

---

[15] The effects of other measures, such as reducing student-to-teacher ratios or additional years of schooling, have differed widely among countries (Evans and Popova 2016; Hanushek and Woessmann 2008).

Health care policies

Average life expectancy in EMDEs is still lower than that in advanced economies: in 2011-21, it averaged 75 and 81 years in the two groups, respectively. While life expectancy in some EMDEs, particularly in SAR and SSA, has risen significantly—by 4-7 years over the past two decades—it remains about one-fifth below advanced-economy levels in SSA and about one-seventh below in SAR.

Policies to improve public health, and to promote longer, healthier, and more productive working lives, range widely. In many EMDEs, better sanitation and access to clean water remain key to improvements in public health. The communities most affected by poor sanitation tend to be the poorest (Andres 2021). However, high sanitation usage and widespread handwashing must accompany improvements in sanitation to yield health benefits such as lower malnutrition and disease burdens (Carter 2017).

Well-defined and regularly monitored performance indicators can spur improvements in health care provision (Bradley et al. 2010). In countries with higher per capita incomes, better health outcomes have followed comprehensive provision of health care services (Maeda et al. 2014). Programs carefully targeted toward local providers of health services or groups of patients have generated considerable improvements in health care services and outcomes. For example, in Rwanda, performance-based incentive payments helped significantly improve health indicators for children (Gertler and Vermeersch 2012). In India, enhanced training of primary health care providers led to better identification and treatment of ailments (Das et al. 2017).

In a stylized scenario of improved health outcomes discussed here, life expectancy is assumed to rise over the course of 2022-30 in each country by as much as its largest improvement in that country over any historical 10-year period during 2000-21. This would imply an increase in average life expectancy in EMDEs of 1.4 years on top of the trend increase of almost 2 years, on average, but an additional increase of 4 years in SSA.

Effects on potential growth

These stylized scenarios suggest that improvements in education and health outcomes—via their effects on the growth of the labor supply and TFP—could lift EMDE potential growth by 0.1 percentage point a year above the baseline, on average, in 2022-30.[16] In EMDEs with strong track records of, and ample room for, improving education and health outcomes, such as many of those in SSA, such improvements could increase

---

[16] This modest effect is in line with the meta-regression analysis of 57 studies of the link between education and growth by Benos and Zotou (2014). They find an economically small, although statistically significant, link between standardized enrollment rates and growth. The small average effect disguises a wide range of impact estimates that also reflect different quality of schooling (Glewwe, Maiga, and Zheng 2014). The empirical literature on the link between life expectancy and labor supply is even more mixed, with results varying widely depending on country circumstances and the direction of causality debated (Acemoglu and Johnson 2007; He and Li 2020; Desbordes 2011).

potential growth by more than twice as much. In contrast, they would have a negligible impact on potential growth for advanced economies.

Raising growth in the supply of labor

Raising the active share of a country's working-age population, through policies to "activate" discouraged workers or groups with historically low participation rates, such as women and younger or older workers, can increase the country's labor supply in advanced economies and EMDEs, higher labor force participation rates have often followed active labor market policies and reforms to social benefits (Betcherman, Dar, and Olivas 2004; Card, Kluve, and Weber 2010). In contrast, less rigid employment protection regulation and lower minimum wages have had mixed effects on employment and labor force participation and, at times, unintended side effects such as lower labor force participation among disadvantaged groups (Betcherman 2014). In any event, the effects of such policies on output will depend on circumstances and country specifics. For example, de Haan and Wiese (2022) find that labor market reforms in 25 OECD member countries in 1985-2013 were associated with higher output growth only when they were introduced during the periods of expansionary fiscal policy.

Data suggest significant scope for increasing labor force participation, particularly among women and older workers. Globally, average female labor force participation in 2011-21, at 54 percent, was three-quarters of that of men, which stood at 72 percent, and the gap between male and female participation was even larger in EMDEs, at 25 percentage points. Similarly, in both EMDEs and advanced economies, the average participation rate of workers aged 55 years or older was about half that of 30- to 45-year-old workers, and labor force participation among those aged 19-29 years was only four-fifths that of 30-45 year olds.

Raising female labor force participation is a formidable task for policy makers because such participation depends on many factors, including economic structure and its transformation over time (especially shifts toward tradable sectors), as well as social norms and values (Klasen 2019; Erten and Metzger 2019). That said, in EMDEs, policies aimed at other objectives have sometimes raised labor force participation among women and older adults. For example, in Nigeria, improved access to finance and training programs increased female labor force participation by encouraging firm start-ups (Brudevold-Newman et al. 2017). In Uruguay, extension of the school day was associated with higher adult labor force participation (Alfaro, Evans, and Holland 2015). In Colombia and Mexico, subsidized day care was associated with increased female labor force participation (World Bank 2013). In ECA, improvements in health care services for the elderly have helped extend productive life spans, and improved support services for women with families has encouraged female labor force participation (Bussolo, Koettl, and Sinnott 2015). Improved transport and communications, including improved road systems and access to power and telecommunications infrastructure, have also facilitated labor force participation and promoted job creation (World Bank 2013).

The upside scenario explored here regarding labor force participation among older workers assumes a reform to social benefits that gradually raises participation rates in each five-year age group from 55-59 years onward. The scenario assumes that in each country and for each gender, participation rates for workers in the age groups of 55-59 years, 60-64 years, and 65 years or older rise to the rates of the age groups that are five years younger: the age groups of 50-54, 55-59, and 60-64 years, respectively. It assumes that these increases occur gradually over 20 years. Such increases in participation—roughly equivalent to raising the average effective retirement age by five years—would be sizable: for comparison, between 2000 and 2020, the effective retirement age in the average advanced economy rose by 2.4 years for men (and fell in EMDEs for which data are available) and 3 years for women.

In this scenario, global and advanced-economy growth in potential output would rise by 0.2 and 0.3 percentage point a year, respectively, on average, in 2022-30. It would have a smaller effect in EMDEs, at 0.1 percentage point a year. EAP and ECA, the two regions with the most rapidly aging populations, would undergo the largest boosts to growth.

Raising TFP growth

The scenario analysis thus far has considered enhancements to the growth of the factors of production, capital, and labor, and how policy action might bring these enhancements about. But in the framework of the production function, faster growth of TFP, which again can be promoted by policies, can also raise output growth. Policies that improve institutional quality, such as stronger application of the rule of law and better control of corruption; increase political stability; and improve business climates can all raise TFP, by encouraging a shift from informal to more productive formal activities, among other ways. Policies that promote spending on research and development can also raise TFP growth by fostering technological progress.

The literature shows broad consensus that market-friendly institutional reforms have been associated with stronger economic growth, albeit with varying results across countries and disagreements about optimal institutional arrangements (Bluhm and Szirmai 2011; Nawaz 2015; Prati, Onorato, and Papageorgiou 2013). Institutional change can raise investment and productivity growth both directly, by raising private returns to productivity-enhancing investment in human and physical capital, and indirectly, by removing obstacles to other drivers of productivity growth, such as innovation, openness to international trade and investment, competition, and financial development (Acemoglu et al. 2005; Botero, Ponce, and Shleifer 2012; Glaeser et al. 2004; Glaeser, Ponzetto, and Shleifer 2007). Institutional reforms can encourage private sector investment and innovation by establishing secure and enforceable property rights, minimizing expropriation risk, promoting competition and limiting market concentration, creating a stable and confidence-inspiring policy environment, lowering the costs of doing business, and encouraging participation in the formal sector, in which productivity tends to be higher (World Bank 2018a, 2019c).

Poor business climates allow anticompetitive practices to flourish, perpetuate corruption, discourage innovation, and distort the efficient allocation of factors of production (Aghion and Schankerman 2004; Bourles et al. 2013; Buccirossi et al. 2013). Burdensome and unnecessary business regulations can amplify the adverse effect of corruption on productivity (Amin and Ulku 2019). Conversely, good governance ensures competitive and flexible markets with limited market concentration, effective regulation, and the efficient and equitable provision of public services, including health care, education, and public infrastructure (Acemoglu and Johnson 2005; Dort, Méon, and Sekkat 2014; Gwartney, Holcombe, and Lawson 2006).

The fact that, in many EMDEs, institutions and governance remain weak underscores the potential benefits of reforms in these areas (World Bank 2018c). The lack of secure and enforceable property rights, pervasive corruption and crime, and large informal sectors often limit the ability of private firms to invest and innovate and thus the ability of many EMDEs to close productivity gaps with advanced economies. This means that institutional reforms provide considerable scope for EMDE governments to stem and reverse the slowdown in the growth of productivity and potential output.

Reforms of institutions and business climates: Literature review

The literature reviewed in annex 5A indicates that substantial improvements in the quality of regulations, institutions, and business climates have often been associated with significant increases in long-term economic growth.

Regulatory reforms have encouraged the entry of more productive firms, including multinational companies, and stimulated research and development spending (Alam, Uddin, and Yazdifar 2019; Egan 2013). Reforms to increase labor market flexibility have helped improve firm-level productivity, increase labor force participation, reduce informality, and encourage a more efficient allocation of labor (see Blanchard, Jaumotte, and Loungani 2013; Bruhn 2011; La Porta and Shleifer 2014; Loayza, Oviedo, and Servén 2005; and Loayza and Servén 2010). EMDEs with business-friendly regulations have tended to have greater economic inclusiveness and smaller informal sectors and have grown faster (Djankov, McLiesh, and Ramalho 2006; World Bank 2014). Conversely, trade restrictions have been associated with lower firm-level productivity, especially when intrusive domestic industrial policy accompanies them (Topalova and Khandelwal 2011). Weak business environments have also diminished complementarities among public, foreign direct, and domestic investment (Kose et al. 2017). Major improvements in business environments have been associated with increased output growth (Divanbeigi and Ramalho 2015; Kirkpatrick 2014).

A number of factors have affected the impact and success of institutional reforms, including a particular country's stage of development and distance to the technological frontier (Dabla-Norris, Ho, and Kyobe 2016). Thus investment in physical and human capital has often been associated with stronger long-term outcomes when the quality of institutions has exceeded certain thresholds (Hall, Sobel, and Crowley 2010; Jude and Levieuge 2017). EMDEs with stronger institutions and better regulations may have achieved greater output gains from financial liberalization and trade openness (Atkin and Khandelwal 2020; Slesman, Baharumshah, and Azman-Saini 2019; Williams 2019).

Governments have often had an uneven ability to maintain the pace of institutional reforms, in part because the growth dividends from reforms have often materialized with substantial lags and reforms may have initially been unpopular and politically costly, including at election times (Alesina et al. 2020). Major growth downturns have sometimes been associated with subsequent reform accelerations; conversely, growth-enhancing reforms have often been delayed or even reversed during times of economic stress and in economies with high debt burdens (Gokmen et al. 2020; Müller, Storesletten, and Zilibotti 2019). Even during more tranquil times, meaningful reforms have often been postponed or abandoned because of their redistributive effects, including their costs to vested interests (Gradstein 2007).

Reforms to institutions and business climates: Empirical estimation

A local-projections approach is used here to estimate the impact of major, sustained institutional reform advances and setbacks on the growth of TFP and investment in EMDEs. The approach defines sustained institutional advances (or setbacks) as increases (or decreases) in the unweighted average of four indicators from the PRS Group's *International Country Risk Guide*—bureaucracy quality, law and order, corruption, and investment profile—provided the increase (or decrease) is not unwound for at least three consecutive years. The local-projections model estimates the effect of a reform event on the cumulative growth of investment and TFP over horizons of two and four years after the start of the event (annex 5B).

The estimates suggest that reform advances have been associated with significant and, in some cases, lasting increases in the growth of TFP and investment, whereas setbacks have had highly heterogeneous impacts. TFP has been, on average, about 1.9 percent above the baseline two years after reform advances (figure 5.11). Over time, this impact becomes more heterogeneous and more difficult to estimate precisely. By contrast, the impact on investment strengthens over time: four years after reform advances, investment has been, on average, 16-17 percent above the baseline. A wide range of outcomes with respect to TFP have followed sustained reform setbacks. Investment has also evolved in too heterogeneous a manner for a well-defined estimate of the impact but has often fallen well below the baseline over several years.

Reforms to fiscal frameworks

Fiscal reforms can also yield important productivity dividends. Several studies have highlighted the long-term growth benefits of fiscal reforms, especially when fiscal reforms are combined with other structural reforms (IMF 2016b). In OECD member countries, the growth-enhancing effects of a budget-neutral shift in government spending toward health, education, and transport often become apparent after five years (Barbiero and Cournède 2013). On the revenue side, a budget-neutral increase in the efficiency of the tax system could raise long-term growth. The IMF (2016a) found that growth acceleration of more than 1 percentage point a year followed 60 percent of fiscal

FIGURE 5.11 **Institutional reforms**

Past institutional reforms have been associated with higher TFP growth and higher investment growth. Reform setbacks have been associated with a wide range of outcomes, but in many cases, growth of both TFP and investment fell steeply.

A. ICRG indicators around sustained reform advances and setbacks in EMDEs

B. Cumulative change in EMDE investment and TFP two and four years after a sustained change in institutional quality

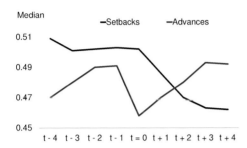

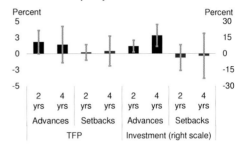

Sources: Penn World Table; World Bank.
Note: Sustained institutional advances or setbacks are defined as increases or decreases, respectively, in the unweighted average of values for four *International Country Risk Guide* (ICRG) indicators—bureaucracy quality, law and order, corruption, and investment profile—provided the increases or decreases are not unwound for at least three consecutive years. Annex 5B details the methodology. EMDEs = emerging market and developing economies; TFP = total factor productivity.
A. Average of value for four indicators: bureaucracy quality, law and order, corruption, and investment profile. *t* = 0 indicates the year when a sustained reform advance or setback started.
B. Sample starts in 1985. Figure shows regression coefficients on TFP and investment growth with dummies for the start of sustained reform advances and setbacks from local-projections estimation for lags of two and four years. Vertical lines show the 90 percent confidence intervals.

reform episodes in 112 countries—such as switching from labor taxation to consumption taxation and shifting spending toward health, education, and infrastructure. Over the longer term, fiscal reforms such as the establishment of fiscal rules have also proven to be growth-enhancing in European Union countries (Afonso and Jalles 2012; Castro 2011; Miyazaki 2014).

Implications of policies in regard to prospects for potential growth

The stylized scenarios presented in the foregoing discussion suggest that a combination of measures—policies to promote investment, better educational and health outcomes, more efficient product and labor markets, an improved business climate, and higher quality of governance—or various subsets of them could more than reverse the projected decline in potential growth in the remainder of this decade. The scenarios with scaled-up physical capital, enhanced human capital, and faster growth of the supply of labor alone are associated, together, with global potential growth that is higher by 0.7 percentage point a year, an increase that is sufficient to reverse the 0.4 percentage-point slowdown projected for 2022-30 (figure 5.9).

Policies could help reverse the projected further slowdown in global potential growth. Reforms associated with higher investment in physical capital, enhanced human capital, and faster growth of the supply of labor could raise potential growth by 0.7 percentage point a year in 2022-30, both globally and in EMDEs. This increase would offset the

0.4 percentage-point decline in global potential growth between 2011-21 and 2022-30 projected in the baseline scenario and most of the 1.0 percentage-point slowdown projected for EMDEs.

One of the options for a major investment boost is climate-related investment, especially if improved spending efficiency accompanies it (figure 5.10). A climate-related investment surge amounting to 2.3 percentage points of GDP alone could raise potential growth globally by 0.1 percentage point per year and in EMDEs by 0.3 percentage point. If improved spending efficiency in EMDEs accompanied the increase in investment, potential growth could rise by another 0.1 percentage point.

Conclusion

Global growth in potential output is projected in the baseline to slow further in 2022-30, by 0.4 percentage point per year from 2011-21, to 2.2 percent per year, with all the main drivers of growth weakening. EMDE potential growth, too, is expected to slow, by 1.0 percentage point per year to 4.0 percent per year in 2022-30. The slowdown would come on the heels of the slowing of potential growth between 2000-10 and 2011-21— globally, by 0.9 percentage point per year. The slowdown in the remainder of this decade could be even more pronounced than projected in the baseline, by 0.2-0.9 percentage point per year, if improvements in education and health outcomes or increases in investment or in female labor force participation, which are assumed in the baseline, fail to occur or if such adverse events as a global recession or more frequent natural disasters materialize.

A comprehensive reform package that replicates past successes could more than reverse the decline in global potential growth projected for the remainder of the 2020s. Such a package could include a boost in investment (for climate-related as well as other purposes); reforms of labor markets, education, and health care; and institutional and business climate reforms.

The design of any reform package should take into account several considerations. First, implementing multiple reforms simultaneously rather than piecemeal can generate mutually reinforcing synergies (annex 5A). For example, in OECD member countries, labor and product market reforms, measures to promote foreign direct investment, and trade liberalization have yielded important synergies (OECD 2017). Also in OECD member countries, labor market reforms have enhanced growth more when combined with an expansionary fiscal stance (de Haan and Wiese 2022). Reforms that are coordinated internationally may also demonstrate cross-country synergies. The potential for growth spillovers puts a premium on reform efforts in advanced economies that can have large beneficial repercussions for their EMDE trading partners.

Second, reform payoffs may take more time to materialize than in the stylized scenarios discussed in this chapter, and they are also likely to depend on the timing of reforms. There is some evidence that well-timed reforms have had the largest growth dividends— at least in the context of advanced economies. For example, labor market reforms may lift growth more during economic upswings or during periods of expansionary fiscal policy, when job entrants can more easily find jobs appropriate to their skills (de Haan and Wiese 2022; IMF 2016a).

Third, reform priorities naturally differ across countries—one of the reasons reform packages have to be tailored to the circumstances and features of individual countries (Dabla-Norris 2016). For example, school enrollment and completion rates in several economies in MNA exceed the EMDE average. However, education reforms continue to be needed to address poor scores on international tests and pervasive skills mismatches in the labor market.

Future research on the questions discussed in this chapter could take several directions, the following among them:

- *Benefits from reforms involving state-owned enterprises.* First, many EMDEs host large state-owned enterprises or poorly regulated private monopolies. Reforms to these entities could trigger increases in productivity as capital and labor are reallocated toward more productive uses. A better understanding of the impact on potential growth for EMDEs (beyond individual case studies) as well as the identification of conducive preconditions and complementary reforms would be helpful.

- *Benefits from improvements of governance and business climates.* Second, many EMDEs have weak governance and business climates. A fuller quantitative assessment of the effects on potential growth of improvements in various dimensions of governance and business climates, including effects that operate through firm productivity and household decisions on labor force participation and informal employment, would also be helpful.

- *Better understanding of longer-term impact of reforms.* Third, the exercises conducted for this chapter rested on as wide a cross-country sample of data as possible, in order to represent the heterogeneity of EMDEs. Data constraints prohibited analysis of developments before 1990. However, for a smaller set of countries, earlier data should be available, which could allow analysis of the longer-term effects of the profound structural policy changes that occurred in the 1970s and 1980s. Analysis of a longer time period may also allow for a better assessment of the possible cleansing effects of adverse shocks at the macroeconomic level.

- *Additional analysis on investment in climate-related infrastructure.* Fourth, the climate change scenario explored in this chapter is based on regional estimates of infrastructure investment needs because for a large number of individual EMDEs, available data are limited. Given the wide heterogeneity in climate challenges, country-specific estimates that can provide more precision should ideally supplement or replace these regional estimates. For some countries, country-specific infrastructure investment goals are available, including, for European Union countries, in the National Recovery and Resilience Plans funded through NextGenerationEU investments. For other regions, however, such country-specific data are for now unavailable.

TABLE 5.1 **Sample and region coverage**

Advanced economies	Emerging market and developing economies	
Austria	**East Asia and Pacific**	**Middle East and North Africa**
Belgium	China	Bahrain
Canada	Indonesia	Egypt, Arab Rep.
Cyprus	Philippines	Iran, Islamic Rep.
Czech Republic	Thailand	Jordan
Denmark	**Europe and Central Asia**	Kuwait
Estonia	Bulgaria	Saudi Arabia
Finland	Croatia	Tunisia
France	Hungary	**South Asia**
Germany	Kazakhstan	India
Greece	Moldova	**Sub-Saharan Africa**
Hong Kong SAR, China	Poland	Benin
Iceland	Russian Federation	Botswana
Ireland	Türkiye	Cameroon
Israel	Ukraine	Côte d'Ivoire
Italy	**Latin America and the Caribbean**	Kenya
Japan	Argentina	Lesotho
Korea, Rep.	Barbados	Mauritius
Latvia	Brazil	Mozambique
Luxembourg	Chile	Niger
Netherlands	Colombia	Rwanda
Norway	Costa Rica	Senegal
Portugal	Ecuador	South Africa
Slovak Republic	Guatemala	Swaziland
Slovenia	Honduras	
Spain	Jamaica	
Sweden	Mexico	
Switzerland	Panama	
United Kingdom	Paraguay	
United States	Peru	
	Uruguay	

Source: World Bank.

ANNEX 5A Literature review: Effects of economic reforms on growth

An extensive literature has explored the effects on economic growth of various structural reforms in recent decades. This annex reviews the main findings of the literature on reforms to enhance human capital, increase and improve infrastructure investment, and raise female labor force participation.

Human capital and growth

Conceptual links. In the production function framework, human capital is a factor of production, and human capital accumulation raises output growth directly (Mankiw, Romer, and Weil 1992). But it can also raise output growth indirectly, by stimulating technological progress, technology adoption, and knowledge spillovers and thus raising TFP growth.[17] In both ways, human capital accumulation is a critical driver of growth in labor productivity, the key to sustained growth in standards (see de la Fuente 2011; Dieppe 2020; Flabbi and Gatti 2018; and World Bank 2018a). The literature is divided on the degree to which human capital accumulation can explain cross-country differences in per capita incomes.[18] Two dimensions of human capital accumulation have been studied for their impact on output growth: education and health.

Education and growth: Empirical evidence. A large literature has established that a better-educated population is associated with higher incomes or faster income growth. Both school enrollment and the quality of education have been shown to benefit growth or levels of income, especially when combined with a supporting environment.

Higher school enrollment or educational attainment—especially in regard to primary and secondary education—has been found to be associated with stronger growth (see Barro 1991, 1997; Krueger and Lindahl 2001; Mankiw, Romer, and Weil 1992; Sala-i-Martin, Doppelhofer, and Miller 2004; Sianesi and Van Reenen 2003; Temple 2001; and Topel 1999).[19] Primary and secondary education appear to be more important for knowledge diffusion and postsecondary education for innovation and creation of new knowledge (Vandenbussche, Aghion, and Meghir 2006). Better-quality education has an even stronger growth-enhancing effect than more schooling, as captured in enrollment and attainment rates (see Barro 2001; Bosworth and Collins 2003; Coulombe and Tremblay 2006; Hanushek 2002; Hanushek and Woessmann 2008; and Woessmann

---

[17] Acemoglu and Autor (2012) discuss the role of education in encouraging technological progress; Che and Zhang (2018), Danquah and Amankwah-Amoah (2017), and Huffman (2020) discuss its role in technology adoption; and Easterly (2005), Ehrlich and Pei (2020), and Klenow and Rodriguez-Clare (2005) discuss its role in knowledge spillovers.

[18] Some studies find that human capital accumulation can explain only 10-50 percent of cross-country income variation (Caselli 2005; Caselli and Ciccone 2013; Klenow and Rodriguez-Clare 1997; Mankiw, Romer, and Weil 1992). Other studies, which differentiate between different types of human capital and skill complementarity, find that the majority of cross-country differences can be attributed to human capital accumulation (Hendricks and Schoellman 2017; Jones 2014; Malmberg 2016; Sasso and Rirzen 2016).

[19] For the impact of primary and secondary schooling, see Barro and Sala-i-Martin (1995).

2003a, 2003b). For example, measures of acquisition of specific skills or academic achievement, such as test scores, are statistically significantly associated with higher growth (see Hanushek and Kimko 2000 and Hanushek and Woessmann 2015a, 2015b, 2016). This is especially true for low-income countries (Hanushek, Ruhose, and Woessmann 2017a, 2017b).

Other factors can slow human capital accumulation or dampen its growth-enhancing effects. These factors include unsupportive household environments (Hanushek 2002; Woessmann 2003a), as well as weak institutional environments that can divert highly skilled labor into unproductive activities such as rent-seeking (see Easterly 2001; Murphy, Shleifer, and Vishny 1991; and Pritchett 2001). Similarly, a stagnating economy with limited job creation may struggle to employ productively a better-educated workforce and thus fail to reap fully the potential gains in terms of growth (World Bank 2018a). Some studies find evidence of self-reinforcing feedback loops from higher growth to higher investment in human capital (see Bils and Klenow 2000; Pritchett 2001, 2006; and Weil 2014).

Health, nutrition, and growth: Empirical evidence. Both at the individual worker level and at the country level, improved health has been found to be associated with greater productivity and higher incomes. Early childhood interventions appear to be particularly beneficial (Grantham-McGregor et al. 2007). For children, better nutrition has been associated with better educational performance and, once they enter the labor market, higher incomes (see Galasso et al. 2017; Luo et al. 2012; and Taras 2005). As with education, there appear to be positive feedback loops as higher incomes allow more investment into health care and related infrastructure (Weil 2014).

Infrastructure and growth

Conceptual links. Like human capital accumulation, infrastructure investment can raise output growth both directly, through growth of the capital stock, which is a factor of production, and indirectly, through its collateral benefits for TFP growth. Good infrastructure investment can encourage innovation and knowledge diffusion, enhance human capital and TFP, and thus lower production costs, improve a country's international competitiveness, and facilitate trade (Agénor 2013; Demetriades and Mamuneas 2000). For example, better transportation networks can reduce the cost of, and time taken to complete, new construction and the installation of new equipment (Turnovsky 1996), while improved access to electricity and better sanitation can help raise educational attainment and public health standards (Agénor 2011; Getachew 2010). The growth-enhancing effects of infrastructure investment depend on its quality and, for some types of infrastructure investment, the interconnectedness of networks and freedom from congestion (see Hulten 1994; OECD 2007; and Sanchez-Robles 1998).

Infrastructure investment and growth: Empirical evidence. Studies of the effects of infrastructure investment spending typically find that it raises output, but only modestly and without accompanying productivity increases (Straub and Terada-Hagiwara

2010).[20] These mixed results have been attributed to uncaptured spillovers, weak institutions, corruption, and inadequate public spending management that impairs the overall efficiency of public investment management.[21] However, studies using physical measures of infrastructure investment have found that it is associated with significantly higher output.[22] Access to specific infrastructure services, such as electricity, better roads, or telephones, has also been found to be associated with higher growth or higher income.[23]

Female labor force participation and growth

Empirical evidence. Greater female labor force participation raises labor supply and thus output. However, women often face restrictions in freely pursuing occupations or engaging in economic transactions or experience gaps in education or health care (Gonzales et al. 2015; World Bank 2012). To the extent that this holds them back from engaging in their most productive employment, it weighs on output. Increased female labor force participation may also generate long-lasting effects by improving education outcomes of children or encouraging other women to enter the labor market (Duflo 2012; Fogli and Veldkamp 2011).

Reinforcing interactions between reforms

Interactions among reforms in multiple areas tend to strengthen their growth dividends. Investment in infrastructure related to safe water, sanitation, electricity, and transportation improves population health, increases school attendance, and improves learning outcomes (Agénor 2010). Healthier students perform better in school and are more likely to attend, while healthier populations are associated with better-qualified staff in the education sector (Behrman 2010). In turn, better education of mothers improves infant health and prospects (Fuchs, Pamuk, and Lutz 2010). Higher

---

[20] Surveys of the literature include Bom and Ligthart (2014), Pereira and Andraz (2013), and Romp and de Haan (2007). The IMF (2014) finds long-term output elasticities of infrastructure investment in excess of 1. In contrast, more recent studies find that infrastructure investment either does not significantly raise output or growth or raises output by less than its cost (Ganelli and Tervala 2016).

[21] In a meta-analysis of 68 studies over 1983-2008, Bom and Ligthart (2014) find that public capital has considerably lower output elasticities at the regional level than at the central government level, suggesting that cross-regional spillovers are not taken into account. The IMF (2015a) argues that countries with stronger public investment management institutions have more predictable, credible, efficient, and productive investments and that strengthening these institutions could close up to two-thirds of the public investment efficiency gap. The IMF (2018) also argues that better management of public sector assets is associated with higher revenues, greater effectiveness and returns on assets, and lower risk. Pritchett (2000) casts doubt on the robustness of econometric estimates of output elasticities.

[22] Canning (1999), Calderon, Moral-Benito, and Servén (2015), and Calderon and Servén (2003) find output gains from electricity generation capacity, transportation networks, and telephone networks. Easterly (2001) finds an association between telephone lines and growth. Fernald (1999) shows that road infrastructure investment raises U.S. productivity. Röller and Waverman (2001) find a positive link between telecommunications networks and growth.

[23] Regarding access to electricity, see Khandker et al. (2012), Kumar and Rauniyar (2011), and Rud (2012). Regarding access to better roads, see Datta (2012), Hu and Liu (2010), and Queiroz and Gautam (1992). Regarding access to telephones, see Canning and Pedroni (2008).

educational attainment is associated with greater labor force participation (Eckstein and Lifshitz 2011; Steinberg and Nakane 2012). Investment in infrastructure in the areas of electricity, clean water, and sanitation also facilitates female labor force participation by freeing women's time for gainful employment (Ghani, Kerr, and O'Connell 2013; Norando 2010). Better governance is also associated with better education (Gerged and Elheddad 2020) and greater and better-quality infrastructure investment (Aghion et al. 2016; Chen, Liu, and Lee 2020; d'Agostino, Dunne, and Pieroni 2016; see also Hulten 1994; OECD 2007; and Sanchez-Robles 1998).

ANNEX 5B Methodology: Impact of institutional reform

The local-projections estimation of changes in potential TFP growth and investment after reform episodes draws on an event study of reform episodes (World Bank 2021a). The identification of institutional reform events is based on the duration of changes in indicators from the PRS Group's *International Country Risk Guide.* After a positive change (for reform advances) or negative change (for reform setbacks) is identified, it is considered an event if no changes in the opposite direction are found within three years of the beginning of changes. The initial years are then chosen as event years. If the initial year of the next episode in the same direction is within five years, the next one is merged with the previous episode. If an episode is ongoing, that episode is used in the analysis, regardless of its length.

Reform events are defined as sustained increases in the average of four indicators of institutional quality produced by the *International Country Risk Guide*: bureaucracy quality, rule of law, corruption, and investment profile. This definition yields 106 episodes of sustained reform advances and 85 episodes of sustained reform setbacks in 100 EMDEs during 2004-19.

A local-projections estimation as in Jordà (2005) using the bias correction specification of Teulings and Zubanov (2014) is estimated to identify the effects of reform events on TFP and real investment growth over time. The main advantages of local-projections estimations include their simplicity of estimation, their robustness to model misspecifications, the ease with which inferences can be made from them, and their flexibility to incorporate highly nonlinear specifications and interactions of various regressors. In impulse responses, the model estimates the effect of reform events in country i in year t (the dummy variable $shock_{it}$) on cumulative growth in TFP or real investment over a horizon h:

$$y_{i,t+h} - y_{i,t} = \alpha^h + \beta^h shock_{i,t} + \sum_j^2 \theta_{1,j}^h shock_{i,t-j}$$

$$+ \sum_j^{h-1} \theta_{2,j}^h shock_{i,t+h-j} + \sum_j^2 \theta_{3,j}^h dy_{i,t-j}$$

$$+ \theta_{4,i}^h X_i + \mu_i^h + \tau_t^h + \varepsilon_{i,t} \, ,$$

in which $y_{i,t}$ refers to the log level of TFP (or real investment) in county i in year t, $dy_{i,t}$ to its annual growth rate, and m_i^h and t_i^h to country and year fixed effects. Additional controls X_i include a dummy indicating whether a country is a commodity exporter, dummies for financial crises occurring during the period h, and the log level of real GDP per capita t. Since $y_{i,t+h} - y_{i,t}$ is cumulative growth in either TFP or real investment over horizon h, the coefficient β_h represents an estimate of the cumulative response of growth in TFP (or real investment) by time $t + h$ to the reform advance (setback) that happened at time t.

The results are robust to using nonoverlapping episodes. That said, as with any regression, it remains possible that the events selected here may coincide with other favorable or adverse developments that spurred or slowed growth and the methodology cannot disentangle these two forces.

References

Abiad, A., M. Debuque-Gonzales, and A. L. Sy. 2018. "The Evolution and Impact of Infrastructure in Middle-Income Countries: Anything Special?" *Emerging Markets Finance and Trade* 54 (6): 1239-63.

Acemoglu, D., and D. Autor. 2012. "What Does Human Capital Do? A Review of Golding and Katz's *The Race between Education and Technology*." *Journal of Economic Literature* 50 (2): 426-63.

Acemoglu, D., and S. Johnson. 2005. "Unbundling Institutions." *Journal of Political Economy* 113 (5): 949-95.

Acemoglu, D., and S. Johnson. 2007. "Disease and Development: The Effect of Life Expectancy on Economic Growth." *Journal of Political Economy* 115 (6): 925-85.

Acemoglu, D., S. Johnson, J. Robinson, and P. Yared. 2005. "From Education to Democracy?" *American Economic Review* 95 (2): 44-49.

Acemoglu, D., and P. Restrepo. 2016. "The Race between Machine and Man: Implications of Technology for Growth, Factor Shares and Employment." NBER Working Paper 22252, National Bureau of Economic Research, Cambridge, MA.

Acemoglu, D., and P. Restrepo. 2017a. "Low-Skill and High-Skill Automation." MIT Department of Economics Working Paper 17-12, Massachusetts Institute of Technology, Cambridge, MA.

Acemoglu, D., and P. Restrepo. 2017b. "Robots and Jobs: Evidence from US Labor Markets." NBER Working Paper 23285, National Bureau of Economic Research, Cambridge, MA.

Acemoglu, D., and P. Restrepo. 2017c. "Secular Stagnation? The Effect of Aging on Economic Growth in the Age of Automation." NBER Working Paper 23077, National Bureau of Economic Research, Cambridge, MA.

ADB (Asian Development Bank). 2016. *Asian Development Outlook 2016: Asia's Potential Growth.* Manila, Philippines: Asian Development Bank.

Adler, G., R. Duval, D. Furceri, S. Kilic Celik, K. Koloskova, and M. Poplawski-Ribeiro. 2017. "Gone with the Headwinds: Global Productivity." Staff Discussion Note 17/04, International Monetary Fund, Washington, DC.

Afonso, A., and J. T. Jalles. 2012. "Fiscal Volatility, Financial Crises and Growth." *Applied Economics Letters* 19 (18): 1821-26.

Agénor, P. 2011. "Schooling and Public Capital in a Model of Endogenous Growth." *Economica* 78 (1): 108-32.

Agénor, P. 2013. *Public Capital, Growth and Welfare.* Princeton, NJ: Princeton University Press.

Aghion, P., U. Akcigit, J. Cagé, and W. R. Kerr. 2016. "Taxation, Corruption, and Growth." *European Economic Review* 86 (C): 24-51.

Aghion, P., and M. Schankerman. 2004. "On the Welfare Effects and Political Economy of Competition-Enhancing Policies." *Economic Journal* 114 (498): 800-24.

Ahmed, S. A., and M. Cruz. 2016. "On the Impact of Demographic Change on Growth, Savings, and Poverty." Policy Research Working Paper 7805, World Bank, Washington, DC.

Aiyar, S., and A. Mody. 2011. "The Demographic Dividend: Evidence from the Indian States." IMF Working Paper 11/38, International Monetary Fund, Washington, DC.

Alam, A., M. Uddin, and H. Yazdifar. 2019. "Institutional Determinants of R&D Investment: Evidence from Emerging Markets." *Technological Forecasting and Social Change* 138 (C): 34-44.

Alesina, A., D. Furceri, J. Ostry, C. Papageorgiou, and D. Quinn. 2020. "Structural Reforms and Elections: Evidence from a World-Wide New Dataset." NBER Working Paper 26720, National Bureau of Economic Research, Cambridge, MA.

Alfaro, P., D. K. Evans, and P. Holland. 2015. "Extending the School Day in Latin America and the Caribbean." Policy Research Working Paper 7309, World Bank, Washington, DC.

Amin, M., and H. Ulku. 2019. "Corruption, Regulatory Burden and Firm Productivity." Policy Research Working Paper 8911, World Bank, Washington, DC.

Andres, L. 2021. "The Economic and Health Impacts of Inadequate Sanitation." In *Oxford Research Encyclopedia of Environmental Science*, edited by L. Hank. Oxford, U.K.: Oxford University Press.

Atkin, D., and A. Khandelwal. 2020. "How Distortions Alter the Impacts of International Trade in Developing Countries." *Annual Review of Economics* 12 (1): 213-38.

Azevedo, J. P., A. Hasan, D. Goldemberg, K. Geven, and S. A. Iqbal. 2021. "Simulating the Potential Impacts of the COVID-19 School Closures on Schooling and Learning Outcomes: A Set of Global Estimates." *World Bank Research Observer* 36 (1): 1-40.

Balleer, A., R. Gomez-Salvador, and J. Turunen. 2014. "Labour Force Participation across Europe: A Cohort-Based Analysis." *Empirical Economics* 46(4): 1385-415.

Banerji, A., C. H. Ebeke, D. Furceri, E. Dabla-Norris, R. A. Duval, T. Komatsuzaki, T. Poghosyan, and V. Crispolti. 2017. "Labor and Product Market Reforms in Advanced Economies: Fiscal Costs, Gains, and Support." IMF Staff Discussion Note 17/03, International Monetary Fund, Washington, DC.

Barbiero, O., and B. Cournède. 2013. "New Econometric Estimates of Long-Term Growth Effects of Different Areas of Public Spending." OECD Economics Department Working Paper 1100, Organisation for Economic Co-operation and Development, Paris.

Barro, R. 1991. "Economic Growth in a Cross Section of Countries." *Quarterly Journal of Economics* 106 (2): 407-43.

Barro, R. 1997. *Determinants of Economic Growth: A Cross-Country Empirical Study*. Cambridge, MA: MIT Press.

Barro, R. 2000. "Inequality and Growth in a Panel of Countries." *Journal of Economic Growth* 5 (1): 5-32.

Barro, R. 2001. "Human Capital and Growth." *American Economic Review* 91 (2): 12-17.

Barro, R., and X. Sala-i-Martin. 1995. *Economic Growth*. New York: McGraw Hill.

Behrman, J. R. 2010. "Investment in Education—Inputs and Incentives." In *Handbook of Development Economics, Volume 5*, edited by D. Rodrik and M. Rosenzweig, 4883-975. Amsterdam: Elsevier.

Benos, N., and S. Zotou. 2014. "Education and Economic Growth: A Meta-regression Analysis." *World Development* 64 (December): 669-89.

Betcherman, G. 2014. "Labor Market Regulations: What Do We Know about Their Impacts in Developing Countries?" *World Bank Research Observer* 30 (1): 124-53.

Betcherman, G., A. Dar, and K. Olivas. 2004. "Impacts of Active Labor Market Programs: New Evidence from Evaluations with Particular Attention to Developing and Transition Countries." Social Protection and Labor Policy and Technical Note 29142, World Bank, Washington, DC.

Bils, M., and P. Klenow. 2000. "Does Schooling Cause Growth?" *American Economic Review* 90 (5): 1160-83.

Blanchard, O., F. Jaumotte, and P. Loungani. 2013. "Labor Market Policies and IMF Advice in Advanced Economies during the Great Recession." IMF Staff Discussion Notes 2013/002, International Monetary Fund, Washington, DC.

Bloom, D. E., and D. Canning. 2004. "Global Demographic Change: Dimensions and Economic Significance." NBER Working Paper 10817, National Bureau of Economic Research, Cambridge, MA.

Bloom, D. E., D. Canning, and P. N. Malaney. 2000. "Population Dynamics and Economic Growth in Asia." *Population and Development Review* 26 (S): 257-90.

Bloom, D. E., and J. G. Williamson. 1998. "Demographic Transitions and Economic Miracles in Emerging Asia." *World Bank Economic Review* 12 (3): 419-55.

Bluhm, R., and A. Szirmai. 2011. "Institutions, Inequality and Growth: A Review of Theory and Evidence on the Institutional Determinants of Growth and Inequality." Innocenti Working Paper 2011/02, United Nations, New York.

Bom, P., and J. Ligthart. 2014. "What Have We Learned from Three Decades of Research on the Productivity of Public Capital?" *Journal of Economic Surveys* 28 (5): 889-916.

Bosworth, B., and S. Collins. 2003. "The Empirics of Growth: An Update." *Brookings Papers on Economic Activity* 34 (2): 113-206.

Botero, J., A. Ponce, and A. Shleifer. 2012. "Education and the Quality of Government." NBER Working Paper 18119, National Bureau of Economic Research, Cambridge, MA.

Botzen, W. W., O. Deschenes, and M. Sanders. 2019. "The Economic Impacts of Natural Disasters: A Review of Models and Empirical Studies." *Review of Environmental Economics and Policy* 13 (2): 167-88.

Bourles, R., G. Cette, J. Lopez, J. Mairesse, and G. Nicoletti. 2013. "Do Product Market Regulations in Upstream Sectors Curb Productivity Growth? Panel Data Evidence for OECD Countries." *Review of Economics and Statistics* 95 (5): 1750-68.

Bradley, E. H., S. Pallas, C. Bashyal, P. Berman, and L. Curry. 2010. "Developing Strategies for Improving Health Care Delivery: Guide to Concepts, Determinants, Measurement, and Intervention Design." Health, Nutrition and Population Discussion Paper 59885, World Bank, Washington, DC.

Brudevold-Newman, A., M. Honorati, P. Jakiela, and O. W. Ozier. 2017. "A Firm of One's Own: Experimental Evidence on Credit Constraints and Occupational Choice." IZA Discussion Paper 10583, IZA Institute for Labor Economics, Bonn, Germany.

Bruhn, M. 2011. "License to Sell: The Effect of Business Registration Reform on Entrepreneurial Activity in Mexico." *Review of Economics and Statistics* 93 (1): 382-86.

Buccirossi, P., L. Ciari, T. Duso, G. Spagnolo, and C. Vitale. 2013. "Competition Policy and Productivity Growth: An Empirical Assessment." *Review of Economics and Statistics* 95 (4): 1324-36.

Bussolo, M., J. Koettl, and E. Sinnott. 2015. *Golden Aging: Prospects for Healthy, Active, and Prosperous Aging in Europe and Central Asia.* Washington, DC: World Bank.

Calderón, C., E. Moral-Benito, and L. Servén. 2015. "Is Infrastructure Capital Productive? A Dynamic Heterogeneous Approach." *Journal of Applied Econometrics* 30 (2): 177-98.

Calderón, C., and L. Servén. 2003. "The Output Cost of Latin America's Infrastructure Gap." In *The Limits of Stabilization: Infrastructure, Public Deficits, and Growth in Latin America*, edited by W. Easterly and L. Servén, 95-118. Palo Alto, CA: Stanford University Press.

Calderón, C., and L. Servén. 2010a. "Infrastructure and Economic Development in Sub-Saharan Africa." *Journal of African Economies* 19 (S1): i13-i87.

Calderón, C., and L. Servén. 2010b. "Infrastructure in Latin America: Dataset." Policy Research Working Paper 5317, World Bank, Washington, DC.

Calderón, C., and L. Servén. 2014. "Infrastructure, Growth, and Inequality: An Overview." Policy Research Working Paper 7034, World Bank, Washington, DC.

Canning, D. 1999. "The Contribution of Infrastructure to Aggregate Output." Policy Research Working Paper 2246, World Bank, Washington, DC.

Canning, D., and P. Pedroni. 2008. "Infrastructure, Long-Run Economic Growth and Causality Tests for Cointegrated Panels." *Manchester School* 76 (5): 504-27.

Card, D., J. Kluve, and A. Weber. 2010. "Active Labour Market Policy Evaluations: A Meta-analysis." *Economic Journal* 120 (548): F452-77.

Carter, R. C. 2017. "Can and Should Sanitation and Hygiene Programmes Be Expected to Achieve Health Impacts?" *Waterlines* 36 (1): 92-103.

Caselli, F. 2005. "Accounting for Cross-Country Income Differences." In *Handbook of Economic Growth*, edited by P. Aghion and S. Durlauf. Amsterdam: Elsevier.

Caselli, F., and A. Ciccone. 2013. "The Contribution of Schooling in Development Accounting: Results from a Nonparametric Upper Bound." *Journal of Development Economics* 104 (C): 199-211.

Castro, V. 2011. "The Impact of the European Union Fiscal Rules on Economic Growth." *Journal of Macroeconomics* 33 (2): 313-26.

Che, Y., and L. Zhang. 2018. "Human Capital, Technology Adoption and Firm Performance: Impacts of China's Higher Education Expansion in the Late 1990s." *Economic Journal* 128 (614): 2282-320.

Chen, C., C. Liu, and J. Lee. 2020. "Corruption and the Quality of Transportation Infrastructure: Evidence from the U.S. States." *International Review of Administrative Sciences* 88 (2): 552-69. https://journals.sagepub.com/doi/abs/10.1177/0020852320953184

Christiaensen, L., L. Demery, and J. Kuhl. 2011. "The (Evolving) Role of Agriculture in Poverty Reduction—An Empirical Perspective." *Journal of Development Economics* 96 (2): 239-54.

Cirera, X., and W. F. Maloney. 2017. *The Innovation Paradox*. Washington, DC: World Bank.

Coulombe, S., and J.-F. Tremblay. 2006. "Literacy and Growth." *Topics in Macroeconomics* 6 (2): Article 4.

d'Agostino, G., J. P. Dunne, and L. Pieroni. 2016. "Government Spending, Corruption and Economic Growth." *World Development* 84: 190-205.

D'Costa, S., and H. G. Overman. 2014. "The Urban Wage Growth Premium: Sorting or Learning?" *Regional Science and Urban Economics* 48 (September): 168-79.

Dabla-Norris, E. 2016. *Structural Reforms and Productivity Growth in Emerging Market and Developing Economies.* Washington, DC: International Monetary Fund.

Dabla-Norris, E., M. S. Guo, M. V. Haksar, M. Kim, M. K. Kochhar, K. Wiseman, and A. Zdzienicka. 2015. *The New Normal: A Sector-Level Perspective on Productivity Trends in Advanced Economies.* Washington, DC: International Monetary Fund.

Dabla-Norris, E., G. Ho, and A. Kyobe. 2016. "Structural Reforms and Productivity Growth in Emerging Market and Developing Economies." IMF Working Paper 16/15, International Monetary Fund, Washington, DC.

Danquah, M., and J. Amankwah-Amoah. 2017. "Assessing the Relationships between Human Capital, Innovation and Technology Adoption: Evidence from Sub-Saharan Africa." *Technological Forecasting and Social Change* 122 (C): 24-33.

Das, S., S. Jain-Chandra, K. Kochhar and N. Kumar. 2017. "Tackling Gender Inequality in Asia: India." In *Women, Work, and Economic Growth: Leveling the Playing Field,* edited by K. Kochhar, S. Jain-Chandra, and M. Newiak, 117-26. Washington, DC: International Monetary Fund.

Datta, S. 2012. "The Impact of Improved Highways on Indian Firms." *Journal of Development Economics* 99 (1): 46-57.

de Haan, J., and R. Wiese. 2022. "The Impact of Product and Labour Market Reform on Growth: Evidence for OECD Countries Based on Local Projections." *Journal of Applied Econometrics* 37 (4): 746-70.

de la Fuente, A. 2011. "Human Capital and Productivity." Working Paper 530, Barcelona Graduate School of Economics, Barcelona.

Demetriades, P., and T. Mamuneas. 2000. "Intertemporal Output and Employment Effects of Public Infrastructure Capital: Evidence from 12 OECD Economies." *Economic Journal* 110 (July): 687-712.

Desbordes, R. 2011. "The Non-linear Effects of Life Expectancy on Economic Growth." *Economics Letters* 112 (1): 116-18.

Dieppe, A., ed. 2020. *Global Productivity: Trends, Drivers, and Policies.* Washington, DC: World Bank.

Dieppe, A., S. Kilic-Celik, and C. Okou. 2020. "Implications of Major Adverse Events on Productivity." Policy Research Working Paper 9411, World Bank, Washington, DC.

Dinlersoz, E. M., and Z. Fu. 2022. "Infrastructure Investment and Growth in China: A Quantitative Assessment." *Journal of Development Economics* 158 (September): 102916.

Divanbeigi, R., and R. Ramalho. 2015. "Business Regulations and Growth." Policy Research Working Paper 7299, World Bank, Washington, DC.

Djankov, S., C. McLiesh, and R. Ramalho. 2006. "Regulation and Growth." *Economics Letters* 92 (3): 395-401.

Dollar, D., T. Kleineberg, and A. Kraay. 2013. "Growth Is Still Good for the Poor." World Bank Policy Research Working Paper 6568, World Bank, Washington, DC.

Dort, T., P. Méon, and K. Sekkat. 2014. "Does Investment Spur Growth Everywhere? Not Where Institutions Are Weak." *Kyklos* 67 (4): 482-505.

Duflo, E. 2012. "Women Empowerment and Economic Development." *Journal of Economic Literature* 50 (4): 1051-79.

Easterly, W. 2001. "The Lost Decades: Explaining Developing Countries' Stagnation in Spite of Policy Reform 1980-1998." *Journal of Economic Growth* 6 (2): 135-57.

Easterly, W. 2005. "National Policies and Economic Growth: A Reappraisal." In *Handbook of Economic Growth*, edited by P. Aghion and S. Durlauf, 1113-80. Amsterdam: Elsevier.

Eckstein, Z., and O. Lifshitz. 2011. "Dynamic Female Labor Supply." *Econometrica* 79 (6): 1675-726.

Egan, P. 2013. "R&D in the Periphery? Foreign Direct Investment, Innovation, and Institutional Quality in Developing Countries." *Business and Politics* 15 (1): 1-32.

Ehrlich, I., and Y. Pei. 2020. "Human Capital as Engine of Growth—The Role of Knowledge Transfers in Promoting Balanced Growth within and across Countries." NBER Working Paper 26810, National Bureau of Economic Research, Cambridge, MA.

Erten, B., and M. Metzger. 2019. "The Real Exchange Rate, Structural Change, and Female Labor Force Participation." *World Development* 117 (May): 296-312.

Espinoza, R., and A. F. Presbitero. 2021. "Delays in Public Investment Projects." *International Economics* 172 (December): 279-310.

European Commission. 2021. *The 2021 Ageing Report: Economic and Budgetary Projections for the EU Member States (2019-2070).* Brussels: European Commission.

Evans, D. K., and A. Popova. 2016. "What Really Works to Improve Learning in Developing Countries? An Analysis of Divergent Findings in Systematic Reviews." *World Bank Research Observer* 31 (2): 242-70.

Fernald, J. 1999. "Roads to Prosperity? Assessing the Link between Public Capital and Productivity." *American Economic Review* 89 (3): 619-38.

Flabbi, L., and R. Gatti. 2018. "A Primer on Human Capital." Policy Research Working Paper 8309, World Bank, Washington, DC.

Fogli, A., and L. Veldkamp. 2011. "Nature or Nurture? Learning and the Geography of Female Labor Force Participation." *Econometrica* 79 (4): 1103-38.

Fuchs, R., E. Pamuk, and W. Lutz. 2010. "Education or Wealth: Which Matters More for Reducing Child Mortality in Developing Countries?" *Vienna Yearbook of Population Research* 8 (1): 175-99.

Galasso, E., A. Wagstaff, S. Naudeau, and M. Shekar. 2017. "The Economic Costs of Stunting and How to Reduce Them." Policy Research Note 17/05, World Bank, Washington, DC.

Ganelli, G., and J. Tervala. 2016. "The Welfare Multiplier of Public Infrastructure Investment." IMF Working Paper 16/40, International Monetary Fund, Washington, DC.

Gerged, A., and M. Elheddad. 2020. "How Can National Governance Affect Education Quality in Western Europe?" *International Journal of Sustainability in Higher Education* 21 (3): 413-26.

Gertler, P., and C. Vermeersch. 2012. "Using Performance Incentives to Improve Health Outcomes." Policy Research Working Paper 6100, World Bank, Washington, DC.

Getachew, Y. 2010. "Public Capital and Distributional Dynamics in a Two-Sector Growth Model." *Journal of Macroeconomics* 32 (2): 606-16.

Ghani, E., W. R. Kerr, and S. D. O'Connell. 2013. "Promoting Women's Economic Participation in India." Economic Premise 107, World Bank, Washington, DC.

Glaeser, E., R. La Porta, F. Lopez-de-Silanes, and A. Shleifer. 2004. "Do Institutions Cause Growth?" *Journal of Economic Growth* 9 (3): 271-303.

Glaeser, E., G. Ponzetto, and A. Shleifer. 2007. "Why Does Democracy Need Education?" *Journal of Economic Growth* 12 (2): 77-99.

Glewwe, P., E. Maiga, and H. Zheng. 2014. "The Contribution of Education to Economic Growth: A Review of the Evidence, with Special Attention and an Application to Sub-Saharan Africa." *World Development* 59 (July): 379-93.

Glewwe, P., and K. Muralidharan. 2015. "Improving School Education Outcomes in Developing Countries: Evidence, Knowledge Gaps, and Policy Implications." Research on Improving Systems of Education (RISE) Working Paper 15/001, University of Oxford, Oxford, U.K.

Gokmen, G., T. Nannicini, M. Onorato, and C. Papageorgiou. 2020. "Policies in Hard Times: Assessing the Impact of Financial Crises on Structural Reforms." IZA Discussion Paper 12932, Institute of Labor Economics, Bonn.

Gonzales, C., S. Jain-Chandra, K. Kochhar, and M. Newiak. 2015. "Fair Play: More Equal Laws Boost Female Labor Force Participation." IMF Working Paper 15/02, International Monetary Fund, Washington, DC.

Gould, E. D. 2007. "Cities, Workers, and Wages: A Structural Analysis of the Urban Wage Premium." *Review of Economic Studies* 74 (2): 477-506.

Gradstein, M. 2007. "Inequality, Democracy and the Protection of Property Rights." *Economic Journal* 117 (516): 252-69.

Grantham-McGregor S., Y. B. Cheung, S. Cueto, P. Glewwe, L. Richter, and B. Strupp. 2007. "Developmental Potential in the First 5 Years for Children in Developing Countries." *Lancet* 369 (9555): 60-70.

Gurara, D., K. Kpodar, A. F. Presbitero, and D. Tessema. 2021. "On the Capacity to Absorb Public Investment: How Much Is Too Much?" *World Development* 145 (September): 105525.

Gwartney, D., R. Holcombe, and R. Lawson. 2006. "Institutions and the Impact of Investment on Growth." *Kyklos* 59 (2): 255-73.

Hall, J., R. Sobel, and G. Crowley. 2010. "Institutions, Capital, and Growth." *Southern Economic Journal* 77 (2): 385-405.

Hanushek, E. 2002. "Publicly Provided Education." In *Handbook of Public Economics*, edited by A. Auerbach and M. Feldstein. Amsterdam: North Holland.

Hanushek, E., and D. Kimko. 2000. "Schooling, Labor Force Quality, and the Growth of Nations." *American Economic Review* 90 (5): 1184-208.

Hanushek, E., J. Ruhose, and L. Woessmann. 2017a. "Economic Gains from Educational Reform by US States." *Journal of Human Capital* 11 (4): 447-86.

Hanushek, E., J. Ruhose, and L. Woessmann. 2017b. "Knowledge Capital and Aggregate Income Differences: Development Accounting for U.S. States." *American Economic Journal: Macroeconomics* 9 (4): 184-224.

Hanushek, E., and L. Woessmann. 2008. "The Role of Cognitive Skills in Economic Development." *Journal of Economic Literature* 46 (3): 607-68.

Hanushek, E., and L. Woessmann. 2015a. *The Knowledge Capital of Nations: Education and the Economics of Growth*. Cambridge, MA: MIT Press.

Hanushek, E., and L. Woessmann. 2015b. *Universal Basic Skills: What Countries Stand to Gain*. Paris: Organisation for Economic Co-operation and Development.

Hanushek, E., and L. Woessmann. 2016. "Knowledge Capital, Growth, and the East Asian Miracle." *Science* 351 (6271): 344-45.

He, L., and N. Li. 2020. "The Linkages between Life Expectancy and Economic Growth: Some New Evidence." *Empirical Economics* 58 (5): 2381-402.

Hendricks, L., and T. Schoellman. 2017. "Human Capital and Development Accounting: New Evidence from Wage Gains at Migration." Working Paper 1, Opportunity and Inclusive Growth Institute, Federal Reserve Bank of Minneapolis.

Herrera, S., and A. Ouedraogo. 2018. "Efficiency of Public Spending in Education, Health, and Infrastructure: An International Benchmarking Exercise," Policy Research Working Paper 8586, World Bank, Washington, DC.

Ho, G., and P. Mauro. 2016. "Growth—Now and Forever?" *IMF Economic Review* 64 (3): 526-47.

Hu, A., and S. Liu. 2010. "Transportation, Economic Growth and Spillover Effects: The Conclusion Based on the Spatial Econometric Model." *Frontiers of Economics in China* 5 (2): 169-86.

Huffman, W. E. 2020. "Human Capital and Adoption of Innovations: Policy Implications." *Applied Economic Perspectives and Policy* 42 (1): 92-99.

Huidrom, R., M. A. Kose, H. Matsuoka, and F. Ohnsorge. 2020. "How Important Are Spillovers from Major Emerging Markets?" *International Finance* 23 (1): 47-63.

Hulten, C. 1994. "Optimal Growth with Infrastructure Capital: Theory and Implications for Empirical Modeling." Working Paper, University of Maryland, College Park.

IMF (International Monetary Fund). 2014. *World Economic Outlook: Legacies, Clouds, Uncertainties*. Washington, DC: International Monetary Fund.

IMF (International Monetary Fund). 2015a. "Making Public Investment More Efficient." Staff Report, International Monetary Fund, Washington, DC.

IMF (International Monetary Fund). 2015b. "Where Are We Headed? Perspectives on Potential Growth." In *World Economic Outlook: Uneven Growth; Short- and Long-Term Factors*. April. Washington, DC: International Monetary Fund.

IMF (International Monetary Fund). 2016a. "Fiscal Policies for Innovation and Growth." In *Fiscal Monitor: Acting Now, Acting Together*. April. Washington, DC: International Monetary Fund.

IMF (International Monetary Fund). 2016b. "Time for a Supply-Side Boost? Macroeconomic Effects of Labor and Product Market Reforms in Advanced Economies." In *World Economic Outlook: Too Slow for Too Long*. Washington, DC: International Monetary Fund.

IMF (International Monetary Fund). 2018. *Fiscal Monitor: Managing Public Wealth*. October. Washington, DC: International Monetary Fund.

IPCC (Intergovernmental Panel on Climate Change). 2022. *Climate Change 2022: Mitigation of Climate Change*. Geneva: Intergovernmental Panel on Climate Change.

Jones, B. 2014. "The Human Capital Stock: A Generalized Approach." *American Economic Review* 104 (11): 3752-77.

Jordà, O. 2005. "Estimation and Inference of Impulse Responses by Local Projections." *American Economic Review* 95 (1): 161-82.

Jude, C., and G. Levieuge. 2017. "Growth Effect of Foreign Direct Investment in Developing Economies: The Role of Institutional Quality." *World Economy* 40 (4): 715-42.

Juhn, G., and P. Loungani. 2002. "Further Cross-Country Evidence on the Accuracy of the Private Sector's Output Forecasts." *IMF Staff Papers* 49 (1): 49-64.

Keilman, N. 2001. "Data Quality and Accuracy of United Nations Population Projections, 1950-95." *Population Studies* 55(2): 149-64.

Khandker, S., H. Samad, R. Ali, and D. Barnes. 2012. "Who Benefits Most from Rural Electrification? Evidence from India." Policy Research Working Paper 6095, World Bank, Washington, DC.

Kirkpatrick, C. 2014. "Assessing the Impact of Regulatory Reform in Developing Countries." *Public Administration and Development* 34 (3): 162-68.

Klasen, S. 2019. "What Explains Uneven Female Labor Force Participation Levels and Trends in Developing Countries?" *World Bank Research Observer* 34 (2): 161-97.

Klenow, P. J., and A. Rodriguez-Clare. 1997. "The Neoclassical Revival in Growth Economics: Has It Gone Too Far?" *NBER Macroeconomics Annual* 12: 73-103.

Klenow, P. J., and A. Rodriguez-Clare. 2005. "Externalities and Growth." *Handbook of Economic Growth* 1: 817-61.

Klomp, J., and K. Valckx. 2014. "Natural Disasters and Economic Growth: A Meta-analysis." *Global Environmental Change* 26 (1): 183-95.

Koh, W. C., M. A. Kose, P. S. Nagle, F. Ohnsorge, and N. Sugawara. 2020. "Debt and Financial Crises." Policy Research Working Paper 9116, World Bank, Washington, DC.

Kose, M. A., F. Ohnsorge, Y. Lei, and E. Islamaj. 2017. "Weakness in Investment Growth: Causes, Implications and Policy Responses." Policy Research Working Paper 7990, World Bank, Washington, DC.

Kozeniauskas, N., P. Moreira, and C. Santos. 2022. "On the Cleansing Effect of Recessions and Government Policy: Evidence from Covid-19." *European Economic Review* 144: 104097.

Kremer, M., C. Brannen, and R. Glennerster. 2013. "The Challenge of Education and Learning in the Developing World." *Science* 340 (6130): 297-300.

Krueger, A., and M. Lindahl. 2001. "Education for Growth: Why and for Whom?" *Journal of Economic Literature* 39 (4): 1101-36.

Kudlyak, M. 2013. "A Cohort Model of Labor Force Participation." *Economic Quarterly* 99 (1): 25-43.

Kumar, S., and G. Rauniyar. 2011. "Is Electrification Welfare Improving? Non-experimental Evidence from Rural Bhutan." MPRA Paper 3148, University Library of Munich, Munich.

La Porta, R., and A. Shleifer. 2014. "Informality and Development." *Journal of Economic Perspectives* 28 (3): 109-126.

Liu, J., and W. Lyu. 2021. "Soft Skills, Hard Skills: What Matters Most? Evidence from Job Postings." *Applied Energy* 300 (October): 117307.

Loayza, N., A. Oviedo, and L. Servén. 2005. "The Impact of Regulation on Growth and Informality: Cross-Country Evidence." Policy Research Working Paper 3623, World Bank, Washington, DC.

Loayza, N., and L. Servén. 2010. *Business Regulation and Economic Performance*. Washington, DC: World Bank.

Luo, R., Y. Shi, L. Zhang, C. Liu, S. Rozelle, B. Sharbono, A. Yue, Q. Zhao, and R. Martorell. 2012. "Nutrition and Educational Performance in Rural China's Elementary Schools: Results of a Randomized Control Trial in Shaanxi Province." *Economic Development and Cultural Change* 60 (4): 735-72.

Maeda, A., C. Cashin, J. Harris, N. Ikegami, and M. R. Reich. 2014. *Universal Health Coverage for Inclusive and Sustainable Development: A Synthesis of 11 Country Case Studies*. Directions in Development 88862. World Bank, Washington, DC.

Malmberg, H. 2016. "Human Capital and Development Accounting Revisited." Job Market Paper, Institute for International Economic Studies, Stockholm University, Stockholm.

Mankiw, G., D. Romer, and D. Weil. 1992. "A Contribution to the Empirics of Growth." *Quarterly Journal of Economics* 107 (2): 407-37.

Miyazaki, T. 2014. "Fiscal Reform and Fiscal Sustainability: Evidence from Australia and Sweden." Discussion Paper 1407, Graduate School of Economics, Kobe University, Japan.

Mizunoya, S., G. Avanesian, S. Mishra, Y. Wang, and H. Yao. 2021. "Education Disrupted: The Second Year of the COVID-19 Pandemic and School Closures." United Nations Children's Fund, New York.

Modis, T. 2013. "Long-Term GDP Forecasts and the Prospects for Growth." *Technological Forecasting and Social Change* 80 (8): 1557-62.

Müller, A., K. Storesletten, and F. Zilibotti. 2019. "Sovereign Debt and Structural Reforms." *American Economic Review* 109 (12): 4220-59.

Murphy, K., A. Shleifer, and R. Vishny. 1991. "The Allocation of Talent: Implications for Growth." *Quarterly Journal of Economics* 106 (2): 503-30.

Nawaz, S. 2015. "Growth Effects of Institutions: A Disaggregated Analysis." *Economic Modelling* 45 (C): 118-26.

Norando, G. C. 2010. *Essays on Infrastructure, Female Labor Force Participation and Economic Development*. PhD diss., University of Iowa, Iowa City. https://doi.org/10.17077/etd.g5h0x4jd.

OECD (Organisation for Economic Co-operation and Development). 2007. *Transport Infrastructure Investment and Economic Productivity*. Paris: OECD Transport Research Centre.

OECD (Organisation for Economic Co-operation and Development). 2014a. "Growth Prospects and Fiscal Requirements over the Long Term." In *OECD Economic Outlook, Vol. 2014/1*. Paris: Organisation for Economic Co-operation and Development.

OECD (Organisation for Economic Co-operation and Development). 2014b. "Long-Term Baseline Projections, No. 95 (Edition 2014)." OECD Economic Outlook: Statistics and Projections (database). https://doi.org/10.1787/data-00690-e.

OECD (Organisation for Economic Co-operation and Development). 2017. *Going for Growth*. Paris: Organisation for Economic Co-operation and Development.

OECD (Organisation for Economic Co-operation and Development). 2018. *The Future of Education and Skills: Education 2030*. Paris: Organisation for Economic Co-operation and Development.

Pereira, A., and J. Andraz. 2013. "On the Economic Effects of Public Infrastructure Investment: A Survey of the International Evidence." Working Paper 108, Department of Economics, College of William and Mary, Williamsburg, VA.

Pham, T. H., and J. Riedel. 2019. "Impacts of the Sectoral Composition of Growth on Poverty Reduction in Vietnam." *Journal of Economics and Development* 21(2): 213-22.

Prati, A., M. G. Onorato, and C. Papageorgiou. 2013. "Which Reforms Work and Under What Institutional Environment?" *Review of Economics and Statistics* 95 (3): 946-68.

Presbitero, A. F. 2016. "Too Much and Too Fast? Public Investment Scaling-Up and Absorptive Capacity." *Journal of Development Economics* 120 (May): 17-31.

Pritchett, L. 2000. "The Tyranny of Concepts: CUDIE (Cumulated, Depreciated, Investment Effort) Is Not Capital." *Journal of Economic Growth* 5 (4): 361-84.

Pritchett, L. 2001. "Where Has All the Education Gone?" *World Bank Economic Review* 15 (3): 367-91.

Pritchett, L. 2006. "Does Learning to Add Up Add Up? The Returns to Schooling in Aggregate Data." In *Handbook of the Economics of Education*, edited by E. Hanushek and F. Welch, 635-95. Amsterdam: North Holland.

Queiroz, C., and S. Gautam. 1992. "Road Infrastructure and Economic Development: Some Diagnostic Indicators." Policy Research Working Paper 921, World Bank, Washington, DC.

Rajah, R., and A. Leng. 2022. "Revising Down the Rise of China." Analyses, March 14. Lowy Institute, Sydney, Australia.

Ravallion, M., and G. Datt. 2002. "Why Has Economic Growth Been More Pro-poor in Some States of India Than Others?" *Journal of Development Economics* 68 (2): 381-400.

Röller, L.-H., and L. Waverman. 2001. "Telecommunications Infrastructure and Economic Development: A Simultaneous Approach." *American Economic Review* 91 (4): 909-23.

Romp, W., and J. de Haan. 2007. "Public Capital and Economic Growth: A Critical Survey." *Perspektiven der Wirtschaftspolitik* 8 (S1): 6-52.

Rozenberg, J., and M. Fay. 2019. *Beyond the Gap: How Countries Can Afford the Infrastructure They Need While Protecting the Planet*. Washington, DC: World Bank.

Rud, J. 2012. "Electricity Provision and Industrial Development: Evidence from India." *Journal of Development Economics* 97 (2): 352-67.

Sala-i-Martin, X., G. Doppelhofer, and R. I. Miller. 2004. "Determinants of Long-Term Growth: A Bayesian Averaging of Classical Estimates (BACE) Approach." *American Economic Review* 94 (4): 813-35.

Sanchez-Robles, B. 1998. "Infrastructure Investment and Growth: Some Empirical Evidence." *Contemporary Economic Policy* 16 (1): 98-108.

Sasso, S., and J. Ritzen. 2016. "Sectoral Cognitive Skills, R&D, and Productivity: A Cross-Country Cross-Sector Analysis." IZA Discussion Paper 10457, Institute of Labor Economics, Bonn.

Shabnam, N. 2014. "Natural Disasters and Economic Growth: A Review." *International Journal of Disaster Risk Science* 5 (2): 157-63.

Sianesi, B., and J. Van Reenen. 2003. "The Returns to Education: Macroeconomics." *Journal of Economic Surveys* 17 (2): 157-200.

Slesman, L., A. Baharumshah, and W. N. W. Azman-Saini. 2019. "Political Institutions and Finance-Growth Nexus in Emerging Markets and Developing Countries: A Tale of One Threshold." *Quarterly Review of Economics and Finance* 72 (C): 80-100.

Squicciarini, M., and H. Nachtigall. 2021. "Demand for AI Skills in Jobs: Evidence from Online Job Postings." OECD Science, Technology and Industry Working Paper 2021/03, Organisation for Economic Co-operation and Development, Paris.

Steinberg, C., and M. Nakane. 2012. "Can Women Save Japan?" IMF Working Paper 12/248, International Monetary Fund, Washington, DC.

Straub, S., and A. Terada-Hagiwara. 2010. "Infrastructure and Growth in Developing Asia." Economics Working Paper 231, Asian Development Bank, Manila.

Taras, H. 2005. "Nutrition and Student Performance at School." *Journal of School Health* 75 (6): 199-213.

Temple, J. 2001. "Growth Effects of Education and Social Capital in the OECD Countries." *OECD Economic Studies* 33 (C): 57-101.

Teulings, C. N., and N. Zubanov. 2014. "Is Economic Recovery a Myth? Robust Estimation of Impulse Responses." *Journal of Applied Econometrics* 29 (3): 497-514.

Topalova, P., and A. Khandelwal. 2011. "Trade Liberalization and Firm Productivity: The Case of India." *Review of Economics and Statistics* 93 (3): 995-1009.

Topel, R. 1999. "Labor Markets and Economic Growth." In *Handbook of Labor Economics*, edited by O. Ashenfelter and D. Card, 2943-84. Amsterdam: Elsevier.

Tsimpo Nkengne, C., A. Etang Ndip, and W. T. Wodon. 2017. "Education and Health Services in Uganda: Quality of Inputs, User Satisfaction, and Community Welfare Levels." Policy Research Working Paper 8116, World Bank, Washington, DC.

Turnovsky, S. 1996. "Fiscal Policy, Adjustment Costs, and Endogenous Growth." *Oxford Economic Papers* 48 (3): 361-81.

UN (United Nations). 2022. 2022 Revision of World Population Prospects (database). New York: UN.

UNCTAD (United Nations Conference on Trade and Development). 2014. "Investment in SDGs: An Action Plan." In *World Investment Report*. New York: United Nations.

UNICEF (United Nations Children's Fund). 2022. "Where Are We on Education Recovery?" United Nations Children's Fund, New York.

Van den bosch, J., and S. Vanormelingen. 2023. "Productivity Growth over the Business Cycle: Cleansing Effects of Recessions." *Small Business Economics* 60 (2): 639-57.

Vandenbussche, J., P. Aghion, and C. Meghir. 2006. "Growth, Distance to Frontier and Composition of Human Capital." *Journal of Economic Growth* 11 (2): 97-127.

Weil, D. 2014. "Health and Economic Growth." In *Handbook of Economic Growth*, edited by P. Aghion and S. Durlauf, 623-82. Amsterdam: Elsevier.

Williams, K. 2019. "Do Political Institutions Improve the Diminishing Effect of Financial Deepening on Growth? Evidence from Developing Countries." *Journal of Economics and Business* 103 (May-June): 13-24.

Woessmann, L. 2003a. "Schooling Resources, Educational Institutions, and Student Performance: The International Evidence." *Oxford Bulletin of Economics and Statistics* 65 (2): 117-70.

Woessmann, L. 2003b. "Specifying Human Capital." *Journal of Economic Surveys* 17 (3): 239-70.

World Bank. 2012. *World Development Report 2012: Gender Equality and Development.* Washington, DC: World Bank.

World Bank. 2013. *World Development Report 2013: Jobs.* Washington, DC: World Bank.

World Bank. 2014. *Doing Business 2014: Understanding Regulations for Small and Medium-Size Enterprises.* Washington, DC: World Bank.

World Bank. 2015. *Global Economic Prospects: Having Fiscal Space and Using It.* January. Washington, DC: World Bank.

World Bank. 2016. *World Development Report 2016: Digital Dividends.* Washington, DC: World Bank.

World Bank. 2017a. *Global Economic Prospects: A Fragile Recovery.* June. Washington, DC: World Bank.

World Bank. 2017b. *Global Economic Prospects: Weak Investment in Uncertain Times.* January. Washington, DC: World Bank.

World Bank. 2017c. *World Development Report 2017: Governance and the Law.* Washington, DC: World Bank.

World Bank. 2018a. *Global Economic Prospects: The Turning of the Tide?* June. Washington, DC: World Bank.

World Bank. 2018b. *Update for East Asia and Pacific: Enhancing Potential.* April. Washington, DC: World Bank.

World Bank. 2018c. *World Development Report 2018: Learning to Realize Education's Promise.* Washington, DC: World Bank.

World Bank. 2019a. *Africa Pulse: An Analysis of Issues Shaping Africa's Economic Future.* April. World Bank, Washington, DC.

World Bank. 2019b. *Malaysia Economic Monitor: Making Ends Meet.* December. Washington, DC: World Bank.

World Bank. 2019c. *World Development Report 2019: The Changing Nature of Work.* Washington, DC: World Bank.

World Bank. 2020a. *Update for East Asia and Pacific: From Containment to Recovery.* October. Washington, DC: World Bank.

World Bank. 2020b. *World Development Report 2020: Trading for Development in the Age of Global Value Chains.* Washington, DC: World Bank.

World Bank. 2021a. *Global Economic Prospects.* January. Washington, DC: World Bank.

World Bank. 2021b. *Update for East Asia and Pacific: Long Covid.* October. Washington, DC: World Bank.

World Bank. 2021c. *Update for East Asia and Pacific: Uneven Recovery.* April. Washington, DC: World Bank.

World Bank. 2022. *Update for East Asia and Pacific: Reforms for Recovery.* October. Washington, DC: World Bank.

World Bank. 2023. *Global Economic Prospects.* January. Washington, DC: World Bank.

World Economic Forum. 2021. "China to Leapfrog U.S. as World's Biggest Economy by 2028," *Economic Progress* (blog), January 11, 2021. World Economic Forum, Geneva.

Yankow, J. J. 2006. "Why Do Cities Pay More? An Empirical Examination of Some Competing Theories of the Urban Wage Premium." *Journal of Urban Economics* 60 (2): 139-61.

CHAPTER 6

Trade as an Engine of Growth: Sputtering but Fixable

International trade has been an important engine of output and productivity growth historically, helping to lift millions out of poverty in recent decades. But since the global financial crisis, world trade growth has slowed, with the slowdown reflecting cyclical and structural forces. The coronavirus disease 2019 (COVID-19) pandemic and the Russian Federation's subsequent invasion of Ukraine have further disrupted global supply chains and the trade that accompanies them. A removal of impediments that raise trade costs could reinvigorate world trade. Trade costs, on average, roughly double the cost of internationally traded goods relative to that of domestically sold goods. Tariffs amount to only one-twentieth of average trade costs; the bulk of those costs are incurred in shipping and logistics and trade procedures and processes at and behind the border. Despite a decline since 1995, trade costs remain about one-half higher in emerging market and developing economies (EMDEs) than in advanced economies; about two-fifths of this gap appears to be due to higher shipping and logistics costs and a further two-fifths to trade policy. A comprehensive reform package to lower trade costs would include trade facilitation measures, deeper trade liberalization, efforts to streamline trade processes and clearance requirements, improvements in transport infrastructure, more competition in domestic logistics and in retail and wholesale trade, and less corruption. Some of these measures could yield large dividends: It is estimated that among the worst-performing EMDEs, a hypothetical reform package to improve logistics performance and maritime connectivity to the standards of the best-performing EMDEs would halve trade costs.

Introduction

Global trade, powered by trade liberalization and falling transport costs, has historically been an important engine of output and productivity growth. In recent decades, it has helped to lift about 1 billion people out of poverty and many developing countries to integrate themselves into the world economy. Empirical studies indicate that an increase in trade openness of 1 percentage point of gross domestic product (GDP) has lifted per capita income by 0.2 percent (World Bank 2020c). The expansion of global value chains can account for a large part of the gains from trade (World Bank 2020c). Participation in global value chains generates efficiency gains and supports the transfer of knowledge, capital, and other inputs across countries, thereby boosting productivity. Integration into global value chains has also been associated with reduced vulnerability of economic activity to domestic shocks, although it has come with increased sensitivity to external shocks (Constantinescu, Mattoo, and Ruta 2020; Espitia et al. 2021).

Note: This chapter was prepared by Franziska Ohnsorge and Lucia Quaglietti, with contributions from Cordula Rastogi.

FIGURE 6.1 Global trade

Global trade in goods and services grew almost twice as fast as global output during 1970-2008, but less than one and one-half times as fast during 2011-19. Goods trade accounted for 75 percent of global trade in goods and services during 2010-19.

A. Global trade and output growth

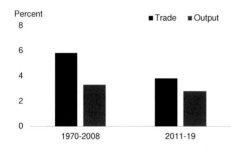

B. Composition of global trade, 2010-19

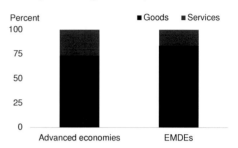

Source: World Bank.
Note: EMDEs = emerging market and developing economies.
A. Bars indicate annual average growth. World output growth is real growth in gross domestic product (GDP) computed as a weighted average (at 2010-19 average prices and exchange rates) as reported in the January 2023 *Global Economic Prospects* report. Trade growth refers to the average growth of import and export volumes.
B. Average of global goods and services trade over the period 2010-19.

In the past decade and a half, global trade growth has slowed as global value chains have matured, investment weakness has weighed on goods trade, and trade tensions have emerged among major economies (World Bank 2015, 2017; chapter 3). As a result, instead of growing twice as fast as global output, as it did during 1990-2011, global trade in goods and services grew just about as fast as global output in 2011-19 (figure 6.1). The COVID-19 pandemic hit global trade particularly hard, and the latter fell by nearly 16 percent in the second quarter of 2020. It subsequently rebounded swiftly, however, especially goods trade, and much faster than it did after the 2007-09 global financial crisis. That said, in 2021, global trade growth slowed again, as lockdowns and closures in the midst of new COVID-19 outbreaks and the emergence of significant supply chain strains in a number of sectors disrupted trade. Russia's invasion of Ukraine in February 2022, which dislocated global commodity markets and manufacturing processes that rely on specialized inputs from Russia or Ukraine dealt a further blow to supply chains and trade.

Absent a major policy effort, trade growth is likely to weaken further over the remainder of the 2020s, given the prospect of slower output growth and the fact that some of the key structural factors that supported rapid trade expansion in the past have largely run their course. Although supply chains have proven remarkably resilient given the magnitude of recent shocks, the COVID-19 pandemic and Russia's invasion of Ukraine could accelerate changes in supply chains that were already under way, through further in-sourcing or regionalizing production networks and increasing digitalization, among other avenues (chapter 4). A contraction of supply chains might lower the output elasticity of trade further, continuing a process that has been under way since 2010 (Timmer et al. 2021). Multinational corporations operating in EMDEs have already increased their use of digital technologies and enhanced their diversification of suppliers and production sites to increase their resilience to supply chain shocks (Saurav et al. 2020). As multinationals seek to diversify, EMDEs may have new opportunities to integrate into global supply chains, provided they can offer a conducive business environment, incorporating such elements as a skilled workforce and adequate infrastructure (Arunyanart et al. 2021; Butollo 2021).

As discussed in chapter 5, growth in potential output is expected to slow in many EMDEs in the coming decade amid unfavorable demographics and slowing investment and productivity growth. One way in which policy makers in EMDEs can boost long-term growth of output and productivity is by promoting trade integration through measures to reduce trade costs.

This chapter examines the following questions:

- What is the link between trade growth and long-term output growth?

- What are the prospects for trade growth in the coming decade?

- How large are trade costs?

- What are the correlates of trade costs?

- Which policies can help to reduce trade costs?

This chapter contributes to the literature in a number of ways. First, it expands on World Bank (2021c) with a new, comprehensive review of the theoretical and empirical literature on the links between trade and output growth. Second, it presents an event study of the evolution of trade in goods and services through global recessions, including the pandemic-induced global recession of 2020.

Third, the chapter revisits an earlier literature that reported estimates of trade costs and their correlates (Arvis et al. 2016; Novy 2013; World Bank 2021c). It uses estimates of the costs of goods trade for up to 180 economies (29 advanced economies and 151 EMDEs) from the UN Economic and Social Commission for Asia and the Pacific (ESCAP)-World Bank Trade Cost Database for 1995-2019 to estimate econometrically the drivers of the costs of goods trade, which accounts for about 75 percent of world and EMDE trade in goods and services. The chapter also quantifies the contribution of one type of services trade—logistics and shipping services—to the costs of goods trade. In addition, the chapter goes further than previously published research in assessing the role of trade policy—tariffs and participation in trade agreements—in trade costs.

Fourth, the chapter builds upon its analytical findings to discuss policy options for lowering trade costs. In particular, it offers scenarios indicating the potential impact of a range of policy measures on trade costs.

This chapter offers the following findings.

First, the theoretical literature indicates that international trade boosts the long-term growth of output and productivity by promoting a more efficient allocation of resources, technological spillovers, and human capital accumulation. The empirical literature supports this theory by finding statistically significant positive relationships between trade openness and output growth, although the statistical significance of these relationships may be conditional on the presence of sound institutions and a supportive business environment in exporting countries. Overwhelmingly, empirical studies find a positive impact of trade on productivity growth.

Second, the COVID-19-induced global recession of 2020 triggered a collapse of global trade in goods and services. Within six months, however, before the end of 2020, global goods trade had recovered to prepandemic levels, and, by September 2021, global services trade had reached prepandemic levels, even though trade in travel and tourism services was still 40 percent lower than before the pandemic. The decline in services trade was considerably more pronounced and the recovery more subdued than in past global recessions, whereas movements in goods trade were broadly comparable to those in past global recessions.

Third, global trade growth is likely to weaken further in the coming decade, owing partly to slower global output growth and partly to the further waning of structural factors that supported rapid trade expansion in the past. The disruptions caused by the pandemic and Russia's invasion of Ukraine may also continue to dampen trade growth over the medium term. A major policy effort to reduce trade costs could help reverse the trade slowdown.

Fourth, trade costs for goods are high: On average, they are almost equivalent to a 100 percent tariff, so they roughly double the costs of internationally traded goods relative to those of domestic goods. Tariffs amount to only one-twentieth of average trade costs; the bulk of trade costs are incurred in transport and logistics, nontariff barriers, and policy-related standards and regulations. Despite a one-third decline since 1995, trade costs in EMDEs remain about one-half higher than those in advanced economies.[1] Analysis of the results of a panel regression suggests that higher shipping and logistics costs can account for about two-fifths of the difference in trade costs between EMDEs and advanced economies explained by the regression, and trade policy (including uncertainty surrounding it) can account for a further two-fifths. Services trade tends to cost considerably more than goods trade; regulatory restrictions can account, to a large extent, for the difference.

Fifth, to reduce elevated trade costs in EMDEs, comprehensive reform packages are needed to streamline trade processes and customs clearance requirements, enhance infrastructure supporting domestic trade, increase competition in domestic logistics and in retail and wholesale trade, lower tariffs, lower the costs of compliance with standards and regulations, and reduce corruption. Trade agreements can also reduce trade costs

---

[1] Differences in trade costs across regions might also stem from differences in domestic trade costs.

and promote trade, especially if they lower nontariff barriers as well as tariffs. The chapter's empirical analysis suggests that an EMDE in the quartile of EMDEs with the highest shipping and logistics costs could halve its trade costs if it improved these high costs to match those in the quartile of EMDEs with the lowest costs of shipping and logistics.

This chapter defines trade costs broadly to include all costs of international trade, whether at the border (such as tariffs), behind the border (such as standards and labeling requirements), or between borders (such as shipping and logistics). It defines trade costs as the excess cost of an internationally traded good compared with those of a similar good traded domestically (box 6.1). Hence, trade costs cover the full range of costs associated with trading internationally, including transportation and distribution costs, tariffs and nontariff barriers arising from policies, costs of information and contract enforcement, and legal and regulatory costs, as well as the costs of doing business across cultures, languages, and economic systems (Anderson and van Wincoop 2003).

The chapter is organized in six sections. Following the introduction presented in this first section, the second section reviews the theoretical and empirical literature on the linkages between international trade and long-term output growth and the main channels of transmission. The subsequent section discusses developments in global trade over the past decade, with a particular focus on developments during the COVID-19 pandemic. The following section presents patterns of trade costs across sectors and regions, while the penultimate section discusses the correlates of trade costs, by means of an estimated gravity panel model, among other methods. The final section focuses on policies to reduce trade costs, presenting a wide range of policy options available to policy makers.

Trade and growth: A review of the literature

An extensive theoretical literature has traced the channels through which international trade can lift output and productivity growth. The empirical literature has largely confirmed a positive association between growth and trade, although some studies have found that the strength of this association depends on country characteristics.

Theoretical literature

The link between international trade and economic activity has long been a major subject of enquiry in theories of international trade and economic growth. Much traditional trade theory explains how trade raises output levels but is silent about effects on long-term output growth (Feenstra 2003; Ricardo 1817). In contrast, more recent trade and growth theories describe a positive relationship between the two, tracing the mechanisms through which trade lifts long-term productivity and output growth (Helpman 1981; Krugman 1979; Lucas 1993).

Three main channels have been explored. First, access to foreign markets allows countries to acquire new technologies, especially when countries with different

BOX 6.1 Understanding the determinants of trade costs

Shipping and logistics, tariffs, and membership in regional trade agreements contribute in a statistically significant way to trade costs.

Introduction

Elevated trade costs remain a significant impediment to cross-border trade. On average, trade costs roughly double the cost of an internationally traded good over that of a similar domestic good. Emerging market and developing economies (EMDEs) have trade costs more than one-half higher than those in advanced economies, despite a decline since 1995.

This box considers the determinants of trade costs empirically by examining the following questions.

- How does the literature measure trade costs?

- What are the main determinants of trade costs empirically?

The results suggest that geographic distance and high bilateral tariff rates are positively associated with trade costs, in the manufacturing sector as well as others. In contrast, common borders (proximity), common language, and membership in a common regional trade agreement tend to reduce trade costs. Policies aimed at facilitating trade, including those promoting better maritime connectivity and stronger logistics performance, are also associated with lower bilateral trade costs.

Measures of trade costs

Conceptually, trade costs may be defined as the excess cost of an internationally traded good compared with that of a similar good traded domestically. By construction, trade costs can therefore move without any change in external costs of trading, simply as a result of changes in domestic trading costs. To measure trade costs, the literature has developed two main types of approaches: direct and indirect (Chen and Novy 2012).

Direct approaches rely on observable data that serve as proxies for individual components. For instance, measures of costs faced at a country's border are often based on counting the average number of days needed for a good to cross the border, while transport costs are often inferred from the costs of ocean and air shipping (Hummels et al. 2007). Information regarding policy barriers such as tariffs and nontariff measures is directly available from a range of statistical sources. Direct approaches suffer from a series of limitations, including the fact the underlying variables are only partially observable and may not be easily converted to plausible ad valorem tariff equivalents, which makes it difficult to compare them, as well as difficult to aggregate them into a summary measure of

BOX 6.1 Understanding the determinants of trade costs *(continued)*

trade costs (Anderson and van Wincoop 2004). Therefore, trade cost estimates taken from such measures tend to be only partial.

Indirect approaches aim to circumvent these difficulties. These approaches infer trade impediments from the top down, from measures of trade flows and aggregate value added. Under these types of approaches, trade costs correspond to the difference between the trade flows that would be expected in a hypothetical "frictionless" world and those that are observed in the data; they are computed relative to domestic trade costs. Measures built through the indirect approach can be tracked over time and include all observed and unobserved factors that explain why trading with another country is more costly than trading domestically. Novy (2013) developed a micro-founded measure of aggregate bilateral trade costs using a theoretical gravity equation for the trade cost parameters that capture the barriers to international trade. The resulting solution expresses trade cost parameters as a function of observable trade data, providing a micro-founded measure of bilateral trade costs. The measure is easy to implement empirically for a number of countries for which data are readily available. One drawback is that simple inspection of the measure cannot easily disentangle the contribution of individual cost measures. A way proposed in the literature to overcome this is to combine indirect and direct measurements into a single regression (Arvis et al. 2013).

Determinants of trade costs

To estimate the contribution of different determinants of trade costs, a gravity model is estimated for a panel of up to 23 advanced economies and 72 EMDEs for which annual data for both trade costs and all determinants of trade costs are available over 2007-18. The sample includes 25 exporters of industrial commodities (energy and metals), all of which are EMDEs.

Data

The estimation relies on bilateral trade costs from the UN Economic and Social Commission for Asia and the Pacific (ESCAP)-World Bank Trade Cost Database. As is done in Novy (2013) and Arvis et al. (2013), bilateral trade costs are obtained as geometric averages of flows between countries i and j. They are computed according to the following formula:

$$(X_{ii} X_{jj})/(X_{ij} X_{ji})^{1/2 \, (\sigma-1)},$$

in which X_{ij} represents trade flows between countries i and j (goods produced in i and sold in j) and σ refers to the elasticity of substitution. This formula captures international trade costs relative to domestic trade costs. Intuitively, trade costs are higher when countries trade more domestically than they trade with each

BOX 6.1 Understanding the determinants of trade costs *(continued)*

other, that is, as the ratio $(X_{ii} X_{jj})/(X_{ij} X_{ji})$ increases. The difference between gross output and total exports proxies intranational (that is, domestic) trade.

Trade costs thus computed implicitly account for a wide range of frictions associated with international trade, including transport costs, tariff and nontariff measures, and costs associated with differences in languages, currencies, and import or export procedures. Trade costs are expressed as ad valorem (tariff) equivalents of the value of traded goods and can be computed as an aggregate referring to all sectors of an economy, but also specifically for its manufacturing and agriculture sectors.

Estimation

Gravity equations are widely used to analyze the determinants of bilateral trade flows. Chen and Novy (2012) and Arvis et al. (2013) also employ a gravity specification to analyze the determinants of bilateral trade costs in a cross-sectional data set. In line with Moïsé, Orliac, and Minor (2011), this study estimates determinants of trade costs in a panel specification.

The regression equation takes the following form:

$$TC_{ijt} = \beta_1 \, RTA_{ijt} + \beta_2 \, tariff_{ijt} + \beta_3 \, LSCI_{ijt} + \beta_4 \, LPI_{ijt}$$
$$+ \beta_5 \, Trade \, Policy \, Uncertainty_{ijt} + \beta_6 \, Gravity_{ij} + \eta_t + \varepsilon_{ijt}, \qquad \text{(B6.1.1)}$$

in which for any given country pair *ij*, bilateral trade costs *TC* observed at time *t* are regressed on a wide range of candidate drivers. These include membership in a regional trade agreement (*RTA* in the equation), sector-specific bilateral tariffs, shipping connectivity (the United Nations Conference on Trade and Development's Liner Shipping Connectivity Index [*LSCI* in the equation]) and logistics (the World Bank's Logistics Performance Index [*LPI* in the equation]), a proxy for trade policy uncertainty, and standard gravity indicators (distance, a common language, and a common border). In line with the approach in Osnago, Piermartini, and Rocha (2018), trade policy uncertainty is defined as the gap between binding tariff commitments and applied tariffs. To ascertain the role of policies aimed at facilitating trade, indexes of logistic performance and maritime connectivity are included.

Specifically, the Logistics Performance Index is based on surveys of global freight operators and express carriers regarding customs, logistics and transport infrastructure, international shipments, logistics competence, tracking and tracing, and delays. The Liner Shipping Connectivity Index is derived from a country's number of ships, their container-carrying capacity, maximum vessel size, the number of services provided, and the number of companies that deploy

BOX 6.1 **Understanding the determinants of trade costs** *(continued)*

container ships in the country's ports. The choice of variables in the panel is informed by Arvis et al. (2013), but also by findings from the stylized facts presented in the chapter text. Table 6.1 presents full details on data and sources.[a]

Since trade costs data are obtained as bilateral geometric averages, trade facilitation indicators available at individual-country level are transformed into bilateral measures by taking the geometric average of each country pair direction. Therefore, the unit of analysis is each individual country pair. Time fixed effects η_t are included in the estimation to control for global trends. As the measures of trade costs already net out multilateral resistance components, in line with Novy (2013), the estimation does not include additional fixed effects.[b] Instead, to control for possible correlation of error terms, clustered standard errors by country pairs are used.

Two models are estimated: a general model for the determinants of trade costs in all sectors of the economy and a sectoral model for the determinants of trade costs in the manufacturing sector. The two models follow the specification presented in equation (B6.1.1), but trade costs and tariff rates are sector specific. Table B6.1.1 shows results from the estimations.

Results

All estimated coefficients have signs and magnitudes in line with prior expectations based on the literature. Geographic distance and high bilateral tariff rates are positively associated with trade costs. In contrast, adjacency, common language, and membership in a common regional trade agreement tend to reduce trade costs. Policies aimed at facilitating trade, including those intended to increase maritime connectivity and generate stronger logistics performance, are also associated with lower bilateral trade costs, both overall and in the manufacturing sector. Trade uncertainty is also positively associated with trade costs, both overall and in the manufacturing sector. With an R-squared value above 50 percent, the regression explains most of the variation in trade costs in the sample.

---

a. Nontariff barriers and exchange rate volatility would ideally have been included in the regression estimation. However, these are difficult to measure, and the panel measures available over time and across countries were too crude to yield statistically significant results. Ideally, the regression would also be applied to services; however, the database does not include trade costs for services.

b. Multilateral resistance captures global trends. Specifically, outward multilateral resistance measures the degree to which trade flows between countries i and j depend on trade costs across all potential markets for country i's exports, while inward multilateral resistance measures the degree to which bilateral trade depends on trade costs across all potential import markets. Therefore, the two indexes summarize third-country effects that might affect bilateral trade flows between countries i and j. Novy (2013) shows that simple algebra makes it possible to eliminate the multilateral resistance terms from the gravity equations, and in so doing he derives an expression for trade costs.

BOX 6.1 Understanding the determinants of trade costs *(continued)*

TABLE B6.1.1 Panel regression results

	All sectors	Manufacturing sector
Liner Shipping Connectivity Index	-0.2299***	-0.2271**
	(0.007)	(0.007)
Logistics Performance Index	-0.5004***	-0.5156***
	(0.032)	(0.356)
Tariffs	0.3449***	0.4265***
	(0.044)	(0.057)
Regional trade agreement membership	-0.0487***	-0.0567***
	(0.006)	(0.006)
Trade policy uncertainty	0.0907**	0.0902**
	(0.004)	(0.005)
Distance	0.2605***	0.2687***
	(0.007)	(0.007)
Common border	-0.4070***	-0.4125***
	(0.033)	(0.035)
Common language	-0.1516***	-0.1369***
	(0.013)	(0.141)
Number of observations	56,038	52,060
R^2	0.569	0.569

Source: World Bank.
Note: Robust standard errors are shown in parentheses. The table shows estimated coefficients from a gravity panel regression estimated for up to 95 countries using annual data for 2007-18 in which the dependent variable is the log of bilateral trade costs. The regression includes time fixed effects. Standard errors are clustered by country pairs.
*$p < 0.05$; **$p < 0.01$; ***$p < 0.001$.

The panel estimation also explains most of the difference in trade costs between the average EMDE and the average advanced economy and attributes about two-fifths of this gap to higher shipping and logistics costs in EMDEs and a further two-fifths to trade policy (including trade policy uncertainty). The regression also explains most of the decline in average trade costs between 2008 and 2018 and attributes three-fourths of it to falling shipping and logistics costs and the remaining one-fourth to trade policy.

There are significant differences in the drivers of trade costs between advanced economies (which are mostly importers of industrial commodities) and EMDEs, and between exporters and importers of industrial commodities. The regression is reestimated for several subsamples of costs of bilateral trade flows: a sample of costs of bilateral trade among EMDEs only, a sample of costs of bilateral trade among advanced economies only, and a sample of costs of bilateral trade between EMDEs and advanced economies. It is also reestimated for a sample of bilateral trade costs between importers of industrial commodities only or exporters of

BOX 6.1 **Understanding the determinants of trade costs** *(continued)*

industrial commodities only, as well as a sample of bilateral trade costs between exporters and importers of industrial commodities. Tables B6.1.2A and B6.1.2B show the results.

For trade among advanced economies only, logistics performance and distance are critical sources of trade costs, whereas tariffs and regional trade agreement membership play negligible roles. By comparison, better logistics performance reduces trade costs between an advanced economy and an EMDE or between a pair of EMDEs by only one-fifth as much as between a pair of advanced economies. On the other hand, membership in regional trade agreements significantly reduces trade costs between pairs of EMDEs (but not in advanced economy-EMDE country pairs or, as noted, between pairs of advanced economies).

Logistics performance and distance are also more important sources costs of trade among commodity importers than between commodity importers and exporters. For tariffs, the reverse is true. For example, an improvement in logistics performance lowers trade costs between commodity importers by almost twice as much as between commodity importers and exporters. Conversely, a cut in tariffs lower trade costs between commodity exporters and importers by twice as much as between commodity importers. These patterns are evident for trade costs both in all sectors and in manufacturing alone.

Robustness

The estimations are robust to different specifications, lag structures, and estimators. An alternative estimation performed with the Poisson maximum likelihood estimator, which is often employed in the literature on gravity models (Santos Silva and Tenreyro 2006) to control for heteroskedasticity, produces similar results to those presented in table B6.1.1.

Adding further variables, including bilateral real exchange rates, gross domestic product (GDP) per capita, institutional variables, and a dummy characterizing landlocked country pairs, does not alter the regression results, and the variables turn out to be statistically nonsignificant. Likewise, adding country fixed effects does not alter the stability of the model, with both the gravity and trade policy variables retaining the expected sign and statistically significant effects. While there are concerns about multicollinearity (regarding the 0.5 correlations between the Logistics Performance Index and Liner Shipping Connectivity Index, among others), a variable inflation factor test (a standard diagnostic test) does not detect the presence of significant multicollinearity among regressors.

A few caveats apply to the analysis. The effect of policies on trade costs can be difficult to disentangle. Changes in trade costs between two countries can be due

BOX 6.1 Understanding the determinants of trade costs *(continued)*

TABLE B6.1.2A Panel regression results for subsamples

	All sectors					
	Advanced economies only	Advanced economies and EMDEs	EMDEs only	Commodity importers only	Commodity importers and exporters	Commodity exporters only
Liner Shipping Connectivity Index	-0.195*** [0.0237]	-0.230*** [0.0111]	-0.209*** † [0.0093]	-0.230*** [0.00886]	-0.231*** ‡ [0.0109]	-0.198*** ‡ [0.0226]
Logistics Performance Index	-1.526*** [0.107]	-0.298*** † [0.055]	-0.277*** † [0.048]	-0.596*** [0.0438]	-0.317*** ‡ [0.0471]	-0.273*** ‡ [0.097]
Distance	0.343*** [0.0157]	0.221*** † [0.0112]	0.233*** † [0.00993]	0.306*** [0.0103]	0.223*** ‡ [0.00962]	0.241*** ‡ [0.0202]
Tariffs	-0.0998 [0.239]	0.517*** † [0.0916]	0.203*** † [0.0488]	0.189** [0.0878]	0.453*** ‡ [0.0647]	0.238*** [0.0682]
Regional trade agreement membership	-0.00793 [0.0125]	-0.0289*** [0.00714]	-0.0850*** † [0.0117]	-0.0326*** [0.00789]	-0.0545*** [0.00844]	-0.0796*** [0.0265]
Trade policy uncertainty	0.0383*** [0.0128]	0.0897*** † [0.00706]	0.0583*** † [0.00684]	0.0799*** [0.00633]	0.0794*** ‡ [0.00666]	0.0103 ‡ [0.0132]
Common border	-0.389*** [0.114]	-0.380*** [0.136]	-0.453*** [0.0334]	-0.327*** [0.0581]	-0.494*** ‡ [0.0566]	-0.356*** [0.0541]
Common language	-0.166***	-0.0878*** †	-0.186***	-0.117***	-0.145***	-0.273*** ‡
Number of observations	504	668	102	802	450	408

Source: World Bank.
Note: Robust standard errors are shown in parentheses. The table shows estimated coefficients from a gravity panel regression estimated for up to 95 countries using annual data for 2007-18 in which the dependent variable is the log of bilateral trade costs. The regression includes time fixed effects. Standard errors are clustered by country pairs.
$*p < 0.05$, $**p < 0.01$, $***p < 0.001$. † indicates the coefficient estimate is different, with statistical significance, from the coefficient estimate for a sample of advanced economies only. ‡ indicates the coefficient estimate is different, with statistical significance, from the coefficient estimate for a sample of commodity importers only.

to actions taken by one government or the other or both together. The fact that the variables featuring in the regression (including the measure of trade costs) are computed as country-pair geometric averages does not allow a disentangling of the source of policy actions. In addition, because of the lack of sufficiently long time-series data, the approach taken here does not take into account the possibility that the regression coefficients have changed over time, as other studies for the effect of distance (Yotov 2012) or trade agreements (de Sousa 2012) have found.

BOX 6.1 **Understanding the determinants of trade costs** *(continued)*

TABLE B6.1.2B **Panel regression results for subsamples**

	Manufacturing					
	Advanced economies only	Advanced economies and EMDEs	EMDEs only	Commodity importers only	Commodity importers and exporters	Commodity exporters only
Liner Shipping Connectivity Index	-0.215*** [0.0266]	-0.235*** † [0.0117]	-0.206*** † [0.0104]	-0.234*** [0.00947]	-0.227*** ‡ [0.0119]	-0.198*** ‡ [0.0258]
Logistics Performance Index	-1.788*** [0.123]	-0.298*** † [0.058]	-0.336*** † [0.0539]	-0.686*** [0.0486]	-0.327*** ‡ [0.0525]	-0.237** ‡ [0.107]
Distance	0.353*** [0.0179]	0.239*** † [0.0122]	0.247*** † [0.0103]	0.303*** [0.011]	0.236*** ‡ [0.0107]	0.255*** ‡ [0.0199]
Tariffs	-0.225 [0.302]	0.804*** [0.11]	0.218*** [0.0569]	0.243** [0.107]	0.621*** [0.0827]	0.258*** [0.099]
Regional trade agreement membership	-0.005 [0.0131]	-0.0243*** [0.00791]	-0.108*** † [0.0122]	-0.0478*** [0.00841]	-0.0515*** [0.00981]	-0.107*** [0.0255]
Trade policy uncertainty	0.0287* [0.0171]	0.0744*** [0.00867]	0.0382*** [0.00701]	0.104*** [0.0069]	0.0615*** [0.00748]	-0.000122 [0.0132]
Common border	-0.283** [0.111]	-0.371** [0.145]	-0.466*** † [0.0364]	-0.325*** [0.0561]	-0.511*** ‡ [0.0609]	-0.354*** [0.0626]
Common language	-0.136***	-0.0924***	-0.183***	-0.153***	-0.146***	-0.254*** ‡
Number of observations	642	538	632	134	382	408

Source: World Bank.
Note: Robust standard errors are shown in parentheses. The table shows estimated coefficients from a gravity panel regression estimated for up to 95 countries using annual data for 2007-18 in which the dependent variable is the log of bilateral trade costs. The regression includes time fixed effects. Standard errors are clustered by country pairs.
*$p < 0.05$, **$p < 0.01$, ***$p < 0.001$. † indicates the coefficient estimate is different, with statistical significance, from the coefficient estimate for a sample of advanced economies only. ‡ indicates the coefficient estimate is different, with statistical significance, from the coefficient estimate for a sample of commodity importers only.

Conclusion

The estimation results suggest that policies can have a statistically significant and economically sizable impact on trade costs. Better shipping connectivity, better logistics performance, and less trade policy uncertainty are associated with trade costs that are lower with statistical significance. More challenging shipping and logistics account for about two-fifths of the predicted gap between trade costs in EMDEs and those in advanced economies, and trade policy accounts for a further two-fifths. Improved shipping and logistics also account for about three-fourths of the predicted decline in trade costs since 2008.

technological endowments trade with one another. Second, openness to international trade offers opportunities to exploit economies of scale and "learning by doing," which enhance both productivity growth and the variety of goods produced and consumed. Third, trade generates competitive pressures that encourage innovation and factor reallocation, including the exit of the least productive firms, thus lifting overall productivity.

Technological progress, by enhancing the productivity of labor and other factors of production, is a critical driver of long-term output growth and poverty reduction. Apart from their immediate impact on productivity, the creation, application, and diffusion of technological advances tend to generate positive externalities and increasing returns to scale (Arrow 1962; Romer 1990). However, as technological innovation tends to occur in a limited number of countries, advances globally depend on international spillovers (Keller 2004). International trade, like foreign direct investment (FDI), is one of the primary channels for diffusion of new technology, as it makes available to importers processes and products that embody foreign knowledge and that would otherwise be unavailable or very costly (Grossman and Helpman 1991; Helpman 1997).

The literature identifies two types of externalities generated through trade: pure knowledge spillovers and rent spillovers. Pure knowledge spillovers arise mostly through licensing agreements or through firms that are multinational. Rent spillovers occur when the prices of imported intermediate and capital goods do not fully reflect the costs of innovation embedded in them, so that part of the rents from innovation are transferred from the innovating firm to trading partners (Keller 2021).

International trade also allows countries to exploit economies of scale and network effects in areas where they have a comparative advantage (Helpman 1981; Helpman and Krugman 1985; Krugman 1979). Trade causes output to expand and, in the presence of increasing returns to scale, firms' fixed costs are spread over a larger number of units produced. This results in more efficient production at smaller average cost. Through a similar mechanism, the output expansion associated with trade may also allow greater product variety, which can enhance productivity (Feenstra 2010). In addition, innovations resulting from international trade often allow workers to acquire new human capital through learning by doing as workers take up new tasks. This also boosts productivity and helps countries move up the product-quality ladder (Lucas 1993).

By increasing competition, trade also promotes productivity growth by reallocating resources toward more efficient firms as the least productive firms are encouraged to exit (Bernard et al. 2007; Melitz 2003). Since entering foreign markets imposes an up-front cost for exporting firms, only relatively productive firms can generally engage in exporting. Once they have entered a new market, exporting firms can expand and attract workers and capital, thus tending to force out firms limited to the domestic market by inferior efficiency. In addition, by raising competitive pressures in the domestic market, international trade lowers firms' markups over marginal cost and encourages organizational change and production upgrades to boost within-firm productivity (Melitz and Ottaviano 2008).

Empirical literature

A large empirical literature using cross-country and firm-level data has investigated the relationship between international trade and long-term output growth. In addition to aggregate effects, studies have identified specific channels through which trade integration boosts productivity, capital accumulation, and employment growth—the fundamental drivers of long-term economic growth.

Trade and output growth. Most cross-country studies have found a positive link between international trade and output growth (see Alesina, Spolaore, and Wacziarg 2000; Dollar and Kraay 2004; Frankel and Romer 1999; Noguer and Siscart 2005; and Sachs and Warner 1995). However, the direction of causality and the role of third factors remain matters of debate. Some studies find clear growth-enhancing effects of trade liberalization (Bhagwati and Srinivasan 2002; Dollar 1992), whereas others find that the effects depend on the measure of trade openness used (Rodríguez and Rodrik 2000). This may, in part, reflect omitted variables. For example, some authors find trade has a large positive impact on growth only when accompanied by high levels of education, well-developed financial systems, and institutional reforms (Chang, Kaltani, and Loayza 2009). Likewise, regulatory reforms have been found to enhance the impact of trade on growth (Bolaky and Freund 2004).

Trade and productivity. A number of cross-country and firm-level studies find a positive link between trade and labor or total factor productivity (see Alcala and Ciccone 2004; Chen, Imbs, and Scott 2009; Edwards 1997; and Frankel and Romer 1999). A cross-country study of 138 countries for 1985 finds that an increase of 1 percentage point in trade openness is associated with 1.2 percent higher labor productivity (Alcala and Ciccone 2004). A more recent study of a large number of advanced economies and EMDEs finds that rising trade openness accounted for about 15 percent of the increase in total factor productivity growth during 1994-2003, but it accounted for a larger proportion—32 percent—in developing countries alone (Broda, Greenfield, and Weinstein 2017). Studies that address firm heterogeneity also point to trade-induced productivity gains. For example, one study finds that firms facing international competition enjoy productivity that is 3-10 percent higher than productivity in those that sell only in domestic markets (Pavcnik 2002). A study for Brazil finds evidence of reductions in inefficiencies in firms that engage in international trade (Muendler 2004).

Trade and capital accumulation. Several studies find evidence of a positive relationship between trade openness and capital accumulation (Alvarez 2017; Sposi, Yi, and Zhang 2019). A study covering the period 1950-98 indicates that countries that liberalized their trade regimes subsequently experienced annual investment growth that was 1.5 percentage points higher than their rates before liberalization, on average (Wacziarg and Welch 2008). The literature also points to a close association between trade openness and FDI inflows, which are a source of funding for investment in addition to domestic saving (Shah and Khan 2016; Sharma and Kumar 2015; Stone and Jeon 2000). For example, one study found that among 36 developing economies between 1990 and 2008, trade openness was associated with higher FDI inflows in the long run (Liargovas and Skandalis 2012). Trade policies and the quality of infrastructure have been found to affect the strength of the link between trade and FDI. Thus, a study of Asian countries during 2008-13 found that countries with fewer restrictions on imports and exports had a higher chance of attracting FDI, with an 8 percent increase in FDI inflows accompanying a 10 percent reduction in bilateral trade costs (Duval, Saggu, and Utoktham 2015).

Trade and employment. Theoretical models often assume long-run full employment, allowing trade to have only limited, short-term effects on jobs. But a number of empirical studies point to positive effects of trade on employment. For example, a cross-country study of member countries of the Organisation for Economic Co-operation and Development (OECD) over 1983-2003 finds that a 10 percent increase in trade openness was associated with a rate of unemployment that was 1 percentage point lower (Felbermayr, Prat, and Schmerer 2009). Country-specific evidence also suggests significant employment creation following greater trade integration, in China, Madagascar, and Singapore, among others (Hoekman and Winters 2005). Another study, however, found that in the United States, rising imports from China raised unemployment and reduced labor force participation in import-competing manufacturing industries and that such imports explained one-quarter of the decline in U.S. manufacturing employment (Autor, Dorn, and Hanson 2013). In general, trade integration has different effects on employment across countries that depend importantly on the functioning of labor markets, the efficiency of capital markets, and social policies (OECD et al. 2010).

Recent trade growth and prospects

The slowdown in trade growth in the decade following the global financial crisis reflected weaker global output growth as well as a lower responsiveness of international trade to global economic activity (the output elasticity of trade). The subsequent COVID-19 pandemic triggered a collapse in goods trade on par with those in earlier global recessions, but the collapse in services trade was much deeper and was followed by an exceptionally slow recovery. All major drivers of trade growth point to a period of prolonged weakness.

Weakness of trade growth in the 2010s

Global trade in goods and nonfactor services grew much more weakly in the prepandemic decade, at just 3.8 percent a year during 2011-19, than during 1970-2008, when it averaged 5.8 percent a year. If global trade had expanded at its 1970-2008 trend rate during 2011-19, it would have been about one-third above its actual level in 2019 (figure 6.2). With the exception of Europe and Central Asia (ECA), the slowdown in trade growth extended across all EMDE regions. Sub-Saharan Africa (SSA) experienced particularly weak trade growth, at about half the EMDE average over the 2010s. The slowdown was concentrated in goods trade; services trade continued to outpace world output growth, by 1.5 percentage points a year on average during 2011-19, before the pandemic hit.

FIGURE 6.2 Factors lowering the elasticity of global trade with respect to global output

Global trade growth has slowed since 2011, in part as a result of slowing output growth. In addition, trade has become less elastic with respect to global economic activity amid slowing global investment, maturing global value chains, and mounting trade tensions.

A. World trade, actual and trend

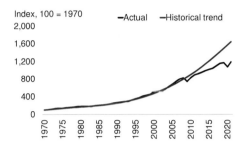

B. Elasticity of global trade with respect to global output

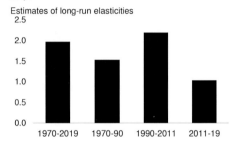

C. Aggregate demand components relative to historical trend, 2019

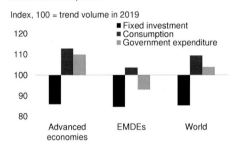

D. Import content of components of aggregate demand, 2014

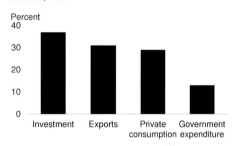

E. Share of global-value-chain-related trade in global trade

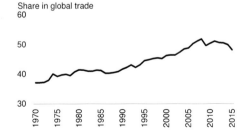

F. New trade measures

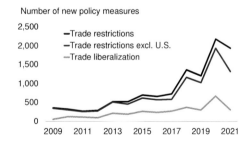

Sources: Auboin and Borino (2018); Constantinescu, Mattoo, and Ruta (2020); Global Trade Alert database; World Bank.
Note: EMDEs = emerging market and developing economies; excl. = excluding.
A. "World trade" refers to the average of imports and exports, indexed to 1970 = 100. The historical trend is computed over 1970-2008 and smoothed using a Hodrick-Prescott filter.
B. Estimates from an error correction model over the period 1970-2019. The model allows trade to have both a long-run elasticity with respect to income (which captures trend, or structural, factors) and a short-run elasticity (which is relevant to short-run or cyclical developments). For further details on the model specification, see Constantinescu, Mattoo, and Ruta (2020).
C. Trend levels in 2019 are obtained on the basis of the historical average trend growth computed over the period 1995-2008 and rebased to 100. Bars below 100 show deviations of actual 2019 levels from trends. Investment is aggregate investment.
D. Data for 2014 as estimated in Auboin and Borino (2018).
E. Share of global-value-chain-related trade in global trade as defined in World Bank (2020c). Data are available through 2015.
F. Data exclude late reports for the respective reporting years (the cut-off date is December 31 of each year).

Estimates of the output elasticity of trade also reflect the slowdown in trade growth. Estimates from an error correction model for 1970-2019 suggest that the long-run output elasticity of trade—the trade increase associated with a 1 percent increase in output—declined from 2.2 during 1990-2011 to about 1.0 during 2011-19.[2] In EMDEs, the ratio of import growth to output growth declined from 1.7 during 1990-2008 to 0.9 during 2011-19. The decline in the global output elasticity of trade in the decade before the pandemic reflected several factors (World Bank 2015).

- *Changes in the composition of global demand.* The composition of global demand shifted away from advanced economies toward EMDEs and toward less trade-intensive components of aggregate demand. EMDEs, which typically have a lower trade intensity than advanced economies, accounted for just under two-fifths of global output during 1980-2008 but for about three-fifths during 2010-19 (Cabrillac et al. 2016; World Bank 2015). Investment, which tends to be more trade-intensive than other components of demand, has been weak over the past decade, especially in EMDEs (Bussière et al. 2013; Kose et al. 2017). This weakness has reflected a number of factors, including a policy-guided shift away from investment-led growth in China and the effects of prolonged weakness of commodity prices on investment in commodity exporters (World Bank 2017, 2019).

- *Maturing global value chains.* Over the past decade, the expansion of global value chains has slowed (Antras and Chor 2021; World Bank 2015, 2020c). The share of global-value-chain-related trade in total world trade grew significantly in the 1990s and early 2000s but has stagnated or even declined since 2011. This stagnation or decline has in part reflected rising labor costs in key emerging market economies, a greater appreciation among firms of supply risks in the wake of natural disasters, and mounting trade tensions over the past five years (Cabrillac et al. 2016; Cigna, Gunella, and Quaglietti 2022; World Bank 2020c). Trade in construction and that in services, which tend not to be embedded in deep global value chains, increased their shares of global trade after 2010 (WTO 2019b).

- *Trade tensions.* A slowing pace of trade liberalization may also have contributed to lower trade elasticity (World Bank 2015). Tariff rates leveled off in both advanced economies and EMDEs in the early 2000s. At the same time, use of regulatory measures and other nontariff barriers such as export subsidies, restrictions on licensing or foreign direct investment, and domestic clauses in public procurement increased (Niu et al. 2018).

Pandemic-triggered collapse and recovery: Historical comparison

The global recession of 2020 was the deepest since World War II and was accompanied by a collapse in global trade in goods and nonfactor services of nearly 16 percent in the

---

[2] The model allows estimation of both the long-run elasticity of trade with respect to income (which captures trend, or structural, factors) and the short-run elasticity (which is relevant to short-run or cyclical developments). For further details on the model specification, see Constantinescu, Mattoo, and Ruta (2020).

FIGURE 6.3 **Trade during global recessions**

Global goods trade collapsed during the pandemic but rebounded quickly. Services trade declined much more sharply than in previous recessions and has recovered much more slowly.

A. Global goods trade

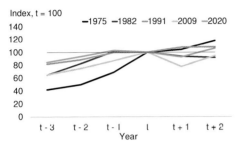

B. Global services trade

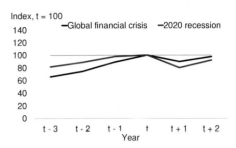

Source: World Bank.
A.B. Figures show annual levels of goods and services trade in the run-up to and aftermath of past recessions and in 2020. *t* refers to the year before the recession.

second quarter of 2020—6 percentage points steeper than the drop in the first quarter of 2009, at the nadir of the global recession triggered by the global financial crisis. In 2020 as a whole, goods trade fell by 7 percent, considerably more than in the average global recession since 1975 (figure 6.3). Unusually for global recessions, global trade in services collapsed more than global trade in goods. The decline in services trade was considerably more pronounced and the recovery more subdued than in past global recessions, with the differences partly reflecting the collapse in global tourism as countries closed their borders to stem the spread of the pandemic. In 2020, services trade fell by 20 percent, more than twice the average drop of 8 percent in global recessions since 1975.

The postpandemic trade recovery fell just a little short of the average recovery following past global recessions. For 2021 as a whole, goods trade stood at 6 percent above its prepandemic level, as compared with 8 percent in the first year of recovery after the average past global recession. The recovery in global trade since 2020 has partly reflected a rotation of global demand toward trade-intensive manufactured goods—especially durable goods—and away from services, which tend to be nontradable. Trade growth has mirrored the increase in industrial production almost one for one. This pattern is consistent with both being lifted by a common factor such as a rebound in global demand (World Bank 2022a). The recovery in goods trade has been fairly broad-based, with global imports of cars, capital goods, consumer goods, and industrial supplies all back at or above prepandemic levels by January 2021 (IMF 2021). However, global goods trade stalled in the second half of 2021, amid slowing demand growth and tightened supply bottlenecks and, in February 2022, due to the impact of Russia's invasion of Ukraine on trade flows.

Through most of 2021, global services trade remained below prepandemic levels, in contrast with what took place in earlier global recessions, in which it typically recovered quite rapidly. Aggregate services trade reached prepandemic levels only in September

2021. By January 2022, most components of services trade, including that in telecommunications and financial services, had fully recovered to prepandemic levels, but trade in travel services remained 40 percent lower. Trade in services recovered most rapidly in East Asia and the Pacific (EAP), as China's services trade had already returned to prepandemic levels by December 2020. Trade in services, including travel and tourism, has played an increasingly important role in the global economy. For example, since 2000, global travel and tourism revenues have nearly tripled, with the sector in 2021 accounting for 10 percent of global GDP, 30 percent of global services trade, and 10 percent of all jobs worldwide (World Bank 2020b).

Spillovers through global value chains are likely to have amplified the fall in world trade associated with the COVID-19 pandemic (Cigna, Gunnella, and Quaglietti 2022). Companies increasingly turned to digital technologies and diversified suppliers and production sites to mitigate disruptions caused by the pandemic (Saurav et al. 2020). In 2021, strains in global supply chains worsened significantly. The rapid recovery in global goods consumption from mid-2020 put acute pressure on the trade-intensive manufacturing sector. At the same time, COVID-19 outbreaks continued to disrupt production at many points along complex global value chains, creating significant obstacles to final goods production. COVID-19 outbreaks have also shut down some key port facilities, disrupting ocean shipping and air freight and leading to an unprecedented lengthening of supplier delivery times (figure 6.4). Regression analysis that controls for the effect of demand conditions suggests that global trade could have been 3.5 percent higher in 2021 were it not for supply chain strains (figure 6.4).[3]

Global goods and services trade was dealt a further blow in February 2022 by Russia's invasion of Ukraine, which has disrupted trade flows from the Black Sea and especially curtailed trade in commodities. Commodity market disruptions—including delays in deliveries of natural gas and coal associated with Russia's invasion of Ukraine—have throttled the production of electricity in several countries, curbing energy-intensive manufacturing activities. Disruptions to wheat shipments from the Black Sea have put pressure on supplies of food staples globally (World Bank 2022b). Some car production lines were temporarily closed down for lack of specific components ordinarily produced in Ukraine, such as car wiring. Shortages and unprecedented increases in the prices of key commodities produced in Russia and Ukraine have rippled through global value chains, leading to production standstills and elevated producer prices globally. Russia's invasion of Ukraine likely dampened trade in services, which had just returned to prepandemic levels in late 2021, once again: The war has disrupted shipping, especially through the Black Sea, driven up insurance and shipping costs globally, diverted trade to more expensive routes, and discouraged tourism from and to several countries in the

---

[3] The impact of supply bottlenecks is estimated here in an ordinary least-squares regression of global trade on the manufacturing purchasing managers' index (PMI) for new export orders, the manufacturing PMI for supplier delivery times (a proxy for supply bottlenecks), and relevant lags of global trade and the PMI for new export orders. Counterfactual scenarios assume that the PMI supply delivery times indicator in the period January 2020-November 2021 remained at the average 2019 level. Regressions are estimated over the period 2000-19. The estimation methodology is similar to the one developed by Celasun et al. (2022).

FIGURE 6.4 Supply chain bottlenecks and trade integration

Global value chains have been severely disrupted since 2020, with that disruption weighing on trade growth and industrial production.

A. Supply chain pressures

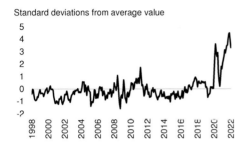

B. Impact of supply bottlenecks on goods trade and industrial production

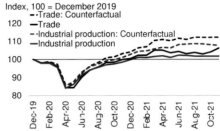

C. Global trade, tariffs, and the Russian Federation's share in global oil production

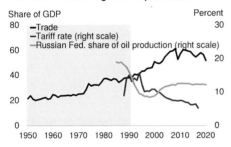

D. Foreign value-added content of gross exports

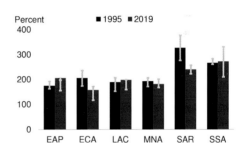

Sources: Benigno et al. (2022); BP, *Statistical Review of World Energy*; Federal Reserve Bank of New York; Organisation for Economic Co-operation and Development (OECD); Penn World Table; World Bank.

Note: EMDEs = emerging market and developing economies. Federation; GDP = gross domestic product.

A. Figure shows the Federal Reserve Bank of New York's Global Supply Chain Pressure Index on a monthly basis since 1998. The index is normalized such that 0 indicates that the index is at its average value, with positive (negative) values representing how many standard deviations the index is above (below) average.

B. The effect of supply bottlenecks is derived from an ordinary least-squares regression of global trade on the manufacturing purchasing managers' index (PMI) for new export orders, the manufacturing PMI for supplier delivery times, and two lags. Dashed lines show counterfactual scenarios derived by assuming that the PMI for supply delivery times (a proxy for supply bottlenecks) in January 2020-November 2021 remained at its average 2019 level. Estimations are performed over the period from 2000-19.

C. Blue line shows global trade in percent of global GDP. Red line shows unweighted average tariffs for all products. Orange line shows oil production in the Russian Federation as a percentage of global oil production. Shaded area indicates cold war period of 1950-90.

D. Figure shows the share of foreign-value-added content of gross exports in advanced economies and EMDEs, as defined in the OECD's Trade in Value Added database.

ECA region. A prolonged conflict in Ukraine could lead to additional dislocations and fragmentation of global value chains, further exacerbating the marked slowdown in the pace of EMDE integration into global value chains since 2008.

Prospects for global trade growth

The January 2023 *Global Economic Prospects* report projected that global trade growth would slow to under 4 percent in 2022 from more than 10 percent in 2021 and then slow further in 2023. This forecast reflects slower projected global output growth, but also the diminished trade intensity of global output: The structural factors that supported the rapid expansion of trade in the decades preceding the global financial crisis seem to have largely lost their force, so that the recently reduced elasticity of global trade with respect to global output seems likely to constitute a "new normal."

Since global output growth itself is projected to be slower by about 0.4 percentage point in the forecast period (2022-30) than in previous decade, world trade growth is also expected to slow (chapter 5; World Bank 2021b). Thus, if the elasticity of trade to output growth is assumed to remain about 1 as it was during the 2010s and no major policy change is assumed, trade growth over the remainder of the 2020s is likely to be slower by another 0.4 percentage point a year than in the preceding decade, an estimate broadly in line with the projected weakening of global growth in potential output (World Bank 2021b). The weakness may be more pronounced in the growth of goods trade. In goods trade, new technologies may allow more localized and more centralized production. In services trade, rapidly growing data services promise a return to rapid expansion as the pandemic is brought under control (chapter 7; Coulibaly and Foda 2020; World Bank 2021a; Zhan et al. 2020).

In the four decades before the global financial crisis, global economic integration through trade increased steadily, assisted partly by falling tariffs (figure 6.4). Since the global financial crisis, however, trade integration has stalled, with the COVID-19 pandemic and Russia's invasion of Ukraine having added further obstacles. With Russia's share of global oil production having increased considerably in recent decades, there is now a material risk that the disruptions caused by Russia's invasion of Ukraine could lead to a major reconfiguration of global trade and investment networks, as countries look for alternative sources of energy. While this may boost trade in some parts of the global economy, it is likely to disrupt trade elsewhere. Since political and security rather than economic considerations would motivate such a reconfiguration, it would likely reduce global economic welfare as well as trade in the long term (Ruta 2022).

Patterns in trade costs

The fading momentum of global trade growth is diminishing its role as an engine of output and productivity growth. Countries therefore need to find new ways to reap the benefits from trade. One possibility is to cut trade costs to boost exports and encourage imports in a manner that enhances growth. A number of studies have documented the negative impact of trade costs on trade growth (for example, Anderson and van Wincoop 2003) and the boost to productivity that can result from lowering trade costs (for example, Bernard, Jensen, and Schott 2006). Trade costs have also been recognized as an important factor in firms' decisions to choose outsourcing over insourcing (Hartman et al. 2017).

Definition

The analysis in this chapter relies on a comprehensive data set of bilateral trade costs, the UNESCAP-World Bank Trade Cost Database. Following Novy (2013), Arvis et al. (2013) derive measures of annual trade costs for the period 1995-2018. For any given country pair i and j, they obtain trade costs as geometric averages of trade flows between countries i and j, computing them according to the formula

$$(X_{ii}X_{jj})/(X_{ij}X_{ji})^{1/2\,(\sigma-1)},$$

in which X_{ij} represents trade between countries i and j (goods produced in i and sold in j) and σ refers to the elasticity of substitution. This measure assumes that international trade flows relative to domestic trade flows reflect international trade costs relative to domestic trade costs: when international trade costs more than domestic trade, countries will trade more domestically than internationally, that is, the ratio $(X_{ii}X_{jj})/(X_{ij}X_{ji})$ will be greater. In the application of this methodology, the difference between gross output and total exports proxies domestic trade. Trade costs thus estimated are expressed as a proportion of the value of traded goods (comparable with an ad valorem tariff rate) and can be computed for the economy as a whole or specifically for such sectors as manufacturing and agriculture.

These trade cost estimates refer to bilateral trade. To obtain country and regional measures of multilateral trade costs, bilateral trade costs from the UNESCAP-World Bank database are aggregated using 2018 bilateral country export shares from the UNCTAD international merchandise trade database. Regional and sectoral aggregates are obtained as unweighted averages of individual-country measures.

Literature view

Trade costs and trade. A growing literature has documented evidence that lower trade costs raise trade growth (for example, Anderson and van Wincoop 2003). Jacks, Meissner, and Novy (2011) study data for the period 1870-2000 and find that declines in trade costs explain roughly 60 percent of the growth in global trade in the pre-World War I period and about 30 percent of trade growth in the period after World War II. Studies of firm-level data have found that lower trade costs encourage firms to locate abroad (for example, Amiti and Javorcik 2008) and to choose outsourcing over insourcing and intrafirm rather than arm's-length trade.

Trade costs and productivity. A link between lower trade costs and higher productivity has also been substantiated. For advanced economies, Ahn et al. (2019) find that a tariff rate that was 1 percentage point lower was associated with a 2 percent gain in total factor productivity during 1997-2007. Analyses of firm-level and sector-level data have shown similar results. Industries with larger declines in trade costs are found to have stronger productivity growth; lower-productivity plants in industries with falling trade costs are more likely to close; and nonexporters are more likely to start exporting in response to falling trade costs (Bernard et al. 2007).

Patterns across regions and sectors

Recent data show that despite a sharp decline in the past two-and-a-half decades, trade costs in EMDEs raise the prices of goods traded internationally to more than double the prices of goods traded domestically and that these costs remain about one-half higher than those in advanced economies (figure 6.5). Among EMDE regions, average trade costs in tariff equivalents range from 96 percent in ECA to 142 percent in South Asia (SAR), with wide heterogeneity within regions. This heterogeneity is particularly pronounced in the Middle East and North Africa (MNA), where trade costs range from 86 to 136 percent in tariff equivalents among different countries. Trade costs have declined since 1995 in all regions except EAP, with the fastest decline occurring in SSA. Within ECA, countries that are members of the European Union or geographically close to it have trade costs that are two-thirds of the average trade costs of other countries, which are less integrated into European Union (EU) supply chains.

Trade costs remain particularly elevated in agriculture: about four-fifths higher than those in manufacturing. Agricultural trade costs are particularly high in SSA where they stand at 270 percent in tariff equivalents. Likewise, SSA and Latin America and the Caribbean (LAC) have particularly high manufacturing trade costs. Trade costs declined less in agriculture—from 194 percent to 170 percent in tariff equivalents—than in manufacturing over 1995-2019, in part because of slower progress in reducing tariffs and the narrower coverage of trade agreements.

Goods and services trade are complementary. Tradable services are key links between stages of value chains and "enablers" of trade in goods, particularly communications, finance, business, and logistics services. As a result, services account for almost one-third of the value added of manufacturing exports (Ariu et al. 2019; OECD 2020). Comparable cross-country data on the costs of trade in services and on policies affecting trade in services are scant. The few attempts in the literature to quantify trade costs in services rely either on observed trade and value-added flows, in a manner akin to the methodology embedded in the UNESCAP-World Bank Trade Cost Database for goods trade costs (Miroudot, Sauvage, and Shepherd 2010), or on an inventory of restrictions on trade in services (Benz 2017). Both types of studies suggest that services have considerably higher trade costs than goods and that unlike those for goods, trade costs for services have not fallen since the 1990s.

Correlates of trade costs

Trade costs include the full range of costs associated with trading across borders: transportation and distribution costs (Marti and Puertas 2019; Staboulis et al. 2020), trade policy barriers (Bergstrand, Larch, and Yotov 2015), the costs of information and contract enforcement (Hou, Wang, and Xue 2021), and legal and regulatory costs, as well as the cost of doing business across cultures, languages, and economic systems (Anderson and van Wincoop 2003). A number of plausible correlates may be considered.

Candidate correlates

A number of possible correlates of trade costs have been identified, including trade policies, shipping and logistics, regulations, uncertainty, and other factors.

FIGURE 6.5 International trade costs relative to domestic trade costs

On average, globally, international trade costs are roughly equivalent to a 100 percent tariff—far above actual average tariff rates. Despite declines over the past three decades, trade costs remain high, especially for agricultural products and in EMDEs. Trade costs for agricultural products are highest, among EMDE regions, in South Asia and Sub-Saharan Africa, while trade costs in the manufacturing sector are highest in Latin America and the Caribbean and Sub-Saharan Africa.

A. Average trade costs in 1995 and 2019

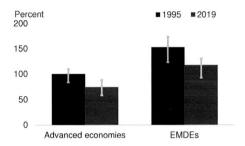

B. Average trade costs in EMDEs in 1995 and 2019

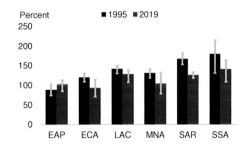

C. Average trade costs for agriculture in 1995 and 2019

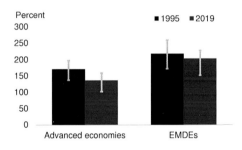

D. Average trade costs for agriculture for EMDE regions in 1995 and 2019

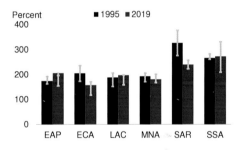

E. Average trade costs for manufacturing in 1995 and 2019

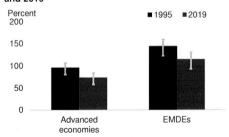

F. Average trade costs for manufacturing for EMDE regions in 1995 and 2019

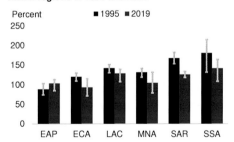

Sources: UN Comtrade; UN Economic and Social Commission for Asia and the Pacific (ESCAP)-World Bank Trade Cost Database; World Bank; World Trade Organization.

Note: Bilateral trade costs (as defined in the UNESCAP-World Bank Trade Cost Database) measure the costs of a good traded internationally in excess of the same good traded domestically and are expressed as ad valorem tariff equivalents. They are aggregated into individual-country measures using 2018 bilateral country exports shares from UN Comtrade. Regional and sectoral aggregates are averages of individual-country measures. Bars show unweighted averages; whiskers show interquartile ranges. Sample in 1995 includes 33 advanced economies and 46 EMDEs (4 in EAP, 8 in ECA, 15 in LAC, 4 in MNA, 2 in SAR, and 13 in SSA). Sample in 2019 includes 23 advanced economies and 53 EMDEs (9 in EAP, 12 in ECA, 16 in LAC, 4 in MNA, 2 in SAR, and 10 in SSA). EAP = East Asia and Pacific; ECA = Europe and Central Asia; EMDEs = emerging market and developing economies; LAC = Latin America and the Caribbean; MNA = Middle East and North Africa; SAR = South Asia; SSA = Sub-Saharan Africa.

Trade policies: Tariffs and trade agreements

Import tariffs raise trade costs. The contribution of tariffs to total trade costs has decreased in the postwar period, through steep reductions since 1990 in tariffs imposed by EMDEs, among other avenues. Thus tariffs in EMDEs averaged 7.7 percent of the value of imports in 2020, down from 16.0 percent in 1995, although this is still much higher than the average tariff of about 1.9 percent in advanced economies (figure 6.6). As a result of tariff reductions, tariffs now amount to a small portion of trade costs: about one-twentieth. Agricultural tariffs remain higher than manufacturing tariffs, by one-fifth in EMDEs and two-fifths in advanced economies.

Establishment and expansion of regional trade agreements has accompanied the decline in tariffs in recent decades. The number of such agreements more than quintupled between the early 1990s and the mid-2010s, and their focus shifted from tariff cuts to the lowering of nontariff barriers (World Bank 2016). The EU alone participates in 46 regional trade agreements, and other advanced economies are members of up to 75. Among EMDEs, membership in regional trade agreements is less common, although all but a handful are members of at least one. Such agreements are most common in ECA, where some countries are EU members and others are members of the free trade area among members of the Commonwealth of Independent States, and in LAC, where most countries are members or associates of Mercado Común del Sur (Southern Common Market, or MERCOSUR) or signatories to trade agreements with the United States, such as the U.S.-Mexico-Canada Agreement and the Dominican Republic-Central America Free Trade Agreement.

Shipping and logistics

The transport of goods and associated administrative border and customs procedures generate a multitude of trade costs (Moïsé and Le Bris 2013). Transport costs, much like tariffs, penalize goods produced in multiple stages across different countries, since producers have to pay to move components at each stage of the production process. They can be thought of as services costs—the costs of services related to shipping and logistics. These costs depend on the efficiency and reliability of transport facilities and the burden of administrative border and customs procedures.

Transit delays have been identified as important deterrents to trade flows, together with poor shipping connectivity and inadequate logistics infrastructure and services (Freund and Rocha 2011). For most U.S. trading partners, transport costs are higher than tariff costs, and for the broader group of advanced economies, poor logistics have resulted in larger trade costs than geographic distance alone (Marti and Puertas 2019; Staboulis et al. 2020). Transport costs, much like tariffs, penalize goods produced in multiple stages across different countries, since producers have to pay to move components at each stage of the production process. Estimates of the tariff equivalent of transit time find that each day in transit is equivalent to a 0.8 percent tariff (Hummels et al. 2007). For a 20-day sea transport route (the average for imports to the United States), this amounts to a tariff rate of 16 percent—much higher than the actual average tariff rate. Using gravity

FIGURE 6.6 International trade policy, border processes, and logistics

Tariffs declined sharply over the 1990s and early 2000s, in part because of regional and multilateral trade agreements, but began to tick upward again in 2017, especially in EMDEs. They are higher in EMDEs than in advanced economies and in agriculture than in manufacturing. Connectivity and logistics tend to be easier, and shipping connectivity better, in advanced economies than in EMDEs.

A. Tariff rates in AEs and EMDEs
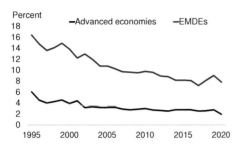

B. Tariff rates by sectors
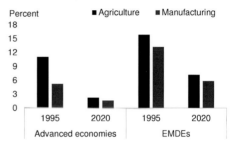

C. Trade uncertainty for AEs and EMDEs
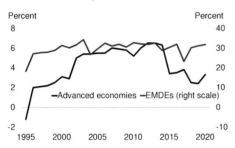

D. Logistics Performance Index
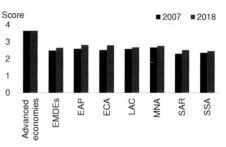

E. Liner Shipping Connectivity Index
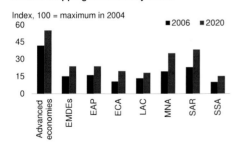

F. Participation in regional trade agreements
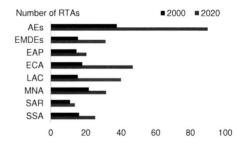

Sources: Centre d'Etudes Prospectives et d'Informations Internationales, Gravity database; Gurevich and Herman (2018); United Nations Conference on Trade and Development (UNCTAD); World Bank; World Trade Organization.
Note: AEs = advanced economies; EAP = East Asia and Pacific; ECA = Europe and Central Asia; EMDEs = emerging market and developing economies; EU = European Union; LAC = Latin America and the Caribbean; MNA = Middle East and North Africa; RTA = regional trade agreement; SAR = South Asia; SSA = Sub-Saharan Africa.
A. B. Average tariff rates are computed as unweighted cross-country averages of applied weighted tariff rates. Sample includes up to 35 advanced economies and 123 EMDEs. Primary tariffs are used as a proxy for agriculture tariffs.
C. Proxy for trade uncertainty is the difference between the bound and applied tariff rates, as defined by the World Trade Organization. Data are through 2020. Sample includes up to 27 advanced economies and 97 EMDEs.
D. The World Bank's Logistics Performance Index is a summary indicator of logistics sector performance combining data on six core performance components into a single aggregate measure. The indicator is available for a sample of 160 countries. Sample includes 36 advanced economies and 123 EMDEs.
E. UNCTAD's Liner Shipping Connectivity Index is an average of five components and captures how well countries are connected to global shipping networks. The index value 100 refers to the country with the highest average index score in 2004. Sample includes up to 30 advanced economies and 118 EMDEs.
F. Regional trade agreements are reciprocal agreements among two or more partners and include both free trade agreements and customs unions. The EU Treaty, United States-Mexico-Canada Agreement, and Pacific Agreement on Closer Economic Relations Plus are included. Regional aggregates are computed as averages of individual-country participation in RTAs.

models, studies find that a 10 percent increase in the time taken to transport exports reduces trade by 5-25 percent, depending on the sector and export destination (Djankov, Freund, and Pham 2010; Hausman, Lee, and Subramanian 2005; Kox and Nordas 2007; Nordas 2006).

Transport costs in real terms have declined over time, as land, sea, and air shipping costs have fallen. Technological improvements in transport services, such as jet engines and containerization, have reduced both transport costs per unit of time and transport times. The average shipping time for imports to the United States declined from 40 to 10 days between 1950 and 1998 (Hummels 2001). Evaluated at an average cost per day of 0.8 percent ad valorem (as noted earlier), this increase in the speed of transport is equivalent to a reduction in the tariff rate of 24 percentage points.

In addition, advances in communication technologies have allowed the development of more effective multimodal transport systems, which have helped both to reduce delivery times and to increase the reliability of deliveries. However, such advances have been uneven among countries, and global shipping connectivity and logistics remain considerably poorer for EMDEs than for advanced economies (figure 6.6), with trade costs correspondingly higher in EMDEs with fewer advances in these areas (figure 6.7).

Regulations

Streamlining trade and customs compliance procedures and processes can lower trade costs significantly (Staboulis et al. 2020). Reductions in regulations have been associated with significantly higher trade volumes: Each additional signature that has to be collected for exports has been found to cost almost as much as the average tariff (Hillberry and Zhang 2015; Sadikov 2007).

Regulatory requirements for trading across borders have been streamlined significantly over the past decade, especially in ECA, SAR, and SSA. In ECA and SSA, this development appears to be linked to automation and digitalization of trade processes in a number of countries, which have reduced the time taken for compliance assessments at the location of customs clearance. In SAR, it appears to be related to the upgrading of port infrastructure in India, coupled with the introduction of a new system of electronic submission of import documents. In EAP, better governance and less burdensome customs procedures have been associated with somewhat lower trade costs.

Trade uncertainty

Uncertainty about the costs associated with transport, customs and border processes, tariffs, and nontariff trade policies can impose significant burdens on investment and output as well as trade. For example, uncertainty about trade policy may have lowered U.S. investment by more than 1 percent in 2018 (Caldara et al. 2020).

One dimension of trade uncertainty is the scope that countries have to raise tariffs without violating World Trade Organization rules—that is, the difference between applied tariffs and bound (maximum) tariffs, the so-called tariff water (Osnago,

FIGURE 6.7 **International trade costs in EMDEs, by country characteristics**

Trade costs are somewhat higher in EMDEs outside of regional free trade agreements, with the poorest logistics performance and the least maritime shipping connectivity. Trade facilitation is stronger in advanced economies than in EMDEs.

A. Trade costs by participation in free trade agreements

B. Trade costs by tercile of Logistics Performance Index

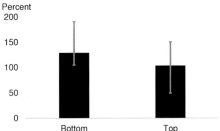

C. Trade costs by tercile of Liner Shipping Connectivity Index

D. Trade facilitation

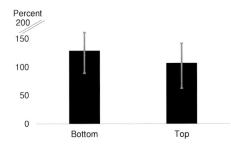
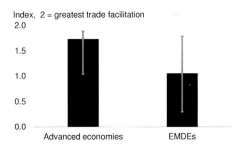

Sources: Gurevich and Herman (2018); Organisation for Economic Co-operation and Development; UN Comtrade; UN Economic and Social Commission for Asia and the Pacific (ESCAP)-World Bank Trade Cost Database; World Bank; World Trade Organization.
Note: Orange whiskers indicate minimum and maximum range. Sample includes 52 EMDEs. EMDEs = emerging market and developing economies; FTA = free trade agreement; LSCI = United Nations Conference on Trade and Development (UNCTAD) Liner Shipping Connectivity Index; LPI = World Bank Logistics Performance Index.
A. Average trade costs (unweighted) of countries based on their membership in regional or global free trade agreements as defined in Gurevich and Herman (2018).
B. Average trade costs (unweighted) for countries ranked in the bottom and top quartiles of scores on the World Bank's Logistics Performance Index.
C. Bars show average trade costs (unweighted) for countries in the bottom and top quartiles of scores on UNCTAD's Liner Shipping Connectivity Index.
D. Unweighted average for 36 advanced economies and 122 EMDEs. The trade facilitation index is an unweighted average of 11 subindexes, all scored on a scale of 0-2. A higher index score indicates greater trade facilitation. The subindexes score countries on information availability, trade consultations, advance rulings, appeals procedures for administrative decisions by border agencies, fees and charges on imports and exports, simplicity of trade document requirements, automation of border procedures and documentation, simplicity of border procedures, cooperation between domestic agencies, cooperation with neighboring agencies, and governance and impartiality. The data are collected from publicly available sources, country submissions, and private sector feedback. Orange whiskers indicate minimum and maximum range.

Piermartini, and Rocha 2015). This dimension of trade uncertainty increased steadily in advanced economies in the two decades to 2013, but it has since declined significantly. In EMDEs, the gap between applied and bound tariffs has remained much wider than that in advanced economies, with little sign of any sustained decline.

Uncertainty about delivery times can also impose significant costs. In Africa, for example, a single-day transit delay for an exporter is estimated to be equivalent to a 2 percent tariff in importing partner countries (Freund and Rocha 2011).

Other factors

Policy-related nontariff barriers may include sanitary, phytosanitary, and other standards (often aimed at protecting consumer health and safety), preshipment inspections, licensing requirements, and quotas. These are important determinants of trade costs. Measuring nontariff barriers is difficult. A common method is to construct a measure of the prevalence of nontariff barriers, such as the percent of product lines covered by nontariff barriers. Kee and Nicita (2016) estimate the average nontariff barrier globally as equivalent to an 11.5 percent tariff, significantly higher than the average tariff rate of 4 percent. Nontariff barriers have risen over time. In 2015, about 2,850 product lines were subject to at least one nontariff barrier, about double the 1,456 product lines in 1997 (Niu et al. 2018). Nontariff barriers affect a higher share of imports in advanced economies than in EMDEs (but a lower share of exports). Almost all agricultural imports face nontariff barriers, compared with about 40 percent on average across all sectors (World Bank and UNCTAD 2018). Nontariff barriers affect low-income countries particularly, because administrative requirements are frequently applied to agricultural products, and firms in low-income countries are less able to comply with such requirements.

Noncompetitive market structures can drive up trade costs. In some countries in SSA, for example, it costs up to five times more to move goods domestically than in the United States (Atkin and Donaldson 2015; Donaldson, Jinhage, and Verhoogen 2017). This difference has in part been attributed to a lack of competition in the domestic transport sector. Elsewhere, excessive competition can drive down the quality of transport services, with high road mortality, deteriorated roads, and poor vehicle quality (Teravaninthorn and Raballand 2008).

Institutional quality and economic infrastructure affect trade costs. Better energy provisioning, more highly developed transport and communication infrastructure and services, financial development, and greater transparency of policy decisions have all been associated with lower trade costs (Calì and te Velde 2011; Hou, Wang, and Xue 2021). Analysis of data for a large sample of countries in the early 2000s indicates that more transparent and effective institutions—as indicated by factors such as the availability of trade-related information, the simplification and harmonization of documents, the streamlining of procedures, and the use of automated processes—were associated with trade costs that were lower by more than 10 percent (Moïsé and Sorescu 2013). Findings on the effects of corruption have been more ambiguous: It may raise trade costs, as when corrupt officials extort bribes, or it may lower trade costs, as when corrupt officials allow tariff evasion (Dutt and Traca 2010). Consistent with concerns about institutional quality, trade finance of a type that reduces risk of nonpayment or nondelivery (such as letters of credit) has been associated with more resilient trade flows during times of economic or financial stress (Crozet, Demir, and Javorcik 2021).

Regulatory restrictions on services trade can add to costs of trade, even goods trade. To a large extent, trade costs in the services sector reflect regulations that create entry barriers,

FIGURE 6.8 Policies restricting trade in services

Services trade in EMDEs faces more restrictions than that in advanced economies. Among EMDE regions, the most restrictive services trade policies are applied in East Asia and Pacific and South Asia.

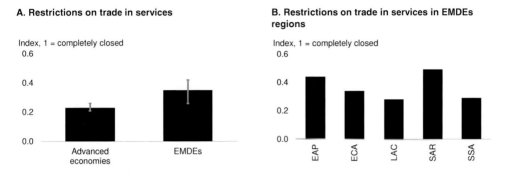

A. Restrictions on trade in services

B. Restrictions on trade in services in EMDEs regions

Sources: Organisation for Economic Co-operation and Development (OECD); World Bank.
Note: EAP = East Asia and Pacific; ECA = Europe and Central Asia; EMDEs = emerging market and developing economies; LAC = Latin America and the Caribbean; MNA = Middle East and North Africa; SAR = South Asia; SSA = Sub-Saharan Africa.
A. B. The OECD's Services Trade Restrictiveness Index helps identify which policy measures restrict trade. It takes values from 0 to 1, with 0 being completely open and 1 being completely closed. Scores on the index are calculated on the basis of information in the database for the index, which reports regulations currently in force. Bars show unweighted averages, and orange whiskers indicate the minimum and maximum range. Sample includes 31 advanced economies and 17 EMDEs in 2020.

such as licensing quotas. The Organisation for Economic Co-operation and Development's Services Trade Restrictiveness Index measures de jure regulatory restrictions on services trade in 44 countries (figure 6.8). As does goods trade, services trade remains more restricted in EMDEs than in advanced economies, especially with respect to the entry of foreign firms. Across regions, the most restrictive policies are applied in EAP and SAR, whereas countries in LAC tend to be more open.

Estimation

Gravity equations are widely used to analyze the determinants of bilateral trade flows. Chen and Novy (2012) and Arvis et al. (2013) employ a gravity specification in analyzing the determinants of bilateral trade costs in a cross-sectional data set. The determinants of trade costs, as defined earlier, are estimated here in a panel specification with time fixed effects, in line with the established literature (Moïsé, Orliac, and Minor 2011). The regression equation takes the following form:

$$TC_{ijt} = \beta_1\, RTA_{ijt} + \beta_2\, tariff_{ijt} + \beta_3\, LSCI_{ijt} + \beta_4\, LPI_{ijt}$$
$$+ \beta_5\, Trade\ Policy\ Uncertainty_{ijt} + \beta_6\, Gravity_{ij} + \eta_t + \varepsilon_{ijt}\,, \tag{6.1}$$

in which for any given country pair *ij*, bilateral trade costs *TC* observed at time *t* are regressed on a wide range of candidate drivers. These candidate drivers include membership in a regional trade agreement, sector-specific bilateral tariffs, shipping connectivity (UNCTAD's Liner Shipping Connectivity Index) and logistics (the World Bank's Logistics Performance Index), a proxy for trade policy uncertainty, and standard gravity indicators (distance, a common language, and a common border). In line with

Osnago, Piermartini, and Rocha (2018), trade policy uncertainty is defined as the gap between binding tariff commitments and applied tariffs. To ascertain the role of policies aimed at facilitating trade, indexes of logistic performance and maritime connectivity are included.

The model is estimated for the economy as a whole and for manufacturing separately. The regression uses bilateral trade data for 2007-18 for up to 2 advanced economies and 72 EMDEs for which data on trade costs and its determinants are available. The choice of variables in the panel is informed by Arvis et al. (2013), as well as by findings from the discussion of the drivers of trade costs presented in the previous sections. Box 6.1 presents full details on data and sources.

In the estimation results, all coefficients have signs and magnitudes consistent with expectations from the literature (table B6.1.1). Geographic distance and bilateral tariff rates are positively associated with trade costs, while proximity, common language, and membership in a common regional trade agreement tend to reduce trade costs. Specifically, membership in a common regional trade agreement lowers bilateral trade costs in a statistically significant way, by just under one-fifth.[4] Greater trade policy uncertainty is also associated with higher trade costs, in the manufacturing sector as well as in the economy as a whole.

The regression results help shed light on the sources of the higher trade costs in EMDEs than in advanced economies and of the decline in trade costs over time. In 2018, the average EMDE in the regression sample had trade costs almost one-quarter higher than the average advanced economy in the sample. The panel estimation explains most of this gap and attributes about two-fifths of it to poorer logistics and shipping connectivity in EMDEs, a further two-fifths to trade policy (including trade policy uncertainty), and just under the remaining one-fifth to the greater remoteness (geographically and culturally) of EMDEs.

Between 2007 and 2018, trade costs fell by one-eighth, on average, in the countries in the sample, somewhat more than the regression predicts. The regression attributes almost three-fourths of this decline to improved shipping connectivity and logistics and one-fourth to trade policy (tariff cuts, membership in regional trade agreements, and uncertainty related to trade policy).[5]

---

[4] This is somewhat smaller than the effect found by Bergstrand, Larch, and Yotov (2015), who estimate that an economic integration agreement lowered trade costs by 30 percent in a smaller and earlier sample (41 mostly advanced economies during 1996-2000). Qualitatively, the results are consistent with those of Brenton, Portugal-Perez, and Regolo (2014), who find that trade agreements help reduce the price differential between domestic and traded foods.

[5] Daudin, Héricourt, and Patureau (2022) decompose the decline in transport costs over 1974-2019 into "pure transport cost" and compositional effects (that is, changes in the composition of origin countries and goods baskets) and find that the decline in pure transport cost accounted for most of the decline in global transport costs over the period studied.

Policies to lower trade costs

A menu of policy options is available to reduce trade costs at the border (OECD and WTO 2015). Some are under the control of individual-country authorities (such as improving border and customs regulations and processes and facilitating shipping and logistics), while others require international agreements (such as regional trade agreements). While some policies can be implemented quickly, others, such as those aimed at increasing competition, can take years to establish.

- Measures that lower trade costs *at the border* include trade facilitation (through reform of customs and border procedures), tariff reductions, and trade agreements.

- Measures that lower trade costs *between borders* include improvements in transport, communications, and energy infrastructure and services networks.

- Measures that reduce trade costs *behind the border* include reforms of trade-related regulations and institutions, improvements in logistics and broader market governance, improvements in domestic transport infrastructure and in the market structure of domestic trucking and port operations, and the lowering of other nontariff barriers (for example, standards, accreditation procedures for standards, and quotas).

- Beyond policies to facilitate trade, a wider set of institutional policies might also be needed to ensure that the benefits are sustainable and widely shared.

At-the-border measures

Possible sources of at-the-border trade costs include tariffs, an absence of or weak trade agreements, poor trade facilitation, and burdensome border processes. A policy package that reduces these at-the-border obstacles could significantly lower trade costs.

Reductions in tariffs, often embedded in broader trade agreements, have contributed to rapid trade growth in much of the period since World War II. However, tariffs have risen over the past five years as trade tensions have mounted, and the rise has contributed to concerns about a protectionist turn among some major economies (World Bank 2021b). Reversing the increases and making further progress in regard to tariff reduction would lower trade costs. Reforms that lower import tariffs have generally been found to be associated with faster economic growth, although effects have been heterogeneous (Irwin 2019). For example, the widespread removal of trade barriers and reduction of import tariffs in the mid-1980s to mid-1990s ushered in a period of rapid global trade integration (Irwin 2022). Removing uncertainty about trade policy by reducing the gap between actual applied and bound tariffs could further lower trade costs: The regression results reported earlier suggest that a 10 percentage-point reduction in this gap would be associated with trade costs that are lower by about one-seventh.

FIGURE 6.9 **Regional trade agreements**

Countries participating in regional trade agreements (RTAs) account for a large part of global GDP. Trade within some of these agreements accounts for a large proportion of member country total trade.

A. Share of members of major RTAs in global GDP and trade

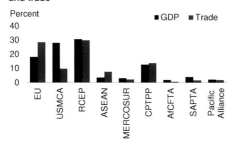

B. Share of intra-RTA trade in members' total trade

Sources: UN Comtrade; World Bank; World Trade Organization.
Note: RTAs are reciprocal trade agreements among two or more partners and include both free trade agreements and customs unions. Data are for 2019.
A.B. AfCFTA = African Continental Free Trade Area; ASEAN = Association of Southeast Asian Nations; CPTPP = Comprehensive and Progressive Agreement for Trans-Pacific Partnership; EU = European Union; GDP = gross domestic product; MERCOSUR = Mercado Común del Sur (Southern Common Market); RCEP = Regional Comprehensive Economic Partnership; SAPTA = South Asian Preferential Trading Arrangement; USMCA = United States-Mexico-Canada Agreement.

The decline in trade costs over the past three decades has stemmed partly from new regional trade agreements and reforms to existing ones. The largest regional trade agreement in terms of the number of member countries, the African Continental Free Trade Area (AfCTA), for example, has raised real incomes among its members mostly by lowering nontariff barriers and implementation of trade facilitation measures (World Bank 2020a). The members of the major regional trade agreements in North America (the United States-Mexico-Canada Agreement) and Europe (the EU) account for more than 40 percent of global GDP (figure 6.9). Such agreements have fostered domestic reforms in EMDEs and generated momentum for greater liberalization and expansion of trade opportunities (Baccini and Urpelainen 2014a, 2014b; Baldwin and Jaimovich 2010).

A multitude of costs are imposed on trade by administrative border and customs procedures. Documentation and other customs compliance requirements, lengthy administrative procedures, and other delays have been estimated to increase transaction costs by 2-24 percent of the value of traded goods. In some countries, governments may lose more than 5 percent of GDP in revenues from inefficient border procedures (Moïsé and Le Bris 2013).

The World Trade Organization's Agreement on Trade Facilitation, adopted in 2014 and ratified by more than 90 percent of the organization's members, provides a framework for streamlining inefficient control and clearance procedures among border authorities, reduce unnecessary border formalities, and cut opaque administrative costs.

Of the commitments made under the agreement to date, 72 percent have been implemented, but progress has been uneven, with that figure less than 40 percent in low-income countries. In West Africa, an initiative is under way to cut trade costs by electronically sharing customs transit data (World Bank 2021d). Guatemala and Honduras have reduced the time it takes traders to cross their common border from 10 hours to 7 minutes by integrating their trade procedures, replacing duplicative processes with a single online instrument (de Moran 2018).

Between-borders measures

The bulk of trade costs arise from the shipping and logistics involved in moving goods between borders. These costs depend in part on the quality of transport infrastructure and the government institutions involved in transport logistics and on market structure in the transport sector. Countries have several avenues for lowering such costs.

High-quality and well-maintained transport infrastructure—at ports, at airports, and on land—and efficient shipping services are associated with lower transport and logistics costs. Thus, policy measures to improve maritime connectivity and logistics performance should help lower trade costs. The regression results reported earlier suggest that if a country's scores on indicators of these two factors were to move up from the bottom quartile to the highest quartile—equivalent to a shift from conditions in Sierra Leone to conditions in Poland—the country would lower its trade costs by between one-tenth and one-third (box 6.1).

Bribes and transport monopolies tend to drive up trade costs. In a pilot study of four African countries, more than two-thirds of survey respondents reported that bribery to accelerate transport services was common (Christie, Smith, and Conroy 2013). Efforts to reduce and eliminate such corruption and to increase competition in the transport sector should help lower transport costs.

Policies that strengthen regional integration can also be beneficial, particularly for small countries and countries that are geographically isolated from trade hubs. Coupled with regional institutions that help to reduce impediments to cross-border trade, improved regional infrastructure can help countries exploit the benefits of regional and global trade networks (Deichmann and Gill 2008). Regional trade agreements can also lower transport-related trade costs (Brenton, Portugal-Perez, and Regolo 2014).

Efforts to improve matching and liaison between providers of trucking services and shippers can also cut trade costs by reducing wait times and empty backhauls. High transport costs may, in part, reflect unbalanced trade flows, since shipping at full capacity in both directions of a route is least costly (Ishikawa and Tarui 2018). At any one time, two-fifths of ships have been estimated to carry no cargo (Brancaccio, Kalouptsidi, and Papageorgiou 2020). Such asymmetries in demand for shipping services have been a major cause of shipping and supply bottlenecks in the wake of the COVID-19 pandemic. While shipping costs from China to Europe and the United

States have risen to historically high levels, costs of shipping on ocean routes to China have remained low. Efforts to reduce wait times and empty backhauls may involve information and communications infrastructure and services to facilitate the timely provision of information about shipping capacity and schedules in order to allow exporters and shippers with available capacity to be matched more efficiently. Over the longer term, and in a favorable business environment more broadly, increased participation in global value chains can expand the volume of bidirectional trade and thus help lower shipping costs.

Behind-the-border measures

Although not included in the empirical exercise discussed earlier because of lack of data, behind-the-border policies such as those involving regulations, standards, and inspection and labeling requirements can impose considerable costs (Moïsé and Le Bris 2013). In Central America, sanitary and phytosanitary requirements, such as inspection requirements and labeling standards for meats and grains, have been estimated to raise import prices by about 30 percent on average (OECD and WTO 2015). Harmonization of standards can significantly reduce or eliminate such costs and increase trade, mutual recognition of standards or conformity assessments can also lead to smaller gains (Chen and Mattoo 2008; World Bank 2016).

A shift from trade-based taxation to income-based or consumption-based taxation can further lower barriers to trade. In middle- and high-income EMDEs, such shifts have not been associated with lasting revenue losses, but revenue losses have occurred in low-income countries (Baunsgaard and Keen 2010).

Comprehensive reform packages

Some of the most successful trade reform programs have covered a wide range of policies. A combination of customs and border improvements, regulatory reform, and streamlined import and export procedures helped Cambodia leap 46 rankings in the World Bank's Logistics Performance Index between 2010 and 2014 (World Bank 2018). In Africa's Great Lakes region, improved trade and commercial infrastructure in the border areas and simplified border-crossing procedures have been credited with improving accountability of officials, reducing rates of harassment at key borders (from 78 percent to 45 percent of survey respondents in south Lake Kivu), extending border opening hours, increasing trade flows, and doubling border crossings (World Bank 2021d).

The regression results reported earlier can be applied to a hypothetical comprehensive reform scenario focusing on pairs of countries that are in the bottom quartiles of the Logistics Performance Index and the Liner Shipping Connectivity Index; three-quarters of these countries are in SSA. The coefficients estimated from the regression suggest that improvements in average logistics performance and shipping connectivity among these country pairs sufficient to place them in the top quartile of the distribution of country pairs would halve their trade costs (figure 6.10).

FIGURE 6.10 **Impact of policy improvements on trade costs**

Better logistics and shipping connectivity could help lower trade costs by more than one-half in the quartile of EMDEs that score worst on indicators of these characteristics.

A. Reduction in overall trade costs associated with policy improvements

B. Reduction in manufacturing trade costs associated with policy improvements

Source: World Bank.
Note: EMDEs = emerging market and developing economies.
A.B. Bars show the fraction of trade costs that would remain after policy improvements. Policy improvements assume that the average EMDE in the quartile of EMDEs with the *poorest* scores on the United Nations Conference on Trade and Development's Liner Shipping Connectivity Index and the World Bank's Logistics Performance Index improves sufficiently that its score matches the score of the average EMDE in the quartile of EMDEs with the *best* scores. The comprehensive package assumes that all three scores are improved simultaneously. Data refer to 2018. Orange line indicates 1 for unchanged trade costs in 2018 among the sample of EMDEs scoring in the poorest quartile on these indicators.

Since manufacturers use services to produce and export goods, policies aimed at lowering trade costs in the services sector can help lower the costs of trading goods. Opening services markets to more competition, including those for road and rail transport services and shipping, may be an effective way to reduce trade costs. Liberal bilateral air services agreements can also help lower trade costs for many goods that form part of global value chains and for high-value-added agricultural products.

Given the perishable nature of agricultural products, measures that accelerate their movement across borders are particularly important (USAID 2019). The Agreement on Trade Facilitation includes several provisions aimed at making agricultural trade faster and more predictable. They involve simplified and more efficient requirements for risk-based document verifications, physical inspections, and laboratory testing. A centralized "Single Window" authority for document processing and coordinating across all relevant agencies can reduce paperwork, too (UNESCAP 2011). Improved storage facilities can reduce spoilage and losses of perishable agricultural goods (UNESCAP 2017; Webber and Labaste 2010). Tracking and monitoring technologies can help accelerate paperwork and improve the monitoring of environmental conditions (Beghin and Schweizer 2020). Such measures to lower agricultural trade costs can also help prevent or reduce food insecurity.

A comprehensive package could also address the potential distributional consequences of trade. The failure of some firms participating in global value chains to pass cost reductions on to consumers and the declining share of labor income in countries integrated into global value chains have contributed to the perception of unequally shared gains from trade (World Bank 2020c). Conversely, growing services trade, global supply chains, and digitalization have offered new economic opportunities to women (World Bank and WTO 2020). Labor market policies that could promote a more equitable sharing the gains from participation in global value chains include policies to facilitate labor mobility, active labor market programs, and wage insurance schemes (World Bank 2020b).

Trade can play a critical role in climate-related transition. It has the potential to shift resources to cleaner production techniques and to promote the production of goods and services necessary for transitioning to low-carbon economies. In addition, trade delivers goods and services that are key for helping countries recover from extreme weather events. However, evidence indicates that in some countries, greater carbon dioxide emissions have accompanied entry into global value chains in manufacturing and that global value chains have contributed to greater waste and increased shipping (World Bank 2020c). Shipping accounts for 7 percent of global carbon dioxide emissions and 15 percent of global emissions of sulfur dioxide and nitrogen oxides (World Bank 2020c). Being heavily concentrated in the electronics sector, global value chains have also contributed to e-waste (discarded electronic devices), which accounts for more than 70 percent of toxic waste in U.S. landfills (World Bank 2020c).

A number of policies can be implemented to reduce trade costs in a climate-friendly way, including policies that remove the current bias in many countries' tariff schedules favoring carbon-intensive goods and that eliminate restrictions on access to environmentally friendly goods and services (Brenton and Chemutai 2021; World Bank 2020c). In addition, multilateral negotiations can focus not only on tariffs on environmental goods but also on nontariff measures and regulations affecting services—access to which is often vital for implementing the new technologies embodied in environmentally friendly goods.

Digital technologies may eventually lower trade costs behind the border, at the border, and borders through a number of channels, including improving transparency and price discovery as well as information flows among exporters, shippers, and country authorities.[6] This may particularly support global supply chains. Robotics can help accelerate port procedures. Artificial intelligence can help lower logistics costs by optimizing route planning, storage, and inventory, as well as by improving tracking and monitoring; three-dimensional printing can help shorten and localize supply chains, thus reducing the environmental footprint of trade; and blockchain technology can help reduce time spent in customs, especially for time-sensitive goods, facilitate cross-border payments by increasing transparency and credibility, and enhance information sharing within supply chains (Fan, Weitz, and Lam 2019; WTO 2018). Such technologies may

---

[6] Digitization can make the enforcement of value-added tax payments of ever smaller payment transactions profitable (World Bank 2021a).

FIGURE 6.11 **Estimated contributions to trade costs**

The panel estimation described in the chapter accounts for much of the difference in average trade costs between EMDEs and advanced economies in 2018 and the change in trade costs between 2008 and 2018. About two-fifths of the predicted difference between average trade costs in EMDEs and advanced economies and three-fourths of the predicted difference between 2008 and 2018 are attributed to costs associated with shipping and logistics.

A. Model-based contributions to differences in overall trade costs

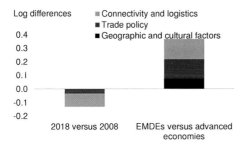

B. Model-based contributions to differences in manufacturing trade costs

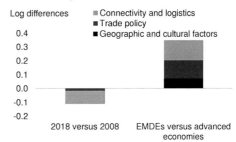

Sources: UN Comtrade; World Bank.

Note: EMDEs = emerging market and developing economies.

A.B. Figures show the difference in predicted contributions to predicted logarithm of overall trade costs (panel A) or manufacturing trade costs (panel B) between 2008 and 2018 in EMDEs and advanced economies. Contributions are computed using coefficient estimates for each variable and the following realizations for each indicator included in the regression: trade-weighted averages for all countries in the sample in 2018 minus equivalent values 2008 (panel A) and trade-weighted averages for EMDEs minus equivalent values for advanced economies in 2018 (panel B). "Trade policy" includes tariffs and membership in regional trade agreements; "Geographic and cultural factors" includes distance, common border, and common language; "Connectivity and logistics" includes connectivity and logistics include lthe United Nations Conference on Trade and Development's Liner Shipping Connectivity Index and the World Bank's Logistics Performance Index.

disproportionately benefit small and medium-sized enterprises, which currently face higher trade costs than large enterprises (WTO 2019a). Shipping supply chains, in particular, could benefit from digitization to improve efficiency (Song 2021).

Conclusion

Despite a decline over the past three decades, international trade costs remain high. In EMDEs, they amount to the equivalent of a tariff of more than 100 percent: Thus they roughly double the price of an internationally traded good relative to that of a similar domestically traded good. Trade costs are on average about four-fifths higher for agricultural products than for manufactured goods and more than one-half higher for EMDEs than for advanced economies.

Trade costs have a number of components. Tariffs amount to only about one-twentieth of trade costs. The remainder are mostly costs of transport, logistics, and adherence to regulations and thus reflect market conditions in the transport sector, administrative practices, and nontariff policy barriers. Differences in the costs of logistics and shipping account for about two-fifths of the difference in trade costs between EMDEs and advanced economies, and differences in trade policies, including trade policy uncertainty, account for another two-fifths (figure 6.11).

Comprehensive packages of reforms have often been successful in reducing trade costs. Such packages can include trade facilitation measures, bilateral and multilateral agreements aimed at deeper trade integration, coordinated efforts to streamline trade procedures and processes at and behind the border, improved domestic infrastructure, increased competition in shipping and logistics, reduced corruption, simplified trade-related procedures and regulations, and the harmonization or mutual recognition of standards. Many of these reforms, especially those relating to the business climate and governance, would stimulate private, trade-intensive investment and output growth more broadly (chapter 3).

Further research and analysis on trade costs is warranted, particularly regarding patterns and correlates of the costs of trade in services. Measures of sthe costs of trade in services remain scant, which makes it difficult to assess and quantify their determinants. In addition, since trade costs in services are largely associated with regulatory barriers, further analysis of the role of regulatory heterogeneity across sectors and regions seems warranted. Trade costs accumulate with multiple border crossings through global value chains. Investigating what policy measures can be most effective in reducing trade costs when countries are involved in complex value chains is also key. Finally, further research could aim to better understand the distributional and climate-related effects of reducing trade costs.

TABLE 6.1 Data employed in the panel regression

Data	Definition	Source
Trade costs	Logarithm of the geometric average of country i's and country j's bilateral trade costs	UN Economic and Social Commission for Asia and the Pacific (ESCAP)-World Bank Trade Cost Database
Tariff rates	Logarithm of the geometric average of country i's and country j's bilateral tariff rates	ESCAP-World Bank Trade Costs Database
Regional trade agreements	Dummy variable equal to unity if countries i and j share a common regional trade agreement	CEPII
Common border	Dummy variable equal to unity if countries i and j share a common land border (adjacency)	CEPII
Common language	Dummy variable equal to unity if countries i and j share a common language	CEPII
Distance	Logarithm of distance (in kilometers) between the largest cities in two countries	CEPII
Logistic Performance Index	Logarithm of the geometric average of country i's and country j's scores	World Bank
Liner Shipping Connectivity Index	Logarithm of the geometric average of country i's and country j's scores	UNCTAD
Trade policy uncertainty	Logarithm of the geometric average of the country i's and country j's gap between bounded and applied tariff rates	World Bank World Development Indicators database

Sources: Centre d'Etudes Prospectives et d'Informations Internationales (CEPII); United Nations Conference on Trade and Development (UNCTAD); World Bank.

References

Ahn, J., E. Dabla-Norris, R. Duval, H. Bingjie, and N. Lamin. 2019. "Reassessing the Productivity Gains from Trade Liberalization." *Review of International Economics* 27 (1): 130-54.

Alcala, F., and A. Ciccone. 2004. "Trade and Productivity." *Quarterly Journal of Economics* 119 (2): 613-46.

Alesina, A., E. Spolaore, and R. Wacziarg. 2000. "Economic Integration and Political Disintegration." *American Economic Review* 90 (5): 1276-96.

Alvarez, F. 2017. "Capital Accumulation and International Trade." *Journal of Monetary Economics* 91 (C): 1-18.

Amiti, M., and B. S. Javorcik. 2008. "Trade Costs and Location of Foreign Firms in China." *Journal of Development Economics* 85 (1-2): 129-49.

Anderson, J. E., and E. Van Wincoop. 2003. "Gravity with Gravitas: A Solution to the Border Puzzle." *American Economic Review* 93 (1): 170-92.

Anderson, J. E., and E. Van Wincoop. 2004. "Trade Costs." *Journal of Economic Literature* 42 (3): 691-751.

Antras, P., and D. Chor. 2021. "Global Value Chains." Discussion Paper 15908, Centre for Economic Policy Research, London.

Ariu, A., H. Breinlich, G. Corcos, and G. Mion. 2019. "The Interconnections between Services and Goods Trade at the Firm-Level." *Journal of International Economics* 116 (January): 173-88.

Arrow, K. 1962. "The Economic Implications of Learning by Doing." *Review of Economic Studies* 29 (3): 155-73.

Arunyanart, S., P. Sureeyatanapas, K. Ponhan, W. Sessomboon, and T. Niyamosoth. 2021. "International Location Selection for Production Fragmentation." *Expert Systems with Applications* 171: 114564.

Arvis, J.-F., Y. Duval, B. Shepherd, C. Utoktham, and A. Raj. 2016. "Trade Costs in the Developing World: 1996-2010." *World Trade Review* 15 (3): 451-74.

Arvis, J.-F., B. Shepherd, Y. Duval, and C. Utoktham. 2013. "Trade Costs and Development: A New Data Set." Economic Premise 104, World Bank, Washington, DC.

Atkin, D., and D. Donaldson. 2015. "Who's Getting Globalized? The Size and Implications of Intranational Trade Costs." NBER Working Paper 21439, National Bureau of Economic Research, Cambridge, MA.

Auboin, M., and F. Borino, 2018. "The Falling Elasticity of Global Trade to Economic Activity: Testing the Demand Channel." CESifo Working Paper 7228, Center for Economic Studies and Ifo Institute, Munich.

Autor, D. H., D. Dorn, and G. Hanson. 2013. "The China Syndrome: Local Labor Market Effects of Import Competition in the United States." *American Economic Review* 103 (6): 2121-68.

Baccini, L., and J. Urpelainen. 2014a. "Before Ratification: Understanding the Timing of International Treaty Effects on Domestic Policies." *International Studies Quarterly* 58 (1): 29-43.

Baccini, L., and J. Urpelainen. 2014b. "International Institutions and Domestic Politics: Can Preferential Trading Agreements Help Leaders Promote Economic Reform?" *Journal of Politics* 76 (1): 195-214.

Baldwin, R., and D. Jaimovich. 2010. "Are Free Trade Agreements Contagious?" NBER Working Paper 16084, National Bureau of Economic Research, Cambridge, MA.

Baunsgaard, T., and M. Keen. 2010. "Tax Revenue and (or?) Trade Liberalization." *Journal of Public Economics* 94 (9-10): 563-77.

Beghin, J. C., and H. Schweizer. 2020. "Agricultural Trade Costs." *Applied Economic Perspectives and Policy* 43 (2): 500-30.

Benigno. G., J. di Giovanni, J. Groen, and A. Noble. 2022. "Global Supply Chain Pressure Index: March 2022 Update." *Liberty Street Economics* (blog), March 3, 2022. Federal Reserve Bank of New York.

Benz, S. 2017. "Services Trade Costs: Tariff Equivalents of Services Trade Restrictions Using Gravity Estimation." OECD Trade Policy Paper 200, Organisation for Economic Co-operation and Development, Paris.

Bergstrand, J. H., M. Larch, and Y. V. Yotov. 2015. "Economic Integration Agreements, Border Effects, and Distance Elasticities in the Gravity Equation." *European Economic Review* 78 (C): 307-27.

Bernard, A. B., J. B. Jensen, S. J. Redding, and P. K. Schott. 2007. "Firms in International Trade." *Journal of Economic Perspectives* 21 (3): 105-30.

Bernard, A. B., J. B. Jensen, and P. Schott. 2006. "Trade Costs, Firms and Productivity." *Journal of Monetary Economics* 53 (5): 917-37.

Bhagwati, J., and T. N. Srinivasan. 2002. "Trade and Poverty in the Poor Countries." *American Economic Review* 92 (2): 180-83.

Bolaky, B., and C. L. Freund. 2004. "Trade, Regulations, and Growth." Policy Research Working Paper 3255, World Bank, Washington, DC.

Brancaccio, G., M. Kalouptsidi, and T. Papageorgiou. 2020. "Geography, Transportation, and Endogenous Trade Costs." *Econometrica* 88 (2): 657-91.

Brenton, P., and V. Chemutai. 2021. *The Trade and Climate Change Nexus: The Urgency and Opportunities for Developing Countries.* Washington, DC: World Bank.

Brenton, P., A. Portugal-Perez, and J. Regolo. 2014. "Food Prices, Road Infrastructure, and Market Integration in Central and Eastern Africa." Policy Research Working Paper 7003, World Bank, Washington, DC.

Broda, C., J. Greenfield, and D. Weinstein. 2017. "From Groundnuts to Globalization: A Structural Estimate of Trade and Growth." *Research in Economics* 71 (4): 759-83.

Bussière, M., G. Callegari, F. Ghironi, G. Sestieri, and N. Yamano. 2013. "Estimating Trade Elasticities: Demand Composition and the Trade Collapse of 2008-2009." *American Economic Journal: Macroeconomics* 5 (3): 118-51.

Butollo, F. 2021. "Digitalization and the Geographies of Production: Towards Reshoring or Global Fragmentation?" *Competition and Change* 25 (2): 259-78.

Cabrillac, B., A. Al-Haschimi, O. B. Kucharčuková, A. Borin, M. Bussiere, R. Cezar, A. Derviz et al. 2016. "Understanding the Weakness in Global Trade—What Is the New Normal?" Occasional Paper 2016-09, European Central Bank, Frankfurt.

Caldara, D., M. Iacoviello, P. Molligo, A. Prestipino, and A. Raffo. 2020. "The Economic Effects of Trade Policy Uncertainty." *Journal of Monetary Economics* 109 (January): 38-59.

Calì, M., and D. W. te Velde. 2011. "Does Aid for Trade Really Improve Trade Performance?" *World Development* 39 (5): 725-40.

Celasun, O., N.-J. Hansen, A. Mineshima, M. Spector, and J. Zhou. 2022. "Supply Bottlenecks: Where, Why, How Much, and What Next?" IMF Working Paper 22/31, International Monetary Fund, Washington, DC.

Chang, R., L. Kaltani, and N. Loayza. 2009. "Openness Can Be Good for Growth: The Role of Policy Complementarities." *Journal of Development Economics* 90 (1): 33-49.

Chen, M. X., and A. Mattoo. 2008. "Regionalism in Standards: Good or Bad for Trade?" *Canadian Journal of Economics* 41 (3): 838-63.

Chen, N., J. Imbs, and A. Scott. 2009. "The Dynamics of Trade and Competition," *Journal of International Economics* 77 (1): 50-62.

Chen, N., and D. Novy. 2012. "On the Measurement of Trade Costs: Direct vs. Indirect Approaches to Quantifying Standards and Technical Regulations." *World Trade Review* 11 (3): 401-14.

Christie, A., D. Smith, and K. Conroy. 2013. "Transport Governance Indicators in Sub-Saharan Africa." Sub-Saharan Africa Transport Policy Program Working Paper 95, World Bank, Washington, DC.

Cigna, S., V. Gunnella, and L. Quaglietti. 2022. "Global Value Chains: Measurement, Trends and Drivers." Occasional Paper 289, European Central Bank, Frankfurt.

Constantinescu, C., A. Mattoo, and M. Ruta. 2020. "The Global Trade Slowdown: Cyclical or Structural?" *World Bank Economic Review* 34 (1): 121-42.

Coulibaly, B. S., and K. Foda. 2020. "The Future of Global Manufacturing." *Up Front* (blog), Brookings Institution, March 4, 2020. https://www.brookings.edu/blog/up-front/2020/03/04/the-future-of-global-manufacturing

Crozet, M., B. Demir, and B. Javorcik. 2021. "International Trade and Letters of Credit: A Double-Edged Sword in Times of Crises." CEPR Discussion Paper 16630, Centre for Economic Policy Research, London.

Daudin, G., J. Héricourt, and L. Patureau. 2022. "International Transport Costs: New Findings from Modeling Additive Costs." *Journal of Economic Geography* 22 (5): 989-1044.

de Moran, M. A. 2018. "Customs Union Between Guatemala and Honduras, from 10 Hours to 15 Minutes!" *Latin America and Caribbean* (blog), World Bank, April 2, 2018. https://blogs.worldbank.org/latinamerica/customs-union-between-guatemala-and-honduras-10-hours-15-minutes

de Sousa, J. 2012. "The Currency Union Effect on Trade Is Decreasing over Time." *Economics Letters* 117 (3): 917-20.

Deichmann, U., and I. Gill. 2008. "The Economic Geography of Regional Integration." *Finance & Development* 45 (4): 45-47.

Djankov, S., C. Freund, and C. S. Pham. 2010. "Trading on Time." *Review of Economics and Statistics* 92 (1): 166-73.

Dollar, D. 1992. "Outward-Oriented Developing Economies Really Do Grow More Rapidly: Evidence from 95 LDCs, 1976-85." *Economic Development and Cultural Change* 40 (3): 523-44.

Dollar, D., and A. Kraay. 2004. "Trade, Growth, and Poverty." *Economic Journal* 114 (493): 22-49.

Donaldson, D., A. Jinhage, and E. Verhoogen. 2017. "Beyond Borders: Making Transport Work for African Trade." IGC Growth Brief 009, International Growth Centre, London.

Dutt, P., and D. Traca. 2010. "Corruption and Bilateral Trade Flows: Extortion or Evasion?" *Review of Economics and Statistics* 92 (4): 843-60.

Duval, Y., A. Saggu, and C. Utoktham. 2015. "Reducing Trade Costs in Asia-Pacific Developing Countries." Studies in Trade and Investment 84, United Nations Economic and Social Commission for Asia and the Pacific, Bangkok.

Edwards, S. 1997. "Openness, Productivity and Growth: What Do We Really Know?" NBER Working Paper 5978, National Bureau of Economic Research, Cambridge, MA.

Espitia, A., A. Mattoo, N. Rocha, M. Ruta, and D. Winkler. 2021. "Pandemic Trade: COVID-19, Remote Work and Global Value Chains." Policy Research Working Paper 9508, World Bank, Washington, DC.

Fan, C. F., A. Weitz, and Y. Lam. 2019. "Blockchain Is Already Transforming Trade and Logistics— And That's Just the Beginning!" *Transport for Development* (blog), World Bank, June 6, 2019. https://blogs.worldbank.org/transport/blockchain-already-transforming-trade-and-logistics-and-thats-just-beginning

Feenstra, R. C. 2003. *Advanced International Trade: Theory and Evidence*. Princeton, NJ: Princeton University Press.

Feenstra, R. C. 2010. *Product Variety and the Gains from International Trade*. Cambridge, MA: MIT Press.

Felbermayr, G., J. Prat, and H. J. Schmerer. 2009. "Trade and Unemployment: What Do the Data Say?" IZA Discussion Paper 4184, Institute for the Study of Labor (IZA), Bonn.

Frankel, J., and D. H. Romer. 1999. "Does Trade Cause Growth?" *American Economic Review* 89 (3): 379-99.

Freund, C., and N. Rocha. 2011. "What Constrains Africa's Exports?" *World Bank Economic Review* 25 (3): 361-86.

Grossman, G., and E. Helpman. 1991. "Trade, Knowledge Spillovers, and Growth." *European Economic Review* 35 (2-3): 517-26.

Gurevich, T., and P. Herman. 2018. "The Dynamic Gravity Dataset: 1948-2016." USITC Working Paper 2018-02-A, U.S. International Trade Commission, Washington, DC.

Hartman, P. L., J. A. Ogden, J. Wirthlin, and B. Hazen. 2017. "Nearshoring, Reshoring, and Insourcing: Moving Beyond the Total Cost of Ownership Conversation." *Business Horizons* 60 (3): 363-73.

Hausman, W. H., H. Lee, and U. Subramanian. 2005. "Global Logistics Indicators, Supply Chain Metrics and Bilateral Trade Patterns." Policy Research Working Paper 3773, World Bank, Washington, DC.

Helpman, E. 1981. "International Trade in the Presence of Product Differentiation, Economies of Scale and Monopolistic Competition: A Chamberlin-Heckscher-Ohlin Approach." *Journal of International Economics* 11 (3): 305-40.

Helpman, E. 1997. "R&D and Productivity: The International Connection." NBER Working Paper 6101, National Bureau of Economic Research, Cambridge, MA.

Helpman, E., and P. Krugman. 1985. *Market Structure and Foreign Trade: Increasing Returns, Imperfect Competition, and the International Economy*. Cambridge, MA: MIT Press.

Hillberry, R., and X. Zhang. 2015. "Policy and Performance in Customs: Evaluating the Trade Facilitation Agreement." Policy Research Working Paper 7211, World Bank, Washington, DC.

Hoekman, B., and L. A. Winters. 2005. "Trade and Employment: Stylized Facts and Research Findings." Policy Research Working Paper 3676, World Bank, Washington, DC.

Hou, Y., Y. Wang, and W. Xue. 2021. "What Explains Trade Costs? Institutional Quality and Other Determinants." *Review of Development Economics* 25 (1): 478-99.

Hummels, D. 2001. "Time as a Trade Barrier." GTAP Working Paper 1152, Center for Global Trade Analysis, Department of Agricultural Economics, Purdue University.

Hummels, D., P. Minor, M. Reisman, and E. Endean. 2007. "Calculating Tariff Equivalents of Time in Trade." Nathan Associates Inc. for United States Agency for International Development, Washington, DC.

IMF (International Monetary Fund). 2021. *World Economic Outlook: Managing Divergent Recoveries.* April. International Monetary Fund, Washington, DC.

Irwin, D. A. 2019. "Does Trade Reform Promote Economic Growth? A Review of Recent Evidence." Working Paper 19-9, Peterson Institute for International Economics, Washington, DC.

Irwin, D. A. 2022. "The Trade Reform Wave of 1985-1995." Working Paper 29973, National Bureau of Economic Research, Cambridge, MA.

Ishikawa, J., and N. Tarui. 2018. "Backfiring with Backhaul Problems: Trade and Industrial Policies with Endogenous Transport Costs." *Journal of International Economics* 111 (March): 81-98.

Jacks, D. S., C. M. Meissner, and D. Novy. 2011. "Trade Booms, Trade Busts, and Trade Costs." *Journal of International Economics* 83 (2): 185-201.

Kee, H. L., and A. Nicita. 2016. "Trade Frauds, Trade Elasticities, and Non-tariff Measures." Paper presented at the Fifth IMF-World Bank-WTO Joint Trade Research Workshop, November 30, 2016, Washington, DC.

Keller, W. 2004. "International Technology Diffusion." *Journal of Economic Literature* 42 (3): 752-82.

Keller, W. 2021. "Knowledge Spillovers, Trade, and FDI." NBER Working Paper 28739, National Bureau of Economic Research, Cambridge, MA.

Kose, M. A., F. Ohnsorge, Y. Lei, and I. Ergys. 2017. "Weakness in Investment Growth: Causes, Implications and Policy Responses." Policy Research Working Paper 7990, World Bank, Washington, DC.

Kox, H., and H. K. Nordas. 2007. "Services Trade and Domestic Regulation." Trade Policy Paper 49, Organisation for Economic Co-operation and Development, Paris.

Krugman, P. 1979. "Increasing Returns, Monopolistic Competition and International Trade." *Journal of International Economics* 9 (4): 469-79.

Liargovas, P., and K. Skandalis. 2012. "Foreign Direct Investment and Trade Openness: The Case of Developing Economies." *Social Indicators Research* 106 (2): 323-31.

Lucas, R. 1993. "Making a Miracle." *Econometrica* 61 (2): 251-72.

Marti, L., and R. Puertas. 2019. "Factors Determining the Trade Costs of Major European Exporters." *Maritime Economics and Logistics* 21 (3): 324-33.

Melitz, M. 2003. "The Impact of Trade on Intra-Industry Reallocations and Aggregate Industry Productivity." *Econometrica* 71 (6): 1695-725.

Melitz, M., and G. Ottaviano. 2008. "Market Size, Trade, and Productivity." *Review of Economic Studies* 75 (1): 295-316.

Miroudot, S., J. Sauvage, and B. Shepherd. 2010. "Measuring the Cost of International Trade in Services." MPRA Paper 27655, University Library of Munich, Germany.

Moïsé, E., and F. Le Bris. 2013. "Trade Costs—What Have We Learned?: A Synthesis Report." OECD Trade Policy Paper 150, Organisation for Economic Co-operation and Development, Paris.

Moïsé, E., T. Orliac, and P. Minor. 2011. "Trade Facilitation Indicators: The Impact on Trade Costs." OECD Trade Policy Paper 118, Organisation for Economic Co-operation and Development, Paris.

Moïsé, E., and S. Sorescu. 2013. "Trade Facilitation Indicators: The Potential Impact of Trade Facilitation on Developing Countries' Trade." OECD Trade Policy Paper 144, Organisation for Economic Co-operation and Development, Paris.

Muendler, M. 2004. "Trade, Technology, and Productivity: A Study of Brazilian Manufacturers, 1986-1998." CESifo Working Paper 1148, Center for Economic Studies and Ifo Institute, Munich.

Niu, Z., C. Liu, S. Gunessee, and C. Milner. 2018. "Non-tariff and Overall Protection: Evidence across Countries and over Time." *Review of World Economics* 154 (4): 675-703.

Noguer, M., and M. Siscart. 2005. "Trade Raises Income: A Precise and Robust Result." *Journal of International Economics* 65 (2): 447-60.

Nordas, H. K. 2006. "Time as a Trade Barrier: Implications for Low-Income Countries." *OECD Economic Studies* 2006 (1): 137-67.

Novy, D. 2013. "Gravity Redux: Measuring International Trade Costs with Panel Data." *Economic Inquiry* 51 (1): 101-21.

OECD (Organisation for Economic Co-operation and Development). 2020. "Trade Policy Implications of Global Value Chains", OECD Trade Policy Brief, Paris: OECD Publishing.

OECD (Organisation for Economic Co-operation and Development), International Labour Organization, World Bank, and World Health Organization. 2010. "Seizing the Benefits of Trade for Employment and Growth." Final Report to the G-20 Summit Meeting, Seoul, November 11-12.

OECD (Organisation for Economic Co-operation and Development) and WTO (World Trade Organization). 2015. "Why Trade Costs Matter for Inclusive, Sustainable Growth." In *Aid for Trade at a Glance 2015: Reducing Trade Costs for Inclusive, Sustainable Growth*. Paris: OECD Publishing.

Osnago, A., R. Piermartini, and N. Rocha. 2015. "Trade Policy Uncertainty as Barrier to Trade." WTO Staff Working Paper ERSD-2015-05, World Trade Organization, Geneva.

Osnago, A., R. Piermartini, and N. Rocha. 2018. "The Heterogeneous Effects of Trade Policy Uncertainty: How Much Do Trade Commitments Boost Trade?" Policy Research Working Paper 8567, World Bank, Washington, DC.

Pavcnik, N. 2002. "Trade Liberalization, Exit, and Productivity Improvements: Evidence from Chilean Plants." *Review of Economic Studies* 69 (1): 245-76.

Ricardo, D. 1817. *On the Principles of Political Economy and Taxation*. London: John Murray.

Rodríguez, F., and D. Rodrik. 2000. "Trade Policy and Economic Growth: A Skeptic's Guide to the Cross-National Evidence." *NBER Macroeconomics Annual* 15: 261-338.

Romer, P. M. 1990. "Endogenous Technological Change." *Journal of Political Economy* 98 (5): S71-S102.

Ruta, M., ed. 2022. *The Impact of the War in Ukraine on Global Trade and Investment*. Equitable Growth, Finance, and Institutions Insights. Washington, DC: World Bank.

Sachs, J., and A. Warner. 1995. "Economic Reform and the Process of Global Integration." *Brookings Papers on Economic Activity* 1: 1-118.

Sadikov, A. 2007. "Border and Behind-the-Border Trade Barriers and Country Exports." IMF Working Paper 07/292, International Monetary Fund, Washington, DC.

Santos Silva, J., and S. Tenreyro. 2006. "The Log of Gravity." *Review of Economics and Statistics* 88 (4): 641-58.

Saurav, A., P. Kusek, R. Kuo, and B. Viney. 2020. "The Impact of COVID-19 on Foreign Investors: Evidence from the Second Round of a Global Pulse Survey." World Bank, Washington, DC.

Shah, M., and Y. Khan. 2016. "Trade Liberalisation and FDI Inflows in Emerging Economies." *Business & Economic Review* 8 (1): 35-52.

Sharma, C., and M. Kumar. 2015. "International Trade and Performance of Firms: Unraveling Export, Import and Productivity Puzzle." *Quarterly Review of Economics and Finance* 57 (C): 61-74.

Song, D. 2021. "A Literature Review, Container Shipping Supply Chain: Planning Problems and Research Opportunities." *Logistics* 5 (41): 1-26.

Sposi, M., M. Yi, and J. Zhang. 2019. "Trade Integration, Global Value Chains and Capital Accumulation." NBER Working Paper 28087, National Bureau of Economic Research, Cambridge, MA.

Staboulis, C., D. Natos, E. Tsakiridou, and K. Mattas. 2020. "International Trade Costs in OECD Countries." *Operational Research* 20 (3): 1177-87.

Stone, S., and B. Jeon. 2000. "Foreign Direct Investment and Trade in the Asia-Pacific Region: Complementarity, Distance and Regional Economic Integration." *Journal of Economic Integration* 15 (3): 460-85.

Teravaninthorn, S., and G. Raballand. 2008. *Transport Prices and Costs in Africa: A Review of the International Corridors.* Washington, DC: World Bank.

Timmer, M. P., B. Los, R. Stehrer, and G. J. De Vries. 2021. "Supply Chain Fragmentation and the Global Trade Elasticity: A New Accounting Framework." *IMF Economic Review* 69 (4): 656-80.

UNESCAP (United Nations Economic and Social Commission for Asia and the Pacific). 2011. "Facilitating Agricultural Trade in Asia and the Pacific." Studies in Trade and Investment 74, United Nations, New York.

UNESCAP (United Nations Economic and Social Commission for Asia and the Pacific). 2017. "Tackling Agricultural Trade Costs in Asia and the Pacific." United Nations, New York.

USAID (United States Agency for International Development). 2019. *Assessing the Benefits of the Trade Facilitation Agreement for Agricultural Trade.* Washington, DC: USAID.

Wacziarg, R., and K. Welch. 2008. "Trade Liberalization and Growth: New Evidence." *World Bank Economic Review* 22 (2): 187-231.

Webber, C. M., and P. Labaste. 2010. *Building Competitiveness in Africa's Agriculture.* Washington, DC: World Bank.

World Bank. 2015. *Global Economic Prospects: Having Fiscal Space and Using It.* January. Washington, DC: World Bank.

World Bank. 2016. *Global Economic Prospects: Spillovers amid Weak Growth.* January. Washington, DC: World Bank.

World Bank. 2017. *Global Economic Prospects: Weak Investment in Uncertain Times.* January. Washington, DC: World Bank.

World Bank. 2018. "Cambodia: Trade Facilitation and Competitiveness." World Bank, Washington, DC. https://projects.worldbank.org/en/projects-operations/project-detail/P089196

World Bank. 2019. *Global Economic Prospects: Heightened Tensions, Subdued Investment.* June. Washington, DC: World Bank.

World Bank. 2020a. *The African Continental Free Trade Area: Economic and Distributional Effects.* Washington, DC: World Bank.

World Bank. 2020b. "Rebuilding Tourism Competitiveness: Tourism Response, Recovery and the Covid-19 Crisis." Markets & Technology Global Tourism Team note, World Bank, Washington, DC.

World Bank. 2020c. *World Development Report: Trading for Development in the Age of Global Value Chains.* Washington, DC: World Bank.

World Bank. 2021a. "Creating Value in the Data Economy: The Role of Competition, Trade, and Tax Policy." In *World Development Report 2021: Data for Better Lives,* 227-64. Washington, DC: World Bank.

World Bank. 2021b. *Global Economic Prospects.* January. Washington, DC: World Bank.

World Bank. 2021c. *Global Economic Prospects.* June. Washington, DC: World Bank.

World Bank. 2021d. "Implementation Status and Results Report: AFR RI-Great Lakes Trade Facilitation." World Bank, Washington, DC.

World Bank. 2022a. *Global Economic Prospects.* January. Washington, DC: World Bank.

World Bank. 2022b. *Global Economic Prospects.* June. Washington, DC: World Bank.

World Bank and UNCTAD (United Nations Conference on Trade and Development). 2018. *The Unseen Impact of Non-tariff Measures: Insights from a New Database.* Washington, DC: World Bank.

World Bank and WTO (World Trade Organization). 2020. *Women and Trade: The Role of Trade in Promoting Gender Equality.* Washington, DC: World Bank.

WTO (World Trade Organization). 2018. *World Trade Report 2018: The Future of World Trade; How Digital Technologies Are Transforming Global Commerce.* Geneva: World Trade Organization.

WTO (World Trade Organization). 2019a. *The Digital Economy: GVCs and SMEs.* Geneva: World Trade Organization.

WTO (World Trade Organization). 2019b. *World Trade Report 2019: The Future of Services Trade.* Geneva: World Trade Organization.

Yotov, Y. V. 2012. "A Simple Solution to the Distance Puzzle in International Trade." *Economic Letters* 117 (3): 794-98.

Zhan, J., R. Baldwinn, B. Casella, and A. S. Santos-Paulino. 2020. "Global Value Chain Transformation to 2030: Overall Direction and Policy Implications." *VoxEU.org,* August 13, 2020. https://voxeu.org/article/global-value-chain-transformation-decade-ahead

CHAPTER 7

Services-Led Growth: Better Prospects after the COVID-19 Pandemic?

The services sector accounted for two-thirds of economic growth in emerging market and developing economies (EMDEs) over the past three decades. In 2019, it accounted for more than half of gross domestic product (GDP) and employment in EMDEs. The sector consists of a wide range of activities, ranging from high-skilled offshorable services, such as information and communications technology (ICT) and professional services, to low-skilled "contact" services, such as retail and hospitality. The pandemic disrupted provision of many low-skilled contact services, which typically require face-to-face interactions between providers and consumers. Provision of high-skilled offshorable services was the least affected, owing to the use of digital technology that enabled remote delivery. Increased digitalization has improved prospects for scale economies and innovation in the services sector that the need for physical proximity and the lack of opportunities to augment labor with capital previously constrained. Policies to support the diffusion of digital technologies could therefore further raise the growth potential of the services sector. Policies to improve market access for, and skills in, ICT and professional services could ease important constraints on growth opportunities in these high-skilled offshorable services that have best withstood the pandemic. The same holds true for policies, including regulatory reforms, that promote investment in low-skilled contact services, such as transportation, which have important linkages with the wider economy.

Introduction

The services sector is large and has been the main source of global economic growth over the past three decades. Services accounted for 66 percent of global output growth and 73 percent of global employment growth between 1995 and 2019 and for 63 percent of global output levels and 57 percent of global employment levels in 2019. While the services sector represented a somewhat lower share of economic activity in emerging market and developing economies than in advanced economies, the difference was small. Even in EMDEs, services made up for 60 percent of output and 52 percent of employment in 2019.

The services sector is diverse. First, it includes high-skilled offshorable services (information and communications technologies, finance, and professional services) that have been internationally traded much like goods since the ICT revolution in the 1990s. Second, it includes generally low-skilled contact services (transportation, hospitality, retail, personal services, arts, entertainment and recreation, and administrative and support) that have typically required physical proximity of providers and consumers. Many services from both these categories provide important inputs for non-services-

---

Note: This chapter was prepared by Gaurav Nayyar and Elwyn Davies.

sector activity. For example, transportation and logistics services form the infrastructure for international trade in agricultural commodities and manufactured goods, while ICT services are increasingly central to data-intensive production processes. Third, it includes a group of social services (education and health) that are largely publicly provided and therefore not a focus of this chapter.

The pandemic has dealt uneven blows to services activity. Social-distancing regulations and precautions against the spread of the virus have hit provision of low-skilled contact services, such as transportation and hospitality, particularly hard. But provision of high-skilled offshorable services, such as ICT and professional services, has been much less affected owing to their amenability to home-based work.

The increased digitalization that firms have implemented to cushion the impact of the pandemic's disruptions can be leveraged to boost growth in the services sector. Baumol (1967) and Hill (1977) argue that the services have limited potential for leading growth because they typically require a simultaneity of production and consumption that precludes economies of scale. In other words, the need for face-to-face interactions between providers of services and consumers inhibits opportunities for the former to serve demand beyond the local market. They also point out that services have less scope for capital-deepening and innovation than does manufacturing. Increased digitalization, however, enables greater scale and innovation in the services sector. The resulting productivity benefits, in turn, can boost overall economic growth owing to the important linkages between the services sector and other parts of the economy.

Against this backdrop, this chapter addresses the following questions:

- How has the services sector shaped global economic growth over the past three decades?

- How has the pandemic affected the services sector?

- How can digitalization enhance the services sector's growth as countries recover from the pandemic?

- Which policies can help harness the services sector's growth potential?

It presents several novel findings. First, although the services sector has led economic growth over the past three decades in both advanced economies and EMDEs, the composition of services sector growth differs significantly between the two groups. While low-skilled contact services make a similar contribution to GDP growth in the two groups, the contribution of high-skilled offshorable services increases with per capita income levels. Thus, high-skilled offshorable services account for about one-third of GDP growth in advanced economies, compared with 15 percent in EMDEs, and for one-half of employment growth in advanced economies, compared with 11 percent in EMDEs. This matters because lower dependence on (1) export growth relative to growth in domestic demand and (2) total factor productivity growth relative to the growth of labor and capital inputs has characterized the growth of low-skilled contact services.

Second, the pandemic has had an uneven impact on the growth of the services sector. Low-skilled contact services reliant on face-to-face interactions with consumers, such as accommodation, food, and transportation services, have been among the most adversely affected sectors, even though there are now signs of recovery. But high-skilled offshorable services, which tend to be amenable to remote work though digital delivery, such as ICT and professional services, were among the sectors least adversely affected, and output and investment have even grown in some—especially ICT services.

Third, the increase in digitalization during the pandemic augurs well for growth prospects in the services sector. Among high-skilled offshorable services, there is a new momentum; the share of digitally deliverable ICT and professional services in total services exports of EMDEs increased to 50 percent in 2020 from 40 percent in 2019. Among low-skilled contact services, streaming platforms such as Netflix and YouTube have increasingly enabled providers of arts and entertainment services to export their creative content to international markets at low cost. Even in regard to services in which physical proximity remains important, intangible capital associated with digitalization has increased opportunities for scale economies. For example, e-commerce platforms have enabled retailers and restaurants to reach customers beyond their local neighborhoods. Additionally, ICT and management practices have facilitated the standardization of production across many establishments.

Fourth, appropriate policy interventions can better enable countries to leverage the potential of the services sector to drive economic growth. Policies to support the diffusion of digital technologies in EMDEs, for example, can bring particularly high returns because of the lack of digitalization in the services sector: The share of firms using email to communicate with clients was less than one-third in several EMDEs as recently as 2018. Investing in ICT infrastructure, updating regulatory frameworks (including those relating to data), and strengthening management capabilities and worker skills can all boost the adoption of digital technologies. Countries can also promote the expansion of high-skilled offshorable services by reducing barriers to international trade and taking measures to improve skills. Last, but not least, countries can support investment and implement regulatory reforms that foster the revival of low-skilled contact services, such as transportation, that can be large employers and important enablers of growth in the wider economy.

This chapter makes several contributions to the literature. First, it presents stylized facts about the role of the services sector in overall economic growth over the past three decades. This presentation draws on and complements a growing literature on structural change and productivity growth in EMDEs that highlights the changing contributions of the manufacturing and services sectors (Fan, Peters, and Zilibotti 2021; Kinfemichael and Mahbub Morshed 2019; McMillan and Rodrik 2011; Nayyar, Hallward-Driemeier, and Davies 2021; Rodrik 2016). The main innovations here are the growth decompositions: Services subsectors are explored; the demand-side contributions of domestic demand, exports, and government consumption are compared; and the supply-side contributions of the growth of factor inputs and total factor productivity are examined.

Second, it analyzes how the pandemic has affected prospects for services-led growth by tracing patterns of recovery and assessing future growth opportunities linked to the acceleration of digitalization. By making a systematic assessment by services subsector, this analysis builds on a spate of recent studies that examine the effects of the pandemic on growth and distribution (Apedo-Amah et al. 2020; Beraja and Wolf 2021; Chetty et al. 2020), as well as the literature on how the digital economy is expanding opportunities to boost productivity.

Third, it discusses policy options and priorities for leveraging the services sector's potential for boosting economic growth after the pandemic. This adds to the policy discussion in Nayyar, Hallward-Driemeier, and Davies (2021) by focusing on developments since the pandemic. Policies considered include the reform of regulatory barriers and the promotion of skill development for both high-skilled offshorable and low-skilled contact services.

The remainder of the chapter is organized as follows. The second section quantifies how the services sector has shaped economic growth over the past three decades. The third section analyzes how the pandemic has affected the services sector's growth. The fourth section examines the potential of digitalization to increase growth in the services sector. The fifth section identifies policy priorities to leverage this potential to drive stronger overall economic growth. The final section presents conclusions.

How has the services sector shaped economic growth?

A general feature of economic development is structural change in national economies. The pioneering work of Fisher (1935), Clark (1940), Chenery (1960), and Kuznets (1971) observed a common pattern of change in the relative sizes of the agricultural, industrial (or manufacturing), and services sectors among industrial or advanced economies in the course of their development. In the early stages of development, the agriculture sector had the dominant share in both output and employment. Subsequently, as industrialization proceeded, the agriculture sector's share fell off, and the industrial (or manufacturing) sector's share rose. Once countries industrialized and reached an advanced stage of economic development, the industrial sector's share also declined, and the services sector's share increased. Interestingly, growth in EMDEs over the past three decades has not conformed to this pattern. Even though most of these economies are in relatively early stages of development, the services sector has offset much of the decline in the share of the agricultural sector in both GDP and employment.

However, there are important differences across services subsectors. Three categories may be distinguished. First, ICT, finance, and business services comprise a group of high-skilled offshorable services. Second, there is a group of low-skilled contact services that are not offshorable. However, some are traded internationally through either their linkages with goods (cargo transportation and wholesale trade) or tourism-related travel (accommodation and food). Education and health services (social services) comprise a third group. High-skilled offshorable and low-skilled contact services differ in two particularly important economic respects. First, lower dependence on export growth, as opposed to growth in domestic demand, has generally characterized growth in the output of low-skilled contract services compared with high-skilled offshorable services. Second, growth in the output of low-skilled contact services has generally been based less on growth of total factor productivity, as opposed to growth of physical capital and labor inputs, than growth in the output of high-skilled offshorable services.[1] High-skilled offshorable services have expanded less in EMDEs than in advanced economies.

Services and structural transformation

Between 1991 and 2019, the services sector's share of total employment in EMDEs increased from 39 to 51 percent, offsetting almost the entire decline in agriculture's share, with little change in the share of industry (figure 7.1.A). Similarly, the services sector's share of GDP rose from 47 percent to 58 percent, offsetting a substantial decline in the share of agriculture together with a smaller decline in the share of industry (figure 7.1.B). These rising shares of the services sector in employment and GDP reflect its central role in driving economic growth in EMDEs over the past three decades. Thus, the services sector accounted for more than half of both employment growth (figure 7.1.C) and value-added growth (figure 7.1.D) between 1991 and 2018 across EMDEs.

In the past, the increasing share of the services sector in employment and GDP in industrial countries was attributed, at least in part, to rising relative prices of services that resulted from lower productivity growth than in industry (Baumol 1967). Labor productivity in the services sector could not be readily increased, either through innovation and capital accumulation, owing to the "intrinsic role of labor," or through economies of scale, because the intensity of face-to-face interactions constrained providers of services from reaching consumers beyond the local market.

This past characterization of the services sector is less relevant for EMDEs today. Labor productivity in the services sector between 1995 and 2018 showed growth similar to, or higher than, that in the industrial sector in four of the six EMDE regions—Latin America and the Caribbean (LAC), the Middle East and North Africa (MNA), South Asia (SAR), and Sub-Saharan Africa (SSA; figure 7.1.E). Only in the East Asia and Pacific (EAP) and Europe and Central Asia (ECA) regions—where export-led manufacturing has been the cornerstone of economic growth—did the growth of labor productivity in industry exceed that in services, as was the case in advanced economies.

---

[1] The relatively large contributions of export growth and total factor productivity growth to the growth in the output of high-skilled offshorable services have, nevertheless, been smaller than their contributions to the growth of manufacturing output.

FIGURE 7.1 The services sector and structural transformation

In recent decades, the services sector's share in output and employment has increased, and the sector has made larger contributions to both employment and output growth than agriculture or industry in both advanced economies and EMDEs. Labor productivity growth in services has been at least similar to that in industry in four out of the six EMDE regions. The services sector has contributed to overall labor productivity growth both through productivity growth within the sector and through the shift of labor to services from the lower-productivity agricultural sector.

A. Shares of individual sectors in employment

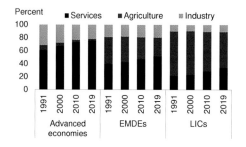

B. Shares of individual sectors in value added

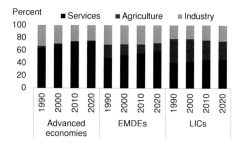

C. Contributions of individual sectors to employment growth, 1995-2019

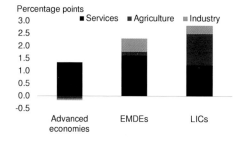

D. Contributions of individual sectors to value-added growth, 1995-2019

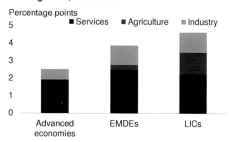

E. Labor productivity growth in services compared with that in manufacturing, 1995-2018

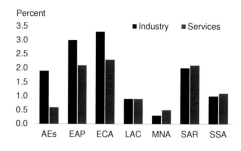

F. Contributions of individual sectors to labor productivity growth, 1995-2018

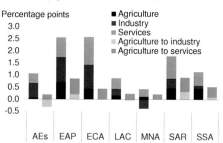

Sources: Nayyar, Hallward-Driemeier, and Davies (2021); World Bank.
Note: EMDEs = emerging market and developing economies; LICs = low-income countries.
A. Sample includes 35 advanced economies, 143 EMDEs, and 26 LICs. Data are until 2019.
B. Sample includes 31 advanced economies, 140 EMDEs, and 23 LICs. Data are until 2020.
C.D. Sample includes 30 advanced economies, 116 EMDEs, and 21 LICs. Bars represent an individual sector's contribution to growth, averaged over 1995-2019.
E.F. AEs = advanced economies; EAP = East Asia and Pacific; ECA = Europe and Central Asia; LAC = Latin America and the Caribbean; MNA = Middle East and North Africa; SAR = South Asia; SSA = Sub-Saharan Africa.
E. Average compounded annual growth rates in labor productivity (value added per worker) across each region between 1995-2018.
F. Bars represent labor productivity growth attributed to each sector, as well as to employment movements from the agriculture sector to the industry and service sector, for the period 1995-2018.

Furthermore, between 1995 and 2018, labor productivity growth in services in all EMDE regions except MNA exceeded that in advanced economies, implying narrowing productivity gaps. This provides encouraging evidence that services growth has been contributing to EMDEs' catch-up in respect to per capita incomes with advanced economies. It is also consistent with evidence of unconditional convergence of productivity across countries: Countries starting from lower labor productivity in the services sector experienced faster productivity growth between 1975 and 2012 than those with higher initial labor productivity in that sector (Enache, Ghani, and O'Connell 2016; Kinfemichael and Mahbub Morshed 2019).

These trends in labor productivity growth, combined with the changing sectoral shares of employment, underlie the contribution of the services sector to overall labor productivity growth. This growth reflects *within-sector* gains in productivity as well as *between-sector* gains as the labor force shifts from low- to high-productivity sectors. Thus, productivity growth within the services sector contributed more than productivity growth within industry to aggregate productivity growth in all EMDE regions other than EAP in the past three decades. Furthermore, although the relative contribution of the between-sector component did not exceed one-third in any region, in each case the bulk of it came from the increasing share of services in total employment (figure 7.1.F).

Increased productivity-enhancing growth opportunities in the services sector include new opportunities for larger-scale production, innovation (including through mechanization), and spillovers through linkages with other sectors—characteristics typically associated with manufacturing-led growth. For example, digital electronic content has made ICT services more storable, codifiable, and transferable and therefore more scalable. Similarly, innovation through research and development since the 1990s has been largely concentrated in ICT multinationals owing to software patents (Branstetter, Glennon, and Jensen 2018). ICT services have also increasingly benefited other sectors as data analytics have improved the quality and efficiency of production processes.

The heterogeneity of the services sector

The services sector comprises a wide range of economic activities.[2] They can be grouped according to the levels of skills that they involve and their amenability to being offshored and internationally traded. Three groups may be distinguished: high-skilled offshorable services, low-skilled contact services, and social services.

The first group, high-skilled offshorable services, comprises ICT, finance, and professional, scientific, and technical services that employ a smaller share of workers in

---

[2] Under the United Nations International Standard Industrial Classification of All Economic Activities, the broad categories of services include, among others, wholesale and retail trade; accommodation and food; transportation and warehousing; ICT services; financial services; real estate; professional, scientific, and technical services; public administration and defense; education and research; health services; arts, entertainment, and recreational services; administrative and support services; and other social, community, and personal services (United Nations 2008). Mining; utilities such as electricity, gas, and water; and construction are typically classified within "industry," together with manufacturing.

FIGURE 7.2 **The heterogeneity of the services sector**

Services subsectors differ in the amount of physical capital they use, their skill intensity, the degree to which they are connected to other sectors, the extent to which they are traded internationally, and how offshorable they are.

A. Offshorability and skill intensity in the United States

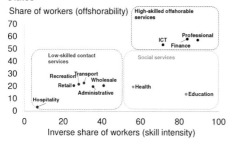

B. Intersectoral linkages in the European Union

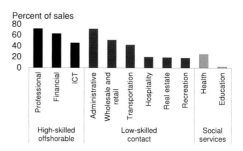

C. Intensity of exports in the United States

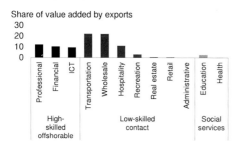

D. Trade by mode of supply

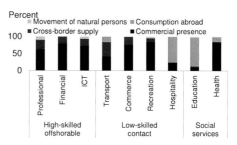

Sources: Blinder and Krueger (2013); Organisation for Economic Co-operation and Development (OECD); U.S. Department of Labor; World Trade Organization.

Note: The services subsectors depicted in the figure are divided by skill intensity and whether the tasks they require can be accomplished remotely or offshored.

ICT = information and communications technology.

A. "Offshorability" is measured as the share of worker tasks in the United States that (1) do not involve face-to-face contact with people other than coworkers, (2) can be completed without the worker's being physically present in a particular location, and (3) will not experience a decline in quality of performance if they can be delivered remotely. It reflects the possibility that tasks can be offshored from the United States to emerging market and developing economies, where labor costs are lower. "Skill intensity" is measured as the inverse of the share of workers in manual-task-intensive occupations among 23 major occupational groups in the U.S. Department of Labor's Occupational Information Network database in 2018. The use of data from the United States provides a lower bound; if a sector's jobs are predominantly filled by unskilled workers in the United States, they are almost certainly likely to be intensive in emerging and developing countries.

B. Share of sales to other domestic sectors in output in European Union countries in 2015. This shows the upside potential for linkages between sectors, since advanced economies have more diversified production structures. Data from the OECD's Trade in Value Added database.

C. Share of value added exported from the United States in 2015. This show the upside potential for scale, since advanced economies have more sophisticated sectors in services that are more likely to be traded internationally. Data are from the OECD's Trade in Value Added database.

D. Share of global trade in services by four modes of supply in 2017. "Commercial presence" refers to foreign direct investment. Data are from the World Trade Organization's Trade in Services by Mode of Supply database.

manual task-intensive occupations and that involve tasks more amenable to offshoring (figure 7.2.A). These services are more offshorable because they rely less on face-to-face interactions with customers and suffer less from losses in quality when delivered remotely. Other firms often also use them as intermediate outputs in the domestic economy, creating opportunities for domestic as well as international trade. For instance, three-fourths of the output of professional services constituted intermediate inputs in other sectors in 2015 (figure 7.2.B).

The second group, low-skilled contact services, relies more on manual labor and are less amenable to offshoring. This group includes transportation; hospitality; wholesale trade; arts, entertainment, and recreation; retail trade; administrative and support services; and personal services. Some of these services—notably transportation, hospitality, and wholesale trade—are highly traded internationally (figure 7.2.C). Transportation services and wholesale trade are often intermediate inputs into internationally traded goods. In contrast, hospitality services—accommodation and food provision—are mostly traded through "consumption abroad" owing to tourism-related travel (figure 7.2.D).

The third group, social services, consists of education and health services that are both relatively skill-intensive and less amenable to offshoring. This group of services is outside the focus of this chapter, since they are largely provided by the public sector.

Low-skilled contact services accounted for about one-third of GDP growth between 1990 and 2019 in each major country group—advanced economies, EMDEs, and low-income countries (LICs). Social services made a similar contribution to overall GDP growth over the past three decades, at about 15 percent, in each of these groups. However, the contribution of high-skilled offshorable services to GDP growth increased with levels of per capita income, ranging from 10 percent in LICs to 15 percent in EMDEs and almost 30 percent in advanced economies (figure 7.3.A).

High-skilled offshorable services also made a larger contribution to employment growth between 1990 and 2019 at higher levels of per capita income, with that contribution ranging from 4 percent in LICs to 11 percent in EMDEs and more than 50 percent in advanced economies. In contrast, the contribution to employment growth of low-skilled services, at about 40 percent, was similar across LICs, EMDEs, and advanced economies (figure 7.3.B).

The nature of services-led growth

The contribution of demand-side factors

The output of a sector caters either to intermediate demand from other sectors in the domestic economy or to final demand, which comprises domestic private consumption and investment, government expenditure, and exports. Among the components of final demand, domestic private demand plays the largest role in many low-skilled contact services, accounting for one-half of output in retail trade and three-fourths of output in hospitality services (figure 7.3.C). The need for physical proximity between providers of services and consumers has typically constrained international trade in these services (Hill 1977). Among low-skilled contact services, exports play a larger role in transportation and wholesale trade, where they are linked to trade in goods.

Exports also have quite a large share in final demand for some high-skilled offshorable services, such as professional services and ICT, in which digital electronic content has

FIGURE 7.3 Employment, value added, and productivity in services subsectors

High-skilled offshorable services and low-skilled contact services have both made key contributions to the growth of value added and employment in advanced economies, while low-skilled services have played a larger role in EMDEs. High-skilled offshorable services tend to be more closely linked to other sectors through input sales, more export-oriented, and more productive. Their growth is also more closely linked to improvements in productivity.

A. Sectoral contributions to value-added growth

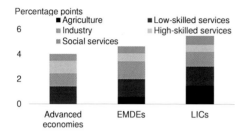

B. Sectoral contributions to employment growth

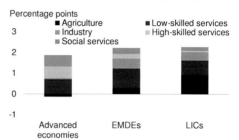

C. Shares of intermediate and final demand

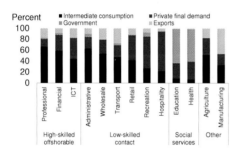

D. Contributions of growth of labor, capital, and TFP to output growth in advanced economies

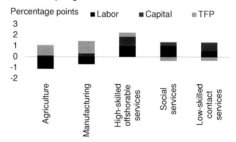

E. Labor productivity compared with that in manufacturing

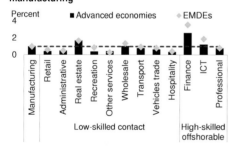

F. Total factor productivity compared with that in manufacturing

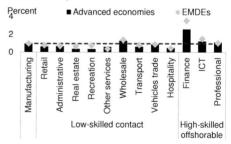

Sources: European Commission; Groningen Growth and Development Center (GGDC), World Input-Output Database (WIOD); Nayyar, Hallward-Driemeier, and Davies (2021).

Note: EMDEs = emerging market and developing economies; LICs = low-income countries; TFP = total factor productivity.

A. Bars represent the average contribution of individual sectors to value-added growth between 1990 and 2018. Sample from the GGDC/United Nations University-World Institute for Development Economics Research (UNU-WIDER) Economic Transformation Database includes 6 advanced economies, 39 EMDEs, and 6 LICs.

B. Bars represent the average contribution of individual sectors to employment growth between 1990 and 2018. Sample from the GGDC/United Nations University-World Institute for Development Economics Research (UNU-WIDER) Economic Transformation Database includes 6 advanced economies, 39 EMDEs, and 6 LICs.

C. "Intermediate consumption" measures sales to other sectors, based on WIOD data from 42 countries for 2014.

D. Based on the European Union KLEMS database because of constraints on data availability in EMDEs.

E.F. Productivity in the manufacturing sector in the same country is normalized to 1 (red line). Data are from 56 countries, including 35 EMDEs, for the latest available year between 2010 and 2017.

made them more storable, codifiable, and transferable. Because the constraint of physical proximity between consumers and providers has become less binding, professional services now have trade costs comparable to those in manufacturing industries (Gervais and Jensen 2019). Yet even these services have a considerably lower share of exports in final demand than do manufactured goods. This may be attributable to a range of policy impediments that have constrained services trade. Government consumption matters most in education and health services, which are often publicly provided.

Intermediate domestic demand—sales to producers in other sectors of the domestic economy—matters greatly for many services, accounting for more than half the output of both high-skilled offshorable services and some low-skilled contact services, such as transportation, wholesale, and administrative and support services (figure 7.3.C). The resulting links with other goods-producing (tradable) sectors also mean that services might be exported indirectly.

Value added by services accounted for 43 percent of world exports in 2009, up from 31 percent in 1980. In fact, more than two-thirds of the growth in services value added in exports between 1995 and 2011 was due to an increase in services embodied in other exports rather than services exported directly (Heuser and Mattoo 2017). This suggests that services such as transportation, telecommunications, finance, and business services have increasingly been used as intermediate inputs in the production and export of goods. In France, Germany, Italy, the United Kingdom, and the United States, services contribute more than half the total value added embodied as inputs in exports. Even in China, often viewed as predominantly an exporter of manufactured goods, more than a third of the value added in its exports comes from services (World Bank 2020). Furthermore, there is evidence that services embodied as inputs improve the productivity of downstream manufacturing (Arnold et al. 2015). These forward linkages highlight the important enabling role that many services play.

The contribution of supply-side factors

The growth of output can be decomposed into the contributions of the growth of factor inputs, such as capital and labor, and the contribution of the growth in the productivity of these factors, known as total factor productivity (TFP). Estimates based on data for 15 European Union countries indicate that growth of factor inputs, particularly labor, accounts for most of the growth of output in most services subsectors between 1991 and 2018 (figure 7.3.D). The low, even negative, contribution of TFP growth may reflect, at least in part, Baumol's "cost disease" hypothesis. Baumol (1967) argued that the productivity of many services sector activities cannot be readily increased through innovation because of their inherently labor-intensive nature. With technological progress in other sectors, the prices of manufactured and agricultural products would tend to fall relative to the price of services, leading to an increasing share of services in total output.[3]

---

[3] The challenges of measuring outputs and inputs in the services sector also raise concerns about the mismeasurement of productivity (Nayyar, Hallward-Driemeier, and Davies 2021).

However, high-skilled offshorable services have contradicted Baumol's hypothesis, with higher labor productivity than in manufacturing. Labor productivity in financial services is 3.5 times higher than that in manufacturing in EMDEs (and about 2.5 times higher in advanced economies), while labor productivity in ICT services is about 2 times higher in EMDEs (and 1.3 times in advanced economies) (figure 7.3.E). Labor productivity in professional services is below that that in manufacturing, but TFP—which corrects for differences in physical capital—is slightly higher than that in manufacturing (figure 7.3.F). Low-skilled contact services tend to have lower labor productivity and TFP than manufacturing.

However, productivity gains still occur in regard to low-skilled contact services. Fan, Peters, and Zilibotti (2021) show that productivity gains have characterized the growth of such contact services—employing large numbers of low-skilled labor—in India over the past three decades. Furthermore, firm-level data from Côte d'Ivoire, North Macedonia, Moldova, and Vietnam show that productivity growth in firms across several low-skilled contact services during their initial years often exceeds productivity growth in manufacturing firms (Aterido et al. 2021).

The relatively large contribution of capital accumulation to output growth in the services sector reflects increasing investments, including through foreign direct investment (FDI).[4] For example, outward FDI from the U.S. in high-skilled offshorable services outpaced that in manufacturing between 2011 and 2020 (figure 7.4.A). Furthermore, employment in U.S. foreign affiliates (outward FDI) increased across all services groups, while employment growth in manufacturing remained more stagnant (figure 7.4.B), despite increasing investment.

How has the COVID-19 pandemic affected the services sector's growth?

In previous recessions, the services sector was resilient despite sharply contracting manufacturing activity (figure 7.5.A). However, this resilience was lacking during the pandemic (figure 7.5.B). In fact, the economic contraction following the coronavirus disease 2019 (COVID-19) pandemic was particularly salient for the services sector (Apedo-Amah et al. 2020; Chetty et al. 2020; OECD 2021; World Bank 2022).

Unlike in previous downturns, the consumption of durable goods was resilient, but the consumption of many services declined owing to lockdown measures and increased caution among consumers (Tauber and Van Zandweghe 2021). This unusual shift in consumption patterns may carry implications for the ongoing recovery: Whereas reduced spending on durables in earlier downturns might just have represented postponed spending, consumers are less likely to catch up on reduced services spending (Beraja and Wolf 2021).

---

[4] Foreign direct investment is the most prevalent "mode" of trade in services ("mode 3" under the General Agreement on Trade in Services framework).

FIGURE 7.4 **Outward foreign direct investment in the services sector from the United States**

Foreign direct investment is an important mode through which services are traded internationally ("mode 3" under the General Agreement on Trade in Services framework). U.S. outward FDI in the services sector has been increasing, and for high-skilled offshorable services it has been outpacing that in manufacturing. Employment in U.S. foreign affiliates has been increasing in both high-skilled offshorable services and low-skilled contact services, while it has been stagnant in manufacturing.

A. Outward FDI from the United States

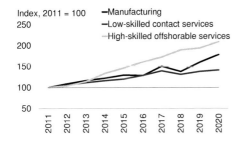

B. Employment in foreign affiliates of U.S. multinational enterprises

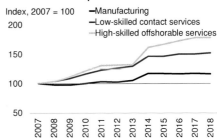

Source: Organisation for Economic Co-operation and Development (OECD).
Note: FDI positions reflect the value of the investment at the end of the reference year. The destination of the outward FDI from the United States is not available in the data but includes both advanced economies and emerging market and developing economies. Data are from the OECD Activity of Multinational Enterprises database. FDI = foreign direct investment.

FIGURE 7.5 **Services and manufacturing activity through recessions**

Recessions that occurred in 2020 at the height of the coronavirus disease 2019 (COVID-19) pandemic were unusual in the disruptions they caused to services activity. In previous recessions, services activity was resilient despite sharply contracting manufacturing activity.

A. Recessions before 2020

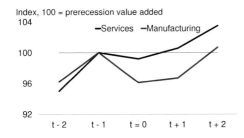

B. Recessions in 2020

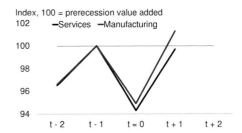

Source: World Bank.
Note: Recessions are defined as output contractions in which output growth is one standard deviation or more below the long-term average. This definition yields 185 recession events that ended before 2020 in 103 countries (for which data are available since 1960) and 76 recession events in 2020 in 76 countries. The average number of events is 1.7 per country. Figures show the unweighted average level of real value added in services (blue) and manufacturing (red) in the years around the recession year t_0, indexed to 100 for the year preceding the recession.

However, the pandemic has not had a uniform impact on the services sector across either subsectors or countries. It has had particularly severe effects on many services in the low-skilled contact services group, especially those most reliant on face-to-face interactions, such as accommodation, food, and transportation services. But the high-skilled offshorable services group, consisting of ICT, professional, and financial services, has generally withstood the pandemic as well as, if not better than, manufacturing, largely because digitalization has helped to make these services amenable to remote delivery and home-based work. Even among some low-skilled contact services, the pandemic has accelerated digitalization, including in countries where the use of digital technologies was low.

Patterns of impact and recovery

Differences across services subsectors

Overall, the pandemic had a somewhat larger impact on output in the services sector than in the manufacturing sector. In 2020, the services sector had a lower growth rate than manufacturing in more than half (87) of the 157 countries for which sectoral value-added data are available (World Bank 2021). In 136 countries, value added of the services sector fell in 2020, compared with 116 countries where there was a decline in that of manufacturing (figure 7.6.A).

However, the overall impact of the pandemic conceals considerable heterogeneity among the various services groups. In the low-skilled contact services group, hospitality (accommodation and food services) and transportation services were the most negatively affected. Gross value added in these sectors declined by 40 and 21 percent, respectively, in the year to April 2020 in a representative group of EMDEs for which data from national accounts are available (figure 7.6.B). Estimates based on data from firm surveys similarly indicate that the largest negative impacts on sales in 2020 and 2021 occurred in accommodation, food services, and transportation (figure 7.6.C), together with "other" services (including personal services).[5] Negative impacts in these sectors continued through 2021 in EMDEs (figure 7.6.D), but some recovery became visible in advanced economies (figure 7.6.E). The concentrated impact of the pandemic contrasts with the more-even effects of the global financial crisis and associated recession across services subsectors.[6]

Similar patterns can also be seen in FDI inflows into EMDEs (figure 7.6.F). For most services subsectors, announced greenfield FDI was lower in 2020 and 2021 than pre-pandemic levels, with the largest declines being in hospitality and "other" services (including personal services). High-skilled offshorable services performed slightly better, although both professional services and financial services saw significant declines. ICT services were the only group that saw an increase in greenfield FDI—of one-third between 2019 and 2021.

---

[5] In classifications of economic activities, personal services are often grouped under "other services" (under International Standard Industrial Classification Revision 4, this corresponds to section S).

[6] For example, in the United States, in the first quarter of 2009, subsectoral impacts in the services sector ranged between -11 percent (for retail and wholesale) and -6 percent (for ICT). In the first quarter of 2020, U.S. services subsectoral impacts ranged from -47 percent (for hospitality) to +1 percent (for ICT).

FIGURE 7.6 The impact of COVID-19 across sectors

Data from national accounts and firm-level surveys indicate that the coronavirus disease 2019 (COVID-19) had negative effects on output in both services and manufacturing and larger effects in services in about half of all countries. But they varied significantly among services subsectors. Hospitality and transportation were the most negatively affected in both EMDEs and advanced economies. FDI also decreased in most services subsectors, with the exception of ICT, which saw growth in value added and investment, as well as FDI, during the pandemic.

A. Value-added growth in manufacturing versus that in services, 2019-20

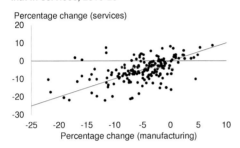

B. Change in value added by services subsector, April 2020 compared with April 2019

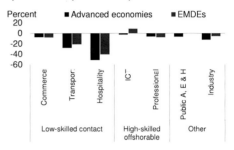

C. Change in sales as reported by firms

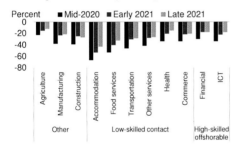

D. Value added by sector in EMDEs

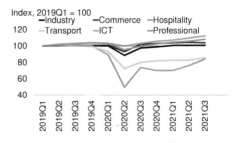

E. Value added by sector in advanced economies

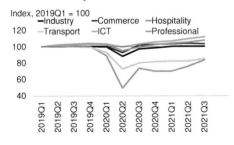

F. Greenfield FDI in EMDEs

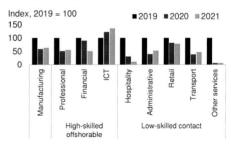

Sources: Financial Times, fDi Markets; Haver Analytics; UN World Tourism Organization; World Bank.
Note: EMDEs = emerging market and developing economies; FDI = foreign direct investment; ICT = information and communications technology.
A. For each individual country in the scatterplot, vertical axis reports percent change in services value added, whereas horizontal axis presents percent change in manufacturing value added.
B.D.E. Sample of advanced economies includes Australia, Canada, Norway, Sweden, and the United States. Sample of EMDEs includes Brazil, Ghana, Indonesia, Kenya, Morocco, and Vietnam. Not all countries in the Haver Analytics database report granular sectoral disaggregation.
B. A, E & H = administration, education, and health.
C. The change in sales reported by firms is a conditional value based on a regression of the change in sales on sector, size, month of interview, and age. Sample from the World Bank COVID-19 Business Pulse Surveys and Enterprise Surveys includes 47 countries (countries with data for three waves). Weights have been applied such that every country carries an equal weight.
F. Greenfield FDI from the fDi Markets database represents the value of new announcements, relative to 2019.

The intensity of face-to-face interactions and amenability to remote work

The importance of physical proximity in delivering services in different subsectors is correlated with the pandemic's adverse impact on sales. Such low-skilled contact services as hospitality took the biggest hit, reflecting their high dependence on face-to-face interactions and the limited possibilities for remote or home-based work.[7] In many countries, hospitality is also highly dependent on tourism-related international travel, which declined significantly; the UN World Tourism Organization estimates a decline of 97 percent at the height of the pandemic (figure 7.7.A).

In contrast, the ICT subsector—part of the high-skilled offshorable services group—was the least adversely affected, being more amenable to home-based work. In EMDEs, output of ICT services grew by 20-25 percent in 2020, while other subsectors contracted or stagnated. Among EMDEs for which data are available, Ghana and Türkiye saw the largest expansion of ICT services (figure 7.7.B). As mentioned earlier, ICT is also the only services subsector that has seen positive investment growth, with FDI in ICT in EMDEs growing by a third between 2020 and 2022.

In general, firms engaged in services activities dependent on face-to-face interactions between providers and consumers, such as hospitality, experienced the largest decline in sales (figure 7.7.C). Similarly, firms engaged in activities that are more amenable to home-based work typically experienced smaller declines in sales. This applies to ICT, financial services, and professional services—all high-skilled offshorable services (figure 7.7.D).

The transportation sector, which is moderately dependent on face-to-face interactions between providers and consumers and among the least amenable to home-based work, has been adversely affected too. This holds not only for passenger transportation services, but also for freight transport, which has been affected not only by border closures but also by impacts upstream in the manufacturing sector, which led to reductions in the capacity of freight transportation. Given the important linkages between freight transportation and goods-producing sectors, this has contributed to prolonged supply chain disruptions.

Since 2020, hospitality and transportation services have experienced partial recoveries, attributable, at least in part, to the phasing out of government restrictions on in-person gatherings and travel. Yet continuing restrictions and social-distancing precautions mean that full recovery has some distance to cover. For example, at the end of 2021, international tourist arrivals were still two-thirds lower than before the pandemic. Furthermore, recovery has been slower in EMDEs than in advanced economies. Thus, while hospitality services in the U.S. in the third quarter of 2021 were about 8 percent lower than in the same quarter of 2020, they were close to 40 percent lower in a group of EMDEs for which data are available.

---

[7] Except in the cases of takeaway and home delivery services, physical proximity has remained central to their provision.

FIGURE 7.7 **COVID-19 and the performance of services subsectors**

Different sectors fared very differently through the pandemic. ICT services, for example, grew in many EMDEs, while tourism-related sectors declined. The need for face-to-face interactions and the possibility for remote delivery explain part of these differences. Sectors relying on face-to-face interactions in the delivery of services fared worse during the pandemic, while those amenable to home-based work—even if traditionally relying on face-to-face interactions (for example, financial services)—fared better.

A. Global tourist arrivals

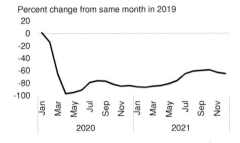

B. Value added of the ICT sector

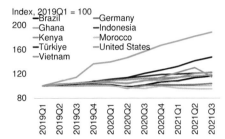

C. Face-to-face index and change in sales

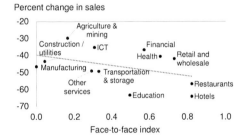

D. Home-based work index and change in sales

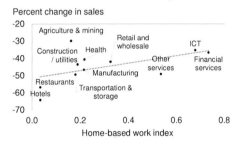

Sources: Avdiu and Nayyar (2020); Dingel and Neiman (2020); Haver Analytics; UN World Tourism Organization; World Bank.
Note: COVID-19 = coronavirus disease 2019; EMDEs = emerging market and developing economies; ICT = information and communications technology.
A. Change in tourist arrivals compared with same month in 2019.
C.D. Year-over-year change in firms' sales between 2019 and 2020, drawn from the first wave of high-frequency data for 47 countries from World Bank COVID-19 Business Pulse Surveys and Enterprise Surveys conducted between March and September 2020. The face-to-face index and home-based work index are, respectively, based on Avdiu and Nayyar (2020) and Dingel and Neiman (2020).

The advent and growth of digitalization

The adoption of digital technologies has increased during the pandemic. The World Bank COVID-19 Business Pulse Surveys and Enterprise Surveys show that nearly 44 percent of businesses globally started or increased their use of digital technologies and that 29 percent invested in digital technologies during the initial months of the pandemic (Apedo-Amah et al. 2020). Even as restrictions were relaxed and firms experienced fewer adverse impacts from the pandemic, firms continued to report increases in the use of digital technologies (figures 7.8.A and 7.8.B).

The adoption of digital technologies was higher in services than in manufacturing, agriculture, mining, construction, and utilities. In these non-services sectors, only roughly one-third of firms reported an increase in the use of these technologies. There

FIGURE 7.8 Adoption of digital technologies in EMDEs

High-frequency surveys of firms in EMDEs during the pandemic highlight that services firms were more likely to start using or increase their use of digital technologies than manufacturing firms. Firms also increased their investment in digitalization.

A. Firms increasing use of digital technologies

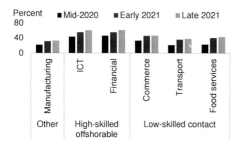

B. Firms investing in digital technologies

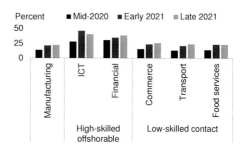

Source: World Bank.
Note: Balanced panel of 47 countries (comprising EMDEs as well as Poland) for which three waves of data were available. Each bar corresponds to a survey wave. For most countries, wave 1 surveys were conducted in the second or third quarter of 2020, wave 2 in early 2021, and wave 3 in late 2021. Data are from World Bank COVID-19 Business Pulse Surveys and Enterprise Surveys. EMDEs = emerging market and developing economies; ICT = information and communications technology.

were also differences across services subsectors. The largest proportions of firms increasing the use of digital technologies were reported in high-skilled offshorable services, including financial services (61 percent in late 2021) and ICT services (60 percent in late 2021).[8]

Use of digital technologies has also increased in some low-skilled contact services. The share of firms in accommodation, food services, and retail trade—services that are among the most dependent on face-to-face interactions—that started or increased their use of digital technologies was 35-45 percent in the most recent (late 2021) survey round. In fact, these services have seen the largest accelerations in digitalization during the pandemic. In fact, the largest change among all industries in the percentage of firms increasing the use of digital technologies between the first and second waves of the survey, at 14 percentage points, was in food preparation and accommodation services. Data for increases in investment in digital technologies show similar patterns. This investment in digitalization reflects adjustments in business models. For example, digital platforms enabled restaurants to offer their food services outside their premises during the pandemic through home-delivery and takeaway meals.[9]

In sum, the pandemic has affected high-skilled offshorable services, which digital technologies permit to be delivered remotely, less adversely than low-skilled contact

---

[8] Firms' investment in digital technologies shows similar patterns across sectors. About 40 percent of firms in ICT and financial services; 25 percent in wholesale and retail trade, food preparation, and accommodation services; and 20 percent in agriculture, mining, construction, manufacturing, and transportation made investments of this type.

[9] For example, in the United States, food delivery apps reported that their revenues more than doubled in 2020 (Sumagaysay 2020).

services, which rely more on face-to-face interactions with customers and have little scope for remote delivery. Among the former group, ICT services have actually experienced positive growth since the beginning of the pandemic. However, even firms in low-skilled contact services have increased their use of, and investment in, digital technologies at a faster pace than firms in manufacturing and agriculture. Furthermore, firms report that they have continued to increase digitalization even since pandemic-related restrictions have been relaxed.

How can digitalization transform opportunities for future services sector growth?

The acceleration of digitalization during the pandemic augurs well for growth prospects in the services sector. In particular, it has shown how digitalization can expand opportunities for scale economies and innovation that dependence on face-to-face interactions between providers and consumers and limits to combining labor with physical capital previously hampered. Even before the pandemic, increased digitalization had expanded these opportunities, albeit mostly for high-skilled offshorable services and a limited number of countries. The recent acceleration raises the question of how much potential the benefits of digitalization may have to spread more widely in the services sector.

Digitalization and exporting opportunities in the services sector

High-skilled offshorable services

The ICT revolution has, since the 1990s, enabled the offshoring of ICT and professional services to lower-cost destinations. Much as in global value chains for manufactured goods, the production of these services is fragmented across countries, as in the case of, for example, preliminary architectural designs and tax returns being put together in one country and finalized and delivered to customers in another (World Bank 2020).[10] The inverse relationship between the share of cross-border delivery (mode 1 trade) in total exports of ICT and professional services and per capita GDP reflects this labor cost arbitrage. Providers of services in EMDEs in which substantial proportions of the population have English-language skills, such as Ghana, India, and the Philippines, have particularly benefited (figure 7.9A).

The rapid expansion of bandwidth with the fifth-generation (5G) technology standard for broadband cellular networks is expected to further increase the quality of data streaming. And new collaborative digital platforms such as Skype for Business, Slack, Trello, and Basecamp have enhanced the remote (digital) delivery of global innovator services. These digital platforms are associated with a new form of online outsourcing for office and other professional services, whereby low search costs enable clients to contract

---

[10] Freund and Weinhold (2002) provided the earliest assessment of the relationship between digital technologies and trade in services, finding that the growth in U.S. exports of services to and imports of services from a partner country increased by 1.1 percentage points as internet penetration in that country increased by 10 percent.

FIGURE 7.9 **Digitalization and services exports**

EMDEs have leveraged offshore ICT and professional services to diversify their export baskets. Many are also among the top 20 countries in terms of the number of online freelancers per capita, which reflects a new form of online outsourcing for computer programming and other professional services through digital platforms. The share of these digitally deliverable services expanded relative to other services during the pandemic. Even for travel-related services, in which in-person delivery remains important, digital technologies have boosted tourist arrivals.

A. Share of cross-border delivery in exports of high-skilled offshorable services versus per capita income, 2017

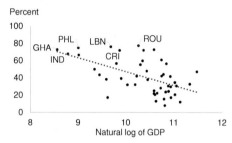

B. Economies with largest number of online freelancers per capita, 2021

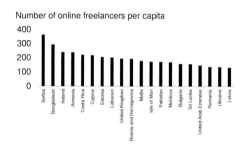

C. Share of digitally deliverable services in total services exports

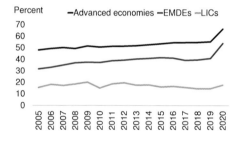

D. Index of internet use for B2C transactions and international tourist arrivals, 2017

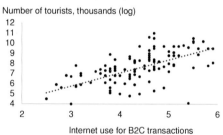

Sources: Lopez-Cordova (2020); United Nations Conference on Trade and Development (UNCTAD); University of Oxford, Oxford Internet Institute, and ILO (2020); World Bank; World Trade Organization (WTO).
A. "Cross-border delivery" refers to services trade through mode 4 of the General Agreement on Trade in Services. Data are from the WTO's Trade in Services by Mode of Supply database. GDP = gross domestic product.
B. Based on data from the five largest English-language online outsourcing platforms from the University of Oxford's iLabour project, representing at least 60 percent of the global market.
C. UNCTAD defines "digitally deliverable services" as an aggregation of insurance and pension services, financial services, charges for the use of intellectual property, telecommunications, computer and information services, other business services, and audiovisual and related services. EMDEs = emerging market and developing economies; LICs = low-income countries.
D. Results show that digital tools may help less traditional destinations overcome information obstacles and reduce travel costs and thereby attract more visitors. Index (with scores from 1 to 7) is based on Lopez-Cordova (2020). Higher index values indicating more transactions. Each scatterpoint indicates a country. The number of tourists is expressed in natural logarithms. B2C = business-to-consumer.

third-party individuals as freelancers. Developing economies have the edge in exporting these services through digital platforms (Baldwin and Dingel 2021).

Based on data from five of the largest English-language online outsourcing platforms between June 2017 and October 2020, the Oxford Internet Institute's iLabour Project estimates that much of the global demand for online outsourcing during that period came from high-income countries, while two-thirds of all online freelancers were in

EMDEs. As of 2021, approximately one-quarter of freelancers were based in India and another quarter in Bangladesh and Pakistan. In per capita terms, the big EMDE suppliers were Bangladesh, Costa Rica, Pakistan, Sri Lanka, and several countries in Eastern Europe (figure 7.9B). Suppliers in Eastern Europe likely benefit from their integration with the European Union market, while those in South Asia leverage the advantage they derive from English being the preferred language for business transactions. This pool of online freelancers is likely to widen geographically as the importance of knowledge of the English language diminishes with the diffusion of artificial-intelligence-enabled machine translation (Baldwin 2019; Brynjolfsson, Hui, and Liu 2019).

The share of digitally deliverable services in total services exports increased steadily between 2005 and 2019 in both EMDEs and advanced economies. The fact that this average share in EMDEs increased from 40 to more than 50 percent in 2020 alone (figure 7.9C) indicates the robustness of these services during the COVID-19 pandemic.

Low-skilled contact services

In the area of low-skilled contact services, streaming platforms such as Netflix and YouTube have enabled providers of arts, entertainment, and recreation services from EMDEs to export their creative content to international markets at low cost. And COVID-19 has provided an impetus for performing artists to devise new ways of sharing their talents with audiences virtually. Even in low-skilled contact services in which in-person delivery has remained important, digital tools have boosted export opportunities. Digital platforms that reduce the costs of searching for, matching, tracking, and verifying information (Goldfarb and Tucker 2019) are particularly relevant here. The digital platforms that travelers and businesses are increasingly using for transactions in accommodation and transportation services are good examples. These digital tools may help less traditional destinations overcome information obstacles and reduce travel costs and thereby attract more visitors. Indeed, countries with higher business-to-consumer internet use have also had higher levels of international tourist arrivals (figure 7.9D). Analyzing population-wide internet use in origin countries and business-to-consumer internet use in destination countries, Lopez-Cordova (2020) finds that digital platforms have boosted the demand for international tourism services in Africa.

Digitalization and innovation in the services sector

High-skilled offshorable services

In the case of high-skilled offshorable services, innovation has occurred largely through the accumulation of ICT capital: computer equipment, telecommunications equipment, computer software, and database assets. Since the 1990s, among member countries of the Organisation for Economic Co-operation and Development, the largest increase in the share of tangible ICT capital in total capital has been in the financial and professional services subsector (figure 7.10.A).

FIGURE 7.10 **ICT and intangible capital**

Firms in the services sector rely more than manufacturing firms on ICT and intangible capital, such as software, research and development, branding, and organizational practices, in their production processes. The shares of ICT capital in total capital and of intangible investment in total fixed investment have been largest among high-skilled offshorable services.

A. Shares of ICT capital in total capital by subsector, advanced economies

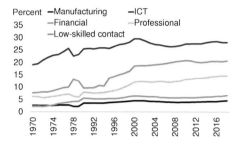

B. U.S. investment in tangible and intangible capital, 2015

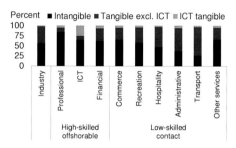

Sources: INTAN-Invest database; Organisation for Economic Co-operation and Development.
Note: EMDEs = emerging market and developing economies; excl. = excluding; ICT = information and communications technology.
A. Includes capital as measured in national accounts and excludes most forms of intangible capital.
B. Intangible capital includes software and databases, intellectual property, and economic competencies, following the methodology of Corrado et al. (2016). The sample is drawn from the INTAN-Invest database, only for the United States, owing to data constraints, but the data may be viewed as indicating the upside potential of ICT-related capital in EMDEs.

The diffusion of digital technologies has also been associated with accumulation of intangible capital—not only computer-related software and data, but also intellectual property acquired through research and development and design, as well as company competencies such as branding, firm-specific training, and business process engineering. Here too, at least in the United States, the largest shares of intangible capital in firms' investment have been in ICT, finance, and professional services (figure 7.10.B). The accumulation of intangible capital in these high-skilled offshorable services is likely to increase further given that artificial-intelligence-driven machine learning algorithms have dramatically increased predictive power in many cognitive tasks such as problem solving, speech recognition, and image recognition (Nayyar, Hallward-Driemeier, and Davies 2021).

Low-skilled contact services

The share of intangible capital in investment is also higher than in manufacturing in several low-skilled contact services, such as commerce and hospitality. For example, in member countries of the Organisation for Economic Co-operation and Development in 2018, hospitality and retail trade had the highest share of businesses with a website allowing online ordering, and almost all services subsectors had higher rates than manufacturing (figure 7.11.A). The increasing sophistication of ICT, through the advent of artificial intelligence and machine learning, among other drivers, is likely to spawn complementary investments in intangible capital (Brynjolfsson, Rock, and Syverson 2021). While ICT services stand out as the services subsector having the largest share of firms using machine learning algorithms, the diffusion of these technologies is

FIGURE 7.11 Digitalization and innovation in the services sector

The use of digital technologies brings greater opportunities for technological innovation in the services sector, including in low-skilled contact services, in which the share of firms using basic ICT and advanced artificial intelligence is higher than in manufacturing. The same holds true for digitalization-related investments in intangible capital that enable marketing and organizational innovation.

A. Share of businesses with a website allowing online ordering

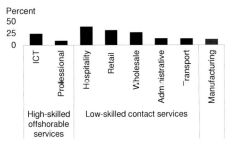

B. Share of businesses using artificial intelligence

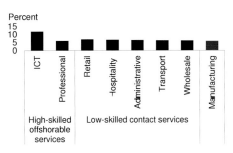

C. Share of businesses introducing new product placement methods

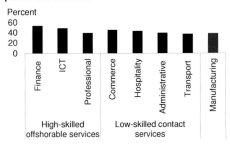

D. Share of businesses introducing new ways of organizing external relations

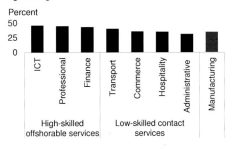

Source: European Union (EU) Community Innovation Survey; Organisation for Economic Co-operation and Development (OECD).
Note: The sample is drawn from advanced economies, owing to constraints on data availability. ICT = information and communications technology.
A.B. Sample includes OECD countries in 2018.
C. New product placement methods help position a firm's product in the market, with the objective of increasing the firm's sales.
C.D. Sample, drawn from the EU Community Innovation Survey, includes EU countries and the U.K. in 2018.

as widespread across many low-skilled services as in manufacturing, if not more so (figure 7.11.B).

New or improved company competencies that accompany digitalization offer similar opportunities for organizational and marketing innovation among low-skilled services. For example, in 2018, most services subsectors had higher shares of firms that introduced new methods for product placement (figure 7.11.C) or new methods for organizing external relations (figure 7.11.D) than manufacturing, and the shares were not very different in low-skilled services than in high-skilled offshorable services.

Increased digitalization and related investments in intangible capital bring opportunities for innovation and productivity gains in low-skilled contact services in three main ways. First, they enable improvements in the efficiency of internal business processes, such as inventory management, accounting practices, marketing, and payments. For example, big data analytics can increase the efficiency of transportation services by making it possible to track shipments in real time, while improved and expanded navigation systems may help route trucks more efficiently on the basis of current road and traffic conditions (World Bank 2020). Second, ICT-related investments can compensate for missing and scarce skills. For example, ICT apps enable Uber drivers to function with limited geographic knowledge and numeracy skills. Third, the expansion of company competencies associated with digital technologies, such as marketing and branding, facilitates the scaling up of low-skilled contact services that are less amenable to remote delivery. For example, restaurant chains have invested in ICT and management practices that help determine optimal staffing, daily food purchases, and new menu items for individual restaurants. This standardization of production over many establishments has enabled restaurants and retail stores to scale up by replicating the same production process in multiple locations near consumers (Hsieh and Rossi-Hansberg 2020).

The adoption of basic ICT in the services sector across EMDEs

Despite the diffusion of digital technologies, the use of basic ICT such as computers and email, which is positively associated with countries' per capita incomes, is far from widespread in EMDEs. In many EMDEs, less than one-third of firms used email to communicate with clients as recently as 2018 (figure 7.12.A). The share of firms with their own websites was even lower (figure 7.12.B).

The positive relationship between the share of firms using email and countries' per capita incomes is much stronger in respect to low-skilled contact services (where it is similar to that of the manufacturing sector) than in respect to high-skilled offshorable services (figure 7.12.C). Firms in retail and hospitality services in EMDEs still rely mostly on manual processes for a range of business functions. For example, in Senegal, 60 percent of such firms use manual costing most frequently for pricing, 80 percent use manual selection most frequently for merchandising, and 62 percent use handwritten records for inventory management (Cirera et al. 2020a). In Senegal, the sophistication of the most widely used technologies across a range of business functions, including business administration, marketing, and inventory management, is similar for firms in retail trade and firms in apparel manufacturing (Cirera et al. 2020b). The share of firms having their own websites is also positively related to countries' per capita incomes, with the relationship being more similar across sectors (figure 7.12.D).

What policies can best harness the services sector's growth potential after the COVID-19 pandemic?

To build on the momentum of digitalization in the services sector, and for the services sector's growth potential to be fully harnessed, policies can play a useful role. First, policies can be used to support the adoption of digital technologies across the services sector, including through promoting investment in ICT infrastructure, reforming regulatory frameworks, and strengthening firms' capabilities. Policies can play an

FIGURE 7.12 Diffusion of ICT among services firms

Services firms use email and websites more widely in countries with higher per capita incomes. Email use has a weaker relationship with per capita income among firms in high-skilled offshorable services than among firms in either low-skilled contact services or manufacturing.

A. Share of firms using email, by country

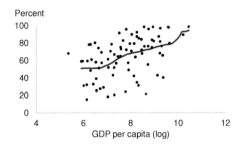

B. Share of firms using their own websites, by country

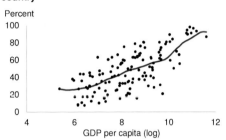

C. Share of firms using email, by sector or subsector

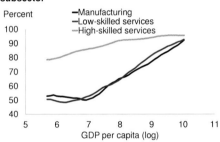

D. Share of firms using their own websites, by sector or subsector

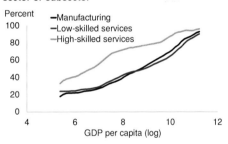

Source: World Bank.
Note: Calculations based on World Bank Enterprise Survey data and World Development Indicators. Gross domestic product (GDP) per capita is in natural logarithms.
A.B. The question regarding on whether firms use email or their own websites was not asked in most high-income countries included in the Enterprise Surveys. Data are for latest available year, ranging from 2006 to 2018. Each dot represents a country. The red line represents a trend line (kernel-weighted local polynomial regression) of the data points shown.
C.D. The lines represent trend lines (kernel-weighted local polynomial regressions) of the share of firms in a country using email or their own websites for three sector groups. Individual country data points are omitted for visual reasons.

especially important role for EMDEs and smaller firms because the greater intensity of digitalization among advanced economies and larger firms during the pandemic has widened the digital divide between countries and firms (Cirera, Comin, and Cruz 2022).

Second, policies can help promote the revival of some low-skilled contact services that the pandemic has hit hardest. The revival of travel-related transportation and hospitality is likely to benefit from the expansion of pandemic-related health services. Supporting infrastructure investments and regulatory reforms in transportation and related distribution services can further help recovery and lay the ground for minimizing supply chain disruptions in the future. Third, policies can be designed to promote the further growth of high-skilled offshorable services that have shown greater resilience to the pandemic, by removing barriers to market access and improving the skills of the workforce.

Supporting the adoption of digital technologies

The use of digital technologies contributed to the resilience of firms in the pandemic. Firms with higher prepandemic levels of technological sophistication saw larger increases in sales during the pandemic and were also more likely to increase their use of digital technologies (Comin et al. 2022). While new technologies have recently been spreading to EMDEs and LICs faster than in the past, only a small share of firms at the technology frontier adopt them (Comin and Mestieri 2018).

Policies that support widespread adoption of the most basic digital technologies in EMDEs can lay the foundation for firms to leverage software applications, digital platforms, and even more advanced machine learning algorithms. But policies supporting investment in broadband infrastructure, while necessary, are not sufficient for greater uptake of digital technologies. In addition, regulatory frameworks must be updated to expand market access, and policies to strengthen worker and management skills are also needed (Cirera and Maloney 2017). Precise policy requirements will vary among countries and across different services subsectors. For example, management practices tend to be particularly weak (but to have the most potential for improvement) among firms in low-skilled contact services, while advanced digital skills matter most in regard to high-skilled offshorable services. Updating regulatory frameworks governing digital markets is especially relevant in regard to high-skilled offshorable services, as technology giants have increasingly dominated markets for these services.

Expanding access to digital infrastructure

Expanding access to the internet is crucial for the services sector. Hjort and Poulsen (2019) show that the arrival of internet cables in Africa predominantly benefited the services sector, spurring the formation of new firms and boosting productivity. Although many countries have been accelerating the rollout of internet access, reliable and affordable access to broadband internet is still not widely available in many EMDEs, and generally much less so than in advanced economies (figure 7.13.A). Fiber-optic cables now reach most countries, but there are big gaps across countries in the provision of "last mile" connectivity. To achieve widespread internet access, public investment may be needed to overcome market failures inherent in the private provision of internet infrastructure (essentially a public good). These failures stem from externalities (including network externalities) and costs that decrease with scale (tending to lead to natural monopolies). Policy interventions can also catalyze complementary private investment by ensuring enough competition between providers, targeting subsidies carefully, and enforcing appropriate performance requirements to ensure coverage in more remote and lower-income locations (World Bank 2021).

Reforming regulatory frameworks for digital markets

The regulation of digital markets also affects the incentives and ability to use digital technologies. Restrictions on digital trade tend to be more stringent, on average, in EMDEs than in advanced economies (figure 7.13.B). Competition authorities face new challenges in the regulation of digital trade in the services sector, particularly in regard to

FIGURE 7.13 Digital technology enablers

Broadband connectivity in EMDEs has increased considerably over the past decade, but it still lags that in advanced economies. Beyond access, relatively high restrictions on international trade in services and digital technology hamper use of digital technologies in EMDEs. The capabilities of firms and workers to adopt new technologies, reflected in management practices, tertiary education rates, and digital skills, are also weaker in EMDEs than in advanced economies.

A. Mobile broadband connections per 100 inhabitants

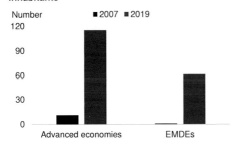

B. Digital trade restrictiveness index

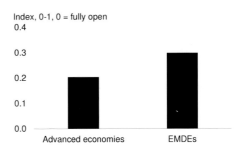

C. Management practices index

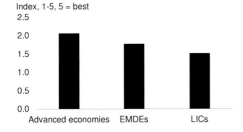

D. Digital skills index

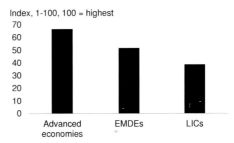

E. Tertiary enrollment rates

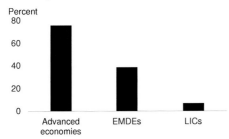

F. Services trade restrictiveness index

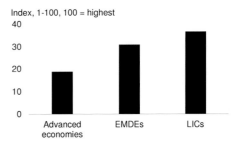

Sources: European Centre for International Political Economy (ECIPE); International Telecommunication Union (ITU); Nayyar, Hallward-Driemeier, and Davies (2021); World Bank; World Economic Forum.

Note: EMDEs = emerging market and developing economies; LICs = low-income countries.

A. Sample from the ITU includes 37 advanced economies and 141 EMDEs in 2019.

B. The ECIPE's Digital Trade Restrictiveness Index provides information on transparency of applied digital trade restrictions across 36 advanced economies and 28 EMDEs in 2017-18.

C. Covers 18 key management practices across 21 advanced economies, 17 EMDEs, and 3 LICs in 2018 or latest year for which data are available.

D. Sample from World Economic Forum includes 34 advanced economies, 71 EMDEs, and 6 LICs in 2019.

E. Sample includes 33 advanced economies, 70 EMDEs, and 7 LICs in 2019.

F. The World Trade Organization-World Bank Services Trade Restrictiveness Index covers five sectors (telecommunications, finance, transportation, retail, and professional services) and key modes of delivery across 22 advanced economies, 67 EMDEs, and 6 LICs in 2008.

high-skilled offshorable services. In this sector, many technology companies own valuable intangible assets (such as software, advertising space, and branding), which derive value from strong network effects and access to data. Ownership and portability of data, especially across international borders, raise issues of privacy and innovation. For example, content providers could place restrictions on the provision of some services to countries that inadequately protect intellectual-property rights (Hallward-Driemeier and Nayyar 2017).

Digital trade in services also poses new challenges for taxation. Traditional tax treaties tend to focus on the question of whether a firm has physical presence in a country. As a result, firms that have "presence without mass" in a particular country through digital business models can avoid significant taxation in that country, denying governments a growing source of potential revenue. International negotiations are seeking to address this issue, through possible formulas for minimum tax payments by multinationals that serve markets only virtually, among other options (World Bank 2021).

Upgrading management and worker skills

Low levels of use of digital technology stem partly from shortcomings in the capabilities of firms, at both management and staff levels. Sound management practices facilitate worthwhile change in production processes, including the adoption of new technologies, which can often be disruptive. Thus, management practices have played a role in the ways firms have, or have not, adapted to the pandemic. Firms with more structured management practices are more likely to adjust their product mixes or to adopt online work arrangements, in the services sector as well as other sectors (Grover and Karplus 2021). Firm-level surveys of the number and type of adopted management practices show that management practices in the services sector are weaker in EMDEs than in advanced economies (figure 7.13.C). Further, evidence for EMDEs and advanced economies shows that structured management practices are particularly uncommon among firms in low-skilled services, such as retail trade and hospitality (Nayyar, Hallward-Driemeier, and Davies 2021). Governments can support technological innovation and the adoption of structured management practices by addressing information failures at the management level—either through the direct provision of training and other business advisory services or through vouchers and awards (Bloom et al. 2013).[11]

Also important for increasing the adoption of digital technology are the skills of a firm's labor force. Digital skills are weaker in EMDEs than advanced economies (figure 7.13.D). Many workers report that their lack of ICT skills is a constraint on employment and higher earnings. For example, about 40 percent of workers in Vietnam reported in 2013 that deficient ICT skills prevented them from finding a job or getting a better-paying job (Nayyar, Hallward-Driemeier, and Davies 2021). Remedying this

---

[11] Not all firms are well positioned to take advantage of management training. Efforts to provide management training to informal enterprises have shown that only a few have the capabilities to use such training (or tap external consulting services) to raise performance significantly. See, for example, Anderson and McKenzie (2022).

type of skill deficiency is less of a priority in firms providing low-skilled contact services, in which basic knowledge of how to use a computer and email is generally sufficient. A skills agenda that is broader than basic information technology is needed for workers to embrace technological change, particularly in high-skilled offshorable services. Education, and particularly tertiary education—in which enrollment rates are lower in EMDEs than in advanced economies (figure 7.13.E)—plays an essential role in equipping workers with the cognitive skills needed for complex problem solving, critical thinking, and adaptability. Tertiary education systems can meet the demand for these skills by incorporating more general education in technical degree programs and facilitating lifelong learning through adult education programs (World Bank 2019). Tuition and training paid for by employers, or by households if access to finance is not a barrier, can supplement public investment in education and training at advanced levels.

Promoting the revival of low-skilled contact services

Investing in widespread rollouts of vaccination against COVID-19 and related health care services is particularly important to enable travel-related services, such as accommodation and passenger transportation, to operate safely again at prepandemic scale. The uneven recoveries of these services from the pandemic thus far—with stronger recoveries in advanced economies than in EMDEs and LICs—is attributable, at least in part, to differences in the pace of vaccine rollouts (World Bank 2022).

While the low vaccination rates in LICs primarily reflect procurement challenges, logistical challenges in vaccine distribution, including insufficient cold chain capacity, are also hampering efforts to scale up inoculations rapidly (Hall et al. 2021). These challenges need to be addressed. Furthermore, testing and access to treatment facilities will need to supplement vaccine rollouts, especially given the uncertainty about the possible emergence of more transmissible or more lethal variants of the coronavirus against which existing vaccines might offer insufficient protection. All this highlights the importance of investing in better health services systems, including through public-private collaboration.

Evidence suggests that countries most dependent on tourism, such as small island economies, often have among the lowest Global Health Security Index scores (AIIB 2020). Increased digitalization, building on the momentum provided by COVID-19, could improve the performance of health services in resource-constrained countries by supporting efforts to revamp health provider education, redesign platforms for care delivery, institute strategic purchasing and management strategies, and develop patient-level data systems (Nimako and Kruk 2021).

Apart from addressing vaccination and other health-related issues, investment in infrastructure (through public-private partnerships, among other avenues) and measures to remove obstacles to competition and associated market distortions can minimize future disruptions in transportation and distribution services. Services trade faces significant regulatory barriers, which are generally higher in EMDEs than in advanced economies (figure 7.13.F). In low-skilled services, such as retail trade, there are both large EMDEs (such as Argentina, India, Indonesia, Malaysia, Thailand, and Vietnam) and advanced economies (such as Belgium, Finland, France, and Greece) among those with the highest trade restrictions, and many have made little progress in reducing them in the past decade (Nayyar, Hallward-Driemeier, and Davies 2021).

The pandemic has highlighted how disruptions in shipping, air transport, trucking, and distribution services at critical trade gateways and hubs can hinder activity in goods-producing subsectors (Celasun et al. 2022). In fact, transportation and distribution services are among the subsectors with the most intensive forward linkages to producers in other sectors—that is, with the largest shares of value added that provide inputs into economy-wide production (Nayyar, Hallward-Driemeier, and Davies 2021). Reducing regulatory restrictions in these upstream services can therefore bring cascading benefits to many downstream sectors. In India, for example, the productivity of downstream manufacturing firms increased following the liberalization of transportation services, through greater foreign direct investment in the 1990s as well as other means (Arnold et al. 2015).

Promoting the expansion of high-skilled offshorable services

High-skilled offshorable services are more amenable to remote delivery and, as a result, have better withstood the COVID-19 pandemic. These are also the services subsectors with the highest total factor productivity, implying that reallocation of resources toward them can raise an economy's total output. In EMDEs, high-skilled offshorable services are 2.7 times more productive than low-skilled services, which account for two-thirds of total services employment. If the composition of the services sector in LICs matched that in advanced economies, overall services productivity would be 35 percent higher. Policy interventions that alleviate constraints on the growth of high-skilled offshorable services may therefore be beneficial.

On the demand side, policy measures could support the growth of trade in ICT, finance, and professional services (see chapter 6). These measures include the easing of trade restrictions. Professional services are among the most protected industries in both EMDEs and advanced economies (Borchert, Gootiiz, and Mattoo 2014). EMDEs stand to gain from liberalizing import restrictions. By allowing more imports of services, with associated foreign know-how and investment, these economies could raise competitive pressures, productivity, and innovation (Fernandes, Rocha, and Ruta 2021; World Bank 2020). Furthermore, trade agreements can provide opportunities for reciprocal reductions in barriers to services. Some progress has already been made through bilateral or regional trade agreements; more than 50 percent of all preferential trade agreements filed with the World Trade Organization through 2017 covered the services sector (Hofmann, Osnago, and Ruta 2019). In 2021, at the multilateral level, 67 World Trade Organization members concluded negotiations on a new set of rules aimed at slashing administrative costs and creating a more transparent operating environment for providers of services in foreign markets.

On the supply side, shortages of technical skills are an important barrier to the growth of high-skilled offshorable services. Education, particularly tertiary education, and technical training are key to equipping workers with the advanced skills necessary to support such growth. Expansion of public-private partnerships could make tertiary education and training programs more responsive to changing industry demands. The use of private providers and incentive contracts (in which participant placement is a condition for payment) can help align incentives in improving the effectiveness of training programs. Having private sector actors involved in setting curricula can also help programs reflect the types of skills future employees will need. Links with industry are a feature of many tertiary education systems that are centers of innovation (World Bank 2019).

Conclusion

The development community's focus on the export-led manufacturing model of growth can divert attention from the fact that the services sector has been the main driver of economic growth in EMDEs over the past three decades. Today, the services sector employs half of all workers in EMDEs. However, except for in the high-skilled offshorable services—ICT, finance, and professional services—increases in domestic consumption have fueled this services-led growth process more than exports, and the growth of factor inputs more than productivity growth. As a result, scale economies and innovation—which formed the basis for growth in the export-led manufacturing model—have been relatively limited in the services sector, especially in regard to low-skilled contact services that employ a large share of regard to low-skilled labor in EMDEs. This has led to pessimism about the longer-term prospects of services-led growth.

At the onset of the COVID-19 pandemic, social-distancing regulations and precautions particularly affected low-skilled contact services—many of which are dependent on face-to-face interactions between providers and consumers. However, providers of services have responded by turning more to digital technologies, including those for online sales in low-skilled contact services in which in-person delivery remains important. Meanwhile digitalization has enabled high-skilled offshorable services to withstand the adverse effects of the pandemic by facilitating remote delivery.

Increased digitalization during the pandemic has provided new momentum to services-led growth and its prospects. For one thing, it has improved opportunities for international trade in services, not only in high-skilled offshorable services, but also, for instance, through streaming platforms that enable the remote delivery of arts, entertainment, and recreation services. For another, it has made possible new and greater efficiency gains: Digitalization can allow otherwise labor-intensive services to be combined with ICT and intangible forms of capital, reduce the importance of physical proximity in market transactions, improve business processes, and facilitate scaling up.

The use of even the most basic digital technologies in EMDEs, however, is far from widespread. To harness the potential of the services sector in shaping the recovery from the COVID-19 pandemic and strengthening future economic growth, policy makers in

EMDEs need to make the wider diffusion of digitalization a priority. Policies to promote digitalization include supporting investment in digital infrastructure, updating regulatory frameworks, and fostering the development of firms' capabilities through education and training. The revival of low-skilled contact services, such as transportation and hospitality, will likely benefit from the expansion of vaccination rollouts and related medical services. Promoting infrastructure investment and regulatory reforms in such services as transportation, which shares important links with goods-producing sectors, is also likely to benefit the wider economy. Last, but not least, policies that improve market access and develop relevant skills can support the expansion of high-skilled offshorable services.

The prospect of long-term services-led growth will also depend on climate change considerations as countries aim to transition to net-zero emissions by 2050-60. The impetus for policy makers in EMDEs to enable structural transformation will be even stronger; agriculture is more vulnerable to changes in climate than nonagricultural sectors (Casey 2020), and rising temperatures are associated with lower shares of workers outside agriculture (Liu, Shamdasani, and Taraz 2019).

The intensity of greenhouse gas emissions varies by sector. In the United States, services produce less than 5 percent of total greenhouse gas emissions directly, and they have much lower direct emission intensities per dollar of output than do physical products (Suh 2006). However, large environmental impacts can be traced to consumption by services workers. Together, these workers account for half of all wages globally, with the highest share of highly paid workers of any sector (Greenford et al. 2020). Simulation models based on hypothetical carbon prices show the net-zero transition will have a limited impact on the shares of manufacturing and services in GDP (Chepeliev et al. 2022). There may also be important differences across services subsectors. On the one hand, travel-related services might contribute more to emissions because of their dependence on transportation. On the other hand, high-skilled offshorable services might contribute more to emissions through consumption, because the workers they employ tend to be more affluent.

The services sector can also play an important role in climate mitigation (reducing emissions of greenhouse gases) and adaptation (building resilience to climate change). For instance, financial services can play a fundamental role in mobilizing the resources needed for necessary climate-related investments (Grippa, Schmittmann, and Suntheim 2019). Similarly, engineering and environmental consulting services will likely be central to enabling energy efficiency improvements (World Economic Forum 2022). The global environmental consulting services market size is expected to almost double from $56.4 billion in 2021 to $93.6 billion in 2026 (TBRC Business Research 2022).

Future research can explore how structural change driven by the manufacturing and services sectors affects climate goals. Analyzing sectoral differences in vulnerabilities to climate change, intensity of emissions, and contributions to climate mitigation and adaptation could help clarify the contribution of the services sector to sustainable economic growth.

References

AIIB (Asian Infrastructure Investment Bank). 2020. "Strengthening Healthcare to Revive Tourism." *AIIB* (blog), July 22, 2022. https://www.aiib.org/en/news-events/media-center/blog/2020/strength ening-healthcare-to-revive-tourism.html

Anderson, S. J., and D. McKenzie. 2022. "Improving Business Practices and the Boundary of the Entrepreneur: A Randomized Experiment Comparing Training, Consulting, Insourcing and Outsourcing." *Journal of Political Economy* 130 (1): 157-209.

Apedo-Amah, M. C., B. Avdiu, X. Cirera, M. Cruz, E. Davies, A. Grover, L. Iacovone, et al. 2020. "Unmasking the Impact of COVID-19 on Businesses: Firm-Level Evidence from Across the World." Policy Research Working Paper 9434, World Bank, Washington, DC.

Arnold, J. M., B. Javorcik, M. Lipscomb, and A. Mattoo. 2015. "Services Reform and Manufacturing Performance: Evidence from India." *Economic Journal* 126 (590): 1-39.

Aterido, R., E. Davies, M. Hallward-Driemeier, and G. Nayyar. 2021. "Revisiting the Size-Production Relationship in Services." Unpublished manuscript, World Bank, Washington, DC.

Avdiu, B., and G. Nayyar. 2020. "When Face-to-Face Interactions Become an Occupational Hazard: Jobs in the Time of COVID-19." *Economics Letters* 197 (December): 109648.

Baldwin, R. 2019. *The Globotics Upheaval: Globalization, Robotics and the Future of Work.* New York: Oxford University Press.

Baldwin, R., and J. Dingel. 2021. "Telemigration and Development: On the Offshorability of Teleworkable Jobs." NBER Working Paper 29837, National Bureau of Economic Research, Cambridge, MA.

Baumol, W. J. 1967. "Macroeconomics of Unbalanced Growth: The Anatomy of Urban Crisis." *American Economic Review* 57 (3): 415-26.

Beraja, M., and C. K. Wolf. 2021. "Demand Composition and the Strength of Recoveries." NBER Working Paper 29304, National Bureau of Economic Research, Cambridge, MA.

Blinder, A. S., and A. B. Krueger. 2013. "Alternative Measures of Offshorability: A Survey Approach." *Journal of Labor Economics* 31 (S1): S97-S128.

Bloom, N., B. Eifert, A. Mahajan, D. McKenzie, and J. Roberts. 2013. "Does Management Matter? Evidence from India." *Quarterly Journal of Economics* 128 (1): 1-51.

Borchert, I., B. Gootiiz, and A. Mattoo. 2014. "Policy Barriers to International Trade in Services: Evidence from a New Database." *World Bank Economic Review* 28 (1): 162-88.

Branstetter, L., B. Glennon, and J. B. Jensen. 2018. "Knowledge Transfer Abroad: The Role of US Inventors within Global R&D Networks." NBER Working Paper 24453, National Bureau of Economic Research, Cambridge, MA.

Brynjolfsson, E., X. Hui, and M. Liu. 2019. "Does Machine Translation Affect International Trade? Evidence from a Large Digital Platform." *Management Science* 65 (12): 5449-60.

Brynjolfsson, E., D. Rock, and C. Syverson. 2021. "The Productivity J-Curve: How Intangibles Complement General Purpose Technologies." *American Economic Journal: Macroeconomics* 13 (1): 333-72.

Casey, G. 2020. "Structural Transformation and Climate Damages." Unpublished manuscript, Department of Economics, Williams College, Williamstown, Massachusetts, and Energy and Climate Economics, CESifo, Munich.

Celasun, O., N.-J. Hansen, M. Spector, A. Mineshima, and J. Zhou. 2022. "Supply Bottlenecks: Where, Why, How Much, and What Next." IMF Working Paper 22/31, International Monetary Fund, Washington, DC.

Chepeliev, M., M. Maliszewska, I. Osorio-Rodarte, M. F. Seara e Pereira, and D. van der Mensbrugghe. 2022. "Towards Net-Zero Emissions: Impacts on Trade and Income across and within Countries." Unpublished manuscript, World Bank, Washington, DC.

Chenery, H. B. 1960. "Patterns of Industrial Growth." *American Economic Review* 50 (4): 624-54.

Chetty, R., J. N. Friedman, N. Hendren, and M. Stepner. 2020. "The Economic Impacts of COVID-19: Evidence from a New Public Database Built Using Private Sector Data." NBER Working Paper 27431, National Bureau of Economic Research, Cambridge, MA.

Cirera, X., D. Comin, and M. Cruz. 2022. *Bridging the Technological Divide: Technology Adoption by Firms in Developing Countries*. Washington, DC: World Bank.

Cirera, X., D. Comin, M. Cruz, and K. M. Lee. 2020a. "Technology Firm-Level Adoption of Technologies in Senegal." Unpublished manuscript, World Bank, Washington, DC.

Cirera, X., D. A. Comin, M. Cruz, and K. M. Lee. 2020b. "Technology within and across Firms." Policy Research Working Paper 9476, World Bank, Washington, DC.

Cirera, X., and W. F. Maloney. 2017. *The Innovation Paradox: Developing-Country Capabilities and the Unrealized Promise of Technological Catch-Up*. Washington, DC: World Bank.

Clark, C. 1940. *The Conditions of Economic Progress*. London: McMillan.

Comin, D., M. Cruz, X. Cirera, K. M. Lee, and J. Torres. 2022. "Technology and Resilience." NBER Working Paper 29644, National Bureau of Economic Research, Cambridge, MA.

Comin, D., and M. Mestieri. 2018. "If Technology Has Arrived Everywhere, Why Has Income Diverged?" *American Economic Journal: Macroeconomics* 10 (3): 137-78.

Corrado, C., J. Haskel, C. Jona-Lasinio, and M. Iommi. 2016. "Intangible Investment in the EU and US before and since the Great Recession and Its Contribution to Productivity Growth." EIB Working Paper 2016/08, European Investment Bank, Luxembourg.

Dingel, J. I., and B. Neiman. 2020. "How Many Jobs Can Be Done at Home?" *Journal of Public Economics* 189 (2): 104235.

Enache, M., E. Ghani, and S. O'Connell. 2016. "Structural Transformation in Africa: A Historical View." Policy Research Working Paper 7743, World Bank, Washington, DC.

Fan, T., M. Peters, and F. Zilibotti. 2021. "Service-Led or Service-Biased Growth? Equilibrium Development Accounting across Indian Districts." NBER Working Paper 28551, National Bureau of Economic Research, Cambridge, MA.

Fernandes, A., N. Rocha, and M. Ruta. 2021. *The Economics of Deep Trade Agreements*. Washington, DC: Centre for Economic Policy Research Press.

Fisher, A. G. B. 1935. *The Clash of Progress and Society*. London: Macmillan.

Freund, C., and D. Weinhold. 2002. "The Internet and International Trade in Services." *American Economic Review* 92 (2): 236-40.

Gervais, A., and J. B. Jensen. 2019. "The Tradability of Services: Geographic Concentration and Trade Costs." *Journal of International Economics* 118 (May): 331-50.

Goldfarb, A., and C. Tucker. 2019. "Digital Economics." *Journal of Economic Literature* 57 (1): 3-43.

Greenford, D. H., T. Crownshaw, C. Lesk, K. Stadler, and H. D. Matthews. 2020. "Shifting Economic Activity to Services Has Limited Potential to Reduce Global Environmental Impacts Due to the Household Consumption of Labor." *Environmental Research Letters* 15 (6): 1-11.

Grippa, P., J. Schmittmann, and F. Suntheim. 2019. "Climate Change and Financial Risk." *Finance & Development* (December): 26-29.

Grover, A., and V. J. Karplus. 2021. "Coping with COVID-19: Does Management Make Firms More Resilient?" Policy Research Working Paper 9514, World Bank, Washington, DC.

Hall, S., L. Kaplow, Y. S. Sun, and T. Z. Holt. 2021. "'None Are Safe until All Are Safe': COVID-19 Vaccine Rollout in Low- and Middle-Income Countries." McKinsey & Company.

Hallward-Driemeier, M., and G. Nayyar. 2017. *Trouble in the Making?: The Future of Manufacturing-Led Development*. Washington, DC: World Bank.

Heuser, C., and A. Mattoo. 2017. "Services Trade and Global Value Chains." Policy Research Working Paper 8126, World Bank, Washington, DC.

Hill, T. P. 1977. "On Goods and Services." *Review of Income and Wealth* 23 (4): 315-38.

Hjort, J., and J. Poulsen. 2019. "The Arrival of Fast Internet and Employment in Africa." *American Economic Review* 109 (3): 1032-79.

Hofmann, C., A. Osnago, and M. Ruta. 2019. "The Content of Preferential Trade Agreements." *World Trade Review* 18 (3): 365-98.

Hsieh, C.-T., and E. Rossi-Handberg. 2020. "The Industrial Revolution in Services." NBER Working Paper 25968, National Bureau of Economic Research, Cambridge, MA.

Kinfemichael, B., and A. K. M. Mahbub Morshed. 2019. "Unconditional Convergence of Labor Productivity in the Service Sector." *Journal of Macroeconomics* 59 (March): 217-29.

Kuznets, S. 1971. *Economic Growth of Nations: Total Output and Production Structure*. Cambridge, MA: Harvard University Press.

Liu, M., Y. Shamdasani, and V. Taraz. 2019. "Climate Change, Structural Transformation, and Infrastructure: Evidence from India." Paper presented at the Annual Meeting of the American Economic Association, January 2020, San Diego.

Lopez-Cordova, E. 2020. "Digital Platforms and the Demand for International Tourism Services." Policy Research Working Paper 9147, World Bank, Washington, DC.

McMillan, M. S., and D. Rodrik. 2011. "Globalization, Structural Change and Productivity Growth." NBER Working Paper 17143, National Bureau of Economic Research, Cambridge, MA.

Nayyar, G., M. Hallward-Driemeier, and E. Davies. 2021. *At Your Service? The Promise of Services-Led Development*. Washington, DC: World Bank.

Nimako, K., and M. E. Kruk. 2021. "Seizing the Moment to Rethink Health Systems." *Lancet* (12): E1758-62.

OECD (Organisation for Economic Cooperation and Development). 2021. *OECD Employment Outlook 2021: Navigating the COVID-19 Crisis and Recovery.* Paris: OECD Publishing.

Rodrik, D. 2016. "Premature Deindustrialization." *Journal of Economic Growth* 21 (1): 1-33.

Suh, S. 2006. "Are Services Better for Climate Change?" *Environment Science Technology* 40 (21): 6555-60.

Sumagaysay, L. 2020. "The Pandemic Has More than Doubled Food Delivery Apps' Business. Now What?" *MarketWatch*, November 27, 2020. https://www.marketwatch.com/story/the-pandemic-has-more-than-doubled-americans-use-of-food-delivery-apps-but-that-doesnt-mean-the-companies-are-making-money-11606340169

Tauber, K., and W. Van Zandweghe. 2021. "Why Has Durable Goods Spending Been So Strong during the COVID-19 Pandemic?" *Economic Commentary* 2021-15, Federal Reserve Bank of Cleveland, Cleveland, OH.

TBRC Business Research. 2022. *Environmental Consulting Services: Global Market Report 2022.* Hyderabad, India: The Business Research Company.

United Nations. 2008. *International Standard Industrial Classification of All Economic Activities. Revision 4.* New York: United Nations.

University of Oxford, Oxford Internet Institute, and ILO (International Labour Organization). 2020. "The iLabour Project: Investigating the Construction of Labour Markets, Institutions and Movements on the Internet." Oxford Internet Institute, Oxford, UK.

World Bank. 2019. *World Development Report 2019: The Changing Nature of Work.* Washington, DC: World Bank.

World Bank. 2020. *World Development Report 2020: Trading for Development in the Age of Global Value Chains.* Washington, DC: World Bank.

World Bank. 2021. *World Development Report 2021: Data for Better Lives.* Washington, DC: World Bank.

World Bank. 2022. *Global Economic Prospects: Slowing Growth, Rising Risks.* Washington, DC: World Bank.

World Economic Forum. 2022. "Davos Agenda 2022: Carbon-Neutral Manufacturing Is Possible: Here's How." January 12.